A HISTORY OF MODERN IRISH WOMEN'S LITERATURE

This book offers the first comprehensive survey of writing by women in Ireland from the seventeenth century to the present day. It covers literature in all genres, including poetry, drama and fiction, as well as life writing and unpublished writing, and addresses work in both English and Irish. The chapters are authored by leading experts in their field, giving readers an introduction to cutting-edge research on each period and topic. Survey chapters give an essential historical overview and are complemented by a focus on selected topics such as the short story. Key figures and their relationship to the narrative of Irish literary history are analysed and reconsidered. Demonstrating the pioneering achievements of a huge number of many hitherto neglected writers, *A History of Modern Irish Women's Literature* makes a critical intervention in Irish literary history.

HEATHER INGMAN is Visiting Research Fellow in the Centre for Gender and Women's Studies in Trinity College, the University of Dublin where she was previously Adjunct Professor in the School of English, teaching and researching in modernist women's fiction, the short story and Irish women's writing. Her publications include *Irish Women's Fiction from Edgeworth to Enright* (2013), *A History of the Irish Short Story* (Cambridge, 2009), *Twentieth-Century Fiction by Irish Women: Nation and Gender* (2007) and *Women's Fiction between the Wars: Mothers, Daughters and Writing* (1998). She has chapters in recent edited collections on Mary Lavin, Virginia Woolf and Elizabeth Bowen. She is currently researching ageing in Irish writing.

CLÍONA Ó GALLCHOIR is a lecturer in the School of English at University College Cork. Her research focuses on Irish writing in the long eighteenth century, women's writing and children's literature. Her publications include *Maria Edgeworth: Women, Enlightenment and Nation* (2005) and numerous articles and book chapters on figures such as Sydney Owenson, Germaine de Stael and Harriet Beecher Stowe. She is currently the literature editor of the journal *Eighteenth-Century Ireland*. She has held research fellowships at the Institute for Advanced Study in the Humanities at Edinburgh University and at the Moore Institute in NUI Galway, and in Autumn 2018 she will be the Peter O'Brien Visiting Scholar in Canadian Irish Studies at Concordia University in Montreal.

A HISTORY OF MODERN IRISH WOMEN'S LITERATURE

EDITED BY

HEATHER INGMAN
Trinity College Dublin

CLÍONA Ó GALLCHOIR
University College Cork

CAMBRIDGE
UNIVERSITY PRESS

CAMBRIDGE
UNIVERSITY PRESS

University Printing House, Cambridge CB2 8BS, United Kingdom

One Liberty Plaza, 20th Floor, New York, NY 10006, USA

477 Williamstown Road, Port Melbourne, VIC 3207, Australia

314–321, 3rd Floor, Plot 3, Splendor Forum, Jasola District Centre, New Delhi – 110025, India

79 Anson Road, #06-04/06, Singapore 079906

Cambridge University Press is part of the University of Cambridge.

It furthers the University's mission by disseminating knowledge in the pursuit of education, learning and research at the highest international levels of excellence.

www.cambridge.org
Information on this title: www.cambridge.org/9781107131101
DOI: 10.1017/9781316442999

© Cambridge University Press 2018

First published 2018

Printed and bound in Great Britain by Clays Ltd, Elcograf S.p.A.

A catalogue record for this publication is available from the British Library.

Library of Congress Cataloging-in-Publication Data

Names: Ingman, Heather, 1953- editor. | O Gallchoir, Cliona, editor.
Title: A history of modern Irish women's literature / edited by Heather Ingman and Clíona Ó Gallchoir.
Description: Cambridge, United Kingdom ; New York, NY : Cambridge University Press, 2018. | Includes bibliographical references.
Identifiers: LCCN 2018009843 | ISBN 9781107131101 (hardback : alk. paper)
Subjects: LCSH: English literature—Irish authors—History and criticism. | English literature—Women authors—History and criticism. | Irish literature—Women authors—History and criticism. | Women and literature—Ireland—History.
Classification: LCC PR8733 .H57 2018 | DDC 820.9/928709417—dc23
LC record available at https://lccn.loc.gov/2018009843

ISBN 978-1-107-13110-1 Hardback

Contents

Notes on Contributors

Susan Cahill is Associate Professor in the School of Irish Studies, Concordia University, Montreal. She is Visiting Research Fellow in the Institute of English Studies, School of Advanced Study, University of London for the academic year 2017–18. Her monograph, *Irish Literature in the Celtic Tiger Years: Gender, Bodies, Memory*, was published in 2011. She has also published two collections of essays on contemporary Irish writers: Anne Enright (edited with Claire Bracken) and Colum McCann (edited with Eoin Flannery). Her research interests include Irish girls' literary cultures, children's and young adults' fiction and contemporary Irish literature, particularly women's writing.

Matthew Campbell is Professor of Modern Literature at the University of York. He is the author of *Irish Poetry under the Union, 1801–1924* (Cambridge, 2013). He has written and published widely on Irish and English poetry of the last 200 years. He is currently editing the volume *Irish Literature in Transition, 1830–1880* for Cambridge University Press.

Valerie Coghlan is an independent researcher and lecturer with a particular interest in Irish children's literature and visual narratives. She has published widely in these areas and is co-editor of *Irish Children's Literature and Culture: New Perspectives on Contemporary Writing* (2011). A former editor of *Inis* magazine and *Bookbird: A Journal of International Children's Literature*, she is the current president of the board of Bookbird, Inc.

Lucy Collins is Associate Professor of English at University College Dublin. Educated at Trinity College Dublin and at Harvard University, where she spent a year as a Fulbright Scholar, she teaches and researches in the area of modern poetry and poetics. Recent books include *Poetry by Women in Ireland: A Critical Anthology 1870–1970* (2012) and a monograph, *Contemporary Irish Women Poets: Memory and Estrangement* (2015). She has published widely on contemporary poets from Ireland, Britain and America, and is co-founder of the Irish Poetry Reading Archive, a national digital repository.

Marie-Louise Coolahan is Professor of English at the National University of Ireland, Galway. She is the author of *Women, Writing, and Language in Early Modern Ireland* (2010), as well as articles and essays about Renaissance manuscript culture, women's writing, early modern identity and textual transmission. She is currently Principal Investigator of the ERC-funded project, *RECIRC: The Reception and Circulation of Early Modern Women's Writing, 1550–1700* (www.recirc.nuigalway.ie). She has recently co-edited two special issues of the journal *Women's Writing* ('Katherine Philips and Other Writers' 2016; 'Katherine Philips: Form and Reception' 2017) with Gillian Wright.

Patricia Coughlan is Emerita Professor, School of English, University College Cork. Her publications include the edited or co-edited books *Spenser and Ireland* (1990), *Modernism and Ireland: The Poetry of the 1930s* (1995) and *Irish Literature: Feminist Perspectives* (2008) and essays on early modern writing (about Ireland). She specializes in Irish poetry and fiction, with a focus on Irish modernism and on gender representations in recent and contemporary writing. Topics include Elizabeth Bowen, Kate and Edna O'Brien, John Banville, Alice McDermott, Anne Enright, Eiléan Chuilleanáin, Seamus Heaney, John Montague and Peig Sayers. She has been a Fulbright Scholar at Fordham and O'Brien Professor of Irish Studies, Concordia University, Montreal.

Anne Fogarty is Professor of James Joyce Studies at University College Dublin, co-editor with Luca Crispi of the *Dublin James Joyce Journal* and Director of the Dublin James Joyce Summer School. She is co-editor with Timothy Martin of *Joyce on the Threshold* (2005), with Morris Beja of *Bloomsday 100: Essays on 'Ulysses'* (2009), with Éilís Ní Dhuibhne and Eibhear Walshe of *Imagination in the Classroom: Teaching and Learning Creative Writing in Ireland* (2013) and with Fran O'Rourke of *Voices on Joyce* (2015). A collection of essays on the novelist, Deirdre Madden, co-edited with Marisol Morales Ládron, is forthcoming. She has published widely on aspects of twentieth-century and contemporary Irish writing.

Patricia Boyle Haberstroh is Emerita Professor of English and of Art History at La Salle University, Philadelphia. She has published two books, *Women Creating Women: Contemporary Irish Women Poets* (1996), recognized by a Choice Award from the American Library Association, and *The Female Figure in Eiléan Ní Chuilleanáin's Poetry* (2013). She has also edited two volumes, *My Self, My Muse: Irish Women Poets Reflect on Life and Art* (2001), and (with Christine St Peter) *Opening the Field: Irish Women Writers, Texts and Contexts* (2007). Haberstroh has been a Fulbright Fellow at University College Dublin, an advisory editor on *Eire-Ireland* and *New Hibernia Review* and a board member of the American Conference for Irish Studies. She holds an MA from Villanova University and a PhD from Bryn Mawr.

Heather Ingman is Visiting Research Fellow in the Centre for Gender and Women's Studies in Trinity College, the University of Dublin where she was previously Adjunct Professor in the School of English, teaching courses on modernist women's fiction, twentieth-century women's writing and Irish women's writing. Her publications include *Irish Women's Fiction from Edgeworth to Enright* (2013), *A History of the Irish Short Story* (Cambridge, 2009), *Twentieth-Century Fiction by Irish Women: Nation and Gender* (2007) and *Women's Fiction Between the Wars: Mothers, Daughters and Writing* (1998). She has chapters in edited collections on Mary Lavin, Virginia Woolf and Elizabeth Bowen. She is currently researching ageing in Irish writing.

James Kelly is a lecturer at the University of Exeter, Cornwall campus. He is the author of *Charles Maturin: Authorship, Authenticity and the Nation* (2011) and editor of *Ireland and Romanticism: Publics, Nations, and Scenes of Cultural Production* (2011). He has published a number of articles on Irish Romanticism and writing in the post-Union period.

Cathy Leeney has lectured in Drama Studies at University College Dublin and co-founded the first MA in Directing in Ireland, now the MA in Theatre Practice. Her research interests are women in Irish theatre, scenography and directing, and feminist and gender theory and performance. She was Chair of the committee that initiated Ireland's first national entry, in 2007, in the Prague Quadrennial Exhibition of Theatre Scenography. Her publications include *Irish Women Playwrights 1900–1939* (2010), *Seen and Heard: Six New Plays by Irish Women* (2001), *The Theatre of Marina Carr* (2003) and articles on Irish theatre in the twentieth and twenty-first centuries.

Caroline Magennis is a lecturer in Twentieth and Twenty-First Century Literature at the University of Salford. She has held research and teaching positions at University College Dublin, the University of Limerick and

Queen's University, Belfast, where she gained her PhD. She sits on the executive boards for the British Association for Irish Studies, the British Association for Contemporary Literary Studies, EFACIS and the editorial board for the *Irish Studies Review*. She has published widely on theoretical approaches to Contemporary Northern Irish Literature and Culture and is currently organizing an international conference and special issue on the cultural legacy of the Good Friday Agreement.

Ellen McWilliams is Senior Lecturer in English Literature at the University of Exeter and has published on Irish, Canadian and American writing. She is the author of *Margaret Atwood and the Female Bildungsroman* (2009) and *Women and Exile in Contemporary Irish Fiction* (2013) and has received a number of awards for research, including an Arts and Humanities Research Council Fellowship and a Fulbright Scholar Award.

Gerardine Meaney is Professor of Cultural Theory and Director of the UCD Centre for Cultural Analytics. She is the author of *Gender, Ireland and Cultural Change* (2010), *Nora* (2004), *(Un)like Subjects: Women, Theory, Fiction* (1993, 2012) and numerous essays on gender and culture. She co-wrote *Reading the Irish Woman: Studies in Cultural Encounters and Exchange, 1714–1960* (2013) with Mary O'Dowd and Bernadette Whelan. She was one of the major co-editors of the *Field Day Anthology of Irish Writing: Women's Writing and Traditions* (2002).

Sinéad Mooney is a senior lecturer in English at De Montfort University, Leicester. She researches on modernism, particularly the work of Samuel Beckett, women's writing and Irish literature, and is currently working on a monograph on Irish women's modernism. Her publications include *A Tongue Not Mine: Beckett and Translation* (2011), which was completed on an Irish Research Council for the Humanities and Social Sciences fellowship and won the American Conference for Irish Studies Robert Rhodes Prize, essays on Elizabeth Bowen, Molly Keane, Mary Lavin and *Waiting for Godot*, and, as editor, with Kathryn Laing and Maureen O'Connor, *Edna O'Brien: New Critical Perspectives* (2006).

Anne Mulhall is a lecturer in the School of English, Drama and Film at University College Dublin, where she teaches and researches in gender, feminist and sexuality studies, twentieth-century and contemporary Irish writing and popular culture and critical migration studies. She is co-director with Ursula Barry of UCD Centre for Gender, Feminisms and Sexualities.

James H. Murphy is Professor of English and Director of the Center for Irish Programs at Boston College. He was previously Professor of English at DePaul University, Chicago. He is the author of five monographs, including *Irish Novelists and the Victorian Age* (2011), and the editor of nine volumes, including the nineteenth-century volume of the *Oxford History of the Irish Book* (2011).

Ríona Nic Congáil is a lecturer in the Irish language in Fiontar and Scoil na Gaeilge, Dublin City University. She has written many essays on aspects of Irish childhood and on the Irish-language revivalist period. Her books include *Úna Ní Fhaircheallaigh agus an Fhís Útóipeach Ghaelach* (2010), *Codladh Céad Bliain: Cnuasach Aistí ar Litríocht na nÓg* (ed.) (2012), *Laethanta Gréine & Oícheanta Sí: Aistí ar Litríocht agus ar Chultúr na nÓg* (co-ed.) (2013), *Litríocht na Gaeilge ar Fud an Domhain, Imleabhar I & II* (co-ed.) (2015), and two new editions of An Seabhac's *Jimín Mháire Thaidhg* (ed.) (2016).

Máirín Nic Eoin is Professor Emerita of Irish, Dublin City University. A literary scholar with a particular interest in the sociological and sociolinguistic context of literary production in Irish, her books include *An Litríocht Réigiúnach* (1982), *Eoghan Ó Tuairisc: Beatha agus Saothar* (1988), *B'ait Leo Bean: Gnéithe den Idé-eolaíocht Inscne i dTraidisiún Liteartha na Gaeilge* (1998) and *Trén bhFearann Breac: An Díláithriú Cultúir agus Nualitríocht na Gaeilge* (2005). She has edited and co-edited literary anthologies and essay collections, including *Litríocht na Gaeilge ar Fud an Domhain, Imleabhar I & II* (2015).

Clíona Ó Gallchoir is a lecturer in the School of English at University College Cork. Her research focuses on Irish writing in the long eighteenth century, women's writing and children's literature. Her publications include *Maria Edgeworth: Women, Enlightenment and Nation* (2005) and numerous articles and book chapters on figures such as Sydney Owenson, Germaine de Stael and Harriet Beecher Stowe. She is currently the literature editor of the journal *Eighteenth-Century Ireland*.

Tina O'Toole is a senior lecturer and programme director of the MA in English at the University of Limerick, Ireland. Her publications include *The Irish New Woman* (2012); a study of the second-wave Irish Women's Movement, *Documenting Irish Feminisms* (co-authored with

Linda Connolly); and several edited books including the recent *Women Writing War: Ireland 1880–1922* (2016; co-edited with Gillian McIntosh and Muireann O'Cinnéide). Her journal publications include essays in *Modernism/Modernity, Irish University Review* and *New Hibernia Review*, and she has edited journal special issues including *Éire-Ireland* (Vol. 47) on 'Irish Migrancies' (2012; with Piaras Mac Éinrí).

Paige Reynolds is Professor of English at the College of the Holy Cross in Worcester, Massachusetts. She is author of *Modernism, Drama, and the Audience for Irish Spectacle* (Cambridge, 2007) and editor of *Modernist Afterlives in Irish Literature and Culture* (2016). Her work has appeared in *Modernism/Modernity* and *Modern Drama*, among other publications, and she has edited special issues of *Éire-Ireland* on material culture (2011) and *Irish University Review* on Kate O'Brien (2018). She is completing a monograph on contemporary Irish women's writing and editing two forthcoming collections for Cambridge University Press, *The New Irish Studies: Twenty-First Century Critical Revisions* and (with Eric Falci) the sixth volume (1980–2020) of the *Irish Literature in Transition* series.

Eibhear Walshe is a senior lecturer in the School of English at University College Cork and Director of Creative Writing. He has published in the area of memoir, literary criticism and biography, and his books include *Kate O'Brien: A Writing Life* (2006), *Oscar's Shadow: Wilde and Ireland* (2012) and *A Different Story: The Writings of Colm Tóibín* (2013). His childhood memoir, *Cissie's Abattoir* (2009), was broadcast on the national radio station RTE's Book on One and his novel, *The Diary of Mary Travers*, was shortlisted for the Kerry Fiction Prize in 2015.

Introduction

Heather Ingman and Clíona Ó Gallchoir

This volume represents the first comprehensive overview of Irish women's literary and cultural production from the early modern period to the present day. Its appearance is timely, in that there is now a solid foundation of research on women's writings across this historical period and a significant number of scholars and critics are working in the field, but it is also undoubtedly belated when considered in relation to the development of feminist literary criticism and feminist literary history in both Britain and America. The reasons for the comparatively slow acknowledgment of the value and importance of women's writing in the Irish context are complex but also instructive, in that an analysis of inhibiting factors has to a degree helped to shape the critical methods and approaches used by scholars of Irish women's writing. In turn, the perspectives and insights produced by critics in the field of women's writing have contributed to a more critical interrogation of the assumptions that have underpinned constructions of the Irish literary tradition in the post-Revival period. In this introduction, we will firstly consider the specific context in which the writing of this history of modern Irish women's literature has taken shape, before outlining some of the themes and interpretative paradigms that emerge across the different chapters of the volume.

In the preface to the 1994 reissue of B. G. MacCarthy's *The Female Pen: Women Writers and Novelists 1621–1818*, Janet Todd remarks that it has, for scholars of early women's writing, 'the kind of status achieved in feminist theory by Simone de Beauvoir's *The Second Sex* or Virginia Woolf's *A Room of One's Own*'.[1] Its significance for scholars and critics of women's writing in Ireland is much less straightforward. MacCarthy, who was Professor of English at University College Cork, was indeed remarkable in her anticipation of feminist methods and perspectives that did not fully emerge in the academy until several decades later. Her book, however, is notable in its inability to celebrate the achievements of Irish women writers. She engages in a pioneering act of what would later be termed

I

feminist recovery, tracing a female tradition that links writers such as Mary Davys, Frances Sheridan, Elizabeth Griffith and Maria Edgeworth – but the fact that all of these women were Irish either by birth or upbringing is never mentioned; their work registers as part of a literary history of women's writing, but its Irish context is invisible. The invisibility is all the more remarkable given MacCarthy's own cultural location and suggests a powerful occlusion of women's role in literary production in Ireland. Some fifty years later, with the publication the *Field Day Anthology*, a landmark in Irish literary studies, Irish women writers were marginalized in a different way, by dramatic under-representation in a work that had set out to redraw the map of Irish literary culture. The apparently unconscious omission was all the more striking, given the anthology's aim of accommodating 'micronarratives', its pioneering coverage of a long historical time span and its inclusion of works in Latin, Irish and English.

The *Field Day* controversy was in many ways indicative of the progress that had been made in the project of recovering women writers excluded from the Irish literary canon. Ann Owens Weekes's groundbreaking study of six writers, *Irish Women Writers: An Uncharted Tradition*, had appeared the year before, in 1990, and the disappointment of many with the anthology stemmed from the fact that it 'coincided with a perceived flowering of women's writing, political activism and feminist scholarship in Ireland'.[2] The controversy was also a significant catalyst for research on women's writing, culminating notably in the publication in 2002 of the 'supplementary' volumes four and five, charting 'women's writing and traditions'. The sheer quantity of material contained in these volumes generated a mixed reception, with some criticizing what they deemed to be an undiscriminating approach and a disregard for aesthetic criteria; the amount of material made available also created something of a lag in terms of its reception. But the impact of *Field Day IV & V* has, with the passage of time, become increasingly significant, as can be seen throughout the chapters of this history, and it has the potential to grow still further when the digitization of all five volumes is completed. The ten years that separated the first three volumes of *Field Day* from its later companion volumes witnessed other significant publications, including *Unveiling Treasures: The Attic Guide to Published Works of Irish Women Literary Writers*, edited by Ann Owens Weekes (1993); Patricia Boyle Haberstroh's *Women Creating Women: Contemporary Irish Women Poets* (1996); Christine St Peter's, *Changing Ireland: Strategies in Contemporary Women's Fiction* (2000); and *Border Crossings: Irish Women Writers and National Identities* (2000), edited by Kathryn Kirkpatrick.

Scholarly output in the field has grown significantly in the twenty-first century, and shows no sign of slowing down. We have seen valuable bibliographical and biographical resources, such as the joint University College Dublin and University of Warwick 'Database of Irish Women's Writing, 1800–2005' together with the *Dictionary of Munster Women Writers 1800–2000* (2005) and *Irish Women Writers: An A to Z Guide* edited by A. G. Gonzalez (2006), as well as anthologies including *The Wake Forest Book of Irish Women's Poetry: 1965–2000* edited by Peggy O'Brien (2011) and *Poetry by Women in Ireland, 1870–1970* edited by Lucy Collins (2012). Book-length studies devoted to different aspects of Irish women's writing include Rebecca Pelan's *Two Irelands: Literary Feminisms North and South* (2005), Heather Ingman's *Twentieth-Century Fiction by Irish Women: Nation and Gender* (2007), Cathy Leeney's *Irish Women Playwrights 1900–30* (2010) and Elke D'hoker's *Irish Women Writers and the Modern Short Story* (2016). Edited collections include Patricia Boyle Haberstroh and Christine St Peter's *Opening the Field. Irish Women: Texts and Contexts* (2007), Patricia Coughlan and Tina O'Toole's *Irish Literature: Feminist Perspectives* (2008), Heidi Hansson's *New Contexts: Re-Framing Nineteenth-Century Irish Women's Prose* (2008) and Elke D'hoker, Raphaël Ingelbien and Hedwig Schwall's *Irish Women Writers: New Critical Perspectives* (2011). Recent years have seen publication of collections of critical essays on writers such as Elizabeth Bowen, Kate O'Brien, Mary Lavin, Edna O'Brien, Molly Keane, Eavan Boland, Éilís Ní Dhuibhne and Anne Enright, as well as studies of individual writers such as Maria Edgeworth (Clíona Ó Gallchoir), Emily Lawless (Heidi Hansson) and Rosamond Jacob (Leeann Lane).

The appearance of such a significant amount of scholarship (of which these titles give only an indicative snapshot) does not in itself mean that the frameworks that led to the erasure of women's writing within the Irish literary canon have disappeared. The root of the issue lies in the concept of the canon itself. One of the chief insights of Anglophone feminist criticism since the 1970s has been the ways in which the construction of literary canons tends almost inevitably to marginalize and exclude women's writing, usually on the grounds of inferior aesthetic quality. Although similar structures can be observed in the Irish case, the desire to align literary expression with the imagined nation has been a further, persistent obstacle to the recognition of women's literary and cultural production in Ireland. Demands for women's rights have often been seen as either in competition with, or even incompatible with, the imperative of national self-determination that dominated Irish political and intellectual life from the late 1800s,[3] and the privileging of the national was reflected in the construction of a 'literary tradition' that could not encompass voices that either challenged the national narrative, or whose primary focus simply lay elsewhere.

The project of writing a history of modern Irish women's literature at this moment in time has however been enabled not only by the achievements of scholars working on women's writing and feminist criticism, but also by a marked shift within Irish literary historiography more generally. In 2006, the editors of the *Cambridge History of Irish Literature*, Margaret Kelleher and Philip O'Leary, in explicit response to the combined achievement of the five-volume *Field Day Anthology*, proposed a much wider and longer view of Irish writing than had ever been offered before. Taking their starting point from 600 AD, they articulated the aim of the history as a way 'to make sense of that long tradition by providing an authoritative chronological history that will enable readers ... to trace in meaningful detail stylistic and thematic developments and influences through time, or to explore the often neglected interrelationships between the two literary traditions that have shared the island over the past five hundred years'.[4] Although the editors' aim of producing an 'authoritative chronological history' is in many respects conventional, the volumes' embrace of a very long historical timeframe and of both language traditions precludes the reliance on 'the nation' as a central structural or conceptual framework, and thus requires a much more expansive understanding of how writing and literary representation have been produced and received in Ireland, and beyond. Broadly speaking, whereas a carefully and selectively constructed national canon once functioned to cover or mask the fracturing that frequently characterizes the relationship between place and identity in Ireland, contemporary scholarship now actively explores how writing has grown in precisely these cracks and fissures.

The development of these more nuanced, flexible and inclusive frameworks has come about in part as a response to feminist critiques of the hegemonic national narrative, which all too often elevated symbols of femininity while erasing and silencing women's voices, lives and experiences. We are now at a point in time where a fruitful dialogue between feminist literary scholarship and new practices in literary history and literary criticism in Ireland can combine to generate a history of modern Irish women's literature. Critics of women's writing have, for instance, benefited from the insights of book history, especially the renewed attention to the popular and to reading as well as writing; the literature of the diaspora has highlighted another cohort of previously invisible women; research on literary and cultural production in Ireland in earlier periods allows for new considerations of how and why women in particular gained access to writing and publication; attention to women's involvement in both language traditions demonstrates that gendered obstacles to women's cultural expression are a constant, while also challenging simplistic constructions of the 'woman writer'.

The research of the past thirty years has thus made critics and readers aware of the important contribution made by women to Ireland's literary cultures, and also provided new perspectives and frameworks through which to discuss this work. As yet, however, there has been no comprehensive attempt to chart and analyse the history of writing by women in Ireland, or to ask what different stories emerge when gender, as a category, shapes and frames the discussion. In order to address what is by now a glaring absence, the contributions to this collection bring together specialists working on women's writing from the seventeenth to the twenty-first centuries, and include writing in both English and Irish. The policy of 'generous inclusion' adopted by the editors of the *Cambridge History of Irish Literature* in relation to the term 'Irish writer' has also been adhered to here, so that in these pages you will find writers who were born in Ireland and those who lived for significant periods of time in Ireland, including women who are part of the increasing immigrant population in Ireland today. The definition used in this volume is in fact even more broadly inclusive, in that it incorporates writers who form part of diaspora communities in Britain and America.

The volume opens with Marie-Louise Coolahan's account of women's writing and literary production in the early modern period, a contribution that is in many ways paradigmatic of how new approaches to women's writing and Irish literary history can illuminate and inform one another. Coolahan outlines the different contexts and purposes of women's writing in different language communities and from different religious backgrounds. With the country's power structures in flux, women from different communities in Ireland wrote for both communal and personal ends. They wrote in Irish, Latin and English, from within both the Old English community and the New English colonial settler class. They composed Irish-language verse, drawing on the native oral tradition, autobiographical narratives, official documents, correspondence, devotional poetry, courtly poetry, religious texts and many other forms. These women were important precursors, contributing to the shaping of genres and carving out new possibilities for female authorship. Coolahan suggests that much material from this earlier period remains to be uncovered, particularly in the genres of letters and life writing.

Beginning the history of women's literature in Ireland in the early modern period highlights the fact that women's involvement in literary culture predates the emergence of the idea of the nation state. This offers an essential grounding for the chapters that follow, in which the expanding range of women's writing took place against a backdrop of successive alterations in Ireland's political status: the 'territory' to which writers related changed profoundly across the eighteenth, nineteenth and twentieth centuries. Coolahan's survey of women's writerly activity in this period also depicts different language communities operating side-by-side, as well as in interaction and at times in competition with one another. A more complete picture of women's participation in the Irish-language tradition across the entire time span of the volume lies to an extent outside the scope of this *History*, given its central focus on written material. The editors are conscious of the neglect of Irish-language material in the nineteenth century in particular, which in general, as Gearóid Denvir has noted, has suffered from a failure to recognize that it 'emanates from a different conceptual framework and from a different world view to modern concepts of the function and aims of the literary act'.[5] One of the many fascinating insights that emerges from the chapter by Ríona Nic Congáil and Máirín Nic Eoin on women's writing in the Irish language from the period of the language revival up to the present day, is that the language revival movement itself was characterized by unresolved tensions over the superior status of modern print culture, coupled with the ideological construction of native speakers, many of whom were illiterate in Irish, as the most authentic sources of Gaelic culture. Prominent Irish-language authors and activists such as Úna Ní Fhaircheallaigh and Máire Ní Chinnéide were highly educated, urban, middle-class women whose sense of affiliation with their female contemporaries in Irish-speaking areas arose from a cultural and political commitment, rather than from meaningful shared experience.

The nuanced picture that emerges from Nic Congáil and Nic Eoin's discussion of women's participation in the language revival movement acts as a vivid example of the fact that nationalism and its centrality to Irish history and culture must be addressed in any history of Irish women's writing, while also exploding the static image of the woman as an icon of national identity. This iconic figure was, in the twentieth century, the focus of much early feminist critique, notably in Eavan Boland's *Object Lessons*, as an obstacle both to the recognition of women as writers and to the representation of lived female experience. But it is vital to recognize that nationalism also facilitated women who wished to write. In the 1780s, writers like Charlotte Brooke and Elizabeth Sheridan explicitly articulated patriot views and aligned themselves as women with the fate of Ireland as a nation while in the nineteenth century, authors such as 'Eva of the Nation' were celebrated for making important contributions to nationalist literature in characteristic genres such as the ballad. In the post-Union period, romantic nationalism was a theme that inspired many women writers, the most celebrated of whom was Sydney Owenson. Other Irish women had solid ties to the British empire, as travellers and settlers in the colonies, as wives and daughters of imperial administrators, as missionaries and social reformers and as members of the increasingly displaced Protestant Ascendancy. Some, like Augusta Gregory, moved between Ascendancy circles and close engagement with the nationalist ideals of the Irish Literary Revival. The intersection between nationalism and women's writing is multilayered, and care must be taken not to distort the politics of the work that is being recovered.

Engagement with the concept of the nation provided some women with a vantage point from which to write, but it is only one strand in a wider movement that sees the legitimization of Irish women's voices in public discourse. In contrast to the turbulence of the seventeenth century, Ireland in the eighteenth century experienced a long period of relative stability. As Clíona Ó Gallchoir shows in Chapter 2, this stability, coupled with the growth of print media that characterized the period in Britain as well as Ireland, and the gradual development of a patriot consciousness among the Anglo-Irish in Ireland, were all factors in the emergence of women not only writing but publishing their work, even if to do so required the negotiation of gender-based objections. The traditional historiography of eighteenth-century Ireland constructs the end of the century as an abrupt termination, with the Act of Union following the failed United Irish uprising. But as James Kelly demonstrates in Chapter 3, devoted to literature under the Union, the story of women's involvement in literary culture is in fact one of continuity and growth. In response to the huge structural changes wrought to Irish political, cultural and social life post-1801 and despite limitations on female agency, Maria Edgeworth, Sydney Owenson and their contemporaries created a body of work that explored the links between female influence, national identity and political involvement and in the process gave women a public voice. A salient feature of their work was the national tale in which the marriage of an English lord to an exotic, though ultimately subordinate, Irish woman took on an allegorical dimension in the aftermath of the 1801 marriage / union between Britain and Ireland. In Chapter 5,

James Murphy discusses Victorian Irish women novelists' refashioning
of this trope of the 'national marriage' into the trope of 'the independent
woman' who is nationally representative. Murphy sees in this the beginnings of New Woman themes, the focus of the following chapter by Tina
O'Toole.

The reader thus begins to discern the emerging acceptance of Irish
women's writing and an acknowledgement of the wish of women writers to enter public discourse; yet it is important not to erase differences.
In Chapter 6, O'Toole stresses that New Woman was not a homogenous
category: coming from a variety of backgrounds, New Woman writers
adopted differing stances on class, politics and even gender. Nevertheless,
common to most New Woman fiction is a central character who, having had her consciousness raised by contact with feminist ideas, feels
sufficiently confident to fight for her rights. O'Toole argues that New
Woman writers mount a challenge in their fiction equal to that posed by
campaigners for women's suffrage.

A volume such as this enables us to trace the gradual development of
women's public voice from official documents, devotional poetry, ballads, autobiographical narratives, from the period before 1700, through
post-Union writers' defiance of limits on femininity in order to enter
the public arena of debate around nation and gender, and Victorian
women novelists' development of this voice, to the newly empowered,
educated and politically active women of New Woman fiction. Yet what
these women writers were saying was often obscured by critical reaction
to their work based on stereotypes about women, Ireland and the Irish
canon, and this holds good for later periods too, notably in the case of
a writer like Edna O'Brien, as Sinéad Mooney highlights in Chapter 13.
In the area of life writing, discussed by Anne Mulhall in Chapter 20,
women have had to battle not only against economic, social and legal
subordination in order to make their voices heard but also against
well-intentioned, though often patronizing, attempts by feminists and
others to appropriate their experiences in order to promote a particular
political agenda. Migrant women in particular have had difficulty being
accepted as part of the literary and cultural community. Women in the
theatre, however, as dramatists, directors, performers and producers, had
the potential to, and often did, assert a public presence with the aim of
changing national, civic and cultural discourses, as Cathy Leeney demonstrates in Chapter 17.

A comprehensive history also allows us to discern certain patterns and
themes in Irish women's writing across the centuries. A single example

may be taken to illustrate this, namely the issues of female sexuality and the body that came to prominence in New Woman writing as a way of expressing women's lived experience. Despite her Catholic upbringing and education, George Egerton was determined to use her writing to portray the hitherto unexplored realm of female sexuality and women's erotic lives, tackling such themes as miscarriage, abortion, post-natal depression and infanticide. Not surprisingly her work fell into neglect in later years when the intertwining of Catholicism and nationalism in the newly independent Ireland produced a homogeneous nation state founded on gender distinctions. Irish men were expected to, and often did, fight for their country while Irish women, with the example of the Virgin Mary set before them, were to embody the purity of the Irish nation: 'The personification of Ireland as "Woman" and "mother" necessitated that the purity of that image was maintained on all levels.'[6]

We have to leap over the decades to the 1960s to find another Irish woman, Edna O'Brien, prepared to tackle the topic of female sexuality with similar frankness. In Chapter 13, Sinéad Mooney explores O'Brien's pioneering themes around women's sexuality and women's bodies, and her political critique of the cultural and religious restrictions on Irish women's lives. In Chapter 12, Eibhear Walshe's highlighting of Kate O'Brien's more veiled depictions of lesbian love, adds another dimension to this theme, as do Mary Lavin's short stories, discussed in Chapter 15. Lavin's stories broke new ground in the Irish short story tradition by dealing with themes such as female sexuality, illegitimacy and the repression of the female body that would be taken up by women writers from the 1970s onwards, a point emphasized both by Patricia Boyle Haberstroh in her chapter on women's poetry and by Anne Fogarty writing on fiction in the period between 1960 and 1995, and extending even into fiction of the Celtic Tiger era, discussed in the final chapter of this volume. Irish women's lack of agency over their bodies and their experiences of various forms of abuse, including institutional abuse, are major themes in their life writing from the 1970s onwards, explored by Anne Mulhall in Chapter 20.

In Chapter 19, Caroline Magennis argues that embodiment is also a feature of Northern Irish women's writing, along with other themes such as domestic confinement, mental illness, discontented motherhood, the unreliability of memory and distrust of patriarchal institutions. Women's fiction from Northern Ireland, Magennis argues, complicates straightforward narratives of sectarian conflict by this focus on gender, class and embodiment. In the theatre too, women writers, directors and performers have often placed the emphasis on the female body, as for example, in Anne Le Marquand Hartigan's *Beds* produced at the Dublin Theatre Festival in 1982 where, as Cathy Leeney describes it, scenes of birth, sex, love and death were represented, including an account of a woman's experience of abortion. Such representations of the body, Leeney argues, disrupted both gender and literary expectations. Leeney's chapter also discusses a group of plays (*On Trial* by Máiréad Ní Ghráda, *Eclipsed* by Patricia Burke Brogan and *Laundry*, created by Anú Productions) that deliberately set out to challenge public discourse around maternity and female sexuality. Ní Ghráda's play, one of the earliest works to explore the treatment meted out to women who fell foul of the rigid and oppressive sexual morality of the Irish state, was in fact first performed in Irish as *An Triail*, illustrating that, as Nic Congáil and Nic Eoin point out in Chapter 18, women's writing in Irish similarly gives voice to women's bodily and lived experience, as is clearly instanced also in the work of poets such as Máire Mhac an tSaoi and Nuala Ní Dhomhnaill. This cluster of writing in different genres and from different periods allows us to identify, without erasing difference, specific themes concerning the body and female sexuality associated with Irish women's writing. It would be possible to perform a similar task across the centuries with themes such as motherhood, the dysfunctional family, the female artist, the nation, travel and female emigration.

Although some of the writers and works discussed in the following chapters are well known, many more are not. In addition to offering the possibility of creating new narratives and asking new questions, the *History* therefore also offers an opportunity to reflect on and understand the varying reasons why so many works by women were forgotten, ignored or dismissed. In Chapter 4, for instance, Matthew Campbell uncovers a rich corpus of women's poetry published between 1845 and 1891 but which subsequently disappeared from the Irish canon partly, he suggests, because in their elegiac poems for the famine dead or the sorrows of exile, and, in their confessional poems expressing anguished conflicts of faith, women writers adopted a gendered subjectivity that in subsequent generations was all too easy to ignore. More generally, one possible reason for this erasure may be that women writers did not always confine themselves to recognizably Irish themes. In Chapter 5, James Murphy points out that Irish Victorian writers, like twenty-first century Irish writers, worked in both national and transnational contexts. In Chapter 6, Tina O'Toole stresses that New Woman writers frequently looked outside Ireland for literary models and topics and for this reason their work was considered insufficiently Irish to be discussed in the context of the Irish canon.

Then there is the question of audience. In the nineteenth century, in common with Irish male authors, large numbers of women migrated to London with its wider publishing opportunities, and wrote for an English readership. In a period notable for the rise of the professional woman writer earning her living by her writing, there developed a particular and damaging association between women writers and commercialism. Murphy sees these middle-class Victorian professional writers as caught between Irishness and Britishness at a time when the literary world still centred on London. Despite this, they demonstrated a willingness to tackle traditional Irish themes such as the land wars and the famine from a point of view that is inflected by gender.

Another factor in the neglect of women's writing has been the centrality of the Irish Revival to the canon. This not only had the effect of marginalizing whatever work, such as the Victorian novel or New Woman writing, that did not fit into the Revivalist imperative of establishing a distinct Irish national identity, but also distorted understanding of women's writing. In her discussion of the prose, drama and poetry written between the *fin de siècle* and 1920, Paige Reynolds argues that women writers' conservatism during this period was partly a reflection of the proscribed roles and limited opportunities available to women who wrote under the shadow of the Literary Revival with its problematic allegorizing of woman and nation and its idealization of self-sacrificing womanhood. Augusta Gregory's willingness to efface her own abilities in favour of foregrounding male achievement is one example of this reflection of societal values. Yet what has been ignored, Reynolds argues, is that even when they were drawing on Revivalist topics writers like Gregory, Eva Gore-Booth, Emily Lawless, Susan Mitchell and Katharine Tynan subtly revised conventional themes and tropes:

> They upheld contemporaneous cultural norms, depicting traditional gender roles and promoting the Revival's imperative that women preserve and transmit national ideals. But they also questioned dominant values and recalibrated limiting tropes, seeking in their writing to advance progressive notions of religion, class, gender, and community in the incipient Irish nation (p. 132).

Their subject matter engaged with multiple different *fin de siècle* discourses including first-wave feminism, anti-imperialism, pacifism and other radical transnational movements that did not fit into the Revival's assumption of Irish exceptionality.[7] The number and diversity of novels, short stories, memoirs and sketches published during these decades leads to a richer understanding of the period's literature and, as Reynolds argues, reveals how interpretations of the Revival based on the forms and topics advocated by Yeats misrepresents the actual breadth of the movement.

The crucial example of the Revival illustrates how often critical opinion on Irish writing has been formed by male critics, scholars and writers. To take another example: the Irish short story has always been central to the Irish canon but critical attitudes towards it were shaped, mid-twentieth century, by Frank O'Connor, a writer notoriously dismissive of women's contribution to the genre. In Chapter 15, Heather Ingman explores the question of why, despite women writers' prominence in the short story from the outset, their presence has until recently been overlooked. Discussing a range of writers from Maria Edgeworth to Claire Keegan, Ingman asks the question whether giving equal weight to women writers modifies our view of the short story itself.

Frank O'Connor was writing at a time when the interaction of patriarchal, Catholic and inherited imperialist values had resulted in a postcolonial culture in Ireland, in the words of Tina O'Toole in this volume, 'characterized by the regulation of sexuality and reproduction, and the concomitant institutionalization of motherhood as women's principal role' (p. 127). Women writers' struggle to maintain creative momentum in the face of critical indifference, or even hostility, is clearly seen in Lucy Collins's discussion of women's poetry. As Collins observes, mid-twentieth-century Irish literary culture was overwhelmingly masculine in character: male writers, editors and journalists dominated debates, both in conversation and in print, and few concerned themselves about the contribution that women might make to the future of Irish letters. In her study of five neglected poets from this period, Collins argues that though these writers were willing to experiment with form and each pursued their unique creative vision despite an environment inhospitable to women's writing in general and poetry in particular, their poetry reveals their anxieties concerning their role as artists and their struggle to hold onto their creative self. In Collins's view, the absence of this generation of women poets from later anthologies has distorted the history, not only of Irish women's writing, but also of modern Irish poetry itself. Their example would certainly have been helpful to the pioneering 1970s generation of women poets, of whom the most notable were Eavan Boland, Eiléan Ní Chuilleanáin and Medbh McGuckian, discussed by Patricia Boyle Haberstroh in Chapter 16. In their search to counteract conventional images by expressing the felt realities of women's lives, these poets found themselves hampered, not only by restrictive views of women imposed by church and state but also by the lack of a strong female tradition in the Irish poetic canon.

Similarly Irish women novelists in the period 1922–60, discussed by Gerardine Meaney in Chapter 10, were largely forgotten by the time feminist criticism emerged in the 1970s, a neglect that has persisted, Meaney argues, into the digital age. She points out that despite the extraordinary range and diversity of these novelists' work, the reissue of their fiction is largely piecemeal, depending on current preoccupations and the particular interests of publishers. In their own time, in the face of public indifference or even hostility and state censorship, they gained much support from the Irish Women Writers' Club, which for twenty-five years provided a literary network for women writing in a variety of genres. Nevertheless, as Meaney highlights, many of these writers were obliged to work and publish abroad. Social criticism where it appears in their writing often takes indirect or unexpected forms, in Dorothy Macardle's Gothic fictions, for instance, or in the interiority of the sacrificial mother's narrative in Kathleen Coyle's *A Flock of Birds*.

In the case of Elizabeth Bowen, as Patricia Coughlan argues in Chapter 11, gender, class, ethnicity and geography combined until the 1980s to marginalize a writer now recognized as one of the finest novelists of the twentieth century. Male-centred definitions of modernism, her perceived lack of 'Irishness' and limiting literary categories (novelist of manners, Big House author) all contributed to downplay Bowen's reputation. The development of feminist theory in the 1970s began the work of reclaiming her writing. In the same decade the establishment of feminist publishing houses in Ireland focused interest on Irish women poets, discussed by Patricia Boyle Haberstroh, and encouraged more explicitly feminist themes in fiction writing from the 1960s onwards, surveyed by Anne Fogarty in Chapter 14.

Cultural difficulties around sexuality also contributed to the neglect of earlier women writers. We have already seen this to be a factor in the case of New Woman writers whose work was all but forgotten during the more repressive years of the new Irish state. In Chapter 12, Eibhear Walshe argues that prejudices around sexuality were part of the reason for the marginalization of Kate O'Brien's work. Walshe regards O'Brien as a figure difficult to categorize, being radical in some respects, for example, in her depiction of gender and sexuality, and conservative in others (her employment of realist narrative forms), with the result that she has been, he argues, a significant, but never straightforward, pioneer for Irish women's writing. Walshe defends the centrality of O'Brien's work in the canon of twentieth-century Irish fiction, seeing her as an enabling voice for the Irish Catholic middle class, despite often being at odds with the dominant political culture of the time. In Chapter 13, Sinéad Mooney argues that a similar gendered prejudice operated until recently in the assessment of Edna O'Brien, obscuring not only the radical nature of her exploration of female sexuality and the body but also the political critique and formal experimentation of her work. The commercial popularity of their fiction also influenced the uncertain literary status of both these writers until recently, while censorship impacted on their careers in different ways.

Reading through the chapters in this volume and their work of recuperation, it becomes apparent that anything that did not fit the narrative of the Irish nation as embodied in the Irish canon was liable to be erased. In Chapter 21, Ellen McWilliams notes that the historical silence around Irish emigration and the lives of women migrants is all the more astonishing given the high numbers of female emigrants from Ireland. She argues that the development of studies on transnationalism and diasporic writing in recent years has expanded not only our understanding of the Irish canon but also particularly of women's writing. A more outward-looking Irish canon will benefit women writers who from the beginning, as this history demonstrates, have exhibited a tendency to work across national boundaries.

Women writers also often work across literary boundaries. Several of our authors appear in different chapters, underlining the range and variety of their work. Maria Edgeworth, for instance, features in chapters concerning literature under the Union, short stories and children's writing, while Edna O'Brien, as well as having a dedicated chapter, is discussed in the context of theatre, short stories, emigrant writing and Celtic Tiger fiction, and Éilís Ní Dhuibhne appears not only under the heading of Celtic Tiger fiction but also in chapters dealing with the Irish language, drama, the short story and writing for children. Patricia Coughlan outlines the diversity of Elizabeth Bowen's work, ranging across novels, short stories, essays, memoirs, reviews, radio broadcasts and travel-writing, and points out that it was only when this diversity began to be acknowledged that Bowen's reputation broke free from the narrow categories into which her work had previously been corralled, allowing her true originality and disruptiveness to be perceived.

This resistance to conventional literary boundaries may have been a contributing factor in the neglect of women writers. Not only did the range of their writing make them often difficult to pigeonhole, but their willingness to embrace popular genres led to an underestimation of their quality. Writing for children may be a case in point. In Chapter 8, Valerie Coghlan discusses the large numbers of Irish women working as children's writers from as far back as 1794, partly as a consequence of women's involvement with children as mothers, sisters and educators. Defending the quality of this work, Coghlan observes the range and extent of serious social problems explored in contemporary writing for children and teenagers, as well as a willingness to experiment stylistically. In Chapter 22, Susan Cahill argues that in chick lit and crime fiction, two flourishing genres of the Celtic Tiger era in which women writers made a strong showing, there is as much of an engagement with the social and cultural changes of the period as in the more literary and innovative fiction of the period. However, as Anne Mulhall notes, the cultural landscape is itself in the process of changing. Internet and digital technologies provide an audience for those without access to traditional publication routes, while blogs, social media platforms and online forums are democratizing the means for women to record and distribute their life stories and testimony.

Gerardine Meaney has said: 'As women claim and change their role and seek a different identity for themselves as women, they will also change the meaning of national identity ... No longer the territory over which power is exercised, women, in exercising power, may redefine the territory.'[8] This insight is borne out in many of the contributions to this *History*. In her examination of women's fiction from Northern Ireland, Caroline Magennis observes that the usual chronology of Northern Irish history does not easily apply to women's writing and that engagement with this body of fiction diversifies the historical context that has informed traditional readings of Northern Irish history. In Chapter 22, Susan Cahill argues that paying attention to women writers gives us a different view of the Celtic Tiger era as a period when some writers were deeply engaged with contemporary socio-economic and cultural transformations, questioning the narratives of Irish progress prevalent at that time and highlighting darker issues persisting into the present, especially around issues of abortion, child abuse, infanticide, ecology, racism and dysfunctional families. The potential for women to challenge the territory of the state is particularly apparent in Anne Mulhall's discussion of the surge in life writing and personal testimony from the 1970s onwards, in which women spoke of their experiences in state-run orphanages, as members of the travelling community, migrants, single mothers, prostitutes and members of the lesbian, gay, bisexual, transgender and queer (LGBTQ) community. Mulhall's account of the power of these diverse voices, as well as of some of the attempts to mediate and manage them, is a very lucid illustration of the dangers of constructing a homogenous image of the 'Irish woman', with the sometimes violent marginalization of women who do not conform to this model.

The chapters in this history bear out Linda Anderson's claim that: 'Women cannot simply be added on to history ... without putting under pressure the conceptual limits that excluded them in the first place.'[9] We began this introduction with an emphasis on the need for a long historical timeframe in order to overcome the myopia that results from the reliance on a single conceptual or ideological perspective. But it is important to note that this history is the product of its particular moment, one in which Ireland and Britain face another reconfiguration of their political relationship, and in which Europe, also, is experiencing a crisis of self-definition, triggered in part by the perceived challenge of migration. The need for nuanced conceptualizations of how the writer or the text relates to its social and political context, and the resistance to unitary definitions of belonging are, we have seen, essential in order to fully appreciate the meanings and the value of women's writing. These insights may have a wider and more urgent resonance as international political structures are redefined.

The largely forgotten work of Irish women reveals some of the critical fault lines that have contributed to the fractured understanding of women's writing in Ireland. Emphasis on national identity rendered their work problematic for early feminist recovery, while the sometimes popular and collaborative nature of their work meant that it had no lasting place within a canon of Irish literature founded on notions of literary greatness epitomized by the individual literary genius. This understanding of literature is in its principles inhospitable to the concept of collective identity and communal experience on which feminism is usually based. Yet it is also important to acknowledge, as Gerardine Meaney reminds us in this volume, that there are often significant differences of language, ethnic identity and political loyalty between women and therefore celebratory identification cannot underpin feminist criticism in Ireland. There is no single story of Irish women's writing, but many fascinating stories. This volume aims to complicate traditional notions of the Irish literary canon by indicating the range and diversity of women's writing. The history of

Irish women's writing is not always a progressive narrative; it has periods of compromises and ambivalences and, as Cathy Leeney points out, all too often it goes through the cycles of erasure and reinvention identified by Adrienne Rich.[10] We hope this volume, rather than closing down debate, will highlight Irish women's writing as a rich and diverse field that merits further research in many different areas.

Notes

1 Janet Todd, preface to B. G. MacCarthy, *The Female Pen: Women Writers and Novelists 1621–1818* (Cork: Cork University Press, 1994), ix.

2 Angela Bourke et al., preface to *The Field Day Anthology of Irish Writing Vols IV & V: Women's Writing and Traditions*, ed. Angela Bourke et al. (Cork: Cork University Press, 2002), 4: xxxii.

3 See for instance C. L. Innes, *Woman and Nation in Irish Literature and Society, 1880–1935* (Athens, GA: University of Georgia Press, 1993).

4 Margaret Kelleher and Philip O'Leary, 'Introduction', in *The Cambridge History of Irish Literature*, ed. Margaret Kelleher and Philip O'Leary (Cambridge: Cambridge University Press, 2006), 1: 2.

5 Gearóid Denvir, 'Literature in Irish, 1800–1890', in *The Cambridge History of Irish Literature*, ed. Kelleher and O'Leary, 1: 546.

6 David Cairns and Shaun Richards, *Writing Ireland* (Manchester: Manchester University Press, 1988), 77.

7 On this topic of the distortions for Irish literary history of the Revival's emphasis on Irish exceptionality, see John Wilson Foster, *Irish Novels 1890–1940: New Bearings in Culture and Fiction* (Oxford: Oxford University Press, 2008), 1–20.

8 Gerardine Meaney, *Sex and Nation: Women in Irish Culture and Politics* (Dublin: Attic Press, 1991), 22.

9 Linda Anderson, *Plotting Change: Contemporary Women's Fiction* (London: Edward Arnold, 1990), 130.

10 Adrienne Rich, *On Lies, Secrets, and Silence: Selected Prose 1966–1978* (London: Virago, 1980), 11.

CHAPTER I

Writing before 1700

Marie-Louise Coolahan

The broad spectrum of literary composition and writerly activity by women in Ireland before 1700 is characterized by diversity in terms of language, form and function. The oral culture of Gaelic tradition centred on vernacular verse and song; exposure to state bureaucracies cultivated literacy; experiences of displacement generated various forms of auto-biographical narratives; efforts to re-establish convents led to the produc-tion of Catholic religious documents; the arrival of settlers proficient in English manuscript culture introduced new poetic and devotional genres; increased literacy and mobility demanded epistolary skills. What women's writing of this period lacks in terms of quantity, it gains in variety. It is the product of different and sometimes overlapping communities inhab-iting the island: the native, or Gaelic Irish; the Old English, descended from the Normans; and the New English, the colonial settler class that arrived from the sixteenth century. It emerged from distinct inherited and new linguistic and literary traditions. Moreover, scholarly under-standing and recovery of female-authored texts has proliferated over the past twenty years, opening up a rich field that invites further research.

Little women's writing, prior to the early modern period, is known to survive. 'Digde's Lament', more commonly known as 'The Lament of the Old Woman of Beare', composed ca. 900, is the only extant exam-ple of female-authored verse from the Old Irish period. As Máirín Ní Dhonnchadha, whose research in this field has provided a definitive map of the terrain, has shown, there is evidence of other early Mediaeval poets by reputation: Laitheog Laídeach; Líadan, wife of Cuirither; Úallach, daughter of Muimnechán; the unnamed daughter of úa Dulsaine; and Gormlaith.[1] The Classical Irish period (ca. 1200–1600) developed and entrenched a sophisticated literary infrastructure across Ireland and Scotland that mitigated against the scribal preservation of verse by non-elite poets. This was dominated by the male hereditary caste of profes-sional poets, known as *fileadha*, of whom the most exalted was the *ollamh*.

These men trained for years in bardic schools, becoming adept in the forms and rules of literary composition – history and genealogy as well as poetry – which were precise and demanding in their codification of metres and rhyme schemes. They were, perhaps understandably, inhospitable to lower-class, untrained versifiers who composed *amhráin* (popular songs). But their expressions of distaste and contempt for such authors have left us some tantalizing glimpses of female authorship. Giolla na Naomh Ó hUiginn, for example, dismissed collectively 'abhrán ban agus bhachlach' ('the song of women and churls') in the fourteenth century.[2] Feidhlim Mac Dhubhghaill, a sixteenth-century Scottish *fileadh*, suggested that, for him, women were the lowest of the low, spitting: 'fuath liom cliar ara mbí bean' ('I hate a poet-band that includes a woman').[3] Further accounts of women's composition of verse emerged as English settlers began to inhabit the island in the sixteenth century. Women figured as 'mannigscoule' (a phonetic rendering of *mná siubhail*, walking women) in a 1561 account by Thomas Smyth, a Dublin-based English apothecary: 'ther order is for to singe and the chyfest of them most haue but one eye'.[4] A list of poets compiled in Cork in 1584 identified among them one 'Mary-ny-Donoghue, a she-barde; and Mary-ny-Clancy, rymer'.[5]

What survives of such women's verse composition derives from a literary culture that was predominantly oral. Even the elite poetry of the *fileadha*, with its intricate and interlocking structures of rhyme, alliteration, assonance and syllabic metre, was designed for oral performance.[6] We know of only one Irish woman, Brighid Fitzgerald (ca. 1589–1682), *inghean iarla Chille Dara* (daughter of the twelfth earl of Kildare), who composed poetry in the elite style. This poem is in *óglachas*, or amateur syllabic verse – bardic poetry, that is, composed by someone outside the hereditary caste of Gaelic poets. Composed between 1603 and 1607, 'A mhacaoimh dhealbhas an dán' ('O young man who composes the poem') is a riposte to a witty love poem addressed to Brighid, from her husband's ally, Cú Chonnacht Óg Mág Uidhir. This instigator poem was in fact commissioned; its real author was the professional poet, Eochaidh Ó hEodhasa. Brighid's answer poem dismantles her interlocutor's arguments through literary critique. She unmasks the author as a professional who betrays himself through his impeccable skill, unable to impersonate an amateur (such as Mág Uidhir or even herself). Her repudiation hinges on Fitzgerald's own competency in *óglachas* and as an interpreter of bardic verse, and there has been some discussion as to the authenticity of her authorship.[7] But she was not without contemporaries in Scotland, which shared the same literary culture until the Reformation and Stuart dynasty caused the fracturing of Gaelic culture. Four amateur syllabic poems by Aithbhreac inghean Coirceadail and Iseabail Ní Mheic Cailéin augment our picture of women's participation in elite bardic culture.[8] Beyond amateur composition, that participation included patronage, as is evident from the many bardic poems in praise of female patrons.[9] That such traditions of benefaction persisted in the face of apparently opposing political and cultural allegiances is clear from the practices of Donough O'Brien, fourth earl of Thomond, of Gaelic descent although raised a Protestant, and Richard Boyle, first earl of Cork who arrived as a penniless New English settler, both of whom retained bardic poets not-withstanding their military and political support of the English crown. That women of Boyle's class were equally immersed and adaptable is evi-dent from the case of Martha Stafford, who married Sir Henry O'Neill of Clandeboye, and whose English nobility as well as active patronage of the *fileadha* is celebrated in the O'Neill family poem-book.[10]

As the seventeenth century progressed and English power became entrenched, Gaelic literary infrastructures such as the bardic schools became unsustainable. The silver lining, for those interested in non-elite verse, is that understanding of the threat to Gaelic culture provoked a greater concern to preserve more vernacular forms. Moves to preserve non-bardic alongside professional verse in manuscript *duanairí* (antholo-gies or family poem-books) escalated among scribes at the turn of the eighteenth century. Hence, the manuscript preservation of verse by women occurred as the formal structures of elite culture were dissipating – orally transmitted forms such as the *caoineadh* (keen or lament), which were dominated by women, were concertedly recorded. A *caoineadh* was traditionally composed and sung by women in order to lament the dead. Its metrical form is based on accentual sounds that reflected the rhythms of speech rather than syllabic schemes. For this particular form, the rhyme scheme is maintained by the final stressed vowel of each line.

Six *caointe* from the seventeenth century are known to survive, all pre-served in manuscript poem-books (*duanairí*) associated with branches of the O'Brien dynasty of Thomond, county Clare. Five keens attributed to a woman named Caitilín Dubh are copied into *Duanaire Uí Bhriain*, the poem-book commissioned by Sir Donough O'Brien (1642–1717) in 1712. Compiled alongside such celebrated professional verse as the series, *Iomarbhágh na bhFileadh* ('The Contention of the Bards'), Caitilín Dubh's poems elegize one generation of O'Briens: Donnchadh (Donough), fourth earl of Thomond; his sister, Máire, and her husband,

Toirdhealbhach Ruadh Mac Mathghamhna (Turlough Roe MacMahon); and Diarmaid (Dermot), Baron Inchiquin – all of whom died in the 1620s.[11] In these poems, Caitilín Dubh exploits the personae available to her as a woman, incorporating the supernatural figure of the *bean sí* (fairy woman, often phonetically anglicized as banshee) to make literary space for her own voice. Aoibheall, the territorial figure associated with Thomond and the O'Briens' claims to its domain, for example, is encountered bereft in the keen on Diarmaid; this imaginative encounter provokes and licenses the female speaker's lament. These poems are remarkable for their fusion of bardic thematic tropes (genealogy, literary patronage, military heroism) with the prosody and materials of lament. This is most pronounced in her poem on the death of Donough, fourth earl – who was a complicated subject for Gaelic poetry, given his simultaneous military support of crown forces (not least during the notorious siege of Kinsale in 1601) and cultural support of Gaelic poets. Caitilín Dubh squares this circle by framing her subject's military exploits according to traditional bardic paradigms. For example, his command of forces against the Gaelic Irish during the Nine Years' War is cast in the traditional terms of a *caithréim*, or battle-roll. Startling at first glance, the female poet's pragmatic accommodation of her addressee's allegiances and military actions was, in fact, a strategy assayed by a number of her contemporaries, seeking to adapt to new realities. Fionnghuala Ní Bhriain's *caoineadh*, also preserved in a family poem-book, articulates a more personal loss: that of her husband, Uaithne Mór Ó Lochlainn (whose descendant Brian Ó Lochlainn had this *duanaire* compiled in 1727). If Caitilín Dubh's poems are gendered in their evocation and manipulation of female voices, Ní Bhriain's is most overtly gendered in its assertion of the widow's vulnerability. Both petition and lament, this poem sets its mourning of her second husband in tandem with the death of her former protector, the third earl of Thomond, to present an inconsolable isolated speaker.[12]

What survives offers only the outlines of the verse that was authored by Gaelic women. Yet the wide evidence of female patronage, and the single surviving syllabic poem by Brighid Fitzgerald – whose attribution was, at the least, deemed credible at the time – points to women's active participation in contemporary literary culture at elite levels of the court as well as with more popular forms of vernacular composition. Sophisticated engagement with that literary culture, and high levels of literacy, can be seen in the compilation of manuscripts for specific female patrons. A fifteenth-century manuscript version of the prose tale, *Cath Finntrágha* ('The Battle of Ventry') was made for Sadhbh Ní Mháille; devotional works were transcribed in 1513 for Máire Ní Mháille (d. 1522) and a life of St Colum Cille in 1608 for another Ulster woman, Róis Óg Ní Dhomnaill (cousin to Rudhraighe Ó Domhnaill, Brighid Fitzgerald's husband).[13] Perhaps most celebrated is the manuscript known as *Leabhar Inghine Í Dhomhnaill* ('The Book of O'Donnell's Daughter') associated with the Irish regiment in Flanders, and compiled in exile between 1622 and 1650. The O'Donnell woman concerned, Nualaidh Ní Dhomhnaill, was sister-in-law to Brighid Fitzgerald. She left for Europe with her brother and nephew in September 1607 as part of the expedition known as the 'flight of the earls'. Nualaidh took charge of her nephew's education at the Franciscan Irish college in Louvain from 1609. Her importance as a figurehead for Gaelic exiles is reflected in five poems concerning her that are transcribed in the poem-book compiled in her name.[14]

The spread of literacy among women and the courting of bilingual audiences, both Old English and native Irish, are further attested in the efforts made by the Poor Clare nuns to have their religious order's foundational documents translated from English into Irish. Five Irish women were professed as members of the order of St Clare at the exiled English convent at Gravelines in the Low Countries, in the 1620s. The order's rule, prescribing the procedures of convent life, had been translated into English and printed in 1621. When they returned to establish a foundation in Ireland, first in Dublin whence they were removed to an island on Lough Ree, near Athlone, the Irish nuns arranged for that rule, and the revisions printed in English as the *Declarations and Ordinances* in 1622, to be translated into Irish. The surviving manuscript was copied in 1636 by no less a figure than Mícheál Ó Cléirigh, the Franciscan who had left Louvain ten years earlier, on a mission to gather historical materials in Ireland (a project that resulted in the monumental *Annals of the Four Masters*).[15] The nuns' enlisting of this eminent scholar demonstrates the expansion of female literacy as well as the increasing demand for written texts and the courting of vocations from the widest range of communities. Female religious orders across Europe required documentation: profession records, obituaries, chronicles and devotional materials. Mother Mary Bonaventure Browne, abbess of the Galway Poor Clare convent from 1647 to 1650, went into exile at the surrender of the city to Cromwellian forces in 1653. Finding sanctuary in the Conceptionist convent, Cavallero de Gracia, in Madrid, she set to writing. According to an eighteenth-century bibliography of Franciscan texts, she composed in

Irish at least eleven distinct works, including biography and hagiography as well as devotional works.[16] Her chronicle of the order's foundation and exile is the only one to survive, in an English translation made in the late seventeenth century.[17] Such developments also lead us beyond traditionally 'literary' genres such as poetry into the many other forms of writing with which women in Ireland engaged.

The 1641 Depositions are a case in point: an enormous body of material comprised of narratives about their own experiences, composed by women and men of the settler class in the immediate aftermath of fleeing their homes following the Catholic insurrection of October that year. Held in thirty-one manuscript volumes at Trinity College Dublin, and recently digitized, the depositions are textual artefacts that capture the encounter of speech with legal process, the moment in which oral narratives were shaped into writing. A royal commission ordered that Protestant victims be examined about their experiences of the insurrection, itemizing losses and identifying culprits. Individuals' depositions were made orally, written down by scribes (usually in the third person), read back to deponents who could then correct any details and finally sworn and witnessed. As writing, these texts preserve the traces of their oral composition; phrases and clauses are crossed out or inserted, details fine-tuned. The process by which deponents signed their depositions in itself reveals a wide range of literacy. Once thought the prime measure of literacy, signature ability is now seen as only one of many indicators of reading and writing competency. Signatories to depositions range from those of the upper and middling classes who could sign their names, to tradespeople who would sign initials, to those who attempted a unique sign on the page.[18] Deponents could see, hear or read – if not write – their depositions. They could insert the writings of others, as Thomas Pickering, curate of Killeigh and Lynally in King's County, did for the siege-letters of Lettice Digby, Baroness Offaly. Offaly had herself circulated the first summons letter she received, along with a defiant reply, to the lords justices in Dublin and to James Butler, earl of Ormond and commander of royalist forces in Ireland; they also found their way to London where they were printed.[19] Pickering ensured that the full set of summonses and Lady Offaly's replies were preserved for the historical record by having them scribally copied into his substantial deposition.[20]

The act of deposing encouraged self-representation and the terms of the commission supplied a narrative structure. Many depositions answered straightforwardly the questions asked but a large number of deponents composed fuller and compelling accounts. The depositions of Elizabeth

Price of Armagh or Mary Hammond of Galway, for example, are substantial and sophisticated accounts that build suspense as well as retribution into their stories.[21] What is more, in the case of Lady Elizabeth
Dowdall, the act of deposing prompted the composition of a separate
first-person account of her military leadership in Limerick – a narrative that is unshackled from the pro-forma constraints of a deposition.[22]
Moreover, as Dowdall's example clearly illustrates, their status as legal
documents, sworn on the Bible and witnessed, makes it unlikely that
anyone but an officer of the commission would be entrusted with the
writing. Always problematic as historical sources, due to their reliance on
hearsay, rumour and subjective interpretation, their very subjectivity and
firsthand perspectives make them valuable as examples of women's (and
men's) writing.[23]

If the fallout of the 1641 rising compelled New English Protestants
of all classes to head for one of the island's ports and frame their experiences in writing, warfare and displacement also drove native Irish and
Old English Catholics into exile and they, too, had to devise narratives of
themselves in order to obtain relief, support and positions. The territories
of Catholic Spain were a draw, not only due to politico-religious affinities
but, more pragmatically, because Irish refugees could apply for a Spanish
pension (*entretenimiento*) on the basis of losses and military or financial
services to the Counter-Reformation cause. As with the 1641 depositions, these texts needed to follow a pre-ordained formula. The successful petitioner to the Spanish king had to establish Gaelic lineage and
specify the nature of service and losses incurred. For women, the bases
on which they petitioned were gendered. Unable to act as soldiers, their
husbands, fathers and sons were often the linchpin of their petitions. But
their gender could be beneficial in terms of persuasive rhetoric: widowhood conferred a moral obligation that was biblically sanctioned; the
picture of a destitute wife and mother drew on long-established tropes of
vulnerability and weakness. Hence, a petition like that of Rose Guegan
in 1607 hit a number of marks – abandonment, as her menfolk enlisted
to serve, established her status as deserving – in order to persuade the
state to move payment from Galicia to Flanders.[24] As Ciaran O'Scea has
argued, exposure to this bureaucratic and creative process inculcated and
spread literacy among members of the exiled community.[25] It directed
language skills not only toward the most successful arguments but also
the Castilian Spanish of the state.

The urgency of confronting and dealing with the English state (as
also the continuity of its institutions of record) meant that women in

Ireland also learnt to frame their needs and positions in petitions. Among the most famous are the petitions addressed to Queen Elizabeth I and her secretary of state, William Cecil, by Gráinne Ní Mháille (Grace O'Malley, known to legend as the pirate queen). Chieftain of sea and land territories in Mayo, Ní Mháille clashed with the queen's governor of Connacht, Richard Bingham, and this drove her to travel to London to entreat the monarch in person. Two visits, in 1593 and 1595, bolstered her submission of petitions. Unable to speak English, as was typical of the chieftain class in the sixteenth century, their composition was collaborative, marshalling and deciding arguments, aided by interpreters and scribes.[26] Eleanor Butler, countess of Desmond, whose first husband was leader of two Munster risings, spent her career as influential wife, widow and mother addressing petitions to the upper branches of the crown. From the earliest days of her first husband's ruptions, Eleanor attempted to soothe tensions by writing conciliatory and explanatory petitions to Elizabeth and her officers. On his execution as a traitor, her petitions shifted gear, aiming to limit the damage by securing some Desmond lands or, failing that, pensions for herself and her children; later, to support her son's claim to the earldom over that of his uncle.[27] Political adversity and warfare drove women of the upper social classes to petition the state and harness the instruments of writerly persuasion, for better circumstances.

Where Ní Mháille was of noble Gaelic descent, and Desmond of Old English as well as Gaelic background, the later seventeenth-century petitions and letters of Elizabeth (née Preston) Butler, countess of Ormond, an English woman who had married into a Protestant ruling branch of the Old English Butlers, demonstrate fluency with Anglophone court and literary culture. Nevertheless, political expediency also drove her writing. By the 1650s, the Ormonds were on the wrong, royalist, side of the Confederate and civil wars. From exile in Caen, France, Elizabeth acted as clearing house and agent, accepting and moving correspondence to her husband, former commander of royalist forces in Ireland. She was one of many who petitioned Oliver Cromwell. Difficult to pitch, this petition alighted on a distinction between petitioner and husband (who remained at large and in service to the exiled King Charles II) with a view to securing independent rights to her lands in Ireland. Deploying flattery and presenting a submissive persona, Butler exploited her gender by downplaying the claim to one of subsistence only, for herself and her children. In fact, her political connections and fame as support to large numbers of victims fleeing through the port of Waterford post-1641, combined with her arguments to deliver success. Ormond was granted livings and land at Dunmore Castle, county Kilkenny, in 1653. The condition – that she discontinue communications with her husband – was surreptitiously ignored. A significant quantity of her letters survived, attesting to her engaged management of her estates in Ireland, as well as her maintenance of courtly and politically influential connections.[28]

As literary scholarship has embraced the study of letter-writing so, too, the large number of letters authored by women in Ireland has come into view. These demonstrate a high degree of political agency as well as literacy; command of argument and contemporary political thought as well as epistolary convention and etiquette. Vincent Carey has shown how Mabel Browne, who had served Queen Mary, acted as mediator between the Geraldine and Tudor courts from her marriage to the eleventh earl of Kildare ca. 1555 through to the 1580s.[29] We gain a glimpse of a Gaelic female leader's political activism through the single surviving letter, in Irish, from Róis Ní Dhochartaigh. Another member of the Ulster expedition to the Continent in 1607, Ní Dhochartaigh was under English surveillance there as a spy. Her second husband, Owen Roe O'Neill, leader of the Irish regiment based at Flanders, returned in July 1642 to lead the Ulster army in the Confederate wars (Elizabeth Price, among others, recounts meeting him in her deposition). Róis's letter, dated 16 September 1642, to an unidentified priest, kept tabs on her husband's movements and shows how instrumental she was (not unlike Ormond) as an agent based abroad.[30] The letters of one Mrs Briver, wife of the mayor of Waterford during that city's siege at the hands of the Confederates in 1641–2, recently edited by Naomi McAreavey, are most notable for their informed manipulation of epistolary form in order to intervene publicly on behalf of her own reputation and that of her husband. Surviving in two different formats (a continuous narrative and a series of four letters), Briver's versions of what had happened in the city – how rebels had behaved, how she and her husband resisted them and defended the English – were addressed to an officer of the English garrison at Duncannon.[31] Writing as a member of the Old English community in the city, Briver evinces the complex entanglements of that hybrid identity. No such qualms of identity affected Susan (née Steynings) Montgomery, wife of the bishop of Derry, Raphoe and Clogher, appointed in 1605, who wrote home to her sister and brother-in-law in Devon. Her nine extant letters trace her experiences as a New English settler, reporting on the new country and encouraging her relatives to visit. Their trajectory runs from the positive outlook of the new arrival through to her isolated situation as the wife of an important man who returned regularly to the London court. Her utter lack of agency, of ability to change her situation, shines through in letters of complaint. Writing was her only recourse, representing her plight to English relatives her only means of improving her lot.[32]

The next generation of settler-class women had been sufficiently educated and economically supported to engage fully with contemporary intellectual culture – although that engagement was predicated on residence elsewhere. Dorothy Moore, whose letters have been edited by Lynette Hunter, left Ireland for London and Utrecht soon after becoming a widow to Arthur Moore in 1635.[33] She used her letters to make connections via the correspondence network centred around Samuel Hartlib. Moore's letters were the means by which she participated, working through her ideas about godly public service for women. Her closest epistolary confidants were the theologian, John Dury, who became her second husband in 1645, and Katherine Jones, viscountess Ranelagh. Jones was the seventh child of Richard Boyle, first earl of Cork. Her father had arrived in Ireland in 1588 with little money and few connections; for him, Ireland opened up vast opportunities and he attained great prominence. His offspring were illustrious and his success enabled them to maintain estates in both Ireland and England, reaching the highest echelons of politics and influence. Ranelagh operated at the centre of intellectual and political circles in London, esteemed and consulted for her expertise in medical, scientific and politico-religious matters.[34]

Ranelagh's younger sister, Mary Rich, was also a prolific author. Her autobiography, composed in 1671–3, recounts her marriage to a younger son of the earl of Warwick as a love match pursued against her father's wishes. Ultimately, this marriage was to deliver both material and spiritual wealth; her husband inherited the title in 1659 and her life narrative interprets her introduction to his family as a prompt to religious conversion. Following the trajectory of spiritual autobiography advocated in puritan culture, this autobiography models life as a journey toward salvation, election and grace, replete with 'backslidings' and a framing of the early life, distracted by books and theatre, as sinful.[35] This narrative structure was replicated in the writings of many radical Protestants, for whom self-examination was a crucial marker of elect identity. The Independent, 'gathered' churches placed great emphasis on such narratives as admission testimonies. The church established by John Rogers at Christ Church, Dublin, in the early 1650s ministered mainly to Cromwellian soldiers and their families. It had a distinctively colonial Irish tenor at

the vanguard of emergent radical culture that differentiated it from similar churches across England – or was presented as such by Rogers in his
Ohel, or, Beth-shemesh (1653). The testimonies required to secure membership of the church followed, like Rich's autobiography, a teleology
from sin through to epiphany, peppered with many fits, starts and backward steps. Rogers published thirty-seven of these in order to stimulate
others to extend that godly work in Ireland. This kind of life writing was
gender-blind; seventeen of Rogers's published testimonies were authored
by female members of his church.[36] Frances Cook, who came to Ireland
with her husband John (the lawyer who led King Charles I's prosecution, recruited by Cromwell for his Irish conquest), was also prompted to
author a narrative of spiritual revelation while in the country. Her near-
death experience in a storm as they travelled by ship from Wexford to
Cork in January 1650 led to a climax of assurance of salvation, for herself
and her husband; they published their accounts together – justifications
for God's work as pursued by the Cromwellian regime.[37]

Other women who lived in Ireland for periods of their lives also
incorporated Irish experiences in their narratives. The Quaker Barbara
Blaugdone travelled to Cork in 1656. Her memoir recounts missions in
that city as well as Dublin and Limerick – all ended in imprisonment
due to the fervour (and even success) of her preaching.[38] Less radical but
equally concerned with personal reputation were the four different versions of her life that were written by Alice Thornton.[39] Her childhood
was spent at the Dublin court, as daughter of Lord Deputy Christopher
Wandesford, who died unexpectedly in 1640. Writing and circulating
her autobiographies in later life, she looked back on her time in Dublin
as idyllic and used it as a literary counterpoint to the trials and tribula-
tions that followed from the family's return to England. Ann Fanshawe
was another traveller whose time in Ireland – an eventful year that saw
the collapse of the royalist army in Ireland and triumphant campaign of
Oliver Cromwell – was recounted in her memoir (ostensibly written as a
biography of her husband, the royalist diplomat Sir Richard Fanshawe).[40]
The more prosaic struggles of life in Ireland may be sampled in the dia-
ristic memoirs of Elizabeth Freke, whose battle with her husband over
whether to live at his family estate in Rathbarry, county Cork, or on hers
at West Bilney, Norfolk persisted for many years in which she repented
her secret marriage of 1672.[41]

For all these Anglophone life writers, Ireland was a potent signifier
of Catholicism – a gift to autobiographers and memoirists whose acts
of writing were moulded and licensed by the tenets of Protestantism.

The island's semantic reach encompassed ideas of the *tabula rasa*, pulsing with possibilities that emerged from warfare and conflict. Their self-representations mined that symbolism and forged new kinds of women's voices and identities on the island itself and for English audiences. But the voluminous diaries of Mary Rich remind us that the protagonist of life writing is no more transparent than any other authorial persona. Unconcerned with life in Ireland, which she had long left behind, focused rather on devotional practice and domestic life, they detail a version of the latter at stark odds with the love match represented in her autobiography.[42] The persona is always a construction, whether framed and shaped for the addressee of a petition or the reader (even oneself) of a diary.

We may more readily read poetry as mediated and the Anglophone poetry produced by women living in early modern Ireland runs the gamut from plain piety to courtly sociability. Frances Cook's near-shipwreck also prompted her to compose poetry. Her 24-stanza poem in ballad metre reworks Psalms 66 and 107 in order to praise God for saving her.[43] The lyricism of the biblical psalms' first-person voice made psalm paraphrase approachable and enabling for women writers, as evidenced also in the verse of Anne Southwell.[44] Anglophone poets such as Southwell and Katherine Philips arrived in Ireland having honed their poetic skills in the court and coterie culture of England and Wales. Southwell arrived at the Munster plantation with her first husband at the turn of the seventeenth century. An accomplished and committed poet, she sought connections with like-minded members of her class, advocating devotional verse, addressing and soliciting poems to and from Bernard Adams, bishop of Limerick; Cecily Ridgeway, countess of Londonderry; and the popular religious poet Francis Quarles, who arrived in 1626 as secretary to James Ussher, archbishop of Armagh. She also composed sequences of Decalogue poetry (poems inspired by the ten commandments). One of these bears the traces of her isolated experience as devout Protestant at a far-flung outpost of the colony as the speaker worries what will happen 'Yf in Hibernia god will haue mee dye'.[45]

The best known today of the writers discussed in this chapter is Katherine Philips, 'the matchless Orinda', whose collected poems and translations were published posthumously in 1667. This Anglo-Welsh poet came to Ireland in 1662 with an already established literary reputation. She accompanied her friend Anne Owen (immortalized as 'Lucasia' in Philips's verse), who had married Colonel Marcus Trevor, viscount Dungannon. She also intended to pursue her father's 1642 investment in Cromwell's 'adventurers' scheme for funding the army in Ireland. Her connections provided Philips with an entrée to the Dublin court, where her literary ambitions were progressed and supported – most prominently by Roger Boyle, earl of Orrery (brother to Mary Rich and Katherine, Lady Ranelagh), who urged her to complete her translation of Corneille's 1643 play, *La Mort de Pompée* ('The Death of Pompey'). Philips's *Pompey* was performed at Smock Alley Theatre, Dublin, in February 1663. A dramatization of the fallout from the Roman civil war, which explores the politics of loyalty and competing interests of periphery (Egypt) and centre (Rome), the play has been analysed in terms of its complex Restoration Irish contexts.[46] The apex of Philips's career, the play was printed both in Dublin and London to great acclaim. Her social verse addressed the aristocratic women of Dublin society; her poems were copied and circulated in manuscript to the London court as well as in print, with those of Abraham Cowley and Orrery, among others, in the miscellany *Poems, by Several Persons* (1663). Her celebrity thus increased, Philips's period in Dublin enhanced her reputation in London. She also inspired a remarkable and substantial praise poem, apparently by a contemporary female poet, known only as Philo-Philippa. Long a source of attraction and bemusement to critics, this poem is strikingly modern in its proto-feminist sensibilities and that very modernity has caused some to question its authenticity as a female-authored poem.[47]

However, the terrain of women's writing before 1700 is substantially populated by single surviving, accomplished and apparently unique texts: Brighid Fitzgerald's syllabic poem, Fionnghuala Ní Bhriain's keen, Róis Ní Dhochartaigh's letter. Their survival suggests they were not the only female-authored texts produced in their communities, nor even the only authors. Another example of seemingly isolated survival is provided by the two Latin praise poems in honour of her father by Eleanora Burnell – the only known Latin poems by an Irish woman in the early modern period. Printed as prefatory poems to her father's play, *Landgartha*, in 1641, they may be unique in an Irish context but, as Jane Stevenson has shown, they are best understood in the wider European context of women and elite cultural practices.[48] These traces of women's participation in a culture of writing, reading and performance point not just to their immersion in the various crosscutting cultures lived on the island but also to their consistency with developments across Europe, themselves varied in form and function – vernacular song and answer poetry, nuns' record-keeping, petitionary and bureaucratic writing, news-gathering and dissemination, coterie and neo-Latin verse.

Women's writing in early modern Ireland problematizes categories of identity, national as well as ethnic or religious. The better-known Anglophone writers discussed in this chapter are more usually considered within an Anglocentric canon of British women's writing. Those women knew both islands and their writing was shaped by their competing origins and destinations. The shift in scholarship toward 'archipelagic' perspectives offers one route for accommodating these forces' influences.[49] For scholars of early modern Ireland, these writers – already occupying marginalized speaking positions due to their sex – can illuminate the interrogation of fluid and emergent ideas of national identity and 'Irishness'. Their multiple poles of identity – language, region, religion and political allegiance – can be interpreted fruitfully through the prism of feminist intersectionality. Finally, the apparent paucity of texts continues to drive recovery research. Prose – particularly the genres of letters and life writing – is most likely to yield new discoveries and scholarly attention. As fields of scholarship that have emerged over the past decade, the rediscovery and reappraisal of such texts is ongoing for historians of early modern women's writing in Europe as well as Ireland.[50] Writing in Irish includes a small but significant body of poetry, as well as documents commissioned by a female religious community as part of the Counter-Reformation drive to provide instruction in vernacular languages. Writing in English ranges from the work of Katherine Philips and Dorothy Moore to petition-letters and depositions. In a context in which structures of power were in flux and new identities were being forged, women from different communities co-existing in Ireland used writing for both communal and individual ends, as a means to conform with and diverge from their social milieus. In the process, they contributed to the reshaping of genres and created new prospects for female authorship.

Notes

1 Máirín Ní Dhonnchadha, 'Courts and Coteries I: c.900–1600' and 'Courts and Coteries II: c.1500–1800', in Angela Bourke et al. eds., *The Field Day Anthology of Irish Writing IV & V: Irish Women's Writing and Traditions* (Cork: Cork University Press, 2002), 4: 293–303, 358–66; for these women, see 111–18, 299–300, 303–5, 133–9.

2 Lambert McKenna, ed., *The Book of Magauran: Leabhar Méig Shamhradháin* (Dublin: DIAS, 1947), 237/379.

3 William J. Watson, ed., *Scottish Verse from the Book of the Dean of Lismore* (Edinburgh: Scottish Gaelic Texts Society, 1937), 244–5.

4 National Archives, London, SP 63/3/67.

5 Lambeth Palace Library, London, MS 627, cited in *Field Day Anthology of Irish Writing*, 4:302.

6 See Michelle O Riordan, *Irish Bardic Poetry and Rhetorical Reality* (Cork: Cork University Press, 2007); Osborn Bergin, *Irish Bardic Poetry* (Dublin: DIAS, 1970).

7 For this discussion and text, see Cathal Ó Háinle, 'Flattery Rejected: Two Seventeenth-Century Irish Poems', *Hermathena* 138 (1985): 5–27; Ní Dhonnchadha, 'Courts and Coteries: II', 384, 388; Jane Stevenson and Peter Davidson, *Early Modern Women Poets (1520–1700): An Anthology* (Oxford: Oxford University Press, 2001), 165; Mícheál Mac Craith, 'Fun and Games among the Jet Set: A Glimpse of Seventeenth-Century Gaelic Ireland', in Joseph Falaky Nagy, ed., *Memory and the Modern in Celtic Literatures* (Dublin: Four Courts, 2006), 15–36.

8 Watson, *Dean of Lismore*, 60–1, 234–5, 307–8; Catherine Kerrigan, ed., *An Anthology of Scottish Women Poets* (Edinburgh: Edinburgh University Press, 1991), 53, 60–1; E. C. Quiggin, *Poems from the Book of the Dean of Lismore*, ed. J. C. Fraser (Cambridge: Cambridge University Press, 1937), 78.

9 For surveys of women's patronage, see Bernadette Cunningham, 'Women and Gaelic Literature, 1500–1800', in Margaret MacCurtain and Mary O'Dowd, eds., *Women in Early Modern Ireland* (Edinburgh: Edinburgh University Press, 1991), 148–52; Ní Dhonnchadha, 'Courts and Coteries: I', 332–40.

10 Tadhg Ó Donnchadha, ed., *Leabhar Cloinne Aodha Buidhe* (Dublin: Irish Manuscripts Commission, 1931), 171, 179, 203–17.

11 Russell Library, Maynooth University, MS M 107, pp. 193–211. Those on Donnchadh and Diarmaid are edited, with translations, by Liam P. Ó Murchú, in *The Field Day Anthology of Irish Writing*, 4:399–405.

12 For editions, see Liam P. Ó Murchú, 'Caoineadh ar Uaithne Mór Ó Lochlainn, 1617', *Éigse* 27 (1993): 67–79; *The Field Day Anthology of Irish Writing*, 4:396–7; Stevenson and Davidson, *Early Modern Women Poets*, 175–8. For discussion of the keen's petitionary aspects, see Máirín Nic Eoin, *B'ait leo bean: Gnéithe den Idé-eolaíocht Inscne i dTraidisiún Liteartha na Gaeilge* (Dublin: An Clóchomhar, 1998), 246–7.

13 Cecile O'Rahilly, ed., *Cath Finntrágha: Edited from MS. Rawlinson B 487* (Dublin: DIAS, 1962); Royal Irish Academy MS 24 P 25; Salvador Ryan, 'Windows on Late Medieval Devotional Practice: Máire Ní Mháille's "Book of Piety" (1513) and the World Behind the Texts', in Rachel Moss, Colmán Ó Clabaigh and Salvador Ryan, eds., *Art and Devotion in Late Medieval Ireland* (Dublin: Four Courts), 1–15; Paul Walsh, *Irish Men of Learning* (Dublin: At the Sign of the Three Candles, 1947), 172–4.

14 Bibliothèque Royale, Brussels, MS 6131–3. See also Jerrold Casway, 'Heroines or Victims? The Women of the Flight of the Earls', *New Hibernia Review: Iris Éireannach Nua* 7 (2003): 64–7; Walsh, *Men of Learning*, 179–205; Nic Eoin, *B'ait leo bean*, 162–5.

15 Royal Irish Academy, MS D i 2; Eleanor Knott, ed., 'An Irish Seventeenth-Century Translation of the Rule of St. Clare', *Ériu* 15 (1948): 1–187.

16 Joanne à s. Antonio Salmantino, *Bibliotheca Universa Franciscana*, 3 vols. (Madrid, 1732; repr. Farnborough: Gregg Press, 1966), 2:328.

17 Chronicle of Mother Mary Bonaventure Browne, MS, Galway Monastery of the Poor Clares; Celsus O'Brien, ed., *Recollections of an Irish Poor Clare in the Seventeenth Century* (Galway: Connacht Tribune, 1993).

18 See Marie-Louise Coolahan, '"And This Deponent Further Sayeth:" Orality, Print and the 1641 Depositions', in Marc Caball and Andrew Carpenter, eds., *Oral and Print Cultures in Ireland 1600–1900* (Dublin: Four Courts, 2010), 72–3.

19 John Temple, *The Irish Rebellion* (London, 1646), sig. Ff2v; Bodleian Library, Oxford, Carte MS II, fol. 305; William Bladen, *A True and Exact Relation of the Chiefe Passages in Ireland, since the First Rising of the Rebels* (London, 1642). See also *Field Day Anthology of Irish Writing*, 5:25–7.

20 Trinity College Dublin, MS 814, fols. 71r–74r; 117, 168r–171v. These texts occur twice in the manuscript; the second iteration is the version available at *1641 Depositions Online*: http://1641.tcd.ie/deposition .php?depID=814117r067a accessed 27 January 2017.

21 TCD MSS 836, fols. 101–5 http://1641.tcd.ie/deposition.php?depID= 836101r054 accessed 27 January 2017; 830, fols. 136–7 http://1641.tcd.ie/ deposition.php?depID=830136r106 accessed 27 January 2017.

22 TCD MS 829, fols. 138–9 http://1641.tcd.ie/deposition.php?depID= 829138r082 accessed 27 January 2017; British Library, London, Sloane MS 1008, fols. 66r–69r; also *The Field Day Anthology of Irish Writing*, 5:22–4.

23 For recent discussions of the depositions, see Nicholas Canny, *Making Ireland British 1580–1650* (Oxford: Oxford University Press, 2001), 461–550; Raymond Gillespie, 'Temple's Fate: Reading The Irish Rebellion in Late Seventeenth-Century Ireland', in Ciaran Brady and Jane Ohlmeyer, eds., *British Interventions in Early Modern Ireland* (Cambridge: Cambridge University Press, 2005), 315–33; David Edwards, Pádraig Lenihan and Clodagh Tait, eds., *Age of Atrocity: Violence and Political Conflict in Early Modern Ireland* (Dublin: Four Courts, 2007); Eamon Darcy, Annaleigh Margey and Elaine Murphy, eds., *The 1641 Depositions and the Irish Rebellion* (London: Pickering & Chatto, 2012); Eamon Darcy, *The Irish Rebellion of 1641 and the Wars of the Three Kingdoms* (London: Boydell Press, 2013).

24 *The Field Day Anthology of Irish Writing*, 5:570.

25 Ciaran O'Scea, 'The Role of Castilian Royal Bureaucracy in the Formation of Early-Modern Irish Literacy', in Thomas O'Connor and Mary Ann Lyons, eds., *Irish Communities in Early Modern Europe* (Dublin: Four Courts, 2006), 200–39.

26 National Archives, London, SP 63/170/64-5; SP 63/179/36; SP 63/170/70. See also *Field Day Anthology of Irish Writing*, 5:21–2; Anne Chambers, *Granuaile: The Life and Times of Grace O'Malley c.1530–1603* (Dublin: Wolfhound, 1988); Brandie Siegfried, 'Queen to Queen at Check: Grace O'Malley, Elizabeth Tudor, and the Discourse of Majesty in the State Papers of Ireland', in Carole Levin, Jo Eldridge Carney and Debra Barrett-Graves, eds., *Elizabeth I: Always Her Own Free Woman* (Aldershot: Ashgate, 2003), 149–75.

27 For examples, see *The Field Day Anthology of Irish Writing*, 5:16–19 and Anne Chambers, *Eleanor, Countess of Desmond, c.1545–1638* (Dublin: Wolfhound, 1986).

28 For examples, see *The Field Day Anthology of Irish Writing*, 5:501–3; British Library, London, Egerton MS 2534, fols. 17, 26, 30–1, 44–5, 57, 129–31. Naomi McAreavey is editing her complete letters for the Renaissance English Text Society.

29 Vincent Carey, '"What's Love Got To Do With It?:" Gender and Geraldine Power on the Pale Border', in Michael Potterton and Thomas Herron, eds., *Dublin and the Pale in the Renaissance c.1540–1660* (Dublin: Four Courts, 2011), 93–103.

30 *The Field Day Anthology of Irish Writing*, 5:30.

31 Naomi McAreavey, 'An Epistolary Account of the Irish Rising of 1641 by the Wife of the Mayor of Waterford', *English Literary Renaissance* 42 (2012): 77–109.

32 Marie-Louise Coolahan, 'Ideal Communities and Planter Women's Writing in Seventeenth-Century Ireland', *Parergon* 29 (2012): 69–91.

33 Lynette Hunter, ed., *The Letters of Dorothy Moore, 1612–64* (Aldershot: Ashgate, 2004).

34 See Michelle DiMeo, '"Such a Sister Became Such a Brother:" Lady Ranelagh's Influence on Robert Boyle', *Intellectual History Review* 25 (2015): 21–36; Carol Pal, *Republic of Women: Rethinking the Republic of Letters in the Seventeenth Century* (Cambridge: Cambridge University Press, 2012), 142–76; Ruth Connolly, 'A Proselytising Protestant Commonwealth: The Religious and Political Ideals of Katherine Jones, Viscountess Ranelagh', *The Seventeenth Century* 23 (2008): 244–64; Betsey Taylor Fitzsimon, 'Conversion, the Bible, and the Irish Language: The Correspondence of Lady Ranelagh and Bishop Dopping', in Michael Brown, Charles McGrath and Thomas Power, eds., *Converts and Conversion in Ireland, 1650–1850* (Dublin: Four Courts, 2005), 157–82; and Evan Bourke, 'Female Involvement, Membership, and Centrality: A Social Network Analysis of the Hartlib Circle', *Literature Compass*, 14 (2017): doi:10.1111/lic3.12388.

35 British Library, London, Additional MS 27,357; Thomas Crofton Croker, ed., *Autobiography of Mary Countess of Warwick* (London: Percy Society, 1848).

36 John Rogers, *Ohel, or, Beth-shemesh* (London, 1653), 393–417 (sigs. Eeer-Hhh3r).

37 Frances Cook, *Mris. Cooke's Meditations* and John Cook, *A True Relation of Mr. Iohn Cook's Passage by Sea from Wexford to Kinsale in that Great Storm* (Cork and London, 1650).

38 Barbara Blaugdone, *An Account of the Travels, Sufferings and Persecutions of Barbara Blaugdone* (London, 1691).

39 Yale University Microfilm no. 326; British Library, London, Additional MS 88, 897; British Library, London, RP2346; British Library, London, RP5757; Charles Jackson, ed., *The Autobiography of Mrs. Alice Thornton* (Durham: Surtees Society, 1875). See Raymond Anselment, 'Seventeenth-Century Manuscript Sources of Alice Thornton's Life', *Studies in English Literature 1500–1900*, 45 (2005): 135–55.

40 John Loftis, ed., *The Memoirs of Anne, Lady Halkett and Ann, Lady Fanshawe* (Oxford: Clarendon Press, 1979).

41 Raymond Anselment, ed., *The Remembrances of Elizabeth Freke: 1671–1714* (Cambridge: Cambridge University Press, 2001).

42 British Library, London, Additional MSS 27, 351–5 and 27, 356 for her diaries and meditations; *Memoir of Lady Warwick: Also Her Diary* (London: Religious Tract Society, 1847); Raymond Anselment, ed., *The Occasional Meditations of Mary Rich, Countess of Warwick* (Tempe, AZ: Arizona Center for Medieval and Renaissance Studies, 2009).

43 Cook, *Meditations*, 14–16; Suzanne Trill, Kate Chedgzoy and Melanie Osborne, eds., *Lay by Your Needles Ladies, Take the Pen: Writing Women in England, 1500–1700* (London: Arnold, 1997), 169–75.

44 Sarah C. E. Ross, *Women, Poetry, and Politics in Seventeenth-Century Britain* (Oxford: Oxford University Press, 2015), 80–96.

45 Jean Klene, ed., *The Southwell-Sibthorpe Commonplace Book: Folger MS V.b.198* (Tempe, AZ: Medieval & Renaissance Texts & Studies, 1997), 132.

46 See, for example, Catharine Gray, 'Katherine Philips in Ireland', *English Literary Renaissance* 39 (2009): 557–85 and Deana Rankin, '"If Egypt now enslav'd or free A Kingdom or a Province be:" Translating Corneille in Restoration Dublin', in Sarah Alyn Stacey and Véronique Desnain, eds., *Culture and Conflict in Seventeenth-Century France and Ireland* (Dublin: Four Courts, 2004), 194–209. For Philips's work, see Patrick Thomas, G. Greer and R. Little, eds., *The Collected Works of Katherine Philips: The Matchless Orinda*, 3 vols. (Essex: Stump Cross, 1990–3).

47 Andrew Carpenter, ed., *Verse in English from Tudor and Stuart Ireland* (Cork: Cork University Press, 2003), 367–73, and unpublished paper, 'Katherine Philips's Dublin Admirers: "Philo-Philippa" Unmasked', Katherine Philips 350: Writing, Reputation, Legacy conference, Marsh's Library, Dublin, 27 June 2014; Kate Lilley, 'Katherine Philips, "Philo-Philippa" and the Poetics of Association', in Patricia Pender and Rosalind Smith, eds., *Material Cultures of Early Modern Women's Writing* (Basingstoke: Palgrave Macmillan, 2014), 118–39.

48 Deana Rankin, ed., *Landgartha: A Tragie-Comedy* (Dublin: Four Courts, 2013), 74–7; Jane Stevenson, *Women Latin Poets: Language, Gender, and Authority from Antiquity to the Eighteenth Century* (Oxford: Oxford University Press, 2005), 384–5.

49 Kate Chedgzoy, *Women's Writing in the British Atlantic World: Memory, Place and History, 1550–1700* (Cambridge: Cambridge University Press, 2007);

John Kerrigan, *Archipelagic English: Literature, History, and Politics 1603–1707* (Oxford: Oxford University Press, 2008).

50 For example, Julie D. Campbell and Anne R. Larsen, eds., *Early Modern Women and Transnational Communities of Letters* (Farnham: Ashgate, 2009); Michelle M. Dowd and Julie A. Eckerle, eds., *Genre and Women's Life Writing in Early Modern England* (Aldershot: Ashgate, 2007); Jane Couchman and Ann Crabb, eds., *Women's Letters Across Europe, 1400–1700: Form and Persuasion* (Aldershot: Ashgate, 2005).

CHAPTER 2

Eighteenth-Century Writing

Clíona Ó Gallchoir

Over the course of the eighteenth century, literary culture in both Britain and Ireland was gradually transformed by the rise to dominance of print. By the end of the century the volume of printed material being produced and consumed had increased enormously, and the concept of authorship was firmly linked to the act of publication. The impact of Enlightenment ideas in this period prompted claims for women's intellectual equality and their shared participation in a culture of reason. At the same time, however, women occupied a problematic position in relation to the 'public' act of authoring a text. In the Irish context, moreover, in the aftermath of the Williamite wars, differences of language and religion, compounded by restrictions on Catholic education and a massively uneven distribution of power and wealth affecting Catholics disproportionately, created very different contexts for women's access to literacy and the printed word. The continuing importance of the manuscript in Irish-language culture and the existence of a vigorous oral Gaelic culture are thus also part of the story of women's literary activity in this period. The eighteenth century also witnessed the emergence of an Irish political and cultural identity amongst the Protestant and Anglo-Irish community, and pioneering attempts to bridge the gap between different cultures and experiences. In this fractured but culturally dynamic context, women in Ireland participated actively over the course of the century, making significant contributions across a range of genres, and finding many ways to express their distinctive concerns as women.

The Irish Language: Written and Oral Culture

The production of written literature in Irish in the eighteenth century was profoundly impacted by the collapse of the central institutions of invariably male professional bardic education and patronage following the Elizabethan reconquest and the Flight of the Earls in 1607.

As damaging as this was for Gaelic literary culture, Mícheál Mac Craith points out that the 'mortal blow' to the institution of the *fileadha* (poet) 'paradoxically resulted in a prolific and impassioned creative outburst'.[1] The disintegration of central literary institutions prompted writers to defend and extol Gaelic culture, while also being less constrained by the elaborate, formal and somewhat archaic modes of bardic poetry. An important element in this 'outburst' was an increase in the number of women who wrote poetry in Irish. Thanks to the work of Máirín Ní Dhonnchadha, non-specialist readers now have access to the small but significant body of work by women poets in this period.[2] None of this work was printed until long after its composition; instead it formed part of the manuscript culture which persisted in Irish-language literary circles. The reliance on manuscript transmission may have contributed to the loss of a significant amount of writing by women, as it is undoubtedly the case that these surviving poems do not represent the entire output by women in Irish in this period. The perception of a rise in the number of women poets, albeit as an indicator of seemingly modern social degeneracy, is evident in 'Éigsíní Ban agus Tae' (translated by Criostoir O'Flynn as 'On Tay-Drinking Poetesses'), by Aindrias Mac Craith (ca. 1709–95). A much more positive indicator of the emergence of women as poets can be seen in poems of tribute, such as those in honour of Máire Ní Chrualaoich, 'the Sappho of Munster' ('Sápphó na Mumhan'). Although none of her works have survived, her achievements can be gauged by the fact that her death in 1761 was marked by poems of praise and tribute by a number of male poets who clearly held her in very high esteem and celebrated her as an honour to her people and country. Another intriguing figure known only through poems which make reference to her is Seón Eana Príor, a writer who travelled Munster and who appeared at times dressed as a man and at others in women's clothing.[3]

Of the women whose work has survived some had close connections to familial and hereditary literary networks. Una Nic Cruitín's poem addressed to Isibéal Ní Bhriain makes it clear that Nic Cruitín, the daughter of Aodh Buí Mac Cruitín and a member of a family which had served as hereditary poets to the Uí Bhriain (O'Brien) family of Thomond, sees herself as having a right to Ní Bhriain's patronage.[4] The Ó Neachtain circle of Irish-language scholars and writers active in Dublin in the first half of the eighteenth century fostered two female poets, Úna Ní Bhroin, the wife of Seán Ó Neachtáin, and Máire Ní Reachtagáin, the wife of Seán's son Tadhg. Liam Mac Mathúna has drawn attention to the urbanity of this circle, and the openness to new ideas and new forms of knowledge in the work these writers and scholars produced.[5] Máire Ní Reachtagáin's poem on the death of her brother Seoirse (George) is indicative of this innovative tendency in that it adapts the oral genre of *caoineadh* (keening), traditionally performed by women, into a reflective, literary form.[6] The small body of poetry that has survived is diverse in its themes and forms. It includes a Jacobite poem by Eibhlín Ní Choillte (fl. 1745), 'Stadaidh Bhur nGéarghol, a Ghasra Chaomhdha' ('Expelling Seán Buí'), which can be found in more than twenty manuscript copies, indicating that it was exceptionally popular.[7] Máire Nic a Liondain's (fl. 1771) lyrical evocation of an earthly paradise for two lovers in 'Coillte Glasa an Triúcha' ('The Green Woods of Triúch') contrasts with Máire Ní Dhonnagáin's (fl. 1760) self-condemnatory confession in her poem 'An Peacach' ('The Sinner'). Communal identification with Catholicism and opposition to the spread of Protestantism are strongly in evidence in Máire Ní Mhurchú's 'An Mhinistir a thug Anbhás dó Fhéin' ('On a Minister Who Killed Himself') (1802).

This body of written work is, however, only a partial representation of women's activity in Irish-language culture. For women, as for the majority of Irish-speakers in Ireland, oral composition and transmission played a much greater role than the written word. As storytellers, singers and keeners, women were active in creating and transmitting oral texts in a tradition that existed into the twentieth century. The oral tradition has given us arguably the most famous female-authored text of the eighteenth century, in any language, 'Tórramh-Chaoineadh Airt Uí Laoghaire' ('The Lament for Art O'Leary'), attributed to Eibhlín Dubh Ní Chonaill (ca. 1743–1800). Art O'Leary's death is framed in the poem in the context of the Penal Laws (he was famously involved in a dispute for owning a horse of greater value than was permitted for Catholics), but it also expresses Ní Chonaill's grief at the loss of a beloved husband and the father of her children, drawing attention, as Neil Buttimer has pointed out, to the ways in which the wider structures of disadvantage and discrimination registered at the level of the home and the family.[8]

The durability and high status of the 'Lament' is instructive, in that not only has the text survived due to multiple modes of transmission, and in numerous translations, but it has also been acclaimed by different audiences for different reasons. The text's origins as an oral composition have been strongly attested to, and there is evidence that the lament achieved acclaim in the oral tradition very rapidly – its ultimate preservation in written form attests to its popularity and durability as an oral text.[9]

As Louis Cullen has pointed out, however, the poem's treatment of 'themes of oppression and conflict' made it particularly popular in the period of the Gaelic revival, when it entered for the first time into an Irish-language print culture. This position was further cemented in the decades following independence, when the poem or extracts from it featured in school anthologies and in state examinations, with an uncomplicated attribution to Ní Chonaill as author.[10] Contemporary critics, however, stress not Ní Chonaill's achievement as the author of a unique text, but the fact that: 'The Lament is part of a long tradition, [and] its excellence derives from the excellence of every keen from which its composers learned their craft.'[11] Furthermore, the significance of the *caoineadh* (keen) as a specifically female form is highlighted by Angela Bourke, who proposes that: 'To the extent that it offers women a licence to speak loudly and without inhibition, and frequently to defend their own interests against those of men, *caoineadh* may be read as a feminist utterance.'[12] The widespread and enduring impact of 'The Lament for Art O'Leary' contrasts with the restricted circulation of and audience for the manuscript poems written in Irish by women in the same period; both these types of composition and circulation, however, are part of the shifting linguistic and social dynamics of eighteenth-century Ireland, and give evidence of women's participation in the evolving Irish-language tradition.

Letters and Unpublished Writing

The most common form of writing by women in Ireland in this period was the letter, rather than any published literary work.[13] We should not, however, always insist on making sharp distinctions between unpublished and published writing, not least because a number of the women who wrote letters or journals in the eighteenth century clearly had a sense of themselves as authors. The most poignant unpublished text to come down to us from the eighteenth century is undoubtedly Dorothea Herbert's *Retrospections*. Herbert (ca. 1768–1829) was the daughter of a clergyman who, following an unhappy love affair, became increasingly isolated from society and was, she claimed, imprisoned by her own family. In addition to writing her *Retrospections*, in which she provides a detailed account of her life and her family and social milieu, Herbert describes herself as the 'Authoress of the Orphan Plays and Various Poems and Novels in Four Volumes'.[14] Herbert prepared her manuscript with all the trappings of a published text (title page, chapter divisions, headings and notes), making it clear that at the very end of the eighteenth century, claiming the title of 'authoress' and positioning her writing as a text for publication held significant appeal for her and was in fact the fulcrum around which she constructed her identity. Elizabeth Sheridan (1758–1837) became known in the twentieth century as the author of a previously unpublished *Journal*, but Sheridan was not in fact simply a woman who wrote for family and friends: not only did she publish novels in the early nineteenth century under her married name, Mrs H. Le Fanu, but she is also (as will be discussed below) the author of two novels published anonymously in the 1780s. Another celebrated letter writer, Mary Granville Delany (1700–88), wrote but never published a Gothic short story entitled 'Marianna'.[15] The preparation of texts for publication that never transpired and the anonymous publication of work testify to the significant conflict that was perceived between the 'public' nature of authorship and proper roles for women in eighteenth-century society.

The public/private distinction was, however, far from absolute: as a form letters occupied a position between public and private and many women, including Mary Delany and, later, Martha McTier (1742–1837), wrote in awareness of the fact that their letters circulated not only among family members but also within networks of friends. Delany's vast output of letters, published in the nineteenth century in six volumes, played an important role in constructing 'a self-conscious community of women friends' in both London and Dublin.[16] These female networks were intellectual, artistic and literary: Delany's lifelong friend Sarah Chapone, for instance, has been identified as the author of *The Hardship of English Laws in Relation to Wives* (1735), and Delany may have played a part in the appearance of a Dublin edition of this work.[17]

Although a world apart from Delany in social and political terms, Martha McTier's letters played a comparable role in constructing an identity that, while not entirely public, was far from exclusively private. From a self-consciously enlightened Presbyterian background, Martha engaged enthusiastically in the philosophical and political debates that animated late eighteenth-century Ireland. Through letters written largely to her brother, the doctor and United Irishman William Drennan, her progressive views would have been known to a wide circle of family, friends and acquaintances, among whom, according to Maria Luddy, she would have had a reputation as a 'political woman'.[18] This identity was highlighted when, as a suspected radical, McTier's correspondence was subject to government surveillance, a fact of which she was aware.[19] Publication therefore is not an infallible benchmark for women's participation in the eighteenth-century 'republic of letters', but it is nonetheless instructive to note how eager McTier was to refute rumours reported to her by William that she was the author of a piece in the *Northern Star* newspaper.[20] Appearing in print, especially in connection with a topic considered controversial or unfeminine, was clearly still something that many women would not have countenanced. This makes it all the more remarkable that the eighteenth century produced so many pioneering female authors.

Prose and the Novel

New research on the early Irish novel and on eighteenth-century women novelists has revealed a much earlier adoption of the novel form in Ireland than was formerly claimed, as well as a much more diverse picture of the types of prose fiction produced in Ireland and by Irish women. The anonymously authored *Virtue Rewarded; or, The Irish Princess* (1693) locates its story of the conflict between love and ambition in the highly contemporary context of the Williamite wars, suggesting that the introduction of a new political order in Ireland was a spur to the emergence of this new genre of prose fiction. If the perspective of *Virtue Rewarded* is broadly speaking that of Protestant Ireland, we have in Sarah Butler's *Irish Tales* (1716), not only the first Irish novel to be ascribed to a female author, but also a text that expresses strong Catholic and Jacobite sympathies. Unfortunately nothing is known of Butler other than her name, but the evidence of the text is that she had access to a manuscript copy in either English or Irish of Geoffrey Keating's historical compendium *Foras Feasa ar Éireann* ('A Basis for a Knowledge of Ireland'), which makes *Irish Tales* an extraordinarily early example of the incorporation of Gaelic manuscript material into a contemporary literary text, together with the use of historical parallels to encode resistance to dominant power structures.[21] This use of Gaelic and historical sources is, however, strikingly ahead of its time and is not found again until the end of the century.

The novels published by Mary Davys (1674–1732), Elizabeth Griffith (1727–93) and Frances Sheridan (1724–66) in the period up to the 1770s are characteristic of women's fiction in this period in their treatment of romance, courtship, sex and marriage as topics of particular significance in women's lives. The moral failings of both sexes are portrayed in a lively and witty manner by Davys, who at the same time displays a sharp awareness of the unequal hand dealt to the majority of women.

Griffith and Sheridan, writing within the genre of sentimental fiction that dominated from the mid-century to the 1770s, dwell to a much greater extent on the emotional suffering that arises as a result of these gendered power structures. As exemplified in the novels of Samuel Richardson, whose work influenced both Sheridan and Griffith, these narratives of distressed virtue also function as critiques of patriarchal oppression. The heightened political awareness and the growth of the Patriot movement in Ireland is reflected in women's fiction in the last quarter of the century, as is the turn towards the Gothic, the national tale and historical settings. In addition to the novel, two remarkable memoirs were published in this period by Irish women, Laetitia Pilkington (ca. 1707–50) and Margaret Leeson (1727–97).

Mary Davys's novels, particularly *The Reform'd Coquet* (1724), *Familiar Letters Betwixt a Lady and Gentleman* (1725) and *The Accomplish'd Rake* (1727), rank alongside those of Aphra Behn, Eliza Haywood and Delariviere Manly, and renewed critical attention to this group of female writers has prompted a significant revision of the history of the novel, traditionally associated with the triumvirate of Defoe, Fielding and Richardson. In the Preface to her *Works*, published in 1725, Davys confidently outlines her views on the strengths and potential of the novel as a form, asserting the advantages of what she calls 'Probable Feign'd Stories' over competing genres including history and travels.[22]

Davys is typical of published women writers in Ireland in this period in a number of ways. She turned to writing as a means of making a livelihood – in this case a need precipitated by the death of her clergyman husband; she left Ireland in order to pursue her plans for a professional literary career; and she displayed a sharp awareness of her position as a woman in the male-dominated literary world. In her *Works*, she defiantly addressed the seeming impropriety of her decision to publish her writing as a means to make a living: she asserts that her work contains nothing that could be morally objectionable, and adds: 'Let them further consider, that a Woman left to her own Endeavours for Twenty-Seven Years together, may well be allow'd to catch at any Opportunity for that Bread, which they that condemn her would very probably deny to give her.'[23] Davys's remarks point both to the new opportunities open to women in an age in which writing was becoming a professional activity, and to the specific obstacles that women had to negotiate as writers, and particularly as published authors.

Like Davys, Laetitia Pilkington left Ireland for Britain in the hopes that her literary gifts would provide her with an income. But whereas

Davys could claim respectability as a clergyman's widow, Pilkington was disgraced, having been divorced by her clergyman husband, Matthew Pilkington, amid accusations of adultery. Pilkington's friendship with Jonathan Swift provided the basis for the success of the first volume of her *Memoirs* (1748–54) which contains several striking first-hand accounts of the Dean. Pilkington certainly deserves recognition as 'Swift's first biographer',[24] but the *Memoirs* are also an important text for those who wish to gain an understanding of the limitations placed on intelligent and talented women in this period. For A. C. Elias, the *Memoirs* are 'an archetypal depiction of the bright woman's lot in the eighteenth-century', showing an 'active mind consigned to passive roles'.[25] Although Pilkington can be as bitter in her criticisms of women as she is of men, she articulates a sharp critique of the gender ideology which had condemned her to a very marginal and precarious existence when she writes that: 'Of all things in Nature I most wonder why Men should be severe in their Censures on our Sex, for a Failure in Point of Chastity: Is it not monstrous that our Seducers should be our Accusers?'[26] Pilkington also reflects on the perceived relationship between her loss of respectability and her literary activity. Her tarnished reputation, financial precarity and identity as an author are compounded when she describes herself as a 'Lady of Adventure', observing that had her husband not cast her off, she would have been 'a harmless household [sic] Dove' and 'should have rested contented with my humble Situation, and, instead of using a Pen, been employed with a Needle'.[27]

In *A Series of Genuine Letters between Henry and Frances* (1757), by contrast, Elizabeth Griffith, together with her husband Richard, based a successful literary venture on her much happier experience of courtship and marriage. This publication drew on the actual letters exchanged between Elizabeth and Richard prior to their marriage, and its popularity is attested to by the number of editions, including later, enlarged editions in which letters were added. The fact that the couple defied the plans of Richard Griffith's father for a more financially advantageous marriage, together with the ample evidence in the letters of a relationship that involved shared intellectual interests, with the couple arguing about ideas and sharing opinions on what they were reading, makes *Letters of Henry and Frances* an important text in the development of the ideal of 'companionate marriage'.[28] After considerable success as the author of numerous plays which will be discussed below, Griffith turned to the novel relatively late in life, and wrote three epistolary novels, *The Delicate Distress* (1769), *The History of Lady Barton* (1771) and *Letters of*

Lady Juliana Harley (1776), as well as editing a three-volume *Collection of Novels* (1777), which included works by Aphra Behn, Eliza Haywood and Penelope Aubin. She also contributed the lion's share of the content to a collection of short stories entitled *Novellettes, Selected for the Use of Young Ladies and Gentlemen* (1780).

Throughout her work, Griffith articulates boldly progressive opinions on women's capacity for reason, the sexual double standard and women's access to education and learning. In her novels, she uses the device of the letter to provide an insight into the psychology of her female protagonists as well as a means to articulate subversive opinions on the patriarchal control of women. The eponymous Lady Barton, for instance, writes to her sister despite the fact that her husband is of the opinion that 'women should be treated like state criminals, and utterly debarred the use of pen and ink'.[29] In the Preface to the same novel, Griffith outlines her views on the aesthetic and moral potential of the novel form, stressing the importance of verisimilitude, originality and the ability to connect emotionally and psychologically with characters. She describes her process of composition as also one of feeling, in which she 'lived along the line' as she wrote.[30]

Griffith's stress on feeling signals the importance in this period of the concept of sensibility and her works belong to the genre of the sentimental novel. The most famous Irish example of this type of novel is undoubtedly *Memoirs of Miss Sidney Bidulph* (1761), by Frances Sheridan (1724–66). As revealed in her daughter Alicia Le Fanu's *Memoirs*, Frances Sheridan's father was hostile even to the idea of women being taught to write, but with the assistance of her brothers Sheridan overcame this obstacle and wrote a romance entitled *Eugenia and Adelaide* when aged only fifteen. When she showed this unpublished tale to Samuel Richardson, he encouraged her to write fiction and the result, *Sidney Bidulph*, which she dedicated to him, was an immediate success on publication. Sheridan also wrote for the theatre, which will be discussed below, but her novel was undoubtedly her most successful work. It is an at times harrowing examination of the suffering endured by a woman who attempts to live according to the contemporary ideal of feminine virtue, and has been described as 'an unspoken but palpable critique of women's lack of marital self-determination under patriarchy'.[31] Elizabeth Griffith hoped that readers would 'catch the infection'[32] of what she felt as she wrote about her characters' experiences, and this was certainly the case with *Sidney Bidulph*: Dr Johnson is reported to have said to Sheridan, 'I know not, Madam, that you have a right, upon moral principles, to make your readers suffer so much.'[33] *Sidney Bidulph* was one of the most popular novels of the later eighteenth century: there were five editions published in London as well as Dublin editions, translations into French and German, and imitations by anonymous authors. Sheridan went on to write a 'continuation', which is in fact a stand-alone story of the second generation of characters, as well as an oriental tale, *The History of Nourjahad*, published posthumously in 1767.

Frances Sheridan's reputation as an author has usually been overshadowed by the success of her son, the playwright Richard Brinsley Sheridan. Until recently, however, what was not known was that her daughter, Elizabeth Sheridan, was the author of two remarkable fictions published in the 1780s, *Emeline* (1780) and *The Triumph of Prudence over Passion* (1781). *The Triumph of Prudence over Passion* is in many respects a striking departure from the conventional concerns of eighteenth-century female-centred fiction, not least her mother's highly acclaimed novel. The primary character, Louisa Mortimer, revels in her independence as a single woman of means, advises her female friends to resist unjust parental interference where necessary and rational, and comments confidently on political events. The novel is in fact notable for the way in which it 'links the state of the Irish nation closely to the position of its women'.[34] Sheridan's novels are indicative of an important shift from the 1770s onwards, in which writers began to engage with Ireland in their work in new and distinctive ways, and women's fiction addressed a more broadly political sphere than had hitherto been the case. Whereas Sheridan's novel is born out of the optimist Patriot politics that animated the Volunteer movement and helped to bring about the short-lived 'independent' Irish parliament that came into being in 1782, other novelists responded to the appeal of the Gothic and the Ossianic, in which the sometimes distant past and wild and remote locations offered alternatives to contemporary life and society.

The use of the term 'historical tale' in the titles of the two novels by Anne Fuller (fl. 1789) gives a clear indication of this new direction. *Alan Fitz-Osborne: An Historical Tale* (1787) is set in the reign of Henry III in the thirteenth century, but *The Son of Ethelwolf: An Historical Tale* (1789) takes as its setting the struggles of the Saxons against the Danish invaders in the ninth century. In her sole novel, *The Hermit of Snowden* (1789), Elizabeth Ryves (1749–97), who was a prolific poet, exploits the associations of the Welsh landscape with the sublime and highlights the growing interest in antiquarianism, when she notes that the customs and traditions of the inhabitants of the remote regions of Wales 'might throw light upon ... the history of those early ages, which are at present exceedingly obscure'.[35] The most successful and influential writer to combine the fascination and appeal of both the Gothic and the Ossianic mood was, however, Regina Maria Roche (ca. 1764–1845) in her *The Children of the Abbey* (1796). This novel combines a tale of persecuted and distressed female virtue with depictions of Welsh, Scottish and Irish locations in which Ossian is explicitly and repeatedly invoked, and which abound in Gothic structures such as the abandoned chapel of Dunreath Castle in Scotland and the ruined Abbey adjacent to Castle Carberry in Northern Ireland. The inclusion of Roche's *Clermont* (1798) in the list of *Northanger Abbey*'s 'horrid novels' contributed to the trivialization of her work, but new critical interest in the early nineteenth-century 'national tale' has led to a re-evaluation of *The Children of the Abbey* in particular as an important forerunner of the fictions of Owenson and Edgeworth.

Drama

Due to the public nature of the form, women who wrote for the theatre in this period were subject to a particularly high degree of scrutiny. This is evident from the prologues and epilogues appended to eighteenth-century female-authored plays, which almost invariably draw attention to the writer's gender. In addition to this, the extent to which a dramatist's success depended on audience approval in a particularly immediate way meant that drama was a more market-driven literary form than either prose or poetry. As Christopher Morash has pointed out, this meant that plays written for a London audience were more likely to succeed than those written for a Dublin audience, and the pull of London meant that many Irish playwrights based themselves there and did not write plays with recognizably Irish characters or locations.[36] Irish female dramatists could thus be said to be doubly marginalized. Mary Davys opens her Prologue to *The Northern Heiress* by claiming that 'When Women write, the Criticks, now-a-days, / Are ready, e'er they see, to damn their Plays'.[37] In many respects, the careers of Davys, Elizabeth Griffith and Frances Sheridan testify to the real nature of the obstacles that they faced as women in the world of theatre, but each of them also succeeded in making a mark in that competitive and sometimes hostile world. It is notable that being based in England appears to have offered these women greater opportunities as dramatists.

Although Davys is now much more often considered as a novelist, she wrote two plays, *The Northern Heiress: Or, the Humours of York* which was performed and published in 1716, and *The Self-Rival*, which was published in her 1725 *Works*, the title describing it 'as it should have been acted at the Theatre Royal in Drury Lane'. Noting that in the *Works* Davys placed her two plays prominently at the beginning of the first volume, Martha Bowden has suggested that the current critical view of Davys as a novelist who started out as a dramatist is mistaken, and Davys should be seen instead as 'a novelist who would have preferred to be known as a dramatist'.[38] The fact that she moved from York to London following the success of *The Northern Heiress* bears out this speculation. The failure to have *The Self-Rival* produced, however, seems to have led to Davys's decision to move to Cambridge and open a coffee house as a means of making a living. Both Davys's plays are lively comedies whose sometimes earthy language contrasts with the turn, later in the century, to sentimental comedy. The nascent culture of politeness is in fact a theme of *The Northern Heiress*, in which the habits and manners of Lady Greasy and her female cronies are contrasted with the younger Isabella who sees in politeness an opportunity for women to cultivate talents outside of the demands of housekeeping.

As the daughter of Thomas Griffith, actor-manager of Dublin's Smock Alley theatre, and an experienced actress who made her stage-debut in 1749 in the role of Juliet, it is not surprising that Elizabeth Griffith's earliest writing was for the stage. Her very first literary effort was not *Letters of Henry and Frances*, but a tragedy entitled *Theodorick, King of Denmark*, which was written in 1752, though it was never performed. Griffith and her husband left Ireland for London in 1764, and this seems to have prompted her to pursue a career as a playwright. Her verse-tragedy *Amana* (1764) was published by subscription but remained unproduced. When she turned to comedy, however, with *The Platonic Wife* (1765), her fortunes changed and the play was produced at Drury Lane. Griffith wrote four further plays over the course of the next 14 years, and she enjoyed considerable success with *The Double Mistake* (1766) and *The School for Rakes* (1769) in particular, both of which belong to the genre of domestic or sentimental comedy which was then hugely popular. Griffith was remarkably successful as a female playwright in this period, but her career was marked by the negative critical reaction to *The Platonic Wife*, her first comedy, in which the wife in question proved too assertive and self-confident for some. Her subsequent work tended to rely on rather than challenge gender stereotypes. Elizabeth Eger comments that: 'While Griffith managed to become a professional playwright by manipulating contemporary opinion rather than allowing herself to be its victim, she was never entirely free from others' sexist prejudice against her work.'[39] Griffith's continuing confidence in her work is, however, illustrated by the fact that she published a work of dramatic criticism, *The Morals of Shakespeare's Drama Illustrated* (1775), and her proto-feminist consciousness is evident in her citation of Elizabeth Montagu as an inspiration on her writing.

Frances Sheridan also had a close connection to the world of Dublin theatre, having married Thomas Sheridan in 1747, at which point he was, like Griffith's father before him, actor-manager of the Smock Alley Theatre. Negative public and critical reaction, however, had a more stifling effect on Frances Sheridan's career as a playwright. As was the case for both Griffith and Davys, Sheridan's work for the theatre was initiated in England, where she moved with her husband and family in 1758. Her first play, *The Discovery* (1763), was produced successfully at Drury Lane, having a run of seventeen nights. It was also produced in the same year in Dublin and proved popular enough to be revived a number of times in the later eighteenth century. A sentimental comedy, *The Discovery* is notable for well-realized characters whose comic quirks and foibles and moral weaknesses are communicated through their particular use of language. Inspired by her success, Sheridan completed a second play, *The Dupe*, within a few months, and it was also staged in Drury Lane in late 1763. The play did not prove popular with audiences, however, and ran for only three nights. The trajectory of Sheridan's career can be contrasted with that of Griffith, who moved away from characters and scenarios that might prove unpalatable to popular taste. *The Discovery*'s Lord Medway is a philandering husband and irresponsible father who manages to emerge unscathed from a mess of his own making, thanks in no small part to the loyalty of both his wife and son. In her Epilogue to *The Discovery*, Sheridan offered a subversive commentary on the character of Lady Medway, the long-suffering wife, accusing her of excessive passivity. In *The Dupe* she went further and left behind the reassuring resolutions of sentimental comedy. The rake at the centre of her next play was not a reformable character like Lord Medway, but the ridiculed 'dupe' of the title, and audiences and critics did not react well to what was perceived as coarseness in the play's satiric humour. Reviews in the *Public Advertiser* and *Gazeteer and London Daily Advertiser* make it clear that the play's alleged 'lowness' in both language and morals was particularly objectionable and shocking in having been written by a woman.[40] Sheridan went on to write her third and final play, *A Journey to Bath*, while living in France in 1766, and submitted it with a view to being produced in

Drury Lane. The play was, however, rejected by Garrick. Sheridan responded to Garrick's criticisms in a letter which gives us some insight into her views on her own work.[41] It has however been suggested that Garrick's rejection of the play may have been motivated in part by Sheridan's 'tarnished reputation' in the wake of the morally inflected criticism of *The Dupe*.[42] What is abundantly clear is that although *A Journey to Bath* was never produced and remained unpublished in any form until the late nineteenth century, it inspired Sheridan's son, Richard Brinsley Sheridan. Mrs Tryfort of *A Journey to Bath* is a social climber whose speech is littered with comically misapplied words and is clearly the model on which R. B. Sheridan based Mrs. Malaprop in his celebrated *The Rivals* (1775).

The relatively small number of Irish women who wrote plays in this period reflects both the gendered nature of the theatre as a public space in which women's presence was only partly tolerated, and the marginal position of Dublin in relation to the dominance of London theatre. Given this highly unfavourable context, the quality of the work produced by these three accomplished playwrights is remarkable. The extent to which their work has been forgotten is, however, a reflection not only of critical amnesia but also of the fact that these plays were not revived and produced in subsequent centuries – this is a work of theatrical recovery that has yet to be accomplished.

Poetry

The earliest published volume of poetry by an Irishwoman in the eighteenth century, *Marinda: Poems and Translations upon Several Occasions* (1716), was the posthumously published work of Mary Monck (ca. 1677–1715). The volume consists of original poems including odes, songs, epigrams, eclogues, and a lengthy landscape poem, addressed to her brother Richard, as well as translations from authors including Petrarch and Tasso. It is prefaced by a long dedication to Princess Caroline by Monck's father, Robert Molesworth, first Viscount Molesworth (1656–1725), in which he stresses that his daughter's poetry was secondary to her domestic duties as a wife and mother. In describing her poems as 'Diversions' rather than 'Labours' and emphasizing that she wrote her poems 'little expecting, and as little desiring the Publick shou'd have any Opportunity either of Applauding or Condemning them', he carefully positions her as conforming to the demands and expectations of femininity.[43] The inclusion in the volume of a number of poems addressed to Mary herself, or 'Marinda', indicates

Monck's membership of a literary coterie, and thus as a writer whose sense of authorship derived from the circulation of manuscript material within a small group, rather than through publication. It can be said, therefore, that in the early part of the century the composition of poetry, within very specific constraints, was not incompatible with ideas of genteel femininity. Significant changes over the course of the century opened up the role of poet to middle-class and even working-class women, and also facilitated women who wished to write poetry on topics previously considered inappropriate or unfeminine.

Mary Barber's *Poems on Several Occasions*, a landmark volume published in 1734, stands at the centre of a decade remarkably rich in work by women poets in Ireland. Barber was part of a network of writers including Elizabeth Sican, Constantia Grierson and Laetitia Pilkington, as well as Pilkington's husband Matthew and Patrick Delany, who have become indelibly associated with Jonathan Swift. Swift was introduced to the figures in this group by his friend Patrick Delany, and he used his considerable influence and fame to assist them and promote their work. His assistance was certainly invaluable to Mary Barber when she sought subscriptions in England and Ireland for the publication of her long-planned volume of poetry, as he allowed a letter of his to the Earl of Orrery on her behalf to be appended to the work, and also wrote to friends in England requesting support. Swift referred to Barber, Grierson and Sican as his 'triumfeminate', and the appropriating tone of this phrase has been reflected in critical commentary on this group, who have until recently been seen as imitative of Swift and depending on him for recognition of their work. Paula Backscheider has, however, pointed out that the women's network existed independently of Swift and that in their work they respond to one another and to other women writers, including Elizabeth Rowe.[44]

Barber was the wife of a woollen draper, and being squarely of the middling class, with restricted time or leisure for writing, it is remarkable that she produced such a significant body of work. She certainly deserves the accolades bestowed on her by Swift, who described her in a letter to Pope as 'our chief Poetess'.[45] Her poems arise largely from reflections and observations on daily life and from her relationships with others, and it is her themes of friendship and the social virtues that are highlighted by Constantia Grierson in a poem addressed to Barber that opens the volume. Barber undoubtedly possessed ambition, so much so that a desire to promote her own work in all likelihood motivated her to forge letters of recommendation addressed to Queen Caroline, allegedly from Swift.[46] In spite of this ill-advised tactic, Barber's volume was resoundingly successful, and boasted the names of over 900 subscribers, including, of course, Swift, but also Samuel Richardson, Elizabeth Rowe and a dazzling array of titled dignitaries from both Britain and Ireland, including the Lord Lieutenant of Ireland, the Duke of Dorset. Any concept of personal or poetic ambition is, however, disclaimed in her Preface, in which she declares that her aim in writing was 'chiefly to form the Minds of my Children'.[47] Although this framing of her work is clearly a somewhat disingenuous performance of feminine modesty and propriety, the several poems written in the voice of her young son Constantine (Con) are among the most striking in her work. In a poem such as 'Written for my Son, and Spoken by Him at School, to Some of the Fellows of the College of *Dublin*, at a Public Examination for Victors', for instance, Barber inserts her voice into a space to which women could not in reality gain access. 'Written for my Son, and Spoken by him on first putting on his Breeches' uses a child's perspective to construct male attire as the imposition of 'Tyrant *Custom*', a trope more commonly reserved for satiric comment on women's fashions.[48]

Barber's inclusion in her volume of six poems by Constantia Grierson also helped to ensure that her poetry survived. Laetitia Pilkington also included a further three poems by Grierson in her *Memoirs*, but Grierson herself did not seek publication for her poetry and some of it remained unpublished until the twentieth century. Included in Barber's *Poems on Several Occasions* is a poem by Grierson addressed to Mrs Percival, celebrating her decision to remain in Ireland rather than to take part in Bishop Berkeley's ultimately ill-fated plan to open a missionary college in Bermuda. Grierson affirms that 'Heav'n will by other Means convert the *West*' and goes on to emphasize Ireland's need for cultivation and improvement. The valuable contribution of patriotic female citizens, such as Mrs Percival, is juxtaposed with the drain of capital, both human and financial, from Ireland to Britain:

> Our Gold may flow to *Albion* with each Tide;
> But let them with that Gold be satisfy'd:
> The want of that we long have learned to bear,
> But Souls like thine accomplish'd, cannot spare.[49]

Poetry was however only a part of Grierson's prodigious literary achievements. From a very modest background and with little formal schooling, she had acquired a mastery of French, Latin, Greek and, it was claimed, Hebrew. Barber described her as 'one of the most extraordinary Women that either this Age, or perhaps any other ever produc'd' not least because 'she rose to this Eminence in Learning merely by the Force of her own Genius, and continual Application'.[50] Laetitia Pilkington likewise admired Grierson, paying her the backhanded compliment of saying that she was the only other woman aside from Katherine Philips whose works were worth reading.[51] Following her marriage to the printer, George Grierson, she prepared editions of Terence and Tacitus and her classical learning was admired by many, including Swift. George Grierson's success in obtaining the position of King's Printer in 1732 has been attributed to the esteem in which Constantia was held.

Grierson's friend and admirer, Laetitia Pilkington, was herself a prolific and accomplished poet, whose *Memoirs* include many examples of her work, including the poem on Swift's birthday through which she managed to secure an introduction to the Dean.[52] Her most accomplished poem is *The Statues; or, A Trial of Constancy*, a reflection on the battle of the sexes that was published separately in 1739 to some acclaim. The ideological tendency to revere women in idealized forms, while punishing them for transgressions both minor and major, is subject to a satiric reversal in the poem, in which the faithless lover is punished for his inconstancy by being transformed into a statue: 'No Sense of Life, no Motions he retains / But, fixed, a dreadful Monument remains.'[53] An alternative to frequently troubled heterosexual relationships can be found in the poems of Charlotte McCarthy (fl. 1745–68). The plot of McCarthy's novel, *The Fair Moralist*, stages scenes of cross-dressing in which the gender confusion opens the possibility of same-sex attraction, and the second edition included a selection of poems described by Emma Donoghue as a celebration of 'idyllic, virtuous love between pairs of women'.[54] McCarthy's writing thus constitutes an early contribution to the depiction of lesbian relationships in Irish writing.

In the second half of the eighteenth century, there are a number of noteworthy developments in the poetry written and published by women. Elizabeth Ryves' *Poems on Several Occasions* (1777) is one of the few female-authored volumes of poetry not to be published by subscription. Ryves was unmarried and was of very slim means; writing was for her as much an economic as a creative activity. Based in London, she produced plays, a novel and translations (including translations of Rousseau) in addition to her seven volumes of poetry. Her economically-precarious position did not prevent her from expressing political opinions however: *The Hastiniad* (1785) is a denunciation of Warren Hastings and of the exploitation of India. *Verses on the Present State of Ireland* (1768) by Margaret Bingham, Countess of Lucan, also explicitly tackles social and political issues, this time closer to home. She deplores Irish poverty and highlights the penal laws and trade restrictions as contributory factors to underdevelopment, warning moreover that 'such wrongs must be redress'd' given that 'whole quarters of the world at once rebel'.[55] Henrietta Battier's poetry is also clearly influenced by the heightened political awareness of the later eighteenth century, and by Patriot perspectives more particularly. The publication in 1792 of a slim volume of poems by Ellen Taylor, 'the Irish Cottager', testifies to the growing sense of poetry as a product of imagination rather than learning, and a 'democratization' of literature that had begun some decades earlier in Britain with the work of labouring class poets including Stephen Duck, Mary Leapor and Ann Yearsley.

The single most significant volume of poetry to appear in this century is Charlotte Brooke's *Reliques of Irish Poetry* (1789). As we have seen, while print became the key medium of communication in English, shaping ideas of authorship and creating an increasingly important space for public opinion, oral and manuscript culture remained dominant in the Irish language. Brooke's work of collecting, editing, anthologizing and translating Irish poetry was based on the work of Gaelic scribes and scholars and the volume thus represents both a collective literary project and a pioneering act of synthesis between two different cultures, 'a new departure in transcultural co-operation'.[56] Brooke's famous metaphor of the Irish and British muses as sisters, 'sweet ambassadresses of cordial union', makes a claim for culture not as an ideological weapon, but a means of mutual understanding. Feminization here is key to a non-combative reshaping of the relationship not just between England and Ireland but between English and Irish language and culture. Overlooked until very recently is the inclusion in *Reliques* of an original work of poetry by Brooke, *Mäon: A Tale*, in which the notorious timidity and self-effacements of Brooke's 'Preface' are replaced by a much more self-assured tone and more explicit alignment with patriotic ideals. Brooke asserts her right to authorship and to advocacy on behalf of her country: 'For oft the Muse, a gentle guest, / Dwells in the female form; / And patriot fire, female breast, / May sure unquestion'd warm.'[57]

Conclusion

Eighteenth-century Ireland was a contested location, in which divisions of language, religion, class, ethnicity and political affiliation created profoundly different experiences for different women. Many Irish women wrote and published abroad, while women such as Mary Delany and Margaret Bingham, born elsewhere, contributed significantly to the literary and cultural sphere in Ireland. Charlotte Brooke's simultaneous claim to poetic authority and to identification with Ireland as a nation in *Mäon* is a landmark moment in women's writing in Ireland, but it should not be read in exclusive terms, as defining the way in which women's writing should position itself in relation to the political nation. As we have seen in this chapter, women's writing and culture display at times expressions of identification with a political or religious community, while at other times, awareness of women's marginalization within political and social structures is strongly articulated. Writing for women in this period in Ireland also functioned variously as vehicle for self-expression, a form of social and political networking, a means to financial independence, an active contribution to generic development and the extension of the boundaries of literary discourse. In Gaelic Ireland, women's roles in composing and transmitting oral culture were vital, and ultimately contributed to the maintenance of a tradition that enriched and transformed Irish literary culture. Over the course of the eighteenth century, print came to play an increasingly important role in social, cultural and political life. Although women's access to print culture was initially restricted, and Irish-speaking women continued to write and read within a manuscript culture, by the end of the century women in Ireland had helped to create a flourishing literary and print culture which had furthermore opened itself to the influence of Gaelic Ireland. The familiar narratives of eighteenth-century Ireland see the 1780s, when Brooke and others such as Elizabeth Sheridan explicitly articulated patriot views and aligned themselves as women with the fate of Ireland as a nation, as a short window of political progress and unity. This unity collapsed with the inability to incorporate Catholics within the political nation and the resulting rise of political radicalism which culminated in the 1798 rebellion. The demise of the Irish parliament in 1801 and the resulting blow to the status of Dublin is also seen as contributing to a weakened literary and cultural sphere. For literary women, however, this narrative of failure and collapse is far from accurate. The pioneering achievements of women across a wide range of genres in the eighteenth century laid the foundations for a consistently expanding sphere of female literary activity into the nineteenth century.

Notes

1 Mícheál Mac Craith, 'Literature in Irish, c.1550–1690', in *The Cambridge History of Irish Literature*, ed. Margaret Kelleher and Philip O'Leary (Cambridge: Cambridge University Press, 2006), 1:219.

2 See Máirín Ní Dhonnchdha, 'Courts and Coteries II: c.1500–1800', in *The Field Day Anthology of Irish Writing IV & V: Women's Writings and Traditions*, ed. Angela Bourke et al. (Cork: Cork University Press, 2002), 4:358–457.

3 See Una Nic Einrí, *Filí Luimnigh gan Iomrá san Ochtú Aois Déag* (Baile Átha Cliath: Coiscéim, 2016).

4 Pádraig A. Breatnach, trans., 'A Bhuime den Bhród Mhórdha ba Rathamhail Réim', in *Field Day Anthology of Irish Writing*, 4:434.

5 Liam Mac Mathúna, 'Getting to Grips with Innovation and Genre Diversification in the Work of the Ó Neachtain Circle in Early Eighteenth-Century Dublin', *Eighteenth-Century Ireland*, 27 (2012): 54.

6 *Field Day Anthology of Irish Writing*, 4:424–7.

7 Ibid., 4:35–6.

8 Neil Buttimer, 'Literature in Irish, 1690–1800', in *The Cambridge History of Irish Literature*, ed. Kelleher and O'Leary, 1:334.

9 With the exception of Brendán Ó Buachalla, in his *An Caoine agus An Chaointeoireacht* (Dublin: Cois Life, 1998), the critical consensus is that the 'Lament' was orally composed and transmitted, and that its form bears clear evidence of this. See Rachel Bromwich, 'The Keen for Art O'Leary, its Background and its Place in the Tradition of Gaelic Keening', *Éigse* 5 (1945–7): 236–52; Seán Ó Coileáin, 'The Irish Lament: An Oral Genre', *Studia Hibernica* 24 (1988): 97–117; Angela Bourke, 'Lamenting the Dead', *Field Day Anthology of Irish Writing*, 4:1365–7; 1372–84; Donna Wong, 'Literature and the Oral Tradition', in *The Cambridge History of Irish Literature*, ed. Kelleher and O'Leary, 1:633–76. Ó Coileáin notes that there is evidence of the poem being 'recognised immediately as something out of the ordinary', and as being widely circulated and spoken of in 1790, only seventeen years after its initially composition ('The Irish Lament', 107).

10 Louis Cullen, 'The Contemporary and Later Politics of Caoineadh Airt Uí Laoire', *Eighteenth-Century Ireland* 8 (1993): 9.

11 Wong, 'Literature and the Oral Tradition', 659.

12 Bourke, 'Lamenting the Dead', 1372.

13 Mary O'Dowd, *A History of Women in Ireland, 1500–1800* (Harlow: Pearson Education, 2005), 226–7.

14 Dorothea Herbert, *Retrospections of Dorothea Herbert, 1770–1806* (Dublin: TownHouse, 2004), n.p.

15 Mary Delany, 'Marianna', in *Mrs Delany and her Circle*, ed. Mark Laird and Alicia Weisberg-Roberts (New Haven: Yale Center for British Art, 2009), 250–61. For a discussion of 'Marianna', see Christina Morin, 'Theorizing Gothic in Eighteenth-Century Ireland', in *Irish Gothics: Genres, Forms, Modes and Traditions, 1760–1890*, ed. Christina Morin and Niall Gillespie (Houndmills: Palgrave Macmillan, 2014).

16 Lisa L. Moore, 'Queer Gardens: Mary Delany's Flowers and Friendships', *Eighteenth-Century Studies* 39, no. 1 (2005): 50.

17 Gerardine Meaney, Mary O'Dowd and Bernadette Whelan, *Reading the Irish Woman: Studies in Cultural Encounter and Exchange, 1714–1960* (Liverpool: Liverpool University Press, 2013), 19.

18 Maria Luddy, 'William Drennan and Martha McTier: A "Domestic" History', in *The Drennan-McTier Letters*, ed. Jean Agnew (Dublin: Women's History Project/Irish Manuscripts Commission, 1998), 1:xlix.

19 Catriona Kennedy, '"Womanish epistles"? Martha McTier, Female Epistolarity and Late-Eighteenth-Century Irish Radicalism', *Women's History Review* 13, no. 44 (2004): 661.

20 Luddy, 'William Drennan and Martha McTier', xlvii–xlix.

21 Ian Campbell Ross, '"One of the Principal Nations in Europe": The Representation of Ireland in Sarah Butler's Irish Tales', *Eighteenth-Century Fiction* 7 (1994): 4.

22 Mary Davys, 'Preface', *The Works of Mrs. Davys* (London, 1725), 1:iii.

23 Ibid., viii.

24 Norma Clarke, *Laetitia Pilkington: Queen of the Wits* (London: Faber, 2008), xvii, 37.

25 A. C. Elias, 'Introduction', in *Memoirs of Laetitia Pilkington*, ed. A. C. Elias (Athens, GA: University of Georgia Press, 1997), 1:xx.

26 Laetitia Pilkington, *Memoirs of Laetitia Pilkington*, ed. Elias, 1:67.

27 Ibid., 1:213–4.

28 For a recent discussion of *Letters of Henry and Frances*, see Meaney, O'Dowd and Whelan, *Reading the Irish Woman*, 20–22.

29 Elizabeth Griffith, *The History of Lady Barton* (London, 1771), 1:2.

30 Ibid., 1:x.

31 Helen Thompson, 'Sentimental Fiction of the 1760s and 1770s', in *The Oxford History of the Novel in English. Vol. 2: English and British Fiction 1750–1820*, ed. Peter Garside and Karen O'Brien (Oxford: Oxford University Press, 2015), 140.

32 Griffith, *The History of Lady Barton*, 1:xi.

33 Qtd. in Jean Coats Cleary, 'Introduction', *Memoirs of Miss Sidney Bidulph* (Oxford: Oxford University Press, 1995), xi.

34 Ian Campell Ross and Aileen Douglas, 'Introduction', in Elizabeth Sheridan, *The Triumph of Prudence over Passion* (Dublin: Four Courts), 10.

35 Elizabeth Ryves, *The Hermit of Snowden: or Memoirs of Albert and Lavinia* (London, 1789), ii.

36 Christopher Morash, 'Theatre in Ireland, 1690–1800', in *The Cambridge History of Irish Literature*, ed. Kelleher and O'Leary, 1:380–81.

37 Davys, *Works*, 1:68.

38 Martha F. Bowden, 'Mary Davys: Playwright as Novelist', *ABOPublic: An Interactive Forum for Women and the Arts, 1640–1830*, 25 August 2014. www .aphrabehn.org/ABO/mary-davys-playwright-novelist/. Accessed 5 March 2016.

39 Elizabeth Eger, 'Elizabeth Griffith', *Oxford Dictionary of National Biography*. Accessed 12 April 2016. https://doi.org/10.1093/ref:odnb/11596

40 See Elizabeth Kuti, 'Rewriting Frances Sheridan', *Eighteenth-Century Ireland* 11 (1996): 125–6.

41 See Robert Hogan and Jerry C. Beasley, 'Introduction', in *The Plays of Frances Sheridan* (Newark: University of Delaware Press, 1984), 25–6.

42 Kuti, 'Rewriting Frances Sheridan', 126.

43 Robert Molesworth, 'Dedication', in Mary Monck, *Marinda: Poems and Translations upon Several Occasions* (London, 1716), n.p.

44 See Paula Backscheider, 'Inverting the Image of Swift's Triumfeminate', *Journal for Early Modern Cultural Studies* 4 (2004): 37–71. For an alternative view of this group, stressing its mixed-gender nature, see Christine Gerrard, 'Senate or Seraglio? Swift's "Triumfeminate" and the Literary Coterie', *Eighteenth-Century Ireland* 31 (2016): 13–28.

45 Bernard Tucker, '"Our Chief Poetess:" Mary Barber and Swift's Circle' *Canadian Journal of Irish Studies* 19, no. 2 (1993): 31–44.

46 See Tucker, '"Our chief poetess,"' 33, and Gerrard, 'Senate or Seraglio', 7.

47 Mary Barber, 'Preface' to *Poems on Several Occasions* (London, 1734), xvii.

48 Ibid., 13, line 3.

49 Grierson, 'To the Hon. Mrs Percival on her desisting from the Bermudan Project', in *The Poetry of Laetitia Pilkington and Constantia Grierson*, ed. Bernard Tucker (Lewiston, NY: The Edwin Mellon Press, 1996), 140–41, line 3; lines 23–6.

50 Mary Barber, 'Preface', in *The Poems of Mary Barber, ?1690–1757*, ed. Bernard Tucker (Lewiston, NY: The Edwin Mellen Press, 1992), 50–51.

51 Pilkington, *Memoirs*, 2:228.

52 Ibid., 1:26.

53 Pilkington, 'The Statues', in *The Poetry of Laetitia Pilkington and Constantia Grierson*, 44, lines 221–2.

54 Emma Donoghue, 'Lesbian Encounters', in *The Field Day Anthology of Irish Writing Vol IV & V*, ed. Bourke et al., 4:1091.

55 Margaret Bingham, Lady Lucan, *Verses on the Present State of Ireland* (Dublin, 1768), 13.

56 Lesa Ní Mhunghaile, 'Introduction', in *Charlotte Brooke's Reliques of Irish Poetry*, ed. Lesa Ní Mhunghaile (Dublin: Irish Manuscripts Commission, 2009), xxi.

57 Charlotte Brooke, 'Mäon: An Irish Tale', in *Charlotte Brooke's Reliques of Irish Poetry*, ed. Lesa Ní Mhunghaile (Dublin: Irish Manuscripts Commission, 2009), 328.

CHAPTER 3

Writing under the Union, 1800–1845

James Kelly

On 1 January 1801, the Act of Union between Great Britain and Ireland passed into law, the culmination of the fraught 1790s that had ended in the uprising and brutal suppression of the United Irish 1798 Rebellion. In debates leading up to and afterwards, the Union was relentlessly figured by both opponents and supporters as either a marriage or a sisterly relationship.[1] It led to profound investigation into the nature of Irish cultural identity, and its figuration as unconsummated marriage lent fictional depictions of courtship and wedlock an explicitly political edge. Maria Edgeworth opened her writing career by noting 'human affairs are chained together; and female influence is a necessary and important link, which you cannot break without destroying the whole.'[2] Edgeworth and her contemporaries would create a body of writing in the post-Union years that would investigate the links between female influence, national identity, and political agency. While the post-Union decades have sometimes been seen as a moribund period in Irish political culture until the movement for Catholic Emancipation in the 1820s, women writers in these decades created an energetic and often experimental literature, testing the extent to which poetry, fiction and travel-writing could convey national character and represent historical change.

This literature emerged as Europe was reeling from the effects of the French Revolution and Napoleonic Wars and female moral propriety was increasingly tied to the stability of the state and society. Both Edgeworth and Sydney Owenson read and responded to Madame de Staël's novel *Corinne; or Italy* (1807). Its tale of a woman of genius giving voice to a nation, but ultimately abandoned by her English lover for her meeker, more domestic sister placed female artistic power at the centre of national life while also demonstrating how inimical conventional morality was to that power. Its themes resonated with both authors, with Owenson worrying as early as 1803 that 'I am *ambitious*, perhaps beyond the power of being happy.'[3] Edgeworth's *Ennui* (1809) compares two women within the public-private binary echoing the dynamics of de Staël's novel: 'One had the envied art of appearing to advantage in public – the other, the more desirable power of being happy in private.'[4] Women entering the public world of print were aware that there would be many critics suspicious of women's writing or claims to a public voice, and in the early decades of the nineteenth century Irish women writers felt the need to balance patriotic sentiment with political circumspection. 'As a woman [I have] avoided any thing like political discussion,' wrote Elizabeth Gunning in her novel, *The Exile of Erin* (1808), 'well aware how ill one of her sex must be qualified to enter on such a topic.'[5] The preface to Olivia Clarke's play, *The Irishwoman* (1819), addressed 'Ye women, in whose swelling bosoms burns / The patriot flame',[6] but the post-Union emergence of a national, if not always nationalist, literature complicated the extent to which private patriotic sentiment could remain apart from sectarian and political arguments. In responding to the violence of recent Irish history, creating a mournful sentimental poetry around Irish material and experimenting with dialect, realism and allegory in fiction, Irish women writers found that as the century progressed, literature increasingly offered and entailed a visible engagement with public issues.

'Rule and Misrule': The Legacy of 1798

Women's literature in the post-Union period was influenced by an eighteenth-century discourse of sensibility which utilized a language of heightened passion and emotional turmoil. As the memoirist Dorothea Herbert expressed it, one could be seized by 'a Passion so forcible that it shook every Sense and Shattered every Nerve'.[7] The culture of sensibility accorded finer emotional sensitivity to women, with the concomitant stress on the importance of learning emotional control and self-possession.[8] 'To possess strong feelings and amiable affections, and to express them with nice discrimination, has been the attribute of many female writers,' declared the preface to a posthumously published 1811 edition of Mary Tighe's long poem, *Psyche* (1805).[9] A literature of powerful emotion encountered a traumatic historical scene in the aftermath of the 1798 Rebellion. 'My mind felt wearied with what appeared to me oppressive in the melancholy state of the times,' wrote the Quaker poet Mary Leadbeater; 'rule and mis-rule fighting with each other, and the country torn to pieces with the strife.'[10] After the cataclysmic events that wracked the country, suffering femininity became a recurrent trope in oral and literary culture. The tragic figure of Mary (occasionally Ellen) le More, a virtuous young woman driven insane by the loss of her lover during the Rebellion, stalked ballad broadsides and chapbooks across Ireland and Britain.[11] Variations on the 1798 widow abound, with Leadbeater's Doro in 'The Ruined Cottage' running from her house lit up by yeomanry to see her Owen 'all bath'd in his gore!'[12]

The destruction of a domestic setting and violated bodies also occur in Amelia Bristow's *The Maniac* (1810). The young hero Albert marries his closest friend Bernardo's sister Mathilda, while his sister Emma marries Bernardo. When the Rebellion breaks out, Albert joins the yeomanry and sees his rebel friend executed and his sister die of grief. The only consolation left is his own home life, but on returning from the Rebellion he finds his wife and children have been slaughtered by rebels:

> His beauteous infants, on the ensanguined ground,
> Lay, sunk in death! deep pierced with many a wound!
> A little further on – racks, tortures, wheels!
> Are bliss, are paradise, to what he feels!
> Of ruffian violence the bleeding prey,
> His soul's rich treasure, his Mathilda lay![13]

Bristow's literary register was familiar from eighteenth-century sentimental literature, her young heroes and heroines having conventional generic names, but when confronted with the horrors of war and rape in 1798, emotional sensitivity easily slips into mania. Bristow placed a coda at the end of her poem noting that 'there is not much exaggeration in this melancholy tale' and that 'scenes similar to that here represented ... were, alas! but too frequent, where activity opposed the popular ferment.'[14]

As Siobhan Kilfeather noted, 1798 marked a moment in which homes were violently invaded, both figuratively by political rhetoric and all too literally by rebels or loyalists, leading to women writers attempting to represent the aftermath of the Rebellion not 'in terms of things seen and felt but in terms of the fears that had been activated and continued to haunt Ireland.'[15] Travellers to Ireland in the post-Union period continued to feel an alarming danger of potential rebellion, with the English writer, Mary Ann Grant, in 1805 noting the 'universal tendency to riot' and danger of French invasion:

> [In] a case so dreadful, I could almost be tempted to wish for a masculine habit and proportionable strength to enable me to face the enemy, rather than be left to the mercy of these unhappy, misguided people.[16]

Narratives of the rebellion from Irish Protestant women register the destruction of safe domestic spaces and the horror of civil conflict,[17] and it is unsurprising that imaginative literature incorporated an imagery and rhetoric of terror, aligning 1798 with the eighteenth-century tradition of the Gothic novel. The rebellion could provide a suitably lurid background to Lady Caroline Lamb's *Glenarvon* (1816), a popular and scandalous *roman á clef* detailing her tempestuous affair with Lord Byron. For Mrs Kelly's *The Matron of Erin* (1816), 1798 represents a more brutal scene of civil war and carnage:

> [That] memorable year ... when impending ruin frowned dire destruction on a devoted land, drenching it with its native blood; when proscription and death stalked abroad, spreading everywhere horror and conflagration.[18]

That Kelly then goes on to describe her national tale as a 'simple narrative of domestic woes'[19] should make us wary of seeing the private and public as anything other than inextricably linked.

The figure of the exiled United Irishman proved attractive to many writers, with the appropriately named Erin Fitzgerald in Gunning's *The Exile of Erin* an early example. Other Irish women writers would return to the character of the exiled, repentant, rebel. Sensibility could lead to mistaken political loyalties, and Irish exiles are often portrayed as figures whose natural benevolence is misdirected into a mistaken political enthusiasm. Alicia Le Fanu's *The Outlaw*, for instance, published in *Tales of a Tourist* (1823), as well as providing a satire of English travellers who misapprehend Irish culture, depicts the return of the Irish heroine's rebel father ('not one of the base or sanguinary inciters of rebellion'[20]) as she herself gradually reacquaints herself with her native culture. Both characters are marked by a strong natural sensibility, but the tale warns against the potential for sensibility to lead to erroneous interpretations of political situations. At the same time it is a text that enjoys indulging in moments of Gothic extravagance. Tellingly, the first meeting between father and daughter takes place in the suitably macabre 'mingled mass of tombs and ruins'[21] of a priory in Kilmallock, Co. Limerick.

In a charged footnote to *The Wild Irish Girl* (1806), Sydney Owenson, eager to 'efface from the Irish character the odium of cruelty', compared the Rebellion of 1798 to the Spanish conquest of South America, aligning British policy with the notoriously cruel colonial policy of the conquistadores:

> Had the *Historiographer* of MONTEZUMA or ATALIBA defended the *resistance* of his countrymen, or recorded the woes from when it sprung, though his QUIPAS was bathed in their blood, or embued with their

tears, he would have unavailingly recorded them; for the victorious *Spaniard* was insensible to the woes he had created, and called the resistance it gave birth to CRUELTY.[22]

Owenson's novel is careful in the level of sympathy it shows to the United Irishmen. That her titular Irish heroine Glorvina chooses an English lover disguised as an artist rather than one disguised as a rebel indicates Owenson's faith in culture rather than violence as the solution to Ireland's problems.

Maria Edgeworth has 1798 provide a backdrop to *Ennui* (1809), published as part of her *Tales of Fashionable Life* (1809–12). In Edgeworth's novel, a dissipated young Anglo-Irish aristocrat travels back to Ireland after meeting his Irish nurse, but due to his defence of his foster-brother against charges of storing rebel weapons, is mistaken for a sympathizer with the United Irishmen. Edgeworth's father, Richard Lovell Edgeworth, had undergone a similar ordeal during the rebellion: his liberal political views setting him at odds with the staunchly loyalist landowning classes of Longford. *Ennui* plays with and satirizes the Gothic expectations attaching to both Ireland and 1798. When Lord Glenthorn visits his Irish estates, he finds his Irish house 'so like ... a haunted castle, that if I had not been too much fatigued to think of any thing, I should have thought of Mrs Radcliffe.'[23] Edgeworth deflates any expectation we might have for a novel along the lines of the famous eighteenth-century Gothic novelist, Ann Radcliffe. Yet after the immediate danger of 1798 passes, Glenthorn is threatened by lingering rebels who meet, according to his Irish nurse, 'at night in the great cave, where the smugglers used to hide formerly, under the big rock, opposite the old abbey'[24]: an accretion of Gothic tropes and locales that knowingly trips into the absurd. '*Unfortunately for me*, the rebellion in Ireland was soon quelled'[25] writes Glenthorn, signalling the ludicrousness of seeing civil strife as entertainment for fashionable society.

Ennui provides, at one level, a satire of uninformed visitors to Ireland while also meditating on the complex negotiations of identity, family history and national character that lie behind land ownership and politics. Glenthorn is revealed to be the son of his nurse, Elinor O'Donoghue, switched at birth with his foster-brother, Christy O'Donoghue. The novel ends with Castle Glenthorn burning down, not as a result of rebel violence, but due to Christy's son, raised in a cottage, causing a fire through drunken ignorance. For Edgeworth, blindly observing hereditary claims to land were insufficient guarantees of stability in a post-rebellion society, and her works emphasize the need for landholding classes to demonstrate an educated, enlightened and committed approach to their tenantry and the social conditions of all classes in post-Union Ireland.

'A Nation of Versifiers': Women and Poetry after the Union

> The idea on which this dream is founded, may appear borrowed from the Pilgrims of the Sun, and Kilmenie, – yet it was nearly finished before I had read those delightful poems. Perhaps it is unnecessary thus to apologise for coincidence, which, as we are a nation of versifiers, or, according to the *Edinburgh Review*, 'a scribbling generation', must perpetually occur.[26]

Melesina Trench's apologetic note to her poem *Laura's Dream: or, The Moonlanders* (1816) sought to distance her work from thematically and stylistically similar works, and in doing so reminds us that, until recently, critical accounts of Irish women's poetry in the post-Union period failed to take account of the sheer quantity of verse produced by women. Some fifty-five women published collections of poetry between 1775 and 1835,[27] ranging across genres from devotional verse, children's literature, satire, love poetry and narrative verse. The sheer breadth of material recovered by recent scholarship has made summaries difficult, but there are noticeable trends in post-Union poetry by women, with many poets blending the personal and political in mournful, melancholic verse.

'My breathing harp! canst thou respire / No other air but grief alone?' asked the Kerry poet Agnes Mahony, with the harp poised for many poets between a sorrowful but glorious past, a debased present, and, at least for some, a potentially hopeful future.[28] Owenson's *The Lay of an Irish Harp: or, Metrical Fragments* (1807) opens with a series of questions that reflect a sense of post-Union national depression:

> Why sleeps the Harp of Erin's pride?
> Why with'ring droops its Shamrock wreath?
> Why has that song of sweetness died
> Which Erin's Harp alone can breathe?[29]

Other poets echoed Owenson's melancholy portrayal of the harp, Jane Susannah Liddiard for instance addressing the 'Aged Harp ... whose tones now seem to mourn their former fame.'[30] Apostrophizing the harp was a way in which women poets could invoke a romantic nationalism and claim a displaced poetic authority. Mary Balfour's 'The Fairy Queen' imagines the harp of Erin waking to 'pour from each raptured string' both the 'thrilling, witching, melting tone' of love, but also a mournful memory of fallen Irish heroes:

> Tell then in loftier, louder strain,
> Of Erin's sons on martial plain,
> And in soft dying murmurs tell,
> How Erin's heroes fell!
> Again the gallant theme pursue.
> Hold to view,
> How Erin's shamrocks crown the brave,
> Her tears bedew their grave.[31]

Melancholic laments could be more pointedly directed at the degraded post-Union state of Ireland. One of the most significant poets for children in the period was the Irish author Adelaide O'Keefe, whose *National Characters* (1818) contained forty poems written as dramatic monologues for children to learn about different national traditions. The offering for Ireland, though, strikes a different tone to others, centring on a wounded Irish officer returning from the Napoleonic wars to find a Dublin denuded of its resident parliament:

> Oh when a youth I took such pride
> Into the House of Parliament to glide,
>   Debates to hear:
>   A member bid me by his side,
>   And archly smiling cried,
>   "A future patriot I fear,
>   A GRATTAN he will grow."
> Tis now a Bank they say – well be it so.
>   And in the Courts and Streets springs grass
>   I'm told;
>   Spirit is dead – its grave-stones we behold.[32]

Other female poets mined ancient Irish history and myth for inspiration, with such long poems as Sarah Steele's *Eva, An Historical Poem* (1816), Vincentia Rodgers *Cluthan and Malvina: An Ancient Legend* (1823) and Hannah Maria Bourke's *O'Donoghue, Prince of Killarney* (1830) using either historical episodes or Ossianic mythology to create romance narratives similar in structure and intent to the national tale. While poems such as these can often seem to present a nationalism that seems quiescent and passively nostalgic, the loss evoked by this poetry can still have a political edge. As Stephen Behrendt suggests, 'such literary gestures … are effective rhetorical strategies for reminding an excluded people of the reality of their exclusion and of the circumstances and institutions responsible for that exclusion.'[33]

The expressive potential of Irish and dialect was noted by a number of Irish women poets, although in general poets were more reluctant to exploit the vernacular than novelists. Owenson felt that 'were Love to draw up a nomenclature of his own technical phrases, the Irish language would perhaps contribute more largely to the undertaking than any other whatever.'[34] The Ulster poet Mary Balfour's *Hope: A Poetical Essay; with Various Other Poems* (1810) contained a number of love songs translated from Irish originals. Balfour had collaborated with the Irish music collector Edward Bunting, and songs such as 'Ellen A Roon,' 'Ceann Dubh Dilis' and 'I am Asleep and Don't Waken Me' are examples of traditional Irish lyrics being brought into alignment with contemporary poetic form and diction:

> And when the dews of eve glistened on ev'ry tree,
>   Fairest of women, I breathed forth my vows to thee;
> Blessed in thy smiles, and from dread of misfortune free,
>   Scenes too enchanting – *Slan leat go bragh!*[35]

Among the many women writing poetry in Ireland after the Union, Mary Tighe garnered the most critical attention both in the nineteenth century and afterwards. Tighe's poetry develops from popular late eighteenth-century poetry on sensibility and solitude. Her long poem *Psyche* (1805) constantly asks the reader if they have truly loved, imagining love as something wrapped in silence and solitude:

> Oh! have you never known the silent charm
> That undisturbed retirement yields the soul,
> Where no intruder might your peace alarm,
> And tenderness hath wept without control,
> While melting fondness o'er the bosom stole?[36]

The poem's rhetorical investment in silence and solitude rewrites the ancient myth of Cupid and Psyche which hinged on the emotional burden of isolation. An awareness of Tighe's own unhappy marriage with her cousin, Henry Tighe, inevitably colours her long poem. Married in 1793, Mary and Henry suffered a loveless marriage that nevertheless involved a heady fashionable life in Dublin and London, although one conducted under Henry Tighe's restrictive controls on his wife's privacy. Tighe's poetry on first reading can often seem claustrophobically introspective, the poetic persona 'with soil and sorrow well nigh spent, / Of sad regret and wasting grief the prey.'[37] Her poetry is however remarkably committed to exploring the life of a woman of sensibility, testing the extent to which a passionate interior self can accommodate itself to the social codes of the wider world. In *Psyche* and her shorter lyrics, an intensely feeling poetic persona grapples with the paradoxical misery and delight of solitude.

However, Tighe was not afraid of direct political comment too. 'There Was a Young Lordling Whose Wits Were All Toss'd Up' attacked the upcoming Union, and her friendship with the anti-Union MP William Parnell is acknowledged in a sonnet of 1808 ('To W. P. Esq. Avondale'). While her published poetry may have courted reticence and solitude, she read avidly and left in manuscript a reading journal, displaying an often caustic critical intelligence that might surprise readers of her poetry. Tighe was at the centre of Dublin literary life in the first post-Union decade despite her physical decline. An avid reader of both foreign literature and Irish history, her death in 1810 left Dublin literary society bereft. While *Psyche* was published privately in 1805, it was the posthumous 1811 edition that secured for Tighe a reputation as a major female poet of the nineteenth century, her comparatively young death from tuberculosis linking her to poets like Henry Kirke White and, increasingly as the century progressed, John Keats.

Language and the Novel

During her visit to Ireland, the English author Anne Plumptre encountered an Irish funeral:

> I had often *heard of* the noise, the sort of yell used by the poorer sort of Catholics on these occasions, but had never till now *heard it*. Indeed it is impossible, without hearing it, to form an idea of any thing so dreadfully discordant. It is to be presumed that, intended by those who utter it as an expression of grief, it is considered by them as extremely plaintive and affecting: but to ears unseasoned to it, nothing could appear less so.[38]

Irish culture was still predominantly oral in this period, and writers after the Union were beginning to explore the potential of incorporating popular speech patterns and traditions into printed literature. The keening of women (and, as Plumptre noted elsewhere, men) at wakes, a perennial topic for visitors to Ireland from the twelfth century on, became a fascinating study for writers in the period who were dealing with a new epistemic interest in emotional authenticity in literary works. Keening (*caointeacháin*) becomes a moment in fiction that can test the bounds of print to capture oral performance, or represent a moment of interpretative doubt about the genuineness of emotional display. As Claire Connolly notes, 'the keen is poised on the knife-edge between performance and sincerity.'[39] Maria Edgeworth's *Castle Rackrent* (1800) describes the 'fine whillaluh' of a keen,[40] while a priest in Sydney Owenson's *The Wild Irish Girl* refers to the old women as 'professional *improvisatori*.'[41]

The most significant series of experiments with dialect were conducted by Edgeworth. In *An Essay on Irish Bulls* (verbal blunders) in 1802, Edgeworth wrote of the 'superfluity of wit and metaphor' which the Irish employ 'in daily conversation about the ordinary affairs of life'.[42] Two years previously, her first novel *Castle Rackrent* employed an Irish servant as narrator. In employing a dialect speaker as narrator and chronicling the history of an Anglo-Irish family, Edgeworth's short novel created a powerful paradigm for subsequent novelists interested in national character and historical change. Through the narration of Thady Quirk, *Castle Rackrent* tells the story of the Rackrents, a formerly Catholic family named the O'Shaughlins, who gradually dissipate their estate through such stereotypical Irish vices as gambling, drinking, litigiousness and over-generosity. 'Honest Thady,' as he is known to the family, creates a narrative open to irony and ambivalence, his motives remaining opaque. Presenting himself as a passive observer, he nevertheless hopes that the last Rackrent, Sir Condy, will marry his daughter Judy. That the estate eventually passes to his legally educated son Jason provides a different model of land transfer than marriage. Indeed, given the extent to which marriage in novels after the Union would be freighted with symbolic resonance, *Castle Rackrent* is anomalous in refusing any positive images of matrimony. Thady interacts with, but never fully understands, any of the Rackrent wives, and the disastrous marriages that lie behind the decline of the Rackrents reinforce the need for a proper domestic settlement to ensure stability of the estate and national community. While the book is laid before the readers as 'a specimen of manners and characters, which are perhaps unknown in England', complete with footnotes and glossary, it ends by asking 'did the Warwickshire militia, who were chiefly artisans, teach the Irish to drink beer, or did they learn from the Irish to drink whiskey?'[43]

Edgeworth incorporated dialect speech into subsequent fiction, concluding both *Ennui* and *The Absentee* (1812) with letters from Irish characters interrupting the standard English of the main narrative. For Edgeworth, dialect allowed for linguistic experimentation without sacrificing realistic representation. The plots of her Irish fiction were often critiqued for relying on coincidence that contradicted the realism of the representation of Irish manners. Her novels, though, were interested not just in literal description but also complex figurative responses to the history of landownership in Ireland and the consequences of Union. That Lord Colambre in *The Absentee* refers repeatedly to his potential marriage to Grace Nugent as a 'union' alerts the reader to the suggestive allegory lying behind erotic entanglements.

Edgeworth would publish a glowing preface to Mary Leadbeater's *Cottage Dialogues Among the Irish Peasantry* (1811) celebrating Leadbeater's ability to capture 'an exact representation of the *manner of being*'[44] of the lower classes in Ireland. Leadbeater's *Cottage Dialogues* contained informative lessons in agricultural practice and moral restraint, and Edgeworth's enthusiastic response to the book was partly connected to Leadbeater's use of dialogue without a mediating third-person narrative point of view to convey practical and moral lessons. As Helen O'Connell has noted, in didactic 'improvement' literature 'decoration, ornamentation, and embellishment are shunned in an effort to achieve transparency in physical bearing, language, and the social and political order as a whole.'[45] The Gothic novelist, Charles Maturin, complained that Edgeworth had a 'sacred horror of anything like exaggerated feeling, or tumid language'.[46] This does not mean, however, that Edgeworth was not preoccupied by style and the language appropriate to literature. While she eschewed the 'exaggerated language' of eighteenth-century sensibility, her life and work was preoccupied by the varieties of language, dialect or otherwise, open to the writer. An interest in dialect speech and everyday language ran alongside a commitment to clear, communicative prose. Writing to the novelist and playwright Elizabeth Inchbald in 1810, Edgeworth outlined the dangers of indulging in 'fine writing':

> You excel, I think, peculiarly in avoiding what is commonly called *fine writing*, – a sort of writing which I detest; which calls the attention away from the *thing* to the *manner*, from the feeling to the language; which sacrifices every thing to the sound, to the mere rounding of a period; which mistakes *stage effect* for *nature*.[47]

From around 1805, Edgeworth began making notes for an essay on the style and language of Edmund Burke. Notes for the essay are found in manuscripts dating from 1805–7, and phrases and ideas from it would reappear in *Essays on Professional Education* (1809) and her novel of English public life, *Patronage* (1814). In particular Edgeworth was attracted to Burke's 'allusions to common life and to mechanic trades' that are required in a country 'where the middle classes have so large a share and influence on the public opinion'.[48] Burke's excellence lay in his ability to draw 'noble allusions from ignoble objects.'[49] And in *Patronage*, when elements of her previous thoughts on Burke are repeated, they are concluded with an observation by one character that links back to her letter to Inchbald:

> Ornaments ... if not kept subordinate, however intrinsically beautiful, injure the general effect, – therefore a judicious orator will sacrifice all such as draw the attention from his principal design.[50]

Something of this suspicion of formulaic and ornamental rhetoric comes across in a letter Edgeworth's father wrote to Sydney Owenson describing Maria's reading of *The Wild Irish Girl* to the family circle:

> Maria, who reads (it is said), as well as she writes, has entertained us with several passages from the *Wild Irish Girl*, which I thought superior to any parts of the book which I had read. Upon looking over her shoulder, I found she had omitted some superfluous epithets.[51]

Edgeworth and Owenson have often been seen as contrasting writers on Ireland, the former heavily didactic and espousing a calm rationality while the latter indulged in an intoxicating romanticism and aligning Irish antiquity with a breathless modern sensibility. While they had significant stylistic and temperamental differences, they both developed fiction that invested in figurative links between erotic and national relations.

Owenson's fiction in the 1800s was heavily invested in a 'tumid language' of sentiment that was linked a self-aware, often ironic, rhetoric of nationality. Later in life she confessed in a preface to a revised edition of *O'Donnell* (1814) that 'every fictitious narrative that has had Ireland for its theme, has assumed a more or less decidedly political colouring.'[52] Starting with *St Clair, or The Heiress of Desmond* (1803), and moving on through *The Novice of St Dominick* (1806), *The Wild Irish Girl* (1806), *Woman; or, Ida of Athens* (1809) and *The Missionary* (1811), her novels of the first decade of post-Union Ireland placed female sensibility and creativity at the centre of the imaginative life of the nation, displacing Irish concerns in the later novels to the similarly colonial locations of Greece and India.

The Wild Irish Girl has been read as a foundational text in the genre of the 'national tale,' a generic category Owenson herself introduced as a subtitle to her novel. Structured for the most part as a series of letters from the young Englishman Horatio to a Member of Parliament correspondent, it demands to be read as a public intervention in debates about Ireland's place in the Union. It is a text that provokes an allegorizing reading even if it remains far more subtle and ambivalent about the happy prospects of Union than its marriage plot might suggest. Horatio's father describes the possibility that the wedding of Horatio and Glorvina will foreshadow wider political rapprochement between Ireland and England as 'a consummation of an event so devoutly to be wished by every liberal mind'.[53] The phrase contains an underlying allusion to Hamlet's famous soliloquy on the wished-for oblivion after suicide, tempering the progressive image of marriage and union.

Woman; or, Ida of Athens rewrites the reconciling marriage plot of the national tale. The novel opens with a young Englishman becoming entranced by the exotic woman of genius, but Owenson gradually sidelines the boorish hero to focus on the love affair between Ida and a young Athenian rebel against Turkish rule. Lord B–, the Englishman, is dismissed at the beginning of the second volume, having been recalled to serve in parliament, and in answer to his proposal that he live as her mistress, Ida states that '[there] can be no individual happiness but that which harmonizes with the happiness of society.'[54] The novel ends with Ida united with her patriot lover, Osmyn, and the contention that 'if it is for man to perform great actions, it is for woman to inspire them.'[55] Owenson published as Lady Morgan after her 1812 marriage, and her fiction moved from sentimental excess to more pointed social satire and political comment in the 1810s and 1820s. In *Florence MacCarthy* (1818), Morgan even includes as an heroine a writer of national tales who declares 'I do trade upon the materials [Ireland] furnishes me; and turning my patriotism into pounds, shillings, and pence endeavour, at the same moment, to serve her, and support myself.'[56] Her travel writing on France (1817, 1830) and Italy (1821) was open in its attacks on the conservative politics of post-Napoleonic Europe and earned stinging criticism. Her last major Irish novel, *The O'Briens and the O'Flahertys*, returns to the 1790s for its setting and combines satire of Dublin fashionable society with angry denunciation of colonial mismanagement. She continued to complain about patriarchal assumptions about women's proper place, noting in *Woman and Her Master* (1840) that '[while] woman is permitted to cultivate the arts which merely please, and which frequently corrupt, she is denounced as a thing unsexed, a *lusus naturae*, if she directs her thoughts to pursuits which aspire to serve, and which never fail to elevate.'[57]

Conclusion

After Catholic Emancipation was achieved in 1828, Owenson predicted 'a change in the character of Irish authorship',[58] with an increasingly prominent number of Catholic (and male) Irish writers. As well as the movement for Catholic Emancipation, the 1820s saw increased Protestant evangelical activity in Ireland, the 'Second Reformation', with women writers taking an active role in sectarian debate both in prose and poetry. Devotional literature offered women a chance to clothe public utterances in narratives of personal salvation. Writers such as Selina Bunbury and Charlotte Elizabeth Tonna included protracted scenes of theological debates within romantic or historical novels respectively, with both developing a strongly pronounced anti-Catholic viewpoint.[59] The intense political and religious pressures released by the movement for Emancipation and, in the 1830s, the Repeal of the Union, led to Maria Edgeworth's famous renunciation of fiction in a letter to her stepbrother:

> It is impossible to draw Ireland as she is now in the book of fiction – realities are too strong, party passions too violent, to bear to see, or care to look at their faces in a looking glass. The people would only break the glass, and curse the fool who held the mirror up to nature – distorted nature in a fever.[60]

This private renunciation of fiction, though, ought to be balanced by her insistence in *Helen* (1834) that the changed historical conditions necessitated a level of engagement with politics by women that would have been frowned upon earlier in the century:

> Let me observe to you, that the position of women in society, is somewhat different from what it was a hundred years ago, or as it was sixty, or I will say thirty years since. Women are now so highly cultivated, and political subjects are at present of so much importance, of such high interest, to all human creatures who live together in society, you can hardly expect, Helen, that you, as a rational being, can go through the world as it now is, without forming any opinion on points of public importance. You cannot, I conceive, satisfy yourself with the common namby-pamby little missy phrase, 'ladies have nothing to do with politics.'[61]

If there is a larger narrative to Irish women's writing in the opening decades of the nineteenth century it might be the gradual emergence of politics from the sometimes-occluded context of private sentimental narratives to the explicit topic of literary writing. Marguerite Power, the Countess of Blessington, had little qualms about moving from her successful anecdotes of high society in the 1820s to politically pointed fiction in the 1830s, describing agitators for repeal of the Union as the 'moral typhus' attacking the country, 'so much more fatal than all the physical fevers that ever attacked it.'[62] Her novel *The Repealers* (1833) has a peasant couple, Jim and Grace, debate repeal and religion, the man inflamed by the rhetoric of agitation (and whiskey) while the woman provides the calm, reflective guidance needed to the country. Blessington's novel ends by arguing that Repealers have 'died a natural death: and the Union between England and Ireland bids fair to become every day more indissoluble.'[63] Yet this positive outcome suggests that the Union was never complete to begin with. Sir Walter Scott suggested in 1829 that the works of Maria Edgeworth 'may be truly said to have done more towards completing the Union, than perhaps all the legislative enactments by which it has been followed up'.[64] The Union was arguably the defining political event of pre-Famine Ireland, and yet its promise of a closer connection between its constituent nations was felt to have remained unfulfilled and in need of supplementation by imaginative writing. Irish women writers responded to the massive structural changes wrought to Irish political, social and cultural life in the early nineteenth century with a fascinating body of work that placed private dramas on a public stage. They wrote in the shadow of the Union as the noisy emergence of a national literature took place.

Notes

1 See Mary Jean Corbett, *Allegories of Union in Irish and English Writing, 1790–1870* (Cambridge: Cambridge University Press, 2000), 3.
2 Maria Edgeworth, *Letters for Literary Ladies (1795)*, ed. Claire Connolly (London: Dent, 1993), 31.
3 Lady Morgan, *Lady Morgan's Memoirs: Autobiography, Diaries, and Correspondence*, ed. William Hepworth Dixon (London, 1862), 1:230.
4 Maria Edgeworth, *Ennui*, in *Castle Rackrent, Irish Bulls, Ennui*, ed. Jane Desmarais, Tim McLoughlin and Marilyn Butler, vol. 1 of *The Novels and Selected Works of Maria Edgeworth*, eds. Marilyn Butler, Mitzi Myers and W. J. McCormack (London: Pickering & Chatto, 1999), 292.
5 Elizabeth Plunkett, *The Exile of Erin* (London, 1808), 1:vii.
6 Lady Olivia Clarke, *The Irishwoman: A Comedy* (London, 1819), vi.

7 Dorothea Herbert, *Retrospections of Dorothea Herbert, 1770–1806*, ed. Louis Cullen (Dublin: Town House Press, 2004), 143.

8 See Janet Todd, *Sensibility: An Introduction* (London: Routledge, 1986); G. Barker Benfield, *The Culture of Sensibility: Sex and Society in Eighteenth-Century Britain* (Chicago, IL: University of Chicago Press, 1992).

9 Henry Tighe, 'To the Reader', in *Psyche: With Other Poems*, 3rd ed. (London, 1811), iii.

10 Mary Leadbeater, *The Annals of Ballitore* (London, 1862), 1:216.

11 Mary Helen Thuente, 'Liberty, Hibernia, and Mary Le More: United Irish Images of Women', in *The Women of 1798*, eds. Dáire Keogh and Nicholas Furlong (Dublin: Four Courts Press, 1998), 20–5.

12 Mary Leadbeater, *Poems* (Dublin, 1808), 262.

13 Amelia Bristow, *The Maniac or, A View of Bethlem Hospital: and The Merits of Women, a Poem from the French* (London, 1810), 15.

14 Ibid., 17.

15 Siobhan Kilfeather, 'Terrific Register: The Gothicization of Atrocity in Irish Romanticism', *Boundary 2* 31, no. 1 (2004): 61.

16 Mary Ann Grant, *Sketches of Life and Manners: With Delineation of Scenery in England, Scotland, and Ireland* (London, 1811), 2:249, 250.

17 See John D. Beatty, ed., *Protestant Women's Narratives of the Irish Rebellion of 1798* (Dublin: Four Courts Press, 2001).

18 Mrs Kelly, *The Matron of Erin: A National Tale* (Dublin, 1816), 1:97.

19 Ibid., 1:97.

20 Alicia Le Fanu, *Tales of a Tourist* (London, 1823), 1:231.

21 Ibid., 1:228.

22 Sydney Owenson, *The Wild Irish Girl*, ed. Kathryn Kirkpatrick (Oxford: Oxford University Press, 1999), 176n.

23 Edgeworth, *Ennui*, in *Novels and Selected Works*, 1:191.

24 Ibid., 258.

25 Ibid., 248.

26 Melesina Trench, *Laura's Dream: or, The Moonlanders* (London, 1816), 45.

27 Stephen Behrendt, 'Ireland and Romanticism', in *Irish Women Poets of the Romantic Period* (Alexandria, VA: Alexander Street Press, 2007), http://lit.alexanderstreet.com/iwrp/view/1000229657. Accessed on 20 April 2016.

28 Agnes Mahony, 'My Harp! My Harp! Once More Resound', in *A Minstrel's Hours of Song; or, Poems* (London, 1825), 102.

29 Sydney Owenson, 'The Irish Harp', in *The Lay of an Irish Harp: or Metrical Fragments*, (London, 1807), 1.

30 J. S. Anna Liddiard, 'Lines Addressed to an Irish Harp of Great Antiquity' in *The Sgelaighe: or, A Tale of Old* (Bath, 1811), 171.

31 Mary Balfour, 'Song: The Fairy Queen', in *Hope: A Poetical Essay; with Various Other Poems* (Belfast, 1810), 163.

32 Adelaide O'Keefe, 'The Irish Officer', in *National Characters Exhibited in Forty Geographical Poems* (London, 1818), 25.

33 Stephen Behrendt, 'Irish Women Poets', in *British Women Poets and the Romantic Writing Community*, (Baltimore, MA: Johns Hopkins University Press, 2009), 276.

34 Sydney Owenson, *Patriotic Sketches of Ireland*, (London, 1807), 2:54.

35 Balfour, 'I am Asleep and Don't Awaken Me,' in *Hope*, 174.

36 Mary Tighe, *Psyche, with Other Poems*, 3rd ed. (London, 1811), Canto III, lines 334–8.

37 Ibid., Canto I, lines 2–3.

38 Anne Plumptre, *Narrative of a Residence in Ireland during the Summer of 1814, and That of 1815* (London, 1817), 248.

39 Claire Connolly, *A Cultural History of the Irish Novel, 1790–1829* (Cambridge: Cambridge University Press, 2012), 190. For a general account of the keen see Patricia Lysaght 'Caoineadh Os Cionn Coirp: The Lament for the Dead in Ireland', *Folklore* 108 (1997): 65–82.

40 Edgeworth, *Castle Rackrent*, in *Novels and Selected Works*, 1:11.

41 Owenson, *Wild Irish Girl*, 183.

42 Edgeworth, *An Essay on Irish Bulls*, in *Novels and Selected Works*, 1:118.

43 Edgeworth, *Castle Rackrent*, in *Novels and Selected Works*, 1:54.

44 Maria Edgeworth, 'Preface', in *Mary Leadbeater, Cottage Dialogues among the Irish Peasantry* (London, 1811), iv. Italics in original.

45 Helen O'Connell, *Ireland and the Fiction of Improvement* (Oxford: Oxford University Press, 2006), 24.

46 Charles Maturin, 'Novel-Writing', *British Review and London Journal* 11 (1818), 57

47 Maria Edgeworth to Elizabeth Inchbald, 14 January 1810, in Marilyn Butler, *Maria Edgeworth: A Literary Biography* (Oxford: Clarendon Press, 1972), 310.

48 Maria Edgeworth, *Essays on Professional Education* (London, 1809), 389, 390.

49 Maria Edgeworth, 'Notes for an Essay on the Genius and Style of Burke' (n.d. c. 1805–7) in *The Absentee*, ed. W. J. McCormack and Kim Walker (Oxford: Oxford University Press, 1988), 282.

50 Edgeworth, *Patronage*, ed. Conor Carville and Marilyn Butler, in *Novels and Selected Works*, 6:2

51 Lady Morgan, *Lady Morgan's Memoirs*, 1:294.

52 Lady Morgan, 'Preface', in *O'Donnell: A National Tale* (London, 1835), 1:viii–ix.

53 Ibid., 250.

54 Sydney Owenson, *Woman; or, Ida of Athens* (London, 1809), 2:4.

55 Ibid., 4:290.

56 Lady Morgan, *Florence MacCarthy; an Irish Tale* (London, 1818), 3:265.

57 Lady Morgan, *Woman and Her Master* (London, 1840), 1:13.

58 Lady Morgan, *The Book of the Boudoir* (London, 1829), 1:vii.

59 See Heidi Hansson, 'Selina Bunbury, Religion, and the Woman Writer', in *The Oxford History of the Irish Book. Vol. IV: The Irish Book in English*,

1800–1891, ed. James H. Murphy (Oxford: Oxford University Press, 2011), 322–30.

60 Maria Edgeworth to Michael Pakenham Edgeworth, 14 February 1834, in Butler, *Maria Edgeworth*, 452.

61 Edgeworth, *Helen*, ed. Susan Manly and Clíona Ó Gallchoir, in *Novels and Selected Works*, 9:214.

62 Countess of Blessington (Marguerite Power Gardiner), *The Repealers* (London, 1833), 1:125.

63 Ibid., 3:320.

64 Walter Scott, 'General Preface' (1829), in *Waverley; or, 'Tis Sixty Years since*, ed. Claire Lamont, rev. ed. (Oxford: Oxford University Press, 2015), 388.

CHAPTER 4

Poetry, 1845–1891

Matthew Campbell

After the early death from consumption of the Irish poet, Rose Kavanagh, in February 1891 – she was just thirty-one – William Butler Yeats wrote her obituary for the Boston Catholic newspaper, the *Pilot*. After quoting a number of stanzas from Kavanagh's best-known poem, 'St Michan's Churchyard', Yeats glossed them thus:

> The manner of such poetry much more closely resembles Kickham and Casey than Davis and Mangan. Like most of the best Irish verse of recent years it is meditative and sympathetic, rather than stirring and energetic: the trumpet has given way to the viol and the flute. It is easy to be unjust to such poetry, but very hard to write it. It springs straight out of the nature from some well-spring of refinement and gentleness. It makes half the pathos of literary history. When one reads some old poem of the sort one says: 'What a charming mind had this writer! How gladly I should have met and talked with such a one!' and then one gathers about one, like a garment, the mist of regret.[1]

Yeats is being fairly precise in the tradition in which he places Kavanagh, of a political poetry sketched out over fifty years. Charles Kickham and John Keegan Casey were poets and activists in the Fenian movement, a nationalist political grouping at times drawn to the exercise of physical force. Its lineage could be traced back to *The Nation* newspaper of the 1840s, and the writing of one of its founders Thomas Davis, and that of a frequent contributor, James Clarence Mangan. Yeats, though, is keen to posit a change to the 'meditative and sympathetic', as if Kickham and Casey – and then Kavanagh – prioritized 'refinement and gentleness' over the 'stirring and energetic'.

But the choice of 'St Michan's Churchyard' to illustrate such a point is an odd one. As Yeats knew, St Michan's in Dublin was long reported to be the burial place of the man with no epitaph, the hanged revolutionary Robert Emmet.[2] It is a grave without a headstone, as Kavanagh says, 'the stone which waits the name / His land must write with Freedom's flame'.[3]

And the non-naming of the subject of a poem which every one of its first readers would recognize, succeeds to a long literary as well as political tradition of the suppressed insurgent: the speaker of Thomas Moore's song, 'Oh! Breathe not his name', published eighty years before Kavanagh's in 1808, also stands mute before Emmet's unmarked grave: 'Sad, silent, and dark be the tears that we shed, / As the night dew that falls on the grass o'er his head'.[4]

What Yeats knew was that whatever the tradition in which she wrote, Kavanagh was writing the national tale in a different register from the writing of her precursors, women as well as men. The poem reaches back into Irish Romantic song and also to the earlier revival of Irish national culture, the movement grouped around the writers of *The Nation*, those who were at first jokingly called 'Young Ireland'.[5] So when, in 1888, the poem could be published in a second time of cultural revival, at the beginning of a period of writing which we now know to have transformed Irish literature, it could be included in a volume called *Poems and Ballads of Young Ireland*.[6] The name was rescued from its associations with Famine, failed insurrection and the decades of imprisonment and exile suffered by at least two subsequent generations of political leaders. Under the tutelage of the returned émigré Fenian, John O'Leary and his sister Ellen O'Leary, this later Young Ireland movement was pacific and cultured. It was now concerned to mount a renewed attempt on the revival of Irish culture in terms which emphasized qualities of literariness rather than political agitation, adverting rather to a late-Victorian poetry of the 'meditative and sympathetic', where pathos and nostalgia might stand in peaceful opposition to decades of martial and patriotic and pious verse. Whether the O'Learys' later Young Ireland project succeeded in such peaceful terms is moot: among those who might have been said to have benefited from its early successes were the revolutionary poets of 1916, and fifty years later one of the volume's contributors, An Craoibhin Aoibhinn (Douglas Hyde), was to become the first President of the newly liberated Free State. But Yeats knew that even given this diversion into the pathos both of 'St Michan's Graveyard' and of Kavanagh's own story, the physical force tradition as theme in Irish poetry was still very much present.

This chapter will be strung between the two cultural movements of Young Ireland – in the 1840s and 1880s to 1890s – and the writing of women poets within them. The readership of *Nation* editor Charles Gavan Duffy's *The Spirit of the Nation* anthologies, first published in 1845 and to go through numerous editions in the nineteenth century, was huge. And if the later *Poems and Ballads of Young Ireland* collection was designed to redress the aesthetic shortcomings of writing for a mass audience, 'the stirring and the energetic' never quite went away from Irish poetry, and they might be thought to be prime characteristics of the women's poetry associated with *The Nation* and later the Fenians and the Land League. Of course, Irish women poets of differing political as well as aesthetic predispositions wrote throughout this period. And it is vital not to underestimate the devotional, whether it be under the sway of Catholicism or the Church of Ireland. But the printed Irish poem of the main years of the rule of Queen Victoria, from about 1845 up to the death of Kavanagh in 1891, occupies a trajectory quite separate from that of the great renaissance of printed women's poetry in Victorian Britain.

Figures in and out of Victorian poetry flitted between varieties of literary naming and identity, not just Irish or English but Romantic or Victorian. Poet and novelist Caroline Sheridan Norton, granddaughter of Richard Brinsley Sheridan, is rarely thought of as Irish. But her sister, Helena Sheridan, later Helena Blackwood, Baronness of Dufferin and Clandeboye, has long been considered an Irish poet. Norton was 'the Byron of modern poetesses', with scandal to match, given that in 1836 her husband sued Lord Melbourne, then Prime Minister, for seducing her. The case was thrown out, but Caroline's husband still claimed custody of their children and his wife's property. Norton's sister Blackwood had more established literary associations: her folly in County Down, 'Helen's Tower', boasts appreciative verses gifted by Tennyson and Browning. The critic Yopie Prins argues that in Norton's poems, 'the Romantic poet turns into the Victorian poetess, who in turn personifies the gradual gendering of lyric as a "feminine" genre in the course of the century'.[7] So, in Prins's terms, where Yeats seems to describe the virtues of a later poet like Kavanagh as refinement and gentleness, he is really describing the development of lyric as a gendered development, that of the 'woman poet'. Prins is careful to say that Norton's 1840 'The Picture of Sappho' is a personification, the dramatic monologue that is the prime lyric invention of the Victorian period. Lyric in Ireland in this period also sought depersonalized forms, cultures of loss and nostalgia cathected into historical subjects, occupying sites of historical defeat, yet also imbricated with anger at great contemporary loss and suffering. The rise of Young Ireland was soon to suffer along with much of the rest of Ireland under the Famine, and thus even a writer like Blackwood, much removed from the politics of Young Ireland, is best known for writing a poem of suffering and exile, 'The Lament of the Irish Emigrant'.[8]

Prins invokes 'Sapphism' in the broadest terms to describe the Victorian woman poet – or the persona of 'poetess', to use the Victorian word she rescues – as an ambivalent lyric example from the classical past. The implicit feminist critique is that the figure has been denied agency in its own literary career, and is written only in posthumous conceptions, from a fragmented text and in many languages and cultures through numerous translations and impersonations, 'a repetition and no longer (if it ever was) a point of origin'.[9] The figure of the Sapphic poetess thus offered a means of exploring an alternative history of subjectivity within the frame of a broadly post-Romantic English poetry; that is, a gendered subjectivity and one suffering unwanted obscurity as a result. Norton's poem ends:

> Fame, to thy breaking heart
> No comfort could impart,
> In vain thy brow the laurel wreath was wearing;
> One grief and one alone
> Could bow thy bright head down –
> Thou wert a woman, and wert left despairing![10]

To such despair, which is the fate of 'a woman' in this poem, alternative models could be found in the public themes and the note of frequent indignation shown by those poets who were born in Ireland. Their predominant mode is the rhetoric of public poetry, but the elegiac remains as a strong feature, either as sorrow for the Famine dead or the self-sorrow of emigration and nostalgia. Even bearing the example of Norton's Sappho in mind, new models of the meditative and sympathetic did persist throughout the period of 'Irish Victorian' poetry.

Was it the case that in Ireland women poets arrived at these new personae and voicings of the new subjectivity? Yeats's view of Rose Kavanagh might suggest it took time to find this new writing of subjectivity. The individuality of the earlier Young Ireland poets has been diagnosed as missing by Gregory Schirmer: 'The project of nationalism in nineteenth-century Ireland demanded the subjection of the individual to the nation, the sacrifice of personal identity to political commitment, and that phenomenon was nowhere more apparent than in the writings of the many women who wrote nationalist poetry.'[11] Whether or not the individual be subject to the national question, there was nevertheless an exploration of persona and subject-status in the women's poetry printed in *The Nation*. A first feature of the women poets of Young Ireland is their pseudonymous publication. This was not unusual for men: Mangan published under a variety of names and personifications and Davis published

as 'The Celt'. But the pseudonyms of Jane Elgee ('Speranza'), Ellen
Mary Downing ('Kate' and then 'Mary of *The Nation*') and Mary Kelly
('Fionnuala' and then 'Eva of *The Nation*') were to assume an important
role in the poetic project of the newspaper in the 1840s as the paper
began to promulgate national feeling and then to seek representative literary forms written by a cast of women poets in a time initially defined
by the ideology of nationalism but then brought into increasingly radical
focus by the mounting catastrophe of Famine. Elgee and Kelly were to
play prominent roles in the more radical publication *United Irishman*,
founded and edited by John Mitchel from 1848. Youthful radicalism
aside, Elgee's life after her marriage to Dublin doctor Sir William Wilde
has meant that she is better known as the mother of Oscar Wilde. But
Kelly was to live the life of the political *emigrée* in France and Australia.
Downing's decision to become a Presentation nun also tells a different
story, a moving between commitments, first national and then confessional. If these life stories tell of distinct careers, they also vacillate
between subjectivity and subjection.

By all contemporary accounts, the gap between the person Jane Elgee
(later Lady Jane Wilde) and the persona 'Speranza' was small, and, as
Horace Wyndham's 1951 biography shows, her personality attracted
much misogynist commentary. Oscar's Trinity tutor, R. Y. Tyrrell,
expressed a common view during the *cause célèbre* of the 1864 libel case
taken against her by a woman involved in an intrigue of her husband's,
Mary Travers, whom Lady Wilde had accused of blackmail. For Tyrrell,
the case showed that Jane was 'a high-falutin' pretentious creature whose
pride was as extravagant as her reputation founded on second-rate verse
making ... She gave herself besides all manner of airs'.[12] A favourite word
in her poetry was 'earnest' (it is used 12 times, once rhymed with 'stern-
est'[13]) a fact not missed by her son. Such unpromising attitudes did have
another side, and it does not mute them so much to express them in
the terms given by Lucy Collins: 'her own work was inflected both by a
Romantic sensibility and a certain religious zeal. [... She regarded] herself as "the acknowledged voice in poetry of all the people in Ireland."'[14]
There is truth in the latter self-characterization, because as Speranza in
the late 1840s, Jane Elgee had written poetry of zealous indignation as
the urban readership of *The Nation* sought succour in representation for
the horrors of the Famine which appeared to be wiping out the rural
population of the West and South West of Ireland. Marjorie Howes has
drawn a nuanced distinction between the affective gendered responses
of these poets as shown in Elgee's imagery of tears and blood: 'She used

Young Ireland's gender conventions to mediate between a bourgeois nationalism's necessary but problematic separation from the people, embodied in the weak feminist tears of the masses and the worthy masculine tears of the true patriot'.[15]

Elgee said that she turned to writing poetry after witnessing the 1845 funeral of Thomas Davis. Out of curiosity she sought out Davis's poetry and began to write in a similar public mode, soon taking Famine for a theme. Critics like Chris Morash or Terry Eagleton have suggested that the immensity of the task of writing about the Famine has resulted in its absence or even repression in history and literature. The adequate representation of trauma is difficult when the event exceeds the capacity of the formal understandings of art. But for writers such as William Carleton, Mangan, Anthony Trollope and even Emily Brontë, the fact of the Famine is never silenced, it inevitably intrudes on fiction or lyric as much as something positioned at the centre.[16] This was not an aesthetic or ethical dilemma about representation for Elgee: her poems on the Famine do not merely intrude, they are focussed on the experience with an effect which approaches shock, drawing into verse images of horror garnered from newspaper sketches and journalistic reports. In tactics that might seem pertinent for a twentieth-century ethics of representation resolved against the flinch from atrocity, her explicitness can appear deliberately to overbalance poetic control. Take these two stanzas from 'The Famine Year':

> No; the blood is dead within our veins – we care not now for life;
> Let us die hid in the ditches, far from children and from wife;
> We cannot stay and listen to their raving, famished cries –
> Bread! Bread! Bread! and none to still their agonies.
> We left our infants playing with their dead mother's hand:
> We left our maidens maddened by the fever's scorching brand:
> Better, maiden, thou were strangled in thy own dark-twisted tresses –
> Better, infant, thou wert smothered in thy mother's first caresses.
> ...
> One by one they're falling round us, their pale faces to the sky;
> We've no strength left to dig them graves – there let them lie.
> The wild bird, if he's stricken, is mourned by the others,
> But we – we die in Christian land – we die amid our brothers,
> In the land which God has given, like a wild beast in his cave,
> Without a tear, a prayer, a shroud, a coffin, or a grave.
> Ha! but think ye the contortions on each livid face ye see,
> Will not be read on judgment-day by eyes of Deity?[17]

Whether or not Elgee herself stared into the faces of the Famine dead, as at the end of the second stanza above, this is a verse which does not avert its gaze. Of course it plays with a discourse of sentimentality as it represents horror: the disgrace of the father leaving his dying family's suffering as he chooses to die alone, the child playing with the dead mother's hand, the invocation of infanticide as preferable to death by starvation. Given the proximity to the images of widespread suffering, the political analysis is basic: the poem ends with the dead transfigured in immortality, an undead horde demanding the eternal punishment of their British rulers: 'A ghastly, spectral army before great God we'll stand / And arraign ye as our murderers, O spoilers of our land!'

In texts like this, Elgee's desire to be 'the acknowledged voice in poetry of all the people in Ireland' can appear to be a fraught and in many ways self-abnegating exercise. According to Morash, this is done by prosopoeia, or personification, and, 'Having been granted a voice, the dead proclaim their contemporaneity with the living reader'.[18] Elgee is quite clearly imagining herself among the 'we' who stand together after death here, an extreme sensibility of sympathy given power by indignation. The projection of self into nation is pathological as much as poetic. The dedication 'To Ireland' at the head of her 1864 *Poems* is to the traumatized in need of Elgee's own brand of selfless shock treatment:

> My country, wounded to the heart,
>   Could I but flash along thy soul
> Electric power to rive apart
>   The thunder-clouds that round thee roll,
> And, by my burning words, uplift
> Thy life from out Death's icy drift,
> Till the full splendours of our age
> Shone round thee for thy heritage –
> As Miriam's, by the Red Sea strand
> Clashing proud cymbals, so my hand
>   Would strike thy harp,
>   Loved Ireland!

That flash of electricity at the start of the poem is something which is more common than might be thought in British Romantic and Victorian writing (Mary Shelley and both Elizabeth Barrett and Robert Browning come to mind). Mixing her metaphors slightly, Elgee offers 'burning words' for Ireland. But the rhymes of 'our age' (the contemporary) and 'heritage' (this traumatized present transfigured for posterity) offer a consoling couplet for past and future. 'My hand' and the object of desire, 'Loved Ireland!' are certainly intimate, and the poem ends with her acknowledged woman's role in this closeness:

> Yet, if thy mighty heart has stirred,
> Even with one pulse-throb at my word,
> Then not in vain my woman's hand
> Has struck thy gold harp while I stand,
>   Waiting thy rise
>   Loved Ireland!

In the title of another of her poems, Elgee, perhaps unusually in Irish national iconography, refers to Ireland as 'Our Fatherland'.

If Elgee's poetry is one without limits, without a sense of artistic or ethical tact, one which assumes the political positions of the converted, this is not always the naïve position of Tyndall's 'high-falutin pretentious creature'. She could acknowledge the limitations of the lyrical position, with the meditative or reflective element turned back on her own poetry, as in 'The Fate of the Lyrist':

> The soul is ever clinging unto form;
> Action, not abstract thought, alone can warm
> The great heart of humanity – in life's fierce storm
>   Pass they the Lyrist by.

The poem about art against action is not without art in its formal activity: the stanza here has ingenuity and the triplet rhyming continues through five stanzas to the end, including the repeated falling or feminine rhymes of the fourth lines: 'Lyrist by' / 'tapestry' / 'mystery' / 'divinity' / 'melody'. This is work which offers the self-realization that not all audiences will be electrified by the lyrical gift of Pindar or Petrarch (or Speranza). The poem ends without an audience, or at least without the desired mass audience. They have been so bowed down by contemporary history that art, and certainly lyric art, cannot be heard:

> Their name, indeed, is echoed by the crowd;
> But from amidst the masses earthward bowed,
> Few lift the head, with kindred soul endowed,
>   To list their Orphic melody.

Elgee fostered the fiction that she was born in 1826, and thus was 21 when she began writing for *The Nation*. She may have been born as much as six years earlier than this, in 1820.[19] But the editors Davis and later Charles Gavan Duffy had no compunction populating the paper with young women, even teenage girls. Mary Kelly was reputedly fifteen when she wrote her first poems for *The Nation* – that is, if an 1830 birth-date is accepted (she may have been born in 1825). Ellen Downing was seventeen when she was first published. If youthfulness was part of the myth of these writers, then love affairs, part-mystery and part-Romance also attached to them. Kelly's engagement to Kevin Izod O'Doherty lasted the five years of his deportation and they were later to live in Paris and Australia as well as Ireland. A number of poems write their personal predicament as that of the larger predicament of the dispersed Young Irelanders, often presented as half-translated fragments 'from the Irish'. For example, 'A Caoine' ends with a scene taken from Kelly and O'Doherty's own separation:

> I never stood within your home – I do not bear your name –
> Life parted us for many a day, but Death now seals my claim;
> In darkness, silence, and decay, and here at last alone
> You're but more truly bound to me – my darling and my own!

Downing's supposed engagement to Joseph Brennan did not last and she entered the Presentation novitiate on 1849, aged twenty-one. Her 'My Owen' may very well be national allegory, but we cannot avoid hearing in its music the despairing voice of one sundered from the loved one by history:

> Proud of you, fond of you, clinging so near to you,
> Light is my heart now I know I am dear to you!
> Glad is my voice now, so free it may sing for you
> All the wild love that is burning within for you!
> Tell me once more, tell it over and over,
> The tale of that eve which first saw you my lover
>   Now I need never blush
>   At my heart's hottest gush –
> The wife of my Owen her heart may discover![20]

Such 'wild love' was not discouraged by *The Nation*, since it is one of the spontaneous qualities of the Romantic Irish. This poem was introduced on 21 February 1846 thus: 'If there be anything in Irish song more pas-sionate, spontaneous, or essentially native, we do not know it. It has the gushing, bounding character which makes its own music, and could not possibly be read tamely'.[21]

In Kelly and Downing's cases, such life stories have perhaps lasted longer than the actual poetry, but they do tell of a recalibration of femi-ninity, family and faith within the Young Ireland circle. Downing's biog-raphy tells of a certain self-reliance even given her chronic illness and decision to take the veil, and Kelly held to Young Ireland politics in her marriage to O'Doherty and their exile in which she continued to write. The poetry remained one which could not feel 'at home', although not always in the expected ways. Settled in Australia, hers is the first recorded use in the Chadwyck Healey Literature Online Database of English poetry of the word 'boomerang', here in a colonist's poem tempered by a diasporic consciousness:

> I go from the soft, bright southern skies,
>   I go from the summer day
> That faints in sweet, voluptuous sighs,
>   In perfume and light away;
> I go, I go, to the ice and snow,
>   Where the cruel north winds clang;
> But I'll come back, on the homeward track, –
>   Come back like the boomerang!
>   Yes, seek your feet, as true and fleet –
>   As true as the boomerang![22]

There is fun here in the bathos of the conceit, but that conceit has cleverness, inverting the theme of the exiled Irish seeking a return to the Australia in which she and O'Doherty settled and to which they returned to die.

In her early poetry, Kelly as 'Eva' wrote in the full mode of outrage that we have seen in Elgee / Speranza. Her collected *Poems by Eva of the Nation* opens with 'Chant: To the Beloved Dead', a lyric addressed to the nationalist past which begins with the invocation, 'Oh Ye Dead'. This repeats the opening of Thomas Moore's 1820 song of the same name and looks forward to James Joyce's 'The Dead', a story with characters haunted in a similar manner by the Irish dead in the West. Unlike Elgee's 'Famine Year', Kelly imagines herself separate from the dead, seeking after sense when disconnected from them. Prins's notion of the posthumous is strong and her poems go on to offer personifications of figures from history – men and women, recent and from the longer past. Ballads like 'The Rebel's Sermon', 'The Patriot Mother: A Ballad of '98' or 'Tipperary' can sound like common *Nation* fare, like 'The Memory of the Dead' or 'The Croppy Boy'. Their origin is as synthetic ballad, designed to sing of the nation's past in new bourgeois contexts. In 'Tipperary', Kelly sets the recent sufferings and depopulation of Connaught against the fecundity of the county she surveys, but over which she has no sovereignty: 'Our land is theirs by plunder, but, by Brigid, ourselves are free'. That freedom includes the friendship and hospitality of the Irish who remain untainted by plunder or xenophobia: the poem ends, 'On the plains of Tipperary the stranger is like a king!'[23] These are tales of national loss and martyrdom, but in Kelly's case, they not only addressed history in deliberately archaic ways, but also began the re-imagining of the contemporary in the same accepted forms.

The sense of coming after the fact is strong within them. In another poem presented as 'From the Irish', 'Glenmaloe', Kelly inhabits a standard mourning for the landscape of Gaelic Ireland and then inflects it with a personal touch which can only be righted by refrain, by a return to Elgee's starting point of lyrics such as these, 'The soul is ever clinging on to form'. Kelly's poem breaks out of its form in small ways:

> Faint are the murmurs humming,
>   Through breeze and stream,
> Dim are the shadows coming –
>   A fairy dream!
> Harp notes are heard to tingle,
> Voices of spirits mingle,
> Deep in each hollow dingle
>   Where violets gleam!
> Ah! but the years are dreary,
>   Since long ago –
> Ah! but this heart is weary,
>   Sweet Glenmaloe!
> Thinking of visions faded,
> Lightsome and glad that made it –
> Hopes that for aye are shaded,
>   So well I know![24]

There is much that is from second-hand stock about this: 'tingle' / 'mingle' / 'dingle', 'lightsome', the 'fairy' and the 'harp'. But the return of the song of place, 'Sweet Glenmaloe!', and then the nostalgist's note, 'So well I know!' no matter how it recycles the poem of place, implicates the self and rises above the sentimental into feeling.

After Emancipation, the lyric project was attuned to the national and the religious, and in the subsequent agitation for Repeal of the Union, an attachment both to the poetry of place and to a renewed confidence in demanding a sovereignty of belief joined as the movers of cultural nationalism. For most of these writers this meant an O'Connellite narrowing of the national into the Catholic. But in another way, a renewed devotionalism implicated these poets in a broad trend in Victorian confessional poetry which placed subjectivity in often anguished relation with divinity and social change. In Irish poetry of the period, the Catholicism of Mangan plays this as a conflict between addiction and faith. But the biography and remaining writing of his contemporary Ellen Downing tells a slightly different version of the story. The forms she decided to cling on to were eventually Catholic. Her decision to become a nun and her subsequent failure in that vocation, was written by Fr Matthew Russell, editor of the *Irish Monthly* as 'saintly' – and he weighed up that word as only a Jesuit might.[25] Russell was a key figure in the later revival (the second Young Ireland, as it were) and looking back to Downing's example, he recognized that her move across from political radicalism to the novitiate was a set of decisions carried out by a distinctive devotional writer and thinker.

Downing's religious and writing career was compromised by a chronic illness, but the events of 1848 clearly traumatised her. Along with Elgee and Kelly, Downing followed John Mitchel out of the *The Nation* into the short-lived *United Irishman*. Elgee, of course, claimed authorship of '*Jacta Alea Est*' ('The Die is Cast', a phrase attributed to Julius Caesar before he crossed the Rubicon), the anonymous *Nation* editorial of 29 July 1848 which counselled revolution and which was to lead to the suppression of the paper and the arrest and trial of the editor, Charles Gavan Duffy.[26] Working from Downing's letters, Russell finds that a combination of the events of 1848 and the subsequent exile of her putative fiancé, led Mary of *The Nation* to become Sister Mary Alphonsus. Downing's decision to take the veil was matched by the change in her preoccupations as a writer: the posthumously collected book, *Voices from the Heart*, gathers nearly 300 pages of the religious poetry written in the thirty years after she entered the Presentation convent in Cork.[27] That poetry deserves its place in Victorian devotional verse, both Catholic and Protestant, along with the verse of Christina Rossetti or John Keble or Gerard Manley Hopkins which has been the subject of much renewed attention in recent British and Irish scholarship. Poems written at, or recalling, the moment of commitment – Rossetti's 'Convent Threshold', Hopkins's *Wreck of the Deutschland* – link back to long traditions of Christian verse.

Downing's best poem, 'The Old Church at Lismore', was, according to Stopford Brooke and T. W. Rolleston, a poem written just before she entered the novitiate in 1849.[28] The poem is at first sight a fairly familiar Young Ireland, post-Emancipation expression of grief for an event which happened long in the past, the Reformation. Downing claims back for Catholicism the then (and still) Protestant St Carthage's cathedral in Lismore, which has suffered the tearing down of its altars, crucifixes, saints and angels. (The medieval church was actually destroyed by an accidental fire in the seventeenth century and rebuilt by Richard Boyle, the scientist.) In answer to such iconoclasm, Downing avers that if the statues have gone, their spirits still haunt the church. Her treatment of the theme is not above sectarianism: the third and fourth stanzas watch the assembled contemporary reformed congregation, wondering how 'so coldly they can pray', and why they are forbidden to pray for the Catholic dead in the graveyard by 'their cruel Church'. This is unpromising stuff, but the poem is saved by the interjection of a personal voice which is allowed to inhabit the long Catholic Irish past of the Church – the building and the institution – and to offer a version of historical memory given rhetorical utterance. The apostrophe in the opening line, 'Old Church, thou still art Catholic!' is followed up by the personal iteration of faith in the fifth stanza: 'My God! I am a Catholic! I grew into the ways / Of my dear Church since my first voice could lisp a word of praise'. In the hands of a contemporary, such as Gerard Manley Hopkins, that exclamation could be a semantically multiple utterance, of profanity or joy or devotional ecstasy, as at the end of one of his Irish poems, 'Carrion Comfort': 'That night, that year of / Now done darkness I wretch lay wrestling with (My God!) my God'.[29] In Downing's hands the apostrophe is performed at nowhere near the same pitch, but it enables an accommodation between the sundering of the historical self, the Irish Church and the Christendom which her faith now restores as a unity of belief:

> Oh, let us lose no single link that our dear Church has bound,
> To keep our hearts more close to Heaven, on earth's ungenial ground;
> But trust in saint and martyr yet, and o'er their hallowed clay,
> Long after we have ceased to weep, kneel faithful down to pray.
>
> So shall the land for us be still the Sainted Isle of old,
> Where hymn and incense rise to Heaven, and holy beads are told;
> And even the ground they tore from God, in years of crime and woe,
> Instinctive with His truth and love, shall breathe of long ago![30]

'The Old Church at Lismore' faces a sectarian and historical divide and seeks to fulfil its author's wish that by averting to things that are outwith poem and culture and place – the long history of the Church and the poet's own faith – a long divide will be healed.

The Christianity of the poets who were contemporaries of Downing or who followed her was ever-present in Irish women's poetry in the decades that followed. The religious poetry of Elizabeth Varian (or 'Finola' of *The Nation*) and Emily Hickey, Northern and Southern Protestants respectively (though Hickey converted to Catholicism in 1901), is fully represented at the beginning of Lucy Collin's anthology of *Poetry by Women in Ireland, 1870–1970*. Collins is quite clear that Christianity and philanthropic activity, charged by nationalist political commitment assumed a feminist teleology as the century went on.[31] There were also conservative powers in play, not least those of the Catholic Church itself, careful as it was to police the possible heretical challenges to faith and family posed by extreme secular movements. The best treatments of this shift in confessional thinking, as in Downing's poetry, turned on the ultimately aestheticizing grasp of the question of belief in broader anglophone Victorian poetry, as fully explored by the critic Kirstie Blair. An intellectual and affective grasp on faith and its emanation through texts and church structures was founded in form: prayer, religious observance, the hymn. Such formal thinking was carried through the great confessional movements in Britain and beyond which followed Emancipation, the challenge to the English Church by the Oxford Movement and the even greater challenge of Charles Darwin.[32]

In his study of Irish poetry and Catholicism, Andrew Auge recognizes that Downing's 'Old Church' evinces 'heartfelt piety' and contrasts it harshly with the 'thin veneer of formal polish' shown by a later Catholic poet such as Katharine Tynan.[33] The poetry of Tynan, friend of Russell and acquaintance of Fr Hopkins, while clearly confessional in tone and outlook and theme, could some decades later find itself seeking a more satisfactory mode for a Catholicism which was not so much 'Roman' as self-consciously 'Irish'. Her second volume, *Shamrocks*, for instance, published in 1887 is as much a book of religious verse as it is on Irish themes, but the religion is Irish, as in her 'Shamrock Song' on the national symbol, which is also St Patrick's symbol of the Trinity.[34] Even her use of Italian themes is not quite Roman Catholic: she wrote a number of poems on St Francis, an invocation of an otherworldly spirituality which is quite in keeping with Arnoldian Celticism and its characterization of the asceticism of the Mediaeval Irish Church as defined by a sort of Atlanticist proto-Franciscan ideal of supernatural naturalism.

Celticism, though, as opposed to the broader Hibernianism or even latter-day Jacobitism which is apparent in the earlier Young Ireland movement, was slow to catch on in women's poetry as the nineteenth century progressed. Tynan's long poem on 'Diarmuid and Grainne' which opens *Shamrocks* is unusual even in the 1880s, though it does predate Yeats's deliberate reclaiming of the Ossianic for Ireland in *The Wanderings of Oisin* of 1889. Before the next and longer-lived revival of Irish women poets in the 1880s, significant voices were either Unionist and sentimental, like Helena Blackwood, or committed and agitatory, in the Speranza mode. Ellen O'Leary was long associated with her brother John's editorship and cultural entrepreneurialism, through his term as an imprisoned Fenian and then editor of the *Irish People*. She was to join Rose Kavanagh and Tynan and Hester Sigerson in the 1888 *Poems and Ballads of Young Ireland* anthology. Yet in America it was the sister of Charles Stewart Parnell, Fanny Parnell, who was to be the most widely read poet of the period between the suppression of Young Ireland and the revival.

Like Kelly before her, Parnell's writing career flourished within a broader Irish diaspora. She was no forced exile: her mother Delia Tudor Stewart Parnell returned from Parnell's Avondale in Wicklow to a large estate at Bordentown New Jersey after separation from her husband. Her father had been an Admiral in the United States navy. Fanny also lived in Bordentown. Landed gentry in both the USA and Ireland, the Parnells were of high Protestant social caste, so Fanny's position as Laureate for the Plan of Campaign, and one of the founders of the Ladies' Land League, told of the ideological commitments of her mother Delia, and of her siblings back in Ireland, sister Anna and brother Charles. She published in the Boston Catholic newspaper, John Boyle O'Reilly's *Pilot* but also in Patrick Ford's New York *Irish World and American Industrial Liberator*, the subtitle of which made explicit its trade union as well as Land League sympathies.

Parnell's memory has suffered when compared to the history of her brother and sister, the one a martyred leader, the other a successful political organizer (who nevertheless failed to find a publisher in her lifetime for her classic account of the Land War, written in much revisionary scorn, *Tale of a Great Sham* – it was eventually published in 1986). But part of the reason for Fanny's obscurity is the loss of her poems from a single volume edition. Her *Land League Songs* was published in pamphlet form in Boston in 1882, but by 1904, the Irish feminist Hannah Sheehy Skeffington could not find a copy on which to base an essay on Parnell's work. No copy has surfaced since, though the poems are sprinkled through the *Pilot* and the *Irish World*.[35] The poems which remain are firmly in the Young Ireland mode, though directed even more explicitly at the campaigns of the land leagues in Ireland. Michael Davitt notoriously said of her 1880 Land League anthem, 'Hold the Harvest', that it was 'the "Marseillaise" of the Irish peasant'. It is a stirring and energetic performance, beginning 'Now are you men or cattle, you tillers of the soil?' Its companion poem, 'Hold the Rent', instils sea shanty rhythms into a similar advocacy of law-breaking which is nevertheless peaceful protest:

Keep the law, oh, keep it well – keep it as your rulers do;
Be not righteous overmuch – when they break it, so can you!
As they rend their pledge and bond, rend you, too, their legal thongs
When they crush your chartered rights, tread you down your chartered wrongs.
    Hold the rents and hold the crops, boys;
    Pass the word from town to town;
    Pull away the props, boys
    So you'll pull Coercion down![36]

This mode lasted for most of the nineteenth century and was to survive in numerous songs and ballads into the twentieth century: Terry Moylan's *Indignant Muse* compiles nearly seven hundred pages of revolutionary song between 1887 and 1926, and while not all are in the Young Ireland / Land League mode, it is hard not to make a direct connection between lyric and nationalist insurgency.

A number of Irish woman poets were to inflect their poetry in other, post-Romantic, ways. *The Poems and Ballads of Young Ireland* volume is maybe an unlikely candidate for the beginnings of a movement we might call modernist, but it did begin to shift the sensibility of the poet, away from the recognizable subjects appropriate for the hustings or the Church or the domestic, initially towards the recognizably post-Romantic (Yeats's praise of Kavanagh as 'meditative and sympathetic') and then towards the self-conscious and innovative. A necessary first step in doing so was the recognition of aesthetic shortcomings, and the writing of Kavanagh and Tynan and O'Leary made small steps to change that. In an impatient account of the aestheticization of politics in the Young Ireland move-ment, its too-easy connection between the *Spirit of the Nation* as literary endeavour and romantic nationalism as obfuscatory, quasi-racist politi-cal ideology, David Dwan has said that Yeats's eventual desire for 'the de-Davisation of literature' was founded in a recognition of aesthetic shortcomings, that Davis was 'a lacklustre poet'.[37] There were other issues, as when the aesthetic shades into the ethical. Those ethics had been strong in the Famine poem or Land League poem, the witness from the offended viewpoint resulting in an indignation aimed at bad government and exploitative landlordism. But there was also the matter of an ethics of representation, of attuning the form of the poem and its linguistic choices for difficult historical material and not-easily-reducible political positions born out of violence and seeming to beget it in turn. Of course, the subsequent career of W. B. Yeats was to prove the strongest model for the poet's ambivalence before a history developing into what might have appeared to be 'mere anarchy' before his eyes. It is smaller matter than this, perhaps, but the principle of selection in the 1888 *Poems and Ballads* contained much that was to persist in the question not just of the quantity of Irish poetry being written but more importantly, its quality, as an ethical as well as a literary question.

This was recognized in the decisions made by the Irish women poets who wrote in the O'Leary anthology and in their successors, still divided between the differing notions of subjectivity as transcribed by Young Ireland and it successors, the politically insurgent or the privately questioning. Highly politicised poetry by women was still written in the decades that followed, most notably by Alice Milligan and Anna Johnston (as Ethna Carbery). Kavanagh and Tynan – and after them Emily Lawless, Dora Sigerson and Susan Mitchel – developed in other ways, seeking poetic voices newly attuned to the British, European and American examples of Victorian and modern poetry, and of how that might be brought within a newly emergent Irish modernism. The reconciliation of a century of experiment in so-called 'Anglo-Irish literature' involved an accommodation with what Thomas MacDonagh would by 1916 call the 'Irish mode', a hiberno-English metric and diction, speaking at once from street ballad and rural lyric, so that Irish poets could succeed in a refashioning of English-language poetry for decolonising ends.[38] Through historical dramatic monologue (Lawless's 1902 *With the Wild Geese*), political elegy and self-elegy (Sigerson's 1918 *The Sad Years*) and satire (Mitchell's 1918 *Secret Springs of Dublin Song*) that Irish mode was developed much by poets who were MacDonagh's contemporaries.

It is a large part of the shame of the partial successes of the decolonising project that the poems written by the women poets discussed here, along with that of a number of their successors, were suddenly to disappear from the poetic canon of the newly 'Free' state. Irish anthology-shaming is maybe no longer a spectator sport, but suffice to say that the rescue of these poets has continued apace after Anne Ulry Colman revealed in 1996 that she had discovered 'in excess of four hundred Irish women poets writing in English, whose birthdates fall between 1800 and 1899'.[39] Her 1996 *Dictionary of Nineteenth-Century Irish Women Poets* is a wonderful bibliographical resource for a posterity which has been newly restored. There may not be in excess of 400 good poems, but readers are now able to read these poems, and rather more good ones than the few discussed here do exist. Reading them we have come to terms with bibliographical, historical and political evidence; while we are at it, the opportunity now exists to seek out their quality.

Notes

1 W. B. Yeats, 'Rose Kavanagh: Death of a Promising Young Irish Poet', in *Letters to the New Island*, eds. George Bornstein and Hugh Witemeyer (London: Macmillan, 1989), 44.

2 See Robert Emmet's speech from the dock, 1803, in *The Field Day Anthology of Irish Writing*, ed. Seamus Deane et al., 3 vols. (Derry: Field Day, 1991), 1:938.

3 Rose Kavanagh, 'St Michan's Churchyard', in John O'Leary, ed. *Poems and Ballads of Young Ireland* (repr.) ed. John Kelly (Otley: Woodstock Books, 2000), 60.

4 Thomas Moore, *Poetical Works*, ed. A. D. Godley (Oxford: Oxford University Press, 1910), 181.

5 They were named after 'Young England', a group of 1840s English Tories grouped around Disraeli.

6 See Kelly, introduction to *Poems and Ballads of Young Ireland*, n.p.

7 Yopie Prins, 'Personifying the Poetess: Caroline Norton, "The Picture of Sappho,"' in *Women's Poetry, Late Romantic to Late Victorian: Gender and Genre, 1830–1900*, ed. Isobel Armstrong and Virgina Blain (Basingstoke: Palgrave Macmillan, 1999), 52.

8 See Stopford Brooke and T. W. Rolleston, eds., *A Treasury of Irish Poetry in the English Tongue* (London: Macmillan, 1915), 226–7.

9 Prins, 'Personifying the Poetess', 53.

10 Caroline Sheridan Norton, *The Dream and Other Poems* (London: Colburn, 1840), 203–5.

11 Gregory Schirmer, *Out of What Began: A History of Irish Poetry in English* (Ithaca: Cornell University Press, 1998), 150.

12 R. Y. Tyrrell to Frank Harris, quoted in Horace Wyndham, *Speranza: A Biography of Lady Wilde* (London: Boardman, 1951), 98.

13 In 'Man's Mission', lines 51 and 53; searched via *Literature Online*. Accessed 10 April 2017.

14 Lucy Collins, 'Introduction' to *Poetry by Women in Ireland: A Critical Anthology 1870–1970* (Liverpool: Liverpool University Press, 2014), 14.

15 Marjorie Howes, *Colonial Crossings: Figures in Irish Literary History* (Dublin: Field Day, 2006), 19.

16 Chris Morash, *Writing the Irish Famine* (Oxford: Oxford University Press, 1995), and Terry Eagleton, *Heathcliff and the Great Hunger* (London: Verso, 1995).

17 Lady Wilde, *Poems by Speranza* (Dublin: Duffy, 1864).

18 Morash, *Writing the Irish Famine*, 182.

19 See Wyndham, *Speranza*, 1, who suggests she was born in 1824.

20 Matthew Russell, 'Ellen Downing. "Mary" of the "Nation"', *The Irish Monthly* 6 (1878).

21 Quoted by Matthew Russell, 'Ellen Downing. "Mary" of the "Nation"', *The Irish Monthly* 6 (1878): 464.

22 Mary Kelly, 'Boomerang', in *Poems of Eva of the Nation*, ed. Seumas MacManus (Dublin: M.H. Gill, 1909), 70–1.

23 Kelly, *Poems and Ballads of Young Ireland*, 78–9.

24 Ibid., 17–18.

25 See Matthew Russell, 'The Late Ellen Downing of Cork: "Mary" of the "Nation"', Part III', *The Irish Monthly* 6 (1878): 577.

26 See Wyndham, *Speranza*, 33–4.

27 Sister Mary Alphonsus Downing, *Voices from the Heart*, new edn., ed. Bishop Leahy (Dublin: Gill, 1881).

28 See Brooke and Rolleston, *A Treasury of Irish Poetry in the English Tongue*, 150.

29 Gerard Manley Hopkins, 'Carrion Comfort', in *Gerard Manley Hopkins*, ed. Catherine Phillips (Oxford: Oxford University Press, 1986), 168.

30 Brooke and Rolleston, *A Treasury of Irish Poetry in the English Tongue*, 151.

31 Collins, *Poetry by Women in Ireland*, 8.

32 See Kirstie Blair, *Form and Faith in Victorian Poetry and Religion* (Oxford: Oxford University Press, 2012).

33 Andrew J. Auge, *A Chastened Communion: Modern Irish Poetry and Catholicism* (Syracuse: Syracuse University Press, 2013), 5.

34 Katherine Tyan, *Shamrocks* (London: Kegan Paul, 1887).

35 Jane M. Coté, *Fanny and Anna Parnell: Ireland's Patriot Sisters* (London: Macmillan, 1991). Coté says that the *Irish World* of 5 August 1882 has twenty of Parnell's poems on its front page. The obituary notice and funeral report are inside.

36 Quoted in Coté, *Fanny and Anna Parnell*, 133.

37 David Dwan, 'Cultural Developments: Young Ireland to Yeats', in *The Princeton History of Modern Ireland*, ed. Richard Bourke and Ian McBride (Oxford: Princeton University Press, 2016), 225.

38 See chapter two of my *Irish Poetry Under the Union, 1801–1924* (Cambridge: Cambridge University Press, 2013).

39 Anne Ulry Colman, *A Dictionary of Nineteenth-Century Irish Women Poets* (Galway: Kenny's, 1996).

CHAPTER 5

Fiction, 1845–1900

James H. Murphy

The dates that contain this chapter gesture neatly to some of the tensions that have existed when it comes to writing about fiction in Ireland in the nineteenth century. The date 1845 clearly refers to the beginning of the Famine in Ireland, while 1900 signals the end of the century and of the Victorian era, though Queen Victoria herself died a few days into 1901. In many Irish literary histories, and, indeed, in chapter seven of this volume, 1891, the year of the death of Charles Stewart Parnell, is used to mark a new period, that of the Irish Literary Revival, following Yeats's belief that at that time people turned away from tainted politics and towards a national culture. Yet much of Irish women's fiction writing, in particular, during the 1890s cannot be contained within the category of the Irish Revival. It relates either to the transnational New Woman movement, as chapter six demonstrates, or to the latter stages of the Victorian age, as this chapter shows.

The culture of Ireland in the second half of the nineteenth century was caught between Irishness and Britishness. Though politically a strengthening nationalism was pulling Ireland away from the United Kingdom, culturally Ireland was converging with Victorian Britain, at least until the 1890s. In spite of the existence of a number of important Dublin and Belfast publishing houses, the literary world centred on London. Cultural analysts from Yeats and the Irish Revivalists to the postcolonial critics of the late twentieth century have wanted to delegitimize Irish Victorian culture. Much of its literature, particularly its fiction, was the work of women. But it has variously been derided as unIrish by the Irish Revivalists and as a failed literature by postcolonialists. The latter were anxious to ignore any signs of a stable social order in Victorian Ireland from which bourgeois realism in fiction might have emerged and to prize Ireland's supposed strangely primitive distinctiveness from which they imagined the radical modernism of James Joyce and others had triumphantly leapt into existence.[1]

The chapter charts the achievement of actual Irish women novelists in the Victorian world. It asserts that the culture of the middle-class Victorian Ireland from which these writers, for all their other diversity, emerged is an important and legitimate part of Irish cultural history. But, equally, it is important not to be carried too far by way of reaction to the Irish revivalists and postcolonialists. The trauma of the Famine and the dislocation of the land struggle were realities for many Irish people but they were ones with which Irish Victorian writers actively engaged, albeit mostly from a middle-class perspective, and gender was a key issue in that engagement.

The work of Loeber and Loeber for the period 1650–1900 reveals that only four in ten Irish novelists were women.[2] Yet it is surely true to say that in the Victorian period, Irish women novelists made a very large contribution and in the most important and essentially pre-Revival anthology of Irish writing there is a rough parity between male and female writers.[3] Even before the scholarly work of the past quarter of a century, the rudimentary canon of nineteenth-century Irish fiction – Edgeworth, Owenson, Lover, Lever, Le Fanu, Lawless, and Somerville and Ross – began and ended with women writers. One of the advantages of the fact that scholarly work on Irish Victorian novelists, both male and female, has been of such recent date, is that the recovery process has eschewed the practice, which still inhibits the study of British Victorian literature, of focusing on a small number of writers. This feminist inclusiveness thus informs the present chapter which considers the work of over forty women writers rather than a small selection.

The relative diversity of Irish Victorian women writers in terms both of their social background and of the topics of their work is impressive and significant. Social class is one important way of understanding them, their world and their work. A clear pattern is discernible, a movement away from writers from wealthy or aristocratic backgrounds and towards writers who were reliant on their work for their income and were thus economically vulnerable. It was a trend though that would lead to the marginalization of Irish women writers throughout much of the following century.

Some Irish women writers, especially in the early part of the period covered in this chapter, were aristocrats or had become aristocrats and had entered London high society. Lady Blessington (1789–1849), the silver-fork novelist, perhaps the best known of these, had been born into a prosperous Catholic family near Clonmel and yet had come to dominate fashionable life in London in the early nineteenth century. Rosina

Anne Doyle Wheeler (1802–82) of Co. Limerick had had an antagonistic relationship with her husband, the prominent novelist, Edward Bulwer Lytton, which is reflected in her novel *Cheveley* (1839). Later in the century, Gertrude Elizabeth Blood of Co. Clare was known as the scandalous Lady Colin Campbell and flaunted her reputation in fiction.[4]

Some of the best remembered novelists of the later nineteenth century were from an Anglo-Irish Ascendancy background, by which time issues of gender had become an explicit theme. Edith Somerville (1858–1949) and Violet Martin (1862–1915), who published as Somerville and Ross, wrote perceptive satires of Ascendancy and middle-class life in rural Ireland which culminated in the magnificent *The Real Charlotte* (1894). Material aspiration and sexual frustration vie in their novels from the 1890s, such as *Naboth's Vineyard* (1891). Emasculation features in their early novel *An Irish Cousin* (1889) and again in *The Silver Fox* (1897). The latter is also the covert story of a same-sex female relationship.[5] Emily Lawless (1845–1913), daughter of Lord Cloncurry, wrote novels about sixteenth-century Irish history – *With Essex in Ireland* (1890) and *Maelcho* (1894) – and about the Irish peasantry – *Hurrish* (1886) and *Grania* (1892). The latter touch on violent antagonism over land and issues of dominance and subservience, in the one instance, and a struggle for freedom against the constraints of gender roles, flavoured with some of the patterns of New Woman fiction, in the other. W. E. Gladstone, the Liberal prime minister, admired Lawless's work, finding in it insights into the apparent intractability of Irish conflict, while W. B. Yeats, perhaps fearing a rival for the role of spokesperson for the peasantry, derided her work as being in 'imperfect sympathy with the Celtic nature'.[6] Irish Victorian novelists of Anglo-Irish backgrounds, including New Woman novelists who will be dealt with in the following chapter, could be found in all kinds of situations. Jemima Baroness von Tautphoeus (1807–1893), who wrote novels in Bavaria, was originally from Donegal and a cousin of Maria Edgeworth. Charlotte Despard (1844–1939), author of a novel about social conditions, was a radical who would eventually turn Irish republican. E. L. Voynich (1864–1960), from Cork, would become one of the most widely read novelists in the Soviet Union.[7]

Upper-class women continued to make a contribution during this period. Most Irish Victorian women novelists, however, were middle class and did not have a cushion of aristocratic financial security. This was thus the period when for the first time middle-class women were able to make a living as writers, albeit often a precarious one, necessitating close attention to the demands of the market in terms of genre and content. They often lived a book-to-book existence. Many found it best to live in London near the larger publishers and to attune their work to the literary requirements and fashions of the day. Many of their novels were set in Britain. Some wrote in the shadow of other writers. There is certainly the feel of a Dickensian childhood to *My Share of the World* (1861) by Frances Browne (1816–79), while her *The Hidden Sin* (1866) is in the tradition of the novel of sensation. The most successful novel by Charlotte Riddell (1832–1906), *George Geith of Fen Court* (1864), was a sensation novel, though she also pioneered a now-forgotten sub-genre, the novel of the city, in *City and Suburb* (1861), which was compared with George Eliot's *Adam Bede* (1859). The novelist with the most overt connection with a writer from among British canonical authors was Julia Kavanagh (1824–77). Her novel *Nathalie* (1850), for example, was both influenced by Charlotte Brontë's *Jane Eyre* (1847) and was itself an influence on Brontë's later work in terms of subject matter. Other novelists who made careers for themselves in popular novel writing in the later part of the century included Annie French Hector (1825–1902, Mrs Alexander), Frances Sarah Johnston (1830–1908, Mrs Cashel Hoey), May Crommelin (1849–1930) and Margaret Wolfe Hungerford (1852–97). The latter was unusual as she conducted her career from Ireland, living in Bandon, Co. Cork.[8]

The writing of fiction on religious and historical topics often proved remunerative. Some Protestant women writers specialized in religious fiction often with both an historical setting and a polemical intent, most notably Selina Bunbury (1802–82) and Deborah Alcock (1835–1913). The former was a frequent recipient of grants from the Royal Literary Fund, which supported hard-up writers during illness or old age. For the most part, Irish Catholic writers did not advance militantly religious themes in their works but were anxious to assert the respectability of Catholicism in a hostile Victorian world. Novels such as *Nanno* (1898) by Rosa Mulholland (1841–1921, Lady Gilbert) focused on issues concerning the moral probity of young women lower down the social scale. A more assertive Catholicism tended only to be advocated by authors who lived abroad. Mary Anne Sadlier (1820–1903) wrote novels to bolster the Catholic identity of Irish immigrants to America. *The Battle of Connemara* (1878) compares favourably the religious faith of Irish peasants with that of Catholics in France where Kathleen O'Meara (1839–88, Grace Ramsay), author of the novel, lived. May Laffan (1850–1916, Lady Hartley) pioneered anti-Catholic social satire in novels such as *Hogan M.P.* (1876). It would be taken up by Somerville and

Ross – in *Naboth's Vineyard*, for example – and others with added sharpness as Catholics came to have a more confident position in society. Laffan and Fannie Gallaher also wrote fiction of urban social concern. Flora Shaw (1851–1929, Lady Lugard) was a children's author, while L. T. Meade (1844–1914, E. T. T. Smith) was a prolific writer of novels about the lives of young women, many of them pioneers in the world of education and work and the professions.[9]

But there was scope for tackling sometimes contentious political topics. Charlotte Grace O'Brien (1845–1905), Attie O'Brien (1840–83), Mary Bradford Whiting and Hannah Lynch (1862–1904) wrote novels about the Fenians, though often within a middle-class social context. It was possible to succeed by writing both for and about a particular region. Several women writers, mostly Protestants, participated in the distinctive fiction relating to Ulster that developed towards the end of the century, though Rose Kavanagh (1859–91), author of *Killaveena, an Ulster Story* (1895), was a Catholic. Letitia McClintock's *The March of Loyalty* (1884) detailed northern Protestant resistance to Irish nationalism. *A Maid of the Manse* (1895) by Erminda Renoul Esler (1860–1924) is about internal theological differences within Ulster Presbyterianism, while *Across an Ulster Bog* (1895) by M. Hamilton (1869–1949, Mary Churchill Luck) is a darker story of sexual exploitation within the Church of Ireland. Some Irish women novelists focused on the British empire, notably B. M. Croker (1849–1920) who wrote about British India.[10]

Almost more important than politics as a public issue in Victorian Ireland was the issue of land. Controversy concerning it culminated in the land wars that began in the late 1870s and that resulted eventually in the passing of ownership of land from landlords to tenants. Women were prominent writers of land novels and, from the 1880s, of land-war novels, though a discussion of the latter is being reserved for a later consideration of feminism in the fiction of Irish women Victorian novelists. Their contribution in the area of land and land-war fiction was until recently ignored not least because some women novelists wrote in a manner sympathetic to landlordism. In many ways the land novel was inaugurated by Anna Maria Hall (1800–81) with *The Whiteboy* (1845). Margaret Brew (1850–1905) was the author of *The Burtons of Dunroe* (1880) and *The Chronicles of Castle Cloyne* (1885) and Annie Keary (1825–79), born to an Irish family in England, was the author of *Castle Daly* (1875). These were important land novels that emerged from the period just before the land war. They also experiment with innovative approaches to the question of realism in Irish Victorian fiction. Then and since the deeply entrenched social, economic and religious differences between landlord and tenant were thought to militate against a realism that relied on an essentially unitary vision of society.[11]

Assessing the impact and influence of Irish women novelists among Victorian readers is difficult because of the general lack of sales figures. It is possible, however, to get a sense of the popularity of individual writers through book reviews. A study of the principal Victorian journals and magazines that reviewed novels reveals the persistent presence of Irish women writers from mid-century. The high points of the careers of Hall and Blessington had passed by 1845. From the 1850s, though, the presence of women, notably Riddell and Kavanagh, begins to make itself felt. They were joined in the 1860s by Hoey and O'Meara and in the 1870s by Keary. By the 1880s the prominent women reviewed were Riddell, Hungerford, Alexander, Laffan, Lawless, Brew, McClintock, Mabel Robinson and E. Owens Blackburne. In the 1890s, however, over twenty Irish women novelists, including several New Woman novelists, were receiving significant attention from reviewers.[12] That decade marked a great expansion in the scope of fiction by Irish authors. Some of the new writers have already been mentioned or will be considered later in this chapter. Others included Alice Milligan (1866–1953), author of the satirical *A Royal Democrat* (1892). The novels of Ella MacMahon (1864–1956) take a generally pessimistic view of women's experience of love and marriage. Many of the novels of this decade, however, address the changing social composition of Irish society in the aftermath of the land struggle. An early novel by Hannah Lynch (1862–1904), *Through Troubled Waters* (1885), explores the decline of the Ascendancy, as do Esler's *The Wardlaws* (1896) and Croker's *Beyond the Pale* (1896). In *Kerrigan's Quality* (1894), a novel by Jane Barlow (1857–1917), who is better remembered as a writer of short stories, newly acquired wealth is unable to replace the Ascendancy. However, in *The Way of a Maid* (1895) by Katharine Tynan (1859–1931) sectarian and class divisions are overcome against all odds.[13]

Thus far we have noted the extent and variety of women's contribution to fiction in Victorian Ireland and we have done so largely in terms of the life context within which that fiction was written. Of course, by the very act of being professional writers in the separate-spheres Victorian world, which ideally confined women to domesticity, these writers were unavoidably feminist in their activities. In general terms, they can be seen as being in contrast to the often more aristocratic women writers of the eighteenth century and Romantic period for whom writing could be an avocation. As we have noted the overwhelming majority were middle-class women who needed to make a living. Many of them lived from hand to mouth and sank into poverty in old age, as novels tended to be bought by publishers with a once-off payment and there was often thus no continuing copyright income. For all its challenges and difficulties, pursuing the life of a professional writer thus itself constituted a progressive, feminist mode of living, at least to a degree.

For the remainder of this discussion, the focus will change from context to content. To what extent then did what these authors write about itself constitute a feminist contribution? The answer is that it is possible to trace the weaving together of several strands of feminist thought in the work of Irish Victorian women novelists. The picture that emerges, and that is presented in direct form here for the first time, is of women detailing – and thus confirming and strengthening – existing struggles against patriarchy; of women imagining the further extension of female activity in the public sphere; and of women challenging and modifying the limiting gendered tropes of political and national identity. Thus, women wrote about what it was like to be a professional, particularly a professional writer. They imagined what it would be like for women to be actively engaged in the central socio-political issue of the century, the land struggle. They took on the trope of the 'national marriage', inherited from fiction in the Romantic age, and morphed it into the trope of the 'independent woman'. Yet, though this was a story of feminist assertion it was not one without its partialities, compromises and ambivalences.

Writing about what you know is a common resort of novel writers. It was not unnatural that women novelists would write about what it was like to be a woman writer or to make one's way in another profession. Quite a few women's novels have this autobiographical or apparently autobiographical dimension to them. *Molly Carew* (1879) by E. Owens Blackburne (Elizabeth Casey, 1845–94) and Riddell's *A Struggle for Fame* (1883) both follow the careers of young Irish women writers who, like their authors, are pursuing their careers in the London publishing world.[14] The eponymous Molly of Blackburne's novel works as a writer for London journals and magazines, though the story revolves around her ill-fated relationship with a male writer whose possible romantic interest in her becomes a greater priority for her than professional success. Riddell's novel is clearly a *roman à clef* with London publishers in particular being quite recognizable in it. Once again the heroine, Glen Westley, has a male author peer but this time Barney Kelly is an unscrupulous rival rather than an exploitative lover, a role which at least is more respectful of Glen's professional position. The demands of the market dictate content and the market is not interested in novels with Irish-themed content. Failure as a writer brings shame as another character attests, describing his subsequent remunerative career as an advertisement canvasser as 'the horrible depths to which I have descended'. Barney's failures as a writer feed his misogyny. He determines to found a review that will exclude women. 'Not a woman ... maid, wife, or widow – shall write a line for it'. Having fallen out of favour with publishers, Glen's career is ironically revived by a positive review by Barney, albeit one he intends primarily as an attack on a publisher rather than as a help for Glen. Glen's career is thus not one of unalloyed or brilliant success. In the unforgiving world of publishing politics it is agreed that her greatest quality is 'her staying powers'.[15] At one low point someone advises Glen to apply for a grant to the Royal Literary Fund. She refuses. Late in life, though, Riddell herself was to rely on a small pension from the Royal Literary Fund. Elizabeth Casey, as Blackburne was known in real life, was not so lucky. Shunned as an obstreperous alcoholic, she died in a house fire.[16]

There were also novels about women in other careers. Blackburne was the author of *The Way Women Love* (1877). In it Moira O'Neill, a young woman of reduced Ascendancy background, goes to London to make her career as an actor. Her most notable role is as Grace O'Malley, the sixteenth-century Irish pirate queen and herself something of a feminist icon. The end of the novel becomes a story of sibling rivalry as the author of the play turns out to be Moira's apparently quieter sister, Honor. Ella MacMahon's *A New Note* (1894), set in London and partly in Ireland, takes on the issues of gender and women's professionalism in a robust and forthright manner.[17] Here Victoria Leathley becomes a professional violist but it is not to the liking of some men: 'Intellect in a woman's face shunts prettiness aside very imperiously. The girl's face was keenly intellectual, otherwise it might possibly have attained to prettiness'. Victoria maintains her determination in the face of such disapproval: 'To me the whole worth of life is my career. It is, to me, as a career in politics, or law, or soldiering is to a man. Marriage is so unnecessary, so needless for me'. For her it is a choice between career and marriage, though for others there is room to manoeuvre in between. 'If Victoria is to end as the orthodox girl ends – in love and marriage – an excursion into another world for a little while first won't hinder that result. If she is not to end so, then she must have some other employment for her faculties.

Victoria, you see, has faculties'. As in the Blackburne novel there is a new play, tellingly entitled 'Sappho' but this time Victoria herself turns out to be the author. In the end she eschews the possibility of marriage though again some opinion holds her choice mistaken, as in this assessment with its clear implications about marriage:

> Victoria Leathley, a great artist, possessed emotional instincts of the strength of which she was not herself yet aware. Victoria Leathley, a woman of the world, the result as well as the creature of civilisation, possessed instincts of self-preservation, a degree so strong as to interfere considerably with the promptings of those other and primary instincts which no order of things has as yet eliminated from human nature.[18]

MacMahon's work was written in the era of the New Woman novel. It is important to recognize that Irish feminist fiction was both formed by and itself helped to form the New Woman movement. But it is also important to recognize that it had roots further back in Irish women's writing, as the similarities between *A New Note* and *The Way Women Love* attest.

Indeed, the first novel of this kind was probably *Dunmara* (1864) which the young Rosa Mulholland published under the name Ruth Murray and which was presumably based on her own early experiences as an art student in London, before she turned to fiction writing. Mulholland was to emerge as a writer of strong if ambivalent feminist instincts, her feminism being sometimes modified by religious, class and social concerns. *Dunmara* gives voice to a fascinating debate between the heroine who, in spite of wishing to be professionally independent as an artist, expresses somewhat conservative views on the role of women in society and another woman art student who had originally wanted to be a doctor:

> I am perfectly sick of the life we girls have to lead. It is nothing at the best but dressing, and dancing, and flirting; and flirting, and dancing, and dressing, I said I would not submit to it ... Why should not a woman give herself to a high calling as well as a man? Why should she not work the powers she has got?

The heroine has chosen an artistic career, however, because she thinks it compatible with the traditional role of a woman:

> I think it is well with the woman who, having sterner inspirations given by Providence for a purpose, can turn on the instant from easel, chisel, or pen, not disgusted and reluctant, but gladly, cheerfully, to do even such common-place things as tending a sick bed, or cleaning a child's stocking.

Even the most isolated life has need of such calls. Obedience to them entails increase of liberty, and for those who live among their kind they are never ceasing.[19]

The autobiographical element in Mulholland's novel is a reminder of two at times overlapping groups of novels by Irish women: those which take the form of an apparent autobiography and those in which there was actually an authorial autobiographical element. Among the former are some significant novels from the 1890s that contain bleak versions of childhood. They include Hannah Lynch's *The Autobiography of a Child* (1899) and *The Beth Book* (1897), by Sarah Grand (1854–1943) who coined the term New Woman. Among the latter is Riddell's *Miss Gascoigne* (1887) about a love affair between an older woman and younger man, which was probably based on an episode in Riddell's own life. Mrs Alexander's *The Frères* (1882) is set in Germany where her family had recently been travelling and her posthumous *Kitty Costello* (1904) may draw on the experiences of her own early move to England in the 1840s.[20]

Of course when it came to the issue of the exercise of power in the public realm by women, the professional advancement of individual women was only one of three arenas in which it was possible to imagine women making an impact. The others were in the realm of politics, which we shall deal with later, and through the inheritance of land. Women were involved on both sides of the land conflict because land involved family, both the families who owned the land and the families of those who rented it.

It should be recalled that a focus on the role of women in the land issue was not just the preserve of female authors. George Moore (1852–1933) was a pioneer in English of Zolaesque naturalism and the author of *Esther Waters* (1894), an English-set novel about the plight of a poor young woman. In *A Drama in Muslin* (1886) he focused on the lives of young marriageable women from landed backgrounds during the land war. In an earlier generation several of the novels of Charles Lever (1806–72), most notably *The Martins of Cro' Martin* (1856) and *Lord Kilgobbin* (1872), include independent-minded women. In the former, for example, Mary Martin, a landlord's niece, exhausts herself and her resources in an attempt to aid the tenants at the time of the Famine when her family has abandoned its traditional responsibilities. The fact that she has to do so is a sign for Lever of the breakdown of that vision of benign Tory feudalism in which he so whole-heartedly believed. Lever may also have identified personally with his apparently marginal women characters in his novels, believing himself to have been marginalized in terms of his career by the assaults of fellow authors on him in the 1840s that had led him to leave Ireland for life on the continent.[21]

Some of the land-war novels written by women, such as *The Plan of Campaign* (1888) by Frances Mabel Robinson (1858–1956) and *The Lloyds of Balymore* (1890) by Edith Rochfort, do not address the issue of gender. Letitia McClintock's *A Boycotted Household* (1881), one of the first books to employ the recent neologism derived from the events surrounding Captain Boycott in 1880, certainly does. Like most land-war novels this remarkable work sees things from the side of a beleaguered landlord family. Its female members join in the struggle. 'Oh, that *I* were a man', wishes one woman character.[22] As in some of these novels though, women's assertiveness is itself seen as proof of the disturbance in the social fabric. McClintock's novel is also prophetic in its depiction of the need for the young women of the family to marry well in order to escape their doomed Anglo-Irish order. In this, McClintock's land-war novel anticipates that later genre, the Big House novel, with its sympathetic depiction of the pathetic plight of the Anglo-Irish which was to culminate in the twentieth century in the work of Elizabeth Bowen (1889–1973) and Molly Keane (1904–96).

In two novels, Fannie Gallaher's *Thy Name is Truth* (1883) and Mulholland's *Marcella Grace* (1886), women become landlords through unexpected inheritance. In both cases the woman landlord comes from humble circumstances in Dublin and is not from a landed background. Gender thus combines with class to enable a way forward for the impasse of rural conflict through sympathy with the tenants. In the case of the first novel the heroine gives away her lands to her tenants; in the case of the second the added dimension of the heroine's pronounced Catholicism enables her to be a good landlord, though the novel ends with her withdrawing into the shadow of her husband. *Marcella Grace* provoked a riposte in the form of the anonymous *Priests and People, a No Rent Romance* (1891), whose heroine, a young Catholic woman of landlord background, aspires to a benign paternalism but who finds the violence of her tenants embittering and disillusioning.[23]

Novels concerning the land, particularly novels of the land war of the 1880s, thus often feature women called on to take leadership roles in a turbulent social and economic situation. The empowerment of the woman leader though is part of an ambivalent discourse of gender. On the one hand, in some instances and in some ways, it can be seen as part of a conservative warning, indicating that the existing and natural social order is in the process of breakdown. On the other hand, it lets the genie out of the bottle. It is surely no coincidence then that several of the most prominent novelists in the New Woman movement were Irish women or that Irish women novelists would channel their energies towards a transnational movement rather than into the less receptive world of the Irish Revival. It is certainly a very suggestive fact that the prominence of active women in Irish land-war novels of the 1880s immediately preceded the prominence of novels by Irish women such as Grand, Iota (Kathleen Hunt, 1852/3–1926) and George Egerton (Mary Chavelita Dunne, 1859–1945) in the New Woman movement.[24] Until very recently, these New Woman writers, as participants in a transnational literary and cultural movement, have not been considered within the ambit of Irish literature because Irish identity has been thought the main matter of interest in the study of Irish literature.

Irish Victorian women writers in general also lived within the literary orbit of a specifically Irish cultural legacy. They worked in both national and transnational contexts. Of the legacies of Romanticism in Irish Victorian fiction the genre of the national tale, centring on the trope of the national marriage, was certainly the most potent. In a national marriage, the marriage of a powerful British man to an exotic though ultimately subordinate Irish woman took on an allegorical dimension in the aftermath of the 1801 marriage/union between Britain and Ireland. There has hitherto been little if any scholarly recognition that the national-marriage trope persisted right down to the end of the nineteenth century and most significantly in the writing of Irish women novelists. Of course they used the convention in very different political and cultural times, sometimes drawing strong attention to it and sometimes allowing it to function in a more allusive fashion. In some cases its basic structure was retained, albeit sometimes in altered and subverted form, with the marriage being not that between Britain and Ireland but that between the two divided religious communities in Ireland. In other cases it was transformed into something else, as part of a feminist analysis, with the subordinate woman marriage partner changing into an independent though no less nationally representative woman leader. Once again, Lever is a rare male writer who deployed the convention. In his work there is a good deal of interaction at the level of family relationships between various forms of Britishness and Irishness, some of which takes the form of implicit national marriages. *The Knight of Gwynne* (1847), for example, illustrates an interesting feature of several of these later nineteenth-century novels inasmuch as the national marriage has taken place in a previous generation. The eponymous knight's wife is English and thus of their daughter the narrative has it that '[f]rom her mother she inherited the placid tenderness of English manner, while from her father her nature imbibed the joyous animation and buoyant light-heartedness of the Irish character'.[25]

Turning to fiction by women, Riddell's *Maxwell Drewitt* (1865), like Lever's novel, rests on a marriage, in this case an inter-religious marriage, that has taken place in a previous generation, though its deleterious effects are still being felt. Having married a Catholic, Maxwell's father is caught between worlds. 'He was not religious, yet he was superstitious and bigoted. He hated the Roman Catholics, yet he was always asking the priest to dinner'. The novel ends with some of the characters expressing their revulsion for Ireland though one character brings himself to continue living in Ireland because of the companionship of the 'bright, loveable English country girl' whom he has married.[26] In this case of a national marriage of sorts, an English bride inoculates against sordid Irish realities. In *Julia Howard, a Romance* (1850), a novel set during the penal laws, by Mary Letitia Martin (1815–50), the notion of a national marriage is deployed though again with a pessimistic turn about the possibility of national reconciliation. The marriage here is between the son of a Gaelic lord, disinherited under the penal laws by the conversion of his brother to Protestantism, and a woman of Ascendancy background. Both die, however, bringing an abrupt end to things.

The Heart of Erin, an Irish Story of To-day (1882) by Blackburne had the misfortune to be published around the time of the Phoenix Park murders of government officials in Dublin and came in for a good deal of criticism in Britain as it seemed to give a positive portrayal of a radical Irish nationalist politician in the character Standish Clinton. At least one of the two women in his life embarks on an active feminist trajectory. From a middle-class background she becomes radicalised and at one point calls on a crowd to avenge an evicted woman and her dead baby. Her new course meets with social disapproval and the disapproval of Clinton. When he deprecates another woman's possible engagement in politics, she retorts, 'who knows but her woman's heart may have urged her to do something Quixotic for Ireland'.[27] Eventually, she marries Clinton but the national marriage element of the novel relates to the revelation that Clinton's parents were a peasant woman and a wealthy landowner and industrialist. Once again it has negative consequences. Having unexpectedly inherited his father's wealth and in spite of his undertakings to the contrary, Clinton seems at the end of the novel poised to exercise his new wealth and position to his own advantage, to the detriment of his previous ideals.

Mary Dominic (1898) by Grace Rhys (1865–1929) also relies on a variant of an ancestral national marriage, though with decidedly negative results. The eponymous Mary is seduced by a member of the Ascendancy and has a child. Her son grows up full of 'undigested resentment and the passion of patriotism'.[28] As in *The Heart of Erin*, however, posthumous inheritance compromises the clarity of national and class resentment. Mary and her son receive money in his late father's will which they accept, in spite of their anger at the conditions attached to it that they emigrate and adopt his surname.

The novel that comes closest to a national tale, or at least to a parody of it, in the style of Sydney Owenson or Maria Edgeworth, wherein an English lord marries an exotic Gaelic princess, is Harriet Jay's *The Queen of Connaught* (1875). Here a contemporary woman tries to live out her romantic ancestral role as Queen of Connaught and also manages to impress a visiting Englishman. 'The delicate refinement underlying the wild romance of her nature, her proud commanding air, and graceful manner, a thousand little things at which he had marvelled, all seemed to be explained'. Aristocratic hauteur causes her to refuse his hand in marriage, and the much-needed money that comes with it, for only so long. She proceeds to live out the role that might have come naturally to a character in an Owenson or Edgeworth novel. 'With the generosity worthy of the race from which she sprang, Kathleen threw open her doors, and welcomed, with lavish hospitality, all those who were pleased to grace the Castle with their presence – in fact, she kept "open house" in the true Celtic sense of the word'. But things do not go well. She encounters tensions with her husband and his modernizing views. The locals exploit her hospitality and flout her self-asserted authority. 'She saw at once that the people laughed at and defied her; the passionate energy of her nature was at once aroused; she felt compelled to meet them with their own weapons, and assert her power before it was too late'. Just before her death, however, she admits defeat: 'I wished to bring back the olden times, to mingle the spirit of the past and the present, but I was wrong, it was impossible'.[29] For all its structural similarity to a national tale then, this novel turns out to be about nostalgia rather than being an allegory of national reconciliation.

Two novels of the 1890s move the convention beyond a negative version of the traditional national marriage and into something else, that

of the independent woman who is representative of Ireland. In this they
were of course competing with versions of an idealized Ireland to be
found in the work of writers of the Irish Revival and later that twentieth-
century Irish women writers would find so problematic. Of the two, the
more significant is *Doreeen, the Story of a Singer* (1894) by Edna Lyall
(1857–1903), which was both dedicated to and admired by Gladstone.
Set in the early 1880s, it is also perhaps the last major land war novel.
It is an irony to note that this central novel for the debate in fiction
between gender and Irish identity was a product of the intermingling of
British and Irish identities and that it was in fact written by an English
author, a supporter of women's suffrage and Irish home rule. Lyall's intent
was clearly that of the original national-marriage novel of the post-union
period, to foster amity between Britain and Ireland. Thus, the *Freeman's
Journal*, Ireland's mainstream nationalist daily newspaper, compared it
positively with *Uncle Tom's Cabin*.[30] It is a novel of national exchange,
with one character who is 'practically an Englishman' becoming a dyna-
miter in the Irish cause and another, whom Doreen eventually marries
(though it does not compromise her independence), a fervent supporter
of the Land League.

Doreen herself is the product of a sort of national marriage, albeit one
unusual in these novels, in which her father is Irish – a Fenian prisoner in
fact – and her mother English. Though there are attempts to sentimen-
talize her by some characters – she is called 'the little Colleen Bawn' by
one – she is an independent woman who earns her living as a singer and
makes no bones about singing Irish nationalist songs to English audiences, even when she is booed for her pains. Her experience is seen as
somehow embodying the Irish national experience. 'Yet the fate of her
nation seems to be upon her ... Think of the troubles that have from her
very childhood persistently beset her!' Tellingly, she is referred to as 'the
national singer'. Her story elicits a proper transnational sense of anger:
'It was the long years of imprisonment which killed him [her father],
and he was imprisoned merely for writing words which every liberty-
loving Englishman would have written had England been under the same
unjust "Castle" system'. It is an anger which good English people such
as her future husband come to share. 'Max, with a feeling of shame and
wrath such as he had never before experienced, realized that these things
were being done in his name, by his own country, and all with the best
of intentions in the world'. Yet, though she suffers imprisonment for her
activism with the Ladies' Land League, she directs that anger into proper
constitutional ends, gaining an interview with the sympathetic prime

minister. The national marriage thus gives birth to the independent woman who is nationally representative.[31]

As its name suggests *Miss Erin* (1898) is written in a similar vein. Its author was M. E. Francis (Mary Sweetman Blundell, 1859–1930), a member of a noted Irish literary family who had married into the Lancashire Catholic gentry. In fact this novel marks an advance on the development of the trope for it does centre around a national marriage but one in which the woman is the dominant partner, to the extent of being wounded while protecting her future husband from violence. It incorporates, too, a feminist feature of some land war novels, inasmuch as Erin is a radical Irish woman landlord who has been brought up among the people. Her love interest is with an English Tory MP for whom she has initial antagonism: 'You and your kind are so used to our miseries that they have even ceased to bore you. You hear them with a sneer, and dismiss them with a gibe – rather glad than otherwise to have the chance of showing off your own wit'. There is no doubt about her intended nationally representative role: 'When you insult my country I feel as though you struck me'. When he proposes marriage she retorts: 'Marriage between us two would only be possible if one of us yielded'. Yet, though it is somewhat ambivalent, this is what happens at the end of the novel with her lover at least promising to let her teach him to love the people.[32]

Irish women's fiction thus furnished the possibility of a feminist alternative to the largely patriarchal imperatives of what was to become the dominating cultural force of the Irish Revival. Ironically, this alternative arose within the very hybridity that would be anathema to the Revivalists. The dominating priority of establishing a distinct Irish national identity has meant virtual critical oblivion for Irish Victorian writers, men as well as women, who lived in a fluid, hybrid world of Irish and British identities. Ironically, their world was a world not unlike that of twenty-first century globalized culture where today leading Irish novelists live in places such as North America and no longer feel bound to Irish identitarian themes. Perhaps the time has come to become better acquainted with and to learn from these antecedents.

Notes

1 James H. Murphy, 'The Dark Arts of the Critic: Yeats and William Carlton', in *Yeats and Afterwords*, ed. Marjorie Howes and Joseph Valente (Notre Dame, IN: Notre Dame University Press, 2014), 80–99.

2 Rolf Loeber and Magda Loeber, *A Guide to Irish Fiction, 1650–1900* (Dublin: Four Courts, 2005), lxxxiv.

3 Charles A. Read and Katharine Tynan Hinkson, eds., *The Cabinet of Irish Literature: Revised and Greatly Extended*, 3 vols. (London: Gresham, 1902).

4 James H. Murphy, *Irish Novelists and the Victorian Age* (Oxford: Oxford University Press, 2011) [hereafter *INVA*], 30–7, 259–60.

5 *INVA* 185–7, 209–11; Julie Ann Stevens, *The Irish Scene in Somerville and Ross* (Dublin: Irish Academic Press, 2007).

6 W. B. Yeats, *The Bookman* 8 (April to September 1895):138; *INVA*, 157–9, 178–81, 211–13, 262–3; Heidi Hansson, *Emily Lawless, 1845–1913: Writing the Interspace* (Cork: Cork University Press, 2007).

7 *INVA* 16, 165, 195–6.

8 *INVA* 5–8, 22–4, 100–9, 112, 140–1, 206, 247–8, 252–4, 256–7, 261; Eileen Fauset, *The Politics of Writing: Julia Kavanagh, 1824–77* (Manchester: Manchester University Press, 2009).

9 *INVA* 28, 116–17, 152, 155, 160–1, 163–5, 175–6, 181–4, 206–8, 227, 245–9, 256, 260; Heidi Hansson, 'Selina Bunbury, Religion, and the Woman Writer', in *The Oxford History of the Irish Book. Volume IV: The Irish Book in English, 1800–1891*, ed. James H. Murphy (Oxford: Oxford University Press, 2011), 322–30; James H. Murphy, *Catholic Fiction and Social Reality in Ireland, 1873–1922* (Westport, CT: Greenwood, 1997), 1–75; Helena Kelleher Kahn, *Late Nineteenth-Century Ireland's Political and Religious Controversies in the Fiction of May Laffan Hartley* (Greenboro, NC: ELT Press, 2005).

10 *INVA* 138–40, 223–4, 232, 240–2, 249–53, 170–1.

11 *INVA* 2–4, 120–3, 125–6, 131–7, 262–4.

12 *INVA* 17–18.

13 *INVA* 208, 230, 232–6.

14 *INVA* 6, 23, 171, 252–3, 255.

15 Charlotte Riddell, *A Struggle for Fame*, 3 vols. (London: Richard Bentley, 1883), 2:14, 3:242, 3:345.

16 *INVA* 253, 255.

17 *INVA* 171, 208.

18 Ella MacMahon, *A New Note* (London: Hutchinson, n.d. [1894]), 6, 8, 72, 173–4.

19 Rosa Mulholland, *Dunmara*, 3 vols. (London: Smith, Edler, 1864), 3:35, 3:38; *INVA* 245–6.

20 *INVA* 249–52, 188–203, 253, 110–11.

21 *INVA* 64–5, 71–91, 123, 215–20, 263.

22 Letitia McClintock, *A Boycotted Household* (London: Smith, Elder, 1881), 232; *INVA* 70–1, 174, 189–90, 233, 251.

23 *INVA* 138, 174–6, 178, 181–4, 233, 245–9, 260.

24 *INVA* 193–206.

25 Charles Lever, *The Knight of Gwynne*, 2 vols. (1847: Boston, MA: Little, Brown, 1899), 1:61; *INVA* 83–5.

26 Charlotte Riddell, *Maxwell Drewitt*, 3 vols. (1865: New York, NY: Garland, 1979), 1:51, 3:260; *INVA* 6–7.

27 E. Owens Blackburne, *The Heart of Erin, an Irish Story of To-day*, 3 vols. (London: Sampson, Low, Marston, Searle and Rivington, 1883), 3:172; *INVA* 156, 171–2, 181, 255.

28 Grace Rhys, *Mary Dominic* (London: J.M. Dent, 1898), 282; *INVA* 237.

29 Harriet Jay, *The Queen of Connaught* (London: Chatto and Windus, 1878), 52, 149, 241, 312; *INVA* 157.

30 *Freeman's Journal*, 14 December 1894.

31 Edna Lyall, *Doreen: The Story of a Singer* (London: Longman, Green, 1894), 231, 1, 98, 146, 182, 284; *INVA* 184, 190–1.

32 M. E. Francis, *Miss Erin* (New York, NY: Benziger, 1898), 173, 182, 229; *INVA* 137–8, 237; Whitney Standlee, *'Power to Observe': Irish Women Novelists in Britain, 1890–1916* (Oxford: Peter Lang, 2015), 171–7.

CHAPTER 6

New Woman Writers

Tina O'Toole

The 'New Woman' polemic gripped the public imagination at the turn of the twentieth century, subverting normative social codes regulating the proper place of men and women in relation to class, gender and nation. Pioneering fiction by key Irish writers in the period animated the New Woman project, particularly that of George Egerton [Chavelita Dunne] (1859–1945), Sarah Grand [Frances Bellenden Clarke] (1854–1943), Hannah Lynch (1859–1904) and L. T. [Elizabeth Thomasina] Meade (1844–1915). Their fictional narratives were premised on a central character who, having her consciousness raised by feminist ideas, gains confidence in her ability to voice her rights, and is ultimately willing to fight for them, as outlined in my study, *The Irish New Woman* (2013). Sarah Grand is a crucial figure in the feminist history of ideas; arguably her deployment of the New Woman in fiction mounted a challenge no less radical than that of contemporary activists in the campaign for women's suffrage. By creating fictional feminists who prevailed against all odds, New Woman novels made way for their readers to follow in the footsteps of their literary heroines; in other words, the imbrication of social activism and literary representation is part of this history. Given the revolutionary context in Ireland at the turn of the twentieth century, the literary New Woman emerged from a discursive nexus comprising political and social movements of various hues. As such, New Woman authors and their readers were part of an emerging generation of newly literate, empowered and, in some cases, politically radical women – writers, artists and educators – who became visible in Irish public discourse and social activism in the period between the Land Wars and partition (ca. 1880–1922).

With varied class, confessional and caste backgrounds, Irish New Woman writers have markedly divergent relationships with their country of origin, and this is reflected in the range of positions they adopted in constructing national and ethnic identities in their work. As such, it is not easy to divide these writers neatly along pro- and anti-imperialist lines. Occupying a double position as both subjects of the 'first colony' and as middle managers of the rest of the British Empire, the Irish were at once agents and subjects of empire by the late nineteenth century. As a white and (by then) mainly English-speaking culture, they were an invaluable source of administrative and military personnel in the colonial world. However, by the turn of the twentieth century, this 'double position' produced hybrid identities and attendant anxieties in Ireland when it came to questions of national and imperial belonging, as we shall see.

Sarah Grand was the product of just such a mixed colonial background; the daughter of a coastguard (i.e. a British naval officer), she was born in Donaghadee, County Down in 1854. She spent her formative years on the remote west coast of County Mayo before moving, following her father's death, to live for a short time near her mother's family in Yorkshire. At sixteen, she married an Irish military doctor, David Chambers McFall, and became a garrison wife, living in various British colonial outposts including Singapore, Ceylon (Sri Lanka since 1972) and the Straits Settlements (now part of Malaysia). However, like many in the period, Grand did not consider her Britishness to be at odds with an Irish national identity that, according to her biographers, she claimed throughout her adult life. Indeed, in old age following her term as Lady Mayor of Bath, she continued to receive a gift of shamrock annually from the town council on St Patrick's Day.[1]

Those years spent in Southeast Asia provided Grand with an opportunity to inhabit and understand British settler colonies and she put this to good use in her later writing. Moreover, her experience as an outsider in a range of cultures enabled her to see the workings of dominant gender formations in different societies. Her first published work was a treatise against footbinding, 'Two Dear Little Feet' (1873); both in it and in short stories such as 'The Great Typhoon' (1881) and 'Ah Man' (1893), her colonial adherence is clear. Grand completed *Ideala*, her pioneering effort to address 'The Woman Question', in 1881 but spent seven years searching for a publisher before she finally raised the funds to self-publish the novel in 1888. Her second novel in this trilogy, the best-selling *The Heavenly Twins* (1893), made her name as a writer and introduced a new feminist protagonist to an international audience. Grand exploited the gap between women's potential and the roles foisted upon them in a patriarchal society; her fictional protagonists are strong, assertive and intelligent, while highly feminine and attractive to men as well as to other women. Grand's rhetorical tactic of taking the reader into her confidence undermined popular caricatures of hysterical, man-hating feminists. Her narrators take for granted an audience comprising reasonable, progressive readers who will treat their analysis seriously as they describe a gendered social hierarchy in which financial inequality, physical abuse and sexual exploitation have kept women in an inferior position. The following year in the landmark essay, 'The New Aspect of the Woman Question' (1894), Grand brought the term 'New Woman' into being.[2]

In her next novel, *The Beth Book* (1897), Grand created a feminist *Bildungsroman*, charting the progress of a young woman through all the stages of nascent adolescent sexuality to maturity. In fact, the novel quickly became notorious in the period for its sexual frankness; contemporary critics accused the author of 'opening sewers' and condemned her 'farcical sex manias'.[3] Despite this opprobrium, Grand encouraged the connections between her own formative experiences and those of Beth; for instance, an 1897 interview with the author is titled 'Just Like Beth'.[4] Even the book's subtitle, 'A Study of the Life of Elizabeth Caldwell McClure: A Woman of Genius', draws attention to its semi-autobiographical status. While contemporary readers knew the author only by her pseudonym, the link between her own name, Frances Bellenden Clarke McFall, and that of the protagonist, is clear. In writing *The Beth Book*, Grand drew on memories of her childhood in the west of Ireland during the 1850s. Ethnic and class divisions were intrinsic to nineteenth-century British society and, nostalgia for her childhood home notwithstanding, Grand's attitude to the Irish indicates an adherence to contemporary discourses of racial determinism. Despite this, her writing betrays an incisive understanding of the workings of the imperial machine and, as I have argued elsewhere, Grand's implicitly contradictory sense of identity in *The Beth Book* betrays a more complicated relationship with imperialism and with her place of birth than has been hitherto understood.[5] This is particularly evident in her discussion of the impact of the Great Famine of the 1840s on Ireland and its people. Grand's efforts to resolve contradictions between her imperialist socialization and her acknowledgment of the devastating outcome of nineteenth-century imperial policy in Ireland, produces significant countercurrents which complicate prevailing critical readings of her New Woman fiction.[6]

L. T. Meade, likewise, had first-hand experience of the British imperial mission; born in 1844 in West Cork where she lived for thirty years, she evinces a strongly-held British identity in most of her writings. As the child of an Anglican clergyman from Bandon, a town that maintained a strong loyalist and Protestant identity in the Famine period, Meade spent her childhood in an atmosphere of confessional and ethnic divisions. Her early writing efforts are indicative of this; she tells us that she scribbled stories in the margins of the *Cork Constitution*, a Unionist newspaper read only by the Protestant minority in the district. Her context in this outpost of empire in rural Cork gave Meade an incisive understanding of, and sympathy with, the identity struggles engaged with by other British colonial girls in more recently 'settled' territories, whom she went on to write about and for in her fiction. Contemporary surveys demonstrate the popularity of her fiction with the children of British settlers overseas; they undoubtedly identified with her protagonists, who were often second-generation children sent 'home' from the colonies to school in Britain.[7] A hugely prolific and successful writer, Meade published over 250 novels; one of her best-known novels, *Polly: A New-Fashioned Girl* (1889), went through three editions in London and was issued by six New York publishers. Perhaps because of this popularity, and because of her reputation as a children's writer, her work has been somewhat neglected in the scholarship until recently.[8]

Meade was a crucial figure in the creation of girls' fiction. Her novel, *A World of Girls: The Story of a School* (1886), was the first girls' school story and many of the tropes she created in her serial school narratives are now considered characteristic of the genre. She is credited with creating the 'New Girl' figure, and disrupting essentialist gender binaries is often central to this character. Two of her best-known novels, *Wild Kitty* (1897) and *The Rebel of the School* (1902), centre on the experience of an Irish girl educated in England. Making common cause between Irish and working-class girls, *The Rebel of the School* foregrounds the distinctly different cultural and ethical values (and mixed loyalties) of a young Irish girl subject to a British institution. Like Sydney Owenson's Glorvina, Meade's wild Irish girls give their schoolfellows valuable lessons in emotional intelligence, in exchange for which they are to learn how to be civilized and become proper imperial subjects (modelled after Arnold's contemporary configuration of an idealized hybrid of Saxon and Celt producing a fully rounded national character). However, unlike the more obviously imperialist plots of her adult fiction, the energy and affective pull of Meade's wild Irish girls disrupt the hegemonic readings we might expect. For regular readers of her work, and there were many, the underlying approbation of the author for these wild girls is evident in the energy with which the characters are drawn. During her editorship of the magazine *Atalanta* (1887–98), Meade created a community of interest through which writing, education and professional careers were legitimated as areas of endeavour for such wild young women.

Having relocated to London in her thirties, Meade quickly became part of New Woman circles there; a committee member of the well-known feminist Pioneer Club, she was an advocate of women's education, and became actively engaged in sports including bicycling, that most New Womanish pursuit.[9] Another keen sportswoman of the period, Beatrice Grimshaw (1870–1953), constructs her feminist coming-to-consciousness via a bicycling narrative: 'I bought a bicycle, with difficulty. I rode it, unchaperoned, miles and miles beyond the limits possible to the soberly trotting horses. The world opened before me. And as soon as my twenty-first birthday dawned, I went away from home, to see what the world might give to daughters who revolted.'[10] Having broken away from her family and their 'big lonely country House' in Co. Antrim, Grimshaw's thirst for adventure led her to travel widely, living for some years in New Guinea before she finally settled in Australia. Her New Woman novels include *Vaiti of the Islands* (1908), *When the Red Gods Call* (1911) and *Nobody's Island* (1917); all set in the South Pacific, her novels are characterized by androgynous protagonists and hybrid language use.

While Grand and Meade had a clear sense of their Irishness as an identity they could subsume and make coherent within a British Protestant one, questions of cultural belonging are foregrounded in Grimshaw's fiction and seem indicative of an uneasiness with her own cultural and confessional background.[11] We find a similarly anxious self-positioning in the writing of George Egerton [Chavelita Dunne]; born 1859 in a British army enclave in Melbourne, Australia, she was the daughter of an Irish Catholic army man, John Dunne, and a Welsh Protestant mother, Isabel George; the Dunnes moved back to live in Dublin during Egerton's childhood. The identity struggles she gives voice to in her letters also find expression in her fictional characters where class and confessional identities are tackled. Elleke Boehmer, discussing anti-colonial intelligentsias, highlights what she terms their 'potentially productive in-betweenness';[12] she describes members of such groups as 'poised between the cultural traditions of home on the one hand and of their education on the other'.[13] This description offers a productive way to approach Egerton's work and that of several other Irish New Women, as we shall see.

The early New Woman novel, *The Prince of the Glades* (1891), by Hannah Lynch (1859–1904) is an example of the kind of 'productive in-betweenness' Boehmer describes.[14] Lynch based her New Woman protagonist on the life and character of her mentor, Anna Parnell, a member of the Protestant Anglo-Irish landowning class whose Irish nationalist activism set her in opposition to the interests of her caste. Parnell was leader of the Ladies' Land League, the first Irish nationalist organization to be directed and managed at all levels by women.[15] There are clear ideological links between Lynch's fictional New Woman, Parnell's textual shaping of the Ladies' Land League in her journalism and public speeches, and the radical ideas emerging from first-wave feminist politics internationally (these connections were underpinned by close contacts between Parnell, Lynch and well-known British feminist activists, Helen Taylor and Jessie Craigen). While an agrarian uprising may seem an unlikely genesis for Irish feminist activism, Parnell's efforts to highlight women's abilities in the public sphere are testament to her belief that this was a moment with potential for social transformation.

Lynch, as Secretary of the Ladies' Land League, had first-hand experience of this potential and the opportunities it offered women to explore active public roles. When the Land League newspaper, *United Ireland*, was proscribed and the printers arrested, Lynch drew on her contacts in France and took the newspaper to be printed in Paris. Given her aspirations to write for a living, the opportunity to manage, edit, distribute and write for a political newspaper in the early 1880s shaped her later career. Her activist experiences formed the basis for Lynch's New Woman fiction; she published a number of other well-known novels in the period, as well as an important study of George Meredith. Describing the central protagonist of *The Prince of the Glades*, Camilla Noyes, the narrator remarks:

> the average woman, if she exercise but moderately her mind, has more occasion for discontent than even the exceptional man. To a girl, throbbing with the inconvenient consciousness of large capabilities and burning enthusiasms, the idiotic existence of the drawing room into which she is compelled at the most intolerant hour of waking youth ... is worse than a slow mental and moral death.[16]

Noyes displays key characteristics of the New Woman type who would become familiar in the culture over the ensuing decade: a marriage resister, she is intelligent, courageous, masculinized (described as a 'fine and manly young woman'[17]), an avid reader and a capable speaker who argues her point with the (male) leaders of the Fenian movement. Moreover, Lynch's novel turns on a woman's search for a meaningful occupation and the concomitant demand to be treated on equal terms with men.

The visibility of the Ladies' Land League on public platforms provided tangible role models for New Woman writers in Ireland, and Anna Parnell's memoir, *The Tale of a Great Sham* (written in 1907), provides us with a case study for emerging first-wave Irish feminist activism. Contemporaries of Parnell and Lynch, including Rosa Mulholland, Emily Lawless, and Somerville and Ross [Edith Somerville and Violet Martin] also combined New Woman and Land War themes in their later novels.[18] Some of this fiction was written from the perspective of women landowners who strove to protect their properties from tenant groups during the rent strikes.[19] Two novels by Emily Lawless, *Hurrish* (1886) and *Grania* (1892), are often included in the nexus of Land War and New Woman fiction too, although, as Heidi Hansson argues in her pioneering study of Lawless, the latter's work is difficult to categorise.[20]

In a New Woman novel written eight years later by E. L. [Ethel Lillian] Voynich (1864–1960), the radical politics of Lynch's *The Prince of the Glades* is transposed overseas.[21] Voynich's *The Gadfly* (1897), foregrounds the Italian *Risorgimento* of the 1840s; the novel is suffused with character disguise and gender dissidence centring on a strong central female figure who is the leader of an activist cell of radical nationalists. Voynich, the Cork-born daughter of mathematician George Boole and scientist Mary Everest Boole, published a number of New Woman novels at the *fin de siècle*, but *The Gadfly* was spectacularly successful. Translated into more than thirty languages, the novel sold over five million copies and was dramatized by G. B. Shaw, among others. Its revolutionary plot was particularly popular in Soviet Russia where it was performed as an opera and filmed in 1955 with a score by Shostakovich.

The transnational setting and reception of *The Gadfly* is echoed in the writing and experience of many of these writers, from Grimshaw's South Sea adventures to those Toronto newspaper audiences who followed the travel writing and adventures of Kit Coleman (1856–1915). Born Catherine Ferguson in Castleblakeney, Co. Galway in 1856, Coleman emigrated to Canada in 1884, having been widowed and having allegedly lost a baby, who may have been fostered by her sister. Reinventing herself in Toronto (where she married twice more and had two children), she became the local celebrity, 'Kit of the *Mail*', by means of her popular 'Woman's Kingdom' pages in the *Daily Mail* and later in the syndicated 'Kit's Column'. Coleman made her name in 1892 for a series of articles on 'Charles Dickens' London'. Her research process was carefully detailed in the series; it involved making forays into the slums of London by night, cross-dressed as a man. She later repeated the trick in

California, visiting the opium dens of Chinatown by night. However, she is perhaps best known today for her reports from Cuba in 1898 during the Spanish-American conflict, becoming the first woman to be accredited as a war correspondent. Adept in Spanish and French, she was acclaimed, especially among other women journalists, for her war reporting but her byline is absent from any of the hard news reports on the war; she later wrote about the extent to which she had been excluded from the war reporters' 'boys' club' in Tampa. Despite challenging gender binaries throughout her career, Coleman had mixed feelings about contemporary organized feminism, as did George Egerton. Like Egerton, Coleman never forgot her early struggles as a penniless migrant to North America, and she was sensitive to her own class origins, carefully covering her tracks when it came to personal information.[22] These experiences doubtless coloured her attitude to the somewhat bourgeois women's movement in 1890s Toronto, where she saw no room for someone like herself. Nonetheless, she was a passionate advocate for equal pay and an outspoken critic of gender discrimination in the workplace, and she frequently made room in her columns for debates about 'women's issues' like suffrage; her main interests were in political, economic and historical matters rather than the traditional fare of women's journalism in the period. Moreover, both by her example and through direct advice given to readers of her column, she became a pioneer for a new generation of Canadian women in the traditionally male-dominated field of journalism.

Like Coleman and Voynich, a considerable number of New Woman writers had long and successful careers in journalism and publishing at the turn of the last century, yet their names are rarely remembered in Ireland today. Dublin author Ella MacMahon (d. 1956), for instance, published almost thirty popular novels in the period, of which *A New Note* (1894) and *A Modern Man* (1895) are the best known. While MacMahon's fame was local, many of her contemporaries achieved international fame, as we have seen, and yet less than a century later their writing had completely fallen into obscurity. Katherine Cecil Thurston (1875–1911), for instance, could readily be described as a celebrity novelist in early twentieth-century Ireland; she became a popular public speaker, her lifestyle was reported on in the fashionable press, and her novels wooed by international film studios. Thurston was the daughter of the nationalist Lord Mayor of Cork, Paul Madden, and she achieved success in her own right as a novelist. In 1904, her novel *John Chilcote M.P.* was a big hit in Ireland and Irish-America; the story was later released as a film, *The Masquerader*, in the USA (Samuel Goldwyn, dir.

Richard Wallace, 1933).[23] Her best-known novel, *The Fly on the Wheel* (1908), was reprinted by Virago Press and continues to be included in anthologies. *Max*, Thurston's most obviously New Woman narrative, is about a young émigrée who cross-dresses as a boy in order to leave 'his' home in St Petersburg and train as an artist in Paris. Following his encounter with an older Irish man, Blake, the two become firm friends; Thurston's depiction of their relationship, which is suggestively homo-erotic, draws on queer subcultures of the *fin de siècle*. Moreover, the gender fluidity of the main protagonist resonates with 'The Tenor and the Boy' episode in Grand's *The Heavenly Twins*. Thurston's main inter-est, however, is not so much in female masculinity, but rather in how femininity was socially constructed and delimited at the end of the nine-teenth century.[24]

Another celebrity figure of the 1890s, George Egerton, has only recently begun to regain her rightful position as one of the most influen-tial writers of her generation.[25] Egerton's name became synonymous with decadence following the Bodley Head's publication of her first collec-tion of short stories, *Keynotes*, in 1893. This ground-breaking collection features a decidedly Scandinavian modernist style and erotically assertive women protagonists, hence its usual designation as a New Woman text. However, like Coleman, Egerton refused invitations to join the Women Writers' Club and, perhaps pointedly, the bourgeois respectability and sexual continence prized by many first-wave feminists are not in evi-dence in her work. Having lived in Australia, the Netherlands, the USA and Norway, as well as in Dublin and rural Cork, Egerton relocated to London in the mid-1890s; nonetheless, the self-identification in her personal and public writing suggests that she was so strongly invested in her Irish origins that today we might describe her as an Irish diasporan.[26] Perhaps because of this background, the Irish characters who feature in her narratives are often transnational migrants like O'Brien, the war correspondent in 'The Chessboard of Guendolen', or Mary Desmond in *The Wheel of God*, an economic migrant who strongly adheres to her Irish ethnicity when living in New York and London (the novel is based on Egerton's own experience of struggling to make a living in New York). However, unlike most other Irish migrant writers, Egerton does not create a diasporic space where the emigrant is bound within an Irish expatriate community – one fixed by ties of culture, class, religion and a predefined relationship to the homeland. Rather, she tends to shape her Irish characters, both women and men, as rootless nomads whose identities are forged in a range of cosmopolitan situations across the colonial world. That 'potentially productive in-betweenness', described by Elleke Boehmer, can certainly be brought to bear on Egerton's migrant figures.[27]

Egerton brings her serial migrants into contact with one another on city streets, such as Fleet Street in 'The Chessboard of Guendolen', where a New Woman may bump into a war correspondent and his *flâneur* friend. Her use of urban contexts is in marked contrast to many of her Literary Revival contemporaries who privilege the rural western seaboard. However, here too Egerton differs from other New Woman writers who favour the London metropolis by setting her narratives in New York, Christiania (Oslo) or Dublin. Her fictional protagonists are often urban creatures who experience the shock of metropolitan existence and anomie on several levels; spatial and temporal shifts are a recurring feature in her fiction. For instance, in her only novel, *The Wheel of God* (1898), she contrasts the torpid atmosphere of pre-industrial Dublin with the modern mass society her protagonist is plunged into in New York:

> Life seemed less concrete, less inside the houses and warehouses; it was everywhere, pounding like a gigantic steam-hammer, full speed, in the air, in the streets – insistent, noisy, attention-compelling. Trains above one's head, one caught glimpses of domestic interiors, intimate bedroom scenes, as one whizzed past second stories in the early cars … Mary Desmond felt that the clocks in America must surely give two ticks to the one of the sedate old timepieces at home.[28]

Highlighting the adverse effects of modernity, the narrator underlines the detrimental impact of this 'monstrous international sifting sieve', including the loss of a private life and of intimate relations when domestic interiors are thus on display. By contrast, the citified sophisticates we encounter in Egerton's European short fiction have made their own accommodations with urban experience. In stories like 'A Lost Masterpiece' (published in the first issue of *The Yellow Book*, 1894), for instance, she demonstrates their strategies for doing so, the social networks they construct and their carefully maintained mental distance from those they encounter.[29]

Described by Austin Clarke as a 'New Irishwoman', Egerton has been overlooked by Irish studies scholars until quite recently.[30] This is despite pioneering work by Margaret Stetz and Lyn Pykett, among others, who clearly identify her Irish origins; the latter compares Egerton's proto-modernist experiments with those of James Joyce's *Dubliners*.[31] Having had similar childhood experiences in the same city in more or less the same period may account for the material similarities between their

Dublin settings. However, as an eldest son, Joyce was protected from the privations endured by his siblings; Egerton, on the other hand, as the eldest girl was expected to take responsibility for the family following her mother's early death. This involved coping with her father's alcoholism and gambling debts, and caring for her siblings – two of whom died in infancy – as they were shunted from one rented accommodation to another across Dublin, often just one step ahead of the bailiffs. In later letters to a cousin, she details her adolescent experiences of having to keep up (petty genteel) appearances when trying to find piecemeal work or beg relief from charitable organizations. Egerton had first-hand experience of being an unchaperoned female on the streets of Dublin in the 1860s and 1870s, a period in which the massive demographic upheaval caused by the Famine resulted in overcrowding in the tenements; urban deprivation is vividly evoked in her fiction, especially in *Flies in Amber* (1905). For instance, her remarkable Dublin story 'Mammy' derives from this social context, and tells the story of a brothel-keeper in Dublin's Monto (the red-light district around Montgomery Street).[32] In it and other stories, such as 'The Marriage of Mary Ascension' and 'Oony', she tackles sectarianism in rural Ireland, and the hypocrisy of the Catholic church when it comes to issues of domestic violence and child welfare.

Despite her Catholic upbringing and education, Egerton is forthright in her fictional representation of women's erotic lives and their right to bodily integrity; her narratives address troubled responses to pregnancy and parturition (including post-natal depression) and tackle issues of 'illegitimacy', miscarriage, abortion and infanticide. There are a striking number of non-traditional families in evidence in Egerton's stories: her fictional children belong to single-parent families, foster families or to nuclear families where the father is the main caregiver. In 'The Regeneration of Two' (1894) she depicts an intentional community comprising only single mothers and their children. Her first-hand experience of social stigma, first as a child-carer in a dysfunctional family and later as a single mother, informed this alternative approach to writing about the Irish family. In her literary writing, Egerton demonstrates an incisive understanding of hegemonic power, and she consistently targets Victorian and Catholic structures designed to keep women in their place. For instance, in the sequence 'A Psychological Moment at Three Periods', the Catholic socialization of young girls and women is held up to scrutiny. The encoding of ignorance is part of this instruction; for example, a mother advises her daughter: 'It's best not to question, lovey – far best. Just trust God as you trust me when I tell you something is for your own good' ('The Child').[33] When we later encounter the same girl, she has grown to distrust such direction: '[the Girl is] too independent a thinker, with too dangerous an influence over weaker souls to find favour with the nuns' ('The Girl').[34] The Girl connects easily with everyone she encounters, and is disciplined by her teacher for chatting to a peasant girl she meets while walking to Mass, 'a disobedience without parallel' in this bourgeois boarding-school environment. Entering into the mindset of the nun who rebukes the child, the narrator comments: 'For to the subdued soul of this still young woman, who has disciplined thoughts and feelings and soul and body into a machine, in a habit, this girl is a *bonnet-rouge*, an unregenerate spirit, the embodiment of all that is dangerous.'[35] The dissident energy of this 'wise child' (to use Angela Carter's later figure), the *bonnet-rouge* permeates Egerton's fiction, providing a blueprint for New Woman writers internationally.

Egerton's fictional experiments range broadly across different 'schools' of European *fin-de-siècle* culture, as we tend to define them today, deploying elements of aestheticism, naturalism and Symbolism, among others. A similar fusion of contemporary avant-garde cultural experiments, including that of the Irish Literary Revival, may be observed in the writing of a second generation of New Woman writers publishing in the first decade of the twentieth century. By the late 1890s, the New Woman had become a well-known phenomenon in popular culture, and an exemplar for a new generation of women writers and activists. Their work on the page and on the streets coincided with a turbulent time of anti-imperial and class agitation in Ireland and internationally. The work of Irish writers such as Eva Gore-Booth (1870–1926), Rosamond Jacob (1888–1960), Alice Milligan (1866–1953), Helena Molony (1883–1967), Úna Ní Fhaircheallaigh [Agnes O'Farrelly] (1874–1951), Ella Young (1867–1956), Dora Sigerson Shorter (1866–1918) and Katharine Tynan (1859–1931) is usually categorized as falling within the Literary Revival; this has distracted attention from their feminist cultural interventions, which clearly draw on the work of earlier New Woman writers. Just as with the work of Egerton et al., we find in their writing an urgent need to resist masculinist hegemonies, subvert gender and sexual stereotypes, and challenge prescribed roles in the family and the state. Their material is multivalent; it evolved from within diverse political interventions at the *fin de siècle*, including first-wave feminism, anti-imperialism, pacifism and other radical movements transnationally.

Among this group of 'New Irishwomen' (to use Austin Clarke's term), the cultural and political activism of Eva Gore-Booth is perhaps the most striking. Taking her lead from earlier role models such as Anna Parnell, Gore-Booth rejected her privileged upbringing as a member of the landowning class and left Ireland in 1897, to move in with her partner, Esther Roper, in a working-class area of Manchester. There, Gore-Booth became involved in community activism on a number of levels, organizing women workers to form trade unions, lobbying politicians on women's working conditions and on the living conditions of Irish emigrant workers in the city, and joining in suffrage organizations (in which she frequently worked at executive level). While she invested much of her energies in such activities, writing numerous speeches, position papers and journalism on a range of social issues, Gore-Booth nonetheless persevered with the literary work she had begun as a young woman in Ireland. She published nine poetry collections in her lifetime, and her poetry frequently featured in American newspapers, including *The New York Times*; she wrote seven plays (some of which were performed at Dublin's Abbey Theatre, and others by the women workers who were members of a dramatic society she set up), and contributed to literary magazines including *The Yellow Book* and *Longman's Magazine*. Consistent with Revival technique, Gore-Booth recast Irish myths for the contemporary stage. However, her version of the Cúchulainn story, *Unseen Kings* (performed in 1912 at the Abbey Theatre), reverses the traditional gender dynamic in Literary Revival myth-making by giving strong, central roles to her women characters. Like her sister, Constance Markievicz, Gore-Booth felt a strong affinity with Queen Maeve;[36] in her version of Maeve's story, *The Triumph of Maeve* (1905), a mother-daughter relationship displaces the usual narrative about a heterosexual relationship. Thus, Irish cultural nationalism and New Woman ideologies are imbricated in Gore-Booth's writing and political activism.[37]

While Eva Gore-Booth and the Revival writers mentioned made the decision to throw in their lot with the 'Irish separatist' struggle, other Irish feminist writers saw no future for political radicalism in a Home Rule Ireland, and fought its advance as a threat to their agenda. These include, for instance, Isabella Tod, Margaret Byers and Mary Bulmer Hobson, as well as Somerville and Ross. Of course, just as there were critics of Irish nationalist feminism, the New Woman had her anti-feminist critics in Ireland, as elsewhere, and among these, other women writers were sometimes the most disparaging. In fact, Irish author Kathleen Mannington Caffyn (ca. 1855–1926),[38] who wrote under the pseudonym 'Iota', produced one of the most notable (and best-selling) anti-feminist novels of the 1890s, *A Yellow Aster* (1893). Mannington Caffyn wrote several novels, but *A Yellow Aster* is the one she is remembered for. Her protagonist, Gwen Waring, conforms to the New Woman type: she is scientifically minded, ambitious and confident, marrying only as an experiment and for want of a fulfilling occupation. While emotionally repressed for much of the novel, ultimately, she is rescued and subsumed by her maternal instinct: 'a whole volume of new life has flowed into me, I could move the world at this moment, not to say carry this mite. I am a woman at last, a full, complete, proper woman and it is magnificent'.[39] Arguably, despite its anti-feminist impetus, *A Yellow Aster* did as much to promote the New Woman as any amount of feminist tracts in the period. As with contemporary *Punch* cartoons designed to delegitimize the Woman Question, novels like *A Yellow Aster* effectively gave the New Woman a platform, albeit in negative terms, and thereby made feminist debates available to a wider public.

Notwithstanding the creative and commercial success of this dynamic group of New Woman writers and feminist political activists, the anti-feminist message of novels like *The Yellow Aster* became a kind of synecdoche for the New Woman in twentieth-century Irish culture. As we know, the interaction of patriarchal, Catholic, and inherited imperialist values ultimately produced a postcolonial culture in Ireland, which was characterized by the regulation of sexuality and reproduction, and the concomitant institutionalization of motherhood as women's principal role. This ideology is exemplified by the work of Alice Curtayne, an extremely well-known and prolific twentieth-century Catholic writer and broadcaster. Her 1934 pamphlet, *The New Woman*, excoriated 'secular feminism' for its attempt to 'suppress the normal and rational division of human labour by removing woman from the family role to fling her into competition with man in public life'.[40] Curtayne's views were consistent with contemporary constructions of gender and sexuality in Ireland, which explains her enormous popularity. Those women whose writing and politics were not consistent with the prevailing ethos chose to emigrate or to subsume their energies into their families; the alternative was to find oneself pilloried and censored, as many well-known twentieth-century writers and activists did. As a result, the Irish *fin de siècle* was perceived through an ideological filter put in place in the more repressive years of the intervening century and, as a consequence, those New Women who had been active agents and cultural producers were written out of the postcolonial grand narrative which prevailed until quite recently. Thus, a cadre of literary feminists (along with their dissident, proto-modern protagonists) who exploded onto the literary scene in the 1890s, were just as quickly erased from the cultural record. Now that the New Woman has reclaimed her rightful place in Irish literary history, we can acknowledge these radical (and sometimes merely liberal) writers and activists at the turn of the twentieth century who produced important, internationally acclaimed and ideologically challenging literary work in and about Ireland.

Notes

1 In Grand's semi-autobiographical novel, *The Beth Book*, the narrator carefully underlines the mixed ethnic background of the protagonist's father. While all biographical material on Grand simply says that her parents were 'English', her father's name was Edward Bellenden Clarke; Bellenden is a Scottish name. This suggested Scottish background, combined with her mother's Yorkshire origins may explain their daughter's affinity with an Irish identity, or at least that sense of having a strong regional identity.

2 See Sarah Grand, 'The New Aspect of the Woman Question', *North American Review* 158 (1894): 270–6.

3 See, for instance, reviews by Frank Danby, Julia Frankau and Frank Harris, *Saturday Review* (20 November 1897): 557–8; for a full account of the novel's reception, see Sally Mitchell, Introduction, *The Beth Book* (Bristol: Thoemmes, 1994), v.

4 Sarah Tooley, 'The Life Story of Sarah Grand', *Review of Reviews* 16 (1897): 595.

5 See Tina O'Toole, *The Irish New Woman* (London: Palgrave Macmillan, 2013), 17–42.

6 Such as, for instance, Iveta Jusová, 'Imperialist Feminism: Colonial Issues in Sarah Grand's *The Heavenly Twins* and *The Beth Book*', *English Literature in Transition* 43, no. 3 (2000): 298–315.

7 See Kate Flint, *The Woman Reader 1837–1914* (Oxford: Clarendon, 1993), 160–1.

8 Beth Rodgers has published several essays on Meade, the most recent of which is 'L. T. Meade, "The Queen of Girls'-Book Makers": The Rise and Fall of a Victorian Bestseller', *Women's Writing* 23, no. 1 (2016): 1–18.

9 For biographical details on Meade, see O'Toole, *The Irish New Woman*, 43–66.

10 Beatrice Grimshaw, 'How I Found Adventure', *Blue Book* (April 1939), see Ulster History Cycle: www.hidden-gems.eu/UHC-grimshawbeatrice.pdf.

11 For biographical details on Grimshaw, including her conversion to Catholicism, see John Wilson Foster, *Irish Novels 1890–1940: New Bearings in Culture and Fiction* (Oxford: Oxford University Press, 2008), 295–300.

12 Elleke Boehmer, *Colonial and Postcolonial Literature: Migrant Metaphors* (Oxford: Oxford University Press, 2005), 21.

13 Ibid., 21.

14 Hannah Lynch was born in Dublin; her father was a member of the Fenian movement. As is evident from her semi-autobiographical *Autobiography of*

a Child (1899; published in *Blackwood's* 1898–9), she attended a Catholic convent boarding school in England before working as a governess in mainland Europe. She travelled widely and earned a living predominantly through her literary writing, translations and journalism; she was Paris correspondent for *The Academy*, for instance. For further information on Lynch see the entry in the Oxford *DNB* by Faith Binckes; see also Faith Binckes and Kathryn S. Laing, 'A Vagabond's Scrutiny: Hannah Lynch in Europe', in *Irish Women Writers: New Critical Perspectives*, ed. Elke D'hoker Raphael Ingelbien and Hedwig Schall (Bern: Peter Lang, 2010), 111–32. See also Binckes and Laing's forthcoming full-length study *Renegade, New Woman, Irish Cosmopolitan: The Life and Writing of Hannah Lynch*.

15 Mobilized in 1880 as a result of the proscription of the Land League and imprisonment of Parnell's brother, Home Rule politician Charles Stewart Parnell.

16 Hannah Lynch, *The Prince of the Glades* (London: Methuen, 1891), 215–16.

17 Ibid., 204.

18 See, for instance, Rosa Mulholland, *Marcella Grace* (1886; Dublin: Maunsel, 2001); Emily Lawless, *Hurrish* (Edinburgh: Blackwoods, 1886); Edith Somerville and Martin Ross [Violet Martin], *Naboth's Vineyard* (London: Spencer Blackett, 1891).

19 See, for instance, Margaret Kelleher, 'Women's Fiction, 1845–1900', in *Field Day Anthology* ed. Angela Bourke *et al.* (vol. IV) (Cork: Cork University Press, 2002), 926–75.

20 See Heidi Hansson, *Emily Lawless 1845–1913: Writing the Interspace* (Cork: Cork University Press, 2007), 5.

21 See Tina O'Toole, *Dictionary of Munster Women Writers* (Cork: Cork University Press, 2005), 306–7, for further information on Voynich.

22 Coleman's origins were humble but she received a good education at Loreto Abbey in Rathfarnham thanks to the patronage of her mother's brother, the prominent Dominican Father Thomas Burke (Burke was a well-known preacher and nationalist; his statue still stands at the entrance to the Claddagh in Galway).

23 For further details on Thurston, see O'Toole, *Dictionary of Munster Women Writers*, 290–1.

24 For further discussion of Thurston's writing, see O'Toole, *The Irish New Woman*, 117–27.

25 Margaret D. Stetz's pioneering research renewed scholarly interest in George Egerton's work in the 1990s. Most studies of New Woman literature address Egerton's work but, with notable exceptions, tend to focus on one or two of the stories from her early collections, *Keynotes* (1893) and *Discords* (1894).

26 For more on Egerton, see O'Toole, *The Irish New Woman*, 88–109; 129–48.

27 For more on Egerton's migrant writing, see Tina O'Toole, 'George Egerton's Translocational Subjects', *Modernism/Modernity* 21, no. 3 (2014): 827–42.

28 Egerton, *The Wheel of God* (London: Grant Richards, 1898), 68–9.

29 See O'Toole, 'George Egerton's Translocational Subjects' and also Kate Krueger Henderson, 'Mobility and Modern Consciousness in George Egerton's and Charlotte Mew's Yellow Book Stories', *English Literature in Transition* 54, no. 2 (2011): 196.

30 See Austin Clarke, *A Penny in the Clouds: More Memories of Ireland and England* (London: Routledge, 1968), 177.

31 See Lyn Pykett, *Engendering Fictions: The English Novel in the Early Twentieth Century* (London: Edward Arnold, 1995).

32 For more on this story, see Tina O'Toole, 'The New Woman Flâneuse or Streetwalker? George Egerton's Urban Aestheticism', in *Reconnecting Aestheticism and Modernism* ed. Bénédicte Coste et al. (London: Routledge, 2016), 19–30.

33 George Egerton, *Keynotes and Discords*, ed. Sally Ledger (London: Continuum, 2006), 69.

34 Ibid., 72.

35 Ibid., 73.

36 While Eva Gore-Booth was a lifelong pacifist, her sister Constance became a leading figure in the Irish struggle for independence and took part in the armed struggle at Easter 1916 as second-in-command at the Stephen's Green battalion. In December 1918, she was the first woman elected to the British House of Commons, but did not take her seat; instead, she became Minister for Labour in the first Dáil (Irish parliament) 1919–22.

37 Maureen O'Connor explores this seam in more depth: 'Eva Gore-Booth's Queer Art of War' focuses on the play *The Death of Fionovar* and illuminates Gore-Booth's pacifism, among other matters. See *Women Writing War: Ireland 1880–1922*, ed. Tina O'Toole, Gillian McIntosh, Muireann O'Cinnéide (Dublin: University College Dublin Press, 2016), 85–102.

38 For more on Iota, see O'Toole, *Dictionary of Munster Women Writers*, 101.

39 Iota, *A Yellow Aster* (Leipzig: Bernhard Tauchnitz, 1894), 304.

40 Alice Curtayne, *The New Woman* (Dublin: Anthonian Press, 1934), 33.

CHAPTER 7

Poetry, Drama and Prose, 1891–1920

Paige Reynolds

During the late nineteenth and early twentieth centuries, radical cultural transformations influenced artists across the globe, transformations from which Irish women writers were not immune. These authors engaged with new understandings of individual consciousness, temporality and perception; they depicted social changes manifest in the rise of feminism and secularism; they considered contemporary wars, labour struggles and other political conflicts at home and abroad. Nonetheless, Irish women's writing from these decades can seem largely traditional in form and conventional in theme. No Gertrude Stein brashly ripped apart literary formulae to celebrate her sexuality. Instead, a writer such as Lady Isabella Augusta Gregory, examined in depth in this essay's conclusion, might discreetly give voice to transgressive passion in a sonnet or subtly critique political ideologies in a realist play. This conservatism was in part a reflection of the proscribed roles and limited opportunities during these decades for women in Irish society who wrote, and sought publication, in the shadows of formidable religious imperatives and a nationalist movement that lionized the vulnerable virgin and self-abnegating mother.

These women also laboured amidst the potent influence of the Irish Literary Revival, a movement advocating the notion that literature, and culture more generally, might stoke in Irish citizens a sense of national pride and inspire demands for political independence. Traditionally understood as spanning the period from the 1890 fall of Charles Stewart Parnell to the end of the Anglo-Irish War and the 1922 publication of James Joyce's *Ulysses*, the Revival urged artists to recover and engage with Irish myth, history, and folklore as sources of inspiration for their work. This tactic enabled new literary articulations of cultural nationalism in which Cúchulainn might serve as the exemplar of heroic nationalism or Deirdre as the embodiment of female sacrifice. An authentic and primitive Ireland, represented in diverse forms such as folklore and peasant plays, became a counter to English imperial and metropolitan logics.

Scholars have profitably highlighted the central importance of women to the institutions and practices of Revivalism.[1] Yet women's literary production of the period still fails to draw the attention it merits, despite the fact that their work was enormously popular with audiences at home and abroad. The complexity, diversity and volume of women's writing during these decades testify to the influence and authority wielded by these authors. They upheld contemporaneous cultural norms, depicting traditional gender roles and promoting the Revival's imperative that women preserve and transmit national ideals. But they also questioned dominant values and recalibrated limiting tropes, seeking in their writing to advance progressive notions of religion, class, gender and community in the incipient Irish nation.

Poetry

The subjects explored in women's poetry from this period were often those found elsewhere in Revivalist literature: events and figures drawn from Irish history and myth, nationalist representations of Mother Ireland, paeans to Irish male heroism at home or abroad. However, these poets – though rarely breaking from traditional forms – frequently presented readers with provocative revisions of conventional themes. For instance, after the success of her late nineteenth-century novels, Emily Lawless (1845–1913) privately published *Atlantic Rhymes and Rhythms* (1898), later reissued with a publisher as *With the Wild Geese* (1902), a collection of historical poems reflecting her reservations about both ascendency conservatism and nationalist fervour.[2] Her most renowned poem, 'After Aughrim', anthologized in *The Oxford Book of Irish Verse* (1958), conveys this ambivalence by giving voice to the nationalist type of the Shan Van Vocht (poor old woman), who appears to endorse the sacrifice of Irish men for political freedom. However, in the final stanza, the 'she' of Mother Ireland can be read as strangely indifferent to, even confused by, the men who die for her:

> She said, 'God knows they owe me nought,
> I tossed them to the foaming sea,
> I tossed them to the howling waste,
> *Yet still their love comes home to me'.*[3]

In her early collections, *Poems* (1898) and *The One and the Many* (1904), Eva Gore-Booth (1870–1926) likewise adhered to Revivalist topics. But in *The Egyptian Pillar* (1906), she drew from her work as a feminist and labour activist in Manchester, England, where she had moved in 1897 with her partner Esther Roper. In rhyming couplets, her poem 'Women's Rights' urges readers to 'Rise with us and let us go / To where the living waters flow' and thus infuses the rural ideal of Yeats's 'The Lake Isle of Innisfree' (1890) with feminist activism. Set near Sligo, 'Women's Rights' represents nature as a feminine contrast to the 'town' of men, and insists 'Men have got their pomp and pride – / All the green world is on our side'.[4]

Skewering the reverential tone of much Revivalist poetry, Susan Mitchell (1866–1926) produced biting satire, harkening to a tradition embodied by Jonathan Swift. Mitchell regularly reviewed for the *Freeman's Journal* and served as assistant editor of George Russell's *Irish Homestead* and *Irish Statesman*, where she published essays and poems. Her *Aids to the Immortality of Certain Persons in Ireland* (1908) mocked the controversies and luminaries of the Revival, including debates over the 1907 Irish Council Bill and the premiere of Synge's *The Playboy of the Western World*, as well as individuals such as George Moore and John Redmond. She sought, in part, to secure their fame through parody, as in her adaptation of Yeats's 'When You Are Old' (1891): 'One Woman loved the foolish souls in you / That made you perfect subjects for Her Art'.[5] Like other women writers of the period, Mitchell worked in an array of literary genres, publishing a biography of George Moore (1916) and writing a short play entitled *Leaguers and Peelers: or, the Apple Cart* (1911).

This sampling of work by Irish women poets underscores the diversity of the period's concerns, which were not limited strictly to Celtic heroes, craggy islands and the daily lives of Irish peasants. For example, spiritual themes abound: Alice Milligan's *The Inalienable Heritage and Other Poems* (1914) is a long poem on the monks of the early Irish church; Eva Gore-Booth's later collections, *The Shepherd of Eternity* (1925) and *The House of Three Windows* (1926), address mysticism and theosophy; Susan Mitchell's collection of lyric poetry, *The Living Chalice and Other Poems* (1908), offers readers complex spiritual meditations, as does her *Frankincense and Myrrh* (1912); Katharine Tynan's *The Rhymed Life of St. Patrick* (1907) commends Famine emigrants for bringing Catholicism to the New World.

Katharine Tynan (Hinkson) (1859–1931) was arguably the major female poet of the Revival. Early collections such as *Shamrocks* (1887) and *Ballads and Lyrics* (1891) prompted George Russell to praise her as 'the earliest singer in that awakening of our imagination which has been spoken of as the Irish Renaissance'.[6] When in lockstep with aims and concerns of the Revival as defined by her friend and colleague Yeats, addressing lofty subjects such as the spirit or heroism, Tynan was embraced. When the representation of the everyday began to occupy her work – as she wrote about her marriage, her move to England, the death of her infant children – she was marginalized by the dominant voices of the Revival. Yet her poetry, like that of her most innovative peers, demonstrates a canny reworking of traditional themes and forms. Written during the early years of her marriage, the paeans to her husband and early marriage in *A Lover's Breast-Knot* (1894) invite comparison with the work of Elizabeth Barrett Browning. As in the admittedly more sophisticated *Sonnets from the Portuguese* (1850), Tynan's poems are ridden with anxieties regarding the constancy and potency of love, and they likewise consider the tension between silence and the articulation of deep feeling. After celebrating the abundant evidence of love found in the sounds and sights of a lush garden, the final stanza of 'Love's Garden' reads: 'Ah no! Love's secrets let us keep, / Lest the winged god / Angered, go seeking, while we sleep, / Some new abode'.[7] The exact a-b-a-b rhyme of the previous stanzas shifts here to the slant rhyme of 'god' and 'abode', formally troubling neat predictability – a complication heightened by the introduction in these lines of a capricious deity who threatens to chase away the pleasures of evanescent affection.

During the First World War, a struggle in which her two sons fought, Tynan published hundreds of war poems focused largely on male hero-ism and female sacrifice, themes also coursing through Revivalism. Many of these were published in newspapers and periodicals, then collected in *The Flower of Peace: A Collection of Devotional Poetry* (1914), *The Flowers of Youth: Poems in War Time* (1915), *The Holy War* (1916), *Late Songs* (1917), and *Herb O'Grace: Poems in War Time* (1918). Other Irish women poets of the period also reflected on modern warfare, whether the First World War or the Easter Rising. They represented the destruc-tion wrought by combat on the battlefield as well as on the home front, largely by engaging a tradition of Irish elegiac poetry that mourned failed insurrections, famine and mass emigration. Like other war poetry of this period, their verse showcases the increasingly complicated role of Irish women writers in a society subject to new forms of violence and trauma. These poems critique as often as praise, mourn as often as rejoice, wit-ness the present as often as lionize the past – complexities evident, for instance, in the pacifist poems of Eva Gore-Booth's collections *The Perilous Light* (1915) and *Broken Glory* (1917).

The war poetry of Winifred M. Letts (1881–1972) offered readers age-old themes peppered with vivid details drawn from contemporary life. The author of short fiction and novels, including *The Rough Way* (1912) and *Christina's Son* (1915), as well as plays produced at the Abbey and Gate Theatres, Letts was popular with readers. Her poetry collection *Songs from Leinster* (1913), which toggled between idyllic rural scenes and portraits of Dublin slum life, was reprinted six times, with some of the poems being scored for music, and was followed by *More Songs from Leinster* (1926). While working as a nurse during the war, Letts published *Hallow-e'en and Poems of the War* (1916), reissued the following year as *The Spires of Oxford* and taking its new title from the most admired poem in the collection. 'The Spires of Oxford (Seen from a Train)' is written from the vantage point of a woman observing Oxford, the alma mater of her lover who was killed in battle, as she travels on a moving train. The sight prompts her to mourn the loss of a generation 'Who took the khaki and the gun / Instead of cap and gown'.[8] The poem 'What Reward?' examines the psychological consequences of male sacrifice with its consideration of a shell-shocked soldier: '*You* gave your life, boy, / And *you* gave a limb: / But he who gave his precious wits, / Say, what reward for him?' (23). In this same collection, 'Pro Patria' reveals the subtle influence of modernism: the regular rhyme and rhythm of the poem is punctuated by stark contemporary images – the top coats and woollen mufflers of office workers practicing a military drill, the 'kindly glow' of the picture palaces replaced by wartime exercises (15).

Dora Sigerson Shorter (1866–1918) also engaged with the devastating political conflicts of this era. The daughter of George Sigerson, she circulated as a young woman among the architects of the Revival. Her early collections of poetry – *Verses* (1893), *The Fairy Changeling and Other Poems* (1898) and *Ballads and Poems* (1899) – offered formally traditional poems suffused with Revivalist themes and Catholic beliefs. Despite living in England after her marriage, Shorter largely attended in her writing to Irish culture and politics, and her late work explored the consequences of war in both countries. In her preface to *The Sad Years* (1918), Shorter's posthumous collection of poems, Katharine Tynan attributes Shorter's death to an 'intense and isolated suffering ... over the events following Easter week', suggesting she died 'for love of the Dark Rosaleen'.[9] This collection represented the cost of war by employing Irish tropes, as in 'Ourselves Alone', addressed to Kathleen ni Houlihan. 'Comfort the Women' invokes Christian imagery, a common tactic in her poetry, to demonstrate the complexities of political conflict. The poem's speaker hopes that 'my neutral prayer' may wend its way past 'scream of shell and mighty cannon's roar' and the 'thunder of the voices that appeal / For His protection' to beg comfort for the women 'in these warring lands / Who through the battles go helpless and frail'.[10]

Drama

Salon culture in Ireland and England, often hosted by women, provided the laboratory for much Revivalist poetry, and the women's political organization Inghinidhe na hÉireann (Daughters of Ireland) (1900–14) was arguably the most important collective engendering Revivalist drama. Inghinidhe made possible the early Abbey Theatre: it pioneered the practice of Irish actors performing Irish plays, it introduced Yeats and the Fays, it hosted performers such as Sara Allgood and Máire Nic Shiubhlaigh. As an organization, Inghinidhe largely adhered to the masculinist ideals of contemporary nationalist movements by celebrating female domesticity as an ideal and urging women to curate and transmit nationalist pedagogy that might foster, protect and convey Irish traditions. In its journal, *Bean na hÉireann* (1908–11), contributors urged readers to buy Irish goods, to learn and speak the Irish language and to propagate ideals embraced by the nationalist project. However, Inghinidhe also published the influential 1909 lecture entitled 'Women, Ideals and the Nation' by Constance Markievicz (1868–1927) in which she insists, 'The old idea that a woman can only serve her nation through her home is gone, so now is the time ... you must make the world look upon you as citizens first, as women after.'[11]

Alice Milligan (1866–1953), who was inspired by the death of Parnell to join the nationalist movement, was one prominent member of Inghinidhe na hÉireann. To advance nationalist ideals, Milligan lectured on behalf of the Gaelic League, published regularly in periodicals including *United Ireland* and *Sinn Féin*, and wrote a political novel entitled *A Royal Democrat* (1892). Over the course of her career, she wrote more than 200 poems, collected in the posthumously published *Poems* (1954), many of which reflect her interests in Gaelic history and contemporary politics. It is difficult to overestimate Milligan's impact on the dramatic revival. In February 1900, her play *The Last Feast of the Fianna* was performed during the second season of the Irish Literary Theatre (ILT). In depicting the struggle between Diarmuid and Finn, the play considered divisive politics and was 'the first drama to draw its characters, setting and theme from Irish saga'.[12] Milligan's use of Irish legend and history as the subject of national drama inspired the founders of the ILT, as did her production of *The Deliverance of Red Hugh* (1901) with dialogue in both

Irish and English. She authored two sequels to the well-received *The Last Feast of the Fianna*, as well as a four-act melodrama about a dispossessed woman, *The Daughter of Donagh* (1905). In much of her drama, Milligan employed new forms to tell old stories. For instance, the innovative scenography and structure of her plays drew from *tableaux vivants* based on Irish myth, history and folklore, and perhaps from the lantern lectures she delivered on Irish history.

Eva Gore-Booth was another writer who understood drama as both literary text and visual performance. As a young woman, she wrote a short sketch entitled *A Daughter of Eve, or, Alphonso's Bride* (1891) in rhyming couplets for performance at her family estate, Lissadell. Between 1902 and 1918, she scripted six full-length plays, though only *Unseen Kings* was produced, appearing at the Abbey in 1912. Like other women writers of the period, she reworked Revivalist themes to suit her interests, as Cathy Leeney has shown in her excellent study of Gore-Booth's drama.[13] In *Unseen Kings*, Gore-Booth focuses on the relationship among Niamh, Eineen the Sorrowful and Cuculain (Cúchulainn), altering the tale of Cuculain's death. In *The Triumph of Maeve* (1902), she infuses her representation of Maeve, also drawn from the Cúchulainn myths, with feminist and pacifist concerns. Like other Revivalist playwrights, female and male, Gore-Booth directly engaged with innovations in European drama.

Maud Gonne (1866–1953) may be the Irish woman writer most affected by the critical tendency to read these decades through Yeats, thanks to his numerous poetic depictions of her. She also provided fodder for subsequent women writers: she was caricatured in Mary Manning's *Mount Venus* (1938) and Iris Murdoch's *The Red and the Green* (1965). Yet Gonne was another Irish writer who ranged among genres, writing journalism, public lectures, drama and autobiography. Her journalism appeared in organs such as *L'Irlande Libre*, which she founded, and her speeches on behalf of Irish nationalism mobilized thousands in the interest of Irish political autonomy. Her one-act play *Dawn* (1904), written for Inghinidhe, was never staged but appeared in the *United Irishman*.[14] It depicts the eviction of three generations of an Irish family, rendering the landlord the villain. A riposte to both *Cathleen ni Houlihan* and *In the Shadow of the Glen*, the latter of whose critical representation of the Irish peasantry inspired Gonne to resign from the Irish National Theatre Society that staged it, *Dawn* was inspired in part by her activism amid evictions and famine. In this production, she used magic lantern slides of actual evictions to achieve the verisimilitude found in subsequent docudramas such as Mary Raftery's *No Escape* (2010).

A century ago, as in the present day, women playwrights had difficulty getting their work staged: among the Abbey Theatre repertoire of this period, for instance, only seven women (not counting Lady Gregory) are credited as sole-author playwrights.[15] Nonetheless, women were the engine of the Irish Dramatic Movement as directors, actresses, patrons, scene and costume designers – and playwrights.

Prose

Poetry and drama have long been considered the dominant modes of the Revival, with some scholarly attention allotted to prose forms, such as folklore, translations and journalism, that resonate with the movement's endeavour to celebrate the indigenous past and inspire the political future. The work of Eleanor Hull (1860–1935) fits neatly within this customary understanding of Revivalist prose. Hull was one of the founders of the Irish Texts Society, which recovered, translated, annotated and published Irish-language manuscripts to promote the study of Irish. Hull's adaptation and translation of native folktales and ancient Irish literature, as published in *The Cuchulain Saga in Irish Literature* (1898) and the children's book *The Boys' Cuchulain* (1904), helped to popularize the folktales, romances and heroic legends that fed the Revival. However, as John Wilson Foster notes, the prose fiction of the Revival is a 'highly diverse and uncooperative body of work' and, since his study of the movement, like most, focuses almost exclusively on male authors, it should come as little surprise that this characterization is amplified when we add to the mix the talented women writers of this period.[16]

The number and diversity of novels, short stories and sketches published during these decades by women reveal how interpretations of the Revival gleaned strictly from the forms and topics condoned by Yeats misrepresents the actual breadth of the movement. Women's fiction demonstrates that Revivalist ideals, easily identifiable in plays set in Mayo or poems about Cúchulainn, are likewise found in social fiction set in Dublin or in utopian novels detailing futuristic technologies. With her portrayals of the rural peasantry and her invocation of mythic tropes, Emily Lawless (1845–1913) appears to fit the category of Revivalist writer. Set in Co. Clare during the Land Wars, her realist novel *Hurrish* (1886) traffics in familiar female types, such as the mother who encourages her son to sacrifice himself for Ireland, but its vivid depiction of peasant life purportedly influenced Gladstone's policies on Ireland. *Grania: The Story of an Island* (1892) focuses on Grania O'Malley, who comes of age amid the harsh natural and economic conditions of the Aran Islands. Her life is filled with personal trauma: her parents and beloved sister Honor die; her future husband Murdough Blake is a disappointment. At the novel's end, Grania drowns sailing from her home of Inis Meáin. The novel, written in dialogue shed of brogue, suggests the psychological impact of the island's harsh natural conditions and of repressive patriarchy on Grania's consciousness.[17] Lawless, another astonishingly productive woman writing across a wide variety of literary forms, also authored two well-regarded historical novels, a collection of *Sketches in Traits and Confidences* (1897), a history entitled *The Story of Ireland* (1897), an autobiography entitled *A Garden Diary* (1901) and a biography of Maria Edgeworth (1904).

The Belfast-born Rosa Mulholland (Lady Gilbert) (1841–1921) also wrote in a diversity of prose forms, publishing more than forty novels, as well as short stories, children's literature, poetry and intellectual prose. Her work exemplifies how Irish women writers cleverly adapted Revivalist archetypes, rather than simply recapitulating them. Her short story 'The Hungry Death', first appearing in Charles Dickens's journal *All the Year Round* (1890) and reprinted in Yeats's *Representative Irish Tales* (1891), embraces Gothic tropes, such as psychological terror, ghostly hauntings and treacherous landscapes, to depict the intense sufferings of the Famine. The story neatly concludes with the self-sacrifice of one female character to save another to highlight its message of Christian charity, as well as its compatibility with a cultural nationalism that celebrated self-abnegation. Her novel *Cousin Sara: A Story of Arts and Crafts* (1909) reflects the Revivalist investment in indigenous, handcrafted art, but turns its eye away from Ireland, portraying the romance between Sara and a young man who rejects a mercantile career in Belfast to pursue life as a painter in Italy. Likewise, in *Father Tim* (1910), Mulholland depicts the career of the titular Catholic priest, offering her readers a vivid account of Irish rural life akin to those found elsewhere in Revivalist literature, but she also depicts Dublin's urban poverty, while offering staunch lessons on the evils of alcoholism and emigration.

Though Irish myth and history, and the rural peasantry, appear throughout women's fiction of these decades, many of these writers also engaged with subtler aspects of Revivalist thinking. Douglas Hyde's *The Necessity for De-Anglicizing Ireland* (1892), a foundational text of the Revival, focuses closely on the importance to the Irish of embracing and publicly performing their Irish identity through the use of the Irish language, the adoption of Irish names, and the consumption of Irish goods. For Hyde, the worst affront to nationalism was incongruency, for the Irish to behave as though they were English rather than Irish. Edith Somerville (1858–1949) and Martin Ross (Violet Martin) (1861–1915) considered this same Revivalist anxiety about the disconnect between authentic identity and public performance in their critically lauded novel, *The Real Charlotte* (1894). This novel harnesses the best tactics of the realist novel to depict the middle-age spinster Charlotte Mullen as she schemes against her vivacious, naive younger cousin Francie Fitzpatrick. Though Charlotte adopts the facade of charitable relative and mentor, her devious nature consistently reveals itself in sinister manifestations of 'the real Charlotte'. The incompatibility between exterior and internal selves results in tragedy: Francie is killed and Charlotte is reviled. The collaborations of Somerville and Ross are among the best-known prose of this period, but may not seem an obvious fit with Revivalist logics. Yet their co-authored fiction, including the popular *Some Experiences of an Irish R.M.* (1899), *Further Experiences of an Irish R.M.* (1908), and *In Mr. Knox's Country* (1915), as well as travelogues documenting their trips through Denmark, France and Wales, exhibit the close attention to local particulars characterizing much of the Revival's folklore and anthropological writing.

The writings of Jane Barlow (1857–1917) span the range of forms that might be labelled Revivalist. Best known for her novels, poems, and sketches about Irish peasant culture, including the enormously popular *Irish Idylls* (1892), *A Creel of Irish Stories* (1897) and *Irish Ways* (1909), she also wrote a utopian novel, entitled *History of a World of Immortals without a God: Translated from an Unpublished Manuscript in the Library of a Continental University*, under the pseudonym Antares Skorpios. This 1891 novel follows the Dutch tradesman and doctor Gervaas van Varken who, inspired by his reading of Swift's *Gulliver's Travels* and his journey to Tibet, travels to the planet Hesperos (Venus), where he encounters a utopian society inhabited by 'one hundred millions of rational and highly-cultured beings'.[18] Seemingly outside the ambit of Revivalist literature, this novel employs the observational tactics of the literary sketch and the travelogue, and due to its rich anthropological detail and its recounting of Hesperian oral history, seems no less fantastic in its approach and form than Synge's *The Aran Islands* (1907).

Many of these women were audaciously prolific, revealing a boundless creativity and the pragmatic need to support themselves financially through regular publication. Katharine Tynan, who like many of these writers engaged in surprising ways with Revivalist themes and forms, provides an exemplar of women writing across a considerable range of forms during these decades. Her collection *A Cluster of Nuts: Being Sketches Among My Own People* (1894) was the first in a series of sketches depicting the practices and vernacular of local peasantry, while *Peeps at Many Lands: Ireland* (1911), a non-fiction introduction to Ireland intended for English children, celebrated the Irish pastoral and 'Celtic' anti-materialism. Tynan also authored numerous popular romances which, while often formulaic, offered insights into the customs and manners of the Irish and English from all classes, as in her first novel *The Way of the Maid* (1895), which focused on a Catholic family in Ireland. Another novel *The Story of Bawn* (1907) exemplified Tynan's 'anti-romantic sentimental novels for the popular audience', a mode that enabled subsequent departures from romanticized Revival literature by Synge and Joyce.[19] Tynan also edited and revised the influential anthology *The Cabinet of Irish Literature* (1902–03) to introduce readers to contemporary Irish literary talents.[20]

During the Revival, journalism offered women a crucial means to publish and widely circulate their ideas. As Tynan observed, 'I think at one time or another I must have written for nearly every paper and magazine in London.'[21] The vast range of periodicals in Ireland, America and England in which Irish women published during these decades demonstrates the diversity of opinions and interests among them: they might publish Irish folklore, offer advice on gardening, advocate hunger strikes to advance women's suffrage or urge violent revolt against England. Several influential Irish periodicals of this period were founded and edited by women writers. Ethna Carbery (Anna Johnston) (1866–1902) published in nationalist organs such as *The Nation* and *Young Ireland*. She also authored the poetry collection, *The Four Winds of Eirinn* (1902), and the short story collections, *The Passionate Hearts* (1903) and *In the Celtic Past* (1904). In 1895, Carbery collaborated with Alice Milligan to edit the monthly nationalist periodical, the *Northern Patriot* (1895). Like Carbery, Milligan had deep experience in journalism. She published in *Sinn Féin* and *United Ireland*, and wrote the column 'Notes from the North' for the *Irish Weekly Independent*. The following year, Carbery and Milligan again collaborated when they founded and edited the literary and political journal *Shan Van Vocht* (1896–9), which first published James Connolly's essay 'Socialism and Nationalism' and featured contributions from Nora Hopper, Russell, Tynan and Yeats. *Bean na hÉireann* (Women of Ireland) (1908–11), the monthly journal of Inghinidhe na hÉireann, was edited by Helena Molony (1883–1967). Molony later became a member of the

Irish Citizen Army and took an active role in the Easter Rising, which she recorded in the contemporary press. These papers served as valuable models for subsequent editors dedicated to feminist concerns. *The Irish Citizen*, a weekly periodical founded in 1912 by James Cousins and Francis Sheehy Skeffington, provided women writers with a platform to disseminate perspectives on suffragism, social welfare and culture.

The articles and essays by Irish women for periodicals afford rich and unexpected insights into social, aesthetic and political culture of this period, as do their autobiographies. Some of these personal chronicles were written during the period, such as Edith Somerville's *Irish Memories* (1917) and Katharine Tynan's *Twenty-Five Years: Reminiscences* (1913) and *The Middle Years* (1916), while others, though published later, nevertheless capture the flavour of the era: W. H. Letts's *Knockmaroon* (1933) offers a detailed portrayal of rural childhood, Maud Gonne's *A Servant of the Queen* (1938) is an intimate record of her early years as an activist, and Máire Nic Shiubhlaigh's *The Splendid Years* (1955) provides one of the most valuable accounts of the early Abbey Theatre as well as of women in the Easter Rising.

During the late nineteenth and early twentieth centuries, Irish women wrote biographies, memoirs, travelogues, children's literature and, as they engaged directly with the political and cultural ferment of the period, pamphlets, speeches, letters, tracts and journalism. They also published a wealth of fiction, a genre that, like the much-lauded poetry and drama of the Revival, spoke potently to the concerns of this era. In their novels, short stories and sketches, they depicted typical Revivalist subjects, such as the triumphs of past Irish heroes and the lives of the rural peasantry. But this was not the whole story: during these decades, they also published social realism and Bildungsroman, as well as religious, Gothic, popular romance and utopian novels. Their adroit fiction and non-fiction obtained for these working women money and acclaim, but has yet to earn them prominence in the Revivalist canon.

Lady Gregory

This essay seeks to complicate traditional notions of literary production in and around the Revival, in part by indicating the diversity of women's writing. It closes, however, with the familiar assertion that Lady Isabella Augusta Gregory (1852–1932) was a vital force in Ireland's literary renaissance. We know her best as the affluent Anglo-Irish patron of Yeats, the doyenne of her Coole Park salon, the barmbrack-baking manager of the Abbey, the mourning mother of her son Robert who was killed during the First World War, and even, thanks in part to the work of Colm Tóibín, as a sensual adulteress. Gregory was also the apotheosis of a Revivalist writer, whose drama, poetry and prose merit as much attention as her fascinating biography.

Throughout her career, Gregory wrote in pursuit of political and social reform at home and abroad. She was uniquely alert to the influence that literature might have in political life, thanks in part to her 1880 marriage to the politician and writer Sir William Gregory. Prior to Gregory's death in 1892, the couple shared a richly cosmopolitan life: in London, their circle included Robert Browning and Henry James, and they travelled to India, Ceylon, Egypt, Spain and Italy. Her first major publication was *Arabi and His Household* (1882), a pamphlet in support of the 1879 Urabi Revolt in Egypt. In 1893, she anonymously published an anti-Home Rule pamphlet entitled 'A Phantom's Pilgrimage: or Home Ruin', a fantasy in which Gladstone returns from the grave ten years after the passage of the Home Rule Bill to find Ireland in chaos. Soon after, her Unionist sympathies transformed into a profound investment in the nationalist ideals espoused by the Revival, a movement she helped to create and sustain. During Ireland's tempestuous early twentieth century, she was an advocate in print for important causes, protesting Dublin Castle's censorship of Shaw's *The Shewing-up of Blanco Posnet* (1909) as well as the abuses of Black and Tans during the Anglo-Irish War, championing Synge's *The Playboy of the Western World* in America (1911–13) and fighting for the return of Hugh Lane's art collection to Dublin.

Another of Gregory's lasting literary achievements was her collecting, editing and translating of Irish myths and folk material. In 1893, she travelled alone to the Aran Islands, after having read Douglas Hyde's *Love Songs of Connacht* (1893), as well as Barlow's *Irish Idylls* and Lawless's *Grania*. Gregory learnt Irish and began recording oral tales and legends from local residents of her Coole estate. These tales, the diverse content of which ranged from fairies and folk medicine to accounts of the Famine and First World War, were published in *A Book of Saints and Wonders* (1906), *The Kiltartan History Book* (1909), *The Kiltartan Wonder Book* (1910) and the two-volume *Visions and Beliefs in the West of Ireland* (1920). She also translated into English various Irish myths, published as the popular *Cuchulain of Muirthemne* (1902) and *Gods and Fighting Men* (1904). These texts, like many of her plays, were written in 'Kiltartanese', a dialect that she created to capture the sound and rhythms of the Hiberno-English spoken by the local Galway people.

Gregory's contributions to Irish theatre are inestimable. She co-founded the Irish Literary Theatre in 1899 with Edward Martyn and Yeats, and the Irish National Theatre Society in 1903 with Synge and Yeats. She served as manager of the Abbey Theatre from its 1904 opening until her retirement in 1928 and her original plays and translations were regularly produced on its stage. Long represented as the Abbey's stern and conservative administrator, the 'old lady' who said no to innovative dramas like those of the playwright Denis Johnston, Gregory was, in fact, one of its most adept and inventive dramatists. Her forty-two plays, which include history, farce and political allegory, among other forms, were generally sympathetic to nationalist ideals and populated with material that audiences recognized from myth, popular melodrama and theatrical realism. Embraced by audiences in part because they offered few of Synge's calculated shocks and little of Yeats's obfuscating poetry, her plays nonetheless featured radical themes and innovative forms.[22]

On the opening night of the Abbey Theatre in 1904, Gregory's *Spreading the News* and *Cathleen ni Houlihan*, which she co-authored with Yeats, appeared on a bill with Yeats's *On Baile's Strand*. *Spreading the News*, a one-act written in the tragi-comedy form she frequently deployed, exposes the foibles of the British constabulary as well as the local Irish community. *Cathleen ni Houlihan* chronicles the seduction of the young Michael by the mythical old woman of Ireland, whose poetry and nationalist ideology lure him to fight in the Irish rebellion of 1798. Her other early Abbey plays – *The Gaol Gate* (1906), *The Rising of the Moon* (1907), *The Workhouse Ward* (1908) and *The Image* (1909) – were in harmony with the concerns of the Abbey's nationalist audiences, even as they offered subtle critiques of their ideals. Her commitment to recording and preserving history is evident in her biographies of family members, her press-cutting books on the Abbey, her meticulous diaries, and her full-length Irish history plays, such as *Kincora* (1905), *The White Cockade* (1905) and *Dervorgilla* (1907). The supernatural aspects of her folklore and mythology suffuse her three 'wonder' plays, *The Jester* (1918), *The Dragon* (1919) and *Aristotle's Bellows* (1921). Her ambitious blending of Irish and international cultures appears in the seven plays she adapted for the Abbey stage: Kiltartanese courses through the dialogue of her translations and adaptations of Molière, Goldoni and Sudermann.

Like other women writers of the period, Gregory invoked the mythology and history central to Revivalism, but recalibrated it to suit her interests. Eva Gore-Booth and Alice Milligan offered feminist revisions of the legendary tragic heroine Deirdre in their drama, and Emily Lawless drew on Grania for her novel of the same name. In the three-act *Grania* (1912), never performed on the Abbey stage, Gregory also invoked the legendary figure of Grania, who was betrothed to Finn, the chief of the Fianna, but eloped instead with the younger and handsomer Diarmuid. Gregory's play underscores Grania's sexual authority.[23] Such is her confidence that Grania urges Diarmuid to fight with Finn, insisting, 'There is nothing will come between us now. You are entirely my own.'[24] When Diarmuid is killed, she maintains her self-assurance and dignity: as the play ends, she opens the door to a jeering off-stage audience that falls silent when she walks out partnered with Finn.

Like many of her peers, Gregory vividly described Irish culture of this era in autobiographies, diaries and personal histories. Her early and unpublished autobiography *An Emigrants' Notebook* (1884) chronicles her coming of age. *Our Irish Theatre: A Chapter of Autobiography* (1913) is partially a history of the Abbey, partially a memoir that covers the founding and early years of the theatre, and *Coole* (1931) is a history of her famous estate. A consummate diarist, Gregory's accounts of her life and times are enormously revealing, showcasing her talents of observation and respectful listening, even as she self-censored her entries.[25] Her autobiography *Seventy Years*, written in the 1920s, was found among family papers and published in 1974.

One factor contributing to the neglect of Gregory's writing, despite her evident talent and productivity, was her willingness to efface her own abilities. Gregory had a brief affair with the English writer Wilfrid Scawen Blunt, and at its conclusion she offered twelve sonnets to Blunt, who published them as *A Woman's Sonnets* (1892) under his name. Using the pseudonym 'Angus Grey', she published two short stories, *A Philanthropist* (1891) and *A Gentleman* (1894). James Pethica observes that Gregory's editorial work reflected 'a tension between the need to assert herself creatively and the ingrained imperatives of her upbringing and culture, which held up womanly self-abnegation as the ideal'.[26] Her first monograph was *Sir William Gregory: An Autobiography* (1894), for which she edited her husband's diaries, making selections from his correspondence and writing the introduction. She also edited *Mr. Gregory's Letter-Box* (1898), a collection of the letters of her husband's grandfather, who had served as Undersecretary to Ireland. Years later, she would memorialize her nephew in *Hugh Lane's Life and Achievement* (1921), after his death in the 1915 sinking of the *Lusitania*.

Gregory's insistent foregrounding of men and male achievement reflects gendered mores drawn from her generation and class, but the continued neglect of her work exposes not only intransigent gender biases but also scholarly biases that fail to regard editing, translation and journalism, among other endeavours, as the serious work of creative genius. As well, it may indicate the privileging of individual virtuosity over collaborative creative labour. Gregory co-authored the plays *The Pot of Broth* (1902) and *Where There Is Nothing* (1902) with Yeats, *The Poorhouse* (1907) with Douglas Hyde, and *The Unicorn from the Stars* (1907) with Yeats and Hyde. And though *Cathleen ni Houlihan* (1902) was written by both Gregory and Yeats, Yeats was long credited with sole authorship of this influential play.[27]

The inattention to Lady Gregory's writing during these decades speaks volumes about the stubborn endurance of conventional readings of the Irish Literary Revival, many put in place by Yeats and his early critics. Long understood as a movement whose ideals were articulated primarily, or even exclusively, by poetry and drama focused on mythic heroes, the rural peasantry, and traditional gender roles, the Revival, read from a century's distance, now demands more sophisticated assessments of the whole of its literary production. We must acknowledge the diversity of forms and themes found among its many texts, as well as the essential role that women played, not only in its cultural practices, but also in its literary production.

Notes

1 For examples, see Karen Brown, *The Yeats Circle: Verbal and Visual Relations in Ireland, 1880–1939* (Surrey: Ashgate, 2011); P. J. Mathews, *Revival: The Abbey Theatre, Sinn Féin, the Gaelic League and the Co-operative Movement* (Cork: Cork University Press, 2003); Sinéad Garrigan Mattar, *Primitivism, Science, and the Irish Revival* (Oxford: Oxford English Monographs, 2004); Timothy McMahon, *Grand Opportunity: The Gaelic Revival and Irish Society, 1893–1910* (Syracuse: Syracuse University Press, 2008); Philip O'Leary, *Ideology and Innovation: The Prose Literature of the Gaelic Revival, 1881–1921* (University Park, PA: Pennsylvania State University Press, 1994); Paige Reynolds, *Modernism, Drama, and the Audience for Irish Spectacle* (Cambridge: Cambridge University Press, 2007); Karen Steele, *Women, Press, and Politics During the Irish Revival* (Syracuse: Syracuse University Press, 2007); Mary Trotter, *Ireland's National Theaters* (Syracuse: Syracuse University Press, 2001).

2 Patrick Crotty, 'The Irish Renaissance, 1890–1940: Poetry in English', in *The Cambridge History of Irish Literature, Vol. 2, 1890–2000*, ed. Margaret Kelleher and Philip O'Leary (Cambridge: Cambridge University Press, 2006), 67.

3 Emily Lawless, 'After Aughrim', in *With the Wild Geese* (London: Isbister and Co, 1902), 5.

4 Eva Gore-Booth, 'Women's Rights', in *The Egyptian Pillar* (Dublin: Maunsel, 1907), 29–30.

5 Susan L. Mitchell, *Aids to the Immortality of Certain Persons in Ireland Charitably Administered*, 2nd ed. (Dublin: Maunsel, 1913), xvii.

6 George William Russell, *Collected Poems* (London: Macmillan, 1913), vii.

7 Katharine Tynan, 'Love's Garden', in *A Lover's Breast-Knot* (London: Elkin Mathews, 1896), 9.

8 Winifred H. Letts, 'The Spires of Oxford', in *The Spires of Oxford and Other Poems* (New York, NY: E. P. Dutton & Company, 1917), 4.

9 Katharine Tynan, 'Dora Sigerson: A Tribute and Some Memories', in Dora Sigerson Shorter, *The Sad Years* (New York, NY: George H. Doran, 1918), xi–xii.

10 Dora Sigerson Shorter, *Comfort the Women: A Prayer in Times of War* (London: s.n., 1915).

11 Constance Markievicz, *A Call to the Women of Ireland: Being a Lecture Delivered to the Students' National Literary Society* (Dublin: Fergus O'Connor, 1918), 12.

12 Antoinette Quinn, 'Introduction', in 'Ireland/Herland: Women and Literary Nationalism', in *The Field Day Anthology of Irish Writing Vol IV & V: Women's Writing and Traditions*, ed. Angela Bourke et al. (Cork: Cork University Press, 2002), 5: 898.

13 Cathy Leeney, *Irish Women Playwrights, 1900–1939: Gender and Violence on Stage* (New York, NY: Peter Lang, 2012), 59–96.

14 Antoinette Quinn, 'Cathleen ni Houlihan Writes Back: Maud Gonne and Irish Nationalist Theater', in *Gender and Sexuality in Modern Ireland*, ed. Anthony Bradley and Maryann Valiulis (Amherst: University of Massachusetts Press, 1997), 39–59.

15 Lucy Collins, *Poetry by Women in Ireland: A Critical Anthology 1870–1970* (Liverpool: Liverpool University Press, 2012), 17.

16 John Wilson Foster, *Fictions of the Irish Literary Revival: A Changeling Art* (Syracuse: Syracuse University Press, 1987), xi.

17 James M. Cahalan, 'Forging a Tradition: Emily Lawless and the Irish Literary Canon', in *Border Crossings: Irish Women Writers and National Identities*, ed. Kathryn Kirkpatrick (Tuscaloosa: University of Alabama Press, 2000), 38–57.

18 Antares Skorpios (Jane Barlow), *History of a World of Immortals without a God: Translated from an Unpublished Manuscript in the Library of a Continental University* (Dublin: William McGee, 1891), 159. This novel is sometimes attributed to her father, James William Barlow, but shares many evident characteristics of her prose.

19 Bonnie Roos, 'Unlikely Heroes: Katharine Tynan's *The Story of Bawn*, the Irish Famine, and the Sentimental Tradition', *Irish University Review* 43, no. 2 (2013): 328.

20 Margaret Kelleher, '*The Cabinet of Irish Literature*: A Historical Perspective on Irish Anthologies', *Éire-Ireland* 38, no. 3–4 (2003): 68–89.

21 Katharine Tynan, *The Middle Years* (New York: Houghton Mifflin, 1916), 122.

22 Recent scholarship acknowledging the more radical aspects of Gregory's drama include Anthony Roche, 'Reworking *The Workhouse Ward*', *Irish University Review* 34, no. 1 (2004): 171–84.

23 Maria-Elena Doyle, 'A Spindle for the Battle: Feminism, Myth, and the Woman-Nation in Irish Revival Drama', *Theatre Journal* 51, no. 1 (March 1999): 33–46; Anne Fogarty, ed., *Irish University Review: Lady Gregory Special Issue* 34, no. 1 (Spring–Summer 2004); Lucy McDiarmid and Maureen Waters, 'Introduction', in *Selected Writings by Lady Augusta Gregory*, ed. Lucy McDiarmid and Maureen Waters (London: Penguin, 1995).

24 Augusta Gregory, 'Grania', in *Selected Writings by Lady Augusta Gregory*, ed. McDiarmid and Waters, 398.

25 See Daniel J. Murphy, ed., *Lady Gregory's Journals* Vol. I (New York, NY: Oxford University Press, 1978); Daniel J. Murphy, ed., *Lady Gregory's Journals*, Vol. II (New York, NY: Oxford University Press, 1987); James Pethica, ed., *Lady Gregory's Diaries 1892–1902* (Gerrards Cross: Colin Smythe, 1995); Lennox Robinson, ed., *Lady Gregory's Journals 1916–30* (New York, NY: Macmillan, 1947).

26 Pethica, *Lady Gregory's Diaries 1892–1902*, xix.

27 James Pethica, '"Our Kathleen:" Yeats's Collaboration with Lady Gregory in the Writing of *Cathleen ni Houlihan*', in *Yeats Annual* 6, ed. Warwick Gould (London: Macmillan, 1988), 3–31.

CHAPTER 8

Writing for Children

Valerie Coghlan

Defining Irish children's literature is not straightforward, and involves questions relating to language, market, national and cultural identity. Irish women's writing for children is even more equivocal and is often perceived as the lesser part of a lesser part. The story of Irish children's literature by women in the eighteenth and nineteenth centuries is entwined with Ireland's history as a British colony with consequent political, social and cultural effects. Writing for children became manifest as a distinctive literary endeavour in England in the 1740s, and the decades that followed witnessed the consolidation of children's books as an identifiable branch of print culture in the English-speaking world.[1] Recognition of childhood as a separate state from adulthood, allied to increased educational opportunities and parents with disposable income to spend on their children contributed to this. Producers of goods for cultural consumption saw an opportunity to increase growth in the production of items likely to appeal to children and their parents, including clothes, toys and books.[2] The middle classes were the target purchasers for these, while the poorer classes were the recipients of cheaply produced didactic and evangelizing publications from English and Irish reforming societies. Irish writing and publishing has always operated in the shadow of a larger, English-speaking neighbour; in the eighteenth century – as today – publications from Britain flooded the Irish market. While Dublin had an active printing trade in the eighteenth century,[3] output was largely didactic, or proselytizing, aimed at countering Roman Catholicism among the poor and uneducated.[4]

Women were largely involved in the creation of literature designed to inform, improve and entertain the young – not necessarily all at once. Norma Clarke observes that 'the second half of the eighteenth century saw a huge expansion of the number of women finding their way into print', attributing this to women's role as mothers, sisters, teachers and governesses.[5] The habits of the better-off in Ireland were similar to those of their counterparts in England, although as Toby Barnard maintains, 'childhood [in Ireland] was commercialized, if not invented, somewhat later than in England'.[6] Barnard states that 'parents high in the economic and social hierarchies can be found buying publications designed for juveniles' – he suggests these households were mostly Protestant initially – and provides an example of books bought for Tom Edgeworth, a brother of Richard Lovell Edgeworth, the educational reformer and father of Maria Edgeworth (1768–1849). Edgeworth, in her collections of stories for children, including *The Parent's Assistant; or, Stories for Children* (1796), set out to impart lessons that would stay with children for their lifetimes. Fiction set in Ireland includes *Orlandino* (1848)[7] and tales such as 'The Orphans' and 'The White Pigeon' from *The Parent's Assistant*. These carry Edgeworth's familiar leitmotifs of hard work and the benefits of education and honesty, enabling even the poorest children to prosper when mindful of these virtues. Edgeworth strove to avoid giving her readers what she saw as false expectations, but she trusted them on occasion to know what was possible and what was a fantasy. Presenting adventure or travel stories to girls was acceptable as they would understand that they were unlikely to have such experiences in their own lives, but such stories for boys – unless they were destined to become sailors or soldiers – were frowned upon by Edgeworth as it might distract them from succeeding in other worthy professions.[8]

There were, however, Irish women writing to entertain rather than to instruct young people. The verse novels for children by Alicia Le Fanu (ca. 1791–ca. 1844), *The Flowers; or the Syphid Queen: a Fairy Tale in Verse* (1809) and *Rosara's Chain, or, the Choice of Life* (1812), were, as Anne Markey comments, fantasies in the mode of French women writers like Madame d'Aulnoy, offering readers fiction that was 'innovative and unusual in its approach to imagination, morality and passion'.[9] Margaret King Moore (1772–1835, Lady Mount Cashell), a somewhat unconventional figure who was a supporter of the United Irishmen and a friend of Lord Edward Fitzgerald, Mary Wollstonecraft and William Godwin, also wrote stories that avoided didacticism, including *Stories for Little Boys and Girls in Words of One Syllable* (1822). *Stories of Old Daniel; or, Tales of Wonder and Delight* (1808) and its sequel, *Continuation of the Stories of Old Daniel* (1820), tales based on Moore's travels, and recounted by ex-soldier 'Old Daniel', were very popular with young readers. Markey suggests this was due to the tales' removal from the more typical domestic setting, and despite Edgeworth's concerns about travel stories, they were underpinned by firm moral principles.[10]

Travel and the lives of people from other lands were popular topics in the publications of the Society for Promoting the Education of the Poor in Ireland, known as the Kildare Place Society because of its Dublin location. The Society was founded in 1811; during its short existence it developed a far-reaching publishing programme with the intention of providing children with more suitable reading material than that commonly available.[11] Schools were encouraged to subscribe to the KPS sets of library books; by 1825 more than a million individual books had been published and more than eighty titles were in print by 1832. The Society's aim was to improve the circumstances of the poor through education, enabling them to become useful members of society, better able to serve those placed above them. Its attention to publications for girls is an example, as literate girls who had skills as needlewomen could better their economic and social status. Some KPS publications were reprints of titles already in print, while others were written for the Society.

One of its authors was Mary Leadbeater (1758–1823, née Shackleton), a well-educated Quaker woman who ran a village post office and a bonnet-making business in Co. Kildare. Her correspondence with Edmund Burke and the Edgeworths influenced her writing. Leadbeater's *Extracts and Original Anecdotes for the Improvement of Youth* (1794), while not a KPS publication, is the earliest-known book for children to be written by an Irishwoman and published in Dublin. Her last work, *The Pedlars* (1826), was designed to encourage thrift and industry on the part of cottagers, as was *The Cottage Fireside* (1821) by Leadbeater's friend, Abigail Roberts (1748–1823), another Quaker. Roberts, a teacher and a shopkeeper in Co. Laois, wrote poetry and stories published by the KPS.

While they may have laid less stress on the acquisition of practical skills, many women writers, including Anna Maria Fielding (1800–81, Mrs Samuel Carter Hall) were equally didactic in intent. Fielding, a close friend of Maria Edgeworth, was born in Dublin but later lived in London where she married an Irish journalist and moved in literary circles. She wrote novels and dramas for adults and children, including *Children of a Schoolroom* (1830) and *Grandmamma's Pockets* (1849), an autobiographical novel set in Ireland.[12] She edited and contributed to a number of magazines, and edited an annual, *The Juvenile Forget-Me-Not* from 1829 to 1837. Frances Browne (1816–79) is remembered for her collection of moralistic fairy stories, *Granny's Wonderful Chair and Its Tales of Fairy Times* (1856). Born in Donegal, she lived in London, where she was known as 'the blind poetess of Donegal', her blindness resulting from childhood smallpox. She wrote a number of poems and novels, some published by the Religious Tract Society, a British publisher of evangelical and moralistic literature widely read by Irish girls. Their list included novels by Elizabeth Hely Walshe (1839–65?) who was born in Co. Limerick but emigrated to America, where she wrote stories for Irish immigrants about villainous acts by the Irish peasantry in famine times counterbalanced by the philanthropy of Irish landlords, including *From Golden Hills: A Tale of the Irish Famine* (1865).

Co. Cork-born Elizabeth Jane Lysaght (?–1894, née Connor) was the author of some twenty-four novels, mostly romances for girls and books for younger children including *Jack-A-Dandy; or the Heir to Castle Fergus; a Story for Boys and Girls* (1889). Jack, the heir to Castle Fergus in Co. Limerick, is initially reluctant to accept his title and his castle. Acceding to his destiny, he defeats a local boy who has wronged his cousin, in a conflict implying the inherent superiority of the ascendancy over the unreliable Irish natives. Lysaght's novel gestures to the binary between the domiciles of the aristocracy and the peasantry. Here it is a castle, but more typically it is a 'big house'. The 'Big House' trope commonly occurs in Anglo-Irish drama and fiction, embodying prevailing political, social and religious dichotomies. It is less apparent in writing for children, but it was employed by Flora Shaw (1852–1929, Lady Lugard) in her first novel, *Castle Blair: a Story of Youthful Days* (1878).[13] Later, in Kathleen Fitzpatrick's (1872–?) *The Weans of Rowallan* (1905), the five Darragh children are left largely to their own devices in a decaying old house by their ailing mother. The children are cared for by servants, allowing the political and religious tensions endemic in Ulster to form a backdrop to their stay. This was republished in 1937 as *They Lived in County Down*.[14] Most of the novels by Louisa Lilias Greene (1833–91, née Plunket) were set in England, but references to tensions in Ireland may be inferred in, for example, *Dora's Dolls' House* (1890) in which Dora's large dolls' house burns, suggesting the burning of Big Houses in Ireland.[15] Greene was related to Edith Somerville (1858–1949), as was Ethel Coghill Penrose (1857–1938). In Penrose's *Clear as the Noonday* (1893), illustrated by Somerville, and which influenced later novels written by Somerville with Martin Ross (Violet Martin), children from the Big House encounter Land League politics.[16]

Somerville wrote and illustrated two picturebooks, *The Story of the Discontented Little Elephant* (1912) and *Little Red Riding Hood in Kerry* (1934). In the early twentieth century, advances in colour printing led to the greater availability of picturebooks for young children. Sophia Rosamond Praeger (1867–1954), a Belfast sculptor, graphic artist and poet, wrote and illustrated picturebooks, all with a distinctive style and appeal for young readers. Unusually for their time, Praeger promoted her images over her written text in stories which included accounts of small children's everyday lives in *How They Went to School* (1903) and in humorous fantasy adventures such as *The Adventures of the Three Bold Babies* (1897).

The 1881 Land Acts giving greater rights to tenants and the rise of Catholic nationalism following the famines of the mid-nineteenth century generated a new market for novels with a Catholic nationalistic emphasis. A growing Roman Catholic middle class created a demand for books by Catholic writers, including Rosa Mulholland (1841–1921, Lady Gilbert) and Mary Anne Sadlier (1820–1903). Sadlier, who emigrated from Ireland to America, wrote for adults, but was popular with younger readers – *Alice Riordan, the Blind Man's Daughter* (1851) was published in Dublin by M. H. Gill in two editions of over 1,000 copies in each.[17] Despite its religious and classist overtones, the romantic elements in Mulholland's fiction endeared it to girl readers. She also wrote for a younger audience with *Four Little Mischiefs* (1882). Mulholland was acquainted with a number of prominent activists in the Irish Revival, including W. B. Yeats who admired her *Hetty Grey; or, Nobody's Bairn* (1884).

The growing confidence and interest in Irish culture during the Literary Revival saw the flourishing of arts of all kinds, and the interest in an imagined heroic past engendered by the Revival influenced writing for children. Retellings of myths, legends and traditional stories for young readers were popular, and collections by Ella Young (1865–1956) and Augusta Gregory (1852–1932) still inspire retellings by present-day writers. Young retold traditional stories, for example *Celtic Wonder-Tales* (1910), illustrated by Maud Gonne, and later adapted tales for imaginative novels, including *The Wonder-Smith and His Son* (1927). She achieved considerable success in the United States where her books were illustrated by the noted artists Boris Artzybasheff and Robert Lawson. Augusta Gregory's children's books include *The Kiltartan Wonder Book* (1910) and *The Golden Apple: A Play for Kiltartan Children* (1916), which was performed in the Abbey Theatre, Dublin in 1920. Both publications were illustrated by Gregory's daughter, Margaret Gregory, and written in Gregory's 'Kiltartanese' adaptation of rural Irish speech. The retellings of Irish myths by Eleanor Hull (1860–1935) were also read by children, and were frequently anthologized.

To a large extent, young readers remained oblivious of the Celtic mists swirling around them, and carried on reading the popular fiction they

enjoyed. For many girls, the school-story provided an escape into an
enticing world. It coincided with an increase in educational opportunities for women, and by the early 1900s female students were enrolled in
Irish universities,[18] supporting the increasingly accepted concept of the
New Woman, exemplified by Elizabeth Thomasina (Lillie) Meade (1844–
1915, L. T. Meade), an Anglican rector's daughter, born in Bandon, Co.
Cork. In London, Meade established a career as a successful novelist,
published over 200 titles, and was the first editor of *Atalanta*,[19] a magazine for girls and young women, featuring high-quality fiction, articles
about the arts and information on education and career opportunities.
Her popular school stories had English settings, and sometimes, a 'wild
Irish girl' who disrupts the established order. The eponymous character
is hoydenish, rejecting conformity to 'civilized' English mores, epitomiz-
ing social and cultural tensions between the two islands in, for example,
A Wild Irish Girl (1910). Meade typified the ambivalence of Irish
Protestant identity in the latter days of colonial rule. Both Tina O'Toole
and Carole Dunbar assert that Meade never moved far from the British
imperialist values engendered by her upbringing, although, as O'Toole
admits, her writing 'germinated new ideas and politics'.[20] Kimberley
Reynolds argues too for Meade's underlying conservatism: although
her 'New Girls' appealed to her readers, Meade assumed that women's
societal roles would largely continue to adhere to the *status quo*.[21]

Irish women writers for children in the early twentieth century reflect
this tendency to conform to the more traditional role of women. While
women were actively involved in the fight for independence, it seems
that Irish women writers were not engaging children in a literary naviga-
tion of the emergent state, with, for example, no counterpart for girls to
the Catholic nationalist magazine *Our Boys,* published by the Christian
Brothers. Declan Kiberd suggests that militant nationalists looked to
the mythical hero Cúchulainn as 'a symbol of masculinity for the Celts,
who had been written off as feminine by their masters' and 'called on
the youth of Ireland to purge themselves of their degrading femininity by a disciplined programme of physical-contact sports'.[22] Catholic
teaching too, emphasizing women's 'purity' and their place in the home,
was hardly conducive to portrayals of girls in active combatant roles, or
even to girls who emulated Meade's 'New Woman'. Katharine Tynan's
(1861–1931) popular novels for adolescent girls were safer; Colette Epplé
describes Tynan's *Heart O' Gold; or, the Little Princess* (1912) and *Bitha's
Wonderful Year* (1921) as 'paens both to social order and to romantic
love', while instructing British children in how to treat the Irish, and

Irish children 'how to resist assimilation and navigate successfully the waters of postcolonial society'.[23] Tynan also wrote fiction, poetry and nonfiction for adults and adolescent girls, sometimes under her married name of Hinkson.

In the post-independence years, cheaply produced books by the Talbot Press were widely read in schools and homes, its broadly conservative social and Catholic thrust chiming with national educational policy. It published a number of female children's authors including Annie M. P. Smithson (1873–1948) and Winifred M. Letts (1882–1972). Dublin-born Smithson was one of the Talbot Press's most prolific authors who, while not writing specifically for a young audience, was very widely read by teenage girls. She trained as a nurse, converted to Roman Catholicism, joined Cumann na mBan and was imprisoned for her Republican activities. Her political beliefs did not impinge, however, on her writing, nor did her predominately romantic fiction empathize with female emancipation. Winifred M. Letts wrote five children's books, the best known of which is *The Gentle Mountain* (1938). She was born in Salford in England, spent most of her life in Ireland and had an Irish husband, W. H. F. Verschoyle. Her first published work was a tale for children, *The Story Spinner* (1907). Letts also wrote plays for the Abbey Theatre, and poetry and novels for adults. Several of Katherine Frances Purdon's (1852–1920) gentle animal stories were republished by the Talbot Press and by Browne and Nolan following Independence – probably because of their apolitical setting in rural Ireland.

In the 1920s, the ebullience of the Revival had waned, giving way to economic difficulty and social conservatism, and the 1929 Censorship of Publications Act had a repressive effect on literature in general. A few authors spanned the didactic/entertainment market with stories set in provincial Ireland, eschewing contemporary politics, and interweaving Irish folk- and fairy-lore into their tales. In the United States, there was a demand for fiction such as Máirín Cregan's (1891–1975) *Old John* (1936) and Anne Casserley's (1881–1961) *The Whins on Knockattan* (1928) and *Barney the Donkey* (1936), appealing to Irish emigrant families holding fast to the notion of Ireland as a country of cosy cottages rather than grim tenements from which many had come.

Patricia Lynch (1894–1972) played a large part in creating a sort of Gaelicized *nostalgie de la boue*. Leeann Lane avers that 'Lynch immediately sets up a vision of arcadian rural simplicity, a repeated image in all her fictions. The cottage is portrayed as an organic offshoot of the landscape rather than an imposition on it'.[24] Lynch was born in Cork, lived in London and settled in Dublin following marriage to journalist R. M. Fox. She became a journalist and her eye-witness accounts of the 1916 Rising in Dublin were among the first to be published in Britain. *A Storyteller's Childhood* (1947) is a version of her childhood which was dominated by insecurity. Lane asserts that this led to a constant search for what she lacked: '[b]elonging to a family is either an accepted fact of her fictional children's lives', or, if they are not initially part of a family, the quest for this permeates her texts. Lane continues: '[m]ost of Patricia Lynch's books end with the home – mostly physical home, but also a state of mind.'[25] Her appeal spread far outside Ireland – she published some 50 titles for children, all in Britain and the United States. Her first book was *The Green Dragon* (1925) and her final was *The Kerry Caravan* (1967). Lynch's best-known work includes *The Turf-Cutter's Donkey* (1934) and its sequels, and her 'Brogeen' books. These feature tropes favoured by Lynch: life on the bog, tinkers, leprechauns and fairy-folk, all stirred with a good dollop of whimsy and stage-Irish brogue, and frequently framed in a quest-style narrative. *Fiddler's Quest* (1941) is one of her few novels without any element of fantasy, and unusually it is not set in the Irish countryside but in Dublin city and expresses Lynch's nationalistic sympathies.

Spurred by Lynch's success, as well as by the prevailing vision of an idealized rural, Catholic nation, authors turned to writing about life in cottages and cabins in the 1930s and 1940s. Rural settings and more than a hint of brogue characterized the novels set in Ireland by Hilda van Stockum (1908–2006). Born in Rotterdam, she lived for much of her young life in Ireland, marrying an Irishman, E. R. Marlin. *The Cottage at Bantry Bay* (1938) is the first title in her series featuring the O'Sullivan family from Cork. Van Stockum, a talented artist, illustrated her own books, and her paintings feature in major collections of Irish art. Maura Laverty's (1907–66) books also gesture to a rural simplicity, combined with gentle adventures. Clair Wills's comments on Laverty's writing for adults are also true of her children's books, the best known of which is *The Cottage in the Bog* (1946): '[i]ts attractiveness undoubtedly had to do with its unbridled nostalgia for an unspoilt Ireland, the simplicity of childhood and youthful innocence, and a land of burgeoning plenty.'[26] Wills also notes that the plentiful supply of food in Laverty's fiction reinforced its attractiveness in the years of rationing, during and following the Second World War. Laverty's collection of seven fairy tales, *The Queen of Aran's Daughter* (1995), published posthumously, was illustrated by her daughter, the artist Barry Castle.

This 'homesickness for the recent past' in the 1930s and 1940s, Wills claims, contributed to the literary 'phenomenon of rural – or at any rate, village – Ireland being recycled for consumption in the cities and towns'.[27] Writing in 1946, Kenneth Reddin makes a plea for fiction that reflects more realistically the lives of Irish children, especially those in urban areas, castigating books for children which are full of pigs in the kitchen, little red hens, tinkers, ass carts, turf and 'heaps of muck';[28] pigs were not the only occupants of the kitchen in mid-twentieth century Irish children's literature – mothers were also ensconced in the domestic sphere.[29] Nevertheless, Reddin acknowledges the bucolic nostalgia demanded by the profitable British and American markets. He made an exception for the lighthearted 'Cornelius Rabbit of Tang' series by Mary Flynn (1911–84), a teacher from Co. Longford, illustrated by Eileen Coghlan who illustrated many children's books of this period. Eileen O'Faolain's (1902–88, née Gould) two 'Miss Pennyfeather' titles, *Miss Pennyfeather and the Pooka* (1940) and *Miss Pennyfeather in the Springtime* (1946) were set in Cork, O'Faolain's birthplace; while they had a fantasy element, they eschewed rural whimsy. O'Faolain's retellings, *Irish Sagas and Folktales* (1954) and *Children of the Salmon and other Irish Folktales* (1965), encouraged children to become familiar with Ireland's ancient past. Sinéad de Valera (1878–1975, née Jane O'Flanagan) also drew on Irish fairy tales and legends in her stories and plays for younger readers, many of which were written in Irish.

Rosamond Jacob (1888–1960), from a Co. Waterford Quaker family, was involved with the republican and suffragette movements, but her activism was not reflected in her only book for children, *The Raven's Glen* (1960). In a typical holiday escapist story, a group of middle-class young people holiday in Co. Wicklow, where they enjoy freedom from the constraints of everyday life. There is a mild fantasy element, but Jacob keeps this in control, and alludes to the prominent role of women in early Celtic life. Janet McNeill (1907–94) was one of the first Irish children's writers to reflect the lives of urban children. Her two books set in a dilapidated city square are realistic, if somewhat formulaic, and are in tune with her adult novels tackling disillusionment in middle-class society. The relationship between children and adults is approached perceptively in *The Battle of St. George Without* (1966) and the sequel, *Goodbye, Dove Square* (1969). McNeill was born in Dublin, but lived for most of her life in Belfast where much of her fiction is set. A journalist, adult novelist and dramatist, she wrote a number of books and plays for children. Best known are the humorous and stylistically somewhat idiosyncratic

My Friend Specs McCann (1955) and its two sequels about schoolboy Specs, which blur the boundaries of fantasy and reality.

Leeann Lane, commenting on 'the repetitive image of the "tinker" in [Patricia] Lynch's fiction', suggests that Lynch 'underscores how close life in the cottage is to life on the road'.[30] As advances were made in rural living conditions, stories featuring tinkers assumed some of the nostalgic romanticism previously nestling under cottages' thatched roofs. Brid Mahon's (1922–) *Search for the Tinker Chief* (1968) was one of several books published in the 1960s with a theme of travelling life. Mahon also wrote a number of factual books on Irish folklore for children. She was one of a number of authors who had brief forays into fiction for children, including Mary Lavin (1912–96) who wrote two children's stories, *A Likely Story* (1957) and *The Second-Best Children in the World* (1972), illustrated by the distinguished artist Edward Ardizzone.

The trope of the island adventure story in an Irish setting is largely associated with Eilís Dillon (1920–94) who published approximately forty books for children, some in Irish, over a forty-year period. Her novels vary in time, theme and setting – some are set in Italy, and her final novel, *The Children of Bach* (1993), is set in Budapest during the Nazi occupation. In most of her children's novels she interrogates life on the western seaboard of Ireland, frequently focusing on young male identity and maturation, and casting girl characters in supporting roles. Dillon first introduces the western islands in *The Lost Island* (1954), one of her earliest books, and between this and her final book in this vein, *The Island of Ghosts* (1990), there is an evident move from a straightforward island adventure story to a greater understanding of character and motivation, chiming with her development as a writer, and with a growing audience for exciting stories that offered more than obvious thrills. Commenting on this, Amanda Piesse suggests that Dillon's treatment of tradition, exploration and emigration drives her books 'into new territories of nuance in children's writing'.[31]

A growing demand for historical fiction, especially in British schools, provided a market for Madeleine A. Polland (1918–). Although born in Co. Cork, Polland lived for most of her life in England. *Fingal's Quest* (1961) begins in Ireland with a young monk's search to find his mentor, Columban, but otherwise her novels have international settings. Born in Yorkshire, Meta Mayne Reid (1905–90) lived in Northern Ireland, where she had long-established family connections and which was the setting for most of her children's books. Her reputation for well-researched historical fiction is evident in *The Two Rebels* (1969), a perceptive account of events following the 1798 Rebellion, which deals effectively with the complications of Irish politics; both rebels are Protestant, but from different social backgrounds, and in other books too, she deconstructs prevailing religious and social binaries. Her realistic fiction explores the meeting of past and present, for example in *The McNeills of Rathcappel* (1959) when from economic necessity, a family moves from a city to an old house in the country. In this and other 'Rathcappel' novels, her characters have adventures where reality and magic intertwine in a romanticized rural setting.

With *The Noguls and the Horses* (1976) Reid offers a perspective on the 'Troubles' in Northern Ireland as a result of a terrorist car-bomb attack. The 'Kevin and Sadie' quintet by Scottish-born Joan Lingard (1932–) is, however, the best known 'Troubles' fiction for children. *The Twelfth Day of July* (1970) introduces protagonists from both sides of the religious divide. The two meet as children, and over the course of the five novels, published over seven years, fall in love, marry and move to England where they find they cannot escape shadows of the Northern conflict. While its 'Romeo and Juliet' approach renders it somewhat stereotypical, the quintet has been praised for an unshrinking presentation of political enmity and violence across divided communities.[32] Drawing on a dark past, Maeve Friel (1950–2015) highlights the 'Troubles' in her first novel, *The Deerstone* (1992), and in the later, more accomplished, *Distant Voices* (1994). This nuanced ghost story captures the isolation felt by the teenage protagonist, and her desire to help the restless spirit of a young Viking she encounters as she cycles from Derry to Donegal, crossing the border between Northern Ireland and the Irish Republic. Border crossings are a recurrent theme here: borders between life and death, between light and dark (the story is set in the Hallowe'en period), and between political entities. By 2004, when Kate MacLachlan's *Love my Enemy* was published, readers were ready for a more sophisticated view of Northern Ireland, reflecting post-Peace Process Belfast. Nevertheless, it is still a romance in which the sectarian divide is breached, but the perceived differences between Protestants and Catholics are wittily – and revealingly – delineated, identifying as Keith O'Sullivan suggests, 'sex as the medium for the transcendence of inherited prejudice'.[33] Sheena Wilkinson's *Taking Flight* (2010) and its sequel, *Grounded* (2012), also broke new ground, showing that fiction set in Northern Ireland did not have to be about war or religion. Instead, tensions revolve around social class, and a young man's desperate efforts to work with the horses he loves are the focus of Wilkinson's uncompromising novels. With

Name Upon Name (2015) Wilkinson turns back to 1916 to explore religious and political tensions in Northern Ireland. Siobhan Dowd's (1960–2007) *Bog Child* (2008) interrogates attitudes in Northern Ireland during the 1980s IRA hunger strikes through the eyes of her 18-year-old protagonist. Dowd skilfully pulls together strands that include the hunger strikes, the unearthing of a first-century bog body and a young man's effort to establish an identity apart from that delineated by the old tribal tensions, revealing the complexities of growing up in Ireland in the 1980s, on either side of the border.

Emer O'Sullivan comments '[t]here is scarcely another European literature whose level of involvement in the production of reading matter for its young was so slight as was Ireland's up until the 1980s. Before then, children's literature was almost exclusively imported'.[34] In the 1980s, however, changes in the school curriculum introduced in the 1970s began to have effect, in particular with a demand for Irish fiction. The Arts Council (ROI) offered grants to encourage writing and publishing for children, and children's literature organizations established awards for Irish authors and illustrators.

Changes in the curriculum meant that schools were now hungry for books with historical themes, and there was a demand for children's books set in contemporary Ireland.[35] The newly established Children's Press responded with the first of Carolyn Swift's (1923–2002) 'Robber' series, *Robbers in the House* (1981), in which a group of children outwit robbers in various Dublin locations. The *Big Guide to Irish Children's Books* (1996) lists thirteen children's publishers, including four publishing in Irish. The *Guide* also names approximately fifty women writing for young people, and the second *Big Guide* (2000) adds more names.[36] Fewer than half of these are now writing and the number of publishers has shrunk considerably. Marita Conlon-McKenna (1956–) with *Under the Hawthorne Tree* (1991) showed that an Irish children's book could become an international as well as a national success in the first of her 'Famine' trilogy which charts the fortunes of three orphaned children from famine-devastated Ireland to better times in the United States. For most of the twentieth century the Famine, and other episodes in Irish history – the 1916 Rebellion, the War of Independence and the Civil War – had been too sensitive for children's books. Now the barriers were down and a slew of publications about these events resulted.[37]

While hitherto taboo events could now feature in books for young readers, both writers and publishers still felt the constraints of a conservative library and schools market in the 1990s. Celia Keenan comments that 'Irish children's writers can be broadly divided in those who see it as their duty to protect children and to transmit heritage, and those who wish to liberate children from the burden of the past and embrace modernity.'[38] Although specifically referencing Joan O'Neill's *Daisy Chain War* (1990), Pádraic Whyte's assertion that O'Neill's text constructs 'a childhood past and a collective past for the child reader, imbuing both the public and the personal with a sense of nostalgia that is often associated with heritage' could apply to other historical fiction set in Ireland.[39] *Daisy Chain War* features Lizzie, a young girl growing up in Dublin during the Second World War. This was the first in a series of four novels that, mainly through Lizzie's voice, charts social changes in Ireland. Marilyn Taylor (1940–) who had earlier published a trilogy featuring girls growing up in contemporary Dublin, focused on the Second World War with the little-known story of Jewish children who came to Northern Ireland from Germany on the *kinder transport* in *Faraway Home* (1999), and Taylor explores Jewish life in central Dublin during the same war in *17 Martin Street* (2011).

Writing as Elizabeth O'Hara, Éilís Ní Dhuibhne (1954–) in her 'Sally' trilogy also examines a subject about which little has been written for children – the lives of working women in Ireland. *The Hiring Fair* (1993) begins in the 1890s and the trilogy concludes in the early days of the twentieth century. Sally Gallagher is 'bought' for domestic service at a hiring fair in Donegal, but dreams of better things, eventually becoming a governess in Dublin. The third book highlights the benefits of education for young women, as Sally establishes her career and becomes involved with the Gaelic League and cultural life at the *fin de siècle*. Siobhán Parkinson's (1954–) *Amelia* (1993) and *No Peace for Amelia* (1994) describe the life of a young Quaker girl living in Dublin prior to and during the 1916 Rebellion. Boys tend to be the protagonists in Morgan Llywelyn's (1937–) historical novels, including *Strongbow* (1992). *The Young Rebels* (2006) is set in Padraic Pearse's St Enda's School in the 1913–16 period, where, unlike other writers who strive for 'balance' in their historical fiction, she is unequivocal in her sympathy for those involved with the Rebellion.

Irish writers in the early 1990s were also beginning to produce realistic fiction which explored the lives of older children and young adults; Kate Thompson (1956–) does this by blending fantasy with realism in her 1990s 'Switchers' trilogy about two Dublin teenagers who have the ability to shape-shift. Subsequently, Thompson has drawn on Celtic mythology and music to explore ecological issues with *The New Policeman*

(2005) and its sequels, and in the poignant teen romance *Annan Water* (2004). Thompson's other work ranges from historical fantasy to science fiction, and with *Creature of the Night* (2008) she examines young male anxieties against a backdrop of Irish folklore, entwining urban dystopia with a dark primitivism still lingering in her rural Co. Clare.

Ita Daly, Bernadette Leech, Geraldine Mitchell and Joan O'Neill were among the authors published in the 1990s by Attic Press, a Cork University Press imprint, in the 'Bright Sparks' series, focusing on realistic fiction for teenage girls set in Ireland. Other publishers too began to produce books in tune with the experiences of Irish young people. Margrit Cruickshank's (1942–) *Circling the Triangle* (1991) was one of the first Irish-published novels to focus on frustrations of an Irish teenage male. Its alternative endings acknowledge the uncertainties of adolescent life, which she also deals with in *The Door* (1996). Cruickshank has also written picturebooks and the S.K.U.N.K series of popular adventure stories. Jane Mitchell (1965–) tackled the gruelling after-effects of alcohol abuse and joy-riding in *When Stars Stop Spinning* (1993) and homelessness in *Different Lives* (1996). More recently she has written about boy soldiers fighting in Kashmir in *Chalkline* (2009). Marita Conlon-McKenna addressed issues faced by the travelling community in *The Blue Horse* (1992), which attracted mild controversy for being too politically correct,[40] and children in institutional care feature in her *A Girl Called Blue* (2003). For Siobhán Parkinson, Ireland's first Children's Laureate, Irish childhood has been a recurring theme. She looks at what happens to children when marriages break down in a witty play on the Cinderella story in *Sisters ... No Way!* (1996). Parkinson, who also writes for adults, frequently experiments both thematically and with the novel form, and neglected children are her focus in *Bruised* (2010) and *Heart Shaped* (2013).

Éilís Ní Dhuibhne's *Hurlamaboc* (2006), published in English under her pen-name of Elizabeth O'Hara, as *Snobs, Dogs and Scobies* (2011), focuses in her typically spare style, on three well-realized urban Dublin teenagers as they prepare for their school Leaving Certificate. Although her coming-of-age novel, *The Dancers Dancing* (1999), was published for adults, it is now considered as a young adult text, a sign of how the parameters of what constitutes young adult literature have changed in Ireland. Siobhan Dowd's first young adult novel, *A Swift Pure Cry* (2006) is set in Co. Cork in the 1980s, but, like *Bog Child*, would have been an unlikely publication for young readers then. Based on two infamous cases in 1984 involving pregnant young single women (one was still a school girl) and the deaths of their babies,[41] it offers chilling insights into attitudes towards women and reproduction. *Solace of the Road* (2009) returns to the theme of maternal loss and its consequences. Dowd's three young adult novels may be regarded as landmark texts in Irish children's literature, because of the excellence of her writing, and because they anticipated a shift in what is considered appropriate for young readers.

Several picturebook creators write their own text, including former Children's Laureate Niamh Sharkey (1972–), best-known for her *Ravenous Beast* (2004). Through a combination of text and image, Marie-Louise Fitzpatrick (1962–) explores situations such as that of a small child who wonders what it will be like when she is 'there' in *There* (2008), and *The Long March* (1997) where she recounts for older readers the story of the Choctaw tribe's empathy with Irish famine victims. Recently she has published several realistic/fantasy novels, including *Timecatcher* (2010) and *Hagwitch* (2013).

The twenty-first century has seen Irish women's writing for young people emerge from big houses and bogland cottages to address serious themes and to experiment with form. Fantasy is still a popular genre, but changes in Irish society, including same sex partnerships, sexual and domestic violence and changes in family structures as well as issues of international concern, are all addressed by Irish women writers for younger readers, who explore the Irish social and cultural landscape, reflecting many aspects of childhood, real and imagined.

Notes

1 Anne Markey, 'Irish Children's Books 1696–1810: Importation, Exportation and the Beginnings of Irish Children's Literature', in *Children's Literature Collections: Approaches to Research*, ed. Keith O'Sullivan and Pádraic Whyte (London: Palgrave Macmillan, 2016), 33–52; M. O. Grenby, *The Child Reader 1700–1840* (Cambridge: Cambridge University Press, 2011), 1–4.

2 See Grenby, *The Child Reader*; Lissa Paul, *The Children's Book Business: Lessons from the Long Eighteenth Century* (New York & Abingdon: Routledge, 2011).

3 See Mary Pollard, *A Dictionary of Members of the Dublin Book Trade 1550–1800. Based on the Records of the Guild of St Luke the Evangelist, Dublin* (London: Bibliographical Society, 2000).

4 Toby Barnard, 'Children and Books in Eighteenth Century Ireland', in *That Woman! Studies on Irish Bibliography. A Festschrift for Mary 'Paul' Pollard*, ed. Charles Benson and Siobhán Fitzpatrick (Dublin: Lilliput Press, 2005), 218–21. Sharon Murphy notes a strong impetus towards education and improvement with the overarching aim of supporting the social order with regard to gender, class and race: Sharon Murphy, *Maria Edgeworth and Romance* (Dublin: Four Courts Press, 2004), 44–5.

5 Norma Clarke, '"The Cursed Barbauld Crew:" Women Writers and Writing for Children in the Late Eighteenth Century', in *Opening the Nursery Door: Reading, Writing and Childhood 1600–1900*, ed. Mary Hilton, Morag Styles and Victor Watson (London: Routledge, 1997).

6 Barnard, 'Children and Books in Eighteenth Century Ireland', 266.

7 See Ciara Ní Bhroin, 'A Divided Union: Reformation and Reconciliation in Maria Edgeworth's *Orlandino*', in *Divided Worlds: Studies in Children's Literature*, ed. Mary Shine Thompson and Valerie Coghlan (Dublin: Four Courts Press, 2007), 22–31.

8 See Murphy, *Maria Edgeworth*, 69, and Grenby, *The Child Reader*, 55.

9 Anne Markey, 'Irish Children's Fiction, 1727–1820', *Irish University Review* 41, no. 1 (2011): 126–8.

10 Anne Markey, ed., *Children's Fiction 1765–1808* (Dublin: Four Courts Press, 2011), 18–19.

11 Titles of books commonly read by children attending hedge schools are listed in Antonia McManus, *The Irish Hedge School 1695–1831* (Dublin: Four Courts Press, 2002). For further information about the Kildare Place Society see Susan Parkes, *The Kildare Place Society* (Dublin: CICE Publications, 2011).

12 Marian Thérèse Keyes, 'Paratexts and Gender Politics: A Study of Selected Works by Anna Maria Fielding Hall', in *Politics and Ideology in Children's Literature*, ed. Marian Thérèse Keyes and Áine McGillicuddy (Dublin: Four Courts Press, 2014), 142–4.

13 See Robert Dunbar, 'Rebuilding Castle Blair: A Reading of Flora Shaw's 1878 Children's Novel', in *Studies in Children's Literature 1500–2000*, ed. Celia Keenan and Mary Shine Thompson (Dublin: Four Courts Press, 2004), 31–7.

14 Robert Dunbar suggests *The Weans of Rowallan* 'inaugurates a tradition in Ulster children's fiction whereby its over-riding concern is with territory, with land, with ownership and expropriation'. He also comments on the book's incorporation of Ulster vocabulary and idiom. '"It's the Way We Tell 'em:" Voices from Ulster Children's Fiction', in *Divided Worlds*, ed. Shine Thompson and Coghlan, 65, 64.

15 This and the work of Ethel Coghill Penrose is discussed in more detail by Julie Anne Stevens in 'The Little Big House: Somerville and Ross's Work for Children', in *Divided Worlds*, ed. Shine Thompson and Coghlan, 41–9.

16 Ibid., 43.

17 Pádraic Whyte, 'Children's Literature', in *The Oxford History of the Irish Book. Vol. IV: The Irish Book in English, 1800–1891*, ed. James H. Murphy (Oxford: Oxford University Press, 2011), 524–5.

18 In 1884 the Royal University (later the National University) conferred degrees on female students for the first time. In 1904 female students were first admitted to Trinity College Dublin.

19 Volumes 1–6, from 1887 to 1892.

20 Carole Dunbar, 'The Wild Irish Girls of L. T. Meade and Mrs George De Horne Vaizey', in *Studies in Children's Literature 1500–2000*, ed. Keenan

and Shine Thompson, 42; Tina O'Toole, *The Irish New Woman* (London: Palgrave Macmillan, 2013), 66.

21 Kimberley Reynolds, *Girls Only? Gender and Popular Juvenile Fiction in Britain 1880–1910* (Hemel Hempstead: Harvester Wheatsheaf, 1990), 14–15.

22 Declan Kiberd, *Inventing Ireland: The Literature of the Modern Nation* (London: Jonathan Cape, 1995), 25.

23 Colette Epplé, '"Wild Irish with a Vengeance": Definitions of Irishness in Katharine Tynan's Children's Literature', in *Divided Worlds*, ed. Shine Thompson and Coghlan, 33, 40.

24 Leeann Lane, '"In My Mind I Build a House": The Quest for Family in the Children's Fiction of Patricia Lynch', *Éire-Ireland* 44, nos. 1–2 (2009): 186.

25 Ibid., 179–80.

26 Clair Wills, 'Neutrality and Popular Culture', in *The Art of Popular Culture: From 'The Meeting of the Waters' to Riverdance*, ed. P. J. Mathews (Dublin: UCDscholarcast, 2008) (Series 1), 5. Accessed 22 February 2016. www.ucd.ie/scholarcast/transcripts/Neutrality_Popular_Culture.pdf.

27 Ibid., 9.

28 Kenneth Reddin, 'Children's Books in Ireland. Were We All Brought Up Behind a Half-door?' *Irish Library Bulletin* 7 (1946): 74.

29 Catholic social thinking, reinforced in the 1937 Constitution, defined women's place as in the home. *Bunreacht na hÉireann*, Articles 41.1 and 41.2.

30 Lane, 'In My Mind I Build a House', 178.

31 A. J. Piesse, 'Islands, Ireland and the Changing State of Writing for Children', in *Treasure Islands. Studies in Children's Literature*, ed. Mary Shine Thompson and Celia Keenan (Dublin: Four Courts Press, 2006), 154.

32 Kate Agnew, 'The Troubled Fiction of the "Troubles" in Northern Ireland: Focus on Joan Lingard and Catherine Sefton', in *The Big Guide 2: Irish Children's Books*, ed. Valerie Coghlan and Celia Keenan (Dublin: Children's Books Ireland, 2000), 116.

33 Keith O'Sullivan, '"Binding with Briars:" Romanticizing the Child', in *Irish Children's Literature and Culture: New Perspectives on Contemporary Writing*, ed. Valerie Coghlan and Keith O'Sullivan (London: Routledge, 2011), 101.

34 Emer O'Sullivan, *Comparative Children's Literature* (London: Routledge, 2005), 58.

35 For more on this see: Jeremy Addis, 'Publishing for Children in Ireland', in *The Big Guide to Irish Children's Books*, ed. Valerie Coghlan and Celia Keenan (Dublin: Irish Children's Books Trust, 1996), 14–19; Valerie Coghlan, 'Ireland', in *The International Companion Encyclopaedia of Children's Literature*, 2nd ed., ed. Peter Hunt (London: Routledge, 2004), 2: 1099–1103; Valerie Coghlan, 'Questions of Identity and Otherness in Irish Writing for Young People', *Neohelicon* 36, no. 1 (2009); Emer O'Sullivan, 'Insularity and Internationalism: Between Local Production and the Global Marketplace', in *Irish Children's Literature and Culture*, ed. Coghlan and O'Sullivan, 183–96.

36 Valerie Coghlan and Celia Keenan, eds., *The Big Guide to Irish Children's Books* (Dublin: Irish Children's Books Trust, 1996); Valerie Coghlan and Celia Keenan, eds., *The Big Guide 2: Irish Children's Books* (Dublin: Children's Books Ireland, 2000). Approximately the same number of male authors are listed.

37 See Celia Keenan, 'The Famine Told to the Children', in *The Big Guide 2*, ed. Coghlan and Keenan, 69–79.

38 Celia Keenan, 'Maeve Friel', in *Irish Children's Writers and Illustrators. A Selection of Essays 1986–2006*, ed. Valerie Coghlan and Siobhán Parkinson (Dublin: Children's Books Ireland and CICE Publications, 2007), 49. Keenan contextualizes this with reference to Maeve Friel's writing.

39 Pádraic Whyte, *Irish Childhoods: Children's Fiction and Irish History* (Newcastle upon Tyne: Cambridge Scholars Publishing, 2011), 53.

40 Eilís O'Hanlon, 'What Shall We Tell the Children?' *The Irish Times*, 8 May 1993, and Bláithín Gallagher, 'Sexing the Bisto', *Children's Books Ireland*, no. 9 (1993), 15.

41 See Valerie Coghlan, '"A Homesick Love:" Emigrant Echoes of Maternal Loss in the Novels of Siobhan Dowd', in *Children's Literature on the Move: Nations, Translations, Migrations*, ed. Nora Maguire and Beth Rodgers (Dublin: Four Courts Press, 2013), 87–99; and various essays in *Irish Children's Literature and Culture*.

CHAPTER 9

Poetry, 1920–1970

Lucy Collins

The middle generation of modern Irish poets, writing between the 1930s and the 1960s, is often marginalized in accounts of twentieth-century poetry. Critical consensus identifies two high points in Ireland's modern literary history: the years of the Irish Revival, from the 1880s to the foundation of the state; and the period from 1970 onwards, a particularly rich time for poetry, both in the Republic and in Northern Ireland. This view has led not only to critical neglect of the poetry of the mid-century years but also to its unavailability to readers: apart from the work of a small number of key figures, little of Ireland's poetic output during this time remains in print. This neglect affected women poets with particular intensity, in part because poetry was becoming a specialist area of publishing and reading, and women constituted a minority of those writing in Ireland. But there were other reasons too. Anne Mulhall notes that the reputation of women writing during this period has 'fallen victim to the particular political investments involved in the construction of an Irish national culture'.[1] The absence of this generation of women poets from later anthologies has radically distorted the history, not only of Irish women's writing, but also of modern Irish poetry itself.[2]

This chapter seeks to reconsider some of these critical assumptions by exploring the work of five women poets from the period, highlighting not only their literary achievements, but also the creative challenges they faced. All these women worked in more than one genre, demonstrating both their formal versatility and the need to make good use of the creative opportunities afforded them. Mary Devenport O'Neill (1879–1967) wrote both drama and poetry. As the wife of Joseph O'Neill, who was a poet and senior civil servant, she moved in literary circles and knew both W. B. Yeats and Æ (George William Russell). Originally trained as a painter, she was an acutely observant poet and

167

her output, though slight, marked a decisive turn towards modern diction. Blanaid Salkeld (1880–1959) also had experience of different art forms. First known as an actress, Salkeld's theatre projects involved both English and Irish language work. The most formally experimental of Irish women poets, she published her first collection at the age of fifty-three. Though her early work was printed in England, the increasingly *avant-garde* nature of her poetry made it difficult for her to find commercial publishers, and in 1937 she co-founded the Gayfield Press in Dublin, which went on to publish an eclectic range of work. This pattern of moving between British and Irish publishers was true of Sheila Wingfield (1906–92) too, whose later work appeared with Liam Miller's Dolmen Press. Wingfield had a privileged upbringing in England, but her marriage to the heir to the Powerscourt estate strengthened her links with Ireland. Though Wingfield's austere poems were praised by critics, she remained on the margins of Irish literary circles. Freda Laughton (1907–?), another poet whose work attracted critical attention, even before her first – and only – collection appeared, was ground breaking in her representation of women's lived experience. Her exploration of the dynamics of human connection and alienation revealed the extent to which women's cultural marginalization could be productive of unique explorations in poetry. A similar degree of innovation can be found in the work of Rhoda Coghill (1903–2000). Coghill, the only one of these poets to publish exclusively in Ireland, was particularly attentive to poetic soundscapes. Better known as a composer and musician than as a poet, Coghill was another woman of great artistic originality whose work was soon forgotten.

These five figures are linked not just by their gender but also by their willingness to challenge the society in which they lived, and to subvert traditional literary modes. Though each woman presented a unique creative vision, their work registered the cultural limitations of mid-century Ireland and the anxieties shared by these poets regarding their reception and literary legacy. The representation of contrasting states of illumination and obscurity in these poems highlights the significance of inspiration even in an environment inhospitable to women's creativity. Uncertain relationships remind us that the poet's practice is essentially a solitary one, and emphasize the contingent nature of artistic affiliations. Yet in spite of these obstacles, women poets from the period pursued their own individual creative goals and made a distinctive contribution to modern Irish culture, which should now be fully acknowledged.

Writing and Publishing in the Irish Free State

The revolutionary period had a deep and lasting effect on Ireland's cultural identity. Though the foundation of the Irish Free State in 1922 was the political realization of a larger movement of Irish cultural nationalism, Ireland's literary development after 1922 did not live up to the promise of the Revival years. It was compromised by the difficult conditions of the time – by economic depression and the challenges of state formation – as well as by the bitter legacy of revolution and civil war. The popularity of poetry declined during this period, reflecting the increased preference for fiction among readers internationally. Many Irish poets, including women, who had built their early reputations in the Revivalist mode, continued to write in this style, but interest from readers both in Ireland and abroad was waning. Debates on the future of Irish poetry centred on a key aesthetic question: should poets build on Revivalist practices and continue to exploit the resources of myth and folklore, or should they prioritize formal innovation and international affinities as a means to distance themselves from the English literary tradition? This was, in many ways, a false binary, since it assumed that writers could be clearly identified with one strategy or the other. In reality, the testing of creative possibilities meant that innovation took many different forms during this period, and even apparently conservative texts sought to breathe new life into established traditions.

As though anticipating later critical neglect, poets and commentators of the time expressed anxiety about the limitations of the Irish literary scene. Such concerns may derive at least in part from the diversity of work produced at this time: the high point of cultural nationalism had passed and there was no particular cause to animate the writers of this generation. Such a deficiency cast doubts on the potential of these poets to produce lasting work and prompted critics to view this as a crisis of artistic inheritance, which could be understood in exclusively male terms. Women poets were disadvantaged by the prevailing social and cultural structures, and their access to readers and audiences for their work was limited. Literary culture was overwhelmingly masculine in character – male writers, editors and journalists dominated debates, both in conversation and in print, and no attention was given by them to the contribution that women might make to the future of Irish letters.[3] Critical anxieties were exacerbated by the lack of publishing opportunities for Irish poetry during this period: Cuala Press, though a significant contributor to the history of modern hand press printing, was committed to limited, high-quality editions; Maunsel Press, which published early collections by a number of significant poets from the mid-century years – including Padraic Colum and Austin Clarke – ceased production in 1926.

Nor was poetry well served in Irish newspaper and periodical culture. The *Irish Homestead* and the *Irish Statesman* continued in production into the Free State years, but poetry did not play a major part in either publication. *The Bell*, by contrast, saw literature as foundational to Irish identity and poetry as 'the most national of the arts ... its colouring must be distinctive'.[4] Sean O'Faoláin, founding editor of *The Bell*, wanted present realities to shape the ethos and content of the magazine, but for Geoffrey Taylor, who took over from Frank O'Connor as poetry editor in July 1941, aesthetic issues were more important than political ones.[5] Despite the strong emphasis on contemporary debate, the editors – in the words of Kelly Matthews – 'failed to challenge the patriarchal structure of mid-twentieth-century society'.[6] *The Bell* published just three women poets in the course of its fourteen-year history. The publication that was most hospitable to women poets was the *Dublin Magazine*, edited by Seumas O'Sullivan – Mary Devenport O'Neill, Sheila Wingfield and Rhoda Coghill were among its contributors.[7] Though viewed negatively by many of the younger writers emerging during the Free State years, the *Dublin Magazine* was a significant literary presence, especially in the 1930s, when economic and cultural decline were especially marked.

The Censorship of Publications Act, passed in 1929, contributed significantly to the limitations of the period. Though few books of poems were among the 1,193 publications banned in the course of the 1930s, the narrowing of artistic horizons led many writers to leave Ireland during these years.[8] This, in turn, impoverished Irish literary culture: Æ found inbreeding to be one of the greatest threats to artistic life. Yet, though editors of the time were committed to resisting the worst excesses of censorship, there was no corresponding desire to reduce the social and political restrictions that curtailed the lives of women at this time. The intense disapproval of sexuality, and the identification of women with their reproductive function, meant that female creativity was channelled into the domestic sphere, making the development of a public role and the exercise of artistic freedom difficult. This tendency was not only evident in Ireland, however. In the British context, Jan Montefiore notes the 'lingering notion of women as private creatures living apart from the public sphere inhabited by male politicians and intellectuals'.[9] This perception can be traced in the reviewing culture of the time, which resisted experimentation by women poets.

In an effort to redress these limitations, women created their own networks and associations in order to support and promote their writing. In 1933, Blanaid Salkeld and Dorothy Macardle founded the Irish Women Writers' Club and its inclusive approach, combining the work of historians and journalists as well as that of poets and fiction writers, testifies to their interest in intellectual breadth. The group gathered regularly and awarded annual prizes for significant achievements by women writers. Though national newspapers, such as the *Irish Times*, covered these events – to which both men and women were invited – they remained essentially separate from the literary mainstream and have received little attention from scholars.[10] Their dependence on circumstance made these women uniquely responsive to social and political environments. Realizing that conventional expectations could only be met by the suppression of creative innovation, many women adopted various literary identities by combining the writing of drama, popular fiction, non-fiction and stories for children, with poetry.[11]

In the course of this process, women poets sought to challenge simplified ideas of national identity and looked for new ways of recording political and personal change. They recognized the need to attend to the role of subjectivity in shaping language, and in turn to the capacity of that language to articulate the experiences of women. Artistic achievement and its legacy became key preoccupations for these women poets; changing modes of self-representation, reflected both in form and subject matter in the poems, revealed uncertainties concerning the status and reception of their work. These women predicted their own disappearance from the canon of Irish writing, a disappearance that has obscured the depth and diversity of their creative talents. Embracing engagement with music and the visual arts as well as a range of languages, histories and cultures far beyond the Irish context, these poets reflected the cosmopolitanism of second-wave modernism in Ireland, at the same time as they spoke of the limitations of its publishing and reading cultures. Attention to their work not only enriches the artistic legacy of the period, but also illuminates a series of complex individual achievements.

A Modernist Gaze: Mary Devenport O'Neill

Mary Devenport O'Neill is an exemplary figure in her representation of the varied cultural challenges facing the woman poet in the early years of the Irish Free State. Born in Loughrea, Co. Galway, she moved to Dublin at the age of nineteen to study at the Dublin Metropolitan School of Art. During this time she became interested in literature, and her skills

as a painter are reflected in her earliest poems.[12] They account for the
'minuteness of insight' noted by an early reviewer,[13] and can be traced too
in the significance of the act of looking, especially at landscapes.[14] Laura
Pomeroy has argued that Devenport O'Neill's response to nature is a contingent one; that she resists identification with nature in favour of 'a focus
on fragmented conceptual frameworks rather than ideas of wholeness
and transcendence'.[15] The resistance to wholeness is also a rejection of the
sentimental that sets Devenport O'Neill apart from poets of the earlier
generation, for whom nature often figured as a restorative power.

Devenport O'Neill had close connections to other writers and artists
and, like many women of her generation, found these networks to be an
important part of her creative development. Her associations with W. B.
Yeats and Æ can be traced to their background in the visual arts but are
indicative of the affinities between different intellectual and artistic circles
in the Dublin of the time. Though her output was small, all her poems
are richly observant of states of mind and articulate the relationship
between the mood of the speaker and her surroundings. This highlights
the importance of the poetic environment as a marker of the creative
mind, at once facilitating its exploration and curtailing its freedoms.
Devenport O'Neill's poetry aspires to heightened experience and understanding, yet it almost invariably describes a process of disappointment,
since what is sought never materializes. These texts try to deflect the feelings of emptiness that this experience prompts. The poem 'Expectation'
at first disavows need – 'I wish for nothing,' the speaker asserts – but the
single stanza with its oscillation of long and short lines tells otherwise.[16]
The act of waiting for a momentous event occurs in a banal present,
which is continuous yet seems to be approaching breaking point, invoking simultaneously the stress of both change and changelessness. The sky
watched by the speaker is a 'monotonous revolving grey', at once unvary-
ing and subject to the Earth's rotations.[17] In looking to the sky for revelation the speaker indicates the hope of transcendence, and registers the
inspirational power of light. The tension of the poem is built around the
opposition between the knowledge that there will be no such revelation,
and the persistent 'hope' of change:

> I know there's nothing,
> But still I use
> Knowledge and reason only as a cloak
> To muffle my preposterous hope –
> A ruse
> To hoodwink some all-cunning eye[18]

The deceptively simple rhyme scheme of the poem weaves these positions together. Half rhymes yield to full rhymes, sometimes alternating, sometimes paired – the halting pace of the poem expresses its oscillating moods. The text's return to its own beginning suggests the cyclical nature of the process, though its final two lines, which indicate the coming of night and the conclusion of the speaker's vigil, also mark the end of hope, at least for a time.

The fluctuating moods of this poem are typical of Devenport O'Neill's work as a whole, in which the dynamics of pride and shame, expectation and disappointment are always in play. This creates a series of unresolved tensions that obliquely express the difficult position of the woman poet in this period of Irish history – inspired to write yet without any certainty of acceptance. For Devenport O'Neill this instability is almost always suggested by the trope of a search, a process that involves a heightened sensitivity to the world in which experiences are magnified: 'It seems to me / I live perpetually / On the cloudy edge of the sound of a bell / For ever listening,' begins 'The Bell'.[19] Caught between memory and anticipation, the poet is unable to live in the present; her contingent state is indicative of a necessary vigilance in the face of change. Devenport O'Neill's poems express a complex temporality: seasonal and diurnal changes are indicated by the dynamics of light and darkness that link mood and sensory experience in fundamental ways. Illumination is always transient: by 'catch[ing] the bars of light' in 'Wishes', the speaker at once articulates her aspirations and confirms their ephemeral nature.[20] Adding these wishes to the path of the blackbirds' flight and the shifting tones of a field at twilight, the poet declares her willingness to 'dissolve' her own desires before reality threatens them. This willingness to participate in, or even pre-empt, her own future disappointment suggests significant anxiety concerning her role as an artist.

Devenport O'Neill's economies of language reflect the creative self's struggle to hold her place in the world. Though time moves slowly, its trajectory is toward dissolution, making memories more imaginatively powerful than projected futures. The poem 'Falling' unites past and present, drawing the speaker into a pattern of constant recollection: 'all there is to do / Is to recall / Thoughts of things that fall / And watch them falling'.[21] Progression is impeded by this retrospection, which unites philosophical contemplation of fallen human nature with the immediacy of the physical world. It is not clear whether an act of present witness prompts these recollections, or whether the past is made real again through memory, and this ambiguity increases the temporal complexity of the work. The merging of the concept and its manifestation draws attention to the relationship between thought and experience, but repetition and containment also express the imaginative limitations of the period in formal terms. Devenport O'Neill's compact oeuvre reflects both her artistic potential and her decisive break with late Revivalism. It signals too the necessity for innovation, not only as a means to engage with wider political and aesthetic changes, but as a way of confronting the specific challenges that women writers faced at this time.

Experimental Forms: Blanaid Salkeld

The formal challenges marked by Devenport O'Neill's work would be taken up by a number of other women poets over the ensuing decades. Blanaid Salkeld was the most radical of these figures, both in the evolving experimentalism of her poetry, and in her engagement with a range of disciplines and cultural contexts. Born in Chittagong, then part of India, Salkeld developed an early interest in poetry, but it was not until she returned to Ireland after the death of her husband, that she became involved in Irish literary circles. Publishing her first collection in 1933, when she was fifty-three years old, Salkeld brought to this process a sophistication of craft and a resistance to conventional lyric modes. This resistance, together with the layering of international influences, has made her work difficult to categorize. Moynagh Sullivan has noted its 'rogue energy ... philosophical restlessness ... and irreverence', all qualities that effectively marginalized Salkeld within the poetry cultures of the time.[22] Her transnationalism was also a crucial point of difference from many of her peers. It emphasized the degree to which she was influenced by her childhood in India – through a writer like Tagore, who was a family friend – as well as by work from Eastern Europe, which she read and reviewed as an adult. Though her first volume, *Hello Eternity!* was positively reviewed, most notably by Samuel Beckett, the full potential of this debut was not recognized, nor could it be realized within the contracting spaces available to Irish women poets in the mid-century years.

Most of the evidence for Salkeld's formal ambition can be gleaned from within the spaces of the poems themselves. Unlike Devenport O'Neill, Salkeld emphasizes the richness of language and complexity of syntax, even as she acknowledges the powerful dynamics of fixed form. The poem 'Absence' is in marked contrast to the sparseness of Devenport O'Neill's aesthetic; it depicts a dynamic self, energized rather than trapped by iambic lines with running rhymes: 'Absence our freedom guilelessly disowns. / On this green sward, this noon, in Spring's clear air – / Flesh tossed aside – our will and thought in hiding'.[23] The rhyming couplet at the centre of the poem (bones … monotones) slows its headlong rush of continuous presence (trembling, rattling, gleaming) at the very moment when the dance of freedom is first explicitly proposed. Both body and intellect are pushed aside, to allow a state of primal innocence to be resumed – to sustain the promise of 'Spring's clear air', these ties must at least be momentarily rejected:

> Yoked to one plough, two horses, you and I –
> Turn Time's soil up behind us, tired advance,
> Side-blinded, blinkered. Absence each bemoans
> From each – gaze set upon Eternity….
> Unlinked by absence, let us strip and prance –
> Come, let us dance here in our innocent bones!
> Absence chains each to each with swaying groans.[24]

Though the subject and her companion move through life together, their failure to connect renders their proximity meaningless. The need to break those restrictions and to find a way of expressing the self to the self – as well as to the other – is a way of asserting human presence against the dehumanizing processes of routine. It also sees the text of the poem as the 'dance' that facilitates connection, moving beyond instrumental language to acknowledge the power of associative expression.

Though the formal developments of modernism offered new creative possibilities for Salkeld, these are often measured against feelings of restriction. In 'Adamant', she considers the dichotomy of freedom and containment, though here the speaker claims to have experienced liberty: 'So, Tyrant, I'll not have you set me free. / Strike not a fetter off. For, liberty / I sampled well.'[25] The ironic acceptance of restraint in preference to 'bright / Unpeopled desolation' suggests an artistic need for discipline, in preference to the 'emptiness and liberty' lamented in another poem from this period, 'Even the Carollers'.[26] Change is necessary, and even the intense pleasure of creativity cannot compensate for an unknowable future. The energies of reinvention are strong in this, Salkeld's first volume, but postponement beyond the frame of the single life or the single poem leads to greater innovation. For her next volume, *The Fox's Covert* (1935), she began to experiment with the form of the sequence, here comprising 163 poems, and characterized by pronounced formal and thematic transitions.

The act of witness, even of revelation, exerts an important shaping force on these poems: between world and body, between earth and air,

new perspectives are generated. Salkeld's unflinching interrogation of
the process of writing is closely linked to these shifts in both physical
and emotional space. As an actor and playwright, she was attuned to the
improvisatory character of performance, and her work was motivated
by the need to challenge inherited forms. Her engagement with print
culture also marked the need to address the presentation of innovative
language. Together with her son, Cecil French Salkeld, she set up the
Gayfield Press in 1937, and this initiative would prove an important
vehicle for her own poetry.[27] Gayfield's *Poets and Artists* series created
a space where she could think further about the relationship between
poetry and the visual arts, and the power of the gaze in shaping the
dynamics of self and world. Obscurity remained an important visual
trope for Salkeld, and in the darkness and light of her poetry the difficulty of seeing things clearly is registered. In 'Homing Joys', a poem
from the late 1940s, the importance of full sensory perception is realized.
Its opening lines highlight the power of sound through the restriction of
sight:

> Fog distances the trees; the rest is lost.
> A gull swims by: there is no breath for flight.
> Why is my mind all music? – left and right,
> Metals are smitten, strings plucked, and the ghost
> Of joy vapours through pipe and reed.[28]

After this ghostly scene, a spark of creativity ignites at the centre of the
sonnet; its resolving sestet answers the call for a sign. The creative urge
must not be wasted, Salkeld suggests, but continually nurtured in the
hope of future inspiration. This openness to new aesthetic possibilities
was a hallmark of Salkeld's poetic career, confirming the process of writing, as much as its completion, to be a sustaining feature in the lives of
these women.

Between States: Sheila Wingfield

The complex intersection of influences that shaped Salkeld's poetry, was
shared – at least in part – by Sheila Wingfield. Wingfield's privileged
upbringing in England facilitated her early reading: from her teenage
years onwards, she had an interest in the classics and in history, and these
sustained her imaginatively as she began to write. In 1932, she married Mervyn Patrick Wingfield, heir to the Powerscourt estate in Co.
Wicklow, and by this time her writing habits were already established,

despite her father's disapproval of her literary interests. Her first collection, published in 1938, reveals her formal versatility. Displaying
imagistic tendencies, but also an interest in narrative history, the volume
exemplifies the objectivist qualities Alex Davis would later trace in her
oeuvre as a whole.[29] In short poems, including the three-line 'Winter' –
as well as in longer works such as 'Chosroe the Second' – Wingfield
worked hard to realize clarity of diction, emphasizing sincerity without
personal revelation: 'The tree still bends over the lake, / And I try to
remember our love, / Our love which had a thousand leaves'.[30] Early
commentators picked up on these qualities, but often interpreted them
according to gender norms. Mona Gooden, for example, argued that
Wingfield 'achieves a fine balance of intellect and feeling, without sacrificing one to the other, that is rare in women poets'.[31]

For personal as well as cultural reasons, Wingfield's early work was
shadowed by death, as poems such as 'Odysseus Dying', 'Chosroe the
Second' and 'The Dead' demonstrate.[32] Yet the stillness, which is so often
to be found at the centre of her work, belies its subtly turbulent character;
this disparity between the observed reality and the inner life is both an
important theme and an enduring formal strategy in the poetry, as the
early 'Sonnet' records: 'All these I feel within me and their scope / Carried
by veins throughout my whole estate, / So quiet is my face and wild my
hope'.[33] This emotional variation transmits a greater cultural, as well as
formal, charge in Wingfield's second book, *Beat Drum, Beat Heart* (1946).
A long poem in four parts, this work draws on the political turmoil of the
1930s, as well as extending Wingfield's capacity for formal innovation.
The self-division that is so clearly a part of the poet's personal and creative self, is expressed in the different sections of the poem which mark the
responses of men and women to the conditions of war and peace:[34]

> Brothers, this is our cloud, our hidden night.
> We, being obscured ourselves, know nothing,
> In this darkness find no frame,
> No ladder to climb in clear air,
> No tap or chip of bricks on a bright day;
> But lean together as if chained to pillars,
> Under scourge from the whole world.[35]

The darkness, moral and actual, in which the soldiers labour, initiates an
exploration of the relationship between singular and collective identities,
between ideas of belonging and exclusion, which shapes the book as a
whole. This darkness can be contrasted to the light energies of the final

section, at 'The dune end / Of the world. / Spiked grass / Loose sand'.[36]
Judged by several critics to be Wingfield's outstanding poetic achievement, *Beat Drum, Beat Heart* presents a more philosophical than experiential approach to conflict, perhaps in keeping with the poet's claims that
much of it was written before the Second World War. Yet its final form
clearly expresses something of Wingfield's own life during the conflict,
when she was separated from her husband for a lengthy period.[37] This
marked a turning point for her, both personally and creatively, affecting
her subsequent development as a poet in significant ways.

There were other events, in the immediate aftermath of the war, which
would have a formative influence on Wingfield's work. In 1947 her
husband inherited the Powerscourt estate and the couple made Ireland
their permanent home. This change is recorded in the subject matter of
her poems from this period onward, a number of which have an explicitly Irish setting.[38] The opening lines of 'Ireland' – 'This is the country /
That has no desolation, no empty feel' – are indicative of Wingfield's
detached treatment of place, in which the subjectivity of the speaker is
scarcely addressed.[39] The intensity of her creative process is belied by
the restraint of the finished work. Rarely autobiographical, Wingfield's
poetry yet manages to critique the constraints under which she was
working – though she described her writing practice as 'tentative' and
'laborious', she was determined to forge a poetic career that would gain
her readers in Ireland and England. Her interweaving of past and present,
and in particular her use of classical material, is not escapist: it deepens
her engagement with the human condition but offers no easy consolation for readers. 'While Satyrs Hunted for a Nymph' contemplates the
limits of philosophical enquiry. A quest, whether motivated by lust or
reason, occurs in the moment, and what is found is contingent – tied to
the materiality of existence. The slippage between real and metaphorical
acts of exploration subtly investigates the role of poetry in crossing these
boundaries: hypotheses are tested through experience and understood in
terms that can be verified by the senses. Ultimately, Wingfield suggests,
abstractions vanish. The philosophers, and 'their counter-pleas / Of proof
have left us, every one, / Like sailors whistling for a breeze – / And still
the breeze drops with the sun'.[40]

Increasingly Wingfield's work came to be dominated by an existential
darkness, expressed through deepening creative difficulties. Though *A
Kite's Dinner: Poems 1938–54* was selected as the Poetry Book Society's
Choice in 1954, it was poorly received by critics. Wingfield's failure,
in the words of Elizabeth Jennings, to 'come to grips with her subject

matter' is in fact evidence of her conviction that epistemology itself is fatally flawed.[41] Wingfield links destructive human behaviour to this discovery. 'Darkness', from her 1964 volume, *The Leaves Darken*, makes this connection clear:

> And what will mitigate my life's long fault,
> I beg you, if authority's black stuffs
> Should fail to reconcile me
> To the final blindfold?
> Cassock and mortar-board
> Are under the same burden,
> Suffer the same problem, as ourselves;
> While conscience comes at night and stings
> The darkness: much as Carthage, ploughed under,
> Was then sown with salt.[42]

Here the existential darkness is figured in material terms – neither spiritual nor intellectual authority can reconcile us to death, as all are subject to the frailty of human mortality. Yet, just as the city of Carthage was destroyed and rebuilt, so darkness waits 'for flourishes of fireworks to exalt / A pitch black sky'.[43] The possibility of meaning beyond human limitation exists: the funerary image with which the poem ends combines stasis and movement – the containment of coffin and grave coexists with the wing beats of disturbed jackdaws.

The vision that informs Wingfield's later poetry is strongly influenced both by the fate of Ireland's landed class, and by her own temperament, which left her vulnerable to criticism and isolation. Yet other women poets of this period share a concern to express dark interior states, suggesting that the constraints of the time could be registered in different situations. The struggle to maintain creative momentum in the face of critical indifference, or even hostility, can also be read in the work of these women, several of whom abandoned their poetic careers despite displaying discipline and originality in their published work.

'Unable to be Born': Freda Laughton

In the context of these challenges, Freda Laughton's career is especially noteworthy. Born in Bristol, Laughton spent much of her adult life in Co. Down. She published regularly in literary journals – especially *The Bell* – during the 1940s, but her involvement with Dublin literary culture in this period remained indirect. Laughton's first collection, *A Transitory House*, appeared from Jonathan Cape in 1945, and though she continued to publish new poems for the remainder of the decade, no further volumes were forthcoming. Laughton's work made a considerable impact on readers and critics during this decade, however. It heralded a newly sensuous approach to free verse forms, as well as a willingness to explore interior states. In spite of her perceived innovation, and the inclusion of her work in anthologies during the mid-century years, Laughton has been almost entirely forgotten by subsequent generations of poets and critics.

Characterized both by a sensuous flexibility and frankness of representation, Laughton's poetry occupies the space between intimacy and isolation that is characteristic of work by women at this time. Uniquely, however, Laughton offers the reader experiential immediacy and symbolic resonance: the place of warmth and light, in which her speakers commune with nature, is always on the brink of being overwhelmed by darkness. Her poem 'Now I am a Tower of Darkness' begins by invoking a child's perspective, recognizing the role of instinct within the crafted space of the poem. This perspective also gives the work its fairytale quality that is at once fanciful and threatening: 'As a child I knew / How, beyond the lamp's circuit, / Lay the Shadow of the shadow / Of this darkness'.[44] In the child's world nighttime visions can be dispelled by the light of the lamp, for the adult poet, though, these fears are internalized:

> Now I am a tower of darkness,
> Whose windows, opening inward,
> Stare down upon tidal thoughts.
> And in this responsive bell,
>
> Hollowed by the silence of the eyes,
> The mind swings its clapper.
> And life resolves into relationships
> Of cadence and dissonance.[45]

The speaking self now confronts what the child instinctively knows: that beyond the reassuring brightness of the lamplight lie unknown, and unknowable, threats. The hollow spaces of tower and bell invoke at once visual and aural frames of reference. These synaesthetic effects reflect the mind's disturbance but also make its expression possible: the space of the poem permits this shifting sense of self to remain at least partially unresolved.

For Laughton, the darkness that suggests instability and despair is confronted in different contexts. 'In a House on the Sea-Shore' combines tidal flows with the fixed materiality of the built space, but in this text the space is shared by the speaker and her lover, and their intimacy balances external threat: 'Pause in our loving for a while and see / The liquid darkness lean against the pane... // And how our light / Repels the pulse of night'.[46] The poem reveals a heightened sensitivity to the boundaries between self and external world, a relationship determined by the rhythm, which is both a distinctive formal element of Laughton's poems and also a key to its interpretation of the inexorable passage of time. In problematizing coherent subjectivity, she highlights larger emotional currents, psychic disturbances that mirror the turbulence of the contemporary world. Written during the Second World War, these poems – though on the margins of conflict – reflect the political instability of the time as well as the concern with subjectivity that shapes the work of many women poets of the period.

In Laughton's case this subjectivity reflects the difficulty in maintaining a coherent sense of self within a world of flux – a consideration born not only of the challenging environment that Ireland presented at the time, but of a creative sensibility attuned to alienation and depression. 'Tombed in Spring' begins:

> The whole of life was figured in a nought,
> You said to me, and any other thought
> Was but a bubble in a desert blown
> To fateful iridescence and undone
> By any wind of reason truly placed.[47]

This opening line confronts the tension at the heart of Laughton's work: the joyous image of the floating bubble, set against the destructive realities of rational thought. Inherent in the title of the poem is the irony of burial in an earth burgeoning with life, and the contrast between the despairing conversation and the space in which it occurs, where 'trees strove upwards and the sunlight paced / Restless among new leaves'.[48] The movement upward, towards light and air, informs the living landscape of the poem; the humans remain rooted in stone – their leaves wither and fall. The gloom of speaker and listener shuts them off from the redemptive potential, much as in Salkeld's work the rigidity of routine stifles personal freedom. In Laughton's poetry, it is often the weight of thought itself that creates negative energy and that renders the speaker 'unable to be born' despite the vigorous renewal that surrounds her in nature. Left alone she vows to 'loose the sap / Locked in my roots beneath the mind's stout stone'.[49]

The contesting energies of instinctive and rational behaviour exerted a powerful force on Laughton's creative process. In this respect, her work addressed a key dichotomy in twentieth-century poetry, as well as challenging a binary that has limited the reception of Irish women's writing. The sensuality of her work is a testament to its resistance to the norms of female representation of the mid-century years, and is evidence of its untapped potential as a liberating model for later generations of poets.

Place, Landscape, History: Rhoda Coghill

Recognition of constraint was an important means by which Laughton could mobilize her own creative voice, but for others such as Mary Devenport O'Neill and Rhoda Coghill these limitations proved more difficult to overcome. Like Blanaid Salkeld, Coghill came to writing late: best known as a composer and pianist, her musical achievements were closely linked to her formal skills as a poet and to her keen ear for rhythmical pattern. Like Laughton, Coghill was drawn to represent the natural world, but her landscapes facilitate a new exploration of the self's relationship to history; placed in the context of evolution, human experience is fleeting:

> Here have I drifted on a quiet wave
> Of happening, that gently washes
> Where Time's slow-flowing ocean flood has shaped
> Age-old valley and hill.[50]

By disturbing the relationship between past and present action, Coghill both initiates, and reflects upon, her departure from lyric norms. Adrift from the co-ordinates of time and space, the speaker in 'Burren, Co. Clare' sees the landscape as simultaneously a place of continuity and one of change, where traces of ancient civilizations are concealed beneath an evolving vista. This awareness yields to shifting powers of perception: like Salkeld's gulls, Coghill's birds 'swim in the liquid air' and 'lichened bushes … [turn] to branching coral'.[51] These mutable spaces are everywhere in *The Bright Hillside* (1948), Coghill's first collection. Shorelines and lakesides not only highlight the boundaries of thought and perception but the intense importance of sound in this poet's work: 'There is a warm, bright silence here,' she observes in 'Summer in Sheephaven', 'which so / Intensifies each tiny stir'.[52]

Water is an important channel for this sensitivity. 'In the City' chooses the River Liffey as a means to link past and future, as well as to consider the relationship between the urban space and its larger hinterland. Again, the bird is a motif for the limits of observation – what cannot be witnessed must be imagined. Coghill at once experiences and recollects the city, capturing childhood memories and registering the space as part of her own body. Her response is strongly visual and draws attention to the changing dynamics of clarity and obscurity within the city space:

> Tonight there are no birds;
> The thickening mist blinds me to all but light.
> By day small painted boats, wings
> Of coloured parrots, tighten their holding ropes
> And lie beside the wall. Pale women
> Hurry across the bridges, dawdle at windows,
> Treasure their handbags, intent on finding bargains.[53]

With her vision obscured, the speaker relies on memory to recreate the urban scene. Yet this is also an intertextual poem: like Louis MacNeice's 'Dublin', Coghill's text combines a dreamlike treatment of the city space with a subtle sense of the bleakness of its history. Hers is a poem of twilight and its monochrome quality brings an air of mystery to the scene, but also an acknowledgment that life endures, even when hidden from observing eyes.

The ghostly quality of this scene finds more direct expression in other poems by Coghill. 'To His Ghost, Seen after Delirium' is concerned with the precarious nature of the subject position, which needs human connection to create meaning. The story of Orpheus and Eurydice is chosen by Coghill to represent the fragility of that bond: Orpheus journeys to the Underworld to rescue his dead wife but fails, at the last moment, through lack of trust. Eurydice's longing here is not only for the sensory world, but also for her own earlier self, whole in mind and spirit. The loss of the symbol is also the loss of language, and from this place the poet must return if she is to write again.

> Since I have fought the pigmy host
> that has besieged me so, those wanton thoughts
> and not-thoughts, which would steal from me
> all memory of being, and at last
> steal me from life: – since I have found
> again my mind's dear garden, will you not praise me?
> will you not give me, victor now,
> a crown of olives? – will you not come
> bearing a flower from fields of asphodel?[54]

As Kathy D'Arcy has argued, this poem confronts the anxieties of the woman poet concerning artistic acceptance.[55] These fears are well founded. Though Seumas O'Sullivan used the occasion of his introduction to *The Bright Hillside* to lament the lack of 'a representative anthology of the women poets of Ireland', this generation of poets was more marginalized than any before them, and became progressively excluded from anthologies from the 1960s onwards.

Conclusion

The perception that there were no women poets of note writing during the mid-century period would be a lasting one, and the poets associated with the literary renaissance of the 1960s rarely looked to this generation of poets for precursors. For women poets, this occlusion is compounded by the challenges they faced in gaining acceptance to the world of writing and publishing in the first place. In order that the narrative of modern Irish literature be told more fully, these women poets must be restored to their place within the creative development of the modern state. Their achievements, as well as their preoccupations, have much to tell later readers about the literary history of these islands.

Notes

1 Anne Mulhall, '"The Well-Known, Old, But Still Unbeaten Track": Women Poets and Irish Periodical Culture in the Mid-Twentieth Century', *Irish University Review* 42, no. 1 (Spring/Summer 2012): 32.

2 Few anthologies of Irish poetry published from the 1980s onwards include any women poets writing original work in English between 1920 and 1970 – Brendan Kennelly's *Penguin Book of Irish Verse* (1981) and Thomas Kinsella's *Oxford Book of Irish Verse* (1986) are cases in point. Even recent anthologies fall short in this respect: Wes Davis's *Anthology of Modern Irish Poetry* (Harvard, 2010) includes no woman poet before Eiléan Ní Chuilleanáin; Patrick Crotty's *Penguin Book of Irish Poetry* (2010) includes only Katharine Tynan and Blanaid Salkeld.

3 Anne Mulhall notes that the desire to reanimate a flagging literary culture in Ireland was also conceived in terms of male succession, 'Women Poets and Irish Periodical Culture', 32–8.

4 Frank O'Connor, 'The Belfry: To Any Would-be Writer', *The Bell* 1, no. 5 (February 1941): 88.

5 For further discussion of Taylor's editorship see Kelly Matthews, *The Bell Magazine and the Representation of Irish Identity* (Dublin: Four Courts, 2012), 74–83.

6 Ibid., 40.

7 For detailed examination of *The Dublin Magazine* see Frank Shovlin, *The Irish Literary Periodical 1923–1958* (Oxford: Oxford University Press, 2003), 39–66.

8 Peter Martin, *Censorship in the Two Irelands 1922–1939* (Dublin: Irish Academic Press, 2006), 193.

9 Janet Montefiore, 'The 1930s: Memory and Forgetting', in *Women Writers of the 1930s: Gender, Politics and History*, ed. Maroula Joannou (Edinburgh: Edinburgh University Press, 1999), 22.

10 Deirdre Brady's forthcoming study of the Irish Women Writers' Club will be the first book-length study of this group.

11 Many women who wrote for a living published across a range of modes and genres: Temple Lane, Winifred Letts and Katharine Tynan were three such figures. Temple Lane, whose real name was Mary Isabel Leslie, published popular fiction under the pseudonym Jean Herbert.

12 Mary Devenport O'Neill's biography is explored in a website devoted to her work: www.marydevenportoneill.org/.

13 Arthur Little, 'Review [*Prometheus and Other Poems*]', *Studies: An Irish Quarterly Review*, 19, no. 73 (1930): 164.

14 See Laura Pomeroy, '"Undisturbed by Leaves": Constructions of Nature in Mary Devenport O'Neill's Poetry', in *Engendering Ireland: New Reflections in Modern History and Literature*, eds. Rebecca Anne Barr, Sarah-Anne Buckley and Laura Kelly (Cambridge: Cambridge Scholars Publishing, 2015), 177.

15 Ibid., 177.

16 Mary Devenport O'Neill, *Prometheus and Other Poems* (London: Jonathan Cape, 1929), 17.

17 Ibid., 17.

18 Ibid.

19 Ibid., 15.

20 Ibid., 19.

21 Ibid., 43.

22 Moynagh Sullivan, '"The Woman Gardener": Transnationalism, Gender, Sexuality and the Poetry of Blanaid Salkeld', *Irish University Review*, 42, no. 1 (Spring/Summer 2012): 54.

23 Blanaid Salkeld, *Hello Eternity!* (London: Elkin Mathews, 1933), 26.

24 Ibid., 26.

25 Ibid., 58.

26 'I hate verse. I have lost faith' from Blanaid Salkeld, 'Even the Carollers,' in *Hello Eternity!*, 55.

27 Deirdre Brady, 'Modernist Presses and the Gayfield Press', *Bibliologia* 9 (2014): 103–18.

28 Blanaid Salkeld, 'Homing Joys', in *Poetry by Women in Ireland: A Critical Anthology 1870–1970*, ed. Lucy Collins (Liverpool: Liverpool University Press, 2012), 217.

29 Alex Davis, '"Wilds to Alter, Forms to Build": The Writings of Sheila Wingfield', *Irish University Review*, 31, no. 2 (Autumn/Winter, 2001): 339–52.

30 Sheila Wingfield, *Poems* (London: Cresset Press, 1938), 15.

31 Mona Gooden, 'Book Reviews', *Dublin Magazine*, 13, no. 4 (October–December 1938): 79.

32 Wingfield lost her brother Guy, to whom she was very close, to tuberculosis in 1925.

33 Wingfield, *Poems*, 61.

34 The four sections are: 'Men in War', 'Men at Peace', 'Women in Love', 'Women at Peace'. These titles juxtapose the physical and emotional turmoil of the sexes.

35 Sheila Wingfield, 'Men in War', in *Beat Drum, Beat Heart* (London: Cresset Press, 1946), 13.

36 Sheila Wingfield, 'Women at Peace', in *Beat Drum, Beat Heart*, 72.

37 Wingfield's father, anxious about the fate of European Jews, dispatched his daughter to Bermuda. Her husband, who served with the 8th Huzzars, spent three years in an Italian prisoner of war camp. See Penny Perrick, *Something to Hide: The Life of Sheila Wingfield, Viscountess Powerscourt* (Dublin: Lilliput Press, 2007), 69–78.

38 Among the poems are: 'Ireland', 'Architectural Tour' and 'Ross Abbey', Sheila Wingfield, *A Cloud Across the Sun* (London: Cresset Press, 1949).

39 Ibid., 8.

40 Ibid., 21.

41 Elizabeth Jennings, Review of *A Kite's Dinner*, *The London Magazine* (April, 1955).

42 Sheila Wingfield, *The Leaves Darken* (London: Weidenfeld and Nicolson, 1964), 11.

43 Ibid., 11.

44 Freda Laughton, *A Transitory House* (London: Jonathan Cape, 1945), 12.

45 Ibid., 12.

46 Ibid., 33.

47 Freda Laughton, 'Tombed in Spring', in *Poetry by Women in Ireland*, ed. Collins, 245.

48 Ibid., 245.

49 Ibid.

50 Rhoda Coghill, *The Bright Hillside* (Dublin: Hodges Figgis, 1948), 3.

51 Ibid., 3.

52 Ibid., 2.

53 Ibid., 6.

54 Ibid., 20.

55 Kathy D'Arcy, '"Almost Forgotten Names:" Irish Women Poets of the 1930s, 1940s and 1950s', in *Irish Literature: Feminist Perspectives*, ed. Patricia Coughlan and Tina O'Toole (Dublin: Carysfort Press, 2008), 118–19.

CHAPTER 10

Fiction, 1922–1960

Gerardine Meaney

The lesser-known women writers of the period 1922 to 1960 occupy a transitional space. They worked in the very long shadow of the conflicts that began in 1914 and ended in exhausted discontent in 1923 and were largely forgotten by the time feminist criticism emerged in the 1970s. The strength, range and topics of their fiction challenge assumptions of the post-independence period as inimical to subversive voices and of the dominance of the short story in critical accounts of the period. The novel by Irish women flourished across diverse genres and was commercially and critically successful internationally. These novels processed the legacy of local and global conflicts, and critiqued the terms of domesticity and the exigencies of gender. Formally, social realism co-existed with and cross-fertilized literary experiment and Gothic atmosphere. Recent work has explored the connections between modernist, realist and popular forms in women's writing between the wars internationally.[1] This is evident in the work of the two best-known Irish women novelists of the mid-twentieth century. Both Kate O'Brien and Elizabeth Bowen moved fluidly between genres, with O'Brien subverting the conventions of historical romance and Bowen creating complex hybrids of modernist style and Gothic atmosphere. This fluidity in relation to genre and style was evident in the work of their lesser-known contemporaries. In the 1930s, marginalization of the radical movements of the pre-war period propelled many former activists from political to cultural activity. The fiction they produced ranged from angry social critique to national romances, but the energetic subversion of literary conventions and multiple stylistic and generic experiments retained a certain revolutionary force.

Political history nonetheless shaped even apparently domestic fictions. The literature of postcolonial disappointment in the period following the Irish Civil War was often characterized by a tragi-comic sensibility in Irish literature, ranging from the elegant wit of Christine Longford to the occasionally dark satires of Norah Hoult through the 'Gothic family romances' of Molly Keane.[2] In the aftermath of the First World War, the War of Independence and the Civil War, and with the 'free state' becoming anything but free, the idea of history as a cruel joke played on idealism was understandably attractive and intimately connected with an often tragi-comic and sometimes black comic sensibility. The novel by Irish women in this period is quite distinct from poetry where there are two clear tendencies, one towards popular verse where women are prominently represented and another towards continuing experiment, still very much in the modernist mode. In fiction, vernacular and late modernism shade into each other, into realism, Gothic, romance and domestic fiction, with evidence of a self-reflexive tendency in popular genres and use of generic convention in literary fiction and a pervasive irony.

Does anything unify this plethora of genres, styles and stratagems for literary innovation and economic survival? Even in Irish literary circles, where few contemporaries have even one degree of separation in society and influence, the fact that so many of these women participated in the Irish Women Writers' Club is very striking. The club was generically democratic, including internationally renowned figures like Kate O'Brien, modernist poets like Blanaid Salkeld, children's writers such as Patricia Lynch and a range of nonfiction writers.[3] Its persistence for twenty-five years indicates it provided more than a support structure for relationships forged in the fiery years of political activism or a literary talking shop. In the decades of extreme state censorship, it appears to have provided a lifeline of contact with other women writers and with literary culture outside the state. It is nonetheless important not to idealize this counterculture. No Irish woman novelist in the twentieth century occupied a position equivalent to the powerful nineteenth-century literary editors based in London, like Mrs S. C. Hall and Charlotte Riddell, and most struggled to make a living from writing. Access to international publishing, specifically in London and New York, was both a sustaining and shaping force for Irish women writers and readers in the period. Most Irish women writers of the 1922–60 period had limited financial resources, but they enjoyed freedom and privileges far beyond that of the population at large and often far beyond that which realism required they bestowed on the protagonists of their fiction. 'I thought with envious admiration of Miss Carroll and Nix Ogilvie,' says Margaret Cullen in Rosamund Jacob's *The Troubled House* (1938) of the women artists to whose lives and lifestyle she is so attracted, 'with their souls in their own work; I would have felt a deeper admiration still had I seen them steering the same course though possessed of husbands and children'.[4] Jacob was a former suffragist and republican activist and a constant campaigner throughout this period on issues from women's rights, international anti-Fascism, school dinners, animal rights and eventually nuclear disarmament. Her interests remind us that these writers engaged with an extraordinary range of historical experience, with many like Jacob, Hoult, Coyle and Macardle being born into Victorian Ireland and registering in their work the effects of local and world wars, the oppressions of post-independence Ireland and the intimate connection between personal lives and political history. The relationship between sexual and aesthetic freedom, which was initially explored by 'New Woman' writers continued to be a residual theme. Margaret's rebelliousness in Norah Hoult's *Holy Ireland* (1935) is initially expressed in her choice of reading material, later in that of her prospective husband.[5] Jacob's Nix paints what she likes, including herself and her lovers, and lives as she pleases. When her paintings are destroyed during a Black and Tan raid, the novel recognizes the precariousness of this freedom, even while it celebrates her ability to endure and start again.

For many women writers in this period, social acceptance and respectability in Ireland became precarious, as censorship tightened its grip. Denunciation from the pulpit was a considerable social and economic risk for writers who lived and worked in Ireland and for their families. Censorship meant that regardless of where they were based, they were at least from the 1930s onwards primarily read and published abroad. This is particularly true of Norah Hoult who was consistently banned in Ireland and well reviewed in London over the course of her career. Una Troy (who later published under the pseudonym Elizabeth Connor) was published in the United Kingdom and United States, popular in German translation and had her work adapted into successful films, but was persistently banned in Ireland.[6] Even women who were deeply embedded in the new Irish establishment found it extremely difficult to maintain the cultural freedoms for which they had fought. By November 1931, Dorothy Macardle, one of the founding executive members of Fianna Fail,[7] complained to her friend Rosamund Jacob of the atmosphere at the party's newspaper, *The Irish Press*, where she was drama critic 'and said how it frightens her for the future, the way things in general are going, trying to stifle non-conformity'.[8] A few weeks later Macardle was 'raging and ... very down hearted over the paper' and 'the sectarian blight over it, and Fianna Fail and the country'.[9] This sense of stifling conformity intensified as the 1930s progressed. With condescending irony, Mr Jiggins in Christine Longford's *Mr Jiggins of Jigginstown*, explains to a visiting relative, 'everything is banned in Ireland.'[10]

Much work remains to be done on the cultural effects and legacy of the disconnection between Irish reading and writing produced by censorship and the effect on literary culture. The Women Writers' Club indicates a high degree of solidarity wrought by this context between modernist experimentalists, children's writers and authors of romance, history and unclassifiable forms. While the club's efforts to overturn the censorship of members' works were ineffective in the short term, with other such groups, like the National University of Ireland (NUI) Women Graduates' Association and Women's Social and Progressive League, it did provide a small alternative public forum within Ireland for work that was either unavailable or of limited interest to the general public.[11] It is easy but ill advised to dismiss these groups as marginal to Irish society and literature: that was the practice of mainstream literary criticism for decades. There is even a danger that this marginalization will be replicated in the digital age. Electronic editions of Irish literature in this period appear to be driven by existing teaching curricula on the one hand and the level of interest of literary estates on the other, so, for example, Liam O'Flaherty is available in digital format and Norah Hoult is not, despite an acclaimed new edition of *There Were No Windows*.[12] Such disparities notwithstanding, the productivity and verve of Hoult and her contemporaries has left an extensive archive of works that are currently attracting a high degree of scholarly interest, a renewed wave of publication and a popular readership through Sinéad Gleeson's innovative new anthologies, *The Long Gaze Back* and *The Glass Shore*.[13]

The sense of a distinct tradition of Irish women's writing in the period is complicated by the fact that so many Irish women writers followed their work abroad. Kathleen Coyle left Derry for London after her divorce, finding a job in publishing, which gave her access to editors and reviewers. Others like Hoult and Kate O'Brien migrated back and forwards between Ireland and England and further abroad. Ireland was already unusual before independence in the prevalence of single women who emigrated. The moral panic around unaccompanied female emigrants led by the church in these years is well documented.[14] Then, as now, easy access to very different regulatory regimes in England both challenged and enabled the strictures of the Irish state. Members of the educated middle class, who might have more persistently challenged censorship if affected more directly, were able to find many ways around it. Rosamund Jacob's diary records Hannah Sheehy Skeffington lending her a copy of *Ulysses*, for example, in 1926, which the author had himself given Hannah. 'Found a lot of interesting, weird and funny stuff in it, but so much plain disgustfullness [sic] that I could not read it at meals', Jacob complained.[15] While relatively few people could depend on a gift of banned books from their authors, censorship only fully applied to those dependent on local bookshops and, especially, public libraries, where almost anything could be removed or blocked from purchase on the whim of the locally easily scandalized. One effect of this was that with the exception of nationalistically minded romance writers such as Annie M. P. Smithson and children's writers such as Patricia Lynch, modern Irish women's writing was almost absent from Irish popular culture. The most popular titles in Irish libraries were often American romances.[16]

Social critique could nonetheless surface in unexpected places. In Patricia Lynch's children's story, *The Bookshop by the Quay*,[17] we get a glimpse into the terrifying precariousness of the lives of orphaned or otherwise vulnerable children through its protagonist, Shane Madden. Shane is initially exploited as child labour. When his one sympathetic relative loses contact, Shane sets out to find him. His initial life on the road puts him at the mercy of both authority figures and of others as hungry and desperate as himself. The bookshop of the title offers Shane refuge in a world of literature and culture and a new family of sorts. Throughout the period, popular genre fiction, whether children's fiction, family saga, historical romances or occasionally crime fiction, offers such fantasy resolutions to dilemmas which, in retrospect, we know to have been intractable. This process is perhaps best exemplified in the persistence of Gothic and supernatural fiction, where generic convention offered both vehicle and camouflage for social criticism. Dorothy Macardle's Gothic fiction offers an oblique critique of conditions and problems which were both well known and unspoken in Ireland, not least because attempts to speak about them were immediately censored. Rosamund Jacob records how her attempt to re-cast the problem of unmarried mothers as a problem of their lack of support by unmarried fathers brought a public meeting to a chaotic close. The unpublished fragment from Jacob's story *Nix and Theo* shows a writer exploring a complex sexual relationship frankly: nothing equivalent appears in her published work. Her friend and one time cell-mate, Dorothy Macardle, was far less outspoken on sexual matters, though her letter protesting about the position of women in the Constitution of the Republic of Ireland, introduced in 1937, indicates the 'tragic dilemma' which allegiances to women's advancement and the Irish state posed for her.[18] Macardle deployed circuitous routes towards protest. Her 1942 novel *Uneasy Freehold* (a.k.a. *The Uninvited*) borrows heavily from the nineteenth-century Gothic tradition. The young Irish

narrator seeks to unravel the mystery of the haunted house he and his
sister have rented in Cornwall, but thinks:

> I was uneasy because I was eavesdropping there. It was an intrusion; this
> house was old; long before we were born it had its occupants, living and
> dying here. We were aliens and trespassers in their hereditary home. Now,
> I knew they were in possession of the house once more, their timelessness
> closing over our intrusion as water over a stone.[19]

This is a reversal of the uneasy freehold of the old ascendancy, but
also the scene of a battle by timeless archetypes of motherhood that represent the regulation of maternity by the Irish state. The ghosts are the
apparently saintly Mary and the apparently fallen Carmel. Mary is the
socially sanctioned adoptive mother of Stella, the young woman whose
presence aggravates the house's spirits. Carmen is Stella's natural, 'illegitimate' mother who was forced to give her up and who died in the house,
possibly of neglect and cruelty. The plot retains its force because every stereotype of the genre leads us to expect that Carmen will be the destructive
ghost,[20] but it is Mary's ghost who tries to kill Stella and fills the house
with her freezing deathly presence. This is not a story that Macardle could
safely set in Ireland. The novel both condemns the cruelty and psychological damage involved in separating mothers from their children born out
of wedlock and displaces its anger to a 'Cliff End' in Cornwall.

Gothic has traditionally been a genre which puts the most frightening
things from home at a safe distance in order to explore them. Conversely,
homes in Irish women's fiction of this period are often haunted by that
which neither censorship nor uneasy peace can obliterate or forget.
The legacy of the Big House tradition in Irish fiction for these writers
is a metonymic relation between domestic and national narrative. The
households of strong farmers, small-town solicitors, bank managers and
shopkeepers are as representative of the state of the nation as Castle
Rackrent and its descendants were in the nineteenth century. Just as
the earlier fine houses in various states of decay represented their owners' relationship to history, the dominance and the insecurity of the
Catholic middle class in the political and economic life of the new state
is represented in Small House fiction between 1922 and 1960. Desperate
smallholders and the urban poor feature infrequently, but the difficulty
of paying for food and heat is often prominent. Norah Hoult's 1930
novel, *Time, Gentlemen, Time*,[21] chronicles the desperation of a middle-
class housewife as she and her children descend into poverty and hunger
when grocers refuse more credit and her husband's alcoholism progresses.

The fatigue and premature ageing brought on by constant childbearing features prominently in the work of Hoult and Elizabeth Connor. The tension and effort involved in keeping up an appearance of respectability in Ireland between the 1930s and 1950s is palpable in these fictions. In Connor's 1938 *Dead Star's Light*[22] it leads to the cover-up of a drunken accident, involving four of the town's pillars of respectability, and the casual disposal of the dead body of the tramp they run over. Like Hoult, Connor is highly critical of the normalization of excessive drinking by men in this society. The full apparatus of censorship was not yet in place so the author was merely denounced from the local pulpit for her critical representation of Irish small town life. This clearly set up the terms of the relationship between literary and official cultures. It was not merely that all critique was considered treachery, but that the literary impulse to speak was intrinsically at odds with a culture defined by the imperative not to tell, precisely the corrosive imperative that *Dead Star's Light* critiques. Decades of reports and historical inquiry into abuse have exposed the cruelty of Irish respectability, silence and repression in this period. In this context domestic fiction becomes haunted by those excluded from domestic space, and women's fiction in this period often blurs the generic boundaries between Gothic and almost every other genre. *Dead Star's Light* is both an exercise in critical realism and a suspense thriller, where we await Gothic retribution to overtake the perpetrators of the crime against the dead committed in the name of respectability at the opening of the novel.

The Gothic tendency is, if anything, redoubled in domestic fiction set in the households of the small-town solicitors, bank managers and farmers as their enemy is always already within, and can at best be externalized onto family, neighbours or previous residents. Exceptions to this tend to be associated with narrative space for new forms of sociality, sexuality and politics. Jacob's *The Troubled House* rehearses the narrative of the nation as tragic to some extent. In this oddly Oedipal novel, depicted from the point of view of Margaret Cullen, a mother coming to terms with her sons' involvement in politics, the rebel Liam mistakenly kills his conservative father. The figure of the New Woman, so old fashioned in the Ireland of the 1930s, nonetheless persists. The artist Nix Ogilvie stands out as an example of what radical women had imagined would be possible in the brave new Ireland. Theo Cullen remarks that Nix's 'mind goes through things like a spear, and she doesn't know how to be false, and she doesn't give a damn for what anyone else thinks'.[23] His optimistic

mother responds: 'She's a new sort of woman, that's all. There will probably be more like her, as time goes on'.[24] The response of his male friends
is more indicative of the attitude of the new southern state: 'One man
told me it was the sign of a lost soul to like her. Said she was an unsexed
monster ... They all say Nix is an unnatural woman.'[25] The viability of
Nix's kind of freedom in the Ireland that the War of Independence and
the Civil War actualized, as opposed to the one the women rebels imagined, is beyond the bounds of plausibility and social realism and there are
few analogies.

While domestic and Gothic fiction set in more modest homes continued the tradition of social and national critique, the Big Houses and
their demise continued to engage the imagination of women writers.
Published in the early 1930s, Pamela Hinkson's *The Ladies' Road* (1932)
and Christine Longford's *Mr Jiggins of Jigginstown* (1933)[26] represent
the two very different modalities in which the tradition flourished.
Longford's novel presents the predicaments of the deposed ascendancy
through a savagely ironic lens. Mr Jiggins eventually leaves his house
to the Irish minister for education to open a school for all the children
of the area, irrespective of creed, though how well this would have
been received in the Ireland of the 1930s is unclear. He leaves size-
able annuities to his servants and there is a strong sense that his relatives have no claim on the land or on Jigginstown House. The idea that
young Geraldine Jiggins would be better off in Ireland is invoked, but
has no hope of fulfilment, though she is treated more sympathetically
than any other character and has more affinity with the old man. Her
young brother is hardly defined, never knowing what his role should be
and dominated by his mother. It is noticeable that the Irish tenants are
represented exclusively by the elderly servants and lunatics Mr Jiggins
supports – he likes the idea of Irish youth and the Irish future but they
are abstractions lacking any characterization in the novel. The possibility
that Mr Jiggins returns to the house in the form of a fox after his death
is both hysterically funny and terribly sad. Even Longford's determination to take a bracingly realistic view of the end of the old order cannot
resist a hint of the uncanny at the end of her Big House novel. Turning
the house into a school at least ensures a resident fox would be safe from
the fox hunting the old man abhorred and, in his confused identification
with the foxes, feared.

The Ladies' Road is more properly a novel of two Big Houses, with the
Irish 'Cappagh' and the English 'Winds' entwined in melancholy symbiosis. Above all it is a novel of post-war trauma. The novel initially hints

at the threat from Irish forces beyond the control of the protagonists in the woods around Cappagh: 'There had been a feeling of menace about the black wall beyond which one could not see'.[27] The English visitor, Edmund, sees the Irish Big Houses as

> so much of a pattern, big and grey, with a suggestion of a fortress against the background of woods. They had been thrown down, he supposed, by the English as they passed through, coming as conquerors and colonialists, and the English influence went just as far as the sunlight went into the woods and no further. Beyond the country lay, unaffected.[28]

That unaffected Ireland poses no existential threat to the inhabitants of Cappagh. Stella, the young girl from whose perspective the story is told, is quite sure, 'If she was Irish ... she would be a rebel'.[29] The great dark force which turns both Cappagh and Winds into sites of melancholy and mourning 'so like, yet unlike' each other,[30] is a bigger war, much further away. Stella loses her oldest brother early in the First World War and David, the beloved sibling closest to her in age, just before the war ends. When she is told, '"Well, it's over,"' she can only reply, '"I don't feel anything ... Do you?"'[31] Remembering her brother and another dead young man she had kissed out of pity before he went to war, she thinks: 'A chapter of life had ended. No one knew how or when the next chapter would begin, or what to do with it.'[32]

In this context, the destruction of Cappagh by the darkness that emerges from the woods is almost an afterthought and is not at all the rebellion Stella imagined as a child. Irene, the character most closely associated with Ireland and the Irish landscape, understands

> for the next generation, no world between two worlds, but only Ireland. And none of this really concerned them, because they had spent everything in the War and so for their lives afterwards must lie on the bank and watch the stream of life go by, unable to go with it or discover clearly where it went.[33]

In effect the novel mourns for a whole generation condemned to the same role as the schoolgirls the novel achingly describes, queuing up with Stella for letters from the front from brothers who may already be dead.[34] History had already happened and they were excluded from it.

A different form of alienation from the time and force of history structures the narrative of mourning in Kathleen Coyle's *A Flock of Birds*,[35] because this is mourning before the fact. The novel begins as Catherine Munster leaves the courthouse where her rebel son Christy has been sentenced to death and ends as she leaves the gaol as he is about to be executed. The narrative registers the efforts of his solicitor brother to save him, but Catherine understands from the start that these are futile and so the novel's suspense is very like Catherine's suspense, a sanity-straining agony of waiting. The novel achieves this in self-reflexive modernist style. Catherine's daughter, called Kathleen, returns from Paris where Kathleen Coyle had also lived to comment on her brother's fate: 'You know, mother, James Joyce says that we have a country that is like a sow that eats its own farrow.'[36] In contrast to his straying siblings, Christy, who 'stayed in the mountains', will die of his fidelity to his place, his ideas and the nice, suitable young woman who wants to marry him in prison before he dies. Coyle takes the defining narrative of cultural national-ism, that of the mother who sacrifices her son for Ireland, and critiques it from inside the consciousness of a mother 'on the edge, the gallows edge with Christie'.[37] Catherine is poised between the madness of grief and an intense lucidity:

> She did not love sacrifice. A waste in the name of heaven was no less waste. It was that that she resented, his waste. To him it was a heroic pur-pose. Heroism or martyrdom was the fashion. What fools they were, these young men, these weavers of wreaths. Other brows bore the thorns … Women had to think it out for a very long time afterwards.[38]

When she agrees with her son to understand his death in heroic terms, it is unclear whether this is simply to ease his mind, just as it is unclear when Christy tells her he has pleaded guilty to exonerate his comrades if he is doing so to relieve her of the burden of thinking her son is a killer. Reality is uncertain, suspended outside the narrative but shaping it, like death itself. When Catherine leaves Christie for the last time she refuses to kneel with the crowd of supporters outside the prison pray-ing for him. She determines to leave Ireland for France: 'She would be a ghost there. A ghost of all the mothers whose sons had been taken.'[39] Unlike the women in *The Ladies' Road*, Catherine's grief unites her with the current of history, but like them she sees no future. Her madness at the end of the novel is both a denial of her son's death and an appropria-tion of his voice, taking him back into herself and repeating the refrain that the black cloud threatening rain is only after all 'a flock of birds'.[40] As in Hinkson, grief unhinges minds and histories, but in Coyle the co-ordinates of reality are at stake. Taking leave of Christie, Catherine finds that: 'Time and place were unsteadied in her.'[41] This sense of dislocation, of living in an afterwards drained of significance, is very strong in the women's fiction from this period dealing with wars global and local, from the perspective, as Coyle puts it, of the women thinking 'it out for a very long time afterwards'.[42]

A decade after Coyle, Hinkson and Longford, Molly Keane revisited this definitive period of Irish history in *Two Days in Aragon*.[43] Aragon is a derangedly matriarchal Big House, one where the legacy of mother to daughter is one of powerlessness. In Aragon, the men have already left, but Nan, the housekeeper and illegitimate daughter of the Big House, is neither female liberator nor maternal presence. Her petty cruelty, especially to the unfortunate Aunt Pidgie, has something in common with the coldness of Macardle's Mary in *Uneasy Freehold* and suggests that the great current of history did not change the fundamental structure of power as it was intimately lived. In this relatively early novel, Keane fuses Gothic excess and historical fiction to explore some of her signature themes, intertwining family dynamics and historical forces. The moral inertia and stupidity of her characters express a profound pessimism, their sensuality completely divorced from the possibility of freedom which is so acutely embodied in Jacob's Nix or the creative potential mourned by Coyle's Catherine. The novel instead explores the violent collapse and reinstatement of psychological and social controls on the female body and feminine power, as the old order is destroyed and the new one both displaces and replicates it.

It is indicative of the political complexity and the dangers of underestimating the dynamic nature of cultural change in a period generally characterized by economic and social stagnation that one of the unifying causes which characterized the Women Writers' Club was protest against the ban on another novel from the early 1940s, Maura Laverty's *Touched by the Thorn*.[44] Laverty was a transitional figure on many levels: between the hegemony of Catholic nationalism in the 1940s and 1950s and the modernization of the 1960s; between the *avant-garde* Gate Theatre and a more vernacular modernism; between theatre, fiction, television and lifestyle writing. Laverty's novels were consistently banned and her plays and the international interest they elicited were subjects of persistent popularity and controversy throughout the 1940s and 1950s, but she moved right into the mainstream of the new Ireland that began to emerge in the 1960s. Laverty wrote the first soap opera, *Tolka Row*, for the state broadcasting corporation RTE.[45] It is tempting to see Laverty as a precursor of the extraordinary success of Irish women writers of popular fiction at the end of the twentieth century, but she is also an inheritor of both the artistic and commercial strategies of the 'ladies of letters' like Katherine Cecil

Thurston in the beginning of the twentieth century. Radio and television played an increasingly significant role in breaching the *cordon sanitaire* erected by the state between what Irish women wished to read and write and what they were supposed to read and write. Just as successful playwrights like Teresa Deevy found a new audience on radio when commissioning policy effectively banished women playwrights from the Abbey stage, novelists like Katherine Keane reached a broad audience in Ireland through radio and Laverty's genius for compelling storytelling made her transition to television almost inevitable.

Our picture of Irish women's writing in the period 1922–60 is shifting and changing as more critical attention is once again focussed on it, this time through a transcultural and transgeneric lens. Feminist recovery projects of fiction in Ireland have primarily sought to connect with the general reader through anthologies, which necessarily does greater justice to the short story than the novel. Nonetheless from the groundbreaking *Woman's Part* anthology in 1984,[46] through the scale of the *Field Day Anthology of Irish Writing* volumes 4 and 5 in 2002 and most recently in sharply focussed anthologies like *The Backward Glance* (2015), it is anthologies that have gradually reintroduced many of these writers to readers who never encountered them in their literary education. The publication of complete novels has been piecemeal in Ireland and, with the heroic exceptions of Blackstaff Press, Arlen House and Tramp Press, was a by-product of London-based feminist publishing, initially by Virago and Pandora, more recently in beautiful new editions by Persephone Books. There are patterns in this re-publication. In the 1980s, Arlen House brought back to print novels that connected with the major concerns of Irish feminism at the time. Anne Crone's *Bridie Steen* (1948),[47] which was re-issued by Arlen House and Blackstaff in 1984, chronicles the destruction of the heroine's life by sectarian forces embodied in the competition to dominate her between her equally unpleasant Catholic and Protestant grandmothers. Norah Hoult's 1935 historical novel *Holy Ireland,* reissued by Arlen House in 1985, recounts the misfortunes, including rejection by her father and the sexual advances of the local priest, which befall its Catholic heroine, Margaret, when she falls in love with a young Protestant man. Such novels offered a context in which to understand not just sexual politics, but also sectarian conflict. Katherine Keane's 1947 *Who Goes Home?*,[48] reissued by Arlen House in 1987, is centrally concerned with issues of independence and equality in work and marriage which resonate strongly with the central concerns of the women's movement of the 1980s, despite being set in the 1880s.

The main couple's decision to stay in Ireland and try to make a difference in the aftermath of Parnell's fall, despite their disillusion with Ireland, similarly echoes debates related to the return of large-scale emigration in the 1980s. Parallel to these Irish concerns, international publishers' choices connected to the evolving preoccupations of feminist criticism and of the women's movement globally. Virago's republication in the 1980s of Molly Keane's early novels and their critical re-evaluation was fuelled by the novels' compatibility with psychoanalytic feminist theory and their rehearsal of the themes of *l'écriture feminine*. Keane's powerful efforts to write the body also connected with the central struggles of the women's movement in the period with the issues of sexuality, reproduction and agency.

While the relationship between nation, gender and sexuality remains a key concern for scholars of Irish women's twentieth-century fiction,[49] these periodic re-evaluations are by no means over. In 2002, Marjorie Howes accurately commented that *Poor Women* (1928) was Norah Hoult's 'best-known and most widely admired work',[50] but that distinction now undoubtedly goes to her 1944 novel, *There Were No Windows*, Hoult's extraordinary depiction of wartime London through the eyes of Claire as she descends into dementia. Howes astutely remarks of Hoult that 'one of her strengths as a writer lies in her ability to create characters whose thoughts and language both inspire the reader's sympathy and a sharp awareness of their limitations without authorial comment'.[51] *There Were No Windows* does this so effectively and forces us to see the world from Claire's point of view so acutely that it is recommended in gerontological practice for those involved in the care of dementia and Alzheimer's sufferers[52]: 'For though I am old, and look old and fearfully shabby, yet my heart still flows with pain just as when I was young, only now there is no one to run to, no letter to expect, no possibility of the long estrangement ending, no one to say goodnight to.'[53] The novel refuses distance and 'Othering' and, as Jeannette King argues, replaces 'dread with empathy'.[54] It also bridges the chasm between 'middlebrow' domestic fiction and modernist women's writing. It is based on the final years of Violet Hunt, whose career spanned New Woman fiction, women's suffrage activism and modernist literary salons. Choosing Hunt as protagonist sets up a critical dialogue with modernism itself and with the scholarly positioning of modernist women as consorts, providers of infrastructure like literary salons, and the relegation of their literary reputation to footnotes. *There Were No Windows* addresses the experience of the London Blitz from the point of view of this confused and yet acerbic old woman,

madly clinging on to her self-importance and her snobbery as the world
around her falls into chaos, but somehow still capable of puncturing the
pomposity of nations. When her former secretary, Sara, lectures her over
tea and toast that, 'the great thing about this war is that since Dunkirk
at any rate all the petty personal things are over. The nation is standing
together as it never has done for centuries. Not since the Napoleonic
wars', Claire responds, 'How interesting you make it all sound. Or if not
interesting, so moral. That is another reason why there is something so
grim about this war. It is an uplift affair, and uplifting things are generally dull and dowdy. Of course, you belong to an uplift society, weren't
you telling me?'[55]

There Were No Windows simultaneously satirizes modernism's elitism
and borrows its techniques, notably with its use of multiple unreliable
narrators. In its central protagonist, it compellingly realizes the terror of
a woman losing her mind and memory – though not her wit – and provides an excoriating allegory of the dissolution of individuality in a world
maddened by war. With Kate O'Brien's historical allegory *That Lady*[56]
and Elizabeth Bowen's *The Heat of the Day*,[57] it is part of an extraordinary trio of novels by Irish and Anglo-Irish women responding to the
experience of women living through the Blitz. Their shared atmosphere
of claustrophobia and encroaching darkness stands in marked contrast
to the broad historical canvas of the ambivalently Irish Olivia Manning,
whose Balkan and Levant trilogies chronicle the Second World War from
the point of view of a woman who is swept around Eastern Europe and
the Middle East by the fortunes of war, but who is consequently is a participant rather than a bystander in historical processes.[58]

Irish women's fiction in the period 1922–60 urgently and centrally
addresses issues of sexuality, gender and nationality. It also analyses the
impact of war on women and societies, critiques many aspects of masculine culture as well as women's social constraints, satirizes and allego-
rizes, stretches genres, uses modernist narrative and stylistic techniques,
engages with international publishing and battles Irish censorship. It is
not always successful in all or any of these things, but sometimes it is
spectacularly so. The strength and diversity of this writing challenges
readers and critics to re-draw the literary map of the novel in Ireland.

Notes

1 See, for example, Lise Jaillant, *Modernism, Middlebrow and the Literary
   Canon: The Modern Library Series, 1917–1955* (London: Pickering & Chatto,
   2014); Martin Hipsky, *Modernism and the Women's Popular Romance in*

Britain, 1885–1925 (Athens: Ohio University Press, 2011); Aaron Jaffe, *Modernism and the Culture of Celebrity* (Cambridge: Cambridge University Press, 2005).

2   Margot Gayle Backus, *The Gothic Family Romance: Heterosexuality, Child Sacrifice, and the Anglo-Irish Colonial Order* (Durham, NC: Duke University Press, 1999).

3   The history of the club has been explored and documented in Deirdre Brady's unpublished doctoral thesis, 'Literary Coteries and the Irish Women Writers' Club (1933–1958)', University of Limerick, 2013. See also Deirdre Brady, 'Modernist Presses and the Gayfield Press', *Bibliologia*, 9, no. 24: 103–18.

4   Rosamund Jacob, *The Troubled House: A Novel of Dublin in the Nineteen Twenties* (Dublin: Browne and Nolan, 1938), 91.

5   Norah Hoult, *Holy Ireland* (London: Heinemann, 1935).

6   *She Didn't Say No* (UK, G.W. Films, Cyril Frankel, 1958), based on Una Troy's story of a dressmaker raising alone her six children by six different fathers, *We Are Seven* (London: Heinemann, 1955), was entered for Britain in Brussels World Film Festival causing a minor diplomatic incident.

7   Macardle's comment on the 1937 constitution that 'I do not see how anyone holding advance views on the rights of women can support it ... it is a tragic dilemma for those who have been loyal and ardent workers in the national cause' was described by de Valera's biographer as 'akin to one of the four Gospel authors falling out with Christ' (Dorothy Macardle to de Valera, May 21, 1937, quoted in Tim Pat Coogan, *De Valera: Long Fellow, Long Shadow* (New York, NY and London: Random House, 1993), 497.

8   The Rosamund Jacob Papers, National Library of Ireland, Ms 32, 582 (68), 14 November 1931.

9   Jacob Papers, Ms 32,582 (68), 7 December 1931. It is noteworthy in terms of the context of the time that, while the atmosphere of conformity was oppressive at *The Irish Press*, Jacob had just come from visiting Hannah Sheehy Skeffington at *An Poblacht*'s offices which were under surveillance by five detectives.

10 Christine Longford, *Mr Jiggins of Jigginstown* (London: Victor Gollancz, 1933), 22.

11 Jacob's diary gives an insight into this milieu. The entry for 24 November 1937, for example, describes how she attended a meeting organized by the NUI Women Graduates Association about the formation of a new organization to protect the political, social and economic status of women. The meeting in Engineers Hall, Dawson Street reported: 'Full, and good speeches from Dorothy, Mrs Kettle, etc ... Hanna spoke well, and Dr Hayden'. MS 32,582 (83).

12 Norah Hoult, *There Were No Windows* (London: Heinemann, 1944; London: Persephone, 2005).

13 Sinéad Gleeson, ed., *The Long Gaze Back: An Anthology of Irish Women Writers* (Dublin: New Island, 2015) and Sinéad Gleeson, ed., *The Glass Shore: Short Stories by Women Writers from the North of Ireland*

(Dublin: New Island, 2016). The popularity and impact of *The Glass Shore* was indicated by it winning the BGE Journal 'Irish published book of the year' award in 2016.

14 See, for example, *The Field Day Anthology of Irish Writing* ed. Angela Bourke et al. (Cork: Cork University Press, 2002) volume 5, 581 and Clair Wills, *That Neutral Island: Ireland in the Second World War* (London: Faber and Faber, 2008).

15 Jacob Papers, MS 32,582 (52), 15 June 1926.

16 See Bernadette Whelan's discussion of the purchasing and borrowing patterns of Irish libraries in this period in Gerardine Meaney, Mary O'Dowd and Bernadette Whelan, *Reading the Irish Woman: Studies in Cultural Encounters and Exchange, 1714–1960* (Liverpool: Liverpool University Press, 2014), 138ff.

17 Patricia Lynch, *The Book Shop by the Quay* (Letchworth: Aldine Press, 1956; Dublin: Poolbeg, 1995).

18 Coogan, *De Valera*, 497.

19 Dorothy Macardle, *Uneasy Freehold* (London: Peter Davies, 1942), 82. Published in the US as *The Uninvited* (New York: Doubleday, Doran, 1942). Reissued under the US title by Tramp Press (Dublin, 2016).

20 The success of Susan Hill's *The Woman in Black* indicates the idea that the woman who has been compelled to give up her child is a dark and dangerous force is still alive and well.

21 Norah Hoult, *Time, Gentlemen, Time* (London: Heinemann, 1930).

22 Elizabeth Connor, *Dead Star's Light* (London: Methuen, 1938).

23 Jacob, *The Troubled House*, 271.

24 Ibid.

25 Ibid.

26 Pamela Hinkson, *The Ladies' Road* (London: Victor Gollancz, 1932); Longford, *Mr Jiggins of Jigginstown*.

27 Hinkson, *The Ladies' Road*, 23.

28 Ibid., 32.

29 Ibid., 27.

30 Ibid., 51.

31 Ibid., 209.

32 Ibid., 211.

33 Ibid., 320.

34 Ibid., 76–83.

35 Kathleen Coyle, *A Flock of Birds* (London: Jonathan Cape, 1930; Dublin: Wolfhound; Chester Springs: Dufour, 1995).

36 Ibid., 10.

37 Ibid., 17.

38 Ibid., 18.

39 Ibid., 158.

40 Ibid., 159.

41 Ibid., 157.

42 Ibid., 18.

43 Molly Keane (M. J. Farrell), *Two Days in Aragon* (London: Collins, 1941; London: Virago, 1985).

44 Maura Laverty, *Touched by the Thorn* (London and New York, NY: Longmans, Green and Co., 1943).

45 See Christopher Fitzsimon, *The Boys: A Biography of Michael MacLiammoir and Hilton Edwards* (Dublin: New Island, 2002), 173 and Meaney et al., *Reading the Irish Woman*, 210–12.

46 Janet Madden Simpson, ed. *Woman's Part: An Anthology of Short Fiction by and about Irish Women 1890–1960* (Dublin: Arlen House, 1984).

47 Anne Crone, *Bridie Steen* (New York, NY: C. Scrubber & Sons, 1948; London: Heinemann, 1949; Dublin: Arlen House, 1984).

48 Katherine Keane, *Who Goes Home?* (Dublin: Talbot Press, 1947).

49 See Heather Ingman, *Twentieth-Century Fiction by Irish Women: Nation and Gender* (New York, NY: Ashgate, 2007) for a very broad-ranging Kristevan exploration of these themes, Claire Bracken, *Irish Feminist Futures* (New York, NY: Routledge, 2016) for an analysis which draws on Deleuzian theory and Susan Cahill, *Irish Literature in the Celtic Tiger Years 1990 to 2008: Gender, Bodies, Memory* (New York, NY: Continuum, 2013) for an account of their continuity and disruption at the end of the century.

50 Bourke et al., *The Field Day Anthology*, volume 4, 933.

51 Ibid.

52 Hannah Zeilig, 'The critical use of narrative and literature in gerontology', *International Journal of Ageing and Later Life*, 6, no. 2 (2012): 7–37.

53 Hoult, *There Were No Windows*, 143.

54 Jeannette King, *Discourses of Ageing in Fiction and Feminism* (Basingstoke: Palgrave Macmillan, 2013), 43.

55 Hoult, *There Were No Windows*, 82.

56 Kate O'Brien, *That Lady* (London: Heinemann, 1946).

57 Elizabeth Bowen, *The Heat of the Day* (London: Cape, 1945).

58 Olivia Manning, *The Great Fortune* (London: Heinemann, 1960); Olivia Manning, *The Spoilt City* (London: Heinemann, 1962); Olivia Manning, *Friends and Heroes* (London: Heinemann, 1965); Olivia Manning, *The Danger Tree* (London: Weidenfield and Nicholson, 1977); Olivia Manning, *The Battle Lost and Won* (London: Weidenfield and Nicholson, 1978); Olivia Manning, *The Sum of Things* (London: Weidenfield and Nicholson, 1980).

CHAPTER II

Elizabeth Bowen

Patricia Coughlan

Elizabeth Bowen (1899–1973), who is among the most important twentieth-century writers in English, flourished over four decades from the 1920s to the 1960s. Beginning in 1923, she published ten novels, seven short-story collections, the family history *Bowen's Court* (1942) and the brief childhood memoir *Seven Winters* (1942); she was also a prolific essayist, reviewer, broadcaster and travel-writer. Her most celebrated novels are *The Last September* (1929), *The House in Paris* (1935), *The Death of the Heart* (1938) and *The Heat of the Day* (1949), but there is now a growing appreciation of previously neglected work from the 1920s and the 1960s, especially *Friends and Relations* (1931) and *Eva Trout* (1968). Some score of her short stories are genre classics, including many of the dozen set in Ireland, and several wartime stories collected in *The Demon Lover* (1946).

Bowen's Themes and Style: Modernity and Modernism

In terms of theme, from her early work onwards Bowen complicates the conventional scripts of monogamous romance, undoes the marriage-plot, repeatedly stages erotic triangles and writes desire as destabilizing and threatening to complacent notions of the orderly self. Her fiction focuses on women's experiences in modernity. Along a timeline from the 1920s to the 1960s, she plays out their striving, in a transformed world, for love, to satisfy their desires, for freedom from the constrictions of inherited rules of behaviour. Frequently her protagonists must resist control by manipulative, dominating mothers and aunts enforcing those rules in the interest of class continuance. This repeated struggle taps into a deep substratum of her personal thematics, namely the child: she is one of the greatest novelists of children. She dwells especially on orphans, sometimes almost as representative twentieth-century figures: isolated, pawns to uncaring adults, displaced, refugees. Bereft but – to an almost frightening degree – resolute, the Bowen child is determined to 'make an impression' on her (less often, his) environment. Notably, this child has unfinished business with a 'Bad Mother' figure, very often cast in a negative light, whether controlling and prohibiting or absent (literally or emotionally); 'Good Mother' versions are scarcer and can offer only ineffectual nurture. These unresolved child-mother contentions make distinctive Bowen's handling of the theme of women's self-realization which she shares with her contemporaries.

Her work has kinship with psychoanalytic perspectives and Proustian insights; her individual characters are divided within themselves and from others, and she anticipates trauma theory in writing memory as an involuntary haunting and as always-already fictional. Her vision is dark, showing human relationships as inextricably entailing power struggles. She registers urban modernity – speed, technology, cinema, bombardment – as galvanizing, yet conveys an acute sense of the growing destabilization after 1914: economic disaster, the collapse of the pre-1914 order of class and family, fascism. Her liminal cultural positioning between national identities, in the moment of Irish rebellion and independence, is vitally connected to the unsettled and unsettling nature of her novels and stories; so too is her attention to both heterosexual and lesbian sexualities.

In terms of form, she creatively hybridizes genres, intertwining, merging and subverting *Bildungsroman*, comedy of manners, Gothic and sensation-fiction. The short stories often deploy motifs from the uncanny and sensational tales she relished in adolescence to disturb psychological complacency or explore twentieth-century social disintegration.

Male-centred conceptions and histories of modernism have tended to exclude Bowen. Yet her writing is unmistakably modernist in withholding the fluent realist reproduction of an empirical world, estranging conventional assumptions about reality. The objects in her décors – clocks, mirrors, pictures – are never mere possessions but are discrete and often, uncannily, seem baleful.[1] Near-eventless scenes, sinuous, cerebral dialogue and startling syntactic inversions constitute her narratives. Once condemned as mannered and viewed as blemishes, these disruptive formal choices have won their due respect, and indeed her late work is beginning to be seen as a form of postmodernism. The question of Bowen's style is, however, a complex one. Her occasional categorization as middlebrow arises from the popularity of her middle novels, which do give more aid and comfort to realist readings than either earlier or later ones, partly because love- and lost-children stories are salient in their plots, and they move beyond elegant irony into more emotionally searching modes.

While Bowen was a prominent literary figure in her lifetime, her reputation till the early 1980s was seriously circumscribed. 'Had she been a man,' John Banville wrote, 'she would have been recognized as one of the finest novelists of the twentieth century'. Other processes of gate-keeping based on ethnicity, class origins and geography have combined with gender to play roles in Bowen's categorization in limiting, some-times patronizing, ways: as a women's writer, a novelist of élite manners between the wars, a Big House writer (each designation ignoring vital facets of her writing to corral her within a limiting classification). In fact, the sheer reach of her work, which encompasses all these characteristics, and the startling strangeness of her vision and style, posed challenges to criticism.[2]

Victoria Glendinning's 1977 biography, Hermione Lee's 1981 critical monograph and her 1986 prose selection marked significant progress in Bowen studies; an ever-broader array of critical viewpoints has since emerged, raising her status.[3] Recent critics such as Maud Ellmann, Andrew Bennett and Nicholas Royle have definitively shown how far Bowen's achievement exceeds her conventional reception. Bennett and Royle (1995) read her work as 'pervaded by the forces of dissolution and mourning', while Ellmann (2003) reveals Bowen's brilliant realization of fractured interiority and her consistently sceptical account of monoga-mous romance. *The Heat of the Day* and the 1940s stories were early recognized as classics of war writing: subsequent criticism has expanded this recognition well beyond the specifics of the Blitz, showing how violent historical process and change from the First World War onwards preoccupies Bowen and plays a key role in her formidable melancholy vision of modernity.[4]

Scholars of women's writing have been foundational in Bowen stud-ies, seeing beyond her own disavowal of social feminism, discerning the unmistakably interrogative character of her gender representations, and pinpointing her lacerating satire of English upper-middle-class self-assurance with its confining rules about sexuality and gender. Psychoanalytic, poststructuralist and feminist perspectives figure impor-tantly among these more capacious and dynamic approaches. In 1994, Renée Hoogland pioneered the study of Bowen's imaginative investment in lesbian affect. Hoogland is sometimes felt to overstate the case, but overly reductionist disclaimers have also appeared, regrettably polarizing feminist and queer approaches. Recent scholarship on lesbian social per-formance in twentieth-century English culture illuminates the insistent presence of lesbian or proto-lesbian characters in the early and late novels and several stories. Moreover, the abiding complexity of sexual choices in Bowen's life has since emerged.[5]

Biography

An only child, Bowen was born in 1899 into the Anglo-Irish landed gentry in North Cork. In 1930 she inherited Bowen's Court, a gaunt eighteenth-century mansion, after the dismantling of landlord wealth and power by successive reforms post-1885. Culminating in the 1923 compulsory government purchase of tenanted lands, these measures removed the economic basis of Protestant Ascendancy. Without the rental income her ancestors enjoyed, Bowen struggled to maintain the house on the proceeds of her writing, eventually selling it in 1959. Her sense of being not quite placed either in geography or in cultural identity – she lived mainly in England and called herself 'hybrid' – accompanied an awareness of historical belatedness.[6] Perhaps paradoxically, the terminal decline of her caste proved, with her personal experiences of displacement, extraordinarily stimulating to her imagination as a writer. The larger breaks and cataclysms, political, economic and social, marking world history 1914–45 are vivid historical contexts for her first seven novels.

Bowen's childhood, alternating till 1907 between Dublin, her birthplace, and Co. Cork, was disturbed by family upheavals. Her birth was difficult and dangerous. A much-desired male heir, already named Robert in anticipation, had been expected: Elizabeth was well loved, but her gender and the absence of siblings breached the customary male lineage. Her fiction dwells on both diminishing gentry natality, and a troubled sense by women of their reproductive obligations, with plots involving infertility and miscarriage.[7] When Florence, her mother, almost died of another lost pregnancy, Henry Bowen began suffering the serious mental illness which, two years later, would occasion Florence's taking Elizabeth to England. Bowen explained Henry's startling self-culpabilization to a 1971 interviewer: 'in 1904 he had failed to give new life to the dead Robert, his father, in the birth of Robert, his son, and he had almost killed his own wife trying'.[8] Mother and daughter lived in intense mutual attachment but, after Henry recovered, a second blow fell: Florence died of cancer. Elizabeth was thirteen. Glimpses of this lost life with Florence appear in the powerful early story 'Coming Home' and in orphaned Portia's memories of travels with her mother in *The Death of the Heart*.[9]

The loss permanently scarred Elizabeth, who developed a lifelong stammer.[10] Contemporary class norms required that strong emotion be contained: kept from Florence's funeral and discouraged from open mourning, Elizabeth learned to suppress her feelings rigorously. Much later she wrote: 'I registered what I loved with such pangs of love ... only out of the corner of my eye ... with an unwilling fraction of my being.' Thus began 'a career of withstood emotion'. Significantly, she wrote, '[s]ensation, I have never fought shy of nor done anything to restrain'; this illuminates her work's distinctive combination of the sensuous and the cerebral.[11] The excoriation of well-bred silences is a major theme in Bowen's work, and burial tropes, incomplete mourning and returns of the repressed pervade her texts. It is as if Florence's grave, unseen by Elizabeth in fact, must continually be revisited in her fiction, though nothing may be found there: in *The Little Girls* (1963) three schoolgirls bury objects in a coffer and decades later find it empty on disinterment; in *To the North* the widowed Cecilia's heart is 'a little coffer of ashes'.[12] Bowen criticism is now productively addressing this cluster of meanings in which she interweaves personal, intimate loss and its suppression with war, displacement and the public-historical ruptures of her lifetime.

In her later teens she attended the progressive school Downe House, which valued girls' intellectual and aesthetic development; her fiction uses funny, mildly satirical versions of this experience. Henry Bowen, happily remarried, lived till 1930 at Bowen's Court, while Elizabeth 'shuttle[ed] between two countries'.[13] A brief 1920 engagement to a Cork-stationed British officer was quietly terminated with an aunt's help (somewhat similar rash betrothals occur in *The Last September* and her first novel *The Hotel* from 1927).[14] Two terms' attendance at a London art school also proved abortive. But Bowen had already begun to write prolifically, and Downe's headmistress Olive Willis enabled her access to London literary circles via Rose Macaulay, who helped her to publication. A first story collection, *Encounters*, appeared in 1923, and she very quickly turned herself into a professional writer, maintaining lifelong dedication to her work. After feeling 'at everyone's disposition' in her motherless adolescence, she struggled to achieve what she called 'a normal relation to society', later remarking that her writing *was* that normal relation, recalling her sense that 'an author, a grown-up, must they not be synonymous?'[15] Also in 1923, she further 'signified her adulthood' by marrying Alan Cameron, a First World War survivor.[16] The marriage was happy and durable though apparently asexual. Through Cameron, employed at the BBC, Bowen, who loved company, soon flourished in elite Oxford and London intellectual circles. During the 1930s the couple gave summer Bowen's Court house-parties for prominent literary friends.

From at least the mid-1930s Bowen led an active extra-marital sexual life. Bisexual in orientation, she then and later had affairs with women and men.[17] Notable among the latter were her first male sexual partner, Oxford critic Humphry House, Irish writer Sean O'Faolain and, from 1941, Canadian diplomat Charles Ritchie.[18] This became her strongest emotional relationship, sustained by correspondence and meetings till her death, though Ritchie married in 1948. Both were colonial semi-outsiders who, coming from relatively remote places (in Ritchie's case Nova Scotia), could, as Glendinning says, 'pass' in upper-class English society.[19] This conduct of social life as multi-layered performance, including the discretion Bowen's married status entailed, contributes significantly to the charged emotional atmosphere of her war novel, *The Heat of the Day*, with conflicted identity and betrayal at its heart. Also significant was Bowen's covert wartime employment gathering intelligence in Ireland for the British Ministry of Information concerning the very vexed question of Ireland's neutrality. I discuss the whole constellation of Bowen and Ireland below.

After 1949, Bowen, widowed in 1952, wrote less fiction but formidable amounts of occasional prose, in addition to broadcasting, lecturing and teaching internationally. From the later 1940s her specifically political ideas grew more fixedly conservative. After the 1959 sale (and rapid demolition) of Bowen's Court, she eventually settled in Hythe, the scene of her happiest childhood years. She died of cancer in 1973, and is buried – as 'Mrs Cameron' – in the Farahy churchyard beside where Bowen's Court stood.

Bowen and Ireland

Within Irish criticism, contrasting reductionist pitfalls have risked distorting Bowen's reception. On one hand, she is found wanting on political grounds for not having disavowed gentry privilege and hegemony. On the other, Ascendancy dispossession is problematically equated with other, far more oppressive, forced displacements, encouraging nostalgia. While a more informed understanding of the nature of her Irishness has emerged, she is still in the process of admission to the Irish canon. Sinéad Mooney rightly likens Bowen's perceived lack of Irish 'credentials' to Beckett's, noting her distinct questioning of a realist 'metaphysics of presence', though the masculinist cast of Irish modernist studies has further functioned to exclude her.[20] Nels Pearson's recent re-conception of her beside Joyce and Beckett as an Irish cosmopolitan indicates, however, a welcome passage beyond such binaries.[21] The 1980s historicist turn in Irish criticism did recruit *The Last September* to this narrative, but

narrowly as the culminating Big House novel, making it amenable to
post-colonialist readings and acknowledging its power, but by a virtual
severance from most of her work and largely ignoring the importance
of gender and sexuality in her vision and how strikingly she combines
gender critique with her end-of-Ascendancy material. Yet not only are
Irish scenes highly significant in two other great novels, *The House in
Paris* and *The Heat of the Day*, the admittedly less compelling *A World of
Love* (1955), and several of her finest stories, but Ireland with its disruptive narratives is an always ghosting presence throughout the work, significant not merely in specifically Irish scenes. The consensus now is that,
far from being important only when explicitly evident in plot or setting,
Bowen's conflicted relationships to Ireland, England and Anglo-Irishness
pervade all her writing and her Irishness, however hyphenated by the
'Anglo-' prefix, deeply underlies and forms her whole vision as a writer of
modernity. Roy Foster observes that she 'lived ambivalently between two
worlds', never being 'quite able to place herself', and that her *oeuvre* is
inseparably tangled with her biography.[22]

This ambivalence, and extensions and exacerbations of it involving
divided allegiance, surveillance, and betrayal, are hallmarks of her imagination, repeatedly appearing in her plots and in her protagonists' experience. Concrete historical contexts – the Anglo-Irish War and the Second
World War – certainly facilitate public instances of these, though illicit
or at least clandestine relations in the private, sexual sphere also figure
prominently. These insistent duplicities combine with tropes of importunate memory and the uncanny to trouble the narrative surfaces, much as
in Sheridan Le Fanu's Irish Gothic, an important influence.

A crux in Bowen's reception has been her wartime reports about attitudes to neutrality among influential Irish people, whom she interviewed
concealing her purpose; some have judged these as espionage and as war-
ranting her complete rejection from Irish belonging. Enlightened scholarship, however, especially by Foster, Clair Wills and W. J. McCormack,
has more productively explored her complex allegiance and shifting
sympathies as the war unfolded, providing a more nuanced understanding of her relation to Ireland.[23] Foster shows how her 1937 connection
with Sean O'Faolain brought her to an extent into the orbit of Irish
cultural criticism – at his instance she contributed to the radical journal
The Bell – and increased her understanding of Irish nationalism. Wills
and McCormack helpfully register the currents and counter-currents of
contemporary opinion about neutrality both inside and outside Ireland.
In *The Heat of the Day*, Bowen represents with affectionate humour the

landlord Francis Morris' self-contradictions, both defending Irish neutrality in 'almost nationalist' terms, and offering to fight for Britain despite his age. Her family history *Bowen's Court* (1942), a minor classic of Irish writing, affords remarkable insights into the Ascendancy as exemplified in a provincial-gentry family living obscurely, intermarrying with equals, alternately provident and improvident. Though the wartime context of composition softens the focus on the settler-colonialist basis of Anglo-Irish culture, Bowen acknowledges the 'inherent wrong' underlying the initial expropriation of indigenous landholders and the maintaining of a privileged caste over centuries at the direct expense of an impoverished population.[24]

The Fiction: Phases

I now explore the trajectory of her developing art, focusing principally on the novels. I group the work in three phases: the four novels published between 1927 and 1932; the 1935, 1938 and 1949 novels (culminating in *The Heat of the Day*, begun in wartime); then the three post-war novels, published between 1955 and 1968. I will attend to the alterations over her career in Bowen's style, narrative strategies and chosen milieus.

Genre, Style and Narrative Strategies: 1927–1932

While Bowen's two 1920s novels adopt the *Bildungsroman* as the point of departure, she significantly modifies its generic features to address violently changed social contexts (in *The Hotel*, aftermaths of the First World War; in *The Last September*, Irish rebellion and the end of Ascendancy). Where Jane Austen's strategy was to create harmony by combining partial reform of the social order with a purge of disruptive figures, Bowen's – emphasized by the *anomie* of the post-1918 world – is to stage negative plot outcomes, flagrantly repudiating the prescribed accommodation of self with society in English realist tradition. All four novels in this group (*The Hotel, The Last September, Friends and Relations, To the North*), moreover, pointedly withhold completion of the heroines' sentimental education. None of these books ends with the promise of a renewed or sustainable social order, but with anti-climactic dispersal, a conflagration, desolate emotional stasis and a fatal car crash respectively. Casting in question both prior social norms and their 1920s slippage, these endings undermine the moral legitimacy of the English upper class, belying Bowen's lingering reputation of society novelist. In style, her first three novels are partly comedy of manners and do dryly maintain that genre's defining irony. But from the start Bowen is forging her distinctive disruptive style, which accords with her fierce questioning of the social order by displacing the characters' interior malaise onto weather, windows and furniture, and making protagonists opaque to themselves so that their being seems dislocated.

The perception that, to reproduce themselves, societies consume the lives of the young bears heavily on her young female characters who struggle to resist that fate and to realize their own – often transgressive – desires. Older women appear as the agents of this social process (leaving her gender constructions troublingly split, posing questions to feminist interpretation).[25] These mothers and aunts are memorably silky, sometimes witchy, sometimes enchantress-like. In *The Hotel*, androgynously handsome Sydney Warren is directionless and too intelligent for an *ingénue*. She is transfixed by her own erotically charged and ultimately destructive attraction to graceful, manipulative Mrs Kerr. The novel's cast of well-heeled English expatriates in Italy inhabit a doll's-house hotel, whose lift, in a mordantly funny scene, leaves them stranded between floors, as between Edwardian and modern worlds, after the Great War's decimation of marriageable men and the still-reverberating shock of the Bolshevik Revolution. For Sydney, heterosexual romance also duly fails: no plot resolution occurs, but an anti-climactic and blackly humorous scattering of the characters.[26]

The Hotel begins by faintly echoing James, Woolf and Forster; but Bowen soon finds her own voice. *The Last September*, among her finest work, makes extraordinarily assured strides forward. Set in Ireland in 1920, it ambitiously merges Big House and *Bildungsroman* fiction. It unfolds Anglo-Irish gentry life as a set of performances of ostensibly undisturbed order in houses 'without weight', 'like cardboard, high and confident in the sun', full of redundant relics of empire. Dining beneath high ceilings, looking 'unconvincingly painted, startled, transitory', they play tennis like 'figures cut out of light green velvet'.[27] Manifestly discontented in this milieu are penniless young cousins, Lois and Laurence, who chafe at their caste's uselessness. The Proust epigraph yokes virginity and idleness with discontent, and Lois is further disaffected with the socially prescribed inactivity of gentlewomen. Tired of 'doing the flowers', longing to experience real desires, she scarcely appreciates the dancing-and-romancing frivolities fostered by the presence of 'all the lovely troops' (Laurence's sarcastic phrase). Chafing to '*do* something', she finds vicarious excitement in the desultory surrounding war.

Laurence shares this sensationalism, entertaining unsuitably positive sentiments, Oxford-nurtured and theoretical, towards Irish republicans. But Laurence has next term to go on with, while watchful Aunt Myra will pack Lois off to France or art school for, as it were, a finishing-coat of lacquer to render her marriageable.

Bowen, however, creates a disturbance – scarcely noted in predominantly post-colonialist critical accounts – at the book's centre, bringing cool, opaque and sexy Marda to visit. Marda casts not only Lois and Laurence, but also Hugo Montmorency (married, old enough to know better), into states of unsatisfied desire. After two or more failed engagements, troublesome Marda at twenty-nine is marrying the symbolically named Mr Lawe: his role will be to integrate her into society, or at least seem to do so, since she palpably lacks sexual interest in him. The reader enjoys Bowen's tragicomedy of socially inappropriate desires: a quadrille-like pattern between Marda, Lois, Hugo and Laurence (Ellmann shows how such patterns pervade Bowen's novels). As in *The Hotel*, this includes woman-to-woman magnetism: Lois's attraction to Marda is far more intensely felt than her ardent soldier-suitor's kiss.[28]

Along with its attention to lesbian attachment, the novel's striking originality is to create a paradoxical and powerful equivalence between the burning restlessness, the unfulfilment, of the young and especially of women, and the physical burning of revolutionary destruction which eventually destroys Danielstown. Lois fantasizes how a fading carpet, sign of this moribund existence, would flame in the night and be seared into Marda's memory of her visit. Bowen powerfully sustains this equivalence with her distinctive writing of inanimate things as sentient, almost bodily, haunted. Figurations of fire and of forces about to heave up and crack everything open energize the whole. The landscape itself threatens, seeming, in a glaring sunset, to close in like an invasion from behind the trees. Meanwhile the characters' schooling in repressive social forms has dissociated them from their own feelings and even bodily experiences. At the centre of *The Last September* is its connection of this psychological repression with the political maintenance, in arms, of the landlord order. This is clearly revealed in a famous passage in which looking down from the hills, Lois and Hugo see the concrete facts of forced plantation. Danielstown with its lawns makes a 'dark formal square like a rug on the green country'. Yet it seems 'smothered ... afraid', its 'isolation apparent', even 'hiding its face' in 'fright and amazement' at the 'wide, light, lovely unloving country, the unwilling bosom whereon it was set'. The edifice of Ascendancy appears evanescent, dissolving into light and water, the

Anglo-Irish presence 'an illusion', 'their passing ... less than a shadow'.[29] With a force pushing beyond realist narrative conventions, carpet, rugs, fire and ashes embody inhibition and its violent sweeping away.

Lois feels like a fly imprisoned inside a glass. Her resistance to the constriction and emptiness of gentry's codes and the imperative that young women relinquish active selfhood in marriage echoes Irish demands for freedom and redress of settler colonialism's intrinsic injustice. The 'routine of living' by the rules is also rejected by the radically disillusioned soldier Daventry, traumatized by active war service. Lois's encounter with him at the officers' dance is what shows her she cannot marry ordinary Home-Counties-bred Gerald who loves his country, his mother and his dog. Anticipating other compelling Bowen misfits (Eddie in *The Death of the Heart*, Max in *The House in Paris*), dark, haunted Daventry brings the harsh outside world into Lois's waking dream. Recognizing his devastation by real, not desultory or fantasized, war, she sees beyond her relations with the callow Gerald. Bowen ironically provides two plot devices to break Lois's unsuitable engagement: first Lois's aunt debars Gerald on grounds of income and class inadequacy, then he is killed in a crossroads ambush. Lois is dispatched to France; the rebels burn Danielstown.

In *Friends and Relations*, the first novel set in England, Bowen changes focus to a marriage-plot: indeed she gets the two marriages over with early on, so as to settle to tracing their undoing. Witty, understated and superficially uneventful, the book tingles, paradoxically, with suspense. It develops *The Last September*'s enquiry into desire and disruption, but now in the ostensibly stable Home Counties, where country gentry and professional classes were merging. A highly conscious artist, Bowen said she always thought first of the design of her plots, and afterwards peopled them with characters: she frames her story with two adulteries, one past but casting a long shadow and one which stays in the realm of potential but produces emotional desolation. Daughters of genteel Cheltenham, Laurel and Janet Studdart both marry, it seems suitably. But the calm of a social world Bowen unmistakably renders as claustrophobic and inward-turned is shattered by a combination of the old 'sin' and the clever lesbian Theodora's desire 'beyond propriety' for Janet. One of Bowen's memorable childlike disrupters, Theodora has the brain her father thinks his son would have had, and a too-large personality, like a punt-pole. She triggers the *dénouement* from malice and emotional desperation combined, an intervention structurally paralleling the conflagration desired by Lois.

Bowen traces the ever-unresolved contention of equal and opposite forces: non-negotiable passion, which can crack open surfaces, and containment: the respectable social order with its 'stiff chintz curtains ... whisper[ing] against [Janet's] window sill', its determination as it were to 'stay indoors with the blinds down because of a funeral always going by'.[30] Not coincidentally, this is also the first of Bowen's novels where determined children with an appetite for sensation figure significantly.[31] Pre-teen Anna can 'guess at nothing of what had not occurred' between the adults (the 'not' is quintessentially Bowen), but will 'feed on' the unacknowledged crisis, 'making her strong young growth, like a tree, from the very thought of ruin'.[32] If Theodora's destructiveness is child-like, it seems almost preferable to the correct, acceptable femininity of the period, which Bowen shows as infantilizing, even as a form of impairment. Caught in the book's impasse of misdirected desire, blame-less Laurel seems arrested in childhood. They had 'married her properly, formally, with a marquee', yet 'not, somehow, married her off', thinks her mother (the marquee an ironic master-stroke). Even Mrs Studdart wishes Laurel could be something other than a woman. This constrict-ing womanliness underpins a psychologically moribund society: none of the four younger generation has been or will be able to free themselves into happiness. At the close, Colonel Studdart walks into Cheltenham along the Promenade, the chestnuts in flower, with a visiting daughter on each arm: appearances are thus charmingly saved, devastating realities unacknowledged.

In *Friends and Relations*, an almost Edwardian stasis anachronistically governs the characters' lives: only Theodora, whose flat has an aggres-sively modernist décor, seems to inhabit the freer, jazzy urban 1920s. But Bowen's next novel, *To the North* (1932), focuses on modern, including modernist, London with its 'aerial glassy white factories'. Change and motion in several senses seem the very theme of the book. Train and air travel and other mechanizing transformations of life match the energy of the plot's catastrophic sexual affair. Traffic glares and vibrates, taxis fling and jerk their occupants. Speed, risk, even recklessness sweep away pro-prieties and restrictions on women's behaviour.

Emmeline and Cecilia share a modern *ménage*. Their 'running about alone' and 'talking too freely' incurs disapproval from Lady Waters, a vintage managing Bowen aunt. Pretty widow Cecilia, apparently a social butterfly, feels unreal when alone, like an unwound clock or breath fad-ing on a mirror, and marries the dull but dependable Julian Tower. By contrast, strong-willed Emmeline is another of Bowen's disturbing and restless seekers. She owns a travel agency and drives her own car: her cool manner flouts gender correctness. Bowen here gives us a far more sexually risky milieu than those of Sydney, Lois or Laurel and Janet. Cecilia encounters (on a train, fittingly) the louche, questionable Markie, a modern type recurrent in Bowen (the 'near cad', in O'Faolain's phrase).[33] Markie occupies an apartment at the top of his sister's house, ordering meals by speaking-tube (a brilliant trope of the age's social dissociation). When Emmeline embarks on a disastrous affair with him, he destroys her. But this is not merely the immemorial plotline of virginal female victim and male rake basely seizing his chance. Emmeline is a modern active woman, delighting in dispatching travellers to risky destinations. Though drawing on distant Jamesian antecedents, she is a resonant figure in Bowen's developing analysis of twentieth-century femininities. Emmeline's desire is unmistakably physical: 'it was not in words [Markie] was writing himself across her'.[34]

In a scene full of brilliantly displaced eroticism, they fly to Paris. But the force of Emmeline's awakened passion outpaces Markie, who recoils from her. Her bewildered suffering is powerfully rendered, producing the catastrophic – and strikingly filmic – ending, an ultimate dangerous journey. Accelerating recklessly northward from London, Emmeline carries them both to destruction in a literal death-drive. Her insistently self-authorized desire destroys her by happening to fall on the despicable Markie. Neither Lady Waters' within-bounds ideas of appropriate behaviour for women, nor Cecilia's listless conformism, carries conviction as an alternative. The pronounced modernism of Bowen's vision has gained momentum.

1935–1949

As Bowen's art and thought develop, the initially adolescent drive towards agency, to 'make an impression' on the world, shown in Emmeline as a specifically sexual desire, changes to encompass deep wishes for loving attachment. *The House in Paris* is a hinge work opening towards this more complex vision, further broadened in the following two novels, *The Death of the Heart* and *The Heat of the Day*. All three contain important representations of mother-child relations; the first and third also see Bowen's finest writing about heterosexual love as a profound transformative experience: these were her most widely appreciated works. This deepening representation of attachment in the personal sphere is accompanied by more attention to history both public and international. Important 1930s stories had registered interwar social change: memorably dystopic, 'The Disinherited' concerns English gentry self-destruction in debt and dissipation, while 'The Tommy Crans' exposes failed Irish Ascendancy fortunes in a Dublin suburb.[35] A masterpiece of sympathetic narration from a young boy's viewpoint, this story prefigures the extraordinary first section of *The House in Paris*.

Moving, erotic and funny, the narration begins near the end of the plot events, which unfold backwards. A one-day encounter of two children, strangers, in the eponymous house, opens the book. Both are displaced, quasi-orphaned ('nobody knows I'm born,' says Leopold, angrily). They are also eagle-eyed and determined not to be merely transported like luggage. Not yet bound up in the Oedipal economy of correct social reproduction – the 'rule of niceness' – they are clear-sighted, not yet unfree, full of potential. Their encounter, part-mutual irritation, part-sympathy, is echoed in the later-disclosed scenes between the clandestine lovers Karen and Max, Leopold's parents. The protagonist Karen struggles against a comfortable, deadening upper-class future, desperate to break out and become herself. She feels that Ray, the suitable (and devoted) English gentleman she is engaged to, will keep her controlled exactly as her – grand, distant – mother has, and acts on the transgressive impulse to sleep with Max, her friend Naomi's fiancé, a Jewish-French-English outsider with questionable prospects and a sensual, unsettling intensity.

The House in Paris notably looks beyond England: to the sinking post-decolonization Co. Cork gentry resettled at the edge of Ireland, to French-bourgeois aspiration as embodied in Madame Fisher, Naomi's ruthless mother, and to the marginal, precarious lives of people designated Jewish that same year.[36] Bowen infuses Karen and Max's impossible love with intense eroticism, but death stalks it. First covertly touching hands in a no-place (the garden of Naomi's dead aunt), they consummate their relations at the edges of France and England (Boulogne, Hythe), in the shadow of the recent death of Karen's aunt. Karen, waking in the night beside Max, understands their future as a 'barred square', inescapable however often or far they travel. Yet, while their hands make no imprint on the grass, their love-making does 'make a mark', embodied in Leopold, their impossible, unplanned son (anticipating, in the longer perspective of Bowen's *oeuvre*, Eva Trout's illegally adopted child Jeremy). Harried by Madame Fisher, Max kills himself. Unable to acknowledge her non-marital child, Karen secretly fosters him out. Later, Ray draws her to retrieve the now nine-year-old Leopold: the book ends, however, without a clear signal of Karen's acceptance of him. In all her pre-war novels, Bowen has in her sights the deforming effect of rigorous prohibitions on the expression of feeling, blocking self-recognition. To exhibit emotion is bad form: Karen's mother has 'not wept for years, and never in the drawing-room': she still does not, even at her sister's death.[37] Strong emotion is felt to be a wrecking force; it is adolescent, not socially appropriate. In a moment of terrible insight, Karen sees that while 'love is obtuse and reckless', her mother shows 'not pity or kindness' but 'worldliness beginning so deep down that it seems to be the heart'.[38]

The Death of the Heart is among Bowen's masterpieces. Her most popular novel in her lifetime, it exposes another motherless child to this 'worldliness', exacerbating her danger by entangling her in a plot of desire. The style is at its most sure-footed, turning the narration's own cool, ironic surfaces against themselves by identifying them with the grand, cold drawing-room which denies feeling and cutting through them with shards of unassuaged emotional pain. Sixteen-year-old orphan Portia, daughter of a disgraced father and *déclassée* mother, sustains herself with memories of her unorthodox but loved childhood in off-season European hotels. She is taken in by her half-brother Thomas Quayne and his wife Anna, who do not love her and whose own union is frozen, like Regent's Park in the superb opening scene. In this portrait of 'an inhibited English marriage', Anna cannot reciprocate Thomas's mute, timid desire.[39] Only the housekeeper Matchett, herself inexpressive, tries to nurture Portia. The irresponsible adult Eddie, another unscrupulous malcontent, exploits her lovelessness with opportunist romantic attention. In desperation Portia seeks improbable refuge with the ex-soldier Major Brutt. A retired soldier and now a socially marginal figure living in a shabby Kensington hotel, he is capable of protective love. This relation and Matchett's clumsy surrogate mothering carry emotional truth. Bowen powerfully contrasts this with both the chill, unloving Quayne *ménage* and the lower-middle-class seaside villa ('Waikiki') of Anna's former governess, brashly modern, slightly raffish, where Portia is summarily dispatched for a summer.

Bowen's social notation of both these milieus is compelling and funny. The historical contexts of the 1930s are recognized; Portia is termed 'displaced' and 'a refugee'; Major Brutt is 'dated, like makes of cars', therefore surplus to social requirements despite his courage; and Thomas, perceiving his class's lack of vitality, expects a working-class revolt.[40] There are evident resonances with Bowen's biography, including Matchett's insisting to Portia that to mourn openly is right. Childless Anna intriguingly suggests how Karen might have stagnated: Charles

Ritchie perceptively discerned in Anna and Portia two halves of a self-portrait by Bowen. The cynical novelist St Quentin famously describes Portia as like 'the lunatic giant in the drawing-room': her eventual flight after Eddie abandons her is a desperate act but, like other such flagrant moves by the disempowered in Bowen, it reveals the polished social surface as bogus, confronting the Quaynes with their own moral abdication. The story ends with Matchett standing on the hotel threshold ready to retrieve Portia, but once again it is hard to see any saving resolution.

The Heat of the Day marks the climax of Bowen's career. It subsumes several major strands of her previous work, and forges an altered style which, in its twists and syntactical strains, seems to enact the very pressure of aerial bombardment, invasive technology and endemic destruction of certainties.[41] Set in wartime London, it presents with unparalleled intensity people's experiences of living in fear, dislodged from secure and predictable lives, daily witnessing death. Some early critics queried the book's public-political aspects, including an English gentleman's covert allegiance to fascism; recent criticism, however, has dispelled these difficulties, using less literal reading strategies. Bowen does not obey spy-thriller conventions, nor provide the satisfactions of that genre, including neat resolution of plot mysteries. Neither (despite fine social notation) does the novel answer entirely to realist reading expectations, with its 'jump-cuts', in Ellmann's phrase, between sensuous description of war streetscapes and demanding, cerebral dialogue. It is a book about epistemological indeterminacy, rendering a claustrophobic psychological climate with solidarity undercut by surveillance and identity requisitioned for a repertoire of roles delineated by propaganda, leaving individual selves violently severed from their mooring.

The main plot concerns Stella Rodney's passionate affair with Robert Kelway, encountered during an air-raid. Stylish and admired, she is a less stunted Anna, a Cecilia with more depth, a Karen who could mother her child. But troubled by Great War loss and 1920s marital breakdown before divorce was respectable, she feels 'she and the century' have deprived her son Roderick of 'organic family life'.[42] Robert and Stella have a rapt mutual involvement. Or so it seems until importunate state agent Harrison appears, asserting that Robert, in high-level secret employment, is an enemy spy. He warns her that to alert Robert will entail his immediate exposure, and offers to spare him or at least defer his arrest if she switches her affections to the egregious Harrison himself. This destroys Stella's emotional security, installing paranoid fears. If Robert is, as Harrison suggests, a good actor, is his love too a performance? He is watching Robert; so, now, inescapably, is she. Meanwhile, if Harrison's disclosure is reliable, Robert too is watching, for intelligence to pass on. At the *dénouement*, Robert admits his betrayal but interrogates Stella about Harrison, catching her in their reciprocal surveillance as if in criss-crossing searchlights. She sees their interchange-ability. Lover and watcher are doubles, both named Robert, undermining the romance-rhetoric ostensibly occupying centre stage; Robert's limp acquired at Dunkirk matches Harrison's stammer (and Bowen's own).

The Heat of the Day also dissolves the apparent *terra firma* of national allegiance, along with the authenticity of romantic love. Radically alien-ated from the England that formed him, Robert declares there are 'no … countries left'; 'words like betrayal can still raise terrific dust in a mind', but 'all that language is dead currency'. Resisting this – 'you cannot say there is not a country!' – Stella can summon only personal memories, as of 'that crystal ruined London morning when she had woken to his face'. But their love, their only remaining habitation, is ripped apart with 'thousands of fluctuations in their own stone country', like bombed London itself.[43]

> Daylight moves round the walls; night rings the changes of its intensity; everything is on its way to somewhere else – there is the presence of move-ment, that third presence, however still, however unheeding in their trance two may try to stay. Unceasingly something is at its work.[44]

Nothing is constant but process. And Harrison is inexorably at *his* work: Stella pictures him almost supernaturally multiplied, watching, all round the house.

Especially in directionless Roderick, *The Heat of the Day* crucially rep-resents identity – a once-clear contract between individual, class expecta-tions, and roles – as sapped by one war, further destabilized by interwar turbulence, and now reduced by another to empty performance. Longing for a script, Roderick eagerly accepts the unexpected Anglo-Irish land-owner role as a 'historic future', despite the economic improbability of its realization. This emotional investment in his inheritance, imagining Mount Morris 'standing outside the war' as 'standing outside the pre-sent', is fantasy. Bowen wittily uses the old caretaker Donovan (echoing Edgeworth's Jason Quirk) to indicate the non-feasibility of Roderick's project, murmuring 'that way, you could sink a terrible lot of money'. This is one strand of a tripartite plot-resolution: the others are Stella's plans to marry 'a brigadier', not even named, and soldier's widow Louie, finally, in a 'now complete life' as mother, showing her infant son three swans flying westwards, after 'our homecoming bombers' have passed 'invisibly high up'. Critics differ as to the force of these resolution(s). While Neil Corcoran celebrates Louie as a hopeful symbol of futurity, and Phyllis Lassner sees Stella as empowered, Gill Plain and Karen Schneider's compelling feminist readings contest such interpretations and see Bowen as critiquing the postwar re-containment of women.

1955–1968

Bowen's 1950s and 1960s novels used to be considered a falling-off from her best work. They have, however, been significantly re-evaluated in work by several recent critics working from different viewpoints. This has revealed the role of these texts in coherently advancing and completing her project as a novelist. Anne Wyatt-Brown has shown Bowen's weaving of mourning (a lifelong preoccupation) with creativity, often notable in artists' late work, while Clare Hanson's Deleuzian reading, focusing on female embodiment, reveals a strong continuity with Bowen's earlier work. The last novel, *Eva Trout*, in particular, is increasingly acknowledged within the canon of important twentieth-century fiction.

A World of Love (1955), less compelling than its three predecessors, is an interesting pendent to *The Last September*, being also set in Ireland. In a baking 1950s summer, a penniless Big House family moulders unregarded: following the heir Guy's First World War death, his illegitimate successor farms with his own hands. The sultry landscape emits uncanny energies, eerily infusing an uneventful plot. An *ingénue* daughter is a pale after-image of rebellious Lois, and history an affair of distance and diminution. After two world wars, life now seems to work at dispossessing the dead, while a (forgotten) male ancestor has erected an obelisk in his memory; a perfunctory romantic ending involving a wealthy American is sketched in. Wills counters previous dismissal of this novel, perceptively showing how Anglo-Irish isolation reflects, not only contrasts with, the condition of Ireland as a whole: decline and depopulation advance both inside and outside Montefort's walls, in grotesque disparity with nouveau-riche expatriate Lady Latterly's rebuilding of a neighbouring castle, but Bowen does register some Irish modernizations, such as Shannon Airport.[45]

The last two novels, *The Little Girls* and *Eva Trout*, challenge inattentive reading and withhold smooth narration, definitively frustrating the passive pleasures of realist style and garnering lively appreciation and respect from readers attuned to postmodernity. They also refuse the

future-orientation of the *Bildungsroman*: one by savage parody, ending in
the heroine Eva Trout's violent death rather than her arrival at satisfactory
integration, the other by unfolding backwards to the age before puberty,
when 'we were entrusted to one another, in the days that mattered'. Both
turn radically inwards, acknowledging the terror and the potential of
self-apprehension: '[n]ow, nothing. There being nothing was what you
were frightened of all the time, eh?'[46] Not coincidentally, both novels
also resume, but in far more pressing terms, Bowen's earlier exploration
of lesbian feeling, 'bracketing' the middle novels' focus on heterosexual
relations.[47]

   If *The Little Girls* is ultimately melancholy, though with piercing
insights, *Eva Trout*, however, has a quality of exhilaration. Practically a
literal embodiment of the 'lunatic giant', the physically awkward and
androgynous-looking Eva Trout is first described as 'the giantess'.[48] Her
characteristics often echo features of one or other of Bowen's earlier characters and plots. An orphaned heiress with no stable single home from
childhood on, who speaks like 'a displaced person', Eva loves technology
(like Emmeline in *To the North*). She uses her wealth to buy consumer
goods avidly, travel afar and, as an adult, to move house repeatedly. She
has experienced a deep and unmistakably lesbian love for a schoolfellow
and is passionately attracted to her teacher, Iseult. Tina O'Toole connects both Eva's physical 'monstrosity' and these transgressive desires with
Rosi Braidotti's conception of the outsider or 'deviant' as a figure both of
abjection and of potential transcendence in her very breaching of conventional norms (as enacted by several previous Bowen characters).[49]

   In a recurrence of Bowen's insistence on the maternal, Eva adopts a
son, the deaf-mute Jeremy, illegally in America. They watch many mov-
ies together, and Eva's awkward, half-fantasy performance of mothering echoes the unrealized, indeterminable Karen-Leopold bond in *The
House in Paris*. Jeremy eventually shoots Eva dead by accident on the
railway platform as she leaves on her wedding journey (how performative or parodic is not clear) with a much younger male friend.[50] A *tour
de force* in several ways, Bowen's final novel movingly draws together key
strands in her life and work. Eva shares with Jeremy an impenetrable, terrifying innocence and an irreparable homelessness, whether in language
or in place: a constellation of all. Discerning its subliminal Irishness,
Claire Connolly argues that it 'confronts contemporary readers with a
memory of an in-between space in literary and cultural history'.[51] This
'in-between'-ness, simultaneously occasioning a volatile unease and sharp
insight, distinguishes much great Irish literature; in *Eva Trout* it expresses

Bowen's self-ascribed Anglo-Irish hybridity, combining vision and pain with renewed intensity. Eva's isolation and displacement – psychological, emotional and sexual – recapitulate Bowen's own lifelong personal, cultural and spatial dislocations, speaking eloquently to her rich, complex, aesthetically incomparable life's work.

Notes

1 See the perceptive discussions by Jacqueline Rose, 'Bizarre Objects: Mary Butts and Elizabeth Bowen', in *On Not Being Able to Sleep: Psychoanalysis and the Modern World* (London: Chatto, 2003), 89–104, and Paul Muldoon, *To Ireland, I* (Oxford: Oxford University Press, 2000).

2 John Banville, 'In Praise of Elizabeth Bowen', *Irish Times*, Saturday 7 March 2015.

3 Victoria Glendinning, *Elizabeth Bowen: Portrait of a Writer* (Harmondsworth: Penguin, 1977); Hermione Lee, *Elizabeth Bowen: An Estimation* (London: Vision, 1981, revised edition London: Vintage, 1999); Hermione Lee, *The Mulberry Tree: Writings of Elizabeth Bowen*, ed. Hermione Lee (London: Virago, 1986). Elizabeth Bowen, *Modern Critical Views*, ed. Harold Bloom (New York, NY: Chelsea House, 1987) has some significant contributions.

4 Heather Bryant Jordan's *How Will the Heart Endure: Elizabeth Bowen and the Landscape of War* (Ann Arbor, MI: University of Michigan Press, 1992) inaugurated this approach, followed by Gill Plain's excellent 'From Alienation to Absence: Avoiding the War in *The Heat of the Day*', in *Women's Fiction of the Second World War: Gender, Power and Resistance* (Edinburgh: Edinburgh University Press, 1996), 166–88.

5 See Laura Doan and Jane Garrity, 'Introduction', in *Sapphic Modernities: Sexuality, Women and National Culture*, ed. Laura Doan and Jane Garrity (London: Palgrave, 2006), 1–13; Patricia Coughlan, 'Women and Desire in Elizabeth Bowen', in *Sex, Nation and Dissent in Irish Writing*, ed. Eibhear Walshe (Cork: Cork University Press, 1997), 104–34 and '"Not like a person at all": Elizabeth Bowen's "The Dancing-Mistress"', in *Elizabeth Bowen: Visions and Revisions*, ed. Eibhear Walshe (Dublin: Irish Academic Press, 2009), 40–65; Tina O'Toole, 'Unregenerate Spirits: The Counter-Cultural Experiments of George Egerton and Elizabeth Bowen', in *Irish Women Writers: New Critical Perspectives*, ed. Elke D'hoker, Raphael Ingelbien and Hedwig Schwall (Oxford: Peter Lang, 2011), 227–44.

6 In 'How I Write: A Discussion with Glyn Jones', and 'A Conversation with Jocelyn Brooke' (both 1950): see Elizabeth Bowen, 'Listening' in *Broadcasts, Speeches and Interviews*, ed. Allan C. Hepburn (Edinburgh: Edinburgh University Press, 2010), 272, 324.

7 See, for instance, Elizabeth Bowen, *The House in Paris* (London: Penguin, 1987); Elizabeth Bowen, *The Death of the Heart* (London: Penguin, 1987); Elizabeth Bowen, *The Heat of the Day* (Harmondsworth: Penguin, 1986);

and Elizabeth Bowen, 'The Inherited Clock' in *Collected Stories* (London: Cape, 1980). Palko innovatively brings perspectives from maternality studies to bear on *The House in Paris*, a promising future direction for Bowen studies; see 'Colonial Modernism's Thwarted Modernity: Elizabeth Bowen's *The House in Paris* and Jean Rhys's *The Voyage in the Dark*', *Textual Practice* 27, no. 1 (2013): 89–108.

8   In the words of the interviewer Edwin Kenney, *Elizabeth Bowen* (Lewisburg: Bucknell University Press, 1975), 25.

9   'Coming Home', Elizabeth Bowen, *Collected Stories, Introduction by Angus Wilson* (London: Penguin, 1983), 95–100.

10 Her cousin Audrey Fiennes said she 'never got over it' (Glendinning, *Bowen*, 28–9).

11 Elizabeth Bowen, *Pictures and Conversations, foreword by Spencer Curtis Brown* (London: Allen Lane, 1974), 9.

12 Elizabeth Bowen, *To the North* (London: Vintage, 1999), 160.

13 'Preface', Elizabeth Bowen, *Early Stories* (New York, NY: Knopf, 1951), x.

14 Elizabeth Bowen, *The Hotel* (London: Penguin, 1987).

15 Bowen, *Early Stories*, x.

16 Kenney, *Elizabeth Bowen*, 30.

17 Virginia Woolf wrote to Vita Sackville-West that Bowen's 'emotions sway in a certain way' (*The Letters of Virginia Woolf*, ed. Nigel Nicolson and Joanne Trautmann, vol. 5 (London: Hogarth,1979), 111; see Glendinning's nuanced discussion (*Bowen*, 188–93 and *Love's Civil War: Elizabeth Bowen and Charles Ritchie: Letters and Diaries from the Love Affair of a Lifetime* (London: Simon and Schuster, 2009), 135); Nicola Darwood, *A World of Lost Innocence: The Fiction of Elizabeth Bowen* (Cambridge: Cambridge Scholars, 2012), 61–4.

18 House wrote: 'Why, Elizabeth, did you not tell me when we first slept together that you were a virgin?' (23 July 1934). Quoted in Deirdre Toomey, 'Elizabeth Bowen', in *New Oxford Dictionary of National Biography* (Oxford: Oxford University Press, 2004). Accessed 19 February 2018. https://doi-org.ucc.idm.oclc.org/10.1093/ref:odnb/30839

19 *Love's Civil War*, ed. Glendinning, 5.

20 Sinéad Mooney, 'Unstable Compounds: Bowen's Beckettian Affinities'. 'Special Issue: Elizabeth Bowen', *MFS: Modern Fiction Studies* 53, no. 2 (2007): 238–56.

21 Nels Pearson, *Irish Cosmopolitanism: Location and Dislocation in James Joyce, Elizabeth Bowen, and Samuel Beckett* (Gainesville: University Press of Florida, 2015).

22 Roy Foster, 'The Irishness of Elizabeth Bowen', in *Paddy and Mr Punch: Connections in Irish and English History* (London: Allen Lane, 1993), 102–33.

23 Ibid., 102–33, and Roy Foster, 'Prints on the Scene: Elizabeth Bowen and the Landscape of Childhood', in *The Irish Story: Telling Tales and Making It Up in Ireland* (London: Allen Lane, 2001), 148–63; Clair Wills,

That Neutral Island: A Cultural History of Ireland during World War II (London: Faber, 2008); W. J. McCormack, *Dissolute Characters: Irish Literary History through Balzac, Le Fanu, Yeats and Bowen* (Manchester: Manchester University Press, 1993).

24 Elizabeth Bowen, *Bowen's Court* (London: Virago, 1984), 453.

25 Though Heather Ingman, drawing on Helene Deutsch, interestingly suggests reading such perverse self-empowerment as an outlet for women frustrated in patriarchal culture. See *Women's Fiction between the Wars: Mothers, Daughters, and Writing* (New York, NY: St Martin's Press, 1998), 73–8.

26 See Petra Rau, 'Telling it Straight: The Rhetorics of Conversion in Elizabeth Bowen's *The Hotel* and Freud's *Psychogenesis*', in *Sapphic Modernities: Sexuality, Women and National Culture*, ed. Doan and Garrity, 217–31.

27 Elizabeth Bowen, *The Last September* (London: Vintage, 1998), 115–16, 24, 48.

28 See Coughlan, 'Women and Desire in Elizabeth Bowen', 123–5.

29 Bowen, *The Last September*, 65.

30 Elizabeth Bowen, *Friends and Relations*, with an Introduction by Candia McWilliam (London: Vintage, 1999), 89–90, 135.

31 But see *The Last September*'s hilarious cameo of the anxious child Hercules Langrishe, last of his name, engaged to retrieve tennis-balls from the hedge, who must overcome his fear of bats before he can go away to school.

32 Bowen, *Friends and Relations*, 152.

33 Sean O'Faolain, *The Vanishing Hero: Studies in Novelists of the Twenties* (London: Eyre and Spottiswoode, 1956), 178.

34 Bowen, *To the North*, 70–1.

35 Muldoon powerfully explores this story's political uncanny in *To Ireland, I*, 18–25.

36 See Jean Radford, 'Late Modernism and the Politics of History', in *Women Writers of the '30s: Gender, Politics and History*, edited and with an introduction by Maroula Joannou (Edinburgh: Edinburgh University Press, 1999), 33–45.

37 Bowen, *The House in Paris*, 126.

38 Ibid., 174.

39 As Lee puts it in *Bowen: An Estimation*, 111.

40 'There was of course his courage', but 'makes of men date, like makes of cars; Major Brutt was a 1914–18 model: there was now no market for that make' (Bowen, *The Death of the Heart*, 90–1).

41 James Purdon, *Modernist Informatics: Literature, Information and the State* (New York, NY: Oxford University Press, 2015), 185.

42 Bowen, *The Heat of the Day*, 61.

43 Ibid., 267–8, 274–5.

44 Ibid., 195.

45 Clair Wills, '"Half different": The Vanishing Irish in *A World of Love*', in *Elizabeth Bowen*, ed. Walshe, 133–49.

46 Elizabeth Bowen, *The Little Girls* (London: Penguin, 1982), 236.

47 Jane Rule, *Lesbian Images* (Garden City: Doubleday, 1976) 119.

48 Elizabeth Bowen, *Eva Trout or Changing Scenes* (London: Jonathan Cape, 1969), 13.

49 See O'Toole, 'Unregenerate Spirits: The Counter-Cultural Experiments of George Egerton and Elizabeth Bowen', in *Irish Women Writers: New Critical Perspectives*, ed. D'hoker, Ingelbien and Schwall, 227–44. O'Toole also revealingly situates the novel in the context of 1960s and earlier lesbian narratives.

50 John Coates cogently argues against interpreting this intended marriage as a mere charade in 'The Misfortunes of *Eva Trout*', *Essays in Criticism* 48, no. 1 (1998): 59–79.

51 Claire Connolly, '(Be)longing: The Strange Place of Elizabeth Bowen's Eva Trout', in *Borderlands: Negotiating Boundaries in Post-Colonial Writing*, ed. Monika Reif Hülser (Amsterdam: Rodopi, 1999), 135–43.

CHAPTER 12

Kate O'Brien

Eibhear Walshe

> Again, a scholar attempting to make a case for including O'Brien in the canon runs up against readings that, while celebrating the author simultaneously refuse to tease out the careful nuances and sophistication of her writing, preferring to remain fixated on only one or two aspects of her work. As a result, she remains, as critics justifiably lament, an under-appreciated figure in literary history despite her contemporary importance and achievement.
>
> (Brad Kent)[1]

Why is Kate O'Brien, as Brad Kent identifies, 'an under-appreciated figure' in Irish literary studies, despite her pre-eminence in the genre of the twentieth-century Irish novel? Is it, as Kent wonders, because of scholarly readings of her fictions, 'preferring to remain fixated on only one or two aspects of her work', or are there other factors coming into play? It is indisputable that her nine realist novels, published between 1931 and 1958, provide the most substantial fictive account of the Irish middle-class during this formative period of twentieth-century national consolidation, a time when, in Derek Hand's words, 'The Catholic middle classes had risen into power within the foundation of the Free State.'[2] More than that, these novels extended the possibilities and also challenged the limits of Irish modernist fiction in the twentieth century. Yet, since her death in 1974, O'Brien's novels and travel books have often been out of print, despite the recovery work of feminist publishing houses like Arlen House and Virago, and critical studies of her work are few and far between. Lorna Reynolds and Adele Dalsimer produced full-length studies in the late 1980s and early 1990s, in parallel with the re-publication of her novels, and my own biography appeared in 2006. Apart from Aintzane L. Mentxaka's 2011 study, an exploration of the importance of *Mary Lavelle* as a modernist, potentially queer text, no other major work has been produced. This is in contrast to the ten monographs and two essay collections on her contemporary, Elizabeth Bowen, whose novels and stories have always remained in print. Why is this?

O'Brien was a modernist in her interest in an enabling aesthetics of erotic transgression and also in her radical representations of gender and of sexual identities but she was, at the same time, a traditionalist in her continued deployment of nineteenth-century realist narrative forms. Her novels depend on intertextual references to Italian opera, English metaphysical poetry, German *lieder* and signifiers of privileged cultural discourse, and she included untranslated French and German phrases and letters throughout her works. By implication, these realist texts were seen as resistant to the emerging experimental forms of the mid-century novel. Another factor in her uncertain status, paradoxical given her interest in 'high' culture, was the commercial popularity and visibility of her work in her own lifetime. Her popularity with book clubs and her excellent critical writings for magazines like *Woman and Beauty* resulted in the perception of O'Brien as best-selling woman writer, in contrast to the more clearly high modernist and thus more assuredly 'literary' Elizabeth Bowen. Finally, and crucially in my opinion, cultural difficulties with her sexuality in Ireland made biographical and critical writing more challenging and thus scarce, perpetuating her ambivalent status within Irish writing. For example, her last, most overtly lesbian novel, *As Music and Splendour*, remained out of print for twenty years after her death.

Scholarly interest in her representations of lesbian and gay desire has led to the objection that these are limited and reductive perspectives in relation to the wider ramifications of her writings. However, such as they are, O'Brien studies have evolved with the rapidly changing cultural modes of thinking around sexuality, feminism and identity in twentieth- and twenty-first-century Ireland. Nearly thirty years ago, Lorna Reynolds wrote that: 'The subject of feminism is never openly raised in Kate O'Brien's work. But the theme of her novels is the necessity for woman to be as free as man.'[3] Since then, O'Brien's feminism has been acknowledged and explored and she can be read as a significant, though never straightforward, pioneer for Irish women's writing. Her literary reputation has suffered the consequences for this pioneering work in many ways.

This chapter will argue for O'Brien's centrality within Irish fiction of the twentieth century, seeing her as the enabling voice of the Irish Catholic middle class, a vital precursor for John Broderick, John McGahern, Mary O'Donnell, Éilís Ní Dhuibhne, Anne Enright, Colm

Tóibín and others, and in doing so it will draw on my own biographical work.[4] I focus on five key O'Brien novels in order to examine the abiding preoccupations within her imagination – the idealization of the Irish middle-class, the subversion of patriarchy, the validation of a European Catholic culture and the articulation of an Irish feminist sensibility. By observing the trajectory of her fictions, the multiplicity of impulses within her work can be seen, many of these impulses contradictory and often at odds with the dominant political culture of the Ireland of her time. These include her insistence on idealizing the physical beauty and material elegance of her Irish bourgeois protagonists, while dissenting from the stifling moral and sexual conformity of the middle class. Her need to valorize her own class clashed with her increasing dissatisfaction towards De Valera's paternalism within the new Irish state, a paternalism that censored her novels. O'Brien's web of references to classical European literature and culture sits side-by-side with her concept of transgressive art. The erotic in O'Brien is both liberating and, at the same time, destructive. Often the experience of romantic love is a transformative one, but one that leads O'Brien's protagonists to inevitable pain, loss and isolation. Overall, her enduring fictive interest is in validating female autonomy and the liberating influence of European civilization and culture for the middle-class Irish protagonist.

A chronological account of the development of her fictions presents her distinct imaginative trajectory away from Ireland and towards a discourse of self-realization for her female characters in Europe. From the publication of her first novel *Without My Cloak* in 1931, O'Brien championed individual freedom against what she perceived as the insularity and repression of the Irish Catholic middle-class culture of her youth. In novels such as *Mary Lavelle* (1936), *The Land of Spices* (1941), *That Lady* (1946) and *As Music and Splendour* (1958), Irish cultural isolationism is juxtaposed with an Europeanized liberal Catholicism, thus providing escape from these constraints for her protagonists. O'Brien was creating new territory for the twentieth-century Irish woman novelist by representing dissident women at odds with the Irish Catholic middle-class ethos. Doing so from England, distance allowed O'Brien's fictive voice to be more direct and more confrontational.

Her own life provided vital areas of influence. Motherless from five, O'Brien was educated for fourteen years in Laurel Hill convent school in Limerick, leaving her with a life-long admiration for Catholic education as a cultural code, and for nuns as figures of female power. Her university education in UCD gave her a sense of education as a necessity in the search for self-actualization, and her working life in London, first as a journalist and then as a novelist, informed her portrayal of the independent female professional life.

Most of O'Brien's career was spent in London, living and working within a network of professional women and she became a visible and popular figure as novelist, reviewer, broadcaster and public speaker. Publishing in London with an identifiably Irish name and with Irish settings in her novels meant that her writing confronts colonial assumptions about Irishness in Britain, leaving her defensive and uneasy about her Irish middle-class protagonists. Therefore Europe, Catholic Spain, Italy, Belgium and France all provide a strategy for evasion, a means of transcending colonial stereotypes. As she writes in a late essay: 'We, a little provincial clutter, as might be thought an outsider, have always had the knack – in our religious history as well as in our literary – of catching on to Europe – of bypassing our British conquerors in our thought and reaching out to Spain and France.'5 'Catching on to Europe' was to be a vital impulse within her imagination, as each of these five novels suggests.

It is worth noting then, that O'Brien's early novels place her Irish protagonists within deadlocked conflicts, where the clash between bourgeois conformity and individual freedom leads to inevitable compromise or tragedy. O'Brien had many links to the new Irish State, through family connections and university friends, but found herself at odds with the increasingly paternalistic cultural climate of Ireland in the 1920s and 1930s. Many of the more radical elements of the Irish Revolution like feminism and socialism were now marginalized and this growing conservatism was clearly to be seen in the censoring of literature. After the establishment of the Irish Free State, the 1929 Censorship of Publications Act provided for the banning of books in Ireland, on the grounds that they were indecent or obscene and O'Brien's writing was to fall under this prohibition. This Censorship Act resulted in the widespread banning of novels and the consequent alienation of Irish writers from their society. Under the 1929 Censorship Act, a Censorship Board of five men considered any publications brought to their attention by custom officials or by a member of the public and judged them on grounds of decency and morality. The composition of this Censorship Board was secret, answerable only to the Minister for Justice. This control of public reading was in line with a number of repressive, paternalistic measures in post-colonial Ireland and, not surprisingly, many writers protested. Despite the fact that the Irish Academy of Letters was set up in 1932 by Yeats and Shaw and others to protest at censorship, the wholesale banning of

novels continued. Between 1930 and 1939, 1,200 books were banned in
Ireland. It is within this context that O'Brien began to publish her work.

Her first novel, *Without My Cloak*, follows the fortunes of the
Considines, a prosperous, Catholic family living in a southern Irish town
called Mellick. This narrative, realistic in form, traces four generations of
Considines, a line of patriarchal descent of father to son, from Anthony,
the horse thief, through Honest John, founder of the family fortune, and
Anthony, late Victorian consolidator of wealth and position, and finally
to Denis, rebel and dissenter. This struggle from poverty towards bourgeois wealth celebrates the resolve and vigour of the family but O'Brien
is ambivalent in this representation of Irish bourgeois family life, partly
because of her impulse to depict an Irish middle-class world that would
challenge colonial prejudice. O'Brien's desire to represent the Irish bourgeoisie as civilized and self-confident is somewhat at odds with conventional literary representations of the bourgeoisie as stolid, prosaic and
oppressive. As her novel opens, O'Brien is at pains to insist that her Irish
protagonists are bourgeois only in name, serenely resistant to colonial
prejudice, secure in their physical beauty and refinement. However, as the
novel progresses, imaginative sympathy moves towards the dissenters and
rebels within the family, and away from the upholders of family worth.
As O'Brien presents it, the price for conforming to Considine communal
values is moral compromise.

A crisis comes when Caroline, the beautiful, unhappily married
Considine sister, leaves her dull lawyer husband behind in Mellick and
runs away to her brother Eddy in London. Her subsequent love affair
with Eddy's lover Richard, 'outs' Eddy as he tells Richard: 'I have never
loved a woman except Caroline; and you love her, and I love her more
perhaps than I love you, more even than I love myself. And these loves of
ours are out of order and come to no good.'[6] Loves 'out of order' become
the radical element in O'Brien's subsequent writings. Throughout, as
Layne Parish Craig argues, 'Emphasis on church doctrine as imposing
a reproductive imperative on sexual relationships reflects not only the
problems of fertility and fulfilment in heterosexual pairings but also the
erasure of homosexual relationships in a culture valuing child-bearing as
the sole purpose of human sexuality.'[7] As the novel progresses, unorthodox relationships outside the heterosexual consensus are erased and this
becomes an imaginative dilemma for O'Brien.

It is for the next generation to attempt another rebellion against
the oppressive conformity of the Considines. The fourth in the line of
Considine males, Caroline's nephew Denis, is destined to inherit the

firm. Denis' slow recognition of the oppressive nature of that inheritance is hampered by the overwhelming love his father, Anthony, has for
him: 'Suddenly it seemed to him that he hated his father, who had compelled from him so womanish and unnatural a love.'[8] It is left to Eddy
to explain to his nephew the very difficult and contradictory nature of
Considine familial love:

> You haven't escaped any more than the rest of us our terrible family affec-
> tion, our cowardly inability to do without each other. Why, our whole
> strength is simply in our instinct to be large and populous and united. We
> cover all our secret misgivings by mass formulation. Already you are liv-
> ing among your uncles and cousins on a kind of compromise, you respect
> them only to compromise. The compromise that will be required of you in
> all your years in Mellick will be a long one.[9]

In resolving this impasse between communal values and individual emotional life, the deadlock is broken when Denis falls in love with Anna
Hennessy, the daughter of a suitable Mellick family, thus satisfying his
desire for a soul mate and allowing him to stay in Mellick. As a novelist, O'Brien is not prepared to break with the conformities of her Irish
middle-class world, and Europe, as yet, is not an imaginative alternative.
The deadlock in her next novel, *The Ante Room*, further demonstrates
this bind for O'Brien. This narrative explores the consequences for the
tormented Vincent, trapped in a loveless marriage and besotted with
his sister-in-law, Agnes, and he takes his own life rather than risk an
elopement from Mellick and a flouting of bourgeois conformity. Derek
Hand notes correctly that 'the atmosphere of unfinished business – of
incompleteness and thwarted desire – is what finally lingers in *The Ante
Room*'.[10]

In O'Brien's next novel, *Mary Lavelle*, escape to Europe offers another
way, mainly via the experience of encountering other cultures and traditions. Amanda Tucker suggests that: 'O'Brien's fictional characters come
to understand that their own positionality as middle-class Irish Catholics
has given them a worldview that they can never entirely abandon;
however, recognizing this does not prevent them from learning about
themselves in relation to women from other cultures and traditions.'[11]
Mary Lavelle provides a new positionality and a reinvented selfhood,
recalibrated in relation to the Mellick selfhood. Set in 1922, the year
O'Brien herself spent as a governess in Bilbao, the novel depicts Mary,
the daughter of a Mellick doctor, journeying out to Spain to work as a
governess or a 'Miss' for a year. She is to be married and her fiancé, a

suitable, conservative, unimaginative Mellick man, John, is very much in love with her. Mary's decision to go abroad troubles John but she insists that she needs 'To go to Spain. To be alone for a little space, a tiny hiatus between her life's two accepted phases. To cease being a daughter without immediately becoming a wife. To be a free-lance, to belong to no one place or family or person.'[12] As she discovers much about this new country, Mary finds herself drawn towards Spanish culture, language and art and starts to question the tenets governing her Mellick identity. Mary's hope of a 'cap of invisibility' is not to be fulfilled when she becomes the focus of obsessive loves from those around her in Spain, her great beauty attracting her employer, Don Pablo, his married son, Juanito and her compatriot, Agatha Conlon.

Despite these intruding loves, Mary Lavelle learns to develop imaginatively and morally in Spain. Crucial to her development is her experience of the bullfight, in company with Agatha, who has also come to love Spain and the *corrida*. In O'Brien's description of the bullfight, there is an eroticized masochism, a celebration of ritualized brutality that characterizes O'Brien's own interpretation of Spanish culture. This aesthetic awakening for her central character through the bullfight is perhaps the most radical element in her fiction up to this point and clashes fruitfully with the conventional form of her novels:

> The matador drew his enemy to his breast, and past it, on the gentle lure; brought him back along his thigh as if for sheer love; let him go and drew him home again ... Again and again in classic passes he allowed the horn to skim him, then drawing back from the great weary but still alert antagonist, he profiled and went over the horn, as gently as an angel might, to kill.[13]

O'Brien constructs the spectacle of the bullfight as a kind of pagan epiphany, a coming to knowledge for the young Mellick woman through the enabling aesthetic of ritualized violence, thus eclipsing the art forms and the beliefs of the bourgeoisie:

> Burlesque, fantastic, savage, all that John had said – but more vivid with beauty and all beauty's anguish, more full of news of life's possible pain and senselessness and quixotry and barbarism and glory than anything ever before encountered by this girl; more real and exacting, more suggestive of wild and high exactions, more symbolic, more dramatic, a more personal and searching arrow to the heart than ever she had dreamed of. Here – and Mary, to whose youth all knowledge was new, received this sudden piece of it as crippling pain – here was art, in its least decent form, its least explainable or bearable. But art, unconcerned and lawless.[14]

With this epiphany, Mary is moved 'outside' herself and is thus empowered to confront the moral problems and conflicts produced by her time in Spain. In the first two Mellick novels, such conflicts end in deadlock and tragedy but, in Spain, a more expansive moral world is possible, for example, in the area of sexual identity. Eddy keeps closeted from his Mellick family but in Spain it is possible for Agatha Conlon to tell Mary: 'I like you the way a man would, you see. I never can see you without – without wanting to touch you.'[15] Mary reacts without shock but with equanimity and acceptance of her friend's sexual identity, a rare occurrence in the few representations of lesbian identity in the 1930s.

O'Brien's representation of the redemptive role of the erotic occurs in a later scene where the ritualization of death at the core of the representation of the bullfight is linked by the scene of illicit lovemaking. O'Brien constructs this forbidden love scene between Mary and Juanito as a necessary rite of pain and sacrifice. Mary decides to consummate her love for the married Juanito before she leaves Spain, in full consciousness of her offence against Catholic doctrine yet the scene is far from liberating or joyful. 'He took her quickly and bravely. The pain made her cry out and writhe in shock, but he held her hard against him and in great love compelled her to endure it.'[16]

From these moments of insight and revelation comes a newly made selfhood for the protagonist. From *Mary Lavelle* onwards, all of O'Brien's novels follow this narrative development, away from Mellick and Ireland and towards voluntary exile and Europe. This aesthetic departure for O'Brien brought her into conflict with the cultural ideology of the Irish state. *Mary Lavelle* was banned by the Irish Censorship Board on the grounds of obscenity on 29 December 1936. It was O'Brien's first novel to be banned in Ireland, and, unlike *The Land of Spices*, it was never the subject of a revocation order and so remained on the list of forbidden works.

Added to this, the outbreak of the Spanish Civil War prevented O'Brien from entering Spain again for another twenty years. The Spanish Civil War broke out in July 1936 when General Franco's Nationalists overthrew the democratically elected government of the Spanish Republic. Like many writers, O'Brien supported the Republican side and felt compelled to respond in print. Her travels in Spain in the 1930s gave her ample material to comment on the conflict and the result was *Farewell Spain*, published in August 1937, just after the fall of Bilbao to Nationalists. This book is a passionate plea against Franco's fascists and for the spirit of democracy but resulted in another bruising encounter for

O'Brien with a second patriarchal state. These experiences of censorship, of the Spanish Civil War and a six-year exile from Ireland during the Second World War, all became influences for the direction O'Brien's writing took in the 1940s.

The war years of the 1940s were a time of upheaval and instability and loss of income for O'Brien but also, at the same time, of great creativity in her writing. Despite continual displacement and impoverishment, she produced novels at the rate of one every two years – *The Land of Spices* (1941), *The Last of Summer* (1943) and, most importantly, *That Lady* (1946). Overall her wartime writing was a kind of resistance writing, a response to censorship, to war and to her unstable working life. Her protagonists in these novels are idealized figures of economic or political independence and of spirited self-assertion.

Written in the light of her enforced absence from Ireland, and published in February 1941, *The Land of Spices* is set in the Mellick convent of Sainte Famille, a French school for Irish girls. It follows the life of the young protagonist, Anna Murphy who, like O'Brien herself, goes to school at the age of six in 1904 and leaves at eighteen in 1916. Apart from autobiographical influences, this novel concerns itself with female agency and Elizabeth Cullingford identifies that: 'The feminist strength of O'Brien's convent, despite its inevitable snobberies and rivalries, is based on the exchange of love and power between older and younger women.'[17]

The paralleling of Anna Murphy and Helen Archer is established in the opening section of the novel when Helen despairs of her life in Ireland: 'She knew, early she had come to know, that at best she was a respected symbol in this house, at worst an Englishwoman.'[18] Partly Helen Archer's isolation is racial, but mostly she is disliked for her prioritizing of a European-slanted education for the young girls of Mellick. The more nationalist-minded nuns and priests of Mellick distrust her cultural ethos and Heather Ingman remarks on 'the interesting juxtaposition of masculinist Irish nationalism with a transnational female network of convents'.[19] For example, the school chaplain, Father Conroy, ('a country boy: fresh from Maynooth') articulates this clash of pedagogies: '"It seems a shame", said Father Conroy, with pointed playfulness, "it seems a shame that our own Irish girls have to go off to do their religious training in a barbarous place like that!"' Reverend Mother counters such attacks with reminders of Ireland's old connections with Europe: '"Certainly Ireland helped in impressing Christianity on Europe. So why should the Irish not go back now, and reclaim for Ireland some of the cultivated thing it planted?'"[20] O'Brien, writing in England in 1940, is here critiquing the narrowing of Irish cultural nationalism in the early twentieth century.

Helen is rescued from her despair when the child Anna recites the poem, 'Peace' by Henry Vaughan, a poem also much loved by Helen's father and this begins the process of connection between the child and the Reverend Mother. The progress of Anna's life towards adulthood and independence from familiar bonds is achieved with Helen's tacit assistance and quiet mentorship. Anna is watched over by Helen, guided through the crisis of her brother's death, and assisted in her desire to attend university, despite family disapproval of female education. In a novel where familial loves bring grief and betrayal, female mentorship is presented as the only viable source for self-actualization.

The novel is filled with references to European literatures and languages, written at a time when Ireland was cut off from Europe by the war. Milton and Schiller are key points of reference and indeed the title of the novel comes from the closing of George Herbert's poem, 'Prayer'. Taken together, all of these poems build up an intertextual web of literary references from seventeenth-century English metaphysical and devotional poetry, imbuing the novel set in a Catholic convent with a Protestant literary sensibility. When O'Brien writes about issues of Catholic faith and conscience, she allows her Irish subjects possession of their own souls, independence of belief and a confidence in their right to moral self-determination. In this, O'Brien was re-inventing her own education at Laurel Hill and re-imagining the reality of the Catholic Church in Ireland in the twentieth century. The system of education portrayed here is her ideal of the intellectual civility of European Catholicism.

This ideal system of education is constructed partly in terms of manners, language, literature and social behaviour but it is also a system of emotional education, where family trauma and shock are contained and made safe. In this context, the central episode in *The Land of Spices* is important for many reasons, not just because a moment of erotic revelation leads Helen Archer into the religious life, subverting the notion of an authentic spiritual vocation for her. Since female education is O'Brien's theme in *The Land of Spices*, Helen's own upbringing as her father, Henry Archer's devoted pupil, is critiqued as an account of the destructive effects of patriarchal and familial identities. Helen's relationship with her father is emotionally intense and excluding: 'In childhood, she thought her father very beautiful. It always delighted her to come on the sight of him suddenly and realize, always with new pleasure that he was different from other men, stronger and bigger, with curly silky hair and eyes that shone like stars.'[21] Henry Archer, a former Cambridge don, who has brought his wife and child to live in Brussels, is a figure from late Victorian decadent literature. Archer sees himself as pagan, reading the Greeks, and represented as a Wildean figure of exquisite Hellenic beauty, of aesthetic and bohemian tastes but with a suspect sexual past. In exile in Europe for some unspecified reason, Henry Archer directs his daughter's liberal, bohemian education and force-feeds her into an understanding of Europe.

Helen's idyllic life ends when she discovers the true nature of her father's sexuality and the reason for his exile from England upon finding him with his male lover:

> She looked into the room. Two people were there. But neither saw her; neither felt her shadow as it froze across the sun. She turned and descended the stairs. She left the garden and went on down the curve of Rue Saint Isidore. She had no objective and no knowledge of what she was doing. She did not see external things. She saw Etienne and her father, in the embrace of love.[22]

This moment of revelation, the sentence that was to be the ostensible reason for the banning of the book, is one of the few moments of sexual directness in O'Brien's fiction. As always in her writings, the erotic is traumatic and destructive in its effect on the unwitting spectator. Henry Archer's sexuality is destructive to those around him but he dies happily, unaware of the damage he has caused. Backus and Valente argue that: 'In *The Land of Spices*, she crafted a beautifully wrought, shimmering account of one educator's unspoken self-appointment as a queer ally who quietly ensures for the next generation that of which her father was bereft.'[23] Part of the alliance between Helen and Anna is the fact that the nun has a vocation based on revenge and punishment for her queer father. However, as the final scene suggests, Helen's religious life enables Anna both as a writer and as a lesbian. Thanks to Helen Archer's intervention against her family, Anna leaves the convent to pursue a life of study. In this final chapter, there is a clear sense that Anna will become a writer and that Helen has enabled the freedom for her to become an artist, suggesting an emergent vocation of female creativity: 'Now, however, she saw Pilar in a new way. She saw her ... ironically, delightedly, as a motive in art.'[24] Anna is also seeing Pilar as one woman desiring another.

Overall, the novel, as Mary Breen suggests, 'questions and criticizes the whole ideology of that period in Irish cultural history ... by its detachment from Irish nationalism, its emphasis on individual freedom and responsibility, its championing of religious and educational structures, detached from patriarchal concerns, its foregrounding of the viability of female identity outside patriarchal family units, and its determinedly outward-looking, European perspective'.[25] These many subversive elements in the novel led to the censoring of *The Land of Spices* for that one sentence illuminating Henry Archer's sexuality and a lively public campaign took place in Ireland against this unwarranted attack on what was considered a cultivated and beautifully civilized novel. The campaign finally led to an eventual amelioration of the censorship laws and the establishment of an appeals board. This realization of the female artist in *The Land of Spices* is paralleled by O'Brien's development of the idealized figure of political dissent, and her next war-time novel, *That Lady*, addresses censorship by focussing on the emblematic figure of an aristocratic, resistant woman, standing up to a totalitarian regime.

That Lady deals with political intrigues within the court of Philip II and focuses on Ana De Mendoza, the widow of Philip's prime minister, a woman of high noble birth and vast independent wealth, at the centre of one very bitter power struggle. Her relationship with her ruler, the devout, complicated Philip II, is complex; she is both his obedient subject and his closest friend, a woman he has admired and desired but never loved. Out of her fictionalizing of this historical relationship, a political metaphor is forged by O'Brien.

Although Ana is the possessor of wealth and position, as a woman in a patriarchal society, she is without political agency. When she finally chooses to assert her individualism, she does so by initiating a love affair with Antonio Perez, the King's Secretary of State and her husband's successor. Ana's love affair with Antonio is the dramatic turning point within the novel, the shaping force in the events that follow. As an authoritarian monarch, Philip acknowledges no limit on his control over both public and private life. He spies on Ana, stealing her love letters and then confronting her with the evidence of her love affair. The scene where Ana faces Philip down dramatizes the clash between public duty and private morality and O'Brien accords the moral victory to Ana. When Philip confronts her with the evidence of sexual misconduct, as he sees it, Ana denies him authority over her private life:

> There have been, Philip, as long as I can remember, thoughts, and even acts in that private life, which, presented to the world, would seem to injure this or that. If I do wrong in it, that wrong is between me and heaven. But here below, so long as I don't try to change it into public life, I insist that I own it.[26]

Not only does Ana assert ownership of her private life, she extends this into a plea for democracy in Spain, subtly linking sexual and political authoritarianism. She asks Philip to: 'Come back to govern us so that we can see what you are doing ... let us feel the movement of government in Spain again.'[27] For Ana, this is a moment of triumph, the opportunity for political change in Spain but for Philip, this is dangerous treason and he punishes her. Ana's resistance to Philip's authoritarian rule is morally successful but politically disastrous for her, leading to her immediate incarceration and loss of family, wealth and freedom. She is shut away in prison, left to die and even her name is expunged from public life; she is henceforth simply referred to as 'That Lady'. In spite of this, her stand against the King is seen as a moral victory for individual conscience, in the face of state control.

In her prison, loyally accompanied by her daughter and her duenna, Ana creates a female commune, a cell of resistance. In some sense, O'Brien again makes suffering a kind of aesthetic validation, constructing Ana as sanctified by this suffering. When Ana's friend, the Cardinal of Toledo, comes to visit her, worn and ill from her incarceration, he observes to himself: 'She looks distinguished and ascetic, he thought, like a very good nun who has been worked too hard.'[28] Ana has become a nun, albeit a secular one, a holy woman beatified by political martyrdom. The novel ends with the King, successful in his prosecution of the rebellious Ana, but alone and stranded in his tyranny:

> He rose painfully from the table and moved without purpose across the room. A bell was ringing from Santa Maria Almudena. He remembered how much more clearly one heard that bell in the Long Room of the Eboli Palace. He looked out at the sunlight towards her empty house and the glare hurt his eyes and the bell seemed to toll for his loneliness and the sins that drove him on, for ever further into loneliness.[29]

As Adele Dalsimer says, 'In the end, Ana has won.'[30] O'Brien has located a key narrative for the realization of female individuality and resistance.

O'Brien's decision to return and live in Ireland in the 1950s coincided with her final novels of female empowerment and artistic vocation, *The Flower of May* and *As Music and Splendour*. From *Without My Cloak* onwards, she had been exploring the possibility for an Irish woman to live independently through art. Her final novel realizes this imaginative ambition. Emma Donoghue suggests *As Music and Splendour* is

> more celebratory in its account of a relationship between two women. Instead of playing a supporting role, the lesbian is one of the two heroines, whose stories are presented equally and in parallel. Set at a safe distance in place (Paris and Rome) and time (the 1880s), *As Music and Splendour*

nonetheless manages to create a modern Irish lesbian and give her a
startling voice.[31]

Published in 1958, the novel is set in the 1880s and traces the fortunes of
two young Irish women, Clare Halvey and Rose Lehane, as they are trained
into independence and success through their talents as singers. Rose and
Clare move from obscurity and relative poverty in Ireland towards fame
and wealth in the opera houses of Europe and North America, by dint of
their talent and artistry. This last novel also charts the growth of Rose and
Clare into sexual selfhood and financial autonomy away from Ireland and
family, eventually becoming part of a liberated bohemian milieu.

One of the consequences of this freedom is that they can now control
their own adult sexual lives and, as the narrative unfolds, this independence brings its own disillusions. Both women assert their autonomy
in sexual terms, Rose with male lovers and Clare with other women.
O'Brien's Catholic background made this challenging for her to represent
and she negotiates this by representing the erotic through the medium
of music. The arias that Rose and Clare sing, from Mozart, Glück and
Verdi, all come to represent, metaphorically, their various loves. As in
her earlier novels, music is deployed to represent the erotic and, more
than this, to validate these bohemian, 'forbidden' loves by investing them
with the mythic quality of their art. So when O'Brien finally presents two
women as lovers, they sing together on stage as husband and wife, Orfeo
and Eurydice, and sexual identity is thus affirmed through artistic ritual.

O'Brien's portrayal of a lesbian character was a risk, especially now that
she was back living in Ireland and yet it is one of the most radical elements in the novel, skilfully integrated into the narrative. Clare and Luisa
sing together in Glück's *Orpheus and Eurydice*, where the two women
singers can legitimately play the part of lovers in public, in operatic
roles originally for female soprano and male castrato. The myth of the
opera gives permission to their subversive love affair: 'Still Orpheus and
Eurydice, their brilliantly made up eyes swept for each the other's face,
as if to insist that this disguise of myth in which they stood was their
mutual reality, their one true dress, wherein they recognized each other.'[32]
Music makes safe the dangerous potential of their sexuality but not completely. At one point, Clare's relationship with Luisa draws attack from
the men who surround them, one sneering at the androgynous quality
of Clare's 'castrato' voice, another calling her: 'beast! You pale, self-loving
ass! You – you stinking lily, you.'[33]

This last novel ends on an open note, with the future of the two girls
still unfolding, the beckoning self-sufficiency of an artistic, bohemian life

in Europe awaiting them. This is no utopian vision but, as Anne Fogarty argues, one of the novel's achievements is the fact that: 'For the first time in O'Brien's *oeuvre*, lesbian love is moved literally and metaphorically centre stage.'[34]

However the novel attracted little critical attention and, possibly as a result, O'Brien published no more novels. In the sixteen years before her death in 1974, she felt a keen sense that her work had outlived its popularity, fallen into obscurity and was ignored by her younger Irish contemporaries. Her instinct, expressed in letters to other writers and friends, was that her form of the novel was now irredeemably old-fashioned. However, for O'Brien's successors, the subsequent chroniclers of the Irish middle-class novel, her fictions provide a rare and welcome precedent, a pioneering series of narratives enabling their own work. One of her last reviews for *The Spectator* was an admiring account of John McGahern's first novel, *The Barracks* but, sadly, when O'Brien did meet the young McGahern himself in Dublin a few years later, he was unaware of her review and had read nothing of her fiction at that point. Later in his career, he did so and came to regard O'Brien as a key influence in his creation of narratives of the Irish Catholic middle-class, particularly in her representations of sexuality, of Catholic belief and of the constraints of family.[35] Colm Tóibín, another writer of the Catholic middle class, was, like O'Brien, an admirer of Spain and his first novel, *The South*, is influenced by *Mary Lavelle*. Crucially, Tóibín, as a later pioneer of Irish lesbian and gay representation, directly linked her writings with his:

> There is a point where you find people who came before you who faced the same difficulties – two gay writers in Ireland in the 1940s and 50s, John Broderick and Kate O'Brien. They played at living in England, coming back here irregularly, they didn't quite put it into their novels. Both were from rich families. They were odd – posh, patrician, Catholics. They stood out since people in those days tended to be poor. Looking at the whole body of their work, it's not as though this particular drama hasn't been enacted here so many times – the question of how one should deal in public with matters which are anathema in private.[36]

Contemporary women novelists like Mary O'Donnell, Mary Morrissy and others draw on her fictions. Anne Enright describes O'Brien as 'an extraordinary resilient writer'[37] while Éilís Ní Dhuibhne identifies O'Brien as 'a master of classic realism. And that's okay now. Mount Parnassus has many mansions'.[38]

To conclude, O'Brien's fictions provide a key element within the development of the Irish novel and remain a vital and enabling presence both for her generation and for subsequent ones. In the words of Emma Donoghue: 'She writes about women who love each other and the realizations and complications that brings; what she does not write about is lesbian identity as such, divorced from context. And this, I suggest, is what gives her such importance as a teacher to my generation.'[39]

Notes

1 Brad Kent, 'Literary Criticism and the Recovery of Banned Books: The Case of Kate O'Brien's *Mary Lavelle*', *Ariel* 41, no. 2 (2011): 55.

2 Derek Hand, *A History of the Irish Novel* (Cambridge: Cambridge University Press, 2011), 165.

3 Lorna Reynolds, *Kate O'Brien: A Literary Portrait* (Gerrard's Cross: Colin Smyth, 1987), 128.

4 See Eibhear Walshe, *Kate O'Brien: A Writing Life* (Cork: Cork University Press, 2006).

5 Kate O'Brien, 'Imaginative Prose by the Irish 1820–1970', in *Myth and Reality in Irish Literature,* ed. Joseph Ronsley (Waterloo: Wilfrid Laurier University Press, 1977), 305.

6 Kate O'Brien, *Without My Cloak* (London: Heinemann, 1931), 158.

7 Layne Parish Craig, 'Passion's Possibilities: Kate O'Brien's Sexological Discourse in *Without My Cloak*', *Eire Ireland* 44, no. 3/4 Winter (2009): 123.

8 O'Brien, *Without My Cloak*, 351.

9 Ibid., 195.

10 Hand, *A History of the Irish Novel*, 167.

11 Amanda Tucker, 'A Space Between: Transnational Feminism in Kate O'Brien's Mary Lavelle', *New Hibernian Review* 12, no. 1 (2008): 84.

12 Kate O'Brien, *Mary Lavelle* (London: Heinemann, 1934), 34.

13 Ibid., 114.

14 Ibid., 116.

15 Ibid., 285.

16 Ibid., 308.

17 Elizabeth Cullingford, 'Our Nuns Are Not a Nation', *Eire-Ireland* 41, no. 1/2 (2006): 24.

18 Kate O'Brien, *The Land of Spices* (London: Heinemann, 1941), 74.

19 Heather Ingman, *Irish Women's Fiction: From Edgeworth to Enright* (Dublin: Irish Academic Press, 2013), 125.

20 O'Brien, *The Land of Spices*, 9.

21 Ibid., 143.

22 Ibid., 158.

23 Margot Backus and Joseph Valente, '*The Land of Spices*, the Enigmatic Signifier and the Stylistic Invention of Lesbian (in) Visibility', *Irish University Review*, 43, no. 1 (2013): 72.

24 O'Brien, *The Land of Spices*, 271/2.

25 Mary Breen, 'Something Understood?: Kate O'Brien and *The Land of Spices*', in *Ordinary People Dancing: Essays on Kate O'Brien*, ed. Eibhear Walshe (Cork: Cork University Press, 1993), (167–90), 188.

26 Kate O'Brien, *That Lady* (London: Heinemann, 1946), 236.

27 Ibid., 245.

28 Ibid., 328.

29 Ibid., 378.

30 Adele Dalsimer, *Kate O'Brien: A Critical Study* (Dublin: Gill and Macmillan, 1990), 98.

31 Emma Donoghue, '"Out of Order": Kate O'Brien's Lesbian Fictions', in *Ordinary People Dancing: Essays on Kate O'Brien*, ed. Walshe, (36–58), 50.

32 Kate O'Brien, *As Music and Splendour* (London: Heinemann, 1958), 175.

33 Ibid., 209.

34 Anne Fogarty, 'The Ear of the Other: Dissident Voices in Kate O'Brien's *As Music and Splendour* and Mary Dorcey's *Noises from the Woodshed*', in *Sex, Nation and Dissent in Irish Writing*, ed. Eibhear Walshe (Cork: Cork University Press, 1997), 60.

35 John McGahern in conversation with the author, May 2002.

36 Colm Tóibín, from Richard Canning, *Hear Us Out: Conversations with Gay Novelists* (New York, NY: Columbia University Press, 2003), 202.

37 Anne Enright, 'A Many Splendoured Love-Story', *The Irish Times*, 20 August 2005, 14.

38 Éilís Ní Dhuibhne, 'In Praise of Kate O'Brien', *The Irish Times*, 7 March 2015, 12.

39 Donoghue, '"Out of Order"', 56.

CHAPTER 13

Edna O'Brien

Sinéad Mooney

Reading Alice Hughes Kernowski's 2013 edited collection *Conversations with Edna O'Brien*, consisting of interviews conducted between 1967, seven years after the publication of *The Country Girls*, and 2012, when O'Brien's memoir *Country Girl* appeared, what is immediately evident is the extent to which the interviews rely on the recirculation of certain tropes. The introduction quips that '[b]efore she was famous, she was infamous';[1] the familiar Edna O'Brien talismanic moments are adverted to – the banning and burning of *The Country Girls*, the social and religious puritanism of rural Ireland against which her work rebelled, the characteristic lyricism of her prose, and the interviewers turning again and again to the apparently irresistible paradox of the physical loveliness of 'the girl who writes about guilt, sex, scandal, and dishevelled lives'.[2] Many interviews assume, scopically, that the author is there to be read alongside her work. Already, in a 1972 interview, O'Brien – at this point the London-based author of seven novels, a collection of short stories, two stage plays and numerous screenplays, and the recipient of the Kingsley Amis Prize and the Yorkshire Post Book of the Year award in 1970 for *A Pagan Place* – is firmly established for an *Irish Times* interviewer as 'Our Edna', 'look[ing] pensive (as doubtless, she had looked in front of a hundred thousand interviewers before)', a 'bittersweet brand'.[3]

The charge of repetition is familiar; O'Brien would frequently be critically excoriated for writing 'the same story over and over again', criticized for her narrowness of theme, an alleged sensationalism and an apparently endless representation of a claustrophobic range of 'women's concerns' and oppression.[4] Further, her stereotyping as a practised, stage-Irish embodiment of the pensive or tempestuous colleen gone to the bad has almost as long a history.[5] For some critics, such as Rebecca Pelan and Amanda Greenwood, it is ongoing constructions of Edna O'Brien as 'Celtic', 'exotic' and sexually dangerous that have severely limited readings of her *oeuvre*, allowing a sidelining of its embedded sociocultural context and political critique.[6] Certainly, the deleterious effects of envisioning Edna O'Brien as a 'Connemara Dietrich' bleed everywhere into the earlier critical descriptions of her literary idiom; personal style is elided into her writing style, in slightly skewed compliments to her 'hypnotically seductive storytelling'.[7] Form and content are particularly closely bound for O'Brien, and many of the misreadings and critical divergences that her work has attracted since 1960 concern misunderstandings of her explorations of a compromised female subjectivity amid the conventions of a denatured or destabilized romance plot whose adequacy as an encoding of women's experience is continually raised even as it is posited.

On the one hand, she has frequently been maligned as a 'lightweight' author of 'women's novels', and her early work in particular has been attacked for its repeated, documentary portrayals of 'throttled, sacrificial women', its relegation of men to grotesquely violent impediments to her protagonists, and for a depiction of the Irish female psyche as defined by suffering and lack.[8] On the other, reviewers who read O'Brien's work as insignificant and repetitive between the 1960s and the early 1990s were curiously resistant to a perceived change and enlargement of her subject matter in mid-career. Having long accused her of a failure 'to move outside the magic circle of women's emotional problems', of being a writer whose work disregards 'social institutions and ties', the overtly political nature of her 1990s trilogy *House of Splendid Isolation* (1994), *Down by the River* (1996) and *Wild Decembers* (1999), together with *In the Forest* (2002), which dealt with abortion, police corruption, Irish terrorism and rural murder, met with a muted, even hostile, reception. O'Brien was violently castigated for being out of touch with the native country she left in the late 1950s, and for taking on subject matter too weighty for a popular writer of 'women's novels'. *House of Splendid Isolation*, which deals with an elderly woman's relationship with an IRA gunman on the run in the Republic, was greeted with the remark by an *Observer* reviewer that O'Brien was the 'Barbara Cartland of long-distance Republicanism', neatly encapsulating both criticisms, as well as the highly gendered disparagement to which her work has long been subject.[9]

Although recent critics have taken O'Brien's work far more seriously, her aesthetic achievements continue to be undervalued, and a certain confusion still attends the question of precisely what kind of writer she might be, even after the publication of seventeen novels, nine short story collections, numerous plays and screenplays, two biographies (of Joyce and Byron) and two memoirs. An uneasy critical vocabulary of disorder, excess and mutability for a long time surrounded her *oeuvre*, which was under-regarded by scholars. Amanda Greenwood still finds it necessary as late as 2002 to preface her monograph on O'Brien by stoutly defending her subject against charges of being merely a 'repetitive chronicler of romantic love'.[10] More recently, O'Brien has been critically recuperated as a writer whose work mounts a 'challenge [to] her nation's particular brand of gendered nationalism'.[11] It is difficult not to conclude, however, that O'Brien's considerable body of work remains productively, even challengingly, 'untidy', and that there is something about her writing which, even as it garners international fame and awards, nonetheless flouts claims to literary 'respectability'.

The uneasy, and heavily gendered, vocabulary that for so long associated her work with the sinful and sensational dates from the banning of her ground-breaking early work. She was one of the most prominent Irish writers to have fallen foul, multiple times, of the Irish Censorship Board. Virtually all of her prolific output of fiction during the 1960s was banned, including her first novel *The Country Girls* (1960), and its sequels *The Lonely Girl* (1962) – reissued in 1964 as *Girl with Green Eyes* – and *Girls in Their Married Bliss* (1964), *August is a Wicked Month* (1965) and *Casualties of Peace* (1966). In addition to the censure of being banned, initially for the depiction of what she termed, more than thirty years later, 'the foolish, not-so-covert sexuality of two young girls',[12] O'Brien, as one of the few prominent banned Irish female writers, was subjected to vicious personal criticism on the grounds of her sex. Famously, she was denounced in 1960 by Archbishop John Charles McQuaid, insistently preoccupied with the censorship of 'obscene' publications, as 'a smear on Irish womanhood'.[13]

Merely by exposing women's struggle for self-determination in the face of the constricting social and religious norms of mid-century Ireland, the *Country Girls* trilogy exploded the prescribed roles for women in Irish society, critiquing at once the way gender roles were constructed in post-independence Ireland, and, as Kristine Byron argues, 'the adequacy of the female romance plot for representing women's experience in fiction'.[14] In 1969, Benedict Kiely characterized the still 'determined persecution of the novels of Edna O'Brien' as due to the feeling, on the part of the Irish censors, that 'while it's bad and very bad for a man to speak out and tell the truth, it is utterly unthinkable that a woman ... should claim any such liberty'.[15] More than thirty years later, when she was strenuously attacked in the Irish media for her use of the real-life murders of Imelda Riney, her son and Father Joe Walsh in rural Clare in her 2002 novel *In the Forest*, a similar rhetoric was applied. Fintan O'Toole, reviewing the novel for the *Irish Times*, while registering O'Brien as an 'honest and astute' novelist, argued that she had 'broken an unspoken rule and crossed the boundary into private grief', rather than recognizing the distinction between private and public realms. Contemporary dramatizations of the Hepatitis C scandal, Bloody Sunday and the career of Charles Haughey, on the other hand, were deemed legitimate as 'major historical and political issues' which 'ask questions about the use of power'. Essentially O'Brien was indicted for a perceived lack of discretion.[16]

Yet this attack, ironically, ignored the fact that, for over forty years, Edna O'Brien had manifested, as Rebecca Pelan notes, 'an almost pathological need to enter the no-go areas O'Toole refers to, precisely for the purposes of asking questions about the use of power, [casting] a forensic eye on the most private aspects of … Irish life'.[17] Her unambiguously, publicly political, fact-based novels of the 1990s and early twenty-first century only make explicit the always implicit politics of her previous work in its foregrounding of women's psychological struggles with the social institutions that seek to constrain them, and their effective silencing via what Helen Thompson calls the overarticulation of their social and sexual roles.[18] As one of the first generation of Irish women raised under the auspices of the 1937 Constitution, a document which significantly limited the civic responsibilities of Irishwomen to the domestic sphere, O'Brien concerns herself with the processes and consequences of such socio-religious indoctrination, and with the adequacy of the literary scripts offered to women by the major writers of the Irish canon.

O'Brien's novels have tended to be divided into phases: the early, autobiographical books about women's struggles and desires; the later state-of-the-nation works about Irish history and politics, but this is to over-schematize a career which has always been difficult to pin down, but, equally, which has always conducted an interrogation of the cultural and political imperatives that reproduce Irish femininity. Rather as Kristine Byron observes of the bleakly unsettling epilogue to *The Country Girls* trilogy, added by O'Brien when the three novels were republished together in 1986, the political novels of the 1990s act as an 'ideological amplifier' to the issues explored earlier in her work.[19] Her earlier interrogations of the romance form and her later novels alike re-imagine foundational nationalist mythologies, critiquing constitutional gender roles and those cognate role models offered by Catholicism, and dismantling static social and sexual identities, even as the romantic fantasies posited in their place are comedically, often disturbingly, exploded in their turn.

O'Brien's status as a political writer was not immediately obvious. Despite being one of the few writers of her generation to publicly protest against censorship, for a long time her work signally failed to attract the kind of aesthetic approval that other writers banned in Ireland often had by virtue of association with Joyce, Beckett and Shaw; the 'prestige' of the ban did not cling to her subsequent output. While Edna O'Brien's work, widely reviewed and translated, received international acclaim – from the 1962 Kingsley Amis award for *The Country Girls* to the 1995 European Prize for Literature and the 2002 American Medal of Honour for literature from the National Arts Club – it for many years failed to achieve anything like the secure canonical status of the *oeuvre* of her contemporary John McGahern, similarly banned for obscenity in the 1960s by the Irish Censorship Board. O'Brien, it seemed, wrote the wrong kind of 'smut', inconveniently feminine, viewed as artlessly confessional – as McGahern's, though drawing equally closely on his own life, was not – dangerously accessible in style, and therefore less akin to the high modernist aesthetic of Joyce and Beckett than to what an American reviewer in 1973 dismisses as a transparently autobiographical 'mucoid odyssey of discovery'.[20] Writing in the 1990s, Rebecca Pelan characterized Edna O'Brien's reception in Ireland as that of 'a likeable, but bold girl who keeps misbehaving, and who regularly has her work assessed on grounds other than its literary qualities'.[21] It is, in fact, difficult to think of another major Irish writer whose work still provokes so much unease, whose reputation is so unsettled and unsettling.

Ambivalence still to an extent shadows her reception today, even after she was honoured as a Saoi of Aosdána in 2015, shortly before the publication of her seventeenth novel, the well-received *The Little Red Chairs*. At her inauguration, President Michael D. Higgins made an official apology for the scorn often heaped on O'Brien in Ireland, and the banning of her books, characterizing her as a 'fearless teller of truth' who, he said, had continued to write 'undaunted, sometimes by culpable incomprehension, authoritarian hostility and sometimes downright malice'.[22] What, therefore, are we to make of this apparently riven and contested, 'untidy' body of writing which is both the work of a 'fearless teller of truth' and, yet somehow, conversely, deemed essentially trivial, inauthentic and insufficiently literary?

'Country Girl' to 'Lyrics of the Loins'

Some account of the development of Edna O'Brien's career is appropriate here. First entering the consciousness of the literary world in the early 1960s as a fresh new literary talent, O'Brien's early work, banned in

Ireland for its sexual frankness, was nonetheless praised overseas for what
reviewers such as V. S. Naipaul, writing in the *New Statesman* in 1960,
viewed as its effortless lyricism.²³ However, by the time the final novel
in the *Country Girls* trilogy, *Girls in Their Married Bliss*, was published
in 1964, critics were already noting 'a move away from the fresh, unself-
conscious charm [and] acute observation of life' towards a sharper, more
cynical tone, as the narrative voice of the first two volumes of the trilogy,
the wistful, romantic Caithleen, gave way in the third volume to an alternating narrative structure featuring Caithleen and her abrasive, ribald
friend Baba, both now in the same predicament: 'enough to eat, married,
dissatisfied'.²⁴ Her next two novels, *August is a Wicked Month* (1965) and
Casualties of Peace (1966), with their emancipated, emotionally scarred
Irish female protagonists launched abroad and adrift in post-marital emotional wrangles, baffled and induced hostility in critics with their lack of
resemblance of tone or subject to *The Country Girls*. Seán McMahon, in
a 1967 essay in *Éire-Ireland*, disapprovingly dubbed them 'committed
writing ... a kind of neo-feminist propaganda',²⁵ though in fact feminist
critics were reluctant to engage with O'Brien for a long time, despite
her position as a culturally marginalized woman writer whose fiction
inscribes the experience of similarly disempowered women. The novelist
Julia O'Faolain, reviewing O'Brien's *A Fanatic Heart* short story collection in 1974, criticized feminists for their rejection of O'Brien's abject,
questing heroines, characterizing her stories as 'bulletins from a front on
which they will not care to engage, field reports on the feminine condition at its most acute'.²⁶ We are back with the problem of O'Brien's difficulty of classification, as Rebecca Pelan views it: 'O'Brien has proved too
"stage-Irish" for the Irish, too Irish for the English and too flighty and
romantic for the feminists of the day.'²⁷

This confusion as to what kind of writer Edna O'Brien might be
was compounded further by the visceral return to the emotional and
geographical terrain of *The Country Girls* in *A Pagan Place* (1970), the
bitter portrait of a marriage of *Zee and Co* (1971) and the consciously
ribald revision of the Joycean and Beckettian interior monologue in the
experimental *Night* (1972), in which Mary Hooligan, an Irish caretaker
in an English house, appropriates the space and identities of her absent
employers in a monologue which both self-consciously plagiarizes James
Joyce's Molly Bloom monologue and indicts him for the shortcomings of his vision of female social and sexual roles, thereby challenging
the hegemony of women's 'scripting' by the Irish canon as well as by
the Constitution.²⁸ *Night* in particular divided critics at the time of its

publication, attracting critical praise for the sensuousness of its language, but also vitriolic condemnation from the *Times Literary Supplement* as 'a mixture of Irishism and whimsy ... gift-wrapped porn ... one long act of public literary masturbation'.[29] In fact, her name frequently suggested an evocative 'brand' of smut in the 1960s and 1970s, exacerbated by the commodification of O'Brien's own image as a paperback cover image for her novels. Stanley Kauffman is typical of reviewers in setting aside O'Brien's remarkable play with genre and writing back to Joyce in *Night*, and viewing it instead as a further instalment of confessional fiction, the novelty only in the change in style from 'impudent charm and wide-eyed mischief' to 'lyrics of the loins'.[30]

As Ireland gave way to metropolitan English, American and continental European settings in the novels and short stories of the 1970s and 1980s, an unthinking conflation of author and heroine is among the most perceptible features of considerations of O'Brien by both reviewers and the first Anglo-American critics to write on her work. Grace Eckley reads O'Brien's work as 'a personal odyssey beginning with the background in Co. Clare, the convent school education, removal to London, birth of children, and dissolution of marriage', arguing for 'a deep personal wound that provokes revenge against men through the diabolical male characters'.[31] Darcy O'Brien, in a 1982 essay, 'Edna O'Brien: A Kind of Irish Childhood', makes the valid point that, because the vast majority of O'Brien's predecessors in Irish women's writing were Anglo-Irish, from Maria Edgeworth through Lady Gregory to Elizabeth Bowen, she was 'the first country girl to write of [her] experience', but this insight is problematic in that the critic cannot conceive of an authorial distance between Edna O'Brien and her 'country girls'.[32] This instability of the relationship between author and characters leads Maureen O'Connor and Lisa Colletta to place O'Brien alongside Lady Morgan and Oscar Wilde 'in a tradition of insurgent, discomposing Irish writers in revolt against the masculinist dominant culture'.[33] Her memoir-cum-travelogue *Mother Ireland* (1976) and her novel *The High Road* (1988) offer parallel insights into her self-stagings as an Irish writer abroad which render porous the boundaries between author and character, and mount an analysis of the constructed nature of national and sexual identities, and the oppressiveness of national gender stereotypes, be they mythological, religious or literary. In the consciously Joycean *The High Road*, a sketchy history of Ireland is mapped onto the alienation, urbanization and eventual departure of a female artist; national and sexual issues cannot be kept separate. Anna is disablingly conscious of her belated cultural position as

Irish emigrant writer, and as a woman in a novel where the Joycean exilic legacy has spawned an expatriate community rife with debased literary imitators, 'wandering nerds, pen-pedlars' who produce 'soulless replicas' which they sell to 'the land of the Stars and Stripes ... to predatory matrons who yearned for homespun, untortured banality' and in which women artists are, bluntly, 'eunuched males'.[34] The Joycean model is here viewed as quite damaging, gendered and all-pervasive as the repressive Irish cultural legacy with which all O'Brien protagonists wrestle.

Mother Ireland likewise explicitly addresses one of the central concerns of her work as a whole, in its fascination with the pervasive figures of Cathleen ni Houlihan, Mother Ireland and their cognate figure, the Virgin Mary, and how the linked mythologies of Catholicism and Irish nationalism allow for the construction of a homogeneous nation state upon foundational gender norms, whereby the policed purity of the Irish female body acts as a conscripted guarantor for the Irish nation state.[35] As such, her outspoken novels, with their female protagonists existing in a close relationship with the commodified 'colleen' archetype (with which O'Brien herself was also frequently aligned), explore the ways in which the sexual continence of this purportedly representative type of Irish femininity is crucial to the maintenance of the nation's boundaries, from *The Lonely Girl*, in which the foreigner Eugene Gaillard's relationship with the protagonist Caithleen is compared by a neighbour to colonization – 'The tragic history of our fair land ... alien power sapped our will to resist'[36] – to *Down by the River* (1996), her trenchant fictionalization of the 'X case', in which a raped teenage girl is forbidden to travel abroad to terminate her pregnancy 'as she and her unborn child symbolize the Irish state's integrity'.[37] Like Joyce, O'Brien insistently figures Ireland as mother. Unlike Joyce's, however, her work interrogates the gendering of the nation. If, as *Mother Ireland* begins, Ireland 'has always been a woman, a womb, a cave, a cow, a Rosaleen, a sow, a bride, a harlot, and of course the gaunt Hag of Beare' then her work foregrounds the ways in which such genderings 'have been told and fabricated by men and by mediums who described the violation of her body and soul'.[38]

Criticism which focused on O'Brien's prolific production of short stories between the 1970s and the early 1990s – nine collections appeared between *The Love Object and Other Stories* (1968) and the 2013 fifty-year retrospective collection, also called *The Love Object* – was quicker than scholarship on her novels to recognize the inherently political nature of her work. Many of her short stories restage elements which appear elsewhere in her work; repetition, far from being an abiding flaw, is crucial to the political and aesthetic effects of O'Brien's *oeuvre*. Rebecca Pelan notes that 'the creation of a recognisable fictional world has been achieved by O'Brien through an extraordinary level of intertextuality'.[39] Characters, settings, motifs and images are repeated and reinterrogated: familiar O'Brien tropes reappear – the beloved, then resented, mother figure, martyred by the alcoholic father, familiar from as far back as *The Country Girls*; the convent crush on the nun, the 'new idol' who replaces the mother and prefigures the distant husband; motifs such as the humble, twine-wrapped food parcels from home, and the slitting of the child's fingers on a discarded razor-blade; while the narrative movement from rural Ireland to exile in England recurs in much of her work. The effect of such dense intertextuality suggests less that O'Brien writes 'the same story over and over again' as Lynette Carpenter phrases it, than that she was engaged in a consciously post-Joycean creation of a recognizable fictional world, the stultifying rural west of Ireland of the mid-twentieth century, and more specifically, in a recovery of the previously unvoiced female experience of that world.[40]

Rebecca Pelan's influential essay 'Edna O'Brien's "World of Nora Barnacle"' begins by citing Philip Roth's much-quoted observation (courtesy of the Joyce scholar Frank Tuohy) from his preface to Edna O'Brien's selected short stories, *A Fanatic Heart* (1985), that, while Joyce was 'the first Irish Catholic to make his experience and surroundings recognisable, the "world of Nora Barnacle" had to wait for the fiction of Edna O'Brien'.[41] For Pelan, in recording that particular world, O'Brien in fact 'performed one of the most important tasks of women's writing – that of turning the female absence into a presence'.[42] For Pelan, and for the critics who came after her – many of whom concentrated less on the novels than on the short stories which formed the majority of O'Brien's output in the 1970s and 1980s – Nora Joyce 'remains symbolic of countless women in post-independence, rural Ireland whose fate was obscurity and powerlessness at the hands of a society which endorsed their continued suppression for reasons of political expediency'.[43] Certainly critics of Edna O'Brien's short stories have generally been responsive to their realist cataloguing of the horrors of rural and small-town Irish life in the mid-twentieth century: a narrow and aggressive Catholic church, a chauvinistic and isolationist government, censorship, uncultivated bourgeois and petty bourgeois classes, vulgarity and provincialism, but particularly – in her most celebrated stories such as 'Irish Revel' (*The Love Object*, 1968), 'A Scandalous Woman' (*A Scandalous Woman and Other Stories*, 1974), and 'A Rose in the Heart of New York' (*Mrs Reinhardt and Other Stories*,

1978) – the social powerlessness and invisibility of women, socially sanc-tioned brutality towards women in the home, and the sexual control of women whose behaviour was considered immoral.

While O'Brien's short stories set in rural Ireland offer an often dead-pan, shockingly detailed, account of the routine brutalization of women within rural communities, they also deploy elements of non-realist modes to enact an alternative mode of scrutinizing female *Bildung* and also, crucially, mother-daughter communion and conflict. If little of the wider world explicitly penetrates these claustrophobic family romances in the short fiction, O'Brien is clearly exposing the violence inherent in the traditional, constitutionally-approved sanctity of the home and the woman's place within the domestic sphere, in which she is brutalized. The Gothic elements in 'A Rose in the Heart of New York', as well as sig-nalling the obviously patriarchal abuses of power – the half-crazed father and his murderous impulses – also emerge in fears of maternal power, the nightmare of female confinement within a domestic space presented as haunted, in states of living death and live burial, family curses and hid-den stories. The happy homestead beloved of De Valera is rewritten as a place of Gothic horror, 'a kind of castle where strange things happened and would go on happening' where decay symbolizes sexual violence, the father is exposed as an alcoholic brute and the mother's mute submission is observed and violently rejected by the daughter who nonetheless fears replicating it.[44] However, the element of the family romance which most engages O'Brien throughout her short stories and novels, culminating in her 2006 mother-daughter novel *The Light of Evening*, is the dark inter-generational conflicts that emerge from the mother-daughter dyad, which her fiction constructs as poised between ecstatic symbiosis – inevitably becoming suffocation – and insurmountable loss. Mothers in O'Brien's work dominate their daughters' material, social and imaginative lives, icons of the daughters' lack of identity and sense of illegitimacy, as well as the almost biological, thanatological pull back towards the mother. More than the god-like father-surrogates sought as husbands and lovers, more even than the fleeting but recurring lesbian relationships evoked in terms of mutual jouissance in *The High Road* and 'The Mouth of the Cave' (*The Love Object*), the mother remains the ultimate 'love object' for the desir-ing subjectivities of O'Brien's heroines, in search of what at the conclu-sion of *Mother Ireland* she calls 'the leap that would restore one to one's original place ... the radical innocence of the moment before birth'.[45] To read this purely in psychoanalytic terms, however, is to ignore the highly overdetermined nature of the mother figure in Irish cultural, political and literary narratives, so that its representation can never be innocent of the maternal iconography of mariolatry and Irish nationalism.

The State of the Nation

O'Brien's return to writing about Ireland in her Irish-set 'state of the nation' novels of the 1990s marks a shift from a consideration of the individual Irish female subject and her pursuit of liberation at home and abroad to a more explicit examination of the national culture that shapes the individual, male and female alike, and a trenchant critique of history. *House of Splendid Isolation* (1994), written in O'Brien's sixties, revisits the relationship between an older woman and a younger man from *Johnny I Hardly Knew You* (1977) – and, to an extent, the evocation of the mother-son relationship of her previous novel, *Time and Tide* (1992) – but, in restaging that relationship between an elderly, childless widow and an IRA gunman on the run who takes refuge in her isolated house, O'Brien is, according to Laura Engel, 'less focused on retelling versions of her own history and more concerned with the way that many stories connect to shape versions of a collective history'.[46] The protagonists, republican terrorist and dying Big House chatelaine, are haunted and constrained by the ghostly 'yoke' constituted by place and 'the chains of history, the restless dead and the restless living, with scores to settle', as the novel, in setting its characters briefly outside known historical scripts, examines the disastrous consequences of a monolithic conception of history.[47] *House of Splendid Isolation* shares with its successors in O'Brien's contemporary Ireland trilogy, a shift in the way the land is portrayed, in a movement away from the lyrical evocation of a beloved landscape (which was also, nonetheless, the location of constricted female lives) of her earlier work, to a more consciously post-colonial synecdoche for an entire Irish history of conquest and rebellion. Further, in a departure from the cipher-like male characters of her earlier work this novel contains a sustained examination of the deformations wrought upon male identity by the extent to which Irish constructs of masculinity are bound up with land ownership and control.

Wild Decembers (1999) revisits the 'land question' via a murderous land dispute between neighbouring farmers fought over the pregnant Breege, whose body is identified with the land, male property to be inscribed and battled over, her sexuality constrained by the Catholic / nationalist / masculinist script and within a problematically seductive relationship between female land and male farmer. That the farmer in question is a returning emigrant whose claiming of the land is ascribed to his mother's instilling in him 'the certainty that one day he must go home'[48] suggests further O'Brien's interrogation of history and memory, and, as a long-term exile herself, analysis of the Irish diaspora and its sponsorship of particular forms of cultural memory, including the way in which, viewed from outside, Ireland retains an indelible association with nature and premodernity.[49] *Down by the River* (1996), O'Brien's controversial fictionalization of the notorious 1992 'X case', shares with *Wild Decembers* a focus on a motherless young woman whose sexuality and pregnancy form a crux, not only for the plot, but, as Eve Stoddard suggests, in symbolic relation to a once-colonized land, 'a female body within a particular landscape marked historically by cultural, national and global events'.[50] For Heather Ingman, its evocation of the teenage girl, raped by her father, and forbidden by the State to travel to England to terminate the resulting pregnancy, constitutes O'Brien's most sustained critique of the connection between Ireland's masculinist nationalism and control of women's bodies.[51] This critique is expanded to include an examination of other masculinist nationalisms, the allied horrors of genocide and the problem of human evil in her 2015 novel *The Little Red Chairs*, which transplants a fugitive Serbian war criminal to a Sligo village where he functions briefly as guru, alternative parish priest and love object for an unhappily married local woman. Yet what is chiefly memorable about the novel is less its evocation of how another Irish rural community expels a female member who has broken the tribal rules on sexual behaviour than its exploration of its protagonist's encounters with other displaced women's voices from the Mothers of Srebernica at The Hague International Criminal Tribunal to those of the immigrant women who people the night-time underworld of London office cleaners and the nameless immigrant drop-in centre which draws the 'nobodies, mere numbers on paper or computer, the hunted, the haunted, the raped, the defeated ... the banished, the flotsam of the world, unable to go home, wherever home is'.[52]

Edna O'Brien and *Field Day*

In 1991, Edna O'Brien was represented in 'Irish Fiction 1965–90' in the original three-volume *Field Day Anthology of Irish Writing*, not by an extract from any of her novels, but by a single, brief short story, an English-set version of 'Bluebeard', 'Number Ten' (*Mrs Reinhardt and Other Stories*, 1978). Even for a publication so famously marked by a virtual absence of women writers, it was a perfunctory nod to a significant Irish woman writer, and an oddly uncharacteristic text by which to represent her within a major anthology implicitly establishing an Irish canon by selecting material to represent and define Irish writing. In the corrective volumes IV and V which emerged almost a decade later as a result of the controversy ignited by the neglect of women's work in the original anthology, O'Brien is far better served. However, it is the multiplicity of editorial headings under which she is represented that is significant: a two-page extract from *Mother Ireland* in 'Recollections of Catholicism 1906–60'; a four-page extract from *The Lonely Girl* and a one-page extract from *Banned in Ireland*, in 'Sexuality: Erosion of the Heterosexual Consensus, 1940–2001'; a two-page short story, 'The Mouth of the Cave', in 'Sexuality: Lesbian Encounters 1745–1997'; a two-page extract from *The Country Girls*, in 'Education in Twentieth-Century Ireland'; a two-and-a-half-page extract from *Girls in their Married Bliss*, in 'Women and Politics in Independent Ireland, 1921–68'; and a two-page extract from Mother Ireland in 'Feminism, Culture and Critique in English'. Her earlier work is still over-represented compared to her mature writing, and that none of her 'state of the nation' novels of the 1990s are extracted is a particularly glaring omission. O'Brien's greater and more multifarious inclusion, however, reconfigures the twentieth-century Irish canon and clears a position for women's voices denied by the grand narratives of the Irish twentieth century. More than simply charting women's struggle for self-determination in the face of constricting social scripts, her work illuminates successive waves of cultural hysteria centring on women's bodies in general and motherhood in particular, and documents Irish women's experiences which have been foreclosed or occluded by the dominant discourses in a post-independence Ireland that continued to be patriarchal and exclusionary; it examines the nexus of inherited fears and anxieties which attend the relationship between women and Irishness. Ultimately, the challenge in anthologizing O'Brien's work is that it continually treats itself as a work in progress, interrogating the cultural and literary scripts with which she works, continually revising itself and questioning and de-authorizing both its own plots and the critical impulse to find closure.

Notes

1 Alice Hughes Kernowski, ed. *Conversations with Edna O'Brien* (Jackson, MI: University of Mississippi Press, 2013), ix.
2 Mary Maher, 'Who's Afraid of Edna O'Brien?' *The Irish Times*, 14 December 1967. In Kernowski, *Conversations with Edna O'Brien*, 3–7, 3.

3 Elgy Gillespie, 'Our Edna – A Song of SW3', *The Irish Times*, 10 June 1972. In Kernowski, *Conversations with Edna O'Brien*, 13–17, 14.

4 Lynette Carpenter, 'Tragedies of Remembrance, Comedies of Endurance: the Novels of Edna O'Brien', in *Essays on the Contemporary Irish Novel*, ed. Albert Wertheim and Hedwig Brock (Munich: Max Hueber, 1986), 263–81, 263.

5 For trenchant analyses of the O'Brien 'persona', see Rebecca Pelan, 'Reflections on a Connemara Dietrich', and Maureen O'Connor, 'Edna O'Brien, Irish Dandy', in *Edna O'Brien: New Critical Perspectives*, ed. Kathryn Laing, Sinéad Mooney and Maureen O'Connor (Dublin: Carysfort, 2006), 12–37, 38–53.

6 See Rebecca Pelan, 'Edna O'Brien's "Stage-Irish" Persona: An "Act" of Resistance', *Canadian Journal of Irish Studies* 19, no. 1 (1993): 67–78, and Amanda Greenwood, *Edna O'Brien* (Plymouth: Northcote House, 2003), 2 and following.

7 *Miami Herald* review, undated. Quoted on New York State Writers' Institute website at www.albany.edu/writers-inst/webpages4/archives/obrien.html. Accessed 20 December 2015.

8 Edna O'Brien, 'A Scandalous Woman', in *A Scandalous Woman and Other Stories* (Harmondsworth: Penguin, 1976), 9–43, 43.

9 Greenwood, *Edna O'Brien*, 2.

10 Ibid., 1, 10.

11 Heather Ingman, 'Edna O'Brien: Stretching the Nation's Boundaries', *Irish Studies Review*, 10, no. 3 (2002): 253–65, 253.

12 Interview with Julia Carlson, 'Edna O'Brien' in *Banned in Ireland: Censorship and the Irish Writer*, ed. Julia Carlson (London: Routledge, 1990), 71.

13 Quoted in Carlson, *Banned in Ireland*, 76.

14 Kristine Byron, '"In the Name of the Mother...": Reading and Revision in Edna O'Brien's *Country Girls Trilogy and Epilogue*', in *Wild Colonial Girl*, ed. Lisa Colletta and Maureen O'Connor (Madison, WI: University of Wisconsin Press, 2006), 14–30, 15.

15 Benedict Kiely, 'The Whores on the Half-Doors', in *Conor Cruise O'Brien Introduces Ireland*, ed. Owen Dudley-Edwards (New York: McGraw-Hill, 1969), 148–61, 158.

16 Fintan O'Toole, 'A Fiction too Far', *Irish Times Weekend Review*, 2 March 2002, 1, 4.

17 Pelan, 'Reflections on a Connemara Dietrich', 14.

18 Helen Thompson, 'Hysterical Hooliganism: O'Brien, Freud, Joyce', in *Wild Colonial Girl*, ed. Colletta and O'Connor, 31–57, 31.

19 Byron, '"In the Name of the Mother..."', 18.

20 Stanley Kauffmann, 'Night', review of *Night* by Edna O'Brien. *World* 30 January 1973, 78. www.enotes.com/topics/edna-obrien/critical-essays/ obrien-edna-1932-2. Accessed online 23 December 2015.

21 Pelan, 'Reflections on a Connemara Dietrich' 19.

22 Quoted in Ed Vulliamy, 'At Last O'Brien Has Her Country under Her Spell', *The Independent* 11 November 2015. www.independent.ie/entertainment/books/book-news/at-last-obrien-has-her-country-under-her-spell-31599401.html. Accessed online 14 December 2015.

23 V. S. Naipaul, 'Review of *The Country Girls* by Edna O'Brien', *New Statesman* 16 July 1960, 97.

24 Edna O'Brien, *Girls in Their Married Bliss* (Harmondsworth: Penguin, 1964), 7.

25 Sean McMahon, 'A Sex by Themselves: An Interim Report on the Novels of Edna O'Brien', *Éire-Ireland* 2, no. 1 (1967): 79.

26 Julia O'Faolain, 'A Scandalous Woman', review of *A Fanatic Heart: Selected Stories by Edna O'Brien, New York Times*, 22 September 1974, 5.

27 Pelan, 'Reflections on a Connemara Dietrich', 24.

28 Thompson, 'Hysterical Hooliganism', 33.

29 Review of Edna O'Brien's *Night, Times Literary Supplement* 6 October (1972): 1184.

30 Kauffmann, 'Night'.

31 Grace Eckley, *Edna O'Brien* (Lewisburg, PA: Bucknell University Press, 1974), 99.

32 Darcy O'Brien, 'Edna O'Brien: A Kind of Irish Childhood', in *Twentieth-Century Women Novelists*, ed. Thomas F. Staley (London: Macmillan, 1982), 179–90, 179.

33 *Wild Colonial Girl*, ed. Colletta and O'Connor, 5.

34 Edna O'Brien, *The High Road* (London: Weidenfeld and Nicolson, 1988), 7.

35 Edna O'Brien, *Mother Ireland* (Harmondsworth: Penguin, 1976).

36 Edna O'Brien, *The Lonely Girl* in *The Country Girls Trilogy and Epilogue* (New York, NY: Farrar, Strauss, Giroux, 1987), 299.

37 Ingman, 'Edna O'Brien: Stretching the Nation's Boundaries', 262.

38 O'Brien, *Mother Ireland*, 11.

39 Rebecca Pelan, 'Edna O'Brien's "World of Nora Barnacle"', *Canadian Journal of Irish Studies* 22, no. 2 (1997): 49–61, 49.

40 Carpenter, 'Tragedies of Remembrance, Comedies of Endurance', 263.

41 Philip Roth, preface to Edna O'Brien, *A Fanatic Heart: Selected Stories* (Harmondsworth: Penguin, 1976), 4.

42 Pelan, 'Edna O'Brien's "World of Nora Barnacle"', 51.

43 Ibid., 49.

44 Edna O'Brien, 'A Rose in the Heart of New York', in *Mrs Reinhardt and Other Stories* (London: Weidenfeld and Nicolson, 1978), 383.

45 O'Brien, *Mother Ireland*, 89.

46 Laura Engel, 'Edna O'Brien', in *British Writers: Supplement V*, ed. George Stade and Sarah Hannah Goldstein (New York, NY: Charles Scribner, 1999), 341.

47 Edna O'Brien, *House of Splendid Isolation* (London: Weidenfeld and Nicolson, 1994), 70, 78.

48 Edna O'Brien, *Wild Decembers* (London: Weidenfeld and Nicolson, 1999), 52.

49 For more on the figure of the Irish emigrant in O'Brien's work, see chapter twenty-one of this volume, and also Ellen McWilliams, *Women and Exile in Contemporary Irish Fiction* (Basingstoke: Palgrave Macmillan, 2013).

50 Eve Stoddard, 'Sexuality, Nation and Land in the Postcolonial Novels of Edna O'Brien and Jamaica Kincaid', in *Edna O'Brien*, ed. Laing, Mooney and O'Connor, 104–21, 106.

51 Ingman, 'Edna O'Brien: Stretching the Nation's Boundaries', 263.

52 Edna O'Brien, *The Little Red Chairs* (London: Faber, 2015), 203.

CHAPTER 14

Fiction 1960–1995

Anne Fogarty

Self-consciously feminist fiction, marketed to meet a new appetite for such work by publishers including Arlen House, Attic Press and Poolbeg Press and fuelled by the endeavours of the women's movement to achieve equality, emerged from the early 1980s in Ireland. However, a survey of the work produced by female authors from 1960–95 reveals that a focus on women's battles for autonomy and their attempt to break free from the confining roles of spouse, carer and mother, conjoined with the project of capturing peculiarly female apprehensions of the various imagined social worlds depicted, feature centrally in all the writing of this period. Notwithstanding the determined endeavour to elicit fiction with a decidedly feminist cast from the 1980s onwards, marked thematic and aesthetic continuities link novels published in the timeframe 1960–95.[1]

The novels under review here exploit what Fredric Jameson has dubbed the 'antinomies of realism' and centre especially on pointing out the gaps between affective states, lived experience and the meaningful, and between the social structures of the family and community and the existential.[2] Inventive re-workings of the *Bildungsroman* and *Künstlerroman*, the historical novel, the Big House novel, the romance, novels of sexual awakening and the marriage plot are also notably undertaken. Politically, a kinship may be discerned between all the fiction of this period resulting from the overarching goals of the first and second waves of the women's movement to promote female independence and to countermand the sexual subjugation of women. Feminist fiction undeniably facilitated the emergence of new voices and modes, but it was less of a breakaway from a confining tradition than a more overt voicing of themes and concerns already fully embedded in novels published between 1960 and 1980. Feminist activism becomes an aspect of the empowerment of the heroines in novels from 1980 onwards; explicit depictions of abuse likewise appear only to have become imaginatively feasible after the women's movement had heightened awareness of its prevalence. Feminist positions and themes, moreover, were not just the province of the literary novel; they were regularly grafted into the popular fiction by Maeve Binchy, Emma Cooke, Mary Rose Callaghan and Marian Keyes from the 1980s onwards. Taboo issues such as extra-marital sex, the costs of sexual permissiveness for women, abortion and divorce were profiled in these texts that often simultaneously upheld conservative communitarian and moral values.

Unsurprisingly, the quandaries posed by pregnancy, inside and outside of marriage, are regularly exposed by these fictions. But contrary to the moral strictures of the Church and Irish society at large, such crises are often depicted as an opportunity for the emotional enlargement and political radicalization of the heroine. The protagonists in many of the novels produced between 1960 and 1995 are represented as resourcefully coping with their pregnancies or single-mindedly choosing to have clandestine abortions in the UK. Self-reliance and beleaguered female solidarity uneasily serve as counterforces to the stigma against single mothers and the patriarchal fear of unbridled female sexuality. The role of the mother is consistently scrutinized but, above all, problematic and lethally engulfing inter-generational bonds between mothers and daughters are highlighted in order to depict the psychic burden of the heroines. Embroiled in irresolvable rivalries or a draining symbiosis with their mothers, they are caught in a deadly compulsion to repeat aspects of female socialization that foil their desire to escape and be different. Moments of homecoming in seemingly perdurable but crumbling homesteads often symbolize such short-circuiting of bids to change the social order while also registering the imperative to implode the family and domesticity from within.

Strikingly, although women are generally conceived of in the fictions from this period in terms of their roles within marriage and the family, a peculiar emphasis is discernible on the solitary female protagonist, whether as worker, lover, widow, unmarried woman or single mother. This trope of the woman alone permits the scrutiny of confining social functions and concretizes the victimization and isolation of women by the misogynist regimes of the Irish state, but it also crucially serves as an emblem of the quest for selfhood and autonomy. It is multiply drawn on to delve into and map the contours of female consciousness and, in some instances, to give voice to an *écriture féminine* as in the work of Dorothy Nelson and Evelyn Conlon. Above all, portrayals of lone, alienated figures facilitate the exploration of female desire and sexuality. Conspicuous continuities in the manner in which the psychic patterns of female experience are rendered interweave the novels considered here: the doomed romantic longings of the suicidal Caithleen in Edna O'Brien's *The Country Girls Trilogy* (1987), the tormented Jessie determinedly preparing for an abortion in London in Emma Cooke's *A Single Sensation* (1981), the haunted Laura reliving the trauma of sexual abuse in Jennifer Johnston's *The Invisible Worm* (1991) and the wry Pen O'Grady tentatively inventing ways of mourning the sudden death of her female lover in Emma Donoghue's *Hood* (1995) belong to distinctive fictional worlds and social moments; yet, they are inherently cross-connected in their conflicted affective states, their experience of constricting sexual conservatism, their thwarted efforts at self-realization and their solitary defiance of the status quo.

'The Problem That Has No Name': Writing Beyond the Marriage Plot

Betty Friedan has argued that the 'strange stirring' or sense of dissatisfaction experienced by women in the mid-twentieth century long remained unvoiced.[3] Finding a means of articulating and combating the nameless malaise of female disempowerment is the besetting preoccupation of Irish novels published from 1960–95. The laying bare of female subservience frequently went hand-in-hand with a querying or even jettisoning of the marriage plot, that is of narratives that posited the nuptials of the heroine as denoting finality and completion. Edna O'Brien's *The Country Girls Trilogy* (1987) and Olivia Manning's two trilogies about the Second World War, *The Balkan Trilogy* (1981) and *The Levant Trilogy* (1982), tracking the fate of the newly married Harriet Pringle who accompanies her husband in 1938 to Bucharest and flees to Athens and then Cairo to avoid the Nazi occupation, evince the increased feminist impetus of women's writing from the 1960s onwards. While O'Brien's novels defiantly probed female sexuality and social formation, Manning's works treated them more obliquely.[4] Subtly insinuating domestic politics into world affairs, her vividly panoramic war novels represent the marriage of Guy and Harriet Pringle almost by default, detailing the latter's pained discovery of her constricted sphere of influence. The petty rivalries and anti-Semitism in the local and British émigré communities in Bucharest 1939–40 in *The Great Fortune* (1960) and *The Spoilt City* (1962) and in Athens 1940–41 in *Friends and Heroes* (1965) act as a counterpoint to Harriet's bleak realization of her limited compass compared to her husband who finds outlets for his artistic and socialist interests in the public sphere. Her fate is cast in world political and existential terms, enervation and a terrible scrabble for survival being its distinguishing features. In *The Levant Trilogy*, Manning widened her ambit to intertwine the story of Simon Boulderstone, a British officer deployed on the front line in the Allies' Middle Eastern campaign against the German army, with that of Harriet adrift in Egypt and confounded by its Otherness. The slow attrition of the desert war and the crumbling of British rule in Egypt are unfurled in parallel with the deterioration of Harriet's relationship with her husband and recognition of her deep-seated unhappiness in *The Danger Tree* (1977), *The Battle Lost and Won* (1978) and *The Sum of Things* (1980). When she runs away to Damascus and Jerusalem, thereby partially embracing the difference of Levantine culture, she gains greater command over herself. But ultimately she capitulates to the necessity of marriage as the inescapable compromise on which female existence is predicated. In *The Rain Forest* (1974), a novel set in the imaginary British colony of Al-Bustan in the Indian Ocean, Manning also uncovers the psychic costs of marriage for women, linking this exploration with the disempowerment attendant on motherhood, colonial misrule and male depredations on the natural environment. Kirsty Foster, a successful novelist, caught in a loveless relationship, is horrified by her dependent condition when in an alien country she unexpectedly finds herself pregnant contrary to the wishes of her husband. The thin dividing lines between love and cruelty are captured in Kirsty's fatalistic embrace of her unborn child on the one hand and her unhesitating but failed attempts to abort it on the other. In a pointed irony, her miscarriage at the end of the novel rescues her from the indignity of the female lot, but it also closes her off from what she had increasingly seen as an escape route from her dissatisfaction with the married state.

Unlike Manning's transnational texts, the novels of Janet McNeill focus on circumscribed provincial worlds in the UK and in Presbyterian Belfast. In these exactingly observed milieus, she lays bare the existential dilemmas that contour female lives and the ambivalent emotional states attendant on them and picks out via acerbic internal monologue the disturbing secrets lurking beneath middle-class gentility. *The Maiden Dinosaur* (1964) in its searing portrayal of the straitened desires of the mannish Sarah Vincent, a single schoolteacher in Belfast, uncovers the brittle existence of someone who refuses the conventions of marriage. A similar dissection of the fate of the solitary, middle-aged woman is undertaken in McNeill's *The Small Widow* (1967) which portrays the difficulties faced by Julia, a Belfast woman living in the UK, in the aftermath of her husband's death.

Perturbed by her inability to play the part of widow, Julia passes her marriage in review, including her husband's affair and the suicide of his lover, concluding that her actions as wife and mother have been entirely at the behest of others. Cold-eyed, she squares up to her expendability and shrinking sexual and emotional prospects. In *As Strangers Here* (1960), McNeill draws out the alienation of post-Second World War Belfast from the viewpoint of a Presbyterian clergyman whose wife has remained bedbound following the loss of a child and cruelly neglects their adopted daughter. Domesticity and marriage in particular are the sources of the unhappiness and ineffectuality of the women in the novel. The young men of the city by contrast seek outlets for their frustrations in evangelical religion, vandalism and sectarian violence. The ending proffers the fragile hope that the next generation may break the endemic cycle of misery.

Setting her plots in Europe or the United States, Julia O'Faolain more than any other writer of her generation imaginatively inspects the ties between female sexuality and Catholic morality. Her protagonists are torn between rebellion and conformity; the pursuit of desire partially frees them but also ends up entrammelling them in values from which they purportedly wish to escape.[5] In *Godded and Codded* (1970), the heroine, Sally Tyndal, recognizing that women remain chameleons until they get married, abandons her PhD and settles for the safe predictability of an affair with an older man following a broken romance with a politically engaged Algerian student in Paris and a self-induced abortion. *The Obedient Wife* (1982) centres on Carla, an unhappily married Italian woman living in California, who embarks on an affair with a priest in a bid to find emotional satisfaction and fulfil the imperatives of the 1960s sexual revolution. Ultimately, she returns to her relationship with her philandering husband, preferring its time-honoured cynicism to modern uncertainty. *The Irish Signorina* (1984) likewise captures points of tension between the drive for liberation and the self-limiting circuitry of desire. Determined not to repeat the female propensity for failure, Anne Ryan visits the Cavalcantis, an Italian family who once employed her mother to act as minder for a wayward daughter. Falling in love with Guido, whom she discovers to have been her mother's lover, Anne determines shockingly to take destiny into her own hands by marrying him, even though it transpires he is actually her father. The closure traditionally represented by marriage is thus rendered grotesque as rivalry with her mother impels Anne to become her surrogate.

Entirely eschewing the framework of marriage, female poverty and dependency are foregrounded in Norah Hoult's novels which variously draw out the social ostracism of single women – the elderly, housebound, Miss Jenkinson living alone in an apartment in London in *The Last Days of Miss Jenkinson* (1962) is conceived of as a tragic grotesque, while the widowed Cusheen Kavanagh, endeavouring to get by in rural Ireland in *Only Fools and Horses Work* (1969), is rendered as a figure of fun who yet manages to salvage her self-respect.[6]

If Hoult depicts women who have outlived their era, Leland Bardwell by contrast conjures up rebellious female characters who are ahead of their time on account of their refusal to conform. Julie de Vraie, the chief protagonist of her picaresque, feminist fable, *Girl on a Bicycle* (1977), is a unique figure in women's fiction in this period, due to her bohemianism, unapologetic assumption of masculine prerogatives and sexual profligacy.[7] Mistreated by her family, she takes up the male occupation of groom and becomes a roving outsider in the world of crumbling Protestant Big Houses. Even though she is frequently subject to predatory male assaults, she moves with a propulsive energy through the country lanes of midlands Ireland during the Emergency, drinks with abandon, flits promiscuously between lovers, empathizes with other female casualties, and remains impervious to the proprieties of romance or sexual possessiveness. In *That London Winter* (1981), Bardwell depicts the ramshackle, experimental lives of a young post-Second World War generation of Irish emigrants living in London and weighs up, in particular, the price exacted of women for a new-found sexual freedom which leaves them immobilized rather than liberated. The opaque plot of Bardwell's *There We Have Been* (1989) unfolds a still more sombre view of women's lives. It centres on Diligence Strong, who has been outlawed by her family for her libertarian ways and returns home to stake her claim in the rundown family farm on the Northern border after the death of her parents. Even though she grapples with the ghosts of the past, including grief for her dead sister, a failed romance and an unfulfilled desire for a child, Diligence is unable to assuage her sense of being a misfit. Bardwell resolutely underscores female difference and draws out the marginality of women who are viewed as transgressive and the emotional destitution that is their fate.

Jennifer Johnston's protagonists are likewise ostracized because they dare to override the sectarian, class and political divisions within Irish society. Her fiction particularly uncovers how war violently disrupts fragile relations formed across ethnic, gender, class and religious boundaries.[8] The chief figures in her novels are routinely sidelined and turned into relics or savagely scapegoated for offending against social sensitivities or

breaching family secrets. In *The Captains and the Kings* (1972), the elderly
Charles Prendergast, a member of a declining Protestant, Anglo-Irish
landowning class, is falsely accused of molesting the young Catholic boy
whom he befriends, while in *The Gates* (1973), a relationship between
Minnie MacMahon and a local Catholic working man proves equally
ill-fated when he absconds to England with the money from the sale of
the gates of her uncle's demesne, thus dashing her hopes of making the
estate profitable again. Minnie's sexual waywardness frees her uncle from
his seigneurial role and her lover from the constrictions of poverty, but
leaves her facing an uncertain future. In *How Many Miles to Babylon?*
(1974), a novel about the First World War, Anglo-Irish officer Alexander
Moore pays an even heavier price for his unorthodox friendship with a
local Irishman and faces execution because he has killed his companion
to save him the anguish of a court martial after he was found guilty of
desertion. Johnston's texts centring on the War of Independence likewise
trace the pressure exerted on the private domain by political ideologies
and the devastation wrought by the crossing of social boundaries. In
Fool's Sanctuary (1987), Miranda, born into a Protestant landed family,
eternally mourns her Catholic lover who was assassinated as an informer
because he warned her brother and his friend, both British army officers,
of an IRA plot to kill them, while in *The Old Jest* (1979), Nancy Gulliver
involuntarily triggers the summary shooting of an IRA man on the run
whom she had befriended.

The ineluctable politicization of the private sphere is also evident in
Johnston's Troubles fictions. Kathleen Doherty in *Shadows on Our Skin*
(1977) is subjected to a punishment beating because of her clandestine
involvement with a British soldier. The Derry schoolboy who has been
her companion betrays Kathleen's secret as he feels ousted by his older
brother who had begun an affair with her. Female desire has even more
disastrous consequences for Helen Cuffe in *The Railway Station Man*
(1985). Curiously liberated by the death of her husband who has been
a victim of a terrorist attack in Derry, Helen pursues a secluded life as
an artist in Donegal but is unable to evade the warring factions in Irish
society as her son and her English lover are killed in an IRA explosion.
Indeed, Johnston's heroines frequently serve as ethical goads and as fero-
cious indicters of the emotional deficits of the past. Constance Keating
in *The Christmas Tree* (1981) returns to Dublin to die in the family
home, confronting in the process her failure to become an artist and
the loveless marriage of her parents. Constance is especially haunted by
her mother's immobile ghost but realizes in a final confrontation that

her mother's cruelty stemmed from her emotional blockages. Constance's determination before she dies that the Eastern European lover from whom she had absconded should be informed about their baby daughter intimates that the cyclical patterns of repression and unvoiced suffering may be cancelled out and that the mother-daughter bond now will become a channel for change.

The Invisible Worm (1991) thematizes the consequences of father-daughter incest in depicting the hallucinatory half-life of Laura Quinlan who has been sexually molested as a child. Haunted by an image of a fleeing woman, Laura comes to the realization that the person on the run is in fact her mother who had shirked the knowledge of her daughter's abuse. The symbolic torching of the summerhouse, the site of her father's first sexual assault on her, allows Laura to vindicate herself, to bury the ghost of the woman who had failed to protect her and to recover a modicum of mental health while recognizing that her pain will never be allayed. A strained relationship between a mother and daughter also forms part of the plot of *The Illusionist* (1995), a novel addressing the emotional and sexual illusions that trap women into subscribing to false ideals of love and marriage. Stella MacNamara leaves Martyn, her manipulative magician husband, to pursue the writing career which he had attempted to bring to a halt, sacrificing in the process the loyalty of her daughter who cleaves to her father. A tentative reconciliation between mother and daughter only becomes possible when Martyn's bigamous marriage is uncovered following his death. Suggestively, Johnston throughout her work implies that the imaginings of the female artist may act as a counter-force to the prestidigitations of patriarchy but that women must first sever the bonds of male power. Her heroines and beleaguered male protagonists undertake determined but anguished reckonings with the past and the loveless families that have scarred them. Their hard-won solitariness is essential to their freedom and the means by which they elude political and familial control.

Sexual and Political Awakenings: The Feminist Novel 1980–1995

A conspicuous upsurge in women's writing occurs from the early 1980s onwards. The fight for greater equality and visibility in the public sphere created the latitude for new writers who openly broached feminist themes. The problematization of motherhood and of women's emotional welfare in sexual relations becomes a recurrent nexus of themes in novels produced in the 1980s in particular. Maura Richards's satirical novel,

Two to Tango (1981), depicts the emotional conflicts and social opprobrium faced by Brig O'Mahony who gets pregnant by her boyfriend.
Determined to bring up her baby alone, Brig is torn between feelings
of shame and defiance. Her future is left in the balance at the end of
the novel as she loses the mobile home in which she planned to live.
Richards presents her heroine as empowered by her solitary battle, but
also indicates that Irish society will not afford her any space and that she
will remain on the margins. Clare Boylan in *Last Resorts* (1984) similarly
uses the twin tools of comedy and satire to appraise the psychic conditions of motherhood and heterosexual love. Having been abandoned
by her husband, her artist-heroine is involved in a desultory affair with
a married man. Taking stock of her situation while on holiday with her
teenage children on a Greek island, she arrives at the recognition that she
has been too beholden to men and to the obligations of domesticity. She
ultimately flees her family yet concedes that her escape alters nothing as
her children have already become caught in the trap of generation building. Consciousness raising is depicted by Boylan as a necessary step in the
liberation of women, but it proves a questionable counter to the ideological grip of the family and patriarchal power.

In the intertwined tragi-comic novels, *Holy Pictures* (1983) and *Home
Rule* (1992), the latter a prequel to the former, Boylan tracks the turbulent and vividly drawn trajectory of the Devlin and Cantwell families
from the 1890s to 1920. Home Rule is less the quest for Irish political independence than a description of the inhibiting regimes that trap
women within the home. In *Home Rule*, the lovelorn Elinore Devlin,
neglected by her husband, tyrannizes over her daughters, one of whom
has been abused by her father, turning them either into domestic slaves
or fating them to become mirror images of herself, while the mother in
Holy Pictures is ineffectual at protecting her daughters from her husband's
petty power. Their penchant for the grotesque allows Nan and Mary
in the latter novel to survive their damaging environment, but they are
still unable to cut loose from domestic and economic dependence and
the poverty of their existences. Boylan fuses fantasia and satire in *Black
Baby* (1988), a portrait of the reclusive, elderly Alice Boyle, who adopts
Dinah in the mistaken belief that she is the African black baby she had
sponsored in school. Part con-artist, part fairy godmother, Dinah, by
reintroducing pleasure into Alice's life, succeeds in rehabilitating her.
Alice faces down in the process an abusive past in which she had been
bullied by her mother and prevented from marrying. Breaking away from
the deleterious effects of biological mothers is an efficacious pathway to

female self-development in Boylan's texts but is rarely sufficient to undo the effects of patriarchy.

The objective of depicting women's lives and perspectives with a new intensity leads to a generic instability in the fiction of the 1980s and the development of jagged plots with disconcerting trajectories. This is the case with the novels of Ita Daly: the eponymous heroine of *Ellen* (1986) transmogrifies from a lonely, cossetted child, who has been the target of her mother's ruinous, over-protective love, into a predatory adult who steals the lives of her friends, resorting in a Gothic subplot to murder in order to protect her romantic interests. The virginal, middle-aged heroine of Daly's *A Singular Attraction* (1987), Pauline Kennedy, is similarly consumed with rage against her recently deceased mother who had dominated her life. Having had sex for the first time in her life, she discovers a new-found confidence and even succeeds in laying the censorious ghost of her mother. Unlike Ellen, who hides behind the borrowed façade of married contentment, Pauline severs all links with the past and faces life alone, freed of the emotional cavilling with which her mother had tormented her. In *The Summerhouse* (1984), Val Mulkerns repurposes the family saga, focalized from the warring viewpoints of several siblings and their spouses. Julia O'Donohue's manipulative favouritism of one of her daughters creates lasting rivalries amongst her other children leading ultimately to Eleanor's suicide despite her mother's lionization of her. Hanny, an outcast daughter, eventually triumphs by inheriting the family home but her malevolent perspective bears witness to the destructive legacy of familial neglect and hatred.

The hidden treacheries subtending the family also dominate the plot of Maeve Kelly's *Necessary Treasons* (1985), a nuanced novel of feminist awakening that foregrounds the struggles of the women's movement in Limerick to provide safe havens for women suffering from marital violence. Eve Gleeson discovers that the sisters of her fiancé, Hugh Creagh, have severed all contact between Eleanor, his sister-in-law, who has been beaten by his brother, and their child. While Eleanor rekindles a love affair with a poet friend and renews her relationship with her lost daughter, Eve abandons her planned marriage and moves to the United States where she continues to work for the feminist movement. The countervailing demands of love and independence lead to differing emotional outcomes for Kelly's heroines, but the text overall presents a pointedly bleak portrait of the commonplace violence experienced by married women in the 1980s. Strikingly, her allied feminist figures are equipped with a greater capacity for survival than the spinsterish, unhappy Creagh sisters who have presided over a damaging family legacy. Uniquely, Kelly's *Florrie's Girls* (1989) concentrates on the working lives of nurses in London and is thus a rare novel to consider feminist issues in the context of emigration. Inventively cast in the form of a diary, it tracks the experiences of Cos (Caitlin Cosgrave) as she trains to be a nurse in London. Even though she feels that her professional training is stifling her real self, Cos is adamant that she needs an independent career as she is unsure whether she will marry. Despite her intense homesickness for rural Ireland, Kelly's heroine is also remarkable because of her heartfelt desire for freedom, noting in the ironic opening and closing sentences that the day she left home was the sunniest day of the summer.

Evelyn Conlon's *Stars in the Daytime* (1989) has a generic kinship with *Florrie's Girls* as it too is a *Bildungsroman* which succeeds in enunciating the point of view of the main protagonist, Rose, capturing the lived textures of her life and insinuating emphatic feminist nuances into her story. Rose rebels against the stifling nature of her rural upbringing and especially questions the predetermined course of female existence, observing acidly that choice and babies do not go hand-in-hand. However, echoing the plots of many other novels of the era, she falls pregnant in France as a consequence of a brief affair and determines to return to Dublin to have her baby alone. Rose finally achieves an uneasy peace with her parents, but recognizes that her current situation belies her earlier quest for freedom and a women's truth.

Mary Beckett's *Give Them Stones* (1987) unfurls a similarly guarded and ironic account of a woman's life in West Belfast from the 1950s to the era of the Troubles. Martha Murtagh, feeling trapped by a loveless marriage and motherhood, decides to take command of her own fate by opening a bakery in the family home. Her business is destroyed by the IRA because she refuses to pay danger money to them. The ending, however, suggests that she has had to compromise on her hard-bitten feminism as she plans to move into a new home with her husband and to reopen her bakery. Dorothy Nelson's experimental novels, *In Night's City* (1982) and *Tar and Feathers* (1987), by contrast, focus on child protagonists who are powerless to change their worlds. Nelson's fragmented, stream-of-consciousness narrations instead capture the ambivalent emotions of children who experience abuse and witness violence in the home and yet feel beholden to the parents who maltreat them. *In Night's City* ends with the tormented daughter's entreaty of her oblivious mother who, even when she fails, remains a fulcrum of her identity. Mary Leland's *Approaching Priests* (1991) profiles the southern reaction to the Northern Troubles and explores a woman's quest for love and her struggles with the constraints of religion in the 1980s. Leland's heroine, a cynical journalist, has been knowingly involved in a violent relationship with a poet-friend, but at the end of the novel she decides to pursue a relationship with the idealistic Damien, a former priest. Love is possible only after independence has been achieved and through the maintenance of a disabused wariness.

Molly Keane's re-toolings of the Big House novel focus centrally on the violence of intimate family relations depicting them with mischievous glee and adding feminist élan to the sexual intrigues that dominated her earlier works. The Big House becomes a site of the grotesque in which poisonous mother-daughter relations above all are writ large. The neglected Aroon St Charles in *Good Behaviour* (1981) turns on the monstrous mother who has tormented her and achieves a deadly revenge on her. In *Time After Time* (1983), three sisters and a brother, all with debilitating physical deformities, are jolted out of their perennial antipathies by the visit of Leda, a Jewish cousin, who aims to destroy their fractious co-existence and to requite herself on their mother who had thwarted her romantic plans in the past. The siblings, however, rally around to drive out this interloper and to restore the lethal energies of their home. *Loving and Giving* (1988) centres on the needy Nicandra, who pursues human and animal substitutes for the love she was denied by her distant mother. After her marriage breaks up, she moves back into the family home, where she is locked into inveterate conflict with a longstanding retainer and an aunt who had sustained the family materially. The Big House in Keane's late iterations is at once a place of emotional deadlock and a *perpetuum mobile* by means of which the psychosexual anxieties and perversities at the heart of the family renew themselves.

Deirdre Madden variously draws on the resources of the novel of ideas, trauma narratives and the *Künstlerroman* to depict the Northern Troubles and to tease out the existential dilemmas of her characters. *Hidden Symptoms* (1986) juxtaposes the passionately engaged viewpoint of Teresa, whose brother has been the victim of a sectarian killing, and Robert, a writer who affects a distanced remove from the political conflicts of Belfast.[9] The text delineates the shadings in their differing worldviews as Catholics caught up in a political struggle not of their own making, but does reconcile them. *The Birds of the Innocent Wood* (1988) is a trauma narrative of a different order that foregrounds the passing on of emotional wounds within families. Mothers and daughters especially in this Gothic text, replete with lost parents, dead babies and incestuous liaisons, are psychically damaged by a foundational female privation. In *Remembering Light and Stone* (1993), Madden's solitary main persona moves restlessly between Ireland, Italy, France and the United States, seeking the metaphysical resources that will help her to make sense of existence. Ultimately, she decides to return to Co. Clare, but this is less of a homecoming than a continuation of her search for a balance between anonymity and the known, the foreign and the familial. *Nothing is Black* (1994) unites Claire, a visual artist, Nuala, an entrepreneur in the throes of an emotional crisis triggered by the death of her mother, and Anna, a Dutch woman who has sought refuge in Ireland after her divorce and the breakdown of her relationship with her daughter. Madden cross-connects their emotional and intellectual worlds while casting doubt on any innate female solidarity. A reconciliation between the estranged mother and daughter is proffered as a possibility but is not a certainty. The burden of this text as of all of Madden's work is that moral and aesthetic attentiveness may buffer us against the fragility of the human condition.

Like Deirdre Madden, Emma Donoghue introduced fresh subjects into the Irish novel and recast the coming-of-age narrative and the tale of sexual awakening. *Stir-Fry* (1994), in part a campus novel and a *Bildungsroman*, wittily delineates the faltering student career of Maria and her gradual discovery of the lesbian relationship between her two housemates, Jael and Ruth. Her desultory attempts to find a boyfriend cede to the recognition that she is in love with Ruth and that the difference which she has cultivated has had implications beyond her ken. Donoghue pointedly makes lesbian love not a coded subplot but an intricate component of the social, emotional and sexual landscapes of her texts. *Hood* (1995), in which Pen mourns her girlfriend who has died in a car accident, canvases the manifold complexities of sexual love and the disparities and points of friction that pattern a relationship. Yet pleasure is nonetheless cross-associated with anxiety and loss in these novels, and a consonance may be seen between the radical Otherness of Donoghue's protagonists and the embattled female subjects that populate many of the fictions produced from 1960–95.

Playing with Genre: Romance, Historical Novels and Fantasy Fiction

The refinement of crucial popular genres contributed to the expansion of women's writing from the 1960s onwards. Maeve Binchy, in particular, created flexible women-centred narratives that, while seemingly preoccupied with romance and marriage, actually prove their overall insignificance. Strikingly, she situates her novels not in the metropolis but in the village or small town and avails of this microworld to scrutinize numerous aspects of women's everyday lives. It is notable that her characters always pursue careers and that female friendship is more central to their wellbeing than heterosexual love. *Light a Penny Candle* (1982) foregrounds the enduring bond between two women who are childhood friends, and the mutual influence of their mothers. Both of their marriages are shown to fail, with key subplots centring on male alcoholism, suicide and abortion, but provincial identity and matriarchal standards ultimately serve as long-term emotional anchors. In *Firefly Summer* (1987), local values similarly win out as a family-run pub survives the misguided endeavours of an Irish-American to turn a Big House into a profitable hotel. *Circle of Friends* (1990) gives precedence to asexual social bonds rather than romance; the heroine abandons an infatuation with a handsome college friend, who has two-timed her, in favour of the rewards of female intimacy and the support of a network of peers.

The novels of Emma Cooke, by contrast, concentrate on the vicissitudes of pregnancy and marriage, and the hypocrisies of liberalism and sexual freedom. The single woman who is the main protagonist of *A Single Sensation* (1981) is determined to abort the child she is carrying as a result of a one-night stand and travels home to confront her mother and sister with her plan. The married heroine of *Eve's Apple* (1985) operates under different constraints finding herself pregnant in her forties by her lover and with a husband who is staunchly Catholic. She is ultimately abandoned by the latter as he too is having an affair but, in a change of heart, feels empowered by the baby she has been forced to bear. Cooke's *Wedlocked* (1994) focuses on the troubled relationships of two couples who have had affairs with each other and scrutinizes their hedonistic values, bleakly revealing women to be especially vulnerable to exploitation in an amoral culture. The heroine's hope for romance nonetheless forlornly survives even though she is abandoned by all the men in her life. Mary Rose Callaghan's *Mothers* (1982) is more optimistic in tenor as it intertwines the stories of women of three different generations and the circumstances they faced during troubled pregnancies. Intergenerational solidarity in the present offsets the harsh treatment meted out to women in the past undergoing pregnancy outside of marriage. Marian Keyes's *Watermelon* (1995), even though it also centres on a foundering marriage, likewise highlights the resilience of the heroine who finds a new partner and builds a different future for herself after having been deserted by her husband during her first pregnancy.

Historical fiction, frequently disparaged because it simplifies 'real' history, is another popular genre regularly practised by women writers in this period. Tellingly, the mode is used to reimagine vital junctures in Irish history and to reconceive female involvement in events usually apprehended as having been entirely driven by men. Iris Murdoch's *The Red and the Green* (1965) daringly rethinks 1916, shifting attention away from the Easter Rising events in the General Post Office to the knotted, erotic, ethnic and religious entanglements of a Dublin family and exploring in the process the psychosexual allure of revolutionary action as well as the sublimations that it demands. Mary Leland's *The Killeen* (1985) also undertakes a dissection of power relations, exposing the authoritarian underpinnings of republicanism when the baby born to a young girl made pregnant by a prominent IRA man on the run during the Civil War is commandeered by his family.[10] The mother's attempt to rescue the infant from this political fate only exposes him to greater danger as he dies of physical maltreatment and is buried in a *killeen*, an unmarked graveyard for unbaptized children. Leland's novel focuses on the non-heroic lives bypassed in official history and reveals the inglorious ideological tussles that obliterate a child who has been rendered an outcast.

Julia O'Faolain's *No Country for Young Men* (1980) similarly depicts republicanism as shackling women since it is controlled by men who pervert its ideals and use their power corruptly to subjugate others.[11] The plot posits a parallel between the struggle of Sr Judith Clancy, an elderly nun, to unearth a traumatic event during the Civil War, namely her murder of a manipulative Irish-American IRA operative, as a consequence of which she had been forced into a convent, and the quest of her grandniece Gráinne to find sexual freedom in the male-dominated Ireland of 1979. Both women achieve freedom at a price; violence is shown to be a collateral effect of their need to fight back against patriarchy. Allied themes are addressed in O'Faolain's *Women in the Wall* (1975), which is set in sixth-century Gaul. The decision of an anchorite to immure herself as an act of expiation reveals the degree to which her convent is still caught up in the conflicts of the external world and subject to the sway of male sexual politics. Éilís Dillon's *Across the Bitter Sea* (1973) and *Blood Relations* (1977) are more sanguine about women's political agency and insurgency. These twinned family sagas delineate events in Ireland from the Famine to the War of Independence. The heroines, who are torn between lovers and spouses affiliated with moderate nationalist and republican stances, undergo a political education and succeed in mediating between these opposing positions and in cross-linking the causes of a meliorist landlord class and of the newly radicalized rural population of the West of Ireland. Republicanism for Dillon is a vital social cement, a catalyst for change and above all the essential means by which her heroines transform themselves.

Éilís Ní Dhuibhne's *The Bray House* (1990) is a dystopian fantasy set in the early twenty-first century, after Ireland has been wiped out by a nuclear disaster. It is a venturesome text, uniting a popular genre with serious literary aspirations.[12] Robin Lagerlof, the cold-blooded leader of a Swedish archaeological expedition to Ireland, ends up in bitter dispute with her comrades about which remnants of Irish society are of most import: the Bray House with its compelling artefacts or a haggard sole survivor, Maggie Byrne, from Wicklow who is a potentially vital link to a now-obliterated past. Ní Dhuibhne's playful text questions the narratives used to depict the social and political dimensions of Irish life. Her figure of the solitary woman survivor mocks tropes of Mother Ireland and fantasies of feminine authenticity, while her version of the ruthlessly ambitious scientist mischievously sends up stereotypes of the modern empowered woman. In toying with and critiquing patriarchal and feminist tropes, *The Bray House* opens up a debate about the cognitive and imaginative gaps in renderings of women's stories, thereby throwing down a gauntlet to writers in future decades.

Notes

1 On the connections between first-wave and second-wave Irish feminism, see Linda Connolly, *The Irish Women's Movement: From Revolution to Devolution* (London: Palgrave Macmillan, 2002), 56–110. For an instructive analysis of women's writing from 1960–90, see Heather Ingman, *Irish Women's Fiction: From Edgeworth to Enright* (Dublin: Irish Academic Press, 2013), 153–236.

2 Fredric Jameson, *The Antimonies of Realism* (London: Verso, 2013), 15–44.

3 Betty Friedan, *The Feminine Mystique* (London: Penguin, 1963), 13–29.

4 On the political themes of Manning's fiction, see Eve Patten, *Imperial Refugee: Olivia Manning's Fictions of War* (Cork: Cork University Press, 2012).

5 For a study of Julia O'Faolain's fiction, see Ann Owens Weekes, *Irish Women Writers: An Uncharted Tradition* (Lexington: University Press of Kentucky, 1990), 174–90.

6 See Sinéad Gleeson, 'A Long Gaze Back at Norah Hoult on Her 117th Birthday', *The Irish Times*, 10 September 2015, for an assessment of Hoult.

7 For an account of this novel, see Christine St Peter, *Changing Ireland: Strategies in Contemporary Women's Fiction* (London: Macmillan, 2000), 53–6.

8 For incisive overviews of Johnston's work, see Teresa Casal, '"Words Bursting, Words Witnessed": Language and Violence in Jennifer Johnston's War Novels', in *New Voices in Irish Criticism*, ed. P. J. Mathews (Dublin: Four Courts Press, 2000), 99–105 and Heather Ingman, 'Nation and Gender in Jennifer Johnston: A Kristevan Reading', *Irish University Review* 35, no. 2 (2005): 334–48.

9 On the themes of Madden's fiction, see Michael Parker, 'Shadows on a Glass: Self-Reflexivity in the Fiction of Deirdre Madden', *Irish University Review* 30, no. 1 (2000): 82–102.

10 See St Peter, *Changing Ireland: Strategies in Contemporary Women's Fiction*, 75–81, for a passionate discussion of Leland's novel.

11 On women's exclusion from history in this novel, see Ellen McWilliams, *Women and Exile in Contemporary Irish Fiction* (Basingstoke: Palgrave Macmillan, 2013), 43–64.

12 On the problematization of identity in this work, see Derek Hand, 'Being Ordinary: Ireland From Elsewhere: A Reading of Éilís Ní Dhuibhne's *The Bray House*', *Irish University Review* 30, no. 1 (2000): 103–16.

CHAPTER 15

The Short Story

Heather Ingman

The short story has always had a central place in the Irish literary canon and it is one genre in which women writers have been prominent from the outset, though their prominence has until recently been somewhat overlooked. Several reasons may be adduced for women writers' enthusiasm for the short story form: when women were running large households, short stories may have seemed to demand less commitment of their time and resources than novels; they could be written and sent off to magazines for a speedy publishing decision. Short stories were a testing ground for women writers lacking confidence in their ability to achieve results in the longer form, notwithstanding the fact that at its best the short story demands as least as much artistic skill as the novel. Frank O'Connor's association of the short story with voices excluded from the ruling narrative of the nation is sometimes claimed as peculiarly appropriate for Irish women, an often submerged population group within Irish public life.[1] Yet O'Connor also associated the short story with the romantic outsider, 'remote from the community',[2] and, as we will see, the stories of Jane Barlow and Somerville and Ross focus on lives within a community, while the work of Mary Lavin and Claire Keegan explores relationships both within the family and in the wider, rural community.[3] There is a need for the canon of the Irish short story to be looked at again in a way that would register the number of distinguished stories by Irish women and would determine whether giving equal weight to women writers modifies our view of the Irish short story itself.

Nineteenth Century

The modern Irish short story emerged in the final decades of the nineteenth century. Before that a tale could embrace the brief sketch, anecdote or fable, a novella or even a three-volume novel. The pressing circumstances of Irish political life meant that for much of the nineteenth-century, short fiction was used for extra-literary purposes.

The tales of two Anglo-Irish writers, Maria Edgeworth and Anna Hall, were primarily didactic, designed to instruct English readers in an understanding of the Irish way of life. Edgeworth's children's tales (*The Parent's Assistant* 1796, *Moral Tales for Young People* 1801 and *Early Lessons* 1801–2), published in London, were part of the predilection for morally uplifting tales for children at the turn of the century. Edgeworth aimed not only to instruct parents in the educational methods proposed by her father and herself in *Practical Education* (1798), but also to give English readers an understanding of what was needed if the Anglo-Irish were to govern Ireland effectively. In Edgeworth's *Popular Tales* (1804) for an artisan readership, stories such as 'The Limerick Gloves' and 'Rosanna' sought to promote favourable feelings towards Ireland in the minds of English readers as well as to encourage landlords to reform their management of Irish estates.

Anna Hall's *Sketches of Irish Character* (1829) were similarly didactic in their bid to explain Ireland to the English, with the aim of benefiting both countries. The network of mutual support and encouragement so often vital to sustaining women writers' careers is evident in the crucial role Maria Edgeworth played in encouraging Anna Hall's literary ambitions.[4] Hall also profited by the rise of the popular penny magazines in the 1830s, finding a ready market for her work in magazines such as *Dublin Penny Journal* (1832–36), the *Irish Penny Magazine* (1833–34) and the *Irish Penny Journal* (1840–41). Hall's *Sketches*, so popular that by 1854 they were into a fifth edition, centre on the parish of Bannow in County Wexford where her early life was spent. They include the type of subject matter expected by her English readers: portraits of dirty and idle Irish peasants, tales of violence in the Irish countryside and local stories of fairy and folklore. As the political situation in Ireland worsened and the successive famines began to take hold, Hall's earlier certainties about how Irish society should develop gave way to a darker portrait of Irish life in *Stories of the Irish Peasantry* (1840). Hall's strengths as a writer lie in her evocative descriptions of the Irish countryside and lively sketches of Irish peasants. Her handling of the form is much less certain in *Stories of the Irish Peasantry* where she can never quite trust the story to tell itself. Not for the first time in the nineteenth century, Ireland's political turbulence had an impact on literary achievement as the contradictions caused by Hall's hybrid national identity proved increasingly difficult to contain within the format of the tale.

Later in the century, stories by Rosa Mulholland and Emily Lawless focus on the famine era. In 'The Hungry Death', selected for publication in Yeats's *Representative Irish Tales* (1891), Mulholland portrays the effects of famine on the 1,000 or 1,200 inhabitants of the island of Innisbofin. An omniscient narrator acts as a kind of Greek chorus, commenting on the gradual disintegration of the community as the crop fails. It is taken for granted that the reader will be outside this community, as the narrator is, and needs detailed explanation of its habits and beliefs, yet the peasants are never condescended to: they speak in quiet and restrained dialect unlike the bombast of Hall's stories. In 'After the Famine' (*Traits and Confidences* 1897), Emily Lawless looks back on the famine of 1846–7 through the memories of a fictitious, unnamed, elderly English gentleman. As often in Lawless's fiction, the male narrator is employed in order to lend her account authority. At the same time, also characteristically, she undermines that authority by presenting him as an unreliable narrator, class-bound and ignorant of the country he is about to exploit.[5] After the famine, Hall's figure of the English tourist who laughs fondly at Irish eccentricities was no longer acceptable, even to an English readership.

The Antrim-born writer, Charlotte Riddell, was inspired by Sheridan Le Fanu to explore the possibilities of the Gothic in her stories: in 'Diarmid Chittock's Story', published in her final collection, *Handsome Phil and Other Stories* (1899), Cyril Danson picks up a copy of Le Fanu's *House by the Churchyard* in his bid to get acquainted with Ireland. The semi-autobiographical 'Out in the Cold' from the same collection is a vivid reminder of the psychological and material obstacles facing nineteenth-century Irish women writers. The story portrays Annabel Saridge as both unappreciated genius and would-be professional author whose struggles to break into print are carefully documented by Riddell. Ignorant of the workings of the publishing world, Annabel sends off her fiction at random to Dublin publishers, all of whom turn her down. Like her creator, Annabel eventually secures a London publisher for her work and in the closing sentences Riddell is unable to resist pointing out what Ireland loses by its discouragement of women writers.

Riddell's melodramatic ending (her heroine dies, worn out by hard work and poverty) is typical of the nineteenth-century story that, under pressure from the turbulent times in Ireland, tended to collapse into Gothic or melodrama, sentimentality or didactics. Nevertheless, as the century wore on, Irish authors began to pay attention to structure, tension and psychological development in a way that intermittently foreshadowed the twentieth-century short story. May Laffan Hartley's stories, 'Flitters, Tatters and the Counsellor' and 'The Game Hen' (*Flitters, Tatters and the Counsellor and Other Stories* 1881), depicting life in the Dublin slums, anticipate the work of Frank O'Connor and James Plunkett in their lively dialogue, urban realism and avoidance of the sentimentality and heavy-handed moralizing characteristic of much nineteenth-century short fiction. A similar lack of condescension marks the presentation of the daily life of impoverished Connemara peasants in Jane Barlow's *Irish Idylls* (1892), a series of interlinking stories that has been compared to a modern short story cycle.[6]

Fin de Siècle

Gregory Schirmer described the *Irish R. M.* stories of Edith Somerville and Martin Ross (*Some Experiences of an Irish R. M.* 1899, *Further Experiences of an Irish R. M.* 1908 and *In Mr Knox's Country* 1915), portraying obtuse Protestant landlords and wily Catholic tenants, as 'the last cry of the nineteenth century'.[7] Other scholars regard the tight formal structure of their stories, their sharp ear for dialogue and consistent narrative voice as marking the beginning of the modern Irish short story.[8] Julie Anne Stevens has emphasized the familiarity of Somerville and Ross with contemporary artistic developments and linked their stories to European traditions of pantomime, carnival and harlequinade.[9] Viewed in this way, the writing of Somerville and Ross seems modern, its European dimension fitting in with turn-of-the-century developments in which the Irish short story opened up to such outside influences as Chekhov, Flaubert, Maupassant, Turgenev and Ibsen. In the specific context of women's writing the modernity of Somerville and Ross may be adduced by their professional approach to the writing and marketing of their work, their strong support for women's rights and the value they placed on the emotional bonds between women. For these reasons Gifford Lewis positions the two writers in the first wave of New Woman writers.[10]

Somerville and Ross's knowledge of the expectations of the British popular press, in which most of these stories of fox-hunting and yachting in County Cork first appeared, allowed them to exploit to the full the comic potential of Irish identity as performance. They experimented with a variety of styles from pure farce in stories such as 'The House of Fahy', 'Occasional Licences', 'The Pug-Nosed Fox' and 'A Royal Command', through to Gothic in 'The Waters of Strife' and tales of ghost hauntings in 'Harrington's' and 'Major Apollo Riggs'. The linking narrative voice of Major Yeates who is of Irish extraction but, as Resident Magistrate, represents the British authorities in Ireland, is seemingly reasonable, self-deprecating and susceptible to women's charm, and thus calculated to appeal to the English reader. Yeates's willingness to admit when he has been gulled shows up the obtuseness of English outsiders like Leigh Kelway in 'Lisheen Races, Second-Hand', Mr Tebbutts in 'The Aussolas Martin Cat' and Maxwell Bruce in 'The Last Day of Shraft', all of whom retreat from Ireland, baffled. In stories such as these, Yeates finds himself allied with the native Irish, and even, in the latter story, on the wrong side of the law in a way that would be inconceivable for a member of the colonial class in Anna Hall's stories. Through their *Irish R. M.* stories Somerville and Ross portray the fractures and uncertainties of Irish life in the first decade of the new century, presenting Ireland as a country of multiple and shifting narratives. Of particular interest in the context of women's writing is the portrayal of the rise of the Dublin middle class woman, Larkie McRory, whose energy so impresses Major Yeates.

New Woman writers, it has been observed, were especially attracted to short fiction because it freed them from the traditional plots of the Victorian novel and made possible the formal innovation necessary for exploring the new subject of women's consciousness.[11] Born Mary Chavelita Dunne, George Egerton spent part of her childhood in Ireland and it was there that she worked on her first two collections of stories, *Keynotes* (1893) and *Discords* (1894). *Keynotes*, published with an Aubrey Beardsley design on the dust jacket, was an immediate success, twice reprinted in the first six months of publication and subsequently translated into seven languages. Inspired by her reading of Ibsen, Egerton created heroines who refuse to be contained by male definitions of womanhood: in 'The Regeneration of Two', the heroine challenges society's judgements on 'fallen' women and proposes entering into a free union with her lover. Where women do cave into convention ('An Empty Frame', 'Her Share'), they are portrayed as leading emotionally sterile lives. 'Virgin Soil' is a forerunner of Mary Lavin's story, 'The Nun's Mother', in depicting the disaster that follows a mother keeping her young daughter ignorant about sexual matters. Egerton was by no means an equal rights feminist, however. Her stories display indifference towards women's education and suspicion of women's professional lives ('The Spell of the White Elf'). Stories like 'Gone Under' and 'Wedlock' portray the dangers of thwarted maternity and Egerton's writing has been interpreted as essentialist for presenting motherhood as the fulfilment of womanhood.[12]

For her exploration of the inner lives and sexuality of women, Egerton drew on the subversive qualities inherent in the short form to do away with conventions of plot, linearity and discursive explanation in favour of dreams, symbolism and stream-of-consciousness. In 'A Cross Line' the complexity of Gipsy's sexuality, misunderstood by both men in the story, is revealed to the reader through a series of daringly erotic reveries describing her dreams and sexual fantasies. 'A Psychological Moment at Three Periods' traces the development of a young woman from a Dublin childhood, through convent school in Holland, to mistress in Paris but, as the title suggests, linear narrative yields to psychological exploration of her heroine's inner consciousness. In this, Egerton was aided by the nature of the short narrative that lends itself to focus on single, crucial moments in the life of the protagonist and in stories such as these it is possible to glimpse an emerging modernist aesthetic. In the urban realist stories of *Flies in Amber* (1905), where the central image of flies trapped in amber aptly reflects Irish women's lives, Egerton's depiction of Ireland as a shabby, backward place under the control of priests anticipates Joyce's *Dubliners*.[13]

Modernism

For Elizabeth Bowen the short story was, like the cinema, a twentieth-century art form: 'The short story is a young art: as we now know it, it is the child of this century. Poetic tautness and clarity are so essential to it that it may be said to stand at the edge of prose.'[14] Bowen's first published work, *Encounters* (1923), was a collection in the modernist style – so much so that when, after submitting her manuscript to publishers, Bowen began to read Katherine Mansfield's stories she worried that readers would say she had copied her New Zealand contemporary.[15] Not only does her subject matter echo Mansfield's – children, family relationships, moving house – but the stories demonstrate from the start Bowen's willingness to explore inconclusive states of mind: 'Impressionism lightly laced with psychology bought one out of needing a plot,' she later admitted.[16]

Many of Bowen's eighty or so stories centre on the dislocation and rootlessness of modern lives and the unpredictability and alienation that haunt even the most middle class of lives. Only nine are set in Ireland but it can be argued that what Bowen is doing even in stories set outside Ireland is combining the Anglo-Irish theme of the supernatural as an external threat with post-Freudian focus on the interior uncanny, using the ghost story to express her contemporaries' unease about identity.[17] 'The Happy Autumn Fields' (1944) is characteristic in its use of ghost themes to juxtapose nineteenth-century Anglo-Ireland with bombed out London, presenting both as places of instability, focused through the anxieties of Anglo-Irish Henrietta and of Mary living through the Blitz. 'In our seeing of ghosts, each of us has exposed our susceptibilities, which are partly personal, partly those of our time', Bowen explained.[18] In 'The Back Drawing-Room' (1926), the stranger's retelling, in a fashionable London drawing room, of his personal ghostly encounter in Ireland has political ramifications that indicate his listeners' guilt and responsibility for their abandonment of the Anglo-Irish after Independence. In Bowen's stories the wider cultural and political context is as important as an individual's psychology. In 'Her Table Spread' (1930), the intensity and isolation of the Anglo-Irish way of life, remarked upon by Bowen in her family memoir, *Bowen's Court* (1942), is revealed in the fantasy the Anglo-Irish heiress, Valeria Cuffe, has woven around English officers who once visited her castle in her absence and whom she expects to return at any moment. Valeria's fantasies are personal – she hopes for a marriage that will save the castle and the line – but her futile dreams also encapsulate the hopeless political situation of the Anglo-Irish expecting rescue from the English that never comes. Taken together, Bowen's two Irish stories from this period have a pointed message for English readers.

Bowen's modernist mode came into its own during the Second World War as a means of expressing the fracturing of identity brought about when homes, and with them entire ways of life, were blown up during the Blitz. This sense of fragmentation was particularly acute in the Anglo-Irish community torn, like Bowen herself, between their Irish identity and their traditional loyalties to England. Such a conflict is experienced by Henry in the semi-autobiographical 'Sunday Afternoon' (1941) where, on a trip back to Ireland after the bombing of his London flat, Henry finds the reluctance of his Anglo-Irish friends to listen to details of life during the Blitz deplorable. Yet he cannot help contrasting the stylized civilities of the Anglo-Irish way of life with the breakdown in language and identity experienced by those living through the war in London. The young Anglo-Irish girl, Maria, is energized by Henry's description of life in wartime London but Henry, who nicknames her Miranda as a gesture to Shakespeare's play, warns her that the brave new world she envisages is one where the brutality of war has caused language, and even personal identity, to all but disappear.

In 'Summer Night', 'Unwelcome Idea' and 'A Love Story, 1939' published in *Look at All Those Roses* (1941), Bowen conveys the combination of claustrophobia and restlessness experienced by many in wartime Ireland. In 'Summer Night', Justin sees the war as a particular threat to Ireland's intellectual life. His apprehension that language is breaking down and must be renewed brings with it a concomitant, almost Beckettian observation that personal identity is also dissolving and will need to be remade: 'On the far side of the nothing – my new form. Scrap "me"; scrap my wretched identity and you'll bring to the open some bud of life. I *not* "I".'[19] Bowen's modernist aesthetic contrasts with her female contemporaries' adoption of the realist mode for their short stories.

The Mid-Twentieth Century

In their stories from the 1930s, Norah Hoult and Olivia Manning employ realism to express their disenchantment with Irish life focalized through such female protagonists as an Irish maid in London (Hoult's 'Bridget Kiernon' 1930) and young professional women in Dublin (Manning's 'A Case of Injury' 1939).[20] Mary Lavin and Maeve Brennan also worked primarily in the realist mode, though an argument has been made for Lavin's use of modernist indeterminacy in her first collection, *Tales from Bective Bridge* (1942).[21]

Lavin published nineteen short story collections during her lifetime, four in the 1940s alone (*Tales from Bective Bridge*, *The Long Ago and other stories* 1944, *The Becker Wives and other stories* 1946 and *At Sallygap and other stories* 1947). Materialism is a prominent theme in her stories, reflecting the economic hardships of mid-twentieth-century Ireland and many of her stories feature a Catholic middle class so consumed by the need to earn a living that the death of the heart ensues. The theme encompasses both urban stories like 'The Little Prince' and 'The Becker Wives', and those that have a rural setting, such as 'Lilacs' and 'The Widow's Son'. Oppressive structures of class ('A Gentle Soul') or religion ('The Convert') are often obstacles to love.

The domestic and seemingly apolitical nature of Lavin's work famously aroused Frank O'Connor's hostility in *The Lonely Voice* (1962) where he describes the discomfort he felt on reading her stories because they seemed to him to bear no relation to the central Irish themes of nationalism and war. He confessed himself disorientated: 'the point of view is perhaps too exclusively feminine'.[22] O'Connor's confusion demonstrates the extent to which Lavin was breaking new ground in the Irish short story. Many of her stories centre on women's lives and deal with themes that would be taken up by later Irish women writers. These include female sexuality and illegitimacy ('Sunday Brings Sunday,' 'Sarah'), the repression of the body ('The Nun's Mother', 'Chamois Gloves'), the portrayal of often fraught mother-daughter relationships ('The Will',

'A Cup of Tea'), as well as her stories of widowhood published in the 1960s ('In the Middle of the Fields', 'In a Café', 'Happiness'). In 'The Becker Wives', Flora Becker seems to offer the possibility of a different, more creative way of living, but she turns out to be schizophrenic, an unsettling conclusion that suggests the choice for women's lives in post-independence Ireland lies between conformity and insanity. Though sometimes rejecting the notion that gender played a significant part in her work ('I write as a person. I don't think of myself as a woman who writes. I am a writer. Gender is incidental to that'),[23] by her exploration of women's emotional lives, Lavin became an important trailblazer for Irish women writers. The extent to which her stories portray Irish women enmeshed in a variety of social restrictions, whilst not classifying her automatically as a feminist, nevertheless highlights her awareness of the severe constraints on mid-century Irishwomen's lives.

Women's lives and the constraints on them feature prominently in the mid-century stories of Maeve Brennan. Born in Dublin, Brennan moved to the United States when she was seventeen and thereafter, like Joyce in exile, endlessly recreated the constricting world of the Dublin in which she had grown up. For nearly thirty years she worked at the *New Yorker* and it was there that her stories depicting her childhood home in Ranelagh began to appear in the 1950s. Based on characters and incidents in Brennan's own family, these stories suited the *New Yorker*'s emphasis on realism, reminiscence and place. Many convey the repressive nature of Irish society at this time: in 'The Devil in Us,' the young girl internalizes the guilt-filled religion inculcated by the nuns into their charges. Brennan followed this with a series of stories about the Derdon and Bagot families, describing unhappy wives trapped in unfulfilled marriages, tyrannized over by neglectful husbands on whom they are financially dependant and living in dark, cramped Dublin houses suggestive of the emotional oppression of their lives. A dominant theme in Brennan's work is empathy with the poor and marginalized: in 'The Poor Men and Women', Rose Derdon's sympathy with the down and outs who turn up at her door is partly compensation for lack of emotional satisfaction in her marriage.

Gender played a part in Brennan's feelings of exclusion from the Ireland that developed after independence – introverted and xenophobic with a narrow definition of femininity that had no place for the sophisticated professional woman she had now become. Such feelings are focussed through the figures of the outsider, Anastasia, and the sexually repressed spinster, Norah Kilbride, in Brennan's novella, *The Visitor*, published posthumously in 2000, but completed in the 1940s.[24] As time went on, Brennan began to feel alienated also from life in America. In six stories published between 1953 and 1956 in the *New Yorker* Brennan takes up a dominant theme in the Irish short story of this period, namely emigration, but focuses on the Irish female emigrant. The power play between wealthy American employers and their envious, rage-driven Irish Catholic maids takes place in a precise social context but opens out in several of Brennan's stories into a generalized loneliness so that being an outsider comes to seem an inescapable part of the human condition. In the hands of writers like Brennan and Lavin, the Irish short story in its realist mode moved towards greater sophistication and psychological complexity, as well as introducing new subject matter around women's lives, family relationships and female sexuality.

1970s and 1980s

Edna O'Brien, whose first collection, *The Love Object*, was published in 1968, pushed these themes to new levels of frankness. Many of her stories feature women routinely brutalized and crushed, not only by their menfolk, but also by the constraints of the patriarchal society in which they live. Though an often ambivalent figure for Irish feminism, O'Brien dealt more openly than before in the Irish short story with such themes as female sexuality ('The Love Object') and lesbianism ('The Mouth of the Cave'). In her later collection, *A Scandalous Woman* (1974), the title story is a bleak and forceful presentation of the sacrifice of a lively young girl, Eily, to social respectability while 'The House of My Dreams' highlights the oppressive religious and social ideologies governing Irish women's lives when the narrator's unmarried sister is banished to a Magdalene laundry to have her baby. The mother-daughter relationship, so often regarded in feminist theory as crucial to female identity, is a central theme in O'Brien's work, challenging the previous dominance of the father-son relationship in the Irish literary canon. O'Brien's stories range from the martyr mother figure seen through the eyes of her young daughter ('A Rug') to the more ambivalent presentation of the rural Catholic mother in 'Cords' and 'A Rose in the Heart of New York' (*Mrs Reinhardt*, 1978). The daughter's sophisticated, cosmopolitan life becomes a source of conflict and misunderstanding that leaves the relationship unhealed even in the late story 'My Two Mothers' (*Saints and Sinners*, 2011).

It has been argued that many of O'Brien's stories reveal a writing back to Joyce's *Dubliners* from a gendered perspective.[25] In 'Irish Revel'

(*The Love Object*) imagery and narrative irony undermine the protagonist's romantic illusions while in 'The Love Object' O'Brien extends Joyce's method by recounting everything from inside her heroine's mind, without authorial commentary. In 'Over' (*A Scandalous Woman*), she experiments with the second person when a stream of consciousness about a love affair gone wrong is directly addressed by the woman to her ex-lover. Extra-literary considerations, such as the focus on her appearance, lifestyle and her supposedly scandalous subject matter, have often hindered serious discussion of O'Brien's writing but her work displays a purposeful attempt to break new ground in the Irish short story, both thematically and stylistically.

With the founding of the Irish Women's Movement in 1970, the feminist note in short stories by Irish women became stronger. Maeve Kelly's *A Life of Her Own* (1976), with its echo of Woolf and its portrayal of the daily thwarting of women's aspirations, reflects the struggles of the Irish feminist movement in this decade. In the title story, Brigid's life is very far from her own, being controlled first by her brother then by her husband, while the protagonist of 'The Vain Woman' has had her artistic talents crushed by her husband and children, but most of all by a religion that has condemned her to constant child-bearing: 'I often find it hard to remember *who* I am. Not just my name. But my self. I look in the mirror and I say, "Who are you?"'[26]

With the strengthening of Catholic opinion in the aftermath of Pope John Paul II's 1979 visit to Ireland, together with the economic recession and high unemployment which reinforced conservative attitudes, short stories by Irish women during the 1980s, like the novels discussed in the previous chapter, registered more explicit protest against the legal and ideological constraints on women's lives. Ita Daly's *The Lady with the Red Shoes* (1980) depicts Irish women deeply entangled in the masculinist values of their society and their often fruitless attempts to break free while Evelyn Conlon's first collection, *My Head is Opening* (1987), highlights women's issues around motherhood and the social unacceptability of unmarried mothers. Other notable collections include Val Mulkerns's *An Idle Woman* (1980), a series of satirical portraits of Irish life, Clare Boylan's *A Nail on the Head* (1983) and *Concerning Virgins* (1989), filled with witty insights into Irish women's attempts to forge new identities for themselves, and *Dublin 4* (1982) by the popular writer, Maeve Binchy, exposing the hypocrisy that lay beneath the supposed liberalism of Dublin's professional classes. Leland Bardwell's *Different Kinds of Love* (1987) focuses on such topics as domestic violence, child abuse and

incest not previously much represented in the Irish short story while the
end of the decade saw the publication of Mary Dorcey's impassioned and
stylistically experimental collection, *A Noise from the Woodshed* (1989),
giving a voice to those defined as marginal in the life of the Irish nation:
battered wives, the elderly and, above all in this collection, lesbians, since
the 'noise from the woodshed' turns out to be the sound of lovemaking
between women.

The 1980s was a decade when Irish women writers broke many
boundaries in the Irish short story, stylistic, as well as thematic. Though
most writers continued to rely on the realist mode, others were more
willing to innovate, as the experiments of Dorcey and O'Brien with
stream-of-consciousness and the second person demonstrate. Irish
women began to feature in anthologies in larger numbers: Ben Kiely's *The
Penguin Book of Irish Short Stories* (1981) was notable for its inclusion of,
alongside Somerville and Ross, Elizabeth Bowen and Mary Lavin, contemporary writers like Val Mulkerns, Edna O'Brien, Julia O'Faolain, Ita
Daly and Eithne Strong.

The Troubles

The choice of the realist mode by women writing on Northern Ireland
has been criticized as unadventurous;[27] within the realist mode, however, writers like Mary Beckett (*A Belfast Woman* 1980) attempted to
demythologize the ideologies behind the violence, portraying the inner
conflicts of women struggling to forge meaningful lives for themselves in
a sectarian society. Beckett's protagonists often fail to fit into stereotypes
of womanhood and, as a consequence, live on the margins of society:
the childless wife in 'The Excursion', the single mother in 'Theresa'. Her
stories probe the psychological attitudes of the region, portraying rural
Northern Ireland as a harsh, repressed society where the only person
capable of showing love is a young girl who is 'wanting' ('Ruth'). Stories
such as 'A Belfast Woman', 'The Balancing of the Clouds', 'Flags and
Emblems' and 'The Master and the Bombs', deal more directly with
political divisions and bigotry in Northern Ireland, while in 'Theresa'
Northern Ireland's racist attitudes are confronted.

Anne Devlin looks at the impact of the Troubles on young women
in her collection, *The Way-Paver* (1986), where 'Naming the Names' is
one of the few stories of this period that attempts to explore the mind
of a female IRA activist. 'Five Notes After a Visit' has autobiographical
overtones as a young Catholic woman from Andersonstown, now living

in England, returns to Belfast on a visit and finds herself in an uneasy in-between position, blamed in England for the bombs her fellow country-men are setting off, threatened in Belfast for staying in a Protestant area. Many stories by women from Northern Ireland express the feeling that to live through the Troubles was to have your life determined by others: in Una Woods's novella, 'The Dark Hole Days' (1984), the attempt of two teenagers to write themselves out of their entrapment is thwarted by violent events.

In 1985 Ruth Hooley's anthology, *The Female Line: Northern Ireland Women Writers*, was published to celebrate ten years of the Northern Ireland Women's Rights Movement. Many of the stories in the anthology explore the impact of the Troubles on women's daily lives in Northern Ireland where, as in Fiona Barr's 'The Wall-Reader', the violence in the streets is shown as spilling into the home. Brenda Murphy's 'A Curse', based on the author's experience of the 1978 dirty protest in Armagh Jail, challenges Catholic and republican attitudes to the female body. Murphy's 'Human Waste' (*The Blackstaff Book of Short Stories* 1988) con-tinues this theme, while 'A Social Call', from the same collection, links male violence in the home with paramilitary activities outdoors.[28]

In the 1990s, contrasting with the transformation of social mores in the Republic, stories set in Northern Ireland continued to record the polarization of national and religious identity: in Briege Duffaud's *Nothing Like Beirut* (1994), Irish emigrants return home to find that, despite superficial changes, people's attitudes have not altered. The dif-ficulties internment created for families are portrayed in Frances Molloy's posthumous collection, *Women Are the Scourge of the Earth* (1998). Short stories by Irish women offering an alternative view on the Troubles and depicting the physical, material and psychological effects on women and families are a small but vital part of the Irish literary canon.

1990 Onwards

The social changes ushered in by Mary Robinson's election as Ireland's first female president in 1990 encouraged Irish women writers to move beyond the angry feminist voice of the 1970s and 1980s to explore the changing nature of femininity and the instability of female identity in a playful, postmodernist style. Anne Enright's witty deconstruction of myths around femininity and marriage in *The Portable Virgin* (1991) was widely acclaimed by Irish commentators as 'a real departure in women's fiction in this country'.[29] 'Fatgirl Terrestrial' is a convincing exploration of why educated and successful women nevertheless feel pressured to conform to society's expectations of femininity, while in Enright's title story the narrator, who endeavours to fit into the feminine ideal by dying her hair blonde, finds ironically that 'the new fake me', conforming to a female stereotype, 'looks twice as real as the old'.[30] In her second collection, *Taking Pictures* (2008), Enright continues her edgy exploration of contemporary life but stories like 'Honey' and 'Little Sister' demonstrate an advance on her earlier collection by combining stylistic subtlety with emotional depth.[31]

In *The Pale Gold of Alaska* (2000), Éilís Ní Dhuibhne employs the voice of an omniscient storyteller to give an overview of changes in Irish society ('The Truth about Married Love'), portray cultural differences between Irish and Americans ('The Day Elvis Presley Died'), or draw parallels between the colonization of nature and the colonization of women ('The Pale Gold of Alaska'). The quality of Ní Dhuibhne's spare, ironic prose probing her characters' fractured states of mind lifts her stories above any tendency to reportage and her constant experiments with the short story form, with unreliable narrators, non-linear plots, complex ironies and lack of closure align her with postmodernism. Ní Dhuibhne's earlier collections, *Blood and Water* (1988) and *Eating Women is not Recommended* (1991), are more overtly feminist. 'Some Hours in the Life of a Witch' and 'Eating Women is Not Recommended' tackle the hitherto almost invisible topic of menstruation, while in 'The Wife of Bath', the narrator's encounter with the Wife and their lengthy discussion of the war between the sexes provides an opportunity for the narrator to assess some of the narratives controlling her life. In stories like 'The Mermaid Legend' and 'Midwife to the Fairies', an indirect comment on the 1984 Kerry babies case, Ní Dhuibhne draws on her expertise in folklore to move into a postmodern, metafictional world, inhabiting the borders between fantasy and reality. *The Inland Ice and Other Stories* (1997) extends this combination of postmodernist literary techniques with the shape-shifting of Irish folklore by interweaving a retelling of a traditional Irish folk tale, 'The Search for the Lost Husband', with contemporary stories of women's disillusionment in love.[32]

Feminist and lesbian rewritings of fairytales are the focus of Emma Donoghue's *Kissing the Witch* (1997) while her second collection, *The Woman Who Gave Birth to Rabbits* (2002), portrays women from various historical periods battling in a patriarchal society to secure their independence. Often they are women like Mary Toft in the title story or Miss F. in 'Cured' who find their stories taken out of their hands by more powerful and better-educated males. Some of Donoghue's stories have a specifically Irish dimension: 'Night Vision' is a recreation of the early life of the blind Donegal poet, Frances Brown, while 'Words for Things' presents Mary Wollstonecraft's brief period as a governess in Ireland when her observation of the idle lives led by Anglo-Irish women provided the catalyst for her views on the educative role of mothers in her *Vindication of the Rights of Woman*. The historical notes at the end of each story underpin the authenticity of these tales and anchor them in the feminist project of recovering women's history.

Claire Keegan has been described as 'reinventing rural Ireland'[33] and stories like 'Men and Women' from her first collection, *Antarctica* (1999), record the shifting of the balance of power between husband and wife, even in conservative rural families. In 'Quare Name for a Boy' the pregnant narrator refuses to submit to the shame traditionally foisted on unmarried mothers in rural Ireland: 'That part of my people ends with me.'[34] In this and her second collection, *Walk the Blue Fields* (2007), traditional Irish themes – the land, the dysfunctional family, emigration, illegitimacy, the celibacy of the priesthood, folk motifs – suggest a time-lessness that is belied by the new twists Keegan brings to them. Keegan's rural women face situations similar to those in Edna O'Brien's stories but changing attitudes and their own resources allow them more choices than they had previously. Walking out of the family home, resisting the power of the Catholic church, challenging male authority, discarding punitive attitudes, Keegan's women are more than capable of fashioning their own lives. Her acclaimed novella, *Foster* (2010), combines an indirect commentary on Irish history with a young girl's coming of age when her stay with a foster family offers her a different and more liberating perspective on life from that of her dysfunctional family.[35]

In the 1990s and beyond, Irish women's short stories gathered pace and became more outspoken. Women writers showed their determination to put women's lives (the mother-daughter relationship, emigration, sexuality) at the centre of their work. The protagonists of Enright, Ní Dhuibhne, Donoghue, Keegan, Mary Morrissy (*A Lazy Eye* 1993), Clare Boylan (*That Bad Woman* 1995), are no longer prepared to endure passively but are shown forging new identities for themselves. In these decades, women writers with their readiness to tackle current topics (immigration, child abuse, national identity, received gender roles, women's history), as well as their willingness to experiment with language and complex, non-linear narratives, established their centrality in the Irish short story canon. Promising first collections by a new generation (Mary

Costello's *The China Factory* 2012, Danielle McLaughlin's *Dinosaurs on Other Planets* 2015 and Clare-Louise Bennett's *Pond* 2015) confirm Irish women writers' commitment to the form.

Notes

1 *Re-reading the Short Story*, ed. Clare Hanson (London: Macmillan, 1989).
2 Frank O'Connor, *The Lonely Voice: A Study of the Short Story* (Cork: Cork City Council, 2003), 6.
3 For a sustained exploration of women writers' challenge to O'Connor around this notion of connectivity and relationality see Elke D'hoker, *Irish Women Writers and the Modern Short Story* (New York, NY: Palgrave, 2016).
4 Maureen Keane, *Mrs S. C. Hall: A Literary Biography* (Gerrards Cross: Colin Smythe, 1997), 121–2.
5 For more on Lawless's use of the male narrator, see Heidi Hansson, *Emily Lawless 1845–1913: Writing the Interspace* (Cork: Cork University Press, 2007), 39–53.
6 Debbie Brouckmans, 'The Short Story Cycle in Ireland: From Jane Barlow to Donal Ryan', unpublished PhD thesis, University of Leuven, 2015, 25–50.
7 Gregory Schirmer, 'Tales from Big House and Cabin: The Nineteenth Century', in *The Irish Short Story: A Critical History*, ed. James Kilroy (Boston, MA: Twayne, 1984), 41.
8 *The Irish Short Story*, ed. Patrick Rafroidi and Terence Brown (Gerrards Cross: Colin Smythe, 1979).
9 Julie Ann Stevens, *The Irish Scene in Somerville and Ross* (Dublin: Irish Academic Press, 2007).
10 Gifford Lewis, *Somerville and Ross: The World of the Irish R. M.* (Harmondsworth: Penguin, 1987), 12.
11 *Daughters of Decadence: Women Writers of the Fin-de-Siècle*, ed. Elaine Showalter (London: Virago, 1993), viii–ix.
12 Ibid., xiv.
13 For further comparison between Egerton and Joyce, see Chapter 6 of this volume.
14 Elizabeth Bowen, 1937 Preface to *Faber Book of Modern Short Stories*, in *The New Short Story Theories*, ed. Charles May (Athens: Ohio University Press, 1994), 256.
15 Elizabeth Bowen, 1949 Preface to *Encounters* reprinted in *The Mulberry Tree: Writings of Elizabeth Bowen*, ed. Hermione Lee (London: Virago, 1986), 120.
16 Elizabeth Bowen, *A Day in the Dark and Other Stories* (London: Jonathan Cape, 1965), 8.
17 For the ghost theme in Bowen's short stories, see particularly Sinéad Mooney, 'Bowen and the Modern Ghost', in *Elizabeth Bowen*, ed. Eibhear Walshe (Dublin: Irish Academic Press, 2009), 77–96.
18 Elizabeth Bowen, 1952 Preface to *The Second Ghost Book*, ed. Cynthia Asquith, in Bowen, *Afterthought: Pieces About Writing* (London: Longmans, Green and Co., 1962), 104.

19 Elizabeth Bowen, *Collected Stories* (London: Vintage, 1999), 591.

20 See Norah Hoult, *Poor Women!* (London: William Heinemann, 1930) and Olivia Manning, *A Romantic Hero* (London: Random House, 2001).

21 See Anne Fogarty, 'Discontinuities: *Tales from Bective Bridge* and the Modernist Short Story', in *Mary Lavin*, ed. Elke D'hoker (Dublin: Irish Academic Press, 2013), 49–64.

22 O'Connor, *The Lonely Voice*, 141.

23 Leah Levenson, *The Four Seasons of Mary Lavin* (Dublin: Marino Books, 1998), 225.

24 Angela Bourke, *Maeve Brennan: Homesick at the 'New Yorker'* (London: Jonathan Cape, 2004), 154.

25 Rebecca Pelan, 'Reflections on a Connemara Dietrich', in *Edna O'Brien: New Critical Perspectives*, ed. K. Laing, S. Mooney and M. O'Connor (Dublin: Carysfort Press, 2006), 12–37. For further details of O'Brien's reworking of Joyce, see Rachel Jane Lynch, '"A Land of Strange, Throttled, Sacrificial Women": Domestic Violence in the Short Fiction of Edna O'Brien', *The Canadian Journal of Irish Studies*, 22, no. 2 (1999): 37–48.

26 Maeve Kelly, *Orange Horses* (Belfast: The Blackstaff Press, 1991), 96.

27 Eve Patten, 'Women and Fiction 1985–1990', *Krino* 8–9 (1990): 1–7.

28 For a gendered approach to women's stories about the Troubles, see Mercedes del Campo del Pozo, 'Alternative Ulsters: Troubles Short Fiction by Women Writers, 1968–1998', unpublished PhD thesis, University of Ulster, 2015.

29 *The Irish Times*, 2 March 1991, 37.

30 Anne Enright, *The Portable Virgin* (London: Vintage, 2002), 87.

31 For the evolution of Enright's style in these two collections, see Elke D'hoker, 'Distorting Mirrors and Unsettling Snapshots: Anne Enright's Short Fiction', in *Anne Enright*, ed. Claire Bracken and Susan Cahill (Dublin: Irish Academic Press, 2011), 33–50.

32 For an examination of how the two narrative forms intertwine, see Anne Fogarty, '"What Matters but the Good of the Story?" Femininity and Desire in Éilís Ní Dhuibhne's *The Inland Ice and Other Stories*', in *Éilís Ní Dhuibhne: Perspectives*, ed. Rebecca Pelan (Galway: Arlen House, 2009), 69–85. For folk themes in Ní Dhuibhne's stories, see Jacqueline Fulmer, *Folk Women and Indirection in Morrison, Ní Dhuibhne, Hurston and Lavin* (New York, NY: Ashgate, 2007).

33 Mary Fitzgerald-Hoyt, 'Claire Keegan's New Rural Ireland: Torching the Thatched Cottage', in *The Irish Short Story: Traditions and Trends*, ed. Elke D'hoker and Stephanie Eggermont (Bern: Peter Lang, 2015), 279–96.

34 Claire Keegan, *Antarctica* (London: Faber and Faber, 1999), 101.

35 See Mary Fitzgerald-Hoyt, 'Claire Keegan's *Foster*: The Child, the Famine, the Future', in *The Country of the Young: Interpretations of Youth and Childhood in Irish Culture*, ed. John Countryman and Kelly Matthews (Dublin: Four Courts Press, 2013), 119–32.

CHAPTER 16

Poetry, 1970–Present

Patricia Boyle Haberstroh

The dramatic rise in interest in women's lives and women's rights in the 1960s and 1970s had repercussions in several areas, including the place of women writers in the Irish literary tradition. Although, as scholars have shown, women poets had been writing in Ireland for centuries,[1] much of their work was not well-known at this time. More emphasis on the woman writer, both present and past, led to the development of feminist publishers like Arlen House, Attic and Salmon, and to the gradual inclusion of women poets on the lists of presses like Gallery, Carcanet, Bloodaxe, Dedalus, Cork and Wake Forest University. Expanding research, critical writing and anthologies of women's poetry have also increased the visibility of the Irish woman poet.[2]

Defining the term 'women's poetry' has not been easy, given competing theories of identity, subjectivity and gender, as these applied to critical reading.[3] The early feminist movement influenced attempts to examine women's poetry in terms of Irish women's experience as well as gender stereotyping. This, however, led to questions of whether the category 'woman writer' marginalized women poets even more and whether one could define 'Irish' or 'woman' in simple terms.[4] Postcolonial approaches to poetry, often helpful, were complicated by the fact that nationalists chose to symbolize the oppression of the colonizer in tropes involving the female body, and ultimately the inferior status of women in Ireland represented a different type of oppression.[5]

Representations of women in poetry lead to further considerations of images of the female body. Seeking alternatives to romanticized or idealized figures, some women poets sought to emphasize the materiality of the body for a more realistic representation.[6] Additional theoretical issues of subjectivity and voice, especially important in poetry, inform postmodern and poststructuralist debates which challenged the idea of a unified poetic voice, including how to read and interpret an 'I' voice in a poem.[7] Constructing a specifically female 'I' in order to establish such a voice in a traditionally male canon, or to represent a communal sense of womanhood, became the focus of debates on subjectivity, the possibility of a specific female language in poetry and the linguistic construction of a gendered voice. All the above theories fall under the general category of self-representation, one of the most important challenges facing women poets. While some theories work more effectively when applied to specific poets, and diverse theories can be applied to a single poet, many have led to a better understanding of the work of contemporary women poets.

Women poets in Ireland share many of the themes, strategies and settings with all poets; one need not necessarily use the qualifying adjective 'women' to consider or judge them as poets. However, certain characteristics distinguish their work and often differentiate their poems from those of male colleagues. And, although they are very different poets, many of these women share similar subjects, images and poetic strategies. A major challenge they face involves the difference between what Eiléan Ní Chuilleanáin has called 'image and achievement',[8] representations of women in Irish culture and literature and the actual lives of women. Women poets respond to this challenge in different ways, and their work shows that, while no single set of characteristics defines women or women's poetry, common experiences unite them. Challenging gender stereotypes propagated by the church and the state, Irish women writers have sought to interrogate the limited 'wife and mother in the home' model embedded in the 1937 Irish Constitution, and to question the sexual taboos imposed upon the culture by both church and state. Given this, how to write as an individual woman poet and at the same time express the commonalities among women became a central issue. Irish tradition and the Irish literary canon provided few well-known examples or models of how to go about this.

The three most visible poets to emerge at this stage, Eavan Boland, Eiléan Ní Chuilleanáin and Medbh McGuckian, as well as others like Eithne Strong, Mary O'Donnell, Anne Le Marquand Hartigan, Susan Connolly and Catherine Phil McCarthy, set into motion a new and broader view of Irish women and Irish poetry. One distinguishing characteristic of this initial group and those to follow was an emphasis on the female body, which had often been objectified and romanticized in poetry. Likewise, in the guise of figures like Mother Ireland and Cathleen ni Houlihan, the early Irish state adopted tropes of the female body to represent the sufferings of the nation. Shifting focus from such gender stereotypes to the material or actual lives of women, women poets created new imagery highlighting the female body. As Lucy Collins notes, writing about the body was both 'an important way for Irish women poets to initiate new forms of self-representation' and 'a way of investigating the link between actual experience and metaphorical understanding'.[9] Women poets took it upon themselves to make a closer connection between their own lives and the ways in which women were imaginatively portrayed.

Eithne Strong's *FLESH The Greatest Sin* (1980), often compared to Patrick Kavanagh's *The Great Hunger*, represented a breakthrough in expressing how the concept of women's bodies as the source of sins of the flesh had dramatic effects on women's lives, including the repression of female sexual desire. Focusing on the church's stress on both sins against the sixth commandment and the virgin / mother as a model for women, Strong's long poem questions traditional images of the Blessed Virgin, asking: 'How does a tower of ivory pray?' 'What is a Mystic Rose?' The poem tells the story of an orphan, Ellen, who marries and bears children she 'conceived with no rejoicing' as she followed the church's demands for procreation. While a priest rails against impurity and exalts Conjugal Rights, Ellen listens, and even as her marriage deteriorates, imparts the lessons against sins of the flesh to her daughter, Nance. Raped at age six by a cousin, Nance, burdened by guilt for many years, eventually marries but subsequently leaves her husband. Rejecting what she has been taught, Nance gradually accepts a positive 'fusion of flesh and spirit' which the poem defines as 'grace'. A radical disapproval of how the church influenced Irish women's sense of their own bodies, Strong's poem rejects images of the temptress and examines the problems created when fear and guilt inculcated in women pass down from generation to generation. A long, narrative prose poem, *FLESH The Greatest Sin* represented a radical departure from accepted mores and introduced a new theme into women's poetry.

Anne Le Marquand Hartigan's work develops similar themes, with the story of Eve as temptress an image in several of her poems. In 'Fruit' from the volume *Long Tongue* (1982), an apple is an apple; it is 'without malice'. Hartigan's long dramatic poem, *Now is a Moveable Feast* (1991), set at the auction of Hartigan's mother's birthplace, builds through the voice of an auctioneer promoting the property's 'old world charm'. Added to his are the voices of her great-grandmother, grandmother, grandfather and other relatives. Interspersed with these are the voice of God from *Ecclesiastes*, other quotations from the Bible, and prayers and hymns to the Blessed Virgin, often used ironically. The poem portrays the lives of patriarchal males, women forced into arranged and unhappy marriages, and a great aunt who died in childbirth with her infant because her husband refused to allow her to get medical treatment. The prescription, 'thou shalt be under thy husband's power', controls all that happens on property that passes from father to son. Hartigan describes this poem as a 'celebration of women'[10] and the interplay of voices demonstrates how cultural and religious views, especially of marriage and sexuality, affect the lives of different generations in Ireland.

Eavan Boland also expresses the importance of, and respect for the female body. Her early volumes, *In Her Own Image* (1980*)* and *Night Feed* (1982), offer images of female sexuality, maternity and domestic life as she attempts to express how her womanhood could connect to her life as a poet, a theme that Boland develops throughout her work.[11] Poems from *In Her Own Image,* like 'Anorexic', 'Mastectomy', 'Solitary' and 'Menses' focus on specific female bodily experiences; the poems in *Night Feed* express a women's view of both the values and problems of domestic life, maternity and marriage. In the collection *Outside History* (1990)*,* the poem 'The Shadow Doll', a figure of a Victorian bride under a glass dome, becomes an emblem of a woman 'under wraps' … 'discreet about / visits, fevers, quickenings and lusts'. Several of Boland's poems serve as 'self-portraits' where she juxtaposes the conditions of her own life to received images of women.[12]

Medbh McGuckian demonstrates a similar but unique vision of the body, exploring multiple selves who undercut concepts of gender identity by blurring lines between femaleness and maleness. As Borbála Faragó and Michaela Schrage-Früh explain, for McGuckian identity becomes 'a construct of continual change and development' which 'incorporates its own undoing', evoking a 'poetic response through reshuffling conventional metaphors of self'.[13] This reshuffling creates sometimes difficult poems where different selves emerge and disappear, often in conflict with one another. Creating numerous images and themes through ever-expanding metaphors, McGuckian's speakers move between selves and genders. Often using an 'I' speaking to a 'you', her speakers allude to twin sisters, dream sisters; one self evolves into another as speakers try to balance the demands of a domestic life with those of a poet. Working with constructed gender stereotypes, for example, McGuckian sees the males in the Maze Prison as feminized because they are powerless;[14] her father's death represents the loss of a maleness in herself. In 'The Potter', a speaker tells her metaphoric, male 'word spouse' self that she is neither the conventional figure of Eve, Helen, Mary nor Sophia, but rather 'the fool of the house' spending time away from her poetry. McGuckian's poems centre on the body, whether in the way violence inscribes the body or in the way the creative act of writing poetry links to a woman's experiences of sexuality, conception, gestation and child-birth. McGuckian's elusive and surrealistic style, with images and meta-phors continually expanding to interrupt narrative flow, is influenced by personal experiences like childbirth, post-partum depression, a parent's death and, quite often, the struggles to integrate such experiences into her work as a poet.

While images of the body appear often in women's poetry, the related characteristic of women's personal experiences informs their work, lead-ing to a wide range of female figures including mothers, sisters, daughters and grandmothers: figures who represent alternatives to narrow images of women's lives. Eiléan Ní Chuilleanáin's poems, for example, often arise from a personal setting or events like her mother's or sister's deaths, and reflect feelings of universal suffering or grief. In her highly imagis-tic style, these do not necessarily appear to be autobiographical poems; objects or places on the surface of her poems ultimately tend to carry the theme. Typical of this are three poems, 'Autun', 'Crossing the Loire', and 'A Hand, A Wood', inspired by the death of Ní Chuilleanáin's sister Máire, a violinist with the London Philharmonic. Ní Chuilleanáin describes the latter poem, set in Máire's home after her death, as factual, 'about the physical absence of Máire from the house in Palmers Green, the sense that every time one washed, one was washing away something of her'.[15] While the poem identifies neither the speaker nor the subject, clues like the 'skill of the left and the right hand' allude to the violinist. The contrast between the living things in the surrounding landscape and the dead sister devel-ops in a short two-stanza poem, the compact images of which suggest the narrative and express feelings of loss central to the poem. Another poem, 'Fireman's Lift', is an elegy for Ní Chuilleanáin's mother, the writer Eilís Dillon. Describing Correggio's painting, 'Assumption of the Virgin' in the dome of the Parma Cathedral which she had visited with her mother, Ní Chuilleanáin imagines her mother ascending to heaven within what the poem calls the 'stone white petticoat' of the dome, an image which sug-gests what is beneath a woman's skirt but also, as Ní Chuilleanáin says, can represent birth and maternity. The 'melted and faded bodies' of Correggio's work, with feet, elbows and body parts floating within the dome, empha-size the dissolution of the material body which death represents.[16]

Eavan Boland, suggesting that women have been 'outside history', more directly focuses on her own life as a way of witnessing women whose lives have not been recorded, while also creating 'self-portraits' to counteract conventional images of Irish women's lives. In many ways a more traditional lyric poet, Boland constructs a specifically female voice, an 'I' derived from her own experiences as wife, mother and poet, making a private life public and placing a woman's lyric 'I' within the predominantly male literary tradition. Over time Boland's poems become a record of one woman's life from an early childhood in London to a home in Dublin, aware of an ageing self. Mother, father, partner, grandparents and children inspire meditations on the ordinary life of a woman in the Dublin suburbs, seeking, as a speaker in 'Muse Mother' says, 'a new language', 'able to speak at last / my mother tongue'. The details of a home's interior, images of a woman in a kitchen or feeding an infant at midnight, love poems to a spouse, a mother's 'Lava Cameo' lead to reflections on the ebb and flow of a woman's life, combining a conversational tone within lyrical language and carefully controlled stanzaic forms.

While autobiographical experience inspires Irish women poets' attempts to express the complexity of women's lives, revising and reconstructing cultural images of the female are also important strategies for these poets, as they begin to bring females from myth, folklore and religion into the spotlight. In Boland's case this means reimagining figures like Mother Ireland, a passive female adopted by nationalists to represent the suffering of the nation and needing the protection of males. In a poem of the same name, Boland creates an alternative to this symbolic figure, giving her a voice: 'I did not see / I was seen. / Night and day / words fell on me ... Now I could tell my story. / It was different / from the story told about me'. Likewise, in the poem 'Anna Liffey' Boland recasts an iconic Irish river goddess from the perspective of an actual woman who experienced the Dublin river as it flowed through her own city and life. In turning to classical myth, Boland juxtaposes recurring images of Demeter and her daughter Persephone with a contemporary speaker telling of her own feelings, such as fear of losing a child. Allusions in Boland's work to Book VI of the *Aeneid* recur; for example, in 'The Journey', the poet Sappho leads the speaker-poet to Virgil's underground where Sappho highlights women and children who had suffered through wars and plagues. Sappho asks the speaker to 'remember it', a metaphor for Boland's attempt to witness the heroic women in Virgil's work and the lives of mothers in general.

Women in folklore and legend also undergo change as Eiléan Ní Chuilleanáin views myth as an entrance into the past, as valuable as historical narrative. Like Boland she sometimes reimagines women characters who played minor roles in major male narratives, bringing them out of silence. In 'Pygmalion's Image', for example, Ní Chuilleanáin animates the artist's statue of Galatea, a stone figure in the landscape, and she receives her own voice as 'A green leaf of language comes out of her mouth'. In 'The Girl Who Married the Reindeer', Ní Chuilleanáin recasts an old myth with a female replacing the male leading figure, and, in several of Ní Chuilleanáin's poems – 'The Informant', 'Borders' and 'Daniel Grose' among them – the *cailleach*, the wise old woman of Irish mythology, plays the roles of both subject and speaker.[17]

While traditional religious images of the female have provided challenges for women poets, religious iconography finds its way into work which often explores imagined liminal space between spiritual and human worlds, what the title of McGuckian's *New Selected Poems* calls *The Unfixed Horizon* (2015). McGuckian's 2004 volume, *The Book of the Angel*, for example, alludes to an ancient Latin text in which St Patrick converses with an angel about his role as mediator with the divine.[18] In McGuckian's reconstruction, her iconoclastic angels and Virgin Mary live both sensual and sexual lives, and the spiritual often merges with the earthly; in 'Four Voices without an Instrument', March arrives and 'the brightening, endangered earth / is the year's first angel'. McGuckian, in whose work the written word always becomes a central theme, focuses on relating the spiritual and creative. As Faragó and Schrage-Früh explain, in these poems 'prayer becomes an alternative language of poetic and political expression, placing the act of composition in the context of divine creation'.[19]

Examining the lives of Biblical figures, women poets seek to recast them into more realistic and less stereotypical figures. In the volume *Spiderwoman's Third Avenue Rhapsody* (1993), Mary O'Donnell turns to the Bible in a series of poems about Eve, seeing her as springing from nature and not from Adam's body. In 'The Rib', Eve asks, 'What gave them the idea / that I was spawned from a rib?' Eve also speaks in her own voice as O'Donnell transforms her from female temptress to Adam's lover, a positive reincarnation of a partner and mother with a premonition of two sons soon to be at war. According to the poem 'Eve's Maternity', Genesis embeds Eve in religious iconography as the first sinner, tempter of Adam with a 'future disabled by scribbling old men / with scrolls and texts / who would write that this was so'. Like the Demeter-Persephone, mother-daughter myth, many women poets reconstruct Eve, turning her from first sinner into a more positive female figure.

To present religious women in more realistic terms, Ní Chuilleanáin has written several poems focused on the communal lives of nuns and the spaces they inhabit, depicting their strength and the often-unrecognized value of their work.[20] In poems like 'J'ai Mal à nos Dents' and 'The Real Thing', nuns live, as Ní Chuilleanáin herself writes, 'in the enclosed world they had chosen, the communities of sisterhood. Their history is no odder, surely', she maintains, 'than the history of armies'.[21] Ní Chuilleanáin's depictions of legendary female saints in poems like 'St. Mary Magdalene Preaching at Marseilles', humanizes them, noting the skin, hair and voice of Magdalene as she preaches after Christ has died. The poem 'St. Margaret of Cortona', focuses on the saint condemned because, unmarried, she bore a child with a man who was eventually murdered. Set at her shrine, the poem depicts a preacher emphasizing that she was 'neither maiden, widow nor wife', with 'the word *whore* prowling silent / Up and down the long aisle'. In the poem, the speaker maintains that St. Margaret is 'still here' and 'refuses / To be consumed', allowing her to be reconstructed. The condemned Margaret – who like Magdalene in legend spent the rest of her life in penance – is remembered here not for her sins but for her suffering.

In their early poems, women poets often avoided issues in Irish history and national politics for many reasons, not the least of which involved the troubled situation within Northern Ireland, as any poet could be accused of writing propaganda for a cause. With their emphasis on women itself an issue, some were already charged with being too political, facing derogatory attempts to label their poetry narrowly as feminist, essentialist or separatist, the kind of backlash women in many other fields also encountered. Inevitably, however, women poets moved towards more overt responses to national issues, illustrating at times how Irish political life affected women. Ní Chuilleanáin's 'On Lacking the Killer Instinct' in *The Sun-Fish* (2009) tells the story of her father's involvement in the Irish Civil War,[22] and poems on the scandals of the Magdalene Laundries in 'Translation' and mother-and-baby homes in 'Bessboro', brought specific attention to the plight of unmarried mothers and the role of the state in the isolation and unjust treatment of these women. In her prose and poetry, Boland also has continually written of problems involving national identity and the woman poet, and her poetry has touched on issues including the effects of colonization and the Irish famines. Her poem 'The Emigrant Irish' in *The Journey* (1987) describes the difficulties faced by past emigrants leaving Ireland, noting 'What they survived we could not even live'. In the same way, Medbh McGuckian in Northern Ireland turned more overtly towards events in Irish history. The poems in *Captain Lavender* (1994) allude to her meetings with internees while teaching in the Maze Prison; those in *Shelmalier* (1998) focus on the 1798 Rebellion, and *The Currach Requires No Harbour* (2006) with violence in contemporary Belfast. 'Drawing Ballerinas' from *Soldiers of Year II* (2002), written as a memorial to Ann Frances Owens, killed in the Abercorn Café bombing in 1972, refers to Matisse's reply when asked how he had survived as an artist in the Second World War. All of these poets connect national issues and political conflict with their concerns about women, the death of Ann Frances Owens being a good example.

By the beginning of the twenty-first century, much had changed in Ireland. Entrance into the European Union led in the Republic to an influx of money and resources, although it would soon be exhausted as the demise of the Celtic Tiger era created economic chaos. Peace accords in the North, cross-border communications, mediations, and cultural and educational activities helped to quell the violence that had wracked Northern Ireland for many years, although the economy of the United Kingdom soon also felt the effects of Europe's monetary crisis. As members of the European Union, however, both countries became part of a larger coalition. Easier passage between European Union countries offered opportunities for a younger generation to move and travel, as well as for citizens from other countries to settle in Ireland. The access to technology and new media, allowing people to communicate within a global audience, opened up avenues unimaginable before. As traditional gender roles came under further scrutiny and more women were educated and joined the workforce, opportunities for women expanded. Allusions in poetry to computers, mobile phones, Skype, Google and other technologies illustrate how possibilities for global communication were changing lives. Women poets took advantage of opportunities to travel to different areas of the world, incorporating into their poetry a larger vision gleaned from other cultures. University residencies and poetry readings became possible for women as they moved beyond home, with the result that their work and their popularity reached larger audiences, both in Ireland and beyond. Nevertheless, their poetry continued to reflect some of the same themes, issues and concerns of the women who began to write in the 1960s. Into the twenty-first century, a new generation of women poets gradually garnered recognition, including over time, Moya Cannon, Mary O'Malley, Rita Ann Higgins, Kerrie Hardie, Catherine Phil MacCarthy, Sara Berkeley, Catherine Walsh, Colette Bryce, Siobhan Campbell, Katie Donovan, Catriona O'Reilly, Enda Wyley, Leontia Flynn, Vona Groarke, Sinéad Morrissey and others.

Of these, Moya Cannon, Mary O'Malley and Rita Ann Higgins centred their poetry on the coastal areas of western Ireland, with much of the landscape of Galway, Connemara and Donegal the setting for their poems. Images of harbours and boats, seascapes and mountains, trees and animals carry Cannon's deep meditations on the beauty and mystery of the natural world, as the changing effects of darkness and light animate her western landscape. Cannon demonstrates how sound, language and music contain the history of a place and a culture, often using Irish place names and phrases in her poems. Emphasizing the importance of music for the people of these regions, she writes in 'Between the Jigs and the Reels' in *The Parchment Boat* (1997) that 'Tunes are migratory / and fly from heart to heart / intimating / that there's a pattern / to life's pulls and draws'. Although the later poems in *Keats Lives* describe settings in different parts of the world, Cannon continues to focus on the smallest details of the natural world as in 'Treasure', where the speaker notes 'a water hen who steered six fistfuls / of black down through a motley of shadows'. The rhythmic music of her lines and the poetic precision of her words reinforce the sounds and music Cannon writes about.

Mary O'Malley might be seen as a quintessentially Galway poet. Although she has written poems about Lisbon, where she lived for several years, and other cities and countries, the Connemara coast and Galway City have been the most prominent settings for her poems, and images of water and shoreline recur. As she writes in 'Shore' from *Valparaiso* (2012), 'the ship, monastic in its matins and vespers / anchors me'. In many ways, O'Malley's poetry presents the opposite of a romanticized domestic life: the death of love, the breakdown of a marriage, leaving a home and watching children move away, domestic violence, madness – the Galway she imagines and records is a difficult place. As the speaker in 'Couplets' in *The Knife in the Wave* (1997) explains: 'This is, after all, a detox programme designed / To knock the prettiness out of my lines'.

Like Boland and Ní Chuilleanáin, O'Malley often turns to myth and legend for her female figures. Variations of the sea maiden, the selkie, the Otter Woman, the Seal Woman and Maighdean Mara are all drawn from coastal legends about a woman who comes ashore to interact with the human world but eventually returns to the water. Adapting Eavan Boland's model of a poet falling asleep and then entering a legend at any point,[23] the speaker in 'The Seal Woman' prepares to write at her desk when the shape-changing seal woman invades her space. Ignored by a man when ashore, the seal woman had returned to the sea, then come back to the town to join a parade at a contemporary festival of Galway citizens, luminaries, and developers. Images of the mermaids high on St Nicholas Church come to life and leave their perches, as these 'girls pack / Combs and mirrors in their purses' one 'heading to Grealy's for lipstick'. In the end, the seal woman kidnaps 'inaction man' and carries him off to Galway's Corrib River, but he surfaces at Nimmo's pier and heads to a pub for a pint of Guinness. The poet-speaker wakes up from her dream and quotes Adrienne Rich, asking 'Did you think I was talking about my life?' This is answered in one sense by the speaker's images of contemporary Galway's poor, of developers demolishing parts of the older city and of the 'two-thirty from Shannon / Bound for Boston'. This seal woman could be any woman, the poem tells us, for 'Behind the chi-chi windows of the town / Who knows what goes on?' As with Moya Cannon, the importance of place and the Irish language, derived from O'Malley's own life on the coast, depicts a culture where landscape and myth closely interrelate. Like Eavan Boland and Ní Chuilleanáin, O'Malley reconstructs mythic women, giving them a contemporary life.

Rita Ann Higgins's milieu, working-class Galway, demonstrates her remarkable ability to transform the rhythm of working-class voices into poetry.[24] From the 'Goddess on the Mervue Bus' to the 'Witch in the Bushes' and the 'God-of-the-Hatch Man', Higgins's cast of characters and places, given names like Plato and Petrarch, Diana, Delphi Lodge and Oracle Readers, struggle to deal with poverty and powerlessness in the face of government and corporate bureaucracies. Single mothers live in poverty, sick people must deal with a 'witch doctor' at the regional hospital, 'The Blanket Man' 'calls / in his / new Volvo / collecting / the pound a week'. Speaking and spoken about are the taxi man, the bus driver and rider, the young girls fascinated by bridesmaids' dresses and rainbow buggies, the workers at the nuts and washers factory whose 'fag breaks / became our summer holidays' when the 'big boys' closed down the factory. As they struggle with rent payments, unemployment, alcohol and drugs, we learn about people like Lizzie Kavanagh who believes her maroon imitation fur coat brings her good luck, and Mona who 'lives / in a house at the back / of her mind'. The homeless sleep in sheds and toilets, while the rent man tells the poet-speaker: 'All I want is fourteen pounds / and ten pence, hold the poesy'.

While Cannon, O'Malley and Higgins portray life in the west of Ireland, the locale for Paula Meehan's poetry is most often Dublin.[25] Like Higgins, she focuses on social and economic injustice, sometimes defined by the lines that divide the north and south sides of the city, North Dublin being Meehan's childhood home. An oral poet, in her readings

Meehan emphasizes the rhythms of voice and lines that flow into one another; nevertheless, her words are tightly framed into couplets, sonnets, villanelles, quatrains. Poems set in tenements on Sean McDermott Street where 'Zeus and Hera battle it out' over money, and homes in Merrion Square and Baldoyle, reflect personal experiences transformed into stories of Dublin's people. In *Pillow Talk* (1994) a drowned man is discovered at the foot of the Capel Bridge ('Good Friday, 1991'), an unnamed woman found raped and 'battered to a pulp' in Glover's Alley ('City'). As the poem 'Nomad Heart' in *Painting Rain* notes, 'Sometimes the soul / just craves a place to rest, safe from earthly wars'.

Family members fill Meehan's poems: a troubled mother, grand-mothers Hannah ('Our Lady of the Facts of Life') and Mary, Auntie Cora and Uncle Peter and Grandfather Wattie who taught her how to read and write. Over time, Meehan's poems chart a personal journey from a traumatic childhood to a reconciliation with the past. Similar to Medbh McGuckian, present and past versions of the self emerge, described variously as the dark twin, a fine twin, the girl lost in the forest, the wounded child, the shape-changer, the other voice. Forcing themselves to confront these ghosts, Meehan's speakers return to the places of the past finding a community gone, fields and flowers replaced by building sites. But memory holds those places and people and all they represent, and, as Meehan's poetry evolves, it also illustrates a way forward. The fist, a metaphor for both abuse and a child's fury, suddenly blooms into a rose, a 'gesture of giving'. The memory of a father's hands when he is out of work, a grandmother's soothing hands which represent home, a loved one's hands appear to counteract the child's memory of hurtful hands. The recurring images of gardens, and especially seeds, also become symbols of rebirth and the possibility of burying the 'troubled dead / with every seed committed to the earth'.

Like Eavan Boland's, Vona Groarke's poetry often focuses on home, transforming ordinary day-to-day life into poetry. While many women use houses and rooms as settings for their poetry, in Groarke's poems homes, families, houses, gardens and flowers predominate as the poet uses this imagery to express larger themes. Never sentimental, Groarke frames her words in formal stanzas, quatrains, tercets, sestets and sonnets, the dexterity of her language and lines giving new perspectives on the commonplace. Her clever and multiple use of a house image in each poem in the volume *Other Peoples' Houses* (1999), reveals how rooms and houses tell us much about people, places, history and culture. Courthouses, workhouses, holiday houses, new homes and caravans contain both memories of the past and insight into the present. In *Flight* (2002), 'Imperial Measure' records the 1916 Rebellion from the kitchens of the Metropole and Imperial Hotels and the College of Surgeons, where Nelly Gifford 'magicked oatmeal and a half-crowned loaf to / make porridge / in a grate' while rifles and gunshots, smoke and fire surrounded those within. Both 'An Teach Tuí', the thatched house, and the Big House appear in Groarke's poems as well. In 'The Game of Tennis in Irish History' from the volume *Juniper Street* (2006), Groarke alludes to the 1873 and 1921 diaries of Lady Alice Howard written at Shelton Abbey, the early home of Charles and Fanny Parnell. The movements and strategies of a tennis game played by 'Charlie' and Fanny, with Lady Alice 'patrolling the white line around the one green space', are compared to the 'volley of shots', 'flurry of late calls', 'service skills', 'foot faults', to the 'ins and outs' of the difficult formation of the Irish Republic.

Many of Groarke's poems revolve around a family's connection to home, the love between partners, the interactions between parents and children, a 'House Style' described in *Other Peoples' Houses* as 'When my grandmother looked into my mother's eyes / she saw what I see in my daughter's'. 'Windmill Hymns' from *Juniper Street* encapsulates what many of these poems express: how a house reflects its owners' plans and dreams until it yields not only to new plans but also to its deterioration. The speaker in 'Windmill Hymns' from (2006) asks: 'How long before the wood / lets itself down on the willowherb at bay in shuttered light; / before doors give up the ghost'. Houses, walls, doors and windows have pasts, presents and futures. Homes, in Groarke's world, keep people 'steady and tied' ('Other People's Houses').

As the women poets in the Republic like Vona Groarke and those discussed above gained recognition, in Northern Ireland the pace was slower. Medbh McGuckian was for some the only well-known poet. Although Joan McBreen, Moyra Donaldson, Janet Fitzpatrick-Simmons, Ruth Hooley Carr, Cherry Smyth and others had been publishing in journals and anthologies, few initial collections by women appeared before the beginning of the twenty-first century, and often those that did went out of print. Alex Pryce demonstrates that, as a consequence of an ingrained bias in anthologies and publishers, women writers in Northern Ireland 'found themselves relegated to the community sphere, producing work perceived as unworthy of mainstream publication, while the men carried on the more lofty, "proper" artistic production'.[26] The ongoing violence in Northern Ireland, Rebecca Pelan argues, also has had an effect in that 'it has always been much more difficult in Northern Ireland than in the Irish Republic to discuss women's lives, their politics, or their cultural practices as distinct from the broader politics of Northern Ireland'.[27] The popularity garnered by Northern poets like Seamus Heaney, Derek Mahon, Paul Muldoon and Ciaran Carson likewise tended to obscure women's poetry. Gradually, however, a younger generation of women poets began attracting attention, and most importantly publication, reviews and awards for their work.

Sinéad Morrissey exemplifies this younger generation. Like the poets who preceded her, much of Morrissey's work deals with female experiences. '"Love, the Nightwatch ..."', a poem about childbirth, in *Through the Square Window* (2009), describes a woman's birthing body as a haystack 'collapsing almost imperceptibly / at first, then caving in spectacularly as you stuttered and came'. In another poem, 'A Matter of Life and Death' from *Parallax* (2013), a woman in labour remembers her grandmother's childbirth story of '*forty-six hours of agony*'; her grandmother's prophetic words that '*when a new life comes into a family, an old life goes out*' come true as her grandmother dies three weeks before her own child is born. Focusing on mothers, grandmothers and daughters, Morrissey presents these figures in elegantly formal poems, with a variety of stanzas, line lengths and shapes, in conversational voices transformed into poetic language.

Morrissey also looks to the past to animate historical and literary women, often connecting them, as do Eavan Boland, Eiléan Ní Chuilleanáin, Mary O'Malley and others, with present-day circumstances and settings. She brings these figures out of the shadows to provide another perspective on women's lives. 'Flight' from *The State of the Prisons* (2005) tells the story of Anne Bridlestone who, defending the king in the Cromwellian era, was subsequently led through the streets in a branks, an iron cage over her head with a piece of iron on her tongue to silence her for 'chiding and scolding'. In Morrissey's poem, the silenced Bridlestone ironically speaks in her own voice, saying 'I have learned to hold my tongue in company.' Literary figures like Dorothy Wordsworth, the subject of '1801' in *Parallax* (2013), or fictional characters like Amelia Sedley, the speaker in 'Vanity Fair' from *Through the Square Window* (2009) also gain voices, in the form of a letter Thackeray's Amelia writes to Dobbin, or in Dorothy Wordsworth's first-person meditation on how she spends her day walking and cooking while William is 'exhausted with altering' his work.

Colette Bryce, another Northern Irish poet, more directly confronts the violence that hung over her childhood in Derry. Car bombs, fires

and riots in the streets are everyday events for children like Hayleigh
or Jamie who live in the high-rise flats. The mute participants at political funerals that mark the days of '1981' in *The Full Indian Rope Trick*
(2005) 'will find a voice for their anger at night' and 'say it with stones,
say it with fire'. With titles like 'Don't speak to the Brits, just pretend
they don't exist', 'Positions Prior to the Arrival of the Military' and 'The
Republicans', Bryce also gives us a look at the insides of homes where
television offers episodes of *Little House on the Prairie*, pictures of the
ruptured Sacred Heart of Jesus adorn the walls and young girls braid one
another's hair as helicopters hover over the city at night. Images of borders appear frequently: Armagh women strip-searched or families on a
beach outing stopped at the North / South border where a head through
the driver's side window demands: 'Where have we come from? / Where
are we going?' Merging the life inside homes, where rubber bullets sit
on a shelf or images of guns hang on the wall, with the violence outside,
Bryce portrays Derry as what one volume calls *The Whole and Rain-
domed Universe*.[28]

Like Morrissey and many of the other poets discussed here, Bryce
most often uses traditional poetic forms, varying line length, end-stopped
and run-on lines with unique topography. She alludes in her titles to
other poets: 'Derry' from Louis MacNeice's poem of the same name,
'Re-entering the Egg' from Anne Sexton, 'Signature' from Sharon Olds,
this intertextuality creating dialogues with the other poets. A William
Carlos Williams' poem echoes in 'Helicopters' in *The Whole and Rain-
domed Universe* (2014) with the lines 'so much depends upon / the way
you choose to look at them'. Bryce uses Williams's poetic transformation
of a red, rain-slicked wheelbarrow into an artistic scene to suggest that
from one perspective the nightly helicopters, their lights among the stars,
are 'almost beautiful'. On the other hand, they can also be imagined,
according to Bryce, as 'a business of flies / around the head wound of an
animal', an apt metaphor for Derry during the Troubles.

The women discussed above represent only a very small sample of
women poets in modern Ireland. We can categorize them in different ways:
as poets from Northern Ireland or the Republic; as writers from cities or
coastal communities; as transnational poets;[29] as practitioners of dramatic
poetry, formalism or free verse; as imagists or lyrical poets. However, their
shared female experience has also united them as poets who bring a unique,
diverse and important vision to Irish poetry. That women have made
large inroads into the Irish literary tradition, changing our views of Irish
poetry, cannot be denied, and is reflected in the expanding publication

and reviewing of their work, as well as prizes like the T. S. Eliot, Patrick Kavanagh, Hennessey and *Irish Times* Poetry Now awards which they have earned. The many universities in which they have taught, Boland directing the Creative Writing Program at Stanford, Ní Chuilleanáin at Trinity, McGuckian at Queens in Belfast, and the positions they have held, Paula Meehan as Ireland's Professor of Poetry, Sinéad Morrissey as the initial Poet Laureate of Belfast, have brought the work of women poets to audiences within and outside of Ireland. Their experiences as women, and the desire to challenge some conventional images of Irish women have been important elements in their success. In the poem 'Poetry in the Making', from her early volume *Eating Baby Jesus* (1993), Enda Wyley's speaker tells us the poet has to 'take pen to huge spider fears / or to late hour ghosts by the window and / record, record, record'. This recording, an important creative act, enlarges our understanding of women's lives and women poets.

Notes

1 For more information on earlier poets, see Maria Luddy and Gerardine Meaney, A Database of Irish Women's Writing 1800–2005 at www2:warwick.ac.uk; Tina O'Toole, *Dictionary of Munster Women Writers 1800–2000* (Cork: Cork University Press, 2005); Anne Colman, *Dictionary of Nineteenth-Century Irish Women Poets* (Galway: Kenney's Bookshop, 1996); and Éilís Ní Dhuibhne, *Voices on the Wind: Women Poets of the Celtic Twilight* (Dublin: New Island, 1995).

2 The controversy over the lack of women writers represented in anthologies, especially the initial three volumes of the *Field Day Anthology* (1991), led to the publication of two more volumes of this anthology, devoted exclusively to women writers: *The Field Day Anthology of Irish Writing IV & V: Women's Writing and Traditions*, ed. Angela Bourke et al. (Cork: Cork University Press, 2002) and opened new areas of literary knowledge which have expanded significantly. Over time, anthologies of women poets have been published, including Ruth Hooley's *The Female Line: Northern Irish Women Writers* (Belfast: Northern Ireland Women's Rights Movement, 1985), A. A. Kelly's *Pillars of the House* (Dublin: Wolfhound, 1987), Joan McBreen's *The White Page* (Co. Clare: Salmon Press, 1999), Peggy O'Brien's *Wake Forest Book of Irish Women's Poetry 1967–2000* (Winston-Salem: Wake Forest University Press, 1999), and Lucy Collins' *Poetry by Women in Ireland: A Critical Anthology, 1870–1970* (Liverpool: Liverpool University Press, 2012).

3 Claire Connolly, *Theorizing Ireland* (London: Macmillan, 2003).

4 Tina O'Toole and Patricia Coughlan, eds., *Irish Literature: Feminist Perspectives* (Dublin: Carysfort Press, 2008).

5 Carmen Llena Zamorano, '(Re)membering the Disembodied Voice: Constructs of Identity in Irish Women's Poetry', in *Bodies and Voices: The Force Field of Representation and Discourse in Colonial and Postcolonial*

Studies, ed. Merete Falck Borch and Anna Rutherford (Amsterdam: Rodopi, 2008), 349–62.

6 Irene Gilsenan Nordin, *The Body and Desire in Contemporary Irish Poetry* (Dublin: Irish Academic Press, 2006).

7 Wanda Balzano, Anne Mulhall and Moynagh Sullivan, eds., *Irish Postmodernisms and Popular Culture* (London: Palgrave Macmillan, 2007). See also Moynagh Sullivan, 'Feminism, Postmodernism and the Subjects of Irish and Women's Studies', in *New Voices in Irish Criticism*, ed. P. J. Mathews (Dublin: Four Courts Press, 2000), 243–50.

8 Eiléan Ní Chuilleanáin, ed., *Irish Women: Image and Achievement* (Dublin: Arlen House, 1985).

9 Lucy Collins, *Contemporary Irish Women Poets* (Liverpool: Liverpool University Press, 2015), 13.

10 Anne Le Marquand Hartigan, 'Introduction', *Now is a Moveable Feast* (Co. Clare: Salmon, 1991), n.p.

11 Eavan Boland's prose in *Object Lessons, The Life of the Woman and the Poet in our Time* (Manchester: Carcanet, NY: Norton, 1995) and Eavan Boland, *A Journey with Two Maps* (New York, NY: Norton, 2011) examine these ideas.

12 Eavan Boland's self-portraits include 'Suburban Woman' (*New Collected Poems* 63–4); 'Self-Portrait on a Summer Evening' (*New Collected Poems* 129); and 'Suburban Woman: A Detail' (*New Collected Poems* 138).

13 Borbála Faragó, Michaela Schrage-Früh, and Medbh McGuckian, eds., *The Unfixed Horizon: New Selected Poems* (Winston-Salem: Wake Forest University Press, 2015), xxx. This edition of McGuckian's *Selected Poems* has a comprehensive introduction. See also Borbála Faragó's *Medbh McGuckian* (Cork: Cork University Press, 2014).

14 The Maze Prison held political internees and was the site of the hunger strikes in 1981.

15 Leslie Williams, '"The Stone Recalls Its Quarry:" An Interview with Eiléan Ní Chuilleanáin', in *Representing Ireland: Gender, Class, Nationality*, ed. Susan Shaw Sailer (Gainesville: University Press of Florida, 1997), 29–44.

16 For more discussion of this point, see Catriona Clutterbuck, 'Good Faith in Religion and Art: The Later Poetry of Eiléan Ní Chuilleanáin', *Irish University Review* 37 no. 1 (2007): 131–56. This special issue of *Irish University Review* is devoted to Ní Chuilleanáin.

17 I discuss this in more detail in 'Fictive Women: Myth and Folklore' in Patricia Boyle Haberstroh, *The Female Figure in Eiléan Ní Chuilleanáin's Poetry* (Cork: Cork University Press, 2013), 60–80.

18 The late seventh-century Latin text is *Liber Angeli*.

19 Faragó, Schrage-Früh, McGuckian, *The Unfixed Horizon*, xxx.

20 Ní Chuilleanáin had three aunts who were nuns. See her essay, 'Nuns: A Subject for a Woman Writer', in *My Self, My Muse: Irish Women Poets Reflect on Life and Art*, ed. Patricia Boyle Haberstroh (Syracuse: Syracuse University Press, 2001), 18–31.

21 Ibid., 21–2.

22 Both sides of Ní Chuilleanáin's family were involved in republican politics; her maternal grandparents, the Dillons and Plunketts, are well known in Irish history.

23 Boland uses this technique in 'The Journey'.

24 Moynagh Sullivan, 'Looking at Being Someone: Class and Gender in the Poetry of Rita Ann Higgins', *Irish University Review* 41 (2001): 112–33.

25 See Luz Mar González-Arias, 'In Dublin's Fair City: Citified Embodiments in Paula Meehan's Landscapes', *An Sionnach: A Journal of Literature, Culture and the Arts* 5 no. 1–2 (2009): 34–49.

26 For more data on this, see Alex Pryce, 'Ambiguous Silences? Women in Anthologies of Contemporary Northern Irish Poetry', *Peer English* 9 (2014), accessed 28 September 2016, www2.le.ac.uk/offices/english-association/publications/peer-english.

27 Rebecca Pelan, *Two Irelands: Literary Feminisms North and South* (Syracuse, NY: Syracuse University Press, 2005).

28 For Bryce's comments, see Susan Haigh, 'An Interview with Colette Bryce', *Dundee University Review of the Arts*, ed. Gail Low, accessed 6 September 2016, https://dura-dundee.org.uk.

29 A further field for study involves both immigrant and emigrant poets. See Eva Bourke and Borbála Foragó, *Landing Places: Immigrant Poets in Ireland* (Dublin: Dedalus Press, 2010).

CHAPTER 17

Women's Traditions in Theatre, 1920–2015

Cathy Leeney

> One serious cultural obstacle encountered by any feminist writer
> is that each feminist work has tended to be received as if it
> emerged from nowhere; as if each of us had lived, thought, and
> worked without any historical past or contextual present.[1]

Plays written by women in Ireland since 1920, although many in number, have had mixed fortunes in their various modes of existence: as the
basis for production, as a live performance in space before an audience,
as a published text in the hands of a lone reader, as a document of dramatic literature in its historical context, as a candidate for the canon and
academic curricula and as a candidate for revival/translation/adaptation.
During almost one hundred years of politically, socially and culturally
complex change in the history of the island, women's writing for theatre
has encapsulated specific and crucial experiences and resistances through
live performance, hence my choice in this chapter to write where possible
about performance values.

The full life of a play is in its staging, and performances have relied
on the genius and dedication of many women directors, producers and
company leaders who have been crucial in making women's (and men's)
visions available to audiences. This account of women writers and practitioners over almost a century is necessarily selective and partial. As a
history, it does not add up to a progressive narrative through the decades
but is continually vulnerable to the cycle of erasure and re-invention that
Adrienne Rich identifies above. The academy, however, has had a central
role in recognizing and analysing women's plays, in developing awareness
and critique of the work, and of how the plays on stage have complicated
and enriched Irish society and its theatrical culture, marking experiences
of exclusion and difference.

A body of scholarship that stretches back to the early decades of the
twentieth century, when women's work often received more serious

consideration than might be assumed, has laid the foundation for identification of a women's Irish theatrical tradition. There has often been
a repeating sense of new beginnings but, notwithstanding vital energies in the twenty-first century, proto-feminism and feminism in Irish
theatre have been issues from the start and continuously. As actress
and Charabanc founder Eleanor Methven announced at 'Waking the
Feminists' on the stage of the Abbey Theatre in 2015, 'I have been awake
for a long time.'[2]

The generally precarious position of women artists in Irish culture
forms the context for the work that follows. This essay might be sub-titled
'Woman in the Public Sphere' since dramatists aim to make interventions
into the public arena to a relatively extreme degree, as compared with the
novelist or the poet, for example. Because gender identities and hierarchies are powerfully asserted through access to space, especially public
space, women place themselves as potentially transgressive solely through
their participation in performance whether through writing, directing
or acting.[3] To be a playwright and a woman is to put words in peoples'
mouths, to dare to make things happen live, to dominate audiences, to
assert a public presence, both literally in theatres, and in the sense of
changing national, civic and cultural assumptions and discourses. Part of
the power of women's writing for the stage is that, more often than not,
it is concerned with change, its energy and pain: women have a stake
in changing accepted values, and exploring new social and gender relations. Ireland's post-colonial past positioned women as doubly othered,
subaltern of the ex-subaltern. Amidst the, at first, isolationist politics of
the Free State and the Republic, and the masculinist social conservatism
affirmed in the Republic's foundation, women as citizens and as artists
found themselves edited out in the consolidating decades after revolution.
The thematic and stylistic history of Irish theatre is substantially changed
through dedicated scrutiny of women's work, and by association, the history of independent Ireland is rewritten as one of initial aspiration and
hope, followed by gendered betrayal and disappointment, and a hard
road back to some incomplete semblance of parity. The particular playwrights and plays in this chapter exemplify this over-arching narrative,
while these authors' re-invention of the staging vocabularies of space, dramatic structure and characterization illustrate a struggle to express what
women experience and think, and the shapes of their lives.

How women's plays occupy and manipulate stage space, and recreate public discourses and resistances is a major focus in the analysis that
follows. In the European theatre tradition, arising from classical Greek

tragic forms, public spaces are dominated by men, while domestic space (the *oikos*) is the realm of women. Theatre that challenges patriarchal or masculinist power has, in Europe, addressed this spatial duality.[4] Irish women playwrights are conscious of how women's experience demands to be accommodated by parodying, twisting, morphing or totally transforming space, theatrical form and character.[5] Through these strategies, the plays tell different stories, reconceiving how theatre reflects and imagines experience, interrogating patriarchal values, defining the losses and erasures of masculinist cultural and social authority, and suggesting possibilities of change.

Theatre Structures and Women's Working Methods

Writing for theatre is only one part of the picture. In Ireland, women have played influential roles in production, training and artistic leadership. From Augusta Gregory on, theatrical institutions and independent companies, as they support and make available the work of playwrights and offer professional training, have often relied on the initiative and organizational generosity of women. For example, individuals such as Daisy (or Toto) Bannard Cogley (real name Helen Carter) was, in the 1910s and 1920s, a cabaret artist, theatrical producer and director of the Little Theatre, a space for new plays that also served as a cabaret venue. In the 1950s, Cogley's Studio Theatre Club was one of Dublin's independent basement theatres.

Having begun her career as an actress at the Abbey Theatre in the 1930s, Phyllis Ryan co-founded Gemini Productions in 1958, one of the key independent companies that, in the 1960s, became associated with the work of John B. Keane. The company played at every major Irish theatre and in London and the United States, and ran the Eblana Theatre in central Dublin, staging new plays, classics and revues. Opportunities for Irish actors to train in their profession were scarce. When Deirdre O'Connell (1939–2001), who trained with Erwin Piscator and at the Actors' Studio in New York, came to Dublin to set up a school for actors based on the Method, the impact was significant. Beginning with the Pocket Theatre run by Ursula White-Lennon, and in 1963 starting Focus Theatre in the mews of a late Georgian house, O'Connell's Stanislavski Studio became a centre for creative training for actors.[6] The theatre made a remarkable contribution to audiences' access to new Irish work (by Mary Elizabeth Burke-Kennedy and Ena May, for example) and to major world plays that stood little chance of being staged elsewhere.

At the National Theatre, the Abbey Theatre, four women have in effect worked as artistic directors. Gregory was a co-founder, manager and artistic leader of the Abbey, writing many of its most successful plays and promoting the work of, for example, Sean O'Casey. Ria Mooney, actress and director at the Abbey from 1936, and director in residence from 1948, oversaw the Abbey's move to the Queen's Theatre after the fire in 1951, and was artistic director of the Peacock Theatre, cleverly working around the prejudices of the managing director Ernest Blythe to produce and revive plays by Teresa Deevy even after the Abbey had rejected Deevy's *Wife to James Whelan* (1942).[7] Lelia Doolan, an award-winning director and producer, was artistic director from 1972 to 1973; her ambitious plans to bring Abbey productions to the country generally were cut short and she turned her considerable energies to film and television production. Garry Hynes, founder of the Druid Theatre Company in Galway, took up the Abbey position from 1991 to 1993. Her first production, of O'Casey's *The Plough and the Stars*, was a brilliant, energizing and inspiring staging in neo-expressionist mode. It deeply disturbed conservative expectations, signalling the extent to which the Abbey was in need of radical change both culturally and theatrically.

Emphasis on the body in performance grew and flourished from the late 1970s onwards, posing a challenge to the literary tradition in Irish theatre. At Project Arts Centre in 1978, Olwen Fouéré worked with Peter Sheridan and others to produce Steven Berkoff's *The Fall of the House of Usher*, adapted from Edgar Allen Poe's story. It was perhaps one of the ground-breaking productions centred on the physical presences and movements of the actors.[8] The 1981 Dublin Theatre Festival featured Wrocław's Teatr Współczesny's *Birth Rate* (1979), based on the play by Tadeusz Różewicz and directed by Kazimierz Braun. The piece introduced Braun's Theatre of Communion to Irish audiences, his aim being to connect performers and spectators in a ritualized event that broke theatrical conventions of representational propriety and bore much in common with a happening. The event had a direct impact on the work of Anne le Marquand Hartigan, whose *Beds* played at the Damer Hall and was a *succès de scandale* of the Dublin Theatre Festival in 1982. Scenes of bodily life – birth, sex, love and death – were represented in ritual form and include a visceral account of a woman's experience of abortion. The performing body, particularly as represented by Hartigan, upset gender and literary horizons of expectation that defined language as the primary site of theatrical meaning. Foregrounding the body increasingly fascinated many practitioners who tested processes of devising, adapting and collaboratively creating performances. Olwen Fouéré has been a crucial figure in reconceiving performance in her creative work overall, with Operating Theatre, and TheEmergencyRoom [sic], founded in 2009.[9] The overlap between theatrical practices, live art and installation has developed through the work of key women such as Fouéré and Amanda Coogan.[10]

Mary Elizabeth Burke-Kennedy, who tested her writing skills at Focus Theatre, set up the Storytellers Theatre Company (1986–2008) to produce and tour new translations of classic plays and adaptations of novels and stories. Stagings were characterized by ensemble performance, spatial experiment and the body of the performer as a site of scenographic meaning, as well as a source of narrative and character.[11] One of the most prominent independent companies in Irish theatre since the 1980s has been the Rough Magic Theatre Company, co-founded in 1984 by Lynne Parker who became artistic director. She and the original manager of the company, Siobhan Bourke, have been pivotal figures in promoting new writing by women, and the company has supported the professional development of many women practitioners through the SEEDS programme (2001) making space for new writers, directors, designers and performers. Parker has directed plays by Gina Moxley, Pom Boyd, Paula Meehan, Morna Regan, Olwen Fouéré and Hilary Fannin.[12] Margaretta Darcy's commitment to theatre as a space to challenge political and social hegemonies is remarkable. Her activism has been culturally and politically enlivening, from the Galway Theatre Workshop through the *Non-Stop Connolly Show* (1978) to her protests against US military use of Shannon Airport. The declaredly feminist Glasshouse Theatre Company (1990–96) staged Emma Donoghue's plays, amongst others, at the Project Arts Centre. Their provocative series 'There Are No Irish Women Playwrights' I and II, ironically exposed the erasure of women's plays from the national theatrical memory.

Exemplary of the kinds of collaborative and interdisciplinary processes through which many women (and men) are making work in the theatre of the twenty-first century is THEATREclub [sic], established in 2008 at a time when economic disaster hit Ireland. Their production *Heroin* (2010) is a case in point, telling 'the story you were never told about the new republic [of Ireland]'.[13] The performance, 'largely unscripted … follows a rigid rules structure that the actors improvise within'.[14] The project was developed in collaboration with the Rialto Community Drug Team and inspired by Rachel Keogh's book *Dying to Survive*.[15] A framework text has been published which provides a basis for future productions

that writer Grace Dyas recommends are informed by research and witness to local conditions.[16] The text is written as free verse, hurtling
through the decades from the 1970s to the 2000s: 'We're watching it
all crash down around us/We can't believe it's happening again/We're
worrying about what we're leaving behind us.'[17] The incantatory use of
'we' asserts a sense of shared futures, shared welfare in the face of individualist neo-liberalism. THEATRE-club's *The Game* (2015) was created
collaboratively by members of the company and women who have exited
prostitution, every performance played by two actors and five men who
volunteered for each performance to play 'the game' without knowing
what the rules were. HotForTheatre [sic] was set up in 2010 by Amy
Conroy, author of I♥Alice♥I (2010), a lesbian romance gently involving
the audience.[18] Practitioners taking multiple roles as writers, actresses,
devisers and producers is increasingly how new work comes into being,
and this creative model has a lot to offer women's gifts for collaboration
and teamwork.

Leaders of the Tradition

In the 1920s, the great energies of the Irish cultural renaissance were
just past, but still resonating; the unpredicted transformative moment of
revolution in 1916 and the end of the First World War fueled expectation, notwithstanding the almost inevitability of the civil war that followed partition of the island. Despite their initial optimistic hopes of
emancipation through national independence and achievement of the
right to vote, women in the Irish Free State made plays that expressed
the tragedy of political violence and the dispiriting continuance of
women's social oppression. Dorothy Macardle was a relatively isolated
figure in the 1920s; her protagonists are not the mythic heroines found
in Gregory's and Gore-Booth's plays. They occupy more modest stations
in life but are deeply involved in the ethics and contradictions of political violence. While a trenchant supporter of the republican movement
and of de Valera in her work as an historian, Macardle the playwright
adopted an open and interrogatory approach to armed struggle in her
Abbey plays of the 1920s, but set them safely in the past. *Ann Kavanagh*
(1922) proposes to the audience a parallel between 1798 and the civil
war moment of 1922, suggesting that both crises share a perplexing clash
of values and loyalties: national, ideological, familial, emotional and
ethical. To Macardle, theatre was an art form with particular communal
qualities, and she believed that: 'Irish drama, even more than that of most

countries, has been conditioned by the nation's history.'[19] As I have argued elsewhere, Macardle's plays open up an argument between conservative theatrical form and disruptive feminist representation.[20] Her playwriting strategies include allegory, irony and the empowerment of her heroines to defy predictable emotional reactions, particularly in the endings of her plays. Thus, Ann Kavanagh does not repent her charity towards a spy; rather she turns the judgement of her husband in her favour, even though he suffers militarily by being implicated in her apparent betrayal of the republican cause. Such endings baffled audiences at the time.

Women's critique of accepted ways that political, institutional or individual violence operated to silence and control, featured repeatedly throughout the decades from the 1920s onwards, and in the late 1920s Macardle's vision grew darker. *Witch's Brew* (1929) is an intense fable of female repression. Una, surveilled by church and family, suffers severe symptoms of a killing hysteria; her alter-ego Blanid is wild, powerful, dangerous and sensuous. Macardle prefigures the gender conservatism of the 1930s through this double woman image and, as the play closes, Una is savagely shut down by the ministrations of her priest and her husband to resume her Kristevan 'drive of forgetfulness and death'.[21]

Like Macardle, several playwrights had complex careers, writing in multiple forms (fiction, poetry, history, journalism). These include Kate O'Brien who had success with plays in London and Dublin through the 1920s to the 1950s, and Molly Keane who co-wrote several comedies of manners for the West End stage. The prominence of Augusta Gregory as the first lady of Irish theatre evaporated quickly enough after her death in 1932, and the light fell on Teresa Deevy, whose stream of plays at the Abbey in that decade seemed to assure her status as part of the Irish canon. Her plays are currently recognized in academic terms, although all except *Katie Roche* (1936) have been ignored on the Irish National Theatre stages.

Deevy's work is stylistically unstable; a gap yawns between the energy and emotional tortion of her protagonists and the various forms of conservatism that fence them in. She explores a patterned, hybrid post-realist form in plays such as *The King of Spain's Daughter*, *Katie Roche* and *Wife to James Whelan*. The dramaturgy displays a combination of self-conscious theatricality, and rituals that structure the action, but are repeatedly left unfinished, botched or abandoned. Restless movement between the scene on stage and the offstage world signals a sense of unhomeliness that throws into doubt the national discourses around the duty of Irish women to contribute to the common good by keeping their place within the home, as wives and mothers.[22] Deevy unrelentingly interrogates the twisted viability of such a supposed refuge. The threat of violence and the actual violence directed at the female protagonists in all three plays express what is clear but unspoken, awareness of an inescapable patriarchal requirement to conform to male desires and to take the blame for transgression.

The settings for all of Deevy's plays expose and intensely test the central characters. In *Temporal Powers* (1932), Min and Michael are taking refuge in an 'old ruin' of a house, an unprotected and porous space that travesties the notion of home. Threatening from the offstage world is the authority of the law and prison, or separation and emigration. The scene is an image of a collapsing state whose citizens are mostly homeless, destitute or surviving on the earnings of emigrant children in the United States. *Temporal Powers* sets the dystopian note that predominates across Deevy's plays for theatre and radio. Deevy's emphasis on broken ritual and on violent force used to intimidate and damage women connects with Mairead Ní Ghráda's work in the 1960s.

Mary Manning (1906–99) was the theatrical *enfant terrible* of the Gate Theatre in 1930s Dublin. She was a creative powerhouse: *Youth's the Season–?* (1931) was her biggest success, appealing to outward-looking audiences, testing Irish lives against the limits of conservative Catholicism and preferring satire and expressionist irony to realist styles.[23] Christine Longford (née Trew) (1900–80), novelist and playwright, worked with Micheál MacLiammóir and Hilton Edwards at the Dublin Gate Theatre between 1931 and 1936. Then she and her husband, Lord Longford, seeking independent use of the Gate stage, established Longford Productions. Over the twenty-four-year life of the company, Longford wrote prolifically.[24] Many of her plays explore Irish history, or the class and identity complexities of the nascent state. She writes wittily and within the conventions of popular West End-style realism of the 1920s and 1930s, but developing their direct relation to Irish contexts. Macardle, Deevy, Manning and Longford made the 1930s a lively decade for women dramatists in Dublin, ironic considering de Valera's 1937 constitution, which augured bleak decades ahead for Irish women, and bleaker outlooks for Europe in general.

1950s and 1960s: Maura Laverty

Maura Laverty's series of three Dublin plays was produced in the 1950s by MacLiammóir and Edwards at the Gate and Gaiety theatres in

Dublin and abroad. They were successful to the point of being crucial
to the financial survival of the MacLiammóir and Edwards company.
Censorship impacted heavily on Laverty's fiction and, as no reasons were
offered for the decision to ban a book, it remains unclear why precisely
Laverty's novels were labelled obscene. What the twenty-first-century
reader notices though, are Laverty's unforgettable expressions of physical
pleasure, whether that is in the relationship between a mother and her
baby, between lovers, or in the love of nature, of health and cleanliness,
or of food.[25] The puritanical ethos of Ireland in the 1950s and 1960s
invaded every aspect of physical experience, destroyed innocence, was
often connected with sexual guilt and was at odds with this frankness.
On stage, Laverty's characters express a rapturous pleasure in the natural
world that counters the stereotype of repressed Irish attitudes. In *A Tree
in the Crescent* (1952), Fintan's love for plants and gardening is never
fulfilled, but in the Prologue to the play, '*he stops to touch the Gloxinia*'
in a surgeon's waiting room and remarks to his wife: 'Feel the touch of
it, May. Sweet and cold. Like a child's lips.'[26] The sensuous body, in this
way, is part of the dramatic space of the play, whether through gesture or
action on stage, subtextually or in the imaginary of the characters.

Laverty's trilogy, *Liffey Lane* (1951), *Tolka Row* (1951) and *A Tree in
the Crescent* ((1952) premiered at the much-larger Gaiety Theatre) dramatized social class and social mobility through the lives of families, with
each play based in a particular area of Dublin, from the slum depriva-
tions of Liffey Lane, through Tolka Row, a Dublin Corporation housing
scheme designed to accommodate those made homeless by inner city
slum clearance, to the aspirational 'Crescent' of the third play. Laverty's
stage strategies mean that the personal issues explored through individual
characters may be understood politically and in material terms through
performance in front of an audience. Until very recently *A Tree in the
Crescent* was the only play for which it was possible to trace a full script,
and it evidences a number of staging choices that clearly indicate a putative performance in this direction.[27] The multiple locations present on
stage, and the tree as a design element are the two focal points in assessing how Laverty's dramaturgy moves the action into the sphere of public/
national space.

The setting for *A Tree* describes a simultaneous scenic space which contains several locations of action: a surgeon's waiting room, a park bench,
the Farrells' living room and in the background a '*vista of decaying houses
given over to boarding houses and flats occupied by respectable poorly-paid
clerks, teachers etc.*'[28] As the scenes move from the private family space

of the living room, to the public park, and then to the upper-middle-class space of professional life in the surgeon's waiting room, the action through the spaces connects the fate of the individual to the family, the municipally bound park and the authority of society's elite. The spaces interact to trap the characters in modes of behaviour that they find impossible to change. In the meantime, the process of the play, as it goes between 1927 and 1952, stopping at points in between, is clarified as a kind of living stasis, a circularity that expresses failure to move ahead. Director Hilton Edwards, who also designed the lighting for the production, was recognized for his expert use of the specific and atmospheric lighting effects upon which this form of staging relies.

It seems, however, that the design for the production did not fully achieve the effect that Laverty describes so carefully in her stage directions.[29] The progress of the play works through an unspoken but visually articulated interconnectivity between the spheres of action. How the scene speaks to frame the action is emphasized by the tree, which Laverty specifies, makes '*a frame for the stage*'. The tree is different in each act, '*young and spindly and sparsely covered with new growth*' at first; in Act II '*big and strong and covered with luxuriant foliage*', and finally in Act III, '*becoming bare but … heavy with golden apples*' (*A Tree* [iii]).[30] The overarching tree invites the spectator to assess its labile meaning as Laverty uncouples its visual narrative from the fate of the Farrells, which is anything but a straightforward one of growth leading to fruition of dreams and ambitions. The green shoots of the tree in Act I promise a great future, but its luxuriant foliage in Act II may be read as deeply ironic, or as a judgement on the couple as they allow the day-to-day to undermine their individuality and their bond. This irony intensifies in Act III. Rosy futures are reserved for the Farrells' children, whose achievements do nothing to change the status quo that excludes Fintan and May.

The stage image of fertile growth frames the play but counters the losses and disillusionment of personal lives; it contrasts starkly with May's and Fintan's lack of fulfilment and defeat. What results, as the audience watches the play within its visual frame, is a dynamic contest between public and private values and aspirations. Individual integrity is pressured by social adherence to the status quo, the requirement for financial success and sexual conservatism. When the tree is covered in rich foliage, the fortunes of May and Fintan are stalled in frustration, alienation and mistimed wishes to recognize their desire for each other. While golden apples weigh its branches (a strangely exaggerated fairy-tale image), May and Fintan are faced with the failure of their dream of a house with a garden, and with the prospect of Fintan's death from cancer. The dramaturgy that emerges through this contradiction between showing and telling, which lifts the play away from the personal into a questioning of the social value of material ambition and success, connects directly into changes in 1950s Ireland, its post-war movements towards industrialization, foreign direct investment and an outward-looking open economy. Although Laverty's dialogue, in the play's last moments, has the potential to close down the debate that the play initiates, all the while the stage has silently asserted the freedom of the spectators to interpret for themselves. The power of theatrical design in performance is exploited to open questions about personal values and to create a space of social argument. Appreciation of Laverty's theatrical work has been compromised by under-valuation and the disappearance of two key scripts – the study of women in Irish theatre is commonly subject to such occlusions. The recent rediscovery of manuscripts for *Liffey Lane* and *Tolka Row* will surely herald a re-evaluation of her status.

Entrapment and Escape: Ní Ghráda, Burke Brogan and Anú

The themes of entrapment and escape take literal and historical form in dramatic representations of maternity, its social discourses and regulation. Patriarchal control of motherhood has a history in Irish society that exposes misogyny in one of its most virulent forms, extending into religion, law and culture. The following have made important interventions into these histories: *On Trial* by Máiréad Ní Ghráda, *Eclipsed* by Patricia Burke Brogan and *Laundry*, created by Anú Productions under Louise Lowe's direction. This short section departs from a chronological account and centres on the theme of maternity and sexuality, outlining how the creators' theatrical strategies have reflected on, challenged and influenced changed public discourses.

Máiréad Ní Ghráda's successful career in radio broadcasting meant she was well known in Ireland from the late 1920s into later decades. She wrote eleven plays in the Irish language.[31] In 1964, *An Triail* was staged at the Damer Hall (on Dublin's St Stephen's Green) as part of the Dublin Theatre Festival.[32] It was a hit, ran for six weeks to packed houses and was acclaimed by Harold Hobson, then critic for the *Times*. The play was subsequently translated into English by the author and produced at the Eblana Theatre by Phyllis Ryan's Gemini Productions. Remarkable for its frank representation of patriarchal Irish familial and social dynamics, *On Trial* recalls the theatrical expressionism seen in Ireland in the 1920s and 1930s in plays by Denis Johnston and Mary Manning. The action is framed as the trial of Maura for killing herself and her baby girl (born outside marriage): 'Every girl grows up to be a woman ... But my child is free.'[33] The legal process challenges those involved in the events that lead to Maura's tragic action; they defend themselves against the accusation of responsibility and complicity. Ní Ghráda brings a personal narrative testingly into the public domain, resisting sentiment and allowing a cool expressionist tone to predominate over emotion.

The structure of *On Trial* in two acts comprises a montage of short scenes that form an uneasily integrated movement. The audience is positioned as a jury, invited to reflect and analyse the connectedness of one sphere of life with another. The play creates an argument between personal responsibility and social forces; the supposedly respectable members of society reveal themselves as morally and economically self-serving and hypocritical. Its analysis is layered but direct, unimpeded by the trappings of realism. In Act I, a Brechtian question rings out; when the Social Worker announces that Maura's baby will be adopted, Maura objects that the adoptive couple want the baby alone, while her employer wants her to return to work alone. 'Separately we're all right, together we're all wrong. Tell me why is that?'[34] Class, religious allegiance, misogyny and the sexual double standard are exposed as intimately connected into social structures of judgement, hierarchy and condemnation. Women caught in this system are often agents of it, internalizing the oppressions that trap them in a Foucauldian machine of circulating power.

Ní Ghráda's representation of the Magdalene Laundries in *On Trial* was pioneering in the 1960s, but focused on their role as temporary locations where the socially unacceptable mother, such as Maura, might give birth, be pressured to have her child adopted, and be released back into society to work for low pay, emigrate or in some way hide her past. The experience is presented as coercive and degrading undoubtedly, and Ní Ghráda succeeds in including social class in her analysis, and making clear how the single mother's stigma was as thoroughly enforced outside the confines of the laundries as within.[35] In 1970, Edna O'Brien's stage adaptation of her novel *A Pagan Place* exemplified how Irish society had, in the late 1930s and early 1940s, constrained and punished girls and women for their aspirations without ever locking them up in institutions.[36] Critic Rebecca Pelan recognizes O'Brien's key role in 'consistently cast[ing] a forensic eye on the most private aspects of ... Irish life in order to show that the distinction between the private and the public realm is a false one.'[37] Space in the play expresses an inescapable invasion of the personal by hegemonic forces that are often brutally patriarchal. The young heroine, Creena, finds in her family and community little refuge from violent coercion. In desperation she chooses exile, both from the home place and from herself.

Patricia Burke Brogan returned in 1988 to 'the Magdalenes' in *Eclipsed* to explore women's experience of long-term confinement. The Laundries offered free labour to religious orders and thus there was an incentive to hold inmates under their control for prolonged periods; Frances Finnegan has articulated the very inconvenient truth that Magdalene Laundries in Ireland remained in operation long after they had closed in other countries (in the United Kingdom and Belgium for example).[38] *Eclipsed* was premiered by Punchbag Theatre Company in Galway and won an Edinburgh Fringe First.[39] It is vividly theatrical and playful in form; its comedic qualities only reinforce its emotional power.

The interior of the laundry is the sole locus of the action. In further contrast with Ní Ghráda's piece, the characterizations in *Eclipsed* are realist and psychologized; two nuns who supervise the women appear and the play reveals the damage done to them as an integrated part of the laundry system. Complex characterization, in confluence with spatial design, marks the women's ownership of the play: their work, their fantasies and metatheatrical games shape and re-shape the stage. Invasions from the outside world, the institution of the Roman Catholic Church and the world of relationship, love and sex are present chiefly through music, whether it is plainchant or Elvis. Psychological cruelty and neglect are daily experienced by the women and the harm they suffer emotionally and physically is central to the narrative, leading to Sister Virginia's revolt and the death of Cathy in her attempt to escape. Through Burke Brogan's Brigit, Cathy, Nellie-Nora, Mandy and Juliet, we experience their humour and imaginative strategies for survival as they repeatedly attempt to transform the space of their confinement, and repeatedly fail. Their fury at injustice, frustration and loss, trap and eclipse them. In the Epilogue to the play the need to forget ironizes the pathos of what has gone before.[40]

Histories of women confined in Magdalene Laundries exemplify how church and state institutions, and the general population effectively failed to resist, challenge or even to acknowledge gendered social injustices and illegalities. The McAleese Report on state involvement with the laundries has been widely criticized, by UNCAT[41] amongst others, as being incomplete, disingenuous and not fully independent.[42] The role of this 'official' history seems to be an incitement to blot out or to minimize.

Anú's intervention, in the form of Louise Lowe's and Owen Boss's site-specific, immersive performance *Laundry* (2011) shifts the ground very significantly; it demands an experiential engagement from each individual member of the audience. It also re-marks the space of Dublin's city centre as a site of state-sponsored, institutional cruelty and illegal imprisonment of women, girls and babies, which persisted well into the twentieth century. Anú, through a remarkable series of performances in Dublin and elsewhere, has addressed public issues of histories, geographies and power, and offered audiences ways of considering how they feel and think about space, community, class and the state.[43] As is clear from Miriam Haughton's detailed account of *Laundry*, the participant is pushed towards an experiential and somatic understanding of what it meant to be subjected to life in a Magdalene Laundry, to meet, touch, speak with performers, who in their named 'characters' give witness to the real identities whose stories have been retrieved from the records and from accounts passed down in the locality.[44] Participants left the abandoned laundry building on Sean McDermott Street with smells, tastes, sounds, sights and haptic memories in contest with their tenuous hold on the consciousness that this was 'only a performance'. *Laundry* poses issues about the power of place and of immersive performance to generate discourse way beyond a numerically restricted theatre-going audience, to open a conduit between the present and past experience, and to relocate the moral weight of past experience physically, to where we live now.

Northern Lights: Overcoming Division

An early female figure in Northern Irish theatre was Patricia O'Connor. Her plays were performed by the Ulster Group Theatre during and after the years of the Second World War. *Voice Out of Rama* (1944), for example, critiques the operations of social and cultural narrowness in Northern Irish life, and travesties the placing of women as icons in the Irish theatrical canon.[45] With civil rights and political strife, and military conflict in the late 1960s and 1970s, Northern Irish theatre by women took on a social and cultural urgency that reveals the tensions around women's relationships with sectarianism and identity. The work of the Charabanc Theatre Company, founded in Belfast in 1983, heralded a sea change in Irish theatre on a number of levels. First was Charabanc's candid recognition that Northern Irish women were disadvantaged in theatre as actresses, as writers and as producers. Then their collaborative approach to making theatre had more in common with processes developed in Europe and in Great Britain, and their politics of gender and class enabled them to challenge sectarian representations: 'Our characters could have been IRA wives or IRA mothers or UDA wives or UDA mothers ... that's what politics was about for us.'[46] The founding members were Marie Jones, Maureen Macauley, Eleanor Methven, Carol Moore Scanlan and Brenda Winter. Two key figures inspired and supported the company: English director Pam Brighton (1946–2015) and writer and director Martin Lynch (1950–).

Highly performative, vividly staged, formally innovative and hugely successful plays were researched and developed collaboratively and/ or written by Marie Jones and others. *Lay Up Your Ends* (1983), which toured widely to new venues and audiences, was written by Martin Lynch in collaboration with the company. The play was set in a Belfast linen mill in 1911, and the cast of five women and one man played a large ensemble of characters, male and female, to brilliant and hilarious effect. *Somewhere Over the Balcony* (Marie Jones, 1987) was researched by the company through personal visits to and interviews with women living in the notorious Divis flats at the edge of west Belfast. The intertext was John Boyd's *The Flats* of 1969.[47] Carol Moore comments on how the play 'signaled the scale of emotional, psychological, physical and economic damage suffered by individuals during the Troubles'.[48]

Charabanc brazened out the considerable discouragement it met; the Arts Council of Northern Ireland did not fund the research, writing or production work of the company, which relied on financial support from Belfast City Council and the Department of Economic Development. Despite this artistic rejection Charabanc successfully drew attention to theatre in Northern Ireland, to women's voices and presences in Irish theatre in general, to different ways of making performances and finding audiences. After Charabanc closed as a company in 1995, Marie Jones co-founded the Dubbeljoint Theatre Company, and has gone on, with work such as *A Night in November* (1994), *Women on the Verge of HRT* (1995) and *Stones in His Pockets* (1996), to draw audiences and awards internationally. Overlapping with Charabanc and in its wake, and consonant with its vigorous creativity are independent northern Irish companies such as Big Telly (1987–), Prime Cut (1992–), Kabosh (1994–), Aisling Ghéar (1997–), Tinderbox (1998–) and, more recently, Macha Productions (2015–); women producers and directors such as Zoe Seaton, Paula McFettridge, Emma Jordan and Jo Egan continue to carve out a space for women in contemporary Northern Irish theatre.

Christina Reid (1942–2015) grew up in Belfast's Ardoyne and wrote for theatre and television. Her plays explore Protestant and Catholic identities during the Troubles in Northern Ireland and latterly she wrote for radio and created Royal National Theatre Young Peoples' Projects such as her *A Year and a Day* (London, 2007). She experimented widely with form, even from her first play, *Tea in a China Cup* (1983), an epic family drama over three generations from 1939 to the early 1970s. The stage is dominated by photographs of the three British soldiers of the family, two who lost their lives in the world wars, and the youngest on duty overseas. The power of discourse to connect and divide over gender and sectarian lines of conflict is central to the two-act structure, as the stage space accommodates competing languages of emotional and identity crisis and loss. Centre stage is devoted to direct address to the audience, a place of witness to the hidden histories of the women of the family. Reid both celebrates and interrogates tradition, loyalty and change, and develops a point of opposition to the view provocatively stated in her later play, *The Belle of the Belfast City* (1989): 'There are no women in Ireland. Only mothers and sisters and wives.'[49]

Anne Devlin has been inspired by the voices of her native Belfast, beginning *Ourselves Alone* through her imagined voices of two women involved at the height of the Troubles; then a third voice joined them and the play began to take shape. Its title, the English translation of Sinn Fein, an early republican movement motto and the name of a republican political party, underlines the play's extraordinarily daring intervention into the discourse surrounding republicanism in Northern Ireland, and the situation of women within that highly patriarchal structure. Devlin's analysis of women's position as peace-makers during the Troubles in Northern Ireland continued in her adaptation for film of Mary Costello's novel, *Titanic Town* (1998). Devlin was drawn to theatre due to its freedom from censorship and her plays challenge received patriarchal sectarian opinion in profound ways.

Ourselves Alone (1985) is set in the Belfast of post-hunger-strike 1980s Andersonstown. Two sisters and their sister-in-law centre the drama, creating a resonance with the triple goddess trope of Celtic mythology. The political context, however, imposes a series of binary oppositions: Republicans versus British forces and unionism, militarism versus democratic process, violence versus life. Devlin refuses this reductive either/or through the complexity of the relationships that run through the play, creating overlapping points of tensions, desires and aspirations that are resolved only in singular utopian moments of ecstasy. In the multiple

spaces of the play, images of dead republican hunger strikers intermittently predominate against a mutable darkness that conceals and reveals
watchers.[50] Surveillance is communicated scenically, clarifying the pressures operating on the female characters in particular. Images of being
watched by male authority figures – priests, policemen, fathers, husbands, the devil – are articulated by Donna and Josie.

Both *Ourselves Alone* and the later *After Easter* (1994) resist the either/
or of tribal conflict and adopt instead the both/and of a feminist imaginary.[51] This is expressed in both plays through language when its energy
goes beyond the real and generates a sense of another space.[52] The development from *Ourselves Alone* to *After Easter* is significantly spatial. Greta,
the central quester of *After Easter* departs from the ambivalent enclosure
of the first scene of the play, saying 'Good bye, room.'[53] The dangers of
rooms to the women in *Ourselves Alone*, repeatedly invaded or infiltrated
by threatening patriarchal figures, is discarded. Greta embarks into a
ritual space of transition, and much of the second play is staged betwixt
and between, just offstage, in hallways, on a bridge, in corridors; there is
a visually unforgettable scene expressing political and emotional precarity, when Greta and her family take tenuous refuge from a street explosion under the table upon which the body of her dead father is being
waked. Change in *After Easter* is at first about exile and England, about
risking return to Ireland, to home, to family; but finally it is about the
relocation of home as something created within the self, through image,
narrative and imagination. As Richard Kearney suggests, for an audience,
the movement between empathy and detachment creates space for 'a
journey beyond the closed ego towards other possibilities of being'.[54] In
these terms, the play's mature journey into identity poses huge questions
of the limiting conditions of ideological and sectarian identity politics.
After Easter extends and deepens the idea of a space of alterity that is a
flow, sloughing off national boundaries to re-imagine the individual in
the midst of culture and nation as a creator of possibility; Devlin's play is
interrogatory and Promethean and one of the most important plays ever
to come out of Northern Ireland.

End of Century and New Futures

From the 1990s, the plays of Éilís Ní Dhuibhne and Paula Meehan have
explored contentious aspects of human experience, and recovered lost
histories and voices of Irish women. Emma Donoghue's stagings of lesbian and queer sexualities in *I Know My Own Heart* (1993) and *Ladies*

and Gentlemen (1996) make an important contribution to gender discourses on the Irish stage. With the increasing globalization of theatre culture, playwrights such as Ursula Rani Sarma, Lisa Tierney-Keogh, Stella Feehily, Stacy Gregg and Nicola McCartney have worked across national and artistic boundaries. Their work thrives in intercultural theatrical and media contexts, exploring information communication technology, the movement of exiled peoples, racial and class identities, and growing up in a so-called post-feminist era. With national and international success, Deirdre Kinahan's plays, such as *Moment* (2011) and *Halcyon Days* (2011), exemplify her free, postrealist theatrical style, emotionally powerful and contemporary.

Since 1989 Marina Carr's work has formed an extraordinarily original, accomplished and theatrically turbulent contribution to Irish and international performance. Her plays situate themselves in relation to mythic tropes, narratives and theatrical styles, ranging from classical Greek tragedy, to renaissance conventions of ghost presences, to Beckettian stringency and a highly anarchic comedy. Added to this are extraordinary characterizations that enhance the repertory of great stage roles for actresses in the theatrical canon. The value of Carr's work includes its sustained and progressively intensifying attack on societal and philosophical patriarchal values, and the machinery of theatrical representation as it operates for women. This comes from within the gates, in the sense that Carr articulates her sense of herself as a writer aligned with European and world literary heritage that is mostly, if not entirely, male. Her strategy, however, does not compromise the power of her work to be an irritant (at its mildest), explosive (at its strongest) and to confront audiences with patriarchal, anthropological and environmental crisis (at its most extreme). *Portia Coughlan* (1996) brings together Celtic myth with a classical Greek sense of human existence persisting in a psychological Hades. Portia's drama is a live experiment, testing the feminist philosophical idea of woman as unmarked and outside the symbolic order, fighting to find a foothold in the world.[55]

Carr reshapes patriarchal myths while she appropriates their powerful cultural heritage. In *By the Bog of Cats*, the Medea story is totally metamorphosed into that of Hester Swane, whose outsider status echoes Medea's, but whose killing of her daughter is not a vengeful action, but a way of breaking a repeating history of separation and mourning for the mother. Carr's play parallels Ní Ghráda's *On Trial* in its repeated refusal of the stereotype of woman as sexually jealous fury. In *Phaedra Backwards* (2011), the story familiar through Seneca and Racine is reversed in order to examine the heroine's heritage, crossing species, entangled with violence and betrayal. The play enacts a collapse of category itself: past/ present, life/death and after death, human species/the monstrous, and foregrounds the oppressive causality of tragedy by countering it with Phaedra's escape from tragic closure. Carr's work has a willingness to go to dark and extreme places, to bring on psychic danger and to show audiences what is not rational, how, as the playwright says, 'we are all, to ourselves, mythological ... our passions are huge'.[56]

It is disturbing but predictable to see the extent to which women playwrights have felt impelled to stage the punitive, demeaning and often-violent exclusions that patriarchal structures have imposed on Irish society. In the male canon we glimpse this reality in, for example, Tom Murphy's *A Whistle in the Dark* (1961) when Michael, provoked beyond endurance by his father and brothers, hits his wife and then reminds his father of 'the years I saw how you treated Mama'.[57] The scene, however, stays with the savagery of the men towards one other. The tragedy remains theatrically theirs. Theatre needs writers who follow the woman, who hold her within sight and earshot, who give her space on stage and in her society, to imagine and to live. It is to be hoped that this essay may lead researchers towards investigations into works and practices created by women that await full exploration. What may emerge as a result, is a sense of how Irish women playwrights share impulses and strategies that link them into a tradition of resistance and challenge, without compromising their individual theatrical voices. Plays by Irish women recover hidden histories, explore human experience from different perspectives, and test and expand the conventions of performance to accommodate 'other' points of view, to show, question and re-imagine the lives of audiences more fully and spaciously.

Notes

1 Adrienne Rich, *On Lies, Secrets, and Silence: Selected Prose 1966–1978* (London: Virago, 1980), 11.
2 In response to the Abbey Theatre 1916 Centenary programme 'Waking the Nation', a campaign for gender equality in theatre was formed, led by Lian Bell, and a public meeting held in the Abbey on 12 November 2015. See www.wakingthefeminists.org
3 Hanna Scolnicov, *Woman's Theatrical Space* (Cambridge: Cambridge University Press, 2004), 8.
4 Scolnicov elaborates on this analysis in depth in *Woman's Theatrical Space*.
5 Geraldine Cousin, *Women in Dramatic Space and Time: Contemporary Female Characters on Stage* (London: Routledge, 1996), 201.

6 Focus Theatre Papers, 1965–2001, National Library of Ireland.

7 Ria Mooney programmed Deevy's *Light Falling* on the Peacock stage in 1948, as well as directed two revivals of *Katie Roche* (1949 and 1954).

8 Olwen Fouéré, 'Interview with Melissa Sihra', *Theatre Talk* (Dublin: Carysfort Press, 2001), 155–66, 156.

9 See Olwen Fouéré's website: www.olwenfouere.com

10 Áine Phillips, *Performance Art in Ireland: A History* (London: Live Art Development Agency and Intellect Books, 2015).

11 Storytellers Theatre Company 1986–2008 [Archive], Irish Theatre Archive, ITA/258, Dublin City Libraries. See Mary Elizabeth Burke-Kennedy, *Women in Arms,* in *Seen and Heard* ed. Cathy Leeney (Dublin: Carysfort Press, 2001), 1–47.

12 Lynne Parker, interviewed by Loughlin Deegan, in *Theatre Talk* (Dublin: Carysfort Press, 2001), 393–408.

13 www.theatreclub.ie Accessed 21 February 2016.

14 Grace Dyas, 'Author's Note', *Heroin* in *Oberon Anthology of Contemporary Irish Plays,* ed. Thomas Conway (London: Oberon Books, 2012), 15–45, 18.

15 Rachel Keogh, *Dying to Survive* (Dublin: Gill &Macmillan, 2009).

16 Dyas, *Heroin,* 18.

17 Dyas, *Heroin,* 44.

18 See www.hotfortheatre.com. Accessed 22 January 2016.

19 Dorothy Macardle, 'Experiment in Ireland', *Theatre Arts,* (1934), 124–33, 124.

20 Cathy Leeney, *Irish Women Playwrights, 1900–1939* (New York, NY: Peter Lang, 2010), 124, and 'Violence on the Abbey Theatre Stage: The National Project and the Critic: Two Case Studies', *Modern Drama,* XLVII, no. 4 (Winter 2004): 585–93.

21 Julia Kristeva, 'Modern Theater Does Not Take (A) Place', *Sub-Stance,* 18/19 (1977): 131–4, 132.

22 Constitution of Ireland (1937), *article 41.2* (Dublin: Government Publications, 2015).

23 Manning edited the Gate house journal *Motley* between 1932 and 1934; see Cathy Leeney, 'Mary Manning (1906–1999)', in *Irish Women Playwrights,* 127–59.

24 John Cowell, *No Profit but the Name* (Dublin: O'Brien Press, 1988), 118.

25 Caitriona Clear, '"I Can Talk About It, Can't I?" The Ireland Maura Laverty Desired, 1942–46', *Women's Studies,* 30, no. 6 (2001): 819–35.

26 Maura Laverty, *A Tree in the Crescent,* unpublished manuscript, Dublin Gate Theatre Archive, Northwestern University Library, Evanston, IL, 6.

27 At the time of writing, *Liffey Lane* and *Tolka Row* were untraced, but manuscripts of the two plays have since come to light and will undoubtedly be the subject of academic commentary in the future.

28 Laverty, *A Tree in the Crescent,* [iii].

29 Ibid.

30 The Gate production at the Gaiety Theatre was designed by Michael O'Herlihy. Drawings of the setting indicate that the tree was placed far

downstage right, and therefore did not, as Laverty describes, 'make a frame for the stage'. The lighting sheets for the production, however, indicate that the stage was defined by light and used as a simultaneous space. See Laverty, *A Tree in the Crescent* [iii], and *A Tree* Production Folder F1, Dublin Gate Theatre Archive.

31 See www.irishplayography.com for details.

32 Máiréad Ní Ghráda, *On Trial* (Dublin: James Duffy, 1966). A rehearsed reading of *An Triail* and *On Trial* took place, half in Irish and half in English (with translations distributed to the audience) at the Project Arts Centre Dublin in March 2015 on the initiative of the Irish Theatre Institute. See the I. T. I. website for further information: www.irishtheatreinstitute.com

33 Ní Ghráda, *On Trial*, 60.

34 Ní Ghráda, *On Trial*, 40.

35 The Irish feminist movement does not escape Frances Finnegan's critique in this regard. See Frances Finnegan, *Do Penance or Perish* (Oxford: Oxford University Press, 2004), 3–4.

36 *A Pagan Place* at the Royal Court Theatre was highly praised by leading critic Harold Hobson. See 'London's Best New Play in a Long Time', *Christian Monitor*, 10 November 1972.

37 Rebecca Pelan, 'Reflections on a Connemara Dietrich', in *Edna O'Brien: New Critical Perspectives*, ed. Kathryn Lang, Sinead Mooney and Maureen O'Connor (Dublin: Carysfort Press, 2006), 12–37 (34).

38 Finnegan, *Do Penance or Perish*, 2, 35.

39 A second play on the Magdalenes by Burke Brogan is *Stained Glass at Samhain* (2002) (Galway: Salmon Press, 2002).

40 Patricia Burke Brogan, *Eclipsed* (Cliffs of Moher: Salmon Publishing, 1994), 75.

41 United Nations Convention Against Torture, 'Consideration of Reports Submitted by States Parties under Article 19 of the Convention, Concluding Observations: Ireland' (17 June 2011), UN Doc CAT/C/IRL/Co/1.

42 *Report of the Interdepartmental Committee to Establish the Facts of State Involvement with the Magdalen Laundries*, Chair: Martin McAleese (Dublin: Government Publications, 2013). See Conall Ó'Fátharta, 'Over 1,600 Women Died in Magdalen Laundries – Over Double the Figure Cited in McAleese Report', *Irish Examiner*, 12 January 2015.

43 Louise Lowe quoted in Miriam Haughton, 'From Laundries to Labour Camps: Staging Ireland's "Rule of Silence" in ANU Productions' *Laundry*', in *Radical Contemporary Theatre Practices by Women in Ireland*, ed. Miriam Haughton and Maria Kurdi (Dublin: Carysfort Press, 2015), 55–69 (60).

44 For a full account of the sequence of the performance, see Miriam Haughton, 'From Laundries to Labour Camps'.

45 Mark Phelan, 'Beyond the Pale: Neglected Northern Irish Women Playwrights, Alice Milligan, Helen Waddell and Patricia O'Connor', in *Women in Irish Drama*, ed. Melissa Sihra (Basingstoke: Palgrave, 2007), 109–29 (117–24).

46 Eleanor Methven and Carol Moore, interviewed by Helen Lojek, in *Theatre Talk*, ed. Lilian Chambers [et al.] (Dublin: Carysfort Press, 2001), 342–54.

47 Imelda Foley, *The Girls in the Big Picture* (Belfast: Blackstaff, 2003), 42.

48 Carol Moore, in 'Eleanor Methven and Carol Moore (Scanlan) in Conversation with Helen Lojek', in *Theatre Talk*, ed. Chambers [et al.], 342–54 (346).

49 Christina Reid, *The Belle of the Belfast City*, in *Reid Plays, 1* (London: Methuen Drama, 2008), 209–10.

50 David Beresford, *Ten Dead Men: The Story of the 1981 Hunger Strike* (London: Grafton Books, 1987).

51 Rachel Blau du Plessis, 'For the Etruscans', in *New Feminist Criticism*, ed. Elaine Showalter (New York: Pantheon Books, 1985), 271–91 (276).

52 Anne Devlin, Interview with Enrica Cerquoni in *Theatre Talk*, ed. Chambers [et al.], 107–23 (114, 119).

53 Anne Devlin, *After Easter* (London: Faber, 1994), 8.

54 Richard Kearney, *On Stories* (London: Routledge, 2002), 12.

55 Peggy Phelan, *Unmarked: The Politics of Performance* (London: Routledge, 1993), 22–4.

56 Marina Carr, *Interview*, www.rcs.org.uk/hecuba. Accessed 3 February 2016

57 Tom Murphy, *Whistle in the Dark* in *Plays 4* (London: Methuen, 1989), 1–87 (76).

CHAPTER 18

Writing in Irish, 1900–2013

Ríona Nic Congáil and Máirín Nic Eoin

The emergence of Irish-language women's literature during the revivalist period appears in retrospect to have been an entirely instrumental phenomenon. By this we mean that there were two overriding goals shared by women writing in Irish at this time: to spread the Irish language and to promote cultural nationalism. The majority of Irish-language women writers were teachers, which explains why so many of the plays, translations and stories published by women during the first decades of the twentieth century were written with children in mind. For the most part, these women writers did not specialize in any one genre; rather, they turned to different genres at different times in their lives. Indeed, several of them freely borrowed plots, structures and themes from contemporary English-language and European literature. Therefore, in terms of Irish-language women's literature, the early twentieth century constituted an age of literary importation rather than literary expression: it was only in the 1920s, when the first two collections of Irish-language women's poetry were published, that literary expression began to emerge in a significant way. Equally, the publication of Irish-language women's fiction and drama was disjointed, with a few of the more prominent women writers falling silent during the 1910s and 1920s, before taking up writing again. In the 1930s, with the Irish language firmly established within the school system, two new initiatives offered a publishing opportunity to Irish-language women writers: a number of children's plays were published by women following the establishment of Cumann Drámaíochta na Scol (The Schools' Drama Association), while the engagement of women writers in children's literature was further facilitated by the attempts of An Gúm – the state publisher – to develop this area of literary production. In spite of these developments, there was no sense of a women's literary movement as such, nor was there any dialogue among women writers as to what they were trying to achieve through their writing.

As the twentieth century progressed, the second generation of Irish-language women writers emerged, and these women continued to work across several literary genres. As was the pattern earlier in the century, women's writing from the 1950s to the 1980s was relatively scarce and can best be narrated as the work of exceptional individuals, who challenged aspects of the status quo, rather than the outcome of a conscious literary movement. It was not until the 1990s that Irish-language women's writing, and poetry in particular, began to flourish as authors individually and collectively confronted further thematic and linguistic boundaries. It is at this time that one can discern the emergence of an Irish-language women's literary movement among what can perhaps be described as the third generation of post-revival Irish-language women writers. This new movement was facilitated, in part, by increased access for women to education from the 1960s onwards and the ascendancy of women's studies in all its forms in academia. The continuing growth in Irish-language women's writing is testified to by authors Anna Heussaff and Éilis Ní Anluain, whose recent report on Irish-language writers reveals that in 1995, women accounted for only 8 per cent in a listing of 254 contemporary published authors; twenty years later, both the percentage of women and the number of Irish-language authors had jumped significantly, with women making up 39 per cent of the 506 living published authors in the language.[1] Interestingly, the research has also established that children's literature is the only genre of creative writing dominated by women writers. This is not a surprise given the correlation between women writers and the teaching profession: throughout the twentieth century, the majority of women writers were engaging with questions of audience, literacy and education, yet this is not often acknowledged by academics. Although children's literature and drama are often alluded to in this chapter, such is the volume and variety of Irish-language material written for children by women, that the subject merits a separate chapter on its own terms.

New Beginnings: Prose, Drama and Poetry 1900–1950

The course of Irish-language women's writing through the first half of the twentieth century can be charted most clearly through the writing careers of two figures: Úna Ní Fhaircheallaigh (1874–1951) and Máire Ní Chinnéide (1878–1967). These women were classmates in St Mary's University College, Dublin, and belonged to the first cohort of women to study the Irish language at university level. Indeed, it was upon Ní

Fhaircheallaigh's request in 1897 that the Irish language was first introduced as a university subject in a women's college, and Eoin Mac Néill
was their first tutor. Between them, these two women engaged in almost
all aspects of the Irish revival – from the Gaelic League, to Inghinidhe
na hÉireann, to promoting the sport of camogie – and they wrote
in almost all the available literary genres. After leaving university, Ní
Fhaircheallaigh would become a teacher, novelist, propagandist, academic
and poet. Ní Chinnéide, for her part, would go on to become a teacher,
dramatist, literary critic, translator and, most notably, the editor in 1936
of the most prominent Irish-language book published by a woman in the
twentieth century: the autobiography of Peig Sayers. Ní Fhaircheallaigh
and Ní Chinnéide were educated, trilingual (English, French and Irish),
middle-class, Dublin-based women, who had essentially learned the Irish
language as adults. The majority of Irish-language women's writers in
the first half of the twentieth century fitted into the same educational,
linguistic, social and geographical categories.

Irish-language women writers were faced with challenges and obstacles far beyond those faced by English-language women writers of the
same period. Firstly, they were not native speakers of the language and
they had few language learning resources available to them: for example,
when Ní Fhaircheallaigh published her first novel, *Grádh agus Crádh*
(1901), which was also the first Irish-language prose fiction published
by a woman, she had only been learning the Irish language for five years.
Secondly, there was no published corpus of Irish-language women's
writing for twentieth-century women writers to draw on. Of course,
Ní Fhaircheallaigh, Ní Chinnéide and the other women writers who
followed them were aware of the rich culture of oral literature among
native Irish-speaking women; however, even the works of celebrated
foremothers such as Eibhlín Dhubh Ní Chonaill (ca. 1743–ca. 1800),
author of the famous lament 'Caoineadh Airt Uí Laoghaire', and Máire
Bhuí Ní Laoghaire (1774–ca. 1848) were not readily available in print.[2] Ní
Fhaircheallaigh and Ní Chinnéide attempted in some of their published
work to emphasize the oral literary tradition of women who were native
speakers of Irish. Both of these university-educated women were well
aware that women who were native speakers of Irish were among the least
likely people in Ireland to have studied Irish in the educational system.

Irish-language women's writing came about through the convergence
of a number of factors: the access of women to university education from
1878 onwards; the willingness of the Gaelic League to accept women
members on a par with men; and the dire need to produce reading

material for the thousands of people learning Irish in classes hosted by the Gaelic League. In 1899, the Gaelic League's Publications Committee was established, with the intention of publishing Irish-language reading material. Ní Fhaircheallaigh was among those appointed to the committee, and she began to address the lack of Irish-language reading material, for female readers in particular, by publishing her own work. *Grádh agus Crádh* was a slim volume that drew on the structure, themes and motifs that abounded in English-language women's literature of the late-Victorian period. Its focus on love and an impossible marriage between people from two very different backgrounds – in this instance, a landlord's daughter and a true Gael – became a recurrent theme in Irish-language women's writing during the first half of the twentieth century. Ní Fhaircheallaigh quickly published two more prose works in 1902: *An Cneamhaire*, an anti-emigration story, and a travelogue entitled *Smuainte ar Árainn*. Both are centred on Inis Meáin, where Ní Fhaircheallaigh learned her Irish during the summers of 1898–1902. *Smuainte ar Árainn* recounts Ní Fhaircheallaigh's time spent on Inis Meáin, the activities of the Gaelic League on the island, and focuses on the lives of the island women. Ní Fhaircheallaigh stayed in the same cottage as J. M. Synge (at a different time) and her travelogue offers a precursor from a female perspective to his *The Aran Islands* (1907).

At the turn of the twentieth century, the Aran Islands were envisaged by revivalists, Dublin-based middle-class Gaelic Leaguers among them, as the last bastion of authentic Irish language and culture. However, as the Aran Islands became populated with language learners who unwittingly increased use of the English language in island interactions, scholars of the language began to turn instead to the Kerry Gaeltacht, most specifically to the Blasket Islands. Máire Ní Chinnéide was one such scholar, and it was through her visit to the Great Blasket with Léan Connellan that Peig Sayers's autobiography came about. Yet this shift in focus from the west to the south west had begun to take place several years before Ní Chinnéide set foot on the Great Blasket. Indeed, the Kerry literary tradition that culminated in Tomás Ó Criomhthain's *An tOileánach* (1929) and Sayers's autobiography (1936) had begun over a decade earlier, in the pages of local Irish-language newspaper *An Lóchrann*, edited by Pádraig Ó Siochfhradha.

Among his other achievements, which would go on to include editing *An tOileánach*, Ó Siochfhradha was responsible for facilitating and promoting the short-lived, yet notable, writing careers of three Kerry schoolgirls: Brighid Stac from Ballyferriter, Máire Ní Shéaghdha from Moorestown, both in the Dingle Peninsula, and Brighid Ní Shíothcháin from the Iveragh Peninsula. These girls were part of the first generation to learn Irish as part of the national school curriculum. Between 1916 and 1918 all three published diaries in *An Lóchrann*, detailing a month in their lives and documenting events such as matchmaking, cutting turf and working as a maid in a wealthier English-speaking household. These diaries were later published as books: Ní Shéaghdha's *Laethanta Geala* (1917); Stac's *Mí dem' Shaoghal* (1918) and *Laethanta Geala: Cunntasaí Cinn Lae do Scríobh Beirt Chailín Sgoile* (1922), which consisted of Ní Shéaghdha's and Ní Shíothcháin's diaries.[3] There is scant information available about these young writers: Stac, the most promising writer of the three, who published several stories in *An Lóchrann*, died as a result of the Spanish flu in 1918, while Ní Shéaghdha emigrated to America. Ní Shíothcháin has not been traced and she did not continue to publish.[4] The short-lived literary careers and fates of the schoolgirl diarists reveal the harsh realities of Irish-speaking women's lives, women who had neither the health (in the case of Stac), the wealth, nor the educational advantages of the likes of Ní Fhaircheallaigh and Ní Chinnéide to further pursue writing in their native language.

Upon Brighid Stac's death, a lament for her was published in *An Lóchrann*, composed by Micheál Ó Gaoithín (1904–74), son of Peig Sayers. Unlike his mother, yet similar to the schoolgirl diarists, Micheál had learned to write in his native language. In spite of being illiterate in the Irish language, Peig Sayers (1873–1958) was well known on the Great Blasket for her rich oral repertoire, and the scholar Kenneth Jackson was the first to transcribe and publish some of Sayers's oral tales in book-format in *Scéalta ón mBlascaod* (1934).[5] Ní Chinnéide was one of the few women to be involved in the Folklore of Ireland Society (est. 1927) and realized that Sayers's life story was worth recording. She persuaded Sayers to narrate her life story and proceeded to edit *Peig* (1936) and *Machtnamh Seana-mhná* (1939).[6] Sayers's publications have generated much debate on the nature of female authorship since the published account was not physically written by the author herself (both Ní Chinnéide and Micheál Ó Gaoithín were involved in transcribing Sayers's autobiography).[7] The role of Ní Chinnéide as one of the few female editors of Gaeltacht autobiography is particularly important, however, and her working relationship with Sayers illustrates the gulf between the two classes of Irish-speaking women most likely to be involved in literary production in the early years of independence.

It is not clear whether Ní Chinnéide had any inkling that Sayers's autobiography would very quickly overshadow all other examples of women's literature published in the first half of the twentieth century. The importance of Sayers's autobiography lay in the fact that it was the first book in the Irish language to provide a detailed and seemingly authentic account of an Irish-speaking woman's life, and to offer new insight into female familial and friendship bonds. It did not belong to an imported genre; indeed, it belonged to a genre that was newly developing in its own direction within the Irish language itself. *Peig* was a work of social realism, and in it, Peig Sayers herself was portrayed as having a remarkable resilience and acceptance of her fate in life. It was no accident that the rise of *Peig* coincided with the rise of the Fianna Fáil party under De Valera and with the curtailment of women's rights in the Irish Free State. Peig Sayers was exactly the type of Irishwoman that De Valera wished to promote: she was a Catholic, Irish-speaking, hard-working and subservient mother, who was not sufficiently schooled to engage in public affairs; yet, as critic Patricia Coughlan has argued, Sayers in her autobiography portrayed herself as an intelligent and creative woman who did challenge aspects of her social situation.[8]

Following the instant success of *Peig* and the other Blasket autobiographies, Nóra Ní Shéaghdha (1905–75) published *Thar bealach isteach: leabhar eile ón mBlascaod Mór* (1940). Ní Shéaghdha was the older sister of the aforementioned schoolgirl diarist Máire Ní Shéaghdha, and spent the years 1927–34 as principal of the national school on the Great Blasket. *Thar bealach isteach* recounts Ní Shéaghdha's experience on the island as an outsider, documenting social events, local customs and the arrival of visitors. Her account has parallels with Ní Fhaircheallaigh's *Smuainte ar Árainn* (1902) although Ní Shéaghdha provides more detail and has a natural command of the Irish language. Ní Shéaghdha then published *Peats na Baintreabhaighe* (1945), a romantic tale set in the Gaeltacht which was not as well received as her first book among critics.[9]

As the Blasket Islands autobiography genre was gaining prominence, another woman novelist was emerging: Úna Bean Uí Dhiosca (1880–1958), who published two novels, *Cailín na Gruaige Duinne* (1932) and *An Seod do-fhághala* (1936). Dublin-born Uí Dhiosca, from a Church of Ireland background, had studied in Switzerland and was a French speaker, and later emigrated to Canada before returning to Ireland and becoming an Irish-language writer. She had learned the language while a student at Alexandra College.[10] The likelihood is that she knew Ní Fhaircheallaigh and Ní Chinnéide from her time at Alexandra College: students from that college had joined the first Irish class in St Mary's University College, and upon receipt of her degree Ní Fhaircheallaigh taught in Alexandra College for a brief spell. Uí Dhiosca was a committed pacifist, a philosophy that is discernible in her two historical novels.[11] *Cailín na Gruaige Duinne* is set in Ireland and Canada between the 1916 Rising and the War of Independence, and shares some common themes with Séamus Ó Grianna's first novel, *Mo Dhá Róisín* (1921). In Uí Dhiosca's novel, the love between Róisín, a Protestant city-woman, and Micheál, a Gaeltacht man, quickly turns into a story of domestic abuse and political violence. She broaches topics that include pregnancy, mistreatment of animals and female emigration to Canada. *An Seod do-fhághala* is also a story of thwarted love, set in the aftermath of the 1798 rebellion. In this work, the leading female character enters a convent and thus exercises her choice of God over her love interest, Bartlaí Ó Séagha, a man who believes that violence is necessary to achieve a free Ireland. Uí Dhiosca's work is noteworthy in its portrayal of strong-minded female characters, and its exploration of the dark domestic aspects of women's lives.

While prose works aimed at adults, such as Uí Dhiosca's novels, remained few and far between, women were more consistent in writing and translating for children. By the turn of the century, many children had begun to study Irish but had little reading material available to them. Máire Ní Chinnéide, as a teacher and later a mother, was well aware of this lacuna and addressed it by translating three Grimm tales in *Scéalta ó Ghrimm* (1923).[12] Prior to this publication, other women worked to fill the gap. They included Máire Ní Chillín (1874–1956), who was involved in the translation of a Danish children's story into an English-Irish bilingual book, *Fuzzy and his Comrades / Mothaláinín agus a Chuideachta* (1912), and Norma Borthwick, who translated several Hans Christian Andersen tales into Irish in *Leabhairín na Leanbh* (1913).[13] From the early 1920s, when Irish became a compulsory school subject, more reading material was needed, and this led to an increase in women writers and translators. Among these figures were: Katherine O'Brien (1886–1938) (sister of Hanna Sheehy-Skeffington and wife of Frank Cruise O'Brien), who wrote *Na Trí Muca: Sgéalta Greannmhara i gCóir na bPáistí* (1925);[14] Brighid Ní Dhochartaigh (1884–1961), a teacher in St Louis Secondary School, Monaghan, and author of *Seamróg na gCeithre nDuilleóg* (1925); Seosaimhín Bean Mhic Néill (1895–1969), translator of *Finnsgéalta ó India* (1933);[15] Máiréad Ní Ghráda (1896–1981), whose early work included *An Giolla Deacair agus Scéalta Eile* (1936) and a translation of J. M. Barrie's *Peter Pan and Wendy*, *Tír na Deó* (1938);[16] Máire Ní Ghuairim (1896–1964), a native speaker of Connemara Irish who published *Ceol na Mara* (1938); Brighid Ní Loingsigh (1894–1974), who translated Edmund Leamy's *Irish Fairy Tales* and a few of Eileen Ó Faoláin's stories;[17] and Maighréad Nic Mhaicín (1899–1983), whose translations of Patricia Lynch's books for children were published by An Gúm in the 1940s.[18] Towards the end of the decade, Eilís Dillon (1920–94), began her writing career by publishing the first of three books of animal adventure tales for younger children with An Gúm: *An Choill Bheo* (1948), followed by *Oscar agus an Cóiste Sé nEasóg* (1952) and *Ceol na Coille* (1955). Dillon was the only one among these women who chose to go on to a writing career in the English language.

In 1909, Máire Ní Chinnéide addressed the genre of drama, along with prose and poetry, in what was the only significant work of literary criticism written by an Irish-speaking woman in the early twentieth century. She claimed that Gaelic culture did not have an indigenous tradition of drama and theatre: in order to fill this artistic chasm, she urged Irish-language playwrights to embrace and import aspects of the dramatic arts from other languages and cultures.[19] Ní Chinnéide herself became involved in drama through Inghinidhe na hÉireann (est. 1900), a nationalist and Dublin-based women's organization. She taught children's Irish classes for Inghinidhe na hÉireann and soon began to compose plays for children, notably *Gleann na Sidheóg* (1905) and *Sidheoga na mBláth* (initially published in *An Claidheamh Soluis* in 1907 and published in book-format in 1909).[20] Both plays recount the tale of two human children who chance upon fairy gatherings, and while the former play reveals a feminist agenda, the latter play equally works as an allegory for colonization. Ní Chinnéide proceeded to write a one-act propagandist play for adults, *An Dúthchas* (1908), that espouses temperance and recounts the disastrous effects of an alcoholic husband on his wife.[21] This play is set in a middle-class home, thereby revealing that alcoholism is not restricted to the working class, and it is clearly influenced by Henrik Ibsen's landmark play, *Ghosts* (1881).

Alongside Ní Chinnéide, but to a lesser extent, Máire Ní Shíthe (1867–1955), Máire Ní Chillín (1874–1956) and Searlot Ní Dhúnlaing (1881–1953), also published Irish-language drama. In 1902, Máire Ní Shíthe's and Eilís Ní Mhurchadha's two-act comic play for adults, *Beart nótaí: dráma suilt*, was staged in Belfast and was published two years later.[22] In early 1912, Máire Ní Chillín (1874–1956) published 'Mairghréad. A topical play for national teachers in two scenes' in *Sinn Féin*.[23] Ní Chillín, a Dublin-based Mayo woman and leading member of Inghinidhe na hÉireann, also saw the need to publish plays for children.[24] While several women, including Ní Shíthe and Ní Chillín, published one or two plays during their lifetime, more productive writers of Irish-language plays would follow. One such woman was Searlot Ní Dhúnlaing, a national school teacher from Dublin, who published at least nine children's plays over a thirty-four-year period, beginning with 'An Leoirghníomh', published by P. H. Pearse in *An Claidheamh Soluis* in 1909.[25] Ní Dhúnlaing's plays were didactic and Christian morality was a recurrent theme in her work.

Ní Chinnéide and Ní Dhúnlaing fell silent in the 1920s, as did other women playwrights. During this state-building decade, several women writers concentrated on developing new institutions and Irish-language organizations. For example, Ní Chinnéide was heavily involved in drawing up the new Irish-language school syllabus in the Free State, and in establishing Cumann na Scríbhneoirí (Association of Writers). One notable exception to this was Úna Bean Uí Dhiosca whose play for adults *Cruadh-chás na mBaitsiléirí, nó, Is éiginteach do dhuine agaibh pósadh* was staged in 1924 and published in 1931.[26] The 1930s marked a resurgence in plays written by women. In 1930, Máire Ní Shíthe translated Molière's comic musical *Le bourgeois gentilhomme* as *An geocach duine uasail: dráma cúig ngníomh*; Máire Ní Dhabhoireann (ca. 1910–90) proceeded to translate Molière's *L'Avare* as *Fear na Sainnte* (1937). The year 1931 saw the staging of *An Udhacht* (published in 1935), the first of Máiréad Ní Ghráda's plays, which she claimed to be loosely based on Puccini's comic musical, *Gianni Schicchi* (1918).[27] Ní Ghráda – whose work for adults will be analysed in more detail later in this essay – had a long and distinguished career as a writer, educational editor and broadcaster, producing nine one-act plays for children, sixteen Irish-language versions of children's classics (including versions of Grimm's *Fairy Tales*), over twenty school textbooks, a science fiction novel and a collection of short stories for young readers. Similar to other women playwrights, she wrote her first Irish-language play due to what she perceived as the lack of suitable plays in Irish for her students.[28]

The renewed interest of Ní Chinnéide, Ní Dhúnlaing and indeed Sinéad de Valera in children's drama in the mid-to-late 1930s, was directly linked to the establishment of Cumann Drámaíochta na Scol in 1934 by Schools' Inspector Proinsias Ó Súilleabháin.[29] This organization initiated a national competition for school drama in the Irish language and new plays were needed to meet the growing interest in children's drama. In 1934, Máire Ní Ghallchobhair and Máire Bean Uí Mhaolmhaoidh co-wrote two children's plays;[30] the following year,

Máire Ní Ghiobúin published a miracle play, *Feichín Fobhair: dráma um mhíorbhailt* (1935). Ní Chinnéide published *An Cochall Draoidheachta* (1938), followed by *Cáit Ní Dhuibhir* (1938), written for the girls attending Louise Gavan-Duffy's and Annie McHugh's all-Irish national school, Scoil Bhríde (est. 1917). In the same year, her play for adults, *Scéal an Tighe*, was first staged by An Comhar Drámaíochta (The Drama Company) in the Peacock Theatre, Dublin.[31] Similar to Ní Chinnéide, Sinéad de Valera (1878–1975) had been involved in Irish-language drama during the 1900s; however, she published the first of her two-dozen Irish-language children's plays in 1934. Her work included newly composed light-hearted plays (e.g. *Buaidhirt agus Bród* (1934)), versions of historical tales (e.g. *Niall agus Gormfhlaith* (1938)) and adaptations of classical European fairytales (e.g. an adaptation of *Bluebeard* as *Féasóg Gorm in Éirinn* (1943)).[32] From 1945–47, Áine Ní Chnáimhín (1908–2001), a teacher and literary critic from Offaly, published ten children's plays in Irish with An Gúm, four of which were newly composed specifically for schoolgirls, and six were translated from English.[33] Ní Chnáimhín's short-term productivity highlights the fact that in the first half of the twentieth century, Irish-language women playwrights, writers and poets often had only short bursts of creative output. The final woman of note, in terms of Irish-language drama, was Áine Ní Fhoghludha, who translated four of M. H. Gaffney's English-language children's plays on aspects of religion.[34]

Ní Fhoghludha (1880–1932) is most significant, however, for being the first female Irish-language poet of the period. Although Irish-language women's poetry was to flourish in the second half of the twentieth century, before then there were only two notable women poets in Irish, both of whose collections were published in the 1920s. Ní Fhoghludha published *Idir na Fleadhanna* in 1922 under her married name, Áine Bean Uí Néill, and Úna Ní Fhaircheallaigh published *Áille an Domhain* in 1927, having previously written an English-language propagandist poetry collection, *Out of the Depths* (1921). It was no coincidence that these women composed their poetry between 1916 and 1927: Ní Fhaircheallaigh herself claimed that her urge to write poetry stemmed from the political unrest in Ireland and the suffering it caused.[35] By writing poetry, these two poets moved towards literary expression rather than the literary importation that defined so many of the prose works and plays by Irish-language women writers in the early twentieth century. Without ready access to the female poetic tradition on which they could draw, these poets were influenced by the male Irish-language poetry tradition and by the male English-language Romantic movement. Ní Fhoghludha was a teacher, from the Ring Gaeltacht, Co. Waterford, and therefore stood apart from the Dublin-based Irish-language women writers. The poems in the collection *Idir na Fleadhanna* were penned between 1916 and 1919, and broached the topics of nature, love, patriotism and piety amongst others.[36] A sense of fragility and loneliness emerges in the poetry of both women, and they both draw heavily on motifs and imagery from the natural world. Since her early writing career, Ní Fhaircheallaigh had become a lecturer in Irish-language poetry in University College Dublin (UCD), and had edited a scholarly edition of poetry, *Filidheacht Sheagháin Uí Neachtain: Cuid a hAon* (1908). Following the Civil War, she turned to the Irish language once more, and the poems in *Áille an Domhain* are more personal than propagandist. As the title suggests, the transient beauty of the natural world is an overarching theme of the collection; however, the suffering of Mother Ireland and her children during the Civil War is also a recurring motif. Ní Fhaircheallaigh's collection embraced the traditional panegyric and elegiac functions of Irish-language poetry by including a poem of praise for Douglas Hyde and an elegy for George Sigerson. Although Ní Fhoghludha and Ní Fhaircheallaigh ventured into traditional male territory by publishing poetry in Irish, there is no clear sense that they did so in a deliberate attempt to challenge or subvert the patriarchal poetic sphere. It took another generation, in the guise of Máire Mhac an tSaoi (1922–), a student of Ní Fhaircheallaigh's in UCD, to firmly establish the idea of a woman poet in the Irish language.

Rising to the Challenge: Prose, Drama and Poetry 1950–2013

The second half of the twentieth century was still a challenging time for female writers in Irish, so much so that the disappearance from view of short-story writer Síle Ní Chéileachair after the publication of the acclaimed co-authored collection *Bullaí Mháirtín* (1955)[37] went un-noted, as did the silence of artist and travel writer Úna Ní Mhaoileoin after the publication of three ground-breaking books between 1958 and 1967. Only from the 1980s onwards was the question of female author-ship raised as an issue worthy of serious debate and analysis.[38] As women poets came to prominence from the 1980s onwards, the dearth of women writing creative prose in Irish was still a cause for concern, with much of the discussion centred on perceived lack of achievement in relation to popular genres such as the novel and the short story.[39] The rest of this chapter will document the emergence of women's writing – prose, drama and poetry – from the 1950s to 2013, when one witnesses the gradual appearance of a number of exceptionally gifted individuals who together set the scene for the flowering of literary activity by women that was to happen in the last decade of the twentieth century and the first decade of the new millennium.

A notable development in Irish autobiographical writing, especially from the 1950s onwards, was the appearance of travel journals of various kinds. The pioneer among women writers in this respect was the artist Úna Ní Mhaoileoin (1927–94) whose first book, *Le grá ó Úna* (1958),[40] a lively collection of impressions of Italy written as letters home to her siblings, was followed by two wonderful travel books, *An Maith Leat Spaigití?* (1965)[41] and *Turas go Túinis* (1969).[42] All three of these books are marked by a sharp wit, a visual artist's keen attention to physical details and a delight in plurilingual and interlingual wordplay. Ní Mhaoileoin, who was closely involved with the publishing house Sáirséal agus Dill, established and run by her brother-in-law Seán Ó hÉigeartaigh and Úna's sister Brighid, disappeared from the Irish literary scene when she moved to London and later Scotland after her marriage. Though Ní Mhaoileoin's light-hearted approach to the genre has never been repeated, women have continued to write engaging travel accounts, such as *Mise agus na Maighigh* (2003),[43] by Nellie Nic Giolla Bhríde, which describes a month-long trip through Guatemala, or *Bealach na Bó Finne* (1994),[44] by Dóirín Mhic Mhurchú (1930–2014), an unusual combination of historical analysis and personal travelogue, based on the tradition of pilgrimage to Santiago de Compostelo.

Gaeltacht-based autobiographical accounts continue to appear, and these include accounts of island life, such as *An tOileán a Bhí* (1978)[45] and *Bean an Oileáin* (1986)[46] by Blasket Islander Máire Ní Ghuithín (1909–88) and *Róise Rua* (1988), an account of her youth and adult life on Árainn Mhór off the Donegal coast by traditional singer Róise Mhic Grianna (1879–1964) as recounted to school teacher Pádraig Ua Cnáimhsí.[47] Autobiographical works by Gaeltacht authors include an account of convent life, *Thar balla isteach* (1982),[48] by West Kerry author Sr de Lourdes Stack, and memoirs such as *Carraig a' Dúin* (1989)[49] by Eibhlín Uí Bheaglaoich that includes a detailed description of emigration to America in the 1920s by a woman who later returned to settle in her place of birth. A more unusual example of the genre is the book *Girseacha i nGéibheann* (1986),[50] an account of the incarceration of Donegal sisters Áine (1949–) and Eibhlín Nic Giolla Easpaig (1952–) in 1975 for alleged involvement in IRA bomb-making activities in Britain.

While certain accounts still involve the mediation of editors and redactors, self-authored memoirs have become more common as literacy levels in Irish increased throughout the century.[51]

Most of the life writing by women in Irish tends to focus on sociological and ethnographic detail rather than on the more personal aspects of the author's youthful formation. The single example of a female *Bildungsroman* in Irish is Éilís Ní Dhuibhne's *Cailíní Beaga Ghleann na mBláth* (2003),[52] a central strand of which is set in a fictional Irish-language college located in the grounds of a Big House in English-speaking east Cork (the details are based on the Trabolgan Estate). The middle-aged narrator Máire, now dealing with the mutism of her own teenage daughter, returns to Gleann na mBláth and to the traumatic event that was to cast a shadow over her life and relationships. This novel has been compared to Ní Dhuibhne's English-language coming-of-age novel *The Dancers Dancing* (2000),[53] set in a summer college in the Donegal Gaeltacht, as both novels successfully exploit the dramatic potential of the Irish college as a site of maturation.[54]

Social realism is the dominant mode employed in Irish-language fiction by women, whether set in rural or urban contexts. The characters that feature in the novels and short stories of Siobhán Ní Shúilleabháin are more often than not rural women, caught between their sense of duty to traditional roles as wives, mothers and carers and their desire for personal fulfilment. Most of her stories depict gender relations as they were before the 1960s and 1980s waves of feminism, and, though the narrating voice is often aware of feminist critique, the domestic dramas that unfold are usually resolved without compromising traditional values or behaviour patterns. One of her best novels is *Aistriú* (2004), which deals with the migration of a West Kerry family to a Gaeltacht colony in Co. Meath in the 1930s. Ní Shúilleabháin sensitively depicts the process of cultural and linguistic displacement experienced by an Irish-speaking community and the effect on the women, in particular, as bonds of kinship and community are sundered.

While the tension in Ní Shúilleabháin's work is often between the romantic and the domestic, women writers of a younger generation, such as Orna Ní Choileáin and Éilis Ní Anluain are bolder in their depiction of young women's sexual desires and social ambitions. Ní Choileáin, who has published two collections of short stories, *Canary Wharf* (2009)[55] and *Sciorrann an t-am* (2014),[56] as well as a series of vampire books for young readers, has broken new ground in creating sharp depictions of young professional men and women often caught dramatically in challenging or compromising social situations. Éilis Ní Anluain, in her debut novel *Filleann Seoirse* (2011)[57], takes Irish-language prose writing into the heart of contemporary urban middle-class life, with its domestic rituals and social pretensions. The central character in Ní Anluain's novel is an educated and emotionally uneasy young wife and mother, attracted by the elusive figure of the bohemian poet Seoirse, but psychologically dependent on the security of her marriage to Muiris who allows her to harbour fantasies of romantic escape.

The debut short story collections of Déirdre Ní Ghrianna and Réaltán Ní Leannáin, both from Belfast, are also firmly located in the realm of urban realism. The stories in Ní Ghrianna's *An gnáthrud* (1999)[58] deal with many of the darker aspects of women's lives, including teenage pregnancy, sexual abuse, marital infidelity, miscarriage and post-natal depression. The title story, which involves the killing of a young father as he returns home with a takeaway meal, is a shockingly dramatic depiction of life lived in the shadow of paramilitary violence, while one of the most moving stories in the collection, 'Súile Gealaí', depicts a young mother coming to terms with her son's diagnosis of autism. The emotional range of the material is more diverse in the stories in Ní Leannáin's collection *Dílis* (2015),[59] many of which are located in Belfast. Whether the focus is on issues such as the mediating role of a mother seeking to prevent her family home becoming a site of conflict in the story 'Teas' or the sense of responsibility of a daughter for her elderly parents in the story 'Codladh Sámh', Ní Leannáin's characters are portrayed with great empathy and humour. The story 'Clic', about a young woman who encounters, in a hospital bed, the man who abused her as a child, shows Ní Leannáin's sense of drama and timing at its best, making an engaging thriller out of what could have been portrayed more simplistically as a tale of morality or revenge.

Women have come to the fore in crime fiction and mystery writing in recent years. Éilís Ní Dhuibhne's murder mysteries, *Dúnmharú sa Daingean* (2000)[60] and *Dún an Airgid* (2008)[61], demonstrate the mastery of plot essential to the genre as well as a keen eye for social detail, especially in her depiction of the lives of professional young women. Similarly, Anna Heussaff, in her series of murder mysteries, *Bás Tobann* (2004),[62] *Buille Marfach* (2010)[63] and *Faoi Scáil an Phríosúin* (2015),[64] manages to create suspense-filled plots while also addressing a range of contemporary social and environmental issues. Poet Biddy Jenkinson, whose first collection of short stories *An Grá Riabhach* (1999)[65] was an ambitious attempt to create a sophisticated, modern and humorous fiction on the foundation of mythical and literary characters and events, has subsequently turned to a more plot-driven and place-specific approach to mystery-writing, using the historical figure of the Irish lexicographer, Pádraig Ua Duinnín, as a central character in the collections *An tAthair Ó Duinnín – Bleachtaire* (2008) and *Duinnín Bleachtaire ar an Sceilg* (2011).[66]

The relationship between academic scholarship and creative writing has been developed by a number of women writers, most notably Máire Mhac an tSaoi whose novella *A Bhean Óg Ón ...* (2001)[67] is a fictional account based on the seventeenth-century poet Piaras Feiritéar's friendship with Meg Russell, the English woman who is the subject of one of his courtly love poems. This is a subject she treats in more detail and in a scholarly style in the book *Cérbh í Meg Russell?* (2008)[68], where her central interest is in the relationship between historical, folkloric and literary sources. The novel *Scéal Ghearóid Iarla* (2011)[69] similarly uses fiction to negotiate the ground between historical evidence and literary and folk tradition, the subject in this instance being the fourteenth-century Gearóid Iarla, Gerald Fitzgerald, 3rd Earl of Desmond and famed love poet.

The development of a vibrant theatre culture in Irish has been challenging and few women emerged as important playwrights for the adult stage in the early decades of independence. It is significant, however, that the single most renowned twentieth-century playwright in Irish to date is still the prolific and hugely talented Máiréad Ní Ghráda (1896–1971), whose play *An Triail* (1978) received immediate and wide critical acclaim, ensuring its canonical position in the history of modern Irish theatre. As well as the three full-length plays for which she is best known, Ní Ghráda's writing for adults also includes an early collection of short stories, *An Bheirt Dearthár agus Scéalta Eile* (1936), and eight one-act plays.[70] These latter works – from early comedies such as *An Grá agus an Garda* (1937), to the later *Lá Buí Bealtaine* (1954), *Úll Glas Oíche Shamhna* (1960), *Súgán Sneachta* (1962) and *Mac Uí Rudaí* (1962), first produced on the Abbey stage as part of Ernest Blythe's strategy of including one-act Irish-language plays alongside the main bill in English[71] – combine humour with astute commentary on gender roles, family relationships and social structures and expectations.

Ní Ghráda has been rightly acknowledged for her long plays *An Triail* (first produced in the Damer in Dublin in 1964) and *Breithiúnas* (first produced in the Peacock stage of the Abbey Theatre in 1968), both of which are scathing in their critique of the hypocrisy and double standards prevailing in Irish life. Based on the story of an unmarried mother who, rejected by her family and the married father of her child, kills herself and her daughter, *An Triail* openly addresses issues of power, sexual predation and hypocrisy and boldly puts the institutions responsible for the care of the young in Ireland on trial. Influenced by Brechtian techniques of addressing the audience directly with a view to eliciting a strong critical response, viewers are forced to decide where the responsibility lies for the death of Máire Ní Chathasaigh and her child. The play was ground-breaking in 1964, and its radical message, particularly its depiction of family relations and of the workings of a mother and babies home where the young women labour in a laundry as adoption arrangements are made for their infants, is still potent. A similar approach is adopted in *Breithiúnas* which scrutinizes the life of an ageing public figure, whose rise to prominence was based on a false narrative of heroism during the war of independence and on the support of women whose own lives were compromised and limited by his powers of manipulation and self-aggrandizement.

The challenging tone of both of these plays is echoed in the work of later Irish-language playwrights and especially in plays that examine the role of women within the family and in Irish society. The central character in the play *Cití* (1975)[72] by Siobhán Ní Shúilleabháin (1928–2013), for example, is a young wife and mother of two who feels trapped in the small Gaeltacht community where she was brought up. Married to Jonathan, an Englishman who came to the region for a film shoot, Cití dreams of escape to London as she can only see death and decay where her husband sees potential for happiness and entrepreneurial success. Effective use is made of choruses to represent the social values with which she must grapple, but ultimately her conflict with Jonathan is unresolved and the play finishes, as it opens, with an image of Cití and her children poised for flight. There are several grounds for comparison between this play, which was first produced as a radio play on Radio Éireann in 1975, and *Dún na mBan Trí Thine* (1997)[73] by Éilís Ní Dhuibhne (1954–), first produced by Amharclann de hÍde in the Peacock stage of the Abbey Theatre in 1994. A sense of incarceration and a debilitating lack of self-esteem mar the life of Leiní, the married woman and mother of two who is the central character in this play. Like Cití, Leiní gives voice to her frustrations and her desires for self-fulfilment, and Ní Dhuibhne draws very self-consciously on a range of folk legends – including legends of fairy abduction, mermaids and transformation – to explore socially induced psychological distress. Ní Dhuibhne's trilingual play *Milseog an tSamhraidh* (1997)[74], first produced by Amharclann de hÍde in the Samuel Beckett Theatre in Trinity College Dublin, is an engaging historical drama, with a range of strong women characters. Set in the time of the Great Famine, it anachronistically presents Irish famine refugees being taken in to the house of the famous 'Ladies of Llangollen', Eleanor Butler and Sarah Ponsonby. Food imagery is employed throughout to explore themes of hunger, sexual desire and the search for fulfilment in another land.

Celia de Fréine (1948–) has written eight Irish-language play scripts,[75] three of which are based on the themes of the classic eighteenth-century poem by Brian Merriman, *Cúirt an Mheán Oíche*, but not all of these have been produced. Typical of her work for the stage is *Anraith Neantóige*, published in *Mná Dána: dornán drámaí* (2009), produced at the Dublin Theatre Festival Fringe in 2004 by Belfast-based theatre company Aisling Ghéar. Set in a stark and desolate environment, the play explores the role of women and the limited potential for human communication in circumstances of perpetual warfare.

It is remarkable, in light of the slow beginnings discussed above, that it is as poets that Irish-language women writers are best known today. It is even more remarkable when one considers the relatively small output of the two most important female poets to emerge in the 1950s and 1960s, Máire Mhac an tSaoi and Caitlín Maude. Máire Mhac an tSaoi (1922–) is unquestionably the most influential woman poet in Irish of the post-Independence generation.[76] Her first collection, *Margadh na Saoire* (1956), a slim volume which consisted of work produced over a twenty-year period, was a ground-breaking collection. It established Mhac an tSaoi as a master of the dramatic love lyric and it demonstrated her strongly held belief in the creative potential of Gaeltacht idiom and traditional metrical forms. Use of material from the Ulster and the Fenian Cycle in this collection – and in particular the interest in powerful female figures such as Deirdre and Gráinne – was to pave the way for a consistent strand of revisionist myth-making in women's poetry in Irish in the 1980s and 1990s.[77] The best-known poem in the collection, 'Ceathrúintí Mháire Ní Ógáin',[78] adopts the mask of tradition to explore the psychological state of a young woman trapped in a transgressive and ill-fated love affair. In this poem, the narrative voice of Máire Ní Ógáin (the female fool of Irish folk tradition) and the form of late Mediaeval love poetry (the courtly Dánta Grádha which were concerned with unrequited love and unrealized passion), are cleverly employed to express female sexual desire and frustration. A marked feature of the poem – and of much of Mhac an tSaoi's later work – is the use of the female body itself as a metaphor for troubling and intense emotional and moral states.[79] Personal and family relationships become central concerns in her later collections, *Codladh an Ghaiscígh* (1973), *An Galar Dubhach* (1980), *An cion go dtí seo* (1987) and *Shoa agus dánta eile* (1999).[80] While many of these poems are conventional expressions of tenderness and domestic and parental responsibility, the complex emotions elicited by different models of motherhood (adoptive motherhood, the relationship between mother and stepdaughters, for example) are also explored in the later volumes, and the field thus opened for more sustained discussion of the complexities of parenting, as well as issues such as miscarriage, stillbirth and childlessness in the work of younger poets like Nuala Ní Dhomhnaill, Biddy Jenkinson, Deirdre Brennan and Bríd Ní Mhóráin.

It is not surprising that politics would feature in the work of a poet raised in a family closely involved both in the Irish revolution and the subsequent nation-building project.[81] Irish politics is approached through a very personal lens in the poems 'Cam Reilige 1916–1966'[82] and 'Fód an Imris',[83] the latter addressed directly to her politician father, Seán Mac Entee. In both poems, the legacy of the revolutionary generation is presented as a conflicted one, and in 'Fód an Imris' in particular it is acknowledged that belief systems and ideals can never be transmitted unproblematically from one generation to another. In light of her experience abroad in the diplomatic service and her sojourns in Africa, London and the United States after her marriage to Conor Cruise O'Brien in 1962, it is not surprising that references to international affairs and conflicts feature regularly in her poetry. Her responses are never simplistic, but instead range from the general to the highly specific and personal. The short poem 'An fuath' (1967),[84] for example, though written for an anti-Vietnam war event in New York, is characteristically ambivalent, acknowledging how non-combatants are implicated in and compromised by the violence of war. Arguably her most compelling comment on international politics is the emotionally charged reflection on human capacity for brutality and abjection, 'Shoa',[85] written in response to a visit to a Holocaust memorial in Vienna in 1988.

Máire Mhac an tSaoi's poetry from the early 1960s onwards could be compared to that of her younger contemporary Caitlín Maude (1941–82), a native of the Connemara Gaeltacht who settled in Dublin where she worked as a teacher and was well-known as a *sean-nós* singer, actor, civil rights activist and writer until her untimely death from cancer in 1982.[86] Poems by Maude appeared in Irish-language and poetry journals from 1963, and were published in a posthumous collection *Caitlín Maude: dánta* (edited by Ciarán Ó Coigligh 1984). Maude can be heard reciting some of the poems on the album *Caitlín* issued by Gael Linn in 1975, where the influence of the rhythms and soundscape of the oral and song tradition is palpable. Maude's is a poetry of intense passion and tenderness, driven by a zest for life and a political idealism whose expression is tempered by a melancholic undertow. Her love poetry is marked by strong physical imagery such as the image of immersion in the love poem 'Aimhréidh'.[87] Like Mhac an tSaoi, she addressed the issue of responsibility for the Vietnam war obliquely in 'Amhrán Grá Vietnam',[88] through the eyes of lovers who can see 'an seabhac ag guairdeall san aer / ag feitheamh le boladh an bháis' ('the hawk hovering in the sky / waiting for the smell of death') but who refuse to bear the burden of guilt for the slaughter, choosing instead the life-enhancing responses of love and laughter.

The period 1980 to 2013 has seen an unprecedented flowering of creativity among women poets in Irish. Major poets like Nuala Ní Dhomhnaill (1952–) and Biddy Jenkinson (1949–) published their first collections in the 1980s and a host of other women poets also emerged as fresh new voices throughout the final decades of the twentieth century. Translation and opportunities for dual-language publication have made certain poets more visible than others, and the work of women poets in Irish has benefited from the more linguistically inclusive approach of feminist presses, women's studies initiatives, and critical feminist revisionist and publication projects.[89] The encouragement of Irish-language publishers, especially Pádraig Ó Snodaigh of Coiscéim, also needs to be acknowledged, as does the feminist turn in Irish-language scholarship.[90] Certain commonalities can be discerned in women's poetry of the period: the conscious reworking from a modern female perspective of material from the literary and oral traditions; a willingness to explore the more traumatic aspects of women's lives; interest in women's social roles both historical and contemporary; ecological awareness and an ethics of care that is both social and environmental; and concern for human rights and for the victims of terror and violence, whether in the home, in institutions or due to political conflict and war.

Nuala Ní Dhomhnaill is undoubtedly the best-known and critically acclaimed female poet in Irish in recent decades. From the publication of her first collections, *An Dealg Draighin* (1981) and *Féar Suaithinseach* (1986), she was recognized as a fresh and distinctive voice, who would exploit rich seams of traditional narrative and imagery in a sustained exploration of issues of identity, alienation and attachment that was consciously female and often overtly feminist.[91] Ní Dhomhnaill's project was informed by a deeply felt belief in the power of the Irish language as a personal creative resource for the exploration of the self and for the release of repressed female voices and experiences.[92] After her return from Turkey, where she spent the early years of her married life, she immersed herself in the oral tradition of the West Kerry Gaeltacht, and mined the folklore of the region for insights that would complement her avid interest in dream images and in Jungian psychology. Referring to the poem 'An Mhaighdean Mhara' from her first collection, she informed folklorist Bo Almqvist in a 1986 interview that the speaker in the poem is 'an mhaighdean mhara go bhfuil a fhios aici na scéalta mar gheall ar na maighdeanacha mara' ('the mermaid who knows the stories about the mermaids'),[93] a remark that could apply to the first-person narrative voice in all those poems that self-consciously draw on imagery from oral legend. Her revisionist myth-making, more overtly feminist than Mhac an tSaoi's, is informed by an interest in Jungian theories of the unconscious,[94] and her exploration of emotional and psychological pain is never simplistic. Her major themes are displacement, alienation, abjection and depression, especially as they affect the lives of women in our own time. Psychological states may be communicated through images of the otherworldly woman ('bean an leasa' or 'an mhaighdean mhara' / 'an mhurúch'), or through a drama of sexual encounter that links the human need for equilibrium with the cosmic, as in the poem sequence 'Feis' from the collection *Feis* (1991),[95] which draws on imagery associated with the winter solstice at Newgrange. Anxieties about mortality are seldom resolved in Ní Dhomhnaill's work, and from poems like 'Gaineamh Shúraic' in *Féar Suaithinseach*,[96] to 'Dún' in *Feis*,[97] to 'Mo Mháistir Dorcha' in *Cead Aighnis*,[98] the transformative power of love and sexual harmony is always only temporary or partial. Ní Dhomhnaill's poetry has been translated into English by a host of fellow-poets – most notably Michael Hartnett, Paul Muldoon and Medbh McGuckian – and her own openness to translation and her collaboration in dual-language publications has meant that her work has reached a very wide audience, making her the most prominent Irish-language poet nationally and internationally.

The reputation of Ní Dhomhnaill's contemporary, the pseudonymous Biddy Jenkinson, has taken a rather different trajectory, mainly due to her playfully defiant authorial stance. She is best known as a poet – having published eight volumes from her debut collection *Baisteadh*

Gintlí (1986) to *Táinrith* (2013) – though she has also published three collections of short stories, as noted above, as well as plays and stories for children. She rejects autobiographical explication of her work, employing a pseudonym not so much as a mask to disguise her personal identity but as a demonstration of her belief in the freedom of the poet to adopt any subject position she chooses. She is reluctant to have her poems translated into English, particularly in Ireland, and she resists being defined as a female or a feminist poet or writer.[99] Nevertheless, her poetry has been subjected to a range of feminist readings, and has been compared to Ní Dhomhnaill's work in its reclamation of powerful female figures from Irish myth and history. Her concerns are often ecological, and while traces of pantheism or images of the earth goddess may meld with Christian symbolism in many of the poems, the ethical position of the human subject is always underpinned by a scientific understanding of biological connectedness. Where other women writers often re-work traditional female images in a manner that exposes patriarchal power structures and ideology, Jenkinson is more often energized by those images and often uses them playfully to challenge and subvert readers' expectations. Though Máire Mhac an tSaoi's characterization of Jenkinson's work as an example of 'imaistriú anama' ('a transmigration of souls')[100] was exaggerated, her recognition that Jenkinson was writing as if the tradition to which she belonged had never been fully ruptured or displaced is apposite. There is a palpable sense throughout her work that the Irish tradition is there to be reclaimed for all, and an assumption that readers will join her in the adventure of discovering and recovering buried strands of that tradition. For example, in the figure of the wild woman of Irish tradition Mis, heroine of the legend 'Mis agus Dubh Rois',[101] Jenkinson re-presents a mythic female character in a manner that allows her to explore the relationship between the natural and the cultural, between sexuality and society, between animal appetite and human desire for comfort and companionship. Her first series of 'Mis' poems, published in the collection *Dán na hUidhre* (1991) included poems that transposed this wild woman to a contemporary urban context, where we see her at the butcher's counter in Superquinn waiting for the leftover bones ('XXX'),[102] or anxiously waiting for her lover at the gates of Trinity College ('Mis ag Geataí na Tríonóide'),[103] or navigating a coastal landscape as far as the traffic lights at Merrion ('Mis ag Caoineadh Dubh Rois').[104] This 'urban' context is absent, however, from the long poem sequence *Mis* (2001), which is, in effect, a first-person retelling of the original tale that modernizes it and attunes it to contemporary concerns about psychological healing, and about the need for equilibrium between animal and human, between the natural and the cultural environment. Natural forces as represented in the landscape are ever-present in Jenkinson's poetry, and an understanding of the empowering potential for women of the Irish sovereignty goddess tradition has been identified by critic Máire Ní Annracháin as a central insight in her work.[105] The physical landscape, both historical and contemporary, animates her re-telling of sixteenth-century Irish history in the dramatic poem 'Gleann Maoiliúra' from the collection *Dán na hUidhre*,[106] where the story of Róis Ní Thuathail, second wife of Fiachaidh McHugh O'Byrne, is related through the consciousness of a contemporary poet visiting the scene ('ag reic dánta le taibhsí'), through the voice of the historical Róis (alert and anxious stepmother and wife), and through the minds of those who survived the battle of Glenmalure and, later, the bloody death of Fiachaidh.

A full discussion of Irish-language poetry from the 1980s onwards would have to acknowledge the sustained engagement with the realities of women's lives throughout the life cycle in the work of bilingual poets Eithne Strong (1923–99)[107] and Deirdre Brennan (1934–),[108] the raw self-scrutiny in the work of Máire Áine Nic Ghearailt (1946–2014)[109] and the combination of razor-sharp intellect and tenderness in the nature poems and love lyrics of Rita Kelly (1953–).[110] Poetry has proven a powerful medium in which to address both controversial issues, such as child sexual abuse, which was the subject of poem sequences by Áine Ní Ghlinn (1955–)[111] and Doireann Ní Ghríofa (1981–),[112] and taboo subjects, such as the pain of infertility, discussed with great courage and honesty by Bríd Ní Mhóráin (1951–).[113] Outstanding individual collections include Celia de Fréine's unforgettable *Fiacha Fola* (2004),[114] where her characteristic surreal lyricism becomes an ideal mode of expression to expose the horrors of the hepatitis C scandal. No longer suffering from a lack of antecedents, there has been a recent flowering of poetry by women writing bilingually or in Irish only, and the work of the most accomplished younger poets such as Dairena Ní Chinnéide (1969–), Colette Nic Aodha (1967–), Ceaití Ní Bheildiúin (1978–), Aifric Mac Aodha (1979–), Caitríona Ní Chléirchín (1978–), Doireann Ní Ghríofa, and Ailbhe Ní Ghearbhuigh (1984–) covers a wide range of material, including love and friendship, the ties of place and kinship, travel and migration and the challenges faced by women in their personal and work lives. Following in the footsteps of Mhac an tSaoi, Ní Dhomhnaill and Jenkinson, younger women poets continue to draw from the Irish literary and folk tradition, while also engaging regularly with international and global issues.

Looking back at over a hundred years of creative activity, it is clear that women's writing in Irish has come a long way from the pioneering efforts of early twentieth-century language revivalists and cultural nationalists. Not only have women broken new ground in all the main literary genres, but many women have excelled in more than one literary field. Other issues of relevance to the discussion, such as women's involvement in Irish-language editing and publishing roles, in writing for young readers and for adult learners, in educational publication, in book promotion and literacy initiatives in general, should also be acknowledged, as should women's roles as literary translators and collaborators in dual-language publication endeavours. The critical reception of new women's writing has been enhanced by the work of several generations of literary scholars and critics who have revised the canon, and rewritten literary history to include consideration of both the recorded and the occluded voices of women. The most salient aspects of recent women's writing in Irish are the honesty with which many intimate and traumatic aspects of women's lives are approached, and the renewed energy with which writers are engaging with Irish cultural and literary history. Though the context has changed utterly since the time of Úna Ní Fhaircheallaigh and Máire Ní Chinnéide, what remains constant is a belief in the language itself as a potent medium of self-expression and as a key to an archive that continues to be a rich source of inspiration for Irish women writers.

Notes

1 Anna Heussaff and Éilis Ní Anluain 'Scríbhneoirí na Gaeilge – cé mhéad acu atá ann, agus cad atá á scríobh acu?', *Tuairisc.ie* 1 November 2016, accessed 12 April 2017, http://tuairisc.ie/scribhneoiri-na-gaeilge-ce-mhead-acu-ata-ann-agus-cad-ata-a-scriobh-acu/

2 A few versions of 'Caoineadh Airt Uí Laoghaire' appeared in *Irisleabhar na Gaedhilge, An Gaodhal* and *An Claidheamh Soluis* at the turn of the twentieth century; however, Shán Ó Cuív was the first to publish this lament in book format. See Eileen O'Connell, *Caoineadh Airt Uí Laoghaire*, ed. Shán Ó Cuív (Baile Átha Cliath: Brún agus Ó Nóláin, 1923). Likewise, though a number of Máire Bhuí Ní Laoghaire's songs were published in the early twentieth century, the earliest substantial collection of her work was in Donncha Ó Donnchú, ed., *Filíocht Mháire Bhuidhe Ní Laoghaire* (Baile Átha Cliath: Oifig Díolta Foillseacháin Rialtais, 1931). See Tríona Ní Shíocháin, *Bláth 's Craobh na nÚdar: Amhráin Mháire Bhuí* (Baile Átha Cliath: Coiscéim, 2012).

3 Máire Ní Shéaghdha, *Laethanta Geala: Cailín Scoile i gCiarraighe Do Scríobh* (Baile Átha Cliath: Muinntir Fheallamhain, 1917); Brighid Stac,

Mí dem' Shaoghal (Baile Átha Cliath: Muinntir Fallamhain, 1918); Máire Ní Shéaghdha and Brighid Ní Shíothcháin, *Laethanta Geala: Cunntasaí Cinn Lae do Scríobh Beirt Chailín Sgoile* (Baile Átha Cliath: Brún agus Ó Nóláin, 1922).

4 These were not the only Irish-speaking girls to write diaries: Eibhlín Ní Shúilleabháin (1900–49), sister of Muiris Ó Súilleabháin, also kept a diary from May to November 1923; this was only published, however, in 2000. See Eibhlín Ní Shúilleabháin, *Cín Lae Eibhlín Ní Shúilleabháin*, ed. Máiréad Ní Loingsigh (Baile Átha Cliath: Coiscéim, 2000).

5 Kenneth Jackson, *Scéalta ón mBlascaod / Kenneth Jackson do scríobh ó bhéal Pheig Sayers* (Baile Átha Cliath: ar n-a fhoillsiú ar son an Chumainn le Béaloideas Éireann ag Comhlucht Oideachais na hÉireann, Teor, 1934).

6 It was Sayers's son, Micheál Ó Gaoithín, who transcribed *Machtnamh Seanamhná* (Baile Átha Cliath: Oifig an tSoláthair, 1939). See www.ainm.ie/Bio.aspx?ID=738.

7 See Patricia Coughlan, 'An Léiriú ar Shaol na mBan i dTéacsanna Dírbheathaisnéise Pheig Sayers', in *Ceiliúradh an Bhlascaoid 3: Peig Sayers Scéalaí 1873–1958*, ed. Máire Ní Chéilleachair (Baile Átha Cliath: Coiscéim, 1999), 20–57; Patricia Coughlan, 'Rereading Peig Sayers: Women's Autobiography, Social History and Narrative Art', *Opening the Field: Irish Women, Texts and Contexts*, ed. Patricia Boyle Haberstroh and Christine St. Peter (Cork: Cork University Press, 2007), 58–73.

8 Coughlan, 'An Léiriú ar Shaol na mBan i dTéacsanna Dírbheathaisnéise Pheig Sayers'.

9 Nóra Ní Shéaghdha, *An Bhlascaod Trí Fhuinneog na Scoile*, ed. Pádraig Ó Héalaí (An Daingean: An Sagart, 2015), 4. See L. O'B., 'Review', *The Irish Monthly*, 73, no. 870 (1945): 539–40.

10 Érin Ní Eaghra, 'Úna Bean Uí Dhiosca: Síochánaí na Réabhlóide', *Comhar* (August 2011): 3.

11 See Úna Bean Uí Dhiosca, *Cailín na Gruaige Duinne* (Baile Átha Cliath: Oifig Díolta Foillseacháin Rialtais, 1932), 23–4.

12 Éilís Ní Dhuibhne, 'Na Deartháireacha Grimm agus Sinne: Tionchar Scéalta na nDeartháireacha Grimm ar Bhéaloideas na hÉireann agus ar Litríocht na nÓg', in *Laethanta Gréine & Oícheanta Sí: Aistí ar Litríocht agus ar Chultúr na nÓg*, ed. Caoimhe Nic Lochlainn and Ríona Nic Congáil (Baile Átha Cliath: LeabhairCOMHAR, 2013), 49.

13 Norma Borthwick (1862–1934), along with Máiréad Ní Raghallaigh (ca. 1867–1945), established an Irish-language printing house, 'Muintir na Leabhar Gaeilge', in 1900. Although best-known for publishing Peadar Ua Laoghaire's *Séadna* (1904), this was also the publisher of Máire Ní Chinnéide's first children's play, *Gleann na Sidheóg* (1905).

14 Katherine O'Brien (Mrs Cruise O'Brien), *Na Trí Muca: Sgéalta Greannmhara i gCóir na bPáistí* (Baile Átha Cliath: Brún agus Ó Nóláin, 1925). Katherine (Cruise) O'Brien is known variously as Kathleen and Katharine in different sources.

15 Seosaimhín Bean Mhic Néill, trans., *Finnsgéalta ó India* (Baile Átha Cliath: Comhlucht Oideachais na h-Éireann, 1933).

16 Lydia Groszewski, 'An Margadh Léitheoireachta i gCás Aistriúchán Gaeilge do Leanaí', and Pádraig de Paor, 'Gnéithe de Théama na hAibíochta i Litríocht do Dhaoine Óga sa Ghaeilge', in *Codladh Céad Bliain: Cnuasach Aistí ar Litríocht na nÓg*, ed. Ríona Nic Congáil (Baile Átha Cliath: LeabhairCOMHAR, 2012), 109–125, 151–171.

17 See www.ainm.ie/Bio.aspx?ID=1911.

18 Caoimhe Nic Lochlainn, 'Asal Fhear na Mónadh: Aistriúchán Mhaighréad Nic Mhaicín ar Shaothar Patricia Lynch', in *Laethanta Gréine & Oícheanta Sí*, ed. Nic Lochlainn and Nic Congáil, 69–93; Máirtín Coilféir, 'Tsechobh, Túrgénebh, agus Púiscín na Gaeilge: Nótaí ar Mhaighréad Nic Mhaicín, Aistritheoir', *Comhar* (September 2016): 14–19.

19 Máire Ní Chinnéide, 'Nuadh-Litridheacht na nGaodhal agus Cionnus is fearr í chur chum cinn,' *Irisleabhar na Gaedhilge* (February 1909), 77.

20 Máire Ní Chinnéide, *Gleann na Sidheóg* (Baile Átha Cliath: Muintir na Leabhar Gaedhilge, 1905); *Sidheoga na mBláth* (Baile Átha Cliath: Connradh na Gaedhilge, 1909).

21 Máire Ní Chinnéide, *An Dúthchas, dráma aonghnímh* (Baile Átha Cliath: Conradh na Gaeilge, 1908).

22 Máire Ní Shíthe and Eilís Ní Mhurchadha, *Beart nótaí: dráma suilt* (Baile Átha Cliath: M. H. Gill agus a Mhac, 1904). This was not the first play to be written by Ní Shíthe but it was the first of her plays to be published. See www.ainm.ie/Bio.aspx?ID=544. Ní Mhurchadha did not continue to compose plays and there is no further information available about her.

23 Máire Ní Chillín, 'Mairghréad. A topical play for national teachers in two scenes', in *Sinn Féin*, 17 February–30 March 1912.

24 See www.ainm.ie/Bio.aspx?ID=0699.

25 *An Claidheamh Soluis*, 21 August 1909. See www.ainm.ie/Bio .aspx?ID=733.

26 Úna Bean Uí Dhiosca, *Cruadh-chás na mBaitsiléirí, nó, Is éiginteach do dhuine agaibh pósadh* (Baile Átha Cliath: Oifig Díolta Foillseacháin Rialtais, 1931). See www.irishplayography.com/play.aspx?playid=3594.

27 Máiréad Ní Ghráda, *An Udhacht* (Baile Átha Cliath: Oifig Díolta Foillseacháin Rialtais, 1935). See www.irishplayography.com/play .aspx?playid=2902.

28 www.ainm.ie/Bio.aspx?ID=76.

29 Proinnsias E. Ó Súilleabháin, ed., *Láimh-Leabhar Drámaidheachta* (Baile Átha Cliath: Brún agus Ó Nualláin, 1938).

30 Máire Ní Ghallchobhair and Máire Bean Uí Mhaolmhaoidh, *Bhfuil leip-reacháin ann?* (Baile Atha Cliath: Tom, 1934); *Geallamhain an tsamhaircín* (Baile Átha Cliath: Tom, 1934).

31 See www.irishplayography.com/play.aspx?playid=3511. Máire Ní Chinnéide, *Scéal an Tighe* (Baile Átha Cliath: Oifig an tSoláthair, 1952).

32 Siobhán Kirwan-Keane, 'Sinéad de Valera agus Drámaíocht Ghaelach na nÓg', in *Codladh Céad Bliain*, ed. Nic Congáil.

33 Ní Chnáimhín also published the first book of criticism on Pádraic Ó Conaire. See Áine Ní Chnáimhín, *Pádraic Ó Conaire* (Baile Átha Cliath: Oifig an tSoláthair, 1947).

34 M. H. Gaffney, *Díthreabhach an tobair; Breacadh an lae; Bréag-riocht Apollo agus cúiteamh .i. Dhá dhráma i gcóir na ngasóg;* and *Róis dhearga agus buadhann Críost*, trans. Áine Ní Fhoghladha. These translations were all published by Oifig an tSoláthair (An Gúm) in 1934.

35 Agnes O'Farrelly [Úna Ní Fhaircheallaigh], *Out of the Depths* (Dublin: Talbot Press, 1921), 7.

36 Áine Bean Uí Néill, *Idir na Fleadhanna* (Baile Átha Cliath: An Gaedheal-Comhlucht, 1922). See Proinsias Ó Drisceoil, '"Eolus na Céirde:" Filíocht Áine Ní Fhoghludha', *An Linn Bhuí: Iris Ghaeltacht na nDéise*, 12 (2008): 101.

37 Síle Ní Chéileachair and Donncha Ó Céileachair, *Bullaí Mhártain* (Baile Átha Cliath: Sáirséal agus Dill, 1955).

38 Seminal publications include Máire Ní Annracháin, '"Ait liom bean a bheith ina file"', *Na Mná sa Litríocht: Léachtaí Cholm Cille* 12 (1982): 145–82; Máirín Nic Eoin, 'Léiriú na mBan sna Leabhair' in *Leath na Spéire*, ed. Eoghan Ó hAnluain (Baile Átha Cliath: An Clóchomhar, 1992), 13–41; Máirín Nic Eoin, 'Gender's Agendas', *Graph* 12 (Summer / Autumn 1992): 5–8; Bríona Nic Dhiarmada, 'An Bhean is an Bhaineann: Gnéithe den Chritic Fheimineach', in *Téacs agus Comhthéacs: gnéithe de chritic na Gaeilge*, ed. Máire Ní Annracháin and Bríona Nic Dhiarmada (Corcaigh: Cló Ollscoile Chorcaí, 1998), 152–82. Hugely influential also were a series of articles by Angela Bourke on issues relating to female oral composition and performance: 'The Irish Traditional Lament and the Grieving Process', *Women's Studies International Forum* 11, no. 4 (1988): 287–91; 'Working and Weeping: Women's Oral Poetry in Irish and Scottish Gaelic', *UCD Women's Studies Forum Working Papers* No. 7 (1988a); 'Performing – Not Writing', *Graph* 11 (1991): 28–31; 'Caoineadh na Marbh: Síceoilfhilíocht', *Oghma* 4 (1992): 3–12; 'More in Anger than in Sorrow: Irish Women's Lament Poetry', in *Feminist Messages: Coding in Women's Folk Culture*, ed. J. Radner (Urbana: University of Illinois Press, 1993), 160–82.

39 See Siobhán Ní Fhoghlú, 'Col ag Mná le Próschruthú i nGaeilge', *Comhar* (August 1991): 4–5; Aisling Ní Dhonnchadha, 'An Grá agus an Ghruaim: Téama an Chaidrimh i nGearrscéalaíocht Ghaeilge na Seachtóidí', *Irisleabhar Mhá Nuad* (1997), 46; Máirín Nic Eoin, 'Léiriú na mBan sna Leabhair', 35; Aisling Ní Dhonnchadha, *Idir Dhúchas agus Dualgas: Staidéar ar Charachtair Mhná sa Ghearrscéal Gaeilge 1940–1990* (Baile Átha Cliath: An Clóchomhar, 2002), 311–13.

40 Úna Ní Mhaoileoin, *Le grá ó Úna* (Baile Átha Cliath: Sáirséal agus Dill, 1958).

41 Úna Ní Mhaoileoin, *An Maith Leat Spaigití?* (Baile Átha Cliath: Sáirséal agus Dill, 1965).

42 Úna Ní Mhaoileoin, *Turas go Túinis* (Baile Átha Cliath: Sáirséal agus Dill, 1969).

43 Nellie Nic Giolla Bhríde, *Mise agus na Maighigh* (Baile Átha Cliath: Coiscéim, 2003).

44 Dóirín Mhic Mhurchú, *Bealach na Bó Finne* (Baile Átha Cliath: Coiscéim, 1994).

45 Máire Ní Ghaoithín, *An tOileán a Bhí* (Baile Átha Cliath: An Clóchomhar, 1978).

46 Máire Ní Ghuithín, *Bean an Oileáin* (Baile Átha Cliath: Coiscéim, 1986).

47 Pádraig Ua Cnáimhsí, *Róise Rua* (Baile Átha Cliath: Sáirséal Ó Marcaigh, 1988). For an interesting discussion on the question of the authorship of this text, see Breandán Ó Conaire, 'Nótaí ar Fhaisnéis Bheatha as Árainn Mhór', *Studia Hibernica* 31 (2001): 147–68.

48 An tSiúr de Lourdes, *Thar Balla Isteach* (Má Nuad: An Sagart, 1982).

49 Eibhlín Uí Bheaglaoich, *Carraig a' Dúin* (Baile Átha Cliath: Coiscéim, 1989).

50 Áine and Eibhlín Nic Giolla Easpaig, *Girseacha i nGéibheann* (Cathair na Mart: FNT, 1986).

51 For examples of both approaches, see Diarmuid Ó Gráinne, ed., *Mo Scéal Féin: Máire Phatch Mhóir Uí Churraoin* (Baile Átha Cliath: Coiscéim, 1995); Cáit Ní Mhainnín, *Cuimhní Cinn Cháit Ní Mhainnín* (Indreabhán: Cló Iar-Chonnachta, 2000).

52 Éilís Ní Dhuibhne, *Cailíní Beaga Ghleann na mBláth* (Baile Átha Cliath: Cois Life, 2003).

53 Éilís Ní Dhuibhne, *The Dancers Dancing* (Belfast: Blackstaff Press, 2000).

54 For example, Brian Ó Conchubhair, 'Éilís Ní Dhuibhne: Is Minic Ciúin Athchruthaithe', in *Éilís Ní Dhuibhne: Perspectives*, ed. Rebecca Pelan (Galway: Arlen House, 2009), 171–96.

55 Orna Ní Choileáin, *Canary Wharf* (Baile Átha Cliath: Coiscéim, 2009).

56 Orna Ní Choileáin, *Sciorrann an tAm* (Baile Átha Cliath: Coiscéim, 2014).

57 Éilís Ní Anluain, *Filleann Seoirse* (Indreabhán: Leabhar Breac, 2011).

58 Déirdre Ní Ghrianna, *An Gnáthrud* (Baile Átha Cliath: Coiscéim, 1999).

59 Réaltán Ní Leannáin, *Dílis* (Indreabhán: Cló Iar-Chonnacht, 2015).

60 Éilís Ní Dhuibhne, *Dúnmharú sa Daingean* (Baile Átha Cliath: Cois Life, 2000).

61 Éilís Ní Dhuibhne, *Dún an Airgid* (Baile Átha Cliath: Cois Life, 2008).

62 Anna Heussaff, *Bás Tobann* (Baile Átha Cliath: Cois Life, 2004).

63 Anna Heussaff, *Buille Marfach* (Indreabhán: Cló Iar-Chonnacht, 2010).

64 Anna Heussaff, *Scáil an Phríosúin* (Indreabhán: Cló Iar-Chonnacht, 2015).

65 Biddy Jenkinson, *An Grá Riabhach* (Baile Átha Cliath: Coiscéim, 1999).

66 Biddy Jenkinson, *An tAthair Pádraig Ó Duinnín – Bleachtaire* (Baile Átha Cliath: Coiscéim, 2008); *Duinnín Bleachtaire ar an Sceilg* (Baile Átha Cliath: Coiscéim, 2011).

67 Máire Mhac an tSaoi, *A Bhean Óg Ón ...* (Indreabhán: Cló Iar-Chonnachta, 2001).

68 Máire Mhac an tSaoi, *Cérbh í Meg Russell?* (Gaillimh: Leabhar Breac / Ionad an Léinn Éireannaigh, Ollscoil na hÉireann, Gaillimh).

69 Máire Mhac an tSaoi, *Scéal Ghearóid Iarla* (Indreabhán: Leabhar Breac, 2011).

70 For a full listing of Ní Ghráda's publications, see Siobhán Ní Bhrádaigh, *Máiréad Ní Ghráda: Ceannródaí Drámaíochta* (Indreabhán: Cló Iar-Chonnachta, 1996), 77–84. For first production details, see www.irishplayography.com. For biography, see Diarmuid Breathnach and Máire Ní Mhurchú 'Máiréad Ní Ghráda (1896–1971)': www.ainm.ie/Bio.aspx?ID=76; and www.irishtheatreinstitute.ie.

71 Hugh Hunt, *The Abbey: Ireland's National Theatre 1904–1979* (Dublin: Gill and Macmillan, 1979), 184.

72 Siobhán Ní Shúilleabháin, *Cití* (Baile Átha Cliath: Sáirséal agus Dill, 1975).

73 Éilís Ní Dhuibhne, *Milseog an tSamhraidh & Dún na mBan Trí Thine* (Baile Átha Cliath: Cois Life, 1997), 73–134.

74 Ibid., 1–67.

75 See: www.celiadefreine.com/drama.htm. Six scripts have been published: Celia de Fréine, *Mná Dána: Dornán drámaí (Anraith Neantóige, Cóirín na dTonn, Tearmann)* (Galway: Arlen House, 2009); *Meanmarc / Desire* (Galway: Arlen House, 2012); *Cúirt an Mheán Oíche / The Midnight Court* (Galway: Arlen House, 2012); *Plight / Cruachás* (Galway: Arlen House, 2012).

76 See essays in Louis de Paor, ed., *Míorúilt an Pharóiste: Aistí ar fhilíocht Mháire Mhac an tSaoi* (Indreabhán: Cló Iar-Chonnacht, 2014).

77 For a discussion of this phenomenon, see Máirín Nic Eoin, 'Athscríobh na Miotas: Gné den Idirthéacsúlacht i bhFilíocht Chomhaimseartha na Gaeilge', *Taighde agus Teagasc* Iml. 3 (2002): 223–47.

78 Máire Mhac an tSaoi, 'Ceathrúintí Mháire Ní Ógáin', *Margadh na Saoire* (Baile Átha Cliath: Sáirséal agus Dill, 1956), 60–3.

79 Patricia Coughlan, '"For nothing can be sole or whole / That has not been rent:" Torn motherhood in Máire Mhac an tSaoi's "Love has pitched his mansion ... "', in *Míorúilt an Pharóiste*, ed. de Paor, 41–62.

80 Máire Mhac an tSaoi, *Margadh na Saoire* (Baile Átha Cliath: Sáirséal agus Dill, 1956); *Codladh an Ghaiscígh* (Baile Átha Cliath: Sáirséal agus Dill, 1973); *An Galar Dubhach* (Baile Átha Cliath: Sáirséal agus Dill, 1980); *An cion go dtí seo* (Baile Átha Cliath: Sáirséal Ó Marcaigh, 1987); *Shoa agus dánta eile* (Baile Átha Cliath: Sáirséal Ó Marcaigh, 1999); *An paróiste míorúilteach / The miraculous parish: Rogha dánta / Selected poems*, ed. Louis de Paor (Dublin / Indreabhán: The O'Brien Press / Cló Iar-Chonnacht, 2011).

81 See Máire Cruise O'Brien, *The Same Age as the State* (Dublin: The O'Brien Press, 2003).

82 Máire Mhac an tSaoi, 'Cam Reilige 1916–1966', *Codladh an Ghaiscígh* (Baile Átha Cliath: Sáirséal agus Dill, 1973), 11.

83 Máire Mhac an tSaoi, 'Fód an Imris', *Shoa agus dánta eile* (Baile Átha Cliath: Sáirséal Ó Marcaigh, 1999), 28–9.

84 Máire Mhac an tSaoi, 'An Fuath (1967)', *Codladh an Ghaiscígh* (Baile Átha Cliath: Sáirséal agus Dill, 1973), 14.

85 Máire Mhac an tSaoi, 'Shoa', *Shoa agus dánta eile* (Baile Átha Cliath: Sáirséal Ó Marcaigh, 1999), 23. For a rigorous analysis of this poem, see Mícheál Mac Craith, 'The same age as the state – ach ní mór filíocht chomh maith', in *Míorúilt an Pharóiste*, ed. Louis de Paor, 109–26, especially 114–18.

86 See Diarmuid Breathnach and Máire Ní Mhurchú, 'Caitlín Maude (1941–1982)': www.ainm.ie/Bio.aspx?ID=35

87 Caitlín Maude 'Aimhréidh', *Caitlín Maude: dánta*, ed. Ciarán Ó Coigligh (Baile Átha Cliath: Coiscéim, 1984), 25.

88 Ibid., 45.

89 This was apparent in anthologies such as *Wildish Things: An Anthology of New Irish Women's Writing*, ed. Ailbhe Smyth (Dublin: Attic Press, 1989), and *The White Page / An Bhileog Bhán: Twentieth-Century Irish Women Poets*, ed. Joan McBreen (Galway: Salmon Poetry, 1999), but particularly in the collaborative project that resulted in the publication of *The Field Day Anthology of Irish Writing Vols. IV & V: Women's Writing and Traditions*, ed. Angela Bourke et al. (Cork: Cork University Press, 2002).

90 See note 38.

91 An important early acknowledgement was Seán Ó Tuama, 'Filíocht Nuala Ní Dhomhnaill: "An Mháthair Ghrámhar is an Mháthair Ghránna" ina cuid filíochta', *An Nuafhilíocht: Léachtaí Cholm Cille* 17 (1986): 95–118. Since then her work has received more critical attention than that of any other contemporary Irish-language poet.

92 Nuala Ní Dhomhnaill, 'Filíocht á Cumadh: Ceardlann Filíochta', *An Nuafhilíocht: Léachtaí Cholm Cille* 17 (1986): 147–79, especially 167–8; 'An Ghaeilge mar Uirlis Fheimineach', in *Unfinished Revolutions: Essays on the Irish Women's Movement*, ed. Mary Nelis (Belfast: Meadbh Publishing, 1989), 22–7; 'Why I Choose to Write in Irish, the Corpse That Sits Up and Talks Back', in *Selected Essays*, ed. Oona Frawley (Dublin: New Island, 2005), 10–24. The influence of her immersion in Turkish culture on her decision to write in Irish is discussed in the essay 'Seal sa Domhan Thoir: Sojourn in the Eastern World', also in *Selected Essays*, 185–201.

93 In Bo Almqvist, 'Of Mermaids and Marriages: Seamus Heaney's "Maighdean Mara" and Nuala Ní Dhomhnaill's "An Mhaighdean Mhara" in the light of folk tradition', *Béaloideas* 58 (1990): 62.

94 The Jungian element in her work was identified from the start by Seán Ó Tuama and has been explored subsequently by many critics writing about Ní Dhomhnaill. See, for example, Bríona Nic Dhiarmada, 'Immram sa tSící: Filíocht Nuala Ní Dhomhnaill agus Próiseas an Indibhidithe', *Oghma* 5 (1993): 78–94; Pádraig de Paor, 'Rún-eolas iarnua-aoiseach an Individithe', in *Tionscnamh Filíochta Nuala Ní Dhomhnaill* (Baile Átha Cliath: An Clóchomhar, 1997), 119–68.

95 Nuala Ní Dhomhnaill, 'Feis' in *Feis* (Maigh Nuad: An Sagart, 1991), 83–109.
96 Nuala Ní Dhomhnaill, 'Gaineamh Shúraic', *Féar Suaithinseach* (Maigh Nuad: An Sagart, 1984), 39.
97 Nuala Ní Dhomhnaill, 'Dún', *Feis* (Maigh Nuad: An Sagart, 1991), 68–9.
98 Nuala Ní Dhomhnaill, 'Mo Mháistir Dorcha', *Cead Aighnis* (An Daingean: An Sagart, 1998), 13–14.
99 For an extensive discussion of Jenkinson's authorial stance, see Caitlín Nic Íomhair, '"Cé hí siúd Biddy Jenkinson?": freagra an fhile ina saothar neamhfhicsin', COMHAR*Taighde* 2 (2016). https://doi.org/10.18669/ct.2016.05
100 Máire Mhac an tSaoi, 'Biddy Jenkinson: sampla d'imaistriú anama?' in *Leath na Spéire*, ed. Eoghan Ó hAnluain (Baile Átha Cliath: An Clóchomhar, 1992), 61–73.
101 Brian Ó Cuív, 'The Romance of Mis and Dubh Ruis', *Celtica* 2, no. 2 (1954): 325–33; Máirín Ní Dhonnchadha, 'The Story of Mis and Dubh Rois (18th Century)' in *The Field Day Anthology of Irish Writing* 4: 238–41; Nuala Ní Dhomhnaill, 'Mis and Dubh Ruis: A Parable of Psychic Transformation' in *Irish Writers and Religion*, ed. Robert Welch (Gerrard Cross, Buckinghamshire: Colin Smythe, 1992), 194–200.
102 Biddy Jenkinson, 'XXX', *Dán na hUidhre* (Baile Átha Cliath: Coiscéim, 1991), 29–31.
103 Ibid., 32–3.
104 Ibid., 26–8.
105 Máire Ní Annracháin, 'Biddy agus an Bandia', in *Saoi na hÉigse: Aistí in Ómós do Sheán Ó Tuama*, ed. Pádraigín Riggs, Breandán Ó Conchúir and Seán Ó Coileáin (Baile Átha Cliath: An Clóchomhar, 2000), 339–57.
106 Biddy Jenkinson, 'Gleann Maoiliúra', *Dán na hUidhre*, 97–108.
107 Eithne Strong, *Cirt Oibre* (Baile Átha Cliath: Coiscéim, 1981); *Fuil agus Fallaí* (Baile Átha Cliath: Coiscéim, 1983); *Aoife faoi Ghlas* (Baile Átha Cliath: Coiscéim, 1990); *An Sagart Pinc* (Baile Átha Cliath: Coiscéim, 1990); *Nobel* (Baile Átha Cliath: Coiscéim, 1998).
108 Deirdre Brennan, *I Reilig na mBan Rialta* (Baile Átha Cliath: Coiscéim, 1984); *Scothanna Geala* (Baile Átha Cliath: Coiscéim, 1989); *Thar Cholbha na Mara* (Baile Átha Cliath: Coiscéim, 1993); *Ag Mealladh Réalta* (Baile Átha Cliath: Coiscéim, 2000); *Swimming with Pelicans / Ag Eitilt Fara Condair* (Galway: Arlen House, 2007); *Hidden Places / Scáthán Eile* (Galway: Arlen House, 2011).
109 Máire Áine Nic Gearailt, *Éiric Uachta* (Baile Átha Cliath: An Clóchomhar, 1971); *Leaca Liombó* (Baile Átha Cliath: Coiscéim, 1990); *Mo chúis bheith beo* (Baile Átha Cliath: Coiscéim, 1991); *Ó Ceileadh an Bhreasaíl* (Baile Átha Cliath: Coiscéim, 1992).
110 Rita Kelly, *Dialann sa Díseart* (Baile Átha Cliath: Coiscéim, 1981); *An Bealach Éadóigh* (Baile Átha Cliath: Coiscéim, 1984); *Fare Well / Beir Beannacht* (Dublin: Attic Press, 1990); *Travelling West* (Galway:

Arlen House, 2000); *Turas go Bun na Spéire: Rogha Dánta is Nua-Dhánta* (Indreabhán: Cló Iar-Chonnachta, 2008).

111 Áine Ní Ghlinn, *Deora nár caoineadh / Unshed tears* (Galway: Arlen House, 1996), 8–49.

112 Doireann Ní Ghríofa, 'Putóga Portaigh', in *Dúlasair* (Baile Átha Cliath: Coiscéim, 2012), 1–21.

113 See especially 'Thíos Seal agus Thuas Seal (Yin agus Yang)' and 'Fé Bhrat Bhríde' in the collection *Fé Bhrat Bhríde* (Baile Átha Cliath: Coiscéim, 2002), 47–8; 81.

114 Celia de Fréine, *Fiacha Fola* (Indreabhán: Cló Iar-Chonnachta, 2004).

CHAPTER 19

Fiction from Northern Ireland, 1921–2015

Caroline Magennis

From partition to the present, female novelists from Northern Ireland have used their fiction to comment on the changing nature of their society. They have employed a range of narrative techniques in their work, from a return to realism to striking postmodernist experimentation. This has been influenced by developments in Irish, British and American fiction but these novels retain a distinctive regional character. Despite women's marginalized role in Northern Irish social and political life, these writers have proven themselves thematic and stylistic innovators. They have developed and presented new representational paradigms for women's experience in Northern Ireland. The remarkable thing about this corpus of novels is the variation of subject matter, setting and political approach of the authors. However, some themes do recur, such as domestic confinement, mental illness, discontented motherhood, the unreliability of memory and distrust of patriarchal institutions. Women's fiction from Northern Ireland has generally been concerned to challenge entrenched ideological positions and inherited patriarchies on both sides of the divide. Their novels powerfully explore the legacy of violence and complicate simple narratives of sectarian conflict with a focus on gender, class and embodiment.

In *The Living Stream*, Edna Longley states that the Ulster Protestant community has 'its cult of male chieftains: Carson, Moses, Paisley the "Big Man"' and that 'the whole country abounds in Ancient Orders of Hibernian Male Bonding: lodges, brotherhoods, priesthoods, hierarchies, sodalities, knights, Fitzwilliam Tennis Club, Field Day Theatre Company'.[1] Vitally, Longley links the entrenchment of cultural, political and religious patriarchal authority, a nexus of influences that many women novelists begin to challenge in their work. Playwright Christina Reid makes a similar point, that 'public faces of Protestant and Catholic paramilitaries are men ... the people who talk about religion and the Church are men. The politicians are men ... Ian Paisley and the Pope are basically in total agreement over what a woman's role in the home should be'.[2] However, the question of challenging these attitudes through fiction-writing without retreating into didacticism is a complex one. Northern Irish women have been writing about a variety of lives since partition, but critics have not always been attentive to this. It is the aim of this chapter to introduce a wide range of novels written by women who were either born in or had strong connection with Northern Ireland, with the hope it will lead the reader to better acquaint themselves with this rich body of work.

From Partition to Civil Rights

In the period following the creation of Northern Ireland in 1921, women's national allegiances are particularly complex and shifting. This is reflected in their fictional responses to the conflicts of the early twentieth century, particularly the First World War, the Easter Rising and the War of Independence. *A Flock of Birds* (1930), by Derry's Kathleen Coyle, focuses on women's suffering during political violence in the aftermath of the Easter Rising. Religious and political beliefs are revealed as fluid, and Catherine's grief for her condemned son is complex, depicted through continual references to the sacrificial body. Belfast novelist and playwright Olga Fielden is best known for her novel *Island Story* (1933), with its 'intriguing generic ambiguity; an ambiguity which in itself makes the work an interesting Irish literary artefact'.[3] A Dundonald Minister's daughter, Agnes Romilly White, wrote the novels, *Gape Row* (1934) and *Mrs Murphy Buries the Hatchet* (1936), which demonstrate a 'sensitive pastoral awareness of poverty and bereavement'[4] but are perhaps less overtly political than other fiction of the period. Olivia Manning was born to an Ulster-Irish mother in Portsmouth in 1908, but travelled with her lecturer husband across Europe and took an active role for the Public Information Office in Jerusalem during the Second World War. *The Wind Changes* (1937) is the first significant work of her thirteen novels and is full of political and sexual intrigue shortly before the end of the War of Independence. Complex allegiances are explored with a careful, ironic touch and an eye for painterly detail. Similar passion is exhibited in Dungannon-educated Margaret Barrington's *My Cousin Justin* (1939). This novel also sets an illicit love-plot against the backdrop of the 1920s, but focuses on the Irish Civil War. The landscape of County Donegal is rendered as harshly beautiful, a contrast to the political world of post-revolution Dublin. Anne Crone was educated in Belfast and chose a Fermanagh setting for her three novels *Bridie Steen* (1948), *This Pleasant Lea* (1951) and *My Heart and I* (1955). Ann Owens Weekes notes that her 'characters are moulded by harsh labour conditions, as well as religious conflict: some few grow as sparse and beautiful as the cotton on the lovely bogs, but the majority shrink like distorted plants'.[5] All of these mid-century novels render the political and personal complexity of Northern Ireland in vivid detail, and all use landscape in metonymically interesting ways. An interesting addition to these Irish-set novels is *Peter Abelard* (1933) from Helen Waddell, one of the first female graduates from Queen's University, Belfast. A translator and Mediaeval scholar, Waddell's work has been reappraised by critics[6] and there was a conference on her work in Belfast in 2012.

The most significant literary voice in this period is Janet McNeill. McNeill was born in Dublin, but eventually married and settled in Northern Ireland. She was involved in the literary culture of Belfast and was prolific in writing novels, plays, short stories and children's books. McNeill's talent is most pronounced in the novels that subtly draw out the ennui behind the net curtains of Protestant life. Owens Weekes describes her portrayal of the middle class: 'No other Irish writer has so clearly and consistently revealed the stark waste and despair beneath the cramped existence of these women.'[7] In flashes, they are profoundly feminist, particularly *The Maiden Dinosaur* (1964), with its discussion of sexual politics and bedroom disappointments, and *The Small Widow* (1967), which portrays a vexed path to independence. The latter's protagonist, Julia, has to renegotiate her place in the world after her husband's death, and McNeill demonstrates a keen eye for the social concerns facing women in this period of early second-wave feminism. McNeill's novels, then, expose an untold story of the period before the Troubles: that sexual and social repression has consequences for women from the community usually perceived as dominant. During these decades, women's fiction drew out the complexities at the heart of the new state: both how women were defined by their domestic and sexual roles but also how they figured the idea of the national.

The Troubles

Following the start of the Troubles in the late 1960s, there has been an array of fictional responses to the conflict by women. This fiction often has a domestic setting and Linden Peach notes that: 'The most obvious point to make about the women who have chosen to write directly or

indirectly about contemporary Northern Ireland is that they are concerned with the impact of the troubles upon people's lives especially
upon the lives of women and children.'[8] Rebecca Pelan states that much
Northern Irish fiction is writing by women from the nationalist community but 'shows very little evidence of an allocation of political responsibility on individuals of the "other" community ... Rather, responsibility
for deprivation is placed firmly on the systems of oppression that keep
both communities in subservience'.[9] While these thematic preoccupations (the domestic and systems of oppression) are present throughout,
Northern Irish novelists deal with violence using a variety of fictional
techniques. Some preferred the use of realism to portray Northern
Irish women's daily experience of living with violence, such as Linda
Anderson's domestic troubles novel *To Stay Alive* (1984), Mary Costello's
autobiographical novel *Titanic Town* (1992) and Joan Lingard's *Sisters by
Rite* (1984). In her influential essay, 'Women and Fiction 1985–1990',
Eve Patten laments the lack of experimentation in novels, citing a 'vested
interest in producing women's writing which is stylistically transparent, reactionary, anti-intellectual, anti-philosophical, and realist to the
point at which it slips easily into journalism or polemic'[10] and notes that
'women have lost out in clinging to realist and autobiographical modes'.[11]
While Patten's critique is valid for early responses to the troubles, some
later novels begin to exhibit an ability to both represent the horrors of
violence and be formally experimental.

Mary Beckett is the author of two collections of short stories and a
children's book, but it is perhaps her only novel that is her most distinct
contribution. *Give Them Stones* (1987) charts the life of Martha from the
Troubles of the 1930s to her role as mother, wife and breadwinner during
the 1970s. The novel does not shy away from political reality: it begins
with a kneecapping at close quarters and highlights socioeconomic deprivation throughout with the refrain of 'No work'. Megan Sullivan sees
the novel through a Marxist lens, noting that because 'she wishes to be
defined as a worker rather than as a Republican or nationalist, Beckett's
protagonist forces a consideration of materialist concerns in Northern
Ireland'.[12] Despite her marginalized position as a working class Catholic
woman, Martha is fiercely independent and determined throughout
and is one of the most distinctive characters in Northern Irish fiction.
Women's lives are bleak in the novel, whether through lack of reproductive choice or because they are medicated to cope with trauma, but their
industriousness and resilience are highlighted. Martha's politics vacillate
between hard-line nationalism and a more conciliatory tone as she sees

the consequences of violence. She is even prepared to stake her bakery, the most powerful sign of her independence, on her principles: 'I'll open or shut as I please and nobody intimidates me.'[13] This novel deals with a remarkable sweep of history and has a well-drawn, sympathetic protagonist.

Other writers were more willing to experiment with postmodernist and metafictional techniques. Anne Devlin's short story 'Naming the Names', in the collection *The Way-Paver* (1986), is rare in featuring women who turn to violence but also innovative in its structure and elliptical narrative. Una Woods's *The Dark Hole Days* (1984) uses 'parallel diary entries' and alternates 'first-person narrators for the most part, except for a protracted section just before its climax in which third-person narration is used'.[14] Briege Duffaud's *A Wreath Upon the Dead* (1993) confronts the tradition of history-writing and conflict in Northern Ireland and beyond, allowing 'characters to tell their stories in internal monologues, reported dialogues, journals, letters, short stories and a one-act drama'.[15] Exploring themes that resonate in later Northern Irish women's fiction, she uses the past in innovative narrative ways, offering a 'post-modern insistence on complexity, ambiguity, plurality, heterogeneity and discontinuity'[16] which has been described as 'historiographic metafiction'.[17]

Frances Molloy's riotous *No Mate for the Magpie* (1985) is recounted entirely in Northern Irish vernacular. Patten describes her work as offering 'major breakthroughs in her use of dialect, her satire, and her development of a perspective which never stopped short of implicating women – the Reverend Mother or the Dublin landlady – within and frequently responsible for the malaise of Irish society'.[18] The protagonist, Ann, with her 'wee screwed up protestant face',[19] presides over a carnivalesque story which features ghosts, child death and a house burning down in the first few pages. While the economic narrative weaves throughout the novel ('the people were so downtrodden that they just shrugged their shoulders'),[20] Ann is a Derry Moll Flanders who adapts to suit her circumstances. She steers away from 'sins of the flesh',[21] though, and is also an instinctive feminist who refuses 'te ate' the priest's 'lavins'[22] and chastises any woman who would feed a man well before herself. Her outspoken attitude leads her to be treated with ECT and strong drugs for depression and she recoils against being labelled a 'full-time tablet eater'.[23] As Ann emerges into adulthood, the pressure of being Catholic in the 1960s grows until she can only get a job by feigning bigotry and complaining about 'fuckin' popish scum'.[24] She is on Derry marches during the ambush at Burntollet Bridge and the violent exchanges are described in visceral detail as she begins to advocate for 'wan man, wan vote'.[25]

The prolific novelist Deirdre Madden's first novel, *Hidden Symptoms* (1986), is concerned with 'psychological, spiritual and cultural health'[26] but aims to discuss 'the intersections of aesthetics, religion and political violence'.[27] Michael Parker and Elmer Kennedy-Andrews have both made the case for Madden as a formally interesting writer, describing the novel as about 'the act of writing fiction'[28] and an 'unstable Machereyan or Derridean text'[29] respectively. The novel is replete with references to the literal and metaphorical suffering body: Belfast is 'a madman who tears his flesh'[30] and Robert, the journalist, describes 'bits of human flesh hanging from barbed wire after a bombing'.[31] Theresa is afflicted with chronic menstrual cramps, but is encouraged by her doctor to bear these silently, as she has borne so much pain in the novel. Like her namesake, St Teresa of Avila ('stunned into ecstasy by union with God'),[32] she tries to make sense of her position through writing and focuses on 'subjectivity – and articulation'.[33] Indeed, characters in the novel regularly discuss the role of art and the politics of form during the Troubles, from the belligerent drunken playwright to Robert's ambivalent relationship to Northern Irish culture. In this way, the novel hovers between the realist mode critiqued by Patten and the move towards something more self-conscious.

Madden's haunting *One by One in the Darkness* (1996) is a family drama that spans the civil rights era to the early stages of the peace process. The range, however, is greater than that, weaving local and national history into an intricate, convincing narrative. Jayne Steel, discussing the problem of representing political violence, notes that Madden 'seems to be aware of this failure of language when she implies how the real trauma of the 1960s, 1970s and early 1980s (being shot, blown up or beaten by paramilitaries) resists repetition through the symbolic order, through media-speak, or through the language of fiction'.[34] The complicated tensions between the sisters are patiently explored, and central to the plot is generational conflict: their grandmother disapproves of their mother Emily's involvement in activism ('Communists, more like'),[35] and Emily in turn disapproves of her unmarried daughters. But, while the conflict between Emily and her own mother is never resolved, she comes to an uneasy peace with Cate's illegitimate child, shortly to be born into this changed political climate ('I know what's required of me, but it'll take time').[36]

Like other Irish novels, the central narrative catalyst of *One by One in the Darkness* is a homecoming and there is a farmhouse at the centre. However, the ways in which Madden carefully depicts the psychological legacy of violence on women's lives are subtly powerful. Each of the sisters has a different approach to dealing with 'the thing that had happened to their father'[37] but they all rebel against traditional concepts of domesticity. Despite her Catholic morality, Emily is also ill-at-ease with traditional roles as she regrets being forced to give up her teaching job and unsentimentally gives away her wedding dress. The novel is particularly subtle as it gradually reveals family dynamics, and Cate speculates on whether this closeness, this 'bubble of maternal affection',[38] is a positive force. This idea recurs later in the text with a character suffocated by the 'small, closed society'.[39] The shadow of men's violence intrudes into this feminist plot. Their father is a benign peacemaker, but we get regular unflinching glimpses of the horrors of war, from Internment to Bloody Friday to his murder. The sisters' girlish focus on kittens, spelling tests and cinema is set against 'images of policemen in Derry, in full riot gear'.[40] Women's sacrifices are voiced throughout the narrative, whether they sacrifice their mental health ('My mother was nearly demented'),[41] their soldier sons ('I'm sure his ma isn't getting a wink of sleep')[42] or are 'left for years to bring up children on their own'.[43] The novel ends with both an acknowledgement of pain but also hope and sisterhood, in every sense.

Anna Burns's powerful, provocative *No Bones* (2001) considers the period 1969–94 from the perspective of Amelia, an anorexic girl whose mental state deteriorates into psychosis. Burns's control of the narrative ensures this is a visceral, disturbing experience that verges, like Molloy's novel, on a carnivalesque disruption of the realist mode of the Troubles novel. The presence of the Troubles is central to the narrative, but this is contrasted with the volatility of Amelia's family, who are depicted through the ambiguous narrative voice as depressives, sexual deviants and prone to indiscriminate violence. The language of psychology is used throughout, but does not help us make sense of the increasingly desperate predicament in which the mentally ill find themselves in a country torn apart by violence. It begins: 'The Troubles started on a Thursday'[44] and from there plunges further and further into renderings of some of the darkest incidents of the conflict as well as the increasingly tenuous grasp that several of the characters have on the world around them as they dissociate from both sectarian and sexual violence.

No Bones opens with Amelia's childhood, where the normal and everyday (sausage, chips and beans for tea) are contrasted with children having their finger prints recorded, the reporting of 'apparently motiveless crimes'[45] and Amelia's plastic bullets, the prized possession in her treasure trove. Burns shows the subtle changes in political currents, from the change in reaction to the presence of the armed forces through to the increasing radicalization of young men. As Mick, Amelia's brother, notes, discussing a device found in the street: 'They're common as petrol bombs, or rubber bullets, or riots, or tea.'[46] He is chief among Amelia's tormentors, as he enjoys confining her and tightening and loosening his grip on her throat. Following a horrifying shooting in her school play yard, Amelia 'can't remember the order of things much after that day'.[47] After this incident, the narrative is carefully controlled to show Amelia's breakdown with hallucinatory effect on the reader, demonstrating clearly that powerful, experimental writing in Northern Ireland is not confined to male writers and also that narrative risks can still be taken to great effect, even on the bleakest of subject matter. This novel, then, refutes attempts to make easy sense of either the Troubles or women's involvement in them as order is frustrated at every turn. In Northern Irish women's Troubles writing, we have many instances of women giving voice to the voiceless of the conflict but Burns's is one of the most powerfully subversive novels written about this period.

Re-writing the Big House

At the same time as these women were exploring the contemporary ramifications of political violence, novelists were also mining another aspect of the North's contested past for their fiction. These historical novels examine the complicated role of the 'Big House' in Northern Irish life and the often deeply ambiguous position of the female denizens. In these novels, as in other Irish representations of the ascendancy, the home is a clear metonym for both the operations of power and the decline of the Anglo-Irish class. However, while the inhabitants of other Big Houses (the Naylors in Elizabeth Bowen's *The Last September* or Aroon in Molly Keane's *Good Behaviour*) are often represented as sexually repressed or sterile, there is a grotesque fecundity about these novels, as women are often placed in the grip of madness by forced child-bearing. Rather than a class in rapid decline after partition, the political context is masculine Unionist dominance in Northern Ireland. This symbolic dominance manifests in the women's lives, as they are confined in their homes, prisons or asylums or by their wombs while political violence rages outside.

Caroline Blackwood's *Great Granny Webster* (1977) charts four generations of women who live in the shadow of the Big House: the formidable eponymous matriarch, her mentally ill daughter, her suicidal flapper grand-daughter and her great grand-daughter. The latter, our unnamed narrator, goes to Mrs Webster's Hove villa in order to convalesce in the sea air but instead gets drawn into investigating the murky, troubled history at the core of her English, Scottish and Irish ascendancy family. Mrs Webster is obsessive about her routines and about protecting the functioning of her 'aged and egotistical heart',[48] while 'her whole personality and aura reeked of barrenness'.[49] The narrator has terrifying dreams about her grandmother, describing her as a 'horrifying witch-like spectre, cursing and gibbering and grimacing'[50] who, when her delusions reached their peak, thought her children had been swopped for changelings and enacted these fears violently in public. The narrator's Aunt Lavinia opens the second chapter with a marked contrast to the austere lifestyle of Great Granny Webster: she is wildly promiscuous and 'reputed once to have gate-crashed a fashionable London party totally naked except for a sanitary towel'.[51] Throughout the novel, women repress their emotions and are horrified when they are expressed involuntarily or inappropriately. At the centre is Dunmartin Hall, which bears striking similarities to Clandeboye, Blackwood's childhood home, but the novel, and the family, stay well away from Irish politics.

Throughout this novel the idea of domestic confinement recurs: whether in a rapidly decaying house or in a psychiatric institution, women are trapped by manacles both of their own and society's making. A decline in several characters' physical and mental health is blamed on the 'stultifying isolation and relentless biting damp of that ancestral Ulster house'.[52] As the house falls apart, so does the narrator's grandmother, and we are told that she only had children 'because conventions of the time demanded that she produce heirs for her husband'.[53] Throughout the novel, due to the mental state of the characters, our trust in the stories relayed by them and by the narrator is undermined constantly. Blackwood has created a memorably, blackly comic grotesquery of a pillar of unionist identity: the ordered estate which, once the fall begins, cannot be tamed again.

Similar themes of maternal horror and grotesquery are found years later in Bernie McGill's 2011 novel, *The Butterfly Cabinet*. It is a fictionalization of the conviction of Annie Margaret Montagu for the death of her daughter by asphyxia. The story is told through the dual perspectives of Maddie, a servant who recounts her part in civil rights-era Northern Ireland, and the pre-partition prison diaries of 'Harriet Ormond, daughter, sister, wife, mother, horsewoman, lepidopterist'[54] (the fictional proxy

for Annie), which are read by her granddaughter, Anna. Throughout the
novel, the central tension is freedom versus confinement: whether in the
prison, the maternal body or in servitude. In both eras, women's relationship to major political events is complex and mediated by their gender.
Harriet's family are Anglo-Irish Catholics, landed but uncertain due
to the Home Rule debates and the rise of the Irish Parliamentary
Party. They have a complicated relationship to the land: they are sur-
prised that their tenants bear them any ill will. In the later period,
Maddie details 'the police in steel helmets and riot shields batonning the
life out of the civil rights marchers, and them all screaming and roaring
and Gerry Fitt's face covered in blood'[55] while she notes that similar battles rage in America against the backdrop of the moon landing. What
is common to both periods are female characters discussing the male
politicians who influence their lives: whether Disraeli and Gladstone or
O'Neill and Fitt. While the usual historical marker in the depiction of
the 1960s is of course the Troubles, the possibility of reproductive choice
following the approval of the contraceptive pill in 1961 is highlighted as
a central moment in women's history. These novels, then, have the opportunity to diversify the historical context that has informed traditional
readings of Northern Irish history to take into account women's experiences and the forces that shaped them.

Kathleen Ferguson's *The Maid's Tale* (1994), which also deals with
confinement and a woman's role in Northern Irish society, has been
described as a 'feminist rewriting of the bildungsroman'.[56] Left in the care
of Catholic institutions after her father beats her mother to death, Brigid
acutely represents the lack of economic opportunity in post-war Derry
but also the ways in which structures of control keep women dominated
and voiceless. She constantly parallels her role as a housekeeper to a
wifely duty, and never questions the authority of 'Father' or the church
hierarchy until they decide she is no longer of use to them. As in the
previous two novels, there are spaces of imprisonment throughout, both
literal and metaphorical: the mental hospital where her father is imprisoned, the orphanage she is raised in, the parochial house and, eventually,
the house in which she cares for her Alzheimer's-ravaged charge. Despite
being set in Derry in the 1960s and 1970s, we are merely told that these
were the 'days of the civil rights marches'[57] and that she was disturbed
by 'sounds of the women banging bin-lids'.[58] Brigid refers to the lack of
opportunity for Catholics in Derry but is not prepared to rock the boat
by joining the protesters. Throughout the novel, the patriarchal nature
of Catholic authority is commented upon. Brigid admits that 'I needed

a man-God with a human face to protect me',[59] she is told that 'To be slow in words is a woman's best virtue'[60] and Tim angrily confirms that a woman is required 'to keep her mouth shut and serve'.[61] Throughout the novel, we see the consequences of this repression as women who serve are doomed to lives burdened by suffering. For Brigid, misery at the hands of one patriarchal agent is merely a woman's lot in life, and she accepts the overt and subtle ways in which she is controlled: 'Father didn't like me talking to people, whatever the reason.'[62] He understands the links between her faith and his dominance in her life: 'I reckon he figured, so long as I was in God's pocket, I was in his pocket as well.'[63] The novel's hopeful ending suggests that, while the structures of patriarchy and religion reinforce each other's dominance in complex ways, liberation is possible.

Twenty-First-Century Fiction

Since the ceasefires of 1998, Northern Irish women's fiction has seen a remarkable formal and thematic diversity. Anne Barnett's *The Largest Baby in Ireland After the Famine* (2000) explores taboo sexual intrigue in rural Tyrone during the First World War and Monica Tracey's *Left of the Moon* (2011) centres on transnational experiences of the Second World War around the Antrim coast. Maeve Davey argues for the political complexity in oft-dismissed popular women's fiction such as Sharon Owens's *The Tavern on Maple Street* (2005) and Anne Dunlop's *The Revenge of Lady Muck* (2010), as well as citing the influence of Niki Hill's *Death Grows On You* (1990).[64] Jan Carson's *Malcolm Orange Disappears* (2014) is set in Oregon and has been lauded by critics as both playful and inventive. Carolyn Jess-Cooke was a prize-winning poet and academic before publishing *The Guardian Angel's Journal* (2011) and *The Boy Who Could See Demons* (2012). Claire McGowan is building a reputation for her crime writing with her novels *The Fall* (2012), *The Lost* (2013) and *The Dead Ground* (2014), as well as a story in the *Belfast Noir* collection (2014). Journalist and novelist Martina Devlin has explored a range of topics in her work, from the banking crisis to witchcraft in her 2014 *The House Where It Happened*, which often blurs the lines between fact and fiction.

With this diversity of writing in mind, however, the rest of this chapter will be concerned chiefly with the growing body of fiction which directly addresses questions of history and memory in 'post'-conflict Northern Irish society. Since the signing of the Good Friday Agreement in 1998, fictional responses by women have focused on both considering the impact of the conflict and also on contesting some of the assumptions of the mechanisms of peace-building. In particular, these novels exhibit scepticism towards grand narratives of memorialization and seek to recover voices that are not always privileged in discourses of 'dealing with the past'. They carefully link public and private spheres to show how the legacy of political violence cannot be untangled from the domestic. But despite this cynicism over homogenizing metanarratives of community memory, these novels are in turn both subversively sensual and occasionally hopeful.

Lucy Caldwell is the author of three novels, *Where They Were Missed* (2006), *The Meeting Point* (2011) and *All the Beggars Riding* (2013) which was chosen for Belfast's and Derry's One City One Book initiative. She is also an award-winning playwright for stage and radio and has recently moved into the short story genre, with a forthcoming collection and inclusion in *Belfast Noir*. All of Caldwell's novels display an interest in desire, memory and the role of women in contemporary Northern Irish society. She is committed to telling stories that are not normally included in the fictional landscape of Northern Ireland. *Where They Were Missed* considers, like Burns's *No Bones*, how children come to terms with political violence and family trauma in Belfast. Irish myth and the psychogeography of Belfast are woven into the narrative which, for all its engagement with suffering, is profoundly hopeful. *The Meeting Point* features an idealistic couple who do missionary work in Bahrain, only to find their relationship and faith are faltering. The novel is deeply sensual and considers the complex interactions of obsession, desire and loss. Ruth's attempt to reconstruct her life and to adjust to her changed reality falter, as she considers her pain 'not a real wound: just the ghost of an old one'.[65] In Caldwell's writing, loss becomes a vocal, active presence in her characters' lives.

All the Beggars Riding deals with the textual mechanics of narrating grief and the protagonist Lara Moorhouse's attempts to make sense of loss. The novel bursts at the seams with different types of grief, whether the victims of the Troubles and Chernobyl or Lara's family tragedy, and considers the different ways in which individuals weave a narrative frame around their experiences. It is a complex meditation on grief and recovery, and of the power of storytelling and empathy in coming to terms with the political and personal past. Memory is an unpredictable, unstable force in the novel: inconvenient memories rise unbidden and characters are often ossified, unable to move forward due to their own partial view of the past. Lara struggles to integrate both her current situation and her parents' torrid relationship into her sense of self: 'I'm writing about my own parents, and how they fucked up, but I'm writing about myself, too, mourning the loss of something I won't now have.'[66] Lara's attempts to tell her mother's story falter and it is only through the empathetic reimagining of the lives of others that she finds some comfort. Caldwell is drawing attention here to the complex processes at the heart of reconciliation: it may not happen in the proscribed way, with the expected participants, it may instead come from unexpected sources.

Michèle Forbes's 2013 novel *Ghost Moth* focuses on two pivotal moments in the life of Katherine: her love affair while starring in a production of *Carmen* in 1949 and the contrast between her domestic life and the violence of the Troubles in 1969. As the novel notes: 'The Past is Not Quite Past.'[67] Against this tale of troubled domesticity, we glimpse reports of petrol bombings, burnt-out vehicles, the deployment of British troops and the sectarian abuse of Katherine's daughters. The novel is chiefly concerned with the operations of memory, and what Katherine terms 'the sweet pattern of compromise. It is love and more than love'.[68] This is contested as the narrative alternates between past and present, particularly in the intensely passionate descriptions of her affair. The vivid memories of her tailor lover, Tom, who took such care with her body, whether making love or her elaborate costumes for the opera, resurface when she sees a seal while swimming with her family: 'Something is happening to her. Something has happened to her in the water. She thinks of the seal's eyes.'[69] She wants to reach out and touch it, even while she is thrilled with the danger and imagines the harm it could do to her. Her dreams return to this object, imagining herself being swallowed up by grotesque sea monsters. Water features throughout and the novel reveals, like Caldwell's work, a fascination with Belfast's topography as Katherine and her lover take night walks along the banks of the Lagan. As Tom's body was found submerged, the novel revolves around the motif of that which has been hidden resurfacing, but Forbes modifies this simplistic interpretation of the past with her complex, difficult ending. Katherine's husband, George, has a different attitude to dealing with things that have been suppressed. His impulse, whether with turnips in the garden or a nest of bees, is to quickly eradicate them. He thinks of them as 'Buried things that he needed to unearth and to destroy. Buried things that he needed to empty himself of. Too many buried things.'[70] What is buried, then, is the guilt both feel for their encounters with Tom: Katherine for her love for him and George for letting him die on the banks of the

Lagan. In this novel, memory cannot be untethered from the sensual. Characters are affected by the past in physical, visceral ways that are underscored by the conflict that rages at the bottom of the hill and edges ever closer to the family as the novel progresses.

Bethany Dawson's debut novel, *My Father's House* (2013), is the story of Robbie's return to care for his dying father and his reconciliation with his family and his own troubled past. As in other recent novels, the Troubles appear as a spectral presence in the novel, which intersect with the narrative but do not overshadow the family plot. The novel, the title of which alludes to the biblical phrase, 'My Father's House has many rooms', shares tonal and thematic similarities with John McGahern's *Amongst Women* as it features both a rural setting and a formidable patriarch in decline. As with other recent Northern Irish fiction, concerns over dealing with the past are never far from the central plot, from Robbie's constant adjusting of the rear view mirror to his column in Dublin as the 'Culture Vulture', who earns his living 'picking through the remains of something that was already dead' while, in his father's dilapidated garden, a 'darker, more malevolent tree was being exposed beneath the silvery bark'.[71] Robbie is a former Troubles reporter whose mentor was murdered for exposing gangland crime. Robbie's mother, Margaret, returns to the motif of 'digging up'[72] when discussing his job and the text circles around the significance of excavating the past through the house and land in which his father becomes more ill. But, in this novel, the past is not simple, and neither is recovery. Margaret's descriptions of the past are at odds with Robbie's memories and unresolved, barely spoken tensions come to the surface when he returns. Around the waking table each family member tries to unburden themselves of their feeling about the 'tyrant' who had been so central to their lives: '"You were a bastard" … "You were a terrible husband" … "You really made my life difficult, Dad" … "I don't even know you."'[73] But even this catharsis is partial as at the wake they hear of his conviviality and sporting prowess, and that he turned to alcohol as a consequence of the decline of the farming trade due to supermarkets and lower food prices. At the end, rather than the rage of the wake table, it is empathy that resolves Robbie to break the cycle and become a good husband and father.

Kelly Creighton's debut novel, *The Bones of Us* (2015), deals with topics more usually considered by male novelists: violence against women and the state of the paramilitary 'hard man' in post-peace process Northern Ireland. Scott McAuley lives in the shadow of his father, Duke, who was released early under the terms of the Good Friday Agreement.

Creighton's novel is an exploration of acceptable forms of violence and of the 'Children of the Troubles'. This phrase, first heard by Creighton at a talk in the John Hewitt Summer School on the Peace Monitoring Report, recurs in a novel concerned with the politics of generations and the competing modes of masculinity evident in father ('big hulking bastard') and son ('poncey, veggie, green-tea-drinking').[74] Like Forbes's turnip-digging, the land is used as a metaphor for an unearthing of difficult, painful memories: 'Things we thought were long buried, that for months and months were pushed under the soil in our heads. Well, the land changes.'[75] Broadly in the crime genre, the novel is told through a diary that a therapist has asked Scott to keep: 'maybe you have a point with this writing malarkey, this writing for therapy'.[76] The picture of post-agreement Northern Ireland is bleak, a contrast between the old guard ('damaged by something he called politics')[77] and the disaffected next generation: 'The recession's over but yet these people are still so very wounded. Why, when life should be getting better, is it not?'[78] The implication in the novel is that wounded men take their frustration out on women ('You had Mum pregnant at seventeen, dead at twenty')[79] and that violence becomes a learned pattern of expression that is meted out from father to son. In Creighton's disturbing vision of contemporary Northern Ireland, we see a female novelist from Northern Ireland prepared to deal with the legacy of conflict in an uncompromising, confrontational manner that also draws attention to the problems facing young men.

Northern Irish women novelists have demonstrated formal innovation, stylistic flair, deft characterization and a willingness to explore difficult subject matter. Some have displayed a concern for the complex intersection of economic concerns and sexual politics, others have dealt with the darkest subject matter with a skilful narrative touch or the blackest humour. Their diverse and challenging work has dealt unstintingly with complex subject matter and deserves recovery.

Notes

1 Edna Longley, *The Living Stream* (Newcastle upon Tyne: Bloodaxe Books, 1994), 187.
2 Quoted in Rebecca Pelan, *Two Irelands* (Syracuse, NY: Syracuse University Press, 2005), 97.
3 Naomi Doak, 'Ulster Protestant Women Authors', *Irish Studies Review* 15, no. 1 (2007): 38.
4 Norman Vance, 'Region, realism and reaction, 1922–1972', in *Cambridge Companion to the Irish Novel*, ed. John Wilson Foster (Cambridge: Cambridge University Press, 2006), 156.

5 Ann Owens Weekes, 'Women Novelists 1930s–1960s', in *Cambridge Companion to the Irish Novel*, ed. Foster, 200.

6 See Jennifer Fitzgerald's '"The Queen's Girl": Helen Waddell and Women at Queen's University Belfast, 1908–1920', in *Have Women Made a Difference*, ed. Claire Rush and Judith Harford (Oxford, Peter Lang, 2010).

7 Owens Weekes, 'Women Novelists 1930s–1960s', 202.

8 Linden Peach, *The Contemporary Irish Novel* (Houndmills, Basingstoke, Hampshire: Palgrave Macmillan, 2004), 58.

9 Pelan, *Two Irelands*, 85.

10 Eve Patten, 'Women and Fiction 1985–1990', *Krino 1986–1996*, ed. Gerald Dawe and Jonathan Williams (Dublin: Gill & Macmillan, 1996), 15.

11 Ibid., 8.

12 Megan Sullivan, '"Instead I Said I Am a Home Baker": Nationalist Ideology and Materialist Politics in Mary Beckett's *Give Them Stones*', in *Border Crossings: Irish Women Writers and National Identities*, ed. Kathryn Kirkpatrick (Tuscaloosa: The University of Alabama Press, 2000), 228.

13 Mary Beckett, *Give Them Stones* (London: Bloomsbury, 1988), 126.

14 Michael Parker, *Northern Irish Literature, 1956–2006* (Basingstoke: Palgrave Macmillan, 2007), 55.

15 Christine St. Peter, *Changing Ireland* (Basingstoke: Palgrave, 2000), 92.

16 Elmer Kennedy-Andrews, 'The Novel and the Northern Troubles', in *Cambridge Companion to the Irish Novel*, ed. Foster, 250.

17 Elmer Kennedy-Andrews, *Fiction and the Northern Ireland Troubles Since 1969* (Dublin: Four Courts, 2003), 139.

18 Patten, 'Women and Fiction', 9.

19 Frances Molloy, *No Mate for the Magpie* (New York, NY, Persea, 1985), 1.

20 Ibid., 7.

21 Ibid., 10.

22 Ibid., 121.

23 Ibid., 102.

24 Ibid., 108.

25 Ibid., 130.

26 Parker, *Northern Irish Literature*, 57.

27 Ibid., 68.

28 Michael Parker, 'Shadows on a Glass: Self-Reflexivity in the Novels of Deirdre Madden', *Irish University Review* 30, no. 1 (Spring/Summer 2000): 82–102, 83.

29 Kennedy-Andrews, *Fiction and the Northern Ireland Troubles since 1969*, 147.

30 Deirdre Madden, *Hidden Symptoms* (London: Faber, 2014), 14.

31 Ibid., 30.

32 Ibid., 55.

33 Ibid., 28.

34 Jayne Steel, 'Politicizing the Private: Women Writing The Troubles', in *Representing the Troubles: Texts and Images, 1970–2000*, ed. Brian Cliff and Eibhear Walshe (Dublin: Four Courts, 2004), 59.

35 Deirdre Madden, *One by One in the Darkness* (London: Faber, 1996), 79.
36 Ibid., 128.
37 Ibid., 9.
38 Ibid., 148.
39 Ibid., 168.
40 Ibid., 95.
41 Ibid., 49.
42 Ibid., 98.
43 Ibid., 174.
44 Anna Burns, *No Bones* (London: Flamingo, 2001), 1.
45 Ibid., 20.
46 Ibid., 51.
47 Ibid., 76.
48 Caroline Blackwood, *Great Granny Webster* (New York, NY: New York Review of Books, 1977), 24.
49 Ibid., 18.
50 Ibid., 18.
51 Ibid., 29.
52 Ibid., 62.
53 Ibid., 86.
54 Bernie McGill, *The Butterfly Cabinet* (London: Headline Review, 2011), Kindle edition.
55 Ibid.
56 Peach, *The Contemporary Irish Novel*, 116.
57 Kathleen Ferguson, *The Maid's Tale* (Dublin: Poolbeg, 1994), 97.
58 Ibid., 138.
59 Ibid., 16.
60 Ibid., 24.
61 Ibid., 189.
62 Ibid., 81.
63 Ibid.
64 Maeve Davey, '"You're Dying for Me": Representations of Masculinity in Contemporary Northern Irish Popular Women's Fiction', in *Irish Masculinities: Reflections on Literature and Culture*, ed. Caroline Magennis and Raymond Mullen (Dublin: Irish Academic Press, 2011), 35–48.
65 Lucy Caldwell, *The Meeting Point* (London: Faber, 2011), 401.
66 Lucy Caldwell, *All the Beggars Riding* (London: Faber, 2013), 72.
67 Michèle Forbes, *Ghost Moth* (London: Weidenfeld and Nicholson, 2013), Kindle edition.
68 Ibid.
69 Ibid.
70 Ibid.
71 Bethany Dawson, *My Father's House* (Dublin: Liberties, 2013), Kindle edition.
72 Ibid.

73 Ibid.
74 Kelly Creighton, *The Bones of It* (Dublin: Liberties, 2015), Kindle edition.
75 Ibid.
76 Ibid.
77 Ibid.
78 Ibid.
79 Ibid.

CHAPTER 20

Life Writing and Personal Testimony, 1970–Present

Anne Mulhall

The decades that have passed since 1970 have witnessed a transformation of women's position in Irish society as women have contested and
significantly weakened their state-enforced economic, social and legal
subordination. The surge in published writing by women in Ireland from
the 1970s on was an important part of that erosion, with life writing and
personal testimony occupying a central place in the political and cultural
ferment of the women's movement and its aftermath. There is perhaps
no field of contemporary writing in Ireland that so explicitly foregrounds
the complex intersections between identity, access to public voice and the
role of genre in mediating the terms of that access as the field of life writing. This emergence of life writing has contributed to a democratization
of auto/biographical studies; it forms part of an expansive and inclusive
strategy that challenges disciplinary divisions between different kinds of
life stories. It also serves to dismantle some of the exclusions attendant
on the critic's limitation to a more or less traditional canon within Irish
auto/biographical studies.

The articulation of experiences and lives formerly unspoken of or
silenced is central to women's life writing in Ireland since 1970. 'The
personal is political' was more than just a second-wave slogan; the truth
of the feminist maxim is attested to by the transformative effects that
women's personal narratives have had in Irish culture and society over the
last half century. This chapter affirms the centrality of feminist politics
and consciousness to the democratization of the autobiographical voice
in Ireland over the last fifty-odd years. It will also foreground those who
do not fit homogenous models of the Irish Woman and highlight some
ways in which marginalized women's lives can be erased or appropri-
ated within the complex politics of the (self) representation of women.
Autobiographical writing by well-known women in the literary and
political fields has helped to erode what seemed an unassailable dominant
Irish male perspective. However, autobiography by established women is

formally and culturally at a remove from the testimonial forms through which most women's personal narratives are articulated. As Gayatri Spivak observes, as distinct from autobiography, 'Testimony is the genre of the subaltern giving witness to oppression to a less oppressed other.'[1] How women get to tell their stories, for what purpose, in what context, within what shaping perimeters, and with what degree of authorial and editorial control is often determined by women's differential positions in terms of class, race, ethnicity, gender, sexuality, citizenship and institutional power. Access to self-representation is in part articulated through generic and disciplinary classifications that are inextricable from the 'interlocking systems of oppression' in which they are constituted, making explicit the co-implication of form, knowledge and power.[2] This chapter, then, seeks to complicate any reductive notion that women's life writing in Ireland allows all women's voices to be heard in the same way.

Woman, Nation and Literary Life Writing

The interconnectedness of the personal and the political is particularly apparent within the Irish autobiographical canon. In giving an account of themselves, writers such as Lady Gregory, W. B. Yeats, George Moore, Elizabeth Bowen or Frank O'Connor also give an account of the 'Nation'.[3] This central trope of the symbiosis between the story of the life and the story of Ireland is one that women writers have interrogated, reworked and transformed in order to undo the masculinist perimeters of both the nation and the authoritative speaking/writing subject. There are, of course, many notable autobiographies by women since 1970 that do not take such re-articulations as their main objective, but most nonetheless address the relation between self and nation from disparate angles. Echoing Elizabeth Bowen, Selina Guinness's *The Crocodile by the Door* (2012) focuses on the struggle to maintain her Anglo-Irish inheritance in the Celtic Tiger present in which most of the narrative is set.[4] Leland Bardwell's *A Restless Life* (2008) resists classification as a characteristic 'Anglo-Irish' autobiography; concluding at the end of the 1960s, it gives a vivid account of the hardships of her upbringing and the difficulties faced by the woman writer at a time when women's options were severely constricted. Bardwell provides a valuable portrait of the male-dominated Irish literary scene that she, along with figures such as Patrick Kavanagh and John Jordan, cultivated in 1960s London and Dublin.[5] The relation between self and nation is declared in the title of Máire Cruise O'Brien's *The Same Age as the State* (2003), where Cruise O'Brien often seems to downplay her own achievements in favour of conventional recollections of the great men of the revolutionary and post-revolutionary period.[6]

These works differ in purpose from personal narratives that self-consciously address and reconfigure the position of the woman writer in the Irish context. This is a central preoccupation in Eavan Boland's *Object Lessons* (1995), a partly autobiographical text that weaves together personal, familial and national mythologies, memories and histories in order to excavate the relationship between gendered embodiment, the poetic self and the national imaginary, revealing the interconnections between the abjection of the woman poet in the national tradition, the exclusion of the woman from the public sphere, and the repression and 'forgetting' of women and other subjugated and exiled populations in Irish history.[7] Ranging from foundation myths of the nation and to the narrator's escape into exile in London, Edna O'Brien's *Mother Ireland* (1975) insists on the centrality of woman and the feminine to the genealogy of the nation. 'Ireland has always been a woman,' the narrator suggests; 'a womb, a cave, a cow, a Rosaleen, a sow, a bride, a harlot, and, of course, the gaunt Hag of Beare.'[8] Despite the lyricism of her memoir, O'Brien depicts a nation in thrall to a demagogic Catholic church. Repressed and sublimated desire influences the texture of everyday life, individual consciousness and the norms which regulate family and community, while self-abnegation is inculcated as the key aspiration for women and girls. Anne Enright's pregnancy memoir *Making Babies* (2005) also touches on the reproductive biopolitics of the nation-state and how women's lives and experiences are shaped through internalized socio-cultural norms. For instance, Enright connects the violent battles over the repressive regulation of women and girls that characterized 1980s Ireland to her own depression and breakdown in her twenties: 'Ireland broke apart in the eighties, and I sometimes think that the crack happened in my own head'.[9] In Rita Ann Higgins's 2010 literary memoir *Hurting God*, critique of the nation is implicit in her depiction of the effects of the hegemonic project of a capitalist theocratic state on self, family and community; the ideology of the state is interwoven with the verbal and physical abuse meted out by 'a father' and the god-fearing moral surveillance of 'the mammies of Baile Crua'.[10] Higgins's memoir demonstrates the interconnectedness of the personal and the political; the more precarious a person's circumstances are, the more that connection is clarified.

Higgins is rare in being an Irish working-class woman who has published a literary memoir. As well as the economic, social and cultural capital that determines such access, it is important too to acknowledge

the abjection of the 'other' woman in Irish women's literary autobiographical writing. The risk of appropriating subaltern women's experience
by 'speaking for' is unavoidably present in Boland's representations of
women 'outside history'. O'Brien's *Mother Ireland* includes photographs
and descriptions of Travellers and the rural and urban poor which share
an ethnographic gaze that positions those depicted as anonymous foils
for her complex autobiographical self. Ambivalence about disparities
of class are also present in Enright's *Making Babies*, which at one point
draws on stigmatizing stereotypes of the Dublin working class mother to
add edge to a passage that satirizes Celtic Tiger class conflict and excess.
Such moments prompt the question of who gets to 'tell their story', and
whose lives are used to add colour or distinction to that story. Who is
granted the platform and capacity to represent herself, and whose self
is shaped and edited by the representational priorities of another? To
encounter self-narratives of women in Ireland speaking from marginalized positions, we generally still must look elsewhere than literary autobiographical writing. We must look to modes of life writing and personal
testimony whose disciplinary origins, shaping purposes and formal constraints at times raise difficult questions about the relation between the
stratified modes of life-narrative and socio-economic stratifications.

The Personal and the Political: Feminist
Memoir/Feminists' Memoirs

Written across a span of thirty-odd years, the memoirs surveyed in this
section share a belief in the transformative effects of women's articulation
of their own experiences. This belief also informs the collective personal
narratives published during the so-called 'second-wave' feminist movement in Ireland – for instance, Rosita Sweetman's interviews with women
about their experiences of patriarchal regulation and changing sexual
mores in two important publications, *On Our Knees* (1972) and *On Our
Backs* (1979), and the profiles and photographs by women published by
Nell McCafferty and Pat Murphy in *Women in Focus: Contemporary Irish
Women's Lives* (1987).

   'The personal is political' is the underlying framework for June Levine's
memoir, *Sisters* (1982). Levine's account of her life and of the women's
movement in Ireland is structured around her awakening as a feminist. She recalls the powerful impact of the Irish Women's Liberation
Movement (IWLM) consciousness-raising sessions and 'discovering
that each one of us was not the oddball, the only one who could not

accept the way things were supposed to be'.[11] Born to a Catholic mother and Jewish father, and raised in a predominantly Jewish community in Clanbrassil Street, Dublin in the 1940s and 1950s, Levine in her memoir focuses on the effects of patriarchal rather than ethno-nationalist structures on her younger self. She emphasizes the universality of patriarchal control of women and women's complicity in this regime across different communities and even continents as she narrates her experiences as a wife and as a single mother in Ireland and North America, recognizing her condition retrospectively in Betty Friedan's *The Feminine Mystique*.

Addressing a feminist movement dominated by white and middle-class women in 1980, Audre Lorde critiqued the 'pretense to a homogeneity of experience covered by the word *sisterhood* that does not in fact exist'.[12] Lorde's observation is relevant too in the context of the Irish women's movement. Keenly aware of women's vulnerability to socio-economic mechanisms of exclusion, Levine is nonetheless ambivalent about the conflicts over class that arose in the IWLM, which contributed to its fracturing and decline. This ambivalence is apparent in anecdotal descriptions of Levine's encounters with Traveller and working-class women. Such moments bring to the surface the norms of class and race that continue to fracture feminist movement-building. The unequal distribution of power and resources between women are manifested in issues of representation and voice that come to the fore when women's life writing is examined.

Maura Richards was the founder of *Cherish*, the first organization for 'unmarried mothers' in Ireland that was run by women for themselves. Published in 1998, *Single Issue* recollects Cherish's early evolution and Richards's life as a single mother and activist during the 1970s. As Richards states: 'One purpose in writing was to record women's stories at a very particular time in Ireland [when] the old order was beginning to give way.'[13] She addresses the operation of normative hierarchies of power within the women's movement as well as Irish society more broadly, framing these in terms of access to self-representation. Even in the IWLM, Richards notes: 'Others were talking on our behalf and patronizingly suggesting we needed "rehabilitation" rather than liberation. The idea of unmarried mothers acting for themselves had not entered their minds.'[14]

Women's lack of agency over their bodies and lives is a recurring theme in life writing from this period. The 1980s witnessed an aggressive battle for the survival of a rigidly patriarchal system that required compulsory reproduction and the punitive regulation of those who transgressed against the heteronormative order. This battle is at the heart of Joanne Hayes's *My Story* (1985), which details her experiences during the 1984 'Kerry Babies' Tribunal. The tribunal to investigate misconduct by the Gardaí became instead an extended public dissection of Hayes herself. Women across Ireland were outraged by her treatment by a hypocritical, misogynist male establishment.

A reading of Hayes's memoir alongside Nell McCafferty's *A Woman to Blame: The Kerry Babies Case* (1985) flags some of the conflicts between the personal and the political in relation to women's life writing. Hayes describes her dehumanization by the tribunal, who 'discussed my capacity to take further punishment ... as somebody would ask a mechanic when the car would be ready'.[15] Her account begins by describing a protest outside Tralee district court during her testimony, organized by women's groups across the country. While buoyed by the outpouring of sympathy and support she received, Hayes's account nonetheless underlines the distance between herself and the protesters: 'Neither I nor any of my family had had anything to do with organizing the protest and we had no control over what was done.'[16] Hayes's life was made public property; telling her own story herself was perhaps her attempt to reclaim ownership of her life. McCafferty's *A Woman to Blame* gives a feminist analysis of the tribunal, situating it in the context of the moral and sexual policing of women in the shadow of the 1983 abortion referendum. Like Hayes, McCafferty describes the outrage and compassion of the thousands who supported Hayes and the 'confessional outpouring' that followed her testimony. McCafferty tell us that over 500 people contacted Hayes, with many sharing their own stories, 'as though the great and fearful silence imposed by the amendment campaign was now being shattered'.[17] McCafferty also notes the unease some protesters felt. She quotes Miriam Killeny, one of the protest organizers, who faced a dilemma on the day of her protest as to whether to approach the Hayes's family or not. She did not want to intrude 'but if we didn't go over it might look as though we were using them, as though they were a handy peg on which to hang the feminist cause'.[18] Hayes's and McCafferty's accounts have necessarily different objectives. Brutally exposed to the public gallery, Hayes is concerned to put her own account on the record. McCafferty's book, whilst of course sympathetic to Hayes, situates her ordeal in the context of the reproductive biopolitics that governed women's lives in Ireland to such an overwhelming extent. The issue of who 'owns' Hayes's story is manifest in McCafferty's rejection of Hayes's 2006 request that she not sell the film rights to her book. McCafferty argued that Hayes's experiences were no longer her own, but that 'Joanne belongs to history. You couldn't write Irish history without referring to Joanne Hayes.'[19]

The outpouring of personal testimony in response to Joanne Hayes's public ordeal and to Ann Lovett's death the same year demonstrates the connections forged between feminist consciousness, social justice and the 'confessional turn' since 1970. The confessional reached an industry apogee in the 'memoir boom' of the 1990s, a 'boom' that was preceded by and co-extensive with speaking out by survivors of abuse in the 1980s, 1990s and after. Nuala O'Faolain's memoirs *Are You Somebody?* (1996) and *Almost There* (2003) are usually analysed in the context of this 'memoir boom'. O'Faolain situates her memoir in the confessional vein and explores the therapeutic function of autobiographical writing. This therapeutic function is public as well as personal in a society where women's accounts of their thoughts and experiences had been rare and self-censoring. O'Faolain received over 5,000 letters from readers of *Are You Somebody?*, mostly women who identified with her book. The memoir was, she says, 'an emotional episode' in Irish public life not because of what she had to say but because of 'the way I wrote about myself' – 'more candid than any Irish woman had yet been' in a non-fictional form, particularly about the difficulties of aging as a woman in a culture where women become invisible at middle-age.[20] On the one hand, O'Faolain describes the Ireland where marriage and motherhood put paid to women's autonomous existence, an Ireland that was 'a living tomb for woman';[21] on the other, she examines her own internalization of the norms and conventional desires instilled by a heteronormative culture.

Feminist Memoirs and the Confessional Turn

Many of the examples of women's life writing from the period in question come from women directly involved in the Women's Movement and document both their personal and political struggles. For example, O'Faolain went public about her fifteen-year relationship with Nell McCafferty in *Are You Somebody?* and McCafferty's own autobiography *Nell: A Disorderly Woman* was published in 2004. Toward its conclusion, she describes her years with O'Faolain, her reaction to *Are You Somebody?* and what she perceived as O'Faolain's diminishing of their relationship. The issue, she concludes, is internalized homophobia. McCafferty's sexuality and her relationship with her mother, Lily, frame her own narrative. Lily is a central, powerful presence in McCafferty's memoir, but her fear of her daughter coming out and the public shame that would ensue demonstrates the rigid heteronormative regime that both O'Faolain and McCafferty came of age in. Being gay was 'a dark secret' and unsurprisingly McCafferty also internalizes this pervasive homophobia.[22] Her descriptions of life in what she calls the 'lesbian ghetto' in the mid-1970s are tinged with shame, with McCafferty admitting that she was 'afraid of looking butch' and that she 'hated the term "lesbian."'[23] Moving between conflicting worlds is a dominant feature of McCafferty's life narrative: between lesbian and heterosexual milieus, between private and public lives, between Derry and Dublin, North and South. The lack of understanding that exists south of the border about the realities of life in the north is clear to her from her first move to Dublin; on viewing bullet holes in the pillars of the GPO, she notes (echoing Bernadette Devlin in her 1969 memoir *The Price of My Soul*[24]) that this 'ancient history was grand, but it had nothing to do with our struggle for civil rights under British rule in the North'.[25] The subject of the North brings the issues of speech and silence to the fore. As the war there escalates, McCafferty finds herself increasingly isolated and ostracized in Dublin. As one of the founding members of the IWLM and subsequently a core member of Irishwomen United (IU), McCafferty notes in her memoir her relief that the IWLM had agreed not to discuss the North and later her relief that in IU, she could talk about the war with like-minded feminist socialists. Ideological conflicts within the Irish women's movement and between feminist groups and male-dominated left politics recur. In the North (with Bernadette Devlin being the exception to many rules), women were excluded from decision-making roles in the civil rights movement and then in the Social Democratic and Labour Party (SDLP). Despite this, because of the work and testimony of McCafferty, Devlin, and others, we know that women like McCafferty's mother, Lily, took central if unsung roles in the struggle for civil rights.

Mary Kenny, another founder member of the IWLM who is equally famous for her dramatic renunciation of the movement, published *Something of Myself* in 2012. The book is not an autobiography but includes some autobiographical writing, such as her 'corrective' to June Levine's account in *Sisters* of the IWLM's 'condom train' from Belfast to Dublin, where she characterizes Kenny, in Kenny's words, 'as someone who went about blowing up condoms like balloons'. To the contrary, Kenny claims that she went to the cinema in Belfast and lingered behind at Connolly Station, anxious to avoid the media glare.[26] Nuala Fennell's *Political Woman – A Memoir* (2010) details the political career,

feminist organizing and personal life of the Fine Gael TD and founding member of the IWLM.[27] Fianna Fail matriarch Mary O'Rourke has
declared her feminist allegiances on many occasions, including in her two
autobiographical publications, *Just Mary: My Memoir* (2012) and *Letters
of My Life* (2016).[28] O'Faolain's books are the sole example from these
feminists' memoirs of 'feminist confession' in the sense that Rita Felski
describes, whereby the author eschews their unique exceptionality in
favour of 'delineating the specific problems and experiences which bind
women together' by emphasizing the representative nature of the teller's
life story and struggles.[29] The texts of McCafferty, Kenny and Fennell
lay claim to their authors' political authority, preserving their accounts
of themselves and others for posterity. O'Faolain's memoirs depart from
this more heroic, individualist approach to self-narrative. Even at her
most solipsistic, the apparent raw honesty of her self-examination forges
an identification between the narrator and the reader. Nonetheless,
despite O'Faolain's downplaying of her position in Irish public life, her
access to the means of autobiographical self-articulation is unavailable
to the majority of women. This material distinction calls into question
the robustness of the shared communal identity that the feminist confessional seeks to construct. A survey of the technologies of mediation in
women's life writing brings to the fore the relation between formal and
disciplinary issues in autobiographical self-representation, and the realities of unequal social, cultural and economic capital between women.

LGBTQ Lives and Personal Narrative

The power of personal testimony and life writing to effect personal and
political change is attested to most recently by the campaign for same-
sex marriage in Ireland. In *Ireland Says Yes* (2015), the authors note the
Yes Equality campaign's strategic choice to 'tap in to the rich vein of
personal stories emerging online and offline'.[30] The personal stories of
public figures such as Ursula Halligan as well as the exhortation to individuals to share positive stories with family and friends were seen as key
to winning the referendum. Such stories partook of the coming-out narrative that has been so central to lesbian, gay, bisexual, transgender and
queer (LGBTQ) identities, activism and community building since the
1970s. The same strategy is evident in the collective LGBTQ testimonies
that have been published since the 1980s, including *Out for Ourselves:
The Lives of Irish Lesbians and Gay Men* (1986), *Lesbian and Gay Visions
of Ireland* (1995), *Coming Out: Irish Gay Experience* (2003) and more

recently *Running Amach in Ireland: True Stories by LGBTQ Women* (2015) and Charlie Bird's *A Day in May: Real Lives, True Stories* (2015), a collection of personal narratives published in the wake of the referendum.[31] In her critique of the coming-out narrative in North American lesbian autobiographical writing, Biddy Martin observes (following Bonnie Zimmerman) that: 'Self-worth, identity and a sense of community have fundamentally depended on the production of a shared narrative or life history and on the assimilation of individuals' life histories into the history of the group'.[32] Shared life stories create a sense of identification and belonging that are vital to people who have been silenced and marginalized; however, 'the production of a shared narrative' can result in its own form of normalization and exclusion, as the lived stories of those who do not fit the narrative are erased in turn. Such erasures are evident in many of the edited collections listed above, which focus on lesbians to the exclusion of trans and bisexual women, for instance, and in the Marriage Referendum campaign where concern with alienating 'the middle ground' meant the silencing of the stories of many queer and trans women.

Questions of Authority in Women's Mediated Life Writing

Collaborative processes in women's life writing raise 'the problem of authority and control over the text', as Carol Boyce Davies notes.[33] Mediated life narratives involve interviewers, transcribers, interpreters, editors and co-writers who inevitably influence the shape of the narrative. The collaborator, usually in the position of expert, translates minority cultural realities and ways of life for a majority audience. Some forms of mediation are clearly interventionist, as in *Lyn: A Story of Prostitution*, a collaboration between Lyn Madden and June Levine. However, no matter how respectful the transcriber-editor's hand (as in the case of Nan Joyce's *Traveller*), translating from oral to written form entails a degree of mediation that inevitably affects the narrative. A survey of these two memoirs indicates the effect mediation can have on ownership of the personal narratives of women from subjugated and stigmatized communities, flagging how class, racialization and socio-cultural status inflect the dynamics of authorial control and voice between the (subaltern) autobiographical 'I' and the (majority community) 'translator'.

Lyn: A Story of Prostitution (1987) tells the life story of Lyn Madden, a former sex worker who testified against John Cullen in his trial for the murder of Dolores Lynch, her mother Kathleen and aunt Hannah.

Levine is credited as both author and editor; Madden's narrative is in the third person, with Levine's narratorial voice mediating between Madden and the reader. Levine's narrative style has a somewhat sensationalizing, fictionalizing, objectifying effect, compounded by her role as what she calls an 'interpreter' of 'a language, a way of life, which is foreign to the average reader'.[34] Madden's story foregrounds the interconnectedness of class inequality, state negligence and widespread indifference to extreme, murderous violence against marginalized women and sex workers. Levine situates Madden's narrative within the dominant second-wave feminist anti-prostitution analysis of sex work. Madden's own position is less clear-cut – reflecting the disjunction between the women's class positions and life circumstances that inflects the position Levine assumes in relation to Madden. She is not just an editor of Madden's story, but also her adviser, a key participant in Madden's journey to self-understanding who imparts feminist and psychological wisdom hitherto hidden from Madden. A similar positioning is repeated in the editorial apparatus of Madden's sequel, *Lyn's Escape from Prostitution* (2008). Madden is credited as the sole author and Levine as editor. However, in the 'Preface', Levine's discussion of Madden and their relationship is uncomfortably proprietorial and paternalistic, with Levine positioning herself as therapist, teacher and guru-figure in relation to Madden. This second memoir, though, is in Madden's voice in the first person, without the confusion between autobiographical self and 'translator' that intervenes between the reader and Madden in *Lyn*.[35]

Nan Joyce's *Traveller: An Autobiography* (1985) was produced in collaboration with Anna Farmar, who transcribed and edited Joyce's taped oral narrative.[36] *Traveller* is a good example of a collaboratively produced, extended autobiographical narrative, the purpose of which is explicitly collective and political. In Joyce's crafted storytelling, individual and communal life are inseparable, reflecting an understanding of the personal as rooted in a collective identity and way of life. While Farmar insisted, according to Martin Shaw, that Joyce's narrative 'be mediated as little as possible', Shaw underlines the effects of collaboration: 'The reader of the life story is not only met with Joyce's urgent, yet reflexive and empathetic, narrating voice, but also a series of words and sentences whose contents are comprised of a complex conflation of voices' and that marshall Joyce's story into a linear narrative for a literate majority culture.[37] Joyce emerged as a leading voice in the Traveller community in the early 1980s, and *Traveller* is perhaps best understood as an act of community advocacy. Joyce's concern is not to construct an autobiographical self or find her personal voice, but to represent a community subjected to systemic racist exclusion, stigmatization and violence, to counter negative stereotypes of Travellers, advance the rights and recognition of her community and foster intercultural understanding in the settled majority population. In anecdotes and portraits of her family and community and in direct address to the reader, Joyce describes how the situation of her community has deteriorated since the state's adoption of a policy of forced settlement and 'assimilation', and its refusal to recognize Travellers as an ethnic minority. The second edition, published in 2000, includes Joyce's 'Afterword', where she describes an ongoing situation of routine violence: 'years of being hunted by the police and being bulldozed down and their trailers being broken ... all the children that died, all the women that died'.[38] While Travellers – particularly Traveller women – have achieved hard-won political visibility and voice, Joyce criticizes the Traveller NGO sector for giving paid positions to settled people over Travellers, who are used for their 'authentic' stories by 'experts' who advocate on their behalf. This demonstrates the strategic centrality of personal testimony to contemporary human rights and social justice advocacy, as well as the sometimes problematic, even exploitative use of people for stories that lend organizations legitimacy.

Bearing Witness: Memoirs and Testimony of Survivors of Institutional Abuse

Memoirs of childhood occupy a defining position in the representation of Ireland's past and its relation to the present. Some, such as Alice Taylor's *To School Through the Fields* (1988)[39] and its sequels, portray an idyllic past remembered with fond nostalgia. As Diarmaid Ferriter has noted, it is difficult to reconcile this idealized version of Ireland with the brutal realities that dominate recent accounts of Irish childhood.[40] First-person accounts by survivors of Ireland's 'architecture of containment' began to be published with increasing frequency in the 1980s and 1990s[41], particularly with the broadcasting of Louis Lentin's documentary *Dear Daughter* (1996). Lentin's work focused on the testimony of Christine Buckley, campaigner, activist and survivor of Goldenbridge industrial school and Mary Raftery's three-part series *States of Fear* (1999)[42] which finally galvanized public attention and government action with Taoiseach Bertie Ahern offering an official state apology and promising to initiate an official enquiry and redress scheme.[43]

Leigh Gilmore notes that in the early 1990s, 'memoirs identified the systemic nature of disenfranchisement' and typically connected personal traumatic experience to structural and ideological causes, linking 'suffering and violence to poverty and state indifference'.[44] The personal narratives of women survivors in 1990s Ireland bear out these observations. Patricia Burke Brogan's play *Eclipsed* (1992), a thinly fictionalized and ground-breaking account of the Magdalene Laundry regime, captured her personal witness as a novice in the Sisters of Mercy of the cruelty suffered by inmates.[45] In *You May Talk Now!* (1994), Mary Phil Drennan describes the violence and deprivation of life in Cobh orphanage and Rushbrooke.[46] Drennan's testimony has a collective objective – to make her experiences known to a public that has been reluctant to listen, and to encourage other survivors to speak. The book's title refers specifically to the total silence demanded during mealtimes, which was broken only when 'Matron' rang her silver bell allowing ten minutes of talk. Bernadette Fahy likewise emphasizes the complexity and significance of silence, speech and being heard in her 1999 memoir, *Freedom of Angels: Surviving Goldenbridge Orphanage*. When she spoke about her experiences, Fahy found that 'some people thought we might be exaggerating ... This made it even more difficult to talk about our lives and we felt that nobody really understood'.[47] Drennan and Fahy emphasize the routine cruelty and regimented discipline they endured, the crippling shame that was inculcated in them and their resultant difficulties in developing a sense of identity and their struggle to establish functional and loving relationships, most particularly with their mothers. For both, a rigidly patriarchal and class-stratified society is the explanatory context for the industrial school system. The ruling class used the system to render the poor docile, fearful and obedient. Both emphasize the continuity between material, structural realities outside and inside the institutions. As Fahy notes, the suffering of most child inmates 'did not begin with the Sisters of Mercy. A significant number of us had been rejected before we ever arrived there'.[48] The interconnected operation of power within the family, society and institutions of incarceration is at the centre of Connie Roberts's poetic testimony, *Little Witness* (2015).[49] First admitted to Mount Carmel in Westmeath when she was five, Roberts and her fourteen siblings grew up in industrial schools. Roberts's poems anatomize Mount Carmel and the mentality of its overseers, while also documenting the continuity of its regime with the violence of family life, dominated by her father's alcoholism and abuse. The poems situate Roberts's experience in relation to the suffering and exploitation of others: children who died horrific deaths as inmates, adults whose fate was suicide or destitution, people on other continents deprived of freedom and dignity and exploited as forced labour. The collection is a literary witness that successfully resists the subsumption of survivors' lives into the depersonalized evidentiary forms of legalistic frameworks, commission reports and research data.

Personal narratives of adult survivors also take the form of collective testimonies that emphasize the widespread, systemic nature of institutional abuse. Such collective testimonies draw on oral history methodologies, with the compiler-author – generally not themselves a survivor – acting as transcriber, editor and commentator. Oral life narratives, as Davies observes, 'facilitate empowerment for women who historically have been silenced, whose words are not accepted as having legitimacy in the realm of accepted public discourse where formal autobiography resides'.[50] As Julia Swindells notes, such projects 'move beyond autobiography as the life story of the key individual' and instead become 'part of a political strategy to produce change'.[51] *Suffer the Little Children* (1999), co-written by Mary Raftery and Eoin O'Sullivan, combines archival research and analysis of the network of industrial schools, reformatories and orphanages with extensive transcriptions from the personal narratives of survivors. Corroborating the witness and analyses of Drennan, Fahy and Roberts, what Raftery and O'Sullivan identify as the networked hierarchy of institutions of detention, demonstrates 'the nuances of the very rigid class system which operated in Ireland' for most of the twentieth century.[52] The cumulative personal narratives powerfully support the explicitly political demand of the book for an adequate response from church and state to survivors' demands in the present. Whilst the Magdalene Laundry Oral History Project has done extensive work in recording interviews with survivors of the Magdalene Laundries the more conventionally published narratives are more problematic. *Whispering Hope: The True Story of the Magdalene Women* (2015) brings together the personal narratives of five women who were incarcerated in the laundries: Kathleen Legg, Marina Gambold, Nancy Costello, Diane Croghan and Marie Slattery, who are all members of Magdalene Survivors Together, a group founded by Steven O'Riordain, director of the 2010 documentary *The Forgotten Maggies*.[53] The women's narratives bear witness to the network of carceral institutions that poor and vulnerable women and children were subjected to, with some women having been inmates of county homes, industrial schools, and mother and baby homes as well as the laundries. The telling of their stories is framed by the women as breaking the imposed silences of their pasts: the silence imposed in the laundries on fear of punishment, the silence in their own lives about their pasts, reinforced by an internalized shame, and the long, culpable silences of the state and church. The memoir aims to transform the lives of the women themselves through the act of telling their stories, while communicating their stories to a wider audience. The book again raises the issue of authorial and editorial control in the shaping of life stories. The women's personal narratives are framed at the beginning, middle and conclusion of the book by chapters by O'Riordain which position him as 'rescuer' and activist at the expense of the centrality of the survivors themselves. Unlike Raftery and O'Sullivan's text, the political objectives in *Whispering Hope* are represented by O'Riordain, especially, as having already been achieved. As such, the book as a whole is structured as a journey from suffering to redemption – a trajectory which is belied by women's narratives, many of which emphasize the ongoing damage the past wreaks on their lives. The redemption trajectory in which the women's stories are embedded suggests a closure that does not exist for many survivors in reality, and obfuscates the continuing government resistance that the Magdalene survivors have experienced in getting full compensation and supports from the state.

As Schaffer and Smith note, commissions, tribunals and hearings offer the possibility for 'previously silenced voices to be heard in new legitimating contexts'. However, in giving testimony in such official contexts, witnesses also relinquish control over their own narratives, giving 'their stories over to institutional shaping'.[54] Personal witness has contributed to progressive social transformation in Ireland, but has also been used against those who give testimony. For instance, the McAleese Report on state culpability for the Magdalene Laundries not only omitted 800 pages of survivor testimony, the committee also ruled out considering such testimony in their deliberations. As framed in the report, it was the committee who did survivors a favour in listening to their stories, rather than the women who did the nation remarkable service in giving evidence of the terrible injustice and suffering inflicted on them by that same nation. This attitude suffuses a statement such as this, for example: 'These women, to a large extent, have not previously had the opportunity to share their memories and experiences.'[55] Such elicitation and dismissal of the 'ordinary witness' demonstrates the cynical uses that the confessional and testimonial imperative can be put to. Commissions, reports and redress schemes are framed by the state as the mechanisms through which the traumatic past can be healed, thus installing a cordon sanitaire between that past and an enlightened present even as the state continues to evade its responsibility to those it has violated. The 2016 report by Justice Harding Clark on the Symphysiotomy Redress Scheme, for instance, derides women's personal testimony as exaggerated, lurid and lacking credibility because of the tainting influence of lawyers and activists. As Mairéad Enright notes, women's testimony is quoted only to represent 'their statements as part of a clumsily orchestrated attempt to mislead the scheme'.[56] The emancipatory effects of 'finding a voice' are not, then, as straightforward or uniform as might be assumed.

Migration, Race and the Politics of Voice

While migration features in much women's life writing in Ireland, equivalents of male-authored memoirs that specifically foreground migrant experience, such as Donal MacAmhlaigh's *An Irish Navvy* (1964), are scarce. Irish women's migration stories are found largely in oral history collections and academic research projects.[57] Similarly, the life stories of migrant women in Ireland are found predominantly in non-literary venues: in academic research, NGO publications, activist campaigns and committee hearings reports. In relation to women's personal narratives of migration, Mary Lennon, Marie McAdam and Joanne O'Brien's *Across the Water: Irish Women's Lives in Britain* (1987) and Íde O'Carroll's *Models for Movers* (1990), the first focused on Irish women in Britain, the second in the United States, were at the vanguard of what Bronwen Walter calls the 'burst of writing about Irish women in the diaspora after the 1980s'.[58] Both are feminist projects that allow women 'who had been "hidden from history"' to tell stories that had been silenced by scholars blind to their value.[59] The issue of authorial control arises again, however. For instance, while O'Carroll observes her ethical commitment 'to respect Irish women's right to narrate their histories in their own words', her interpretation of those narratives does not necessarily coincide with her informants' perspectives. 'While I frame the situation in Ireland as patriarchal oppression,' O'Carroll states: 'The women I talked to describe how there was no paying work and life on the farm held little for them.'[60]

Migrant women writers in Ireland face multiple barriers in reaching the 'majority' population. These same barriers – constituted by diverse manifestations of systemic racism and marginalization from normative cultural gatekeeping to border securitization and enforcement – explain why the life narratives of migrant women in contemporary Ireland are seldom found outside of publications with social justice and 'intercultural' objectives, publications in which the women themselves are rarely credited as authors. In an interview with Jody Allen Randolph in 2009,

Olutoyin Pamela Akinjobi observes that: 'There appear to be ethnic boundaries in Irish literature, which set conditions as to who can be included in it and who cannot.'[61] Similarly, novelist Ifedinma Dimbo remarks that she 'was told by a reputable bookshop that nobody is interested in what a Nigerian has to say'.[62] Having spent three years in the Irish asylum system, deprived of the right to work and warehoused out of sight in direct provision, Dimbo articulates the connection between the racist dehumanization of people in the asylum system and her exclusion from Irish literary platforms.

The exclusion of migrant women from the category 'woman' in Ireland is critiqued by Ebun Joseph Akpoveta. When migrant women are taken into account in 'mainstream discourse', they are generally 'added on', as the objects of analysis and sources of personal testimony rather than as analysts and commentators in their own right. As Akpoveta explains:

> when one looks at the different issues that concern women, migrant women are not part of the mainstream discourse … if the issue were migration, then migrant women are added or, should I say, they are the quintessential subjects of this discourse. Migrant women are always added in, not part of … If you understand what I mean. And, accordingly, if these women continue to be added on as an afterthought, then the solutions to their issues will always be secondary … In Ireland, migrant women still have to fight for their problems outside the mainstream of women's issues.[63]

In her blog *Steal This Hijab*, Farah Mokhtareizedah incorporates autobiographical elements in her analysis of coloniality and in generating a decolonial feminist politics and theoretics that is grounded in but not confined to her own position and experience as a woman of Iranian-Irish-American background. As she argues,

> the capacity for feminists to aspire towards changing the societies in which we live is not separate from the political and cultural regimes within which our lives are intertwined. By understanding the complex dynamics of our identities and their contexts we can transform the dominant narratives that frame our personal and political lives and make genuine solidarity possible.[64]

Many women of colour and of migrant background in Ireland incorporate autobiographical elements in their writing and analysis, insisting on the inseparability of the personal and the political in ways that challenge the normative scripts of feminism and gendered identity in contemporary Ireland. For instance, in a piece produced for RTÉ Radio One's Documentary on One, writer, journalist and activist Neltah

Chadamoyo tells the story of her brother-in-law's life and death. In this piece, Chadamoyo draws on interwoven memories and conversations with her sister and nieces, a process of personal storytelling that goes beyond the kind of testimony elicited by both 'advocates' and the media, 'to access people, to tell stories from different places', reclaiming voice, experience and analysis that can be erased by what Ebun Akpoveta calls 'the single story' that women of migrant background are often confined within.[65] In her one-woman play *Broken Promise Land* (2013), Mirjana Rendulic draws on her personal narrative in a way that challenges the 'single story' that informs normative mainstream feminist scripts in Ireland about migrant women's experiences of and reasons for working in the sex industry.[66] Rendulic particularly critiques the stereotypes of women from eastern Europe in the industry as invariably exploited victims and without agency: 'The play isn't embracing [the sex industry]. Nor is it saying, "we are victims." It's just saying, "this is what happens."'[67]

The majority of published and readily accessible women's personal narratives of their experiences as migrant women in Ireland are published by NGOs as part of specific campaigns, or as collective life narratives with the objectives of cultural visibility, intercultural education and personal and collective empowerment.[68] Critiques of the confessional turn often focus on how the heroic, redemptive, individualist trajectory that such narratives can take masks the structural drivers of inequality. At the same time, narratives that focus solely on suffering and trauma can reinforce a racialized neo-colonial dynamic that reduces women to passive victims to be rescued. Three volumes of life stories published between 2006 and 2013 by AkiDwA, a migrant-led organization for African and migrant women in Ireland, seek to challenge marginalization and silencing by creating a platform for migrant women to tell their own stories. While their stories foreground their strength, resilience and hopes for the future, the women in these collections are not apolitical or silent about the operations of the racist state. Many of the women's narratives eloquently critique the social death imposed by the Direct Provision system, for instance. Heather notes that in Ireland 'as a migrant woman I ultimately was not allowed to do anything. I was really being locked up for so many years'.[69] Betty concurs: 'You just start feeling that you are nothing, and they tell you that you are nothing.'[70]

Herstory: Migration Stories of African Women in Ireland (2006) mediates the personal narratives of ten women.[71] Two key tenets of post-1970s feminist life writing are central to the collection: that 'finding a voice' is transformative on a personal and political level; and that trauma can be processed by telling one's story. The circumstances of the women's migration journeys are narrated in some detail so that we get a sense of the individual women and what they have faced and overcome, rather than subsuming different women's lives into a generalizing stereotype or reducing them to evidence. However, the women's stories are narrated in the third person, foregrounding Akinjobi as author and cultural mediator. Most of the eleven personal narratives included in *Home and Away: Migrant Women Transforming Ireland* (2011) address the administrative and cultural difficulties of negotiating life in Ireland and the precarious position of migrant women who are denied the right to work or work in industries vulnerable to exploitation – domestic work, the service industry and the sex industry, for instance.[72] The different obstacles faced by migrant women in Ireland are determined largely by race, status and the asylum and the Direct Provision system. Mary Ann Wangari Mullen, who came to Ireland in 1988, observes that 'Ireland has changed into a very racist country' and that 'integration is getting harder and harder'.[73] Zuzana Tesarova notes the contrast between her own experience and that of the young women she has worked with in the asylum system. The contrast hinges on race, class and cultural capital: 'I am a middle-class, white, educated, good-looking woman with fluent English … I didn't present any challenge to the status quo.'[74] The collection emphasizes the importance of voice. Yasmin Kutub, a Bangladeshi-British woman working in Ireland, considers the lack of minority-led NGOs in Ireland as a neo-colonial situation that is part of the infrastructure of systemic racism in Ireland. Established as a specifically migrant woman-led organization with a key objective to create a platform for migrant women to speak for themselves rather than be spoken for, AkiDwA has sought to challenge this situation, and narratives such as Kutub's demonstrate the critical role of women's personal narratives in migrant justice activism. *Between Two Cultures: Inspirational Stories of Young Migrant Women in Ireland* (2013), a collection of six young women's personal narratives arising from the 'Inspirational Stories Project', again emphasizes the importance of platforms that amplify women's voices, particularly platforms created and sustained by migrant women and women of colour by and for themselves. As Julia writes: 'Being able to tell my story here is giving me a voice.'[75] However, speech and silence are complex for those vulnerable to expulsion from the state and whose stories are subject to legal adjudication and cultural delegitimation. As Wangari Mullen observes in *Home and Away*: 'You are afraid to talk in case you are thrown out.'[76] Betty,

who lived in Somalia and Yemen before coming to Ireland, complicates
the notion that telling the story of a traumatic past is a simply liberating act: 'Sometimes I don't want to go back to those thoughts. I feel like
going back there can be a barrier to me in what I want to do, where I
want to go, to moving forward.'[77]

Media interviews and reports, community arts projects and government committee reports have also been key venues for the personal narratives of women of migrant backgrounds. Activists such as Ellie Kisyombe,
Patricia Murambinda and Donnah Vuma have used personal narrative
and testimony in the media to push for change to the asylum and the
Direct Provision system in Ireland.[78] Based on the life stories of people
living in Direct Provision, Carl O'Brien's 'Lives in Limbo' series ran in
the *Irish Times* in August 2013. The Migrants Rights Centre Ireland
(MRCI) Domestic Workers Support Group's 2007 exhibition 'Opening
Doors: Migrant Domestic Workers Speak Through Art' arose from their
collaboration with artist Susan Gogan. 'Undocumented in Ireland: Our
Stories' (2007) and 'Direct Provision in Ireland: Nine Stories' are collaborative digital storytelling projects directed by Darcy Alexander that give
a multimedia platform to migrant women's personal narratives. Despite
legitimate fears of repercussions for speaking out, migrant women have
also managed to put aspects of their life stories on public record in recent
years by using the platform of testifying in front of Oireachtas commit-
tees with the political aim of effecting change in the state's migration
apparatus, thereby using their own life stories in the struggle for migrant
justice and once more linking autobiography with the nation.[79]

The story of women's life writing and personal testimony in Ireland since
1970 demonstrates the symbiotic relationship between women's public
claiming of their diverse voices and women's achievement of social change.
Nonetheless, anxiety about disciplinary divisions between different forms
of personal narrative can translate into anxieties about what constitutes
(for instance) properly literary and sociological 'evidence'. In their work on
life narratives and human rights, Schaffer and Smith note that while two
dominant contemporary modes for the articulation of life writing – human
rights testimony and published memoirs – 'have commonly been understood to exist within the separate domains of politics and literature', an
interdisciplinary and socially engaged approach 'understands "the political"
as inclusive of moral, aesthetic and ethical aspects of culture' and personal
narrative in this context as a multidimensional domain where these different
modes of address intersect in both emancipatory and problematic ways.[80]
The stratifications of class, citizenship, race and ethnicity, gender and sexual

normativities are reflected in the hierarchies of genre and authorial credit. However, the cultural landscape is in a process of profound transformation. The affordances of internet and digital technologies have given unprecedented access to audience for those excluded from traditional publication routes, with blogging and social media platforms, online forums and communities democratizing the means for women to record and distribute their life stories and testimony. It is in these areas which this chapter has not had space to explore that the future direction of life writing lies.

Notes

1 Gayatri Spivak, 'Three Women's Texts and Circumfession', in *Postcolonialism and Autobiography*, ed. Alfred Hornung and Ernstpeter Ruhe (Amsterdam: Editions Rodopi, 1998), 7.

2 Patricia Hill Collins, *Black Feminist Thought: Knowledge, Consciousness, and the Politics of Empowerment* (Boston, MA: Unwin, 1990), 221.

3 On the dominance of the self-nation trope in Irish autobiography, see Michael Kenneally, 'The Autobiographical Imagination and Irish Autobiographies', in *Critical Approaches to Anglo-Irish Literature*, ed. Michael Allen and Angela Wilcox (Totowa, NJ: Barnes and Noble, 1989), 123; Seamus Deane, 'Introduction' to 'Autobiography and Memoir', *The Field Day Anthology of Irish Writing*, ed. Andrew Carpenter et al., 3 vols. (Cork: Field Day, 1991), 3: 380; Roy Foster, *The Irish Story: Telling Tales and Making It Up in Ireland* (Oxford: Oxford University Press, 2002); Claire Lynch, *Irish Autobiography: Stories of Self in the Narrative of a Nation* (Bern: Peter Lang, 2009); Liam Harte, 'Introduction', in *Modern Irish Autobiography: Self, Society and Nation* (Basingstoke: Palgrave, 2007); Taura Napier, *Seeking a Country: Literary Autobiographies of Twentieth-Century Irishwomen* (Lanham, MD: University Press of America, 2001), 37.

4 Selina Guinness, *The Crocodile by the Door: The Story of a House, a Farm and a Family* (Harmondsworth: Penguin, 2012).

5 Leland Bardwell, *A Restless Life* (Dublin: Liberties Press, 2008).

6 Máire Cruise O'Brien, *The Same Age as the State* (Dublin: The O'Brien Press, 2003). Other important literary autobiographical writing published since 1970 ranging across different genres and modes includes *A Portrait of the Artist as a Young Girl*, ed. John Quinn (London: Methuen, 1986), a collection of childhood memoirs by Irish women writers such as Maeve Binchy, Clare Boylan, Polly Devlin, Jennifer Johnston, Molly Keane, Mary Lavin, Joan Lingard, Dervla Murphy and Edna O'Brien; Jessie Lendennie, *Daughter* (Galway: Salmon Poetry, 1988); Nuala Ní Dhomhnaill's essays which typically use autobiographical elements (see *Selected Essays*, ed. Oona Frawley (Dublin: New Island, 2005); Edna O'Brien, *Country Girl: A Memoir* (London: Faber and Faber, 2012); Julia O'Faoláin, *Trespassers: A Memoir* (London: Faber and Faber, 2013); Vona Groarke, *Four Sides Full: A Personal Essay* (Loughcrew: Gallery Press, 2016).

7 Eavan Boland, *Object Lessons: The Life of the Woman and the Poet in Our Time* (Manchester: Carcanet, 1995).

8 Edna O'Brien, *Mother Ireland: A Memoir* (Harmondsworth: Penguin, 1976), 1.

9 Anne Enright, *Making Babies: Stumbling into Motherhood* (London: Vintage, 2005), 186.

10 Rita Ann Higgins, *Hurting God: Part Essay, Part Rhyme* (Cliffs of Moher: Salmon Poetry, 2010), 18.

11 June Levine, *Sisters: The Personal Story of an Irish Feminist*, afterword by Nell McCafferty, 2nd edn, Kindle edn (Cork: Attic Press, 2009), loc. 2035.

12 Audre Lorde, 'Age, Race, Sex and Class: Women Redefining Difference', in *Sister Outsider: Essay and Speeches* (New York, NY: Crossing Press, 1984), 116.

13 Maura Richards, *Single Issue* (Dublin: Poolbeg, 1998), 3.

14 Ibid., 46.

15 Joanne Hayes, *My Story* (Dingle, Co. Kerry: Brandon, 1985), 96.

16 Ibid., 102.

17 Nell McCafferty, *A Woman to Blame: The Kerry Babies Case*, new edn, Kindle edn (Dublin: Attic Press, 2010), loc. 1771.

18 Ibid., loc. 1958.

19 Aidan O'Connor, 'Joanne Breaks 20-Year Silence with Plea to Stop Film', *Irish Independent*, 2 June 2006. www.independent.ie/regionals/kerryman/news/joanne-hayes-breaks-20year-silence-with-plea-to-stop-film-27359498.html

20 Nuala O'Faolain, *Are You Somebody?* (Dublin: New Island, 1996), 221; *Almost There: The Onward Journey of a Dublin Woman* (New York, NY: Riverhead Books, 2003), 59.

21 O'Faolain, *Are You Somebody?*, 10.

22 Nell McCafferty, *Nell: A Disorderly Woman* (Dublin: Penguin, 2004), 1.

23 Ibid., 283, 284.

24 Bernadette Devlin, *The Price of My Soul* (London: Pan Books, 1969).

25 McCafferty, *Nell*, 193.

26 Mary Kenny, 'All Aboard the Condom Train: My Side of the Story', in *Something of Myself and Others: Memories and Reflections* (Dublin: Original Writing, 2012), 53.

27 Nuala Fennell, *Political Woman: A Memoir* (Kildare: Curragh Press, 2010).

28 Mary O'Rourke, *Just Mary: My Memoir* (Dublin: Gill Books, 2012); *Letters of My Life* (Dublin: Gill Books, 2016).

29 Rita Felski, 'On Confession', in *Beyond Feminist Aesthetics: Feminist Literature and Social Change* (Harvard: Harvard University Press, 1989), 94.

30 Grainne Healy, Brian Sheehan and Noel Whelan, *Ireland Says Yes: The Inside Story of How the Vote for Marriage Equality was Won* (Dublin: Irish Academic Press, 2015), 40.

31 Clodagh Boyd et al., eds., *Out for Ourselves: The Lives of Irish Lesbians and Gay Men* (Dublin: Dublin Lesbian and Gay Men's Collective, 1986); Íde

O'Carroll and Eoin Collins, eds., *Lesbian and Gay Visions of Ireland: Towards the Twenty-First Century* (London and New York, NY: Cassell, 1995); Maureen Looney, ed., *Running Amach in Ireland: True Stories by LGBTQ Women* (Dublin: Orpen Press, 2015); Charlie Bird, *A Day in May: Real Lives, True Stories* (Dublin: Irish Academic Press, 2016).

32 Biddy Martin, 'Lesbian Identity and Autobiographical Difference[s]', in *The Lesbian and Gay Studies Reader*, ed. Henry Abelove, Michele Aina Barale and David Halperin (New York and London: Routledge, 1993), 278.

33 Carol Boyce Davies, 'Collaboration and the Ordering Imperative in Life Story Production', in *De/Colonizing the Subject: The Politics of Gender in Women's Autobiography*, ed. Sidonie Smith and Julia Watson (Minneapolis, MN: University of Minnesota Press, 1992), 3.

34 June Levine, in Lyn Madden and June Levine, *Lyn: A Story of Prostitution* (Cork: Attic Press, 1987), 3. It is interesting to note that in the section on 'The Women's Movement in the Republic of Ireland, 1968–1980' in *The Field Day Anthology*, vol. 5, edited by June Levine, it is Madden's letters to Levine that are excerpted rather than the published memoir. See Angela Bourke, et al., eds., *The Field Day Anthology of Irish Writing Vols. IV & V: Irish Women's Writing and Traditions* (Cork: Cork University Press, 2002), 5: 219–20.

35 Lyn Madden, *Lyn: My Escape from Prostitution* (Cork: Cork University Press, 2008).

36 Nan Joyce, *Traveller: An Autobiography*, ed. Anna Farmar (Dublin: Gill Books, 1985). For other examples of Traveller women's personal narratives, see the collective life stories included in *Moving Stories: Traveller Women Write* (London: Southwark Traveller Women's Group, 1992) and *Traveller Ways, Traveller Words*, ed. Gearóid Ó Riain (Dublin: Pavee Point Publications, 1992).

37 Martin Shaw, 'Warning Signs: Hybridity and Violence in Nan Joyce's "Traveller" and "My Life on the Road"', *Nordic Irish Studies* 11, no. 1 (2012): 63.

38 Nan Joyce, *My Life on the Road: An Autobiography*, ed. Anna Farmar (Dublin: A. & A. Farmar 2000), xv.

39 Alice Taylor, *To School through the Fields: An Irish Country Childhood* (Dingle: Brandon, 1988).

40 Ferriter Diarmaid, 'Suffer Little Children? The Historical Validity of Memoirs of Irish Childhood', in *Childhood and Its Discontents: The First Seamus Heaney Lectures*, ed. Joseph Dunne and James Kelly (Dublin: The Liffey Press, 2003), 69–107.

41 See, for instance, Mannix Flynn, *Nothing to Say* (Dublin: Ward River Press, 1983) and Paddy Doyle, *The God Squad* (Dublin: Raven Arts Press, 1988). This overview focuses on women's personal narratives of institutional abuse, but other childhood memoirs include Christina McKenna, *My Mother Wore a Yellow Dress: An Irish Childhood in the 1960s* (Glasgow: Neil Wilson Publishing, 2004); Lily O'Connor, *Can Lily O'Shea Come Out to Play?*

(Dingle: Brandon Books, 2000); Edith Newman Devlin, *Speaking Volumes: A Dublin Childhood* (New York, NY: E. P. Dutton, 2000).

42 *Dear Daughter*, directed by Louis Lentin (Crescendo Concepts for RTÉ, 1996); *States of Fear*, produced by Mary Raftery (RTÉ, 1999).

43 The work of survivors of institutional abuse and their supporters has led to various commissions of enquiry resulting in the Ferns Report (2005); the Ryan Report (2009); the Murphy Report (2009) and the McAleese Report (2013). Given space constraints, the personal testimony in these reports and collected by projects such as the Magdalene Oral History Project (www .magdaleneoralhistory.com/oralhistories.htm) and the Waterford Memories Project (www.waterfordmemories.com/) along with some important single-author personal narratives of institutional abuse cannot be discussed in detail here. Further published memoirs include Hanna Greally, *Bird's Nest Soup: Locked Up in an Irish Psychiatric Hospital* rev. ed. 1971 (Cork: Cork University Press, 2008); Kathy Beirne, *Kathy's Story: A Childhood Hell Inside the Magdalen Laundries* (Edinburgh: Mainstream Publishing, 2005); Frances Reilly, *Suffer the Little Children* (London: Orion, 2010); Kathleen O'Malley, *Childhood Interrupted: Growing Up in an Industrial School* (London: Virago, 2011); Irene Kelly, *Sins of the Mother* (London: Pan Macmillan, 2015).

44 Leigh Gilmore, 'American Neoconfessional: Memoir, Self-Help, and Redemption on Oprah's Couch', *Biography* 33, no. 4 (2010): 659.

45 See Patricia Burke Brogan, *Memoir with Gyrkes and Turloughs* (Galway: wordsonthestreet, 2014), for an account of her time in the Sisters of Mercy and the writing of *Eclipsed* (Galway: Salmon Publishing, 1994). See also Burke Brogan, 'The Magdalene Experience', in *Motherhood in Ireland: Creation and Context*, ed. Patricia Kennedy (Cork: Mercier Press, 2004), 160–9.

46 Mary Phil Drennan, *You May Talk Now!* (Blarney: On Stream, 1994).

47 Bernadette Fahy, *Freedom of Angels: Surviving Goldenbridge Orphanage* (Dublin: The O'Brien Press, 1999), 178.

48 Ibid., 14.

49 Connie Roberts, *Little Witness* (Dublin: Arlen House, 2015).

50 Davies, 'Collaboration and the Ordering Imperative', 15.

51 Julia Swindells, 'Autobiography and the Politics of the "Personal,"' in Julia Swindells, ed. *The Uses of Autobiography* (London: Routledge, 1995).

52 Mary Raftery and Eoin O'Sullivan, *Suffer the Little Children: The Inside Story of Ireland's Industrial Schools*, Kindle edn (Dublin: New Island, 2001), loc. 5076.

53 Nancy Costello, Kathleen Legg, Diane Croghan, et al., *Whispering Hope: The True Story of the Magdalene Women* (London: Orion, 2015). See also *The Forgotten Maggies*, directed by Steven O'Riordain (2009).

54 Kay Schaffer and Sidonie Smith, *Human Rights and Narrated Lives: The Ethics of Recognition* (Basingstoke: Palgrave Macmillan, 2004), 40.

55 Report of the Inter-Departmental Committee to establish the facts of State involvement with the Magdalen Laundries 2013 (McAleese Report), 925. Accessed 23 March 2017. On women's testimony, see chapter 19, 'Living and Working Conditions', www.justice.ie/en/JELR/Pages/MagdalenRpt2013.

56 Mairéad Enright, 'Notes on Judge Harding Clark's Report on the Symphysiotomy Payment Scheme', *Human Rights in Ireland*. Accessed 24 November 2016. http://humanrights.ie/law-culture-and-religion/notes-on-judge-harding-clarks-report-on-the-symphysiotomy-payment-scheme/

57 See, for instance, the UCC Irish Centre for Migration Studies project 'Breaking the Silence: Staying at Home in an Emigrant Society' and Breda Gray's analysis of women's personal narratives compiled during the project in 'Breaking the Silence: Emigration, Gender and the Making of Irish Cultural Memory', in Liam Harte, ed., *Modern Irish Autobiography: Self, Nation and Society* (Basingstoke: Palgrave, 2007), 111–31; the final report of the Émigre project on contemporary emigration from Ireland: Irial Glynn, Tomás Kelly and Piaras MacÉinrí, *Irish Migration in an Age of Austerity* (Cork: Émigré/The Irish Research Council, 2013); Roisín Ryan-Flood, 'Sexuality, Citizenship and Migration: the Irish Queer Diaspora in London' (Full Research Report ESRC, 2009). Women's personal narratives of migration experiences are often threaded through academic studies of women and migration; see for example Bronwen Walter, *Outsiders Inside: Whiteness, Place and Irish Women* (London: Routledge, 2001); Breda Gray, *Women and the Irish Diaspora* (London and New York: Routledge, 2004).

58 Bronwen Walter, 'Personal Lives: Narrative Accounts of Irish Women in the Diaspora'. *Irish Studies Review* 21, no. 1 (2013): 37.

59 Íde O'Carroll, *Models for Movers: Irish Women's Emigration to America* (Cork: Attic Press, 2015), 12.

60 Ibid., 43. For excellent discussions of this point, see Bronwen Walter, 'Personal Lives' and Breda Gray, 'Breaking the Silence'.

61 Olutoyin Pamela Akinjobi, 'Women Writers in the New Ireland Network', in Jody Allen Randolph, *Close to the Next Moment: Interviews from a Changing Ireland* (Manchester: Carcanet, 2010), 196.

62 Sara Martín-Ruiz, '"The Way the Irish Asylum System Turns People into Un-human is My Problem:" An Interview with Ifenema Dimbo', *Estudios Irlandeses* 10 (2015): 114.

63 Asier Altuna-García de Salazar, '"Migrant Women are Always Added in:" In Conversation with Ebun Joseph Akpoveta', *Estudios Irlandeses* 12 (2017): 160.

64 Farah Mokhtareizedah, 'The Political is Personal', *Steal This Hijab – Feminism Without Borders*. Accessed 18 March 2017. https://stealthishijab.com/2017/03/08/in-2017-the-political-is-personal/

65 Neltah Chadamoyo, 'Neltah Tells a Love Story'. *Documentary on One: The Curious Ear*. RTÉ Radio One, February 2010. www.rte.ie/radio1/doconone/2010/0209/646341-the-curious-ear-neltah/

66 Mirjana Rendulic, 'Broken Promise Land (2013)', in *Staging Intercultural Ireland: New Plays and Practitioner Perspectives*, ed. Charlotte McIvor and Matthew Spangler (Cork: Cork University Press, 2014).

67 Colin Murphy, 'How Mirjana Went from Pole Dancer to Playwright on Her Journey of Discovery', *Irish Independent*. Accessed 3 March 2013. www .independent.ie/entertainment/books/how-mirjana-went-from-pole-dancer-to-playwright-on-her-journey-of-discovery-29104297.html

68 Personal narratives of women's migrant experience in Ireland in addition to the texts to be discussed here include Mary Valarasan-Toomey, *The Celtic Tiger: From the Outside Looking In* (Dublin: Blackhall, 1998); Susan Knight, *Where the Grass is Greener* (Cork: Oak Tree Press, 2001).

69 *Between Two Cultures: Inspirational Stories of Young Migrant Women in Ireland*, compiled by Aedín Kelly, ed. Patrick Guerin (Dublin: AkiDwA, 2013), 28.

70 Ibid., 41.

71 *Herstory: Migration Stories of African Women in Ireland*, compiled by Olutoyin Pamela Akinjobi (Dublin: AkiDwA, 2006).

72 See for instance *We Lived to Tell* (Dublin: AkiDwA, 2012); *A Public Concern: The Experience of Twenty Migrant Women Employed in the Private Home in Ireland* (Dublin: MCRI, 2004); *Part of the Family? The Experiences of au Pairs in Ireland* (Dublin: MRCI, 2012); *Who Cares? The Experience of Migrant Care Workers in Ireland* (Dublin: MRCI, 2012). *Changing Ireland*, compiled by Kate Morris, photographs by Derek Speirs (NCCRI and Equality Commission for Northern Ireland 2006) also contains personal narratives of migrant women in Ireland.

73 *Home and Away: Migrant Women Transforming Ireland*, collected by Frini Makadi and Melatu Okorie (Dublin: AkiDwA, 2011), 32.

74 Ibid., 90.

75 *Between Two Cultures*, 38.

76 *Home and Away*, 43.

77 *Between Two Cultures*, 52.

78 See for instance Kitty Holland and, 'Direct Provision is Killing Our Souls, Protest Hears', *The Irish Times*. Accessed 12 November 2016. www .irishtimes.com/news/social-affairs/direct-provision-is-killing-our-souls-protest-hears-1.2865960; *In the Wings – Our Table*, with Ellie Kisyombe. Drama on One. RTÉ Radio One. 27 January 2017. www.rte.ie/drama/ radio/plays/2017/0127/848213-in-the-wings-our-table/; Kitty Holland, 'My Children Have the Same Needs as All Others at Christmas – I Dread It', *The Irish Times*. Accessed 3 December 2016. www.irishtimes .com/news/social-affairs/my-children-have-the-same-needs-as-all-others-at-christmas-i-dread-it-1.2889387. Many women in the Direct Provision system gave personal testimony and analysis in a series of *Liveline* episodes given over to the topic in 2016: 'Direct Provision', *Liveline*, RTÉ Radio One. Accessed 19–21 September 2016. www.rte.ie/radio1/

liveline/programmes/2016/0919/817624-liveline-monday-19-september-2016/?clipid=2287475

79 See for instance the testimony of Patricia Murambinda and Josephine Bakaabatsile to the Joint Oireachtas Committee on Finance, Public Expenditure and Reform: Freedom of Information (Amendment) Bill 2012 – Discussion. Accessed 6 February 2013. http://oireachtasdebates .oireachtas.ie/Debates%20Authoring/DebatesWebPack.nsf/committee takes/FIJ2013020600018?opendocument. Also the testimony of Pako Mokoba to the Joint Oireachtas Committee on Public Oversight and Petitions: Discussion on Direct Provision. Accessed 23 October 2014. http://oireachtasdebates.oireachtas.ie/debates%20authoring/debatesweb pack.nsf/committeetakes/NVJ2014102200002?opendocument#A00100

80 Schaffer and Smith, *Human Rights and Narrated Lives*, 2.

CHAPTER 21

Diasporic and Transnational Writing, 1950–Present

Ellen McWilliams

Maeve Brennan's novella, *The Visitor*, written in the 1940s, dramatizes the relationship between the Irish woman emigrant and Ireland, and anticipates some of the primary preoccupations of diasporic and transnational Irish women's writing in the later decades of the twentieth century. The opening pages sound a cautionary note: 'Home is a place in the mind. When it is empty, it frets. It is fretful with memory, faces and places and times gone by.'[1] Brennan's triangulation of home, place and memory has proven to be a powerfully anxious and productive formula in post-1950s Irish writing and prefigures new ways of thinking and writing about Ireland's often-contentious history of engaging with its diaspora.

The development of transnational and diasporic writing since the mid-twentieth century has expanded the provenance of women's writing and generated new and vital currencies in critical conversations about the boundaries of Irish literature and the Irish literary canon. The rise of public and academic interest in representations of women's experiences of migration and women in the Irish diaspora has been especially striking given historical silences around Irish emigration and the lives of women migrants in particular. Up until the 1990s, the Irish woman migrant remained what one historian called 'the great unknown'[2] of Irish emigrant history, but since then historians and social scientists have been assiduous in addressing that missing history. The reason for such belated attention, which is all the more surprising given the consistently high rates of female emigration,[3] has been explained, in part, as an effect of a larger public anxiety and embarrassment about the scale of emigration, and particularly the emigration of women, from post-independence Ireland. According to one estimate, three out of every five children born in Ireland in the 1950s left the country at some point[4] and Mary Hickman goes so far as to suggest that the reality of emigration in the Irish Republic into the later decades of the twentieth century was for many people 'a life event as "normal" as leaving school or getting married'.[5]

The story of the Irish woman emigrant has been recovered in the work of social scientists and historians in the last two decades and literary critics have followed suit in developing new models for thinking about women in the diaspora and their representation in literature.[6] President Mary Robinson's call to cherish the previously forgotten Irish diaspora in 1995 – one of the many important changes she enacted as Ireland's first woman president – awoke a new awareness of the need to remember and retain connection with those who left, as well as to foster a greater understanding of the experience of generations of emigrants and acknowledge the estimated seventy million people of Irish descent worldwide[7]: 'The men and women of our diaspora represent not simply a series of departures and losses. They remain, even while absent, a precious reflection of our own growth and change, a precious reminder of the many strands of identity which compose our story.'[8] That discussion took on a new dimension as Ireland became a destination for the establishment of new immigrant communities during the economic prosperity of the late 1990s and 2000s.[9] Debates about emigration from Ireland found new emphasis after the collapse of this 'Celtic Tiger' economy, which saw the emergence of a new kind of rhetoric about the necessity of harnessing the Irish diaspora.[10] One manifestation of this took the form of the cultural initiative, 'The Gathering', in 2013, a recapitulation of earlier attempts to call home the diaspora, such as the An Tóstal festivals of the mid-twentieth century, the first of which was held in 1953.

In the decades between the first An Tóstal and 'The Gathering', Irish women writers were preoccupied with reclaiming the story of the Irish woman migrant in ways that challenged the myth of what historians Patrick Fitzgerald and Brian Lambkin describe as the misleading cultural trope of the 'stay-at-home female'.[11] These writers have given voice to the challenges, anxieties and rewards of establishing a life elsewhere and forging a new relationship with the idea of Ireland as home. This vibrant strand of Irish women's writing often returns to a number of competing and sometimes contradictory problems and possibilities – the loss and dispossession that attends being forced to leave Ireland out of economic necessity or because of oppressive social structures hostile to the individual's self-realization or creative life; the freedom to fashion an autonomous life away from the limits set by family and community; the hazards encountered in acclimatizing to the hostland and the rewards the same has to offer; and the lure of home and difficulty of return. Irish women writers and women writers of Irish descent have taken up these issues as a means of recovering the history of Irish women migrants on their own terms and at a remove from the powerful, male-centred archetype of the Irish writer in exile, so strongly associated with canonical figures such as Joyce and Beckett. While Irish emigration in the twentieth century was too often greeted with what Piaras Mac Éinrí describes as 'palpable public silence'[12] at the same time George O'Brien makes the case that, given the dominance of exile as a literary theme, 'without exile there would be no contemporary literature'.[13]

This essay argues that for women writers post-1950, to write about migrant and diasporic experience in Britain – and, specifically, England – was to write an as-yet-untold story. Dominant modes of representation of the Irish migrant in Britain centred on male archetypes such as the navvy[14] that too often rendered Irish women in Britain invisible. On the other hand, the story of the Irish woman migrant in America has been underwritten by publicly visible and often troubling stereotypes, some of which seek to romanticize, others to diminish, such as the 'strong Irish mother';[15] 'Bridget', the Irish domestic servant so often caricatured in mid-to-late nineteenth-century American magazines;[16] and what Sally Barr Ebest identifies as the popular image of the unruly Irish woman, who posed a danger to the status quo.[17] I will focus on Britain (primarily England) and the United States as these have been the primary destinations for Irish women's migration, but will also consider other destinations, including Canada, Australia, South America and continental Europe, before going on to offer a brief account of how narratives of return have their own place in this literary history. In doing so, I will show how the female returnee appears as a powerful and unsettling figure in writing about Ireland's migrant history; one that – in distinctive ways – holds up a mirror to the country she left behind.

The Vanishing Irish: Representing Irish Women's Lives in Britain

The historical absence of women from scholarly work on migration may be best understood as one of a number of elisions addressed by historians and social scientists as well as writers and literary critics in recent decades. Mary Robinson's gesture of lighting a lamp in Áras an Uachtaráin to commemorate Ireland's emigrant history finds striking affinity with Eavan Boland's poetic sensibility. Boland's poem 'The Emigrant Irish' inspired Robinson's speeches addressing the Irish diaspora and is a rallying cry to attend to the history of lost generations: 'Like oil lamps we put them out the back, / of our houses, of our minds.'[18] Furthermore, Boland's work refashions the idea of exile, which is so powerfully associated with the male-centred paradigm and with James Joyce in particular. Boland's poetry calls attention to how Irish women poets have had to create room for themselves in a tradition that so heavily relied upon the figure of woman as muse, as an icon of the nation: 'Over a relatively short time – certainly no more than a generation or so – women have moved from being the objects of Irish poems to being the authors of them.'[19] Her concern with this transition and with the meaning of exile for the woman writer has an intimately autobiographical dimension, given her experience of leaving Ireland at a young age and the losses she incurred. In 'An Irish Childhood in England: 1951' she recalls herself as a child alienated and made strange by her Hiberno-English: 'when all of England to an Irish child / was nothing more than what you'd lost and how: / was the teacher in the London convent who / when I pronounced "I amn't" in the classroom / turned and said – "you're not in Ireland now"'.[20] The exploration of alternative meanings of exile for the woman writer is part of a larger project in Boland's work, what Adrienne Rich described in a 1971 essay as the necessity of 'writing as revision';[21] Boland's work is celebrated for the reclamation of the suburban and the ordinary and domestic as spaces for poetry as well as for its movement between classical myth and Irish myth and the recovery of untold stories of Irish women's lives. In one of her best-known poems, 'Mise Eire', which freeze-frames the lived experiences of women against the mythical celebration of woman as national muse, she includes an abject figure of the Irish woman emigrant 'holding her half-dead baby to her / as the wind shifts East / and North over the dirty / waters of the wharf' amongst those figures she rescues from the margins of the grand narrative of Irish history.[22] These are just a few representative poems that resonate with broader patterns in recent Irish women's poetry and, as argued by Deirdre O'Byrne, speak in important ways to the work of Irish-born and second-generation Irish women poets such as Catherine Byron and Maura Dooley.[23]

The place of women in earlier popular accounts of Irish emigration is exemplified in John A. O'Brien's compendium of essays, *The Vanishing Irish: The Enigma of the Modern Age*, which first appeared in the United States in 1953 and was published in Britain a year later. It comprises essays that studied and sought to explain Ireland's emigration crisis and rural depopulation – it is most anxious about Irish women emigrants who forfeit their identity in marrying English men: 'Too often these marriages are mixed, and the children grow up as young English boys and girls in an alien faith, and with no particular interest in the "quaint and comic" sister isle that gave birth to their mother.'[24] Published in Britain just two years before the 'Report of the Commission on Emigration and Other Population Problems' in 1956, it gave expression to a pervasive contemporary anxiety about marriage patterns and the possibility of religious conversion that might lead to the disappearance of Irish women into British society. In *Outsiders Inside: Whiteness, Place and Irish Women* (2000), Bronwen Walter attributes the relative lack of visibility of women in the public sphere to the dominance of male stereotypes such as that of the Irish 'Paddy' and to reductive attitudes towards the Irish in post-war debates about race, migration and national identity: 'The Irish have become invisible in the discourse of "race" in Britain, despite ongoing evidence of undisguised anti-Irish hostility. The construction of this invisibility is gendered according to the representational and material places occupied by Irish people.'[25]

If the 1950s represented a period of particular anxiety over Irish depopulation, in 1960 Edna O'Brien's *The Country Girls* unsettled more pious narratives of the naïve young Irish woman lost to English society. The first book in the trilogy, *The Country Girls*, plots the movement of Caithleen Brady and her friend and nemesis, Baba, as they escape the limits of their rural home place for the relative freedoms of Dublin. In the second book in the trilogy, *The Lonely Girl* (1962), they leave for England, but neither Dublin nor England are presented as sites of uncomplicated refuge as in each phase of the journey, from the west of Ireland to Dublin and their move to England, they encounter different obstacles to their pursuit of freedom and, in Caithleen's case, her ambitions to write. O'Brien's fierce letter back to Ireland in the form of her memoir, *Mother Ireland* (1976), belongs to a Joycean tradition of writing home to Ireland from a safe distance; as was the case for her influential predecessor, Ireland remains at the centre of O'Brien's imagination even though she has spent the greater part of her life away from the country, something she expounds on in both her biography of Joyce (1999) and her memoir, *Country Girl* (2012). She returns to the dilemma of the Irish writer in exile in *The Light of Evening* (2006), which revisits some of the terrain of *The Country Girls* trilogy. It features an Irish woman writer in England whose achievements as a novelist are accompanied by another literary history in the form of her letters to and from her mother: 'My mother not wanting ever to let me go, but having to let me go, having to bear it, having to bear everything, her one indulgence the letters she wrote on the Sunday nights, asking to be heard, asking to be understood, crossing the sea to be with me.'[26] Her mother's letters provide a vital link to home, but this woman writer also takes refuge in the English literary tradition – the novel is replete with references to Rossetti, Woolf and the Brontës in particular, and the hybrid influences at work in the novel offer a reminder of the complicated affinities of the Irish woman writer in search of tradition. The figure of the navvy is given less than sympathetic treatment in O'Brien's work in *The Country Girls* trilogy, but receives a more nuanced characterization in her recent short story, 'Shovel Kings' in *Saints and Sinners* (2011), a collection that is particularly concerned with estrangement, alienation and reconciliation. O'Brien's writing *oeuvre* is, then, a careful excavation of her changing relationship with Ireland over time and her preoccupation with the emigrant experience has found different articulations across different writing modes throughout her career.

Anne Enright's work brings O'Brien's narrative of Irish migration and women in the diaspora closer to the contemporary moment, particularly in novels such as *What Are You Like?* (2000) and *The Gathering* (2007). Her first novel, *The Wig My Father Wore* (1996), is set partly in England but her later work is especially concerned with examining the fashioning of identity in different diasporic contexts. *What Are You Like?* is about twins separated at birth – one of whom moves to New York where she discovers that she has a sister, Rose, who was adopted and raised by an English family. At one moment, a crass comment from Rose's English boyfriend offers a reminder of the oppressive social forces behind the decision of many Irish women to leave Ireland: 'William was very excited by the fact that Rose was Irish. This she discovered when he took her out to dinner and said: "This place used to be an abortion clinic," for no reason at all ...'[27]

The Gathering features another Irish woman on the move in tracing Veronica Hegarty's journey to England to make arrangements to have her brother's body brought home to Dublin for burial. She leaves Celtic Tiger Dublin behind and, in the course of her journey, pieces together the complex mosaic of the Hegarty family history. Her alcoholic brother's suicide is part of the larger narrative of the abandoned emigrant and a history of excluding emigrants from the story of the nation in spite of the contribution of the remittances of the 1950s generation to the building of Ireland's economy and the prosperity enjoyed during the Celtic Tiger years. In *The Green Road* (2015), Enright further advances her interest in family and diasporic connections as the Madigans return to the West of Ireland, called home by family duty.

Alongside these dramatizations of the relationship between Ireland and its emigrant generations, writers such as Juanita Casey have confronted other elided and missing histories. A writer of Irish traveller descent on her mother's side, Casey's poetry and prose represents an often-overlooked strand in Irish migrant history. Episodic and innovative in form, *The Horse of Selene* (1971) is a lyrical account of traveller life that weaves back and forth across the Irish sea and engages directly with the hostility and prejudice encountered by traveller people: 'And the tinkers, on the edges of the island, always on the edges of the lands and the settled society, prepared to move on ... The Dorans were off for the ferry over to the mainland, none of them bothered by the stares and the withdrawings of their fellow travellers on board, fearful of their cars touching the high-wheeled carts, the shaggy heads of the horses resting against their rear windows.'[28] The need to bear witness to the lived experience of Irish women in Britain has been addressed by a number of anthologies of first-person testimonies such as those published in *Across the Water: Irish Women's Lives in Britain*. The collection appeared in 1988, towards the end of another decade marked by mass emigration and comprises cross-generational first-person testimonies by Irish women about their experience of moving to and settling in Britain. Íde O'Carroll's *Models for Movers: Irish Women's Emigration to America*, published just two years later in 1990, achieved the same in capturing stories of emigration to the United States.[29]

The strain of being torn between two competing identities is of special concern to second- and third-generation Irish writers in England. Maude Casey's *Over the Water* (1987) is a coming-of-age novel about a young Irish girl in England – a summer in Ireland leads to a delicate negotiation with and enhanced understanding of her dual identity. Gretta Mulrooney explores a different version of this dislocation in her novel, *Crossing the Line* (1997), in which the teenage protagonist is uprooted from her home in Dublin and moves with her family to London.

Moy McCrory's stories of a Liverpool-Irish childhood in *The Water's Edge* (1985) contribute another important chapter to this history. McCrory is especially concerned with dramatizing intergenerational tensions and feelings of dislocation experienced by second-generation Irish women in England. She sums up the dilemma as follows:

> Wary about claiming one identity over another, a shared sense of difference from which there is no one-size-fits-all identity emerges. The second generation might express national identity as a fluid construct which is responsive to background but which defies clear definitions ... Indeed a subversion of 'easy' national identification is at the heart of the second generation who have long existed between two land masses, connected and simultaneously disconnected to both.[30]

This concern with simultaneous connection and disconnection and the suspension between two cultures is a key marker in writing about the lives of Irish women in Britain.

Outsiders Inside: Imagining Irish Women in America

In *Women and the Irish Diaspora* (2004), Breda Gray argues that Irish migration to the United States has dominated the narrative of emigration and has a considerably more confident timbre to it when compared to the story of the Irish in Britain:

> It is hard to emerge from the shadow of the United States as the emblematic locus of the diaspora and the classic Irish migrant narrative of crossing the Atlantic and following the 'American Dream' ... The varying status of Britain as a transitional, seasonal or permanent destination, combined with the legacy of colonial relations may have rendered it too contested a site to be emblematic of the Irish diaspora.[31]

As previously mentioned, within this narrative a number of visible tropes in popular culture and literature emerge – they include the 'strong Irish mother', the working-class Irish 'Bridget' and the image of the Irish woman as rebellious and a threat to the status quo. Irish and Irish-American women writers have deployed different strategies of resistance in undoing the damaging legacy of such stereotypes as well as offering their own stories of self-realization in the American context.

Mary Anne Sadlier's *Bessy Conway; or, The Irish Girl in America* (1861) is an early example of the public visibility of the Irish woman servant in the literary marketplace and the popularity of the Irish 'Bridget' archetype in nineteenth-century American literary culture. In her short stories for *The New Yorker* in the 1950s, Maeve Brennan shows an alertness to the same history of imagining the Irish woman migrant as domestic servant. Brennan's writing history divides into stories set in Dublin and those played out in a New York suburb, as well as essays written under the pseudonym the Long-Winded Lady for the 'Talk of the Town' column of *The New Yorker*. In her Dublin stories, Brennan conjures up intimate scenes of Irish family life while her short stories, set in the fictional New York suburb of Herbert's Retreat, are explicitly satirical in the way they pitch the Irish woman servant, so long a beleaguered figure of fun, against her American middle-class employers. The story of Brennan's life and her rise to prominence amongst the mid-century, New York literati, fully captured in Angela Bourke's biography, *Maeve*

Brennan: Homesick at the New Yorker, is its own powerful counterpoint to those jaded stereotypes. At the same time, the worlds of Dublin and New York overlap in the Joycean aspects of Brennan's project of mapping New York. An epiphany in one of her final essays as the Long-Winded Lady published in 1981 offers a vivid metaphor for the way in which the two cities encounter each other in her work: 'Yesterday afternoon, as I walked along Forty-second Street directly across from Bryant Park, I saw a three-cornered shadow on the pavement in the angle where two walls meet ... I recognized it at once. It was exactly the same shadow that used to fall on the cement part of our garden in Dublin, more than fifty-five years ago.'[32]

More recently, other Irish-born women writers have taken up the history of Irish women in America in various ways – examples include Nuala O'Connor's *Miss Emily* (2015) and Mary Costello's *Academy Street* (2014). O'Connor casts an Irish domestic servant as companion to Emily Dickinson – the novel emphasizes her shared sensibility with the poet and so provides a counter narrative to more familiar images of the Irish servant in the United States. Costello's *Academy Street* is the story of Tess Lohan's migration to the United States in the 1960s. The novel centres on the changing interior life of Tess and her attempt to engage with the world on her own terms and, like so many of the previously mentioned works, is deeply concerned with the possibilities of self-determination away from the limits of home. Paula McGrath's 2015 novel, *Generation*, can be added to the list of works that examine the lives and afterlives of Irish women in the United States and imagines how family connections are fashioned and altered by the butterfly effect of emigrant histories on future generations.

Irish-American women writers have found their own modes of imagining a relationship with Ireland on new terms. Of the generation that came of age in the earlier decades of the century, Mary McCarthy stands out as especially prolific and path-breaking. Her work does not rest easily in any tradition of Irish-American literature and cannot be said to celebrate Irish-American life. Her 1957 memoir, *Memories of a Catholic Girlhood*, is a searing account of the suffering of McCarthy and her siblings at the hands of cruel guardians when they are orphaned – it is both an indictment of religious hypocrisy and at the same time shows a profound appreciation of the cultural and literary riches of Catholicism. McCarthy's autobiography demonstrates an alertness to the meaning of her Irish and Jewish ancestry. In *How I Grew* (1986), she recalls:

> By senior year I was well aware of having a Jewish grandmother and aware of it – let me be blunt – as something to hide ... In Waterbury, whenever

I visited Ginny, I had to live down being Irish. To Ginny's admirers, just out of Yale, it was a rich joke that a girl named Mary McCarthy should be drinking cocktails with them at the country club: Irish were mill workers at the Chase and the Scovill and American brass plants.[33]

Aside from her life writing and her satire on university life, *The Groves of Academe* (1951), which follows the hapless efforts of an Irish-American Joyce scholar, McCarthy's fiction tends to shy away from Irish-American themes. At the same time, the sustained interest in self-invention in her writing and her perennial focus on the fate of the autonomous, self-creating heroines who hold their own amidst a formidable intelligentsia adds a new voice to the Irish-American canon – one that often risks being overlooked because it refuses to be readily categorized as Irish American. McCarthy's *The Group* (1963), an autobiographical novel about a group of Vassar graduates in the 1930s, anticipates and makes a foundational contribution to the literature of the women's movement in addressing female sexuality, contraception, marriage, women in the workplace and in the literary marketplace. New York novelist Mary Gordon takes up some of these questions in her acclaimed 1978 novel, *Final Payments*, which centres on the negotiation of personal desire and family duty and the inheritances of the previous generation. Elizabeth Cullinan's work is marked by similar concerns. Many of the stories collected in *The Time of Adam* (1970) and *Yellow Roses* (1977) are carefully executed dissections of lower-middle-class and middle-class life, as is her best-known novel, *House of Gold* (1971), which portrays the lives and intergenerational tensions of the Irish-American Devlins.

Alice McDermott is perhaps the most acclaimed of Irish-America's contemporary women writers. Her work usually centres on New York from *That Night* (1987), set in Long Island in the 1960s, to her most recent novel, *Someone* (2013), which starts out in Brooklyn in the 1920s. In *A Bigamist's Daughter* (1982), *At Weddings and Wakes* (1992), *Child of My Heart* (2003) and *Charming Billy* (1997), McDermott moves through different chapters of Irish-American experience. She sets the domestic lives of Irish-American families against larger unfolding histories, from America in the decades after the Second World War in *Charming Billy* (1997) to the spectre of the Vietnam War in *After This* (2006). Her work is known for its particular concern with the lives of ordinary girls and women and is characterized by a controlled, ruminative explication of individual and national histories.

Other Places, Other Voices

Britain and America loom large on the literary landscape of Irish transnational and diasporic writers, but they do not preclude other stories of
migration that play out in Canada, Australia, South America and continental Europe. Since English pioneer writer Susanna Moodie, a recent
arrival to Canada herself, recorded in 1852 with some distaste the Irish
scrambling over the rocks at Grosse Isle,[34] Irish women have had a significant place in the development of Canadian literary culture. One of
Canadian writer Margaret Atwood's most celebrated novels *Alias Grace*
(1996), tells the story of an Irish woman accused of murder in the 1840s –
another Irish domestic servant who, in Canadian popular culture, came to
represent an altogether more alarming threat than the 'Bridget' figure of
nineteenth- and early-twentieth-century America. Canadian-Irish novelist
Jane Urquhart's *Away* (1993) moves between Ireland and Canada during
the years of the Great Famine, and Irish-Canadian history is of special
interest across all Urquhart's work. Of Scots-Irish descent, Alice Munro's
early writing bears signs of Joycean influence and her 1971 short story
cycle, *Lives of Girls and Women*, can be read as a portrait of the artist as a
young Canadian woman.

More recently Emma Donoghue, who was born in Dublin but holds
Irish and Canadian citizenship, has offered her own take on arriving
in Canada in her novel, *Landing* (2007). An earlier engagement with
migrant themes appears in her short story, 'Going Back' (1993), in
which a character realizes that her lesbian identity made her 'more of an
exile for twenty years in Ireland than I ever have in the twelve I've been
out of it'.[35] Donoghue's more recent writing about Ireland and North
America has taken her interest in transnational networks in new directions. If Brian Moore offered a reanimation of Leopold Bloom in the
figure of Ginger Coffey in his landmark coming-to-Canada novel, *The
Luck of Ginger Coffey* (1960), in Donoghue's *Landing* (2007), Síle is a
citizen of an increasingly globalized Celtic Tiger Ireland who falls in love
with a Canadian woman. Donoghue's literary interest in transnational
migration recurs in her collection of stories, *Astray* (2012). The line
between fiction and history is deliberately blurred as Donoghue reveals
her source texts for each literary experiment in writing different migrant
histories that criss-cross North America. Dublin-born, Vancouver-based
Anakana Schofield in her novel, *Malarky* (2012), offers a letter home to
Ireland from Canada in a work marked by the clear influence of Irish literary modernism. Schofield, like Donoghue, transcends any easy national

categorization and represents another innovative turn in transatlantic literary culture.

Irish women writers have also looked to Europe in seeking out alternative settings for their work. Much as Kate O'Brien before her found inspiration in the cultural landscape of Spain as offering a mirror-image of Irish Catholicism, Julia O'Faolain sets her 1984 novel, *The Irish Signorina*, in Italy and follows the main character's re-enactment of her mother's sojourn as an au pair. She leaves Ireland behind but Italy reproduces aspects of Irish family life and religious conformism.

Anne Enright locates *The Pleasure of Eliza Lynch* (2002) in nineteenth-century South America, although as Susan Cahill notes, it serves as a vivid example of a historical novel that holds a mirror up to anxieties about the present; for instance, Eliza Lynch's predilection for luxury serves as a wry refraction of the hyper-consumerism that marked the Celtic Tiger years.[36] Evelyn Conlon's *Not the Same Sky* (2013) addresses a lacuna in narratives of the Great Famine. Set in 1848 it charts the voyage of a group of young women who are transported as migrant labourers to Australia. Given the relative paucity of writing about the famine, it represents an unusual intervention in terms of both the underrepresented histories of Irish women migrants and larger cultural anxieties about representing the famine years. These more recent works were prefigured by the flamboyantly experimental take on Irish women and nomadism that is to be found in Emer Martin's novel, *Breakfast in Babylon* (1995). This is a novel about life on the margins punctuated by stories of squatting and drug smuggling, which sees the nomadic Isolt move from Israel to France to the United States. It offers a new narrative of the relationship between the Irish woman and Ireland as Isolt is cut adrift from any meaningful emotional connection to home.

Homecomings: The Returnee in Post-1950s Irish Women's Writing

Irish women writers and writers of Irish descent have offered narratives of return as well as of departure and exploration. Fitzgerald and Lambkin emphasize the impact of emigration on those who stayed and the effect of the 'American parcel', a staple of emigrant culture until the 1960s, which served as a material reminder of the possibilities of life elsewhere. They argue that: 'Successful returned emigrants, embodying this difference, were particularly effective agents of social change, which included a new, unsettling, attitude of "independence" among tenants and employees, and further emigration.'[37] Breda Gray offers an alternative reading of the returnee in mapping out the emotional currents of the emigrant's return: 'Return visits stage an emotional encounter between migrants and those who stayed. In this encounter, migrants find themselves positioned as outside the national community (settled elsewhere) but harbouring a desire to return, and stayers are seen as policing the (narrow) terms of belonging in Ireland.'[38] Early versions of the returnee can be seen in the work of writers such as Maurice Walsh whose story, 'The Quiet Man', first published in *Green Rushes* in 1933, gave rise to John Ford's film of the same name that reached an international audience in 1952. Kate O'Brien first took up the dilemma of the returnee in her novel, *Pray for the Wanderer* (1938), which follows the fate of an Irish playwright home from England and Julia O'Faolain followed suit decades later with her version of the returned Irish-American in Ireland in *No Country for Young Men* (1980). Anne Haverty's Celtic Tiger satire, *The Free and Easy* (2006), builds on the by-now-recognizable tradition of the well-meaning Irish-American who returns full of fixed notions about the homeland; a tradition that stretches back as far as Sean O'Faolain's satire on the returned 'Yank' in his 1940 novel, *Come Back to Erin*.

Alongside this stands an alternative tradition of the female returnee. Maeve Brennan's previously mentioned novella, *The Visitor*, reads like a parable about the impossibility of return, as her character Anastasia King is banished afresh by her grandmother. Gretta Mulrooney explores a similar dynamic in *Out of the Blue* (2007), in which the main character makes the journey home from England to claim the cottage inherited from her grandmother and to seek respite from her alcoholic husband and unhappy marriage. Kate O'Riordan turns to Paris as a site of cultural escape from Ireland in *The Memory Stones* (2003) from where Nell Hennessy meditates on the sacrifices of motherhood. Nell is forced to leave the hard-won freedom and cosmopolitanism of her life in France to return to Ireland to rescue her daughter from crisis. In this case, the returnee is further alienated by the newly prosperous culture of Celtic Tiger Ireland, as is revealed in a knowing nod to a familiar conflation of gender and nation: 'This motherland is wearing lipstick ... She drives a sleek silver car with last year's registration plates. She drapes expensive cotton sweaters across her shoulders.'[39]

Elizabeth Cullinan and Alice McDermott have also written novels that focus on the emotional bristle of an Irish-American character's return and the unsettling effect of the same. Cullinan's *A Change of Scene* (1982) sees Ann Clarke return from New York to 1960s Dublin while McDermott's *Charming Billy* (1997) charts the visit of her eponymous character to

Ireland to untangle a decades-old romantic betrayal. He returns to the United States restored but also unnerved by his first visit: "'Another thing about Ireland,' he said. 'We're all over there. All our faces'" … "'Good Lord, I saw my mother in almost every shop I went into, usually behind the counter. And my father's face was on one of the priests who said Mass at the retreat house.'"[40] Edna O'Brien's *Wild Decembers* (1999), a novel about an Australian's return to Ireland to claim his inheritance, ends in deadly violence, but her own account of her attempted return to the west of Ireland in her memoir *Country Girl* (2012) is perhaps the most powerful and moving returnee narrative of all, for the way it vividly recounts the hostility that awaited her when she tried to make a home in Donegal in the 1990s.

Whether imagining departure, acculturation or the difficulty of return, these women writers, although writing out of different historical moments and from diverse cultural perspectives, have illuminated the forgotten lives of Irish women emigrants and women in the Irish diaspora. In doing so they have made a vital contribution to the outward expansion of the Irish literary canon. The emergence of this powerful generative strand in Irish writing has cultivated a new consciousness of the sometimes-fraught relationship between Ireland and its diaspora and the place occupied by women in the history of Irish emigration.

Notes

1 Maeve Brennan, *The Visitor* (London: Atlantic, 2001), 8.
2 Donald Harman Akenson, *The Irish Diaspora* (Belfast: Institute of Irish Studies, 1996), 157.
3 According to Fitzgerald and Lambkin, from 1871 to 1971 the number of women migrants from Ireland consistently outnumbered men. Patrick Fitzgerald and Brian Lambkin, *Migration in Irish History, 1607–2007* (Basingstoke: Palgrave Macmillan, 2008), 56.
4 Ibid., 244.
5 Mary Hickman, 'Migration and Diaspora', in *The Cambridge Companion to Modern Irish Culture*, ed. Joe Cleary and Claire Connolly (Cambridge: Cambridge University Press, 2005), 117.
6 Patrick O'Sullivan, *Irish Women and Irish Migration* (Vol. 4), *The Irish World Wide* (Leicester: Leicester University Press, 1995); Bronwen Walter, *Outsiders Inside: Whiteness, Place and Irish Women* (London: Routledge, 2000); Breda Gray, *Women and the Irish Diaspora* (London: Routledge, 2004); Ellen McWilliams and Bronwen Walter, 'New Perspectives on Women and the Irish Diaspora', *Special Issue of Irish Studies Review* 21, no. 1 (2013); Ellen McWilliams, *Women and Exile in Contemporary Irish Fiction* (Basingstoke: Palgrave Macmillan, 2013).

7 Akenson, *The Irish Diaspora*, 15.

8 Mary Robinson, 'Cherishing the Irish Diaspora', An Address to the Houses of the Oireachtas, 2 February 1995.

9 For a comprehensive and multi-faceted study of the same, see Sinéad Moynihan, *"Other People's Diasporas": Negotiating Race in Contemporary Irish and Irish American Culture* (Syracuse, NY: Syracuse University Press, 2013).

10 David McWilliams, 'Harnessing Diaspora Will Help Us Rebuild the Economy', *Irish Independent*, 27 October 2010. www.independent.ie/opinion/columnists/david-mcwilliams/david-mcwilliams-harnessing-diaspora-will-help-us-rebuild-economy-26693338.html.

11 For a discussion of the 'stay-at-home female', see Fitzgerald and Lambkin, *Migration in Irish History*, 55–6.

12 Piaras Mac Éinrí, 'Introduction', in *The Irish Diaspora*, ed. Andrew Bielenberg (Harlow: Pearson, 2000), 3.

13 George O'Brien, 'The Aesthetics of Exile', in *Contemporary Irish Fiction: Themes, Tropes, Theories*, ed. Liam Harte and Michael Parker (Basingstoke: Macmillan, 2000), 35. For a recent discussion of the relationship between emigration and exile in the American context, see Elizabeth Butler Cullingford's article, 'American Dreams: Emigration or Exile in Contemporary Irish Fiction?', *Eire-Ireland: An Interdisciplinary Journal of Irish Studies* 49, nos. 3–4 (2014): 60–94.

14 For further discussion of the figure of the navvy, see Tony Murray, 'Navvy Narratives', in *London Irish Fictions: Narrative, Diaspora and Identity* (Liverpool: Liverpool University Press, 2012), 42–56.

15 Gray, *Women and the Irish Diaspora*, 51.

16 Margaret Lynch-Brennan, *The Irish Bridget: Irish Immigrant Women in Domestic Service in America, 1840–1930* (Syracuse, NY: Syracuse University Press, 2009).

17 Sally Barr Ebest, *Banshees: A Literary History of Irish American Women Writers* (Syracuse, NY: Syracuse University Press, 2013), 1.

18 Eavan Boland, 'The Emigrant Irish', in *Eavan Boland: Collected Poems* (Manchester: Carcanet, 1995), 129.

19 Eavan Boland, *Object Lessons: The Life of the Woman and Poet in Her Time* (Manchester: Carcanet, 1995), 126.

20 Boland, 'An Irish Childhood in England: 1951', in *Collected Poems*, 127.

21 Adrienne Rich, 'When We Dead Awaken: Writing as Revision', in *On Lies, Secrets, and Silences: Selected Prose 1966–1978* (London: Virago, 1980), 33–49.

22 Boland, 'Mise Eire' in *Collected Poems*, 102–3.

23 O'Byrne offers a careful and thorough analysis of loss and dispossession in the work of Boland, Byron and Dooley in relation to the history of Irish women in England in '"You're Not in Ireland Now": Landscape and Loss in Irish Women's Poetry', in *Affective Landscapes in Literature, Art and Everyday Life: Memory, Place and the Senses*, ed. Christine Berberich, Neil Campbell and Robert Hudson (Farnham: Ashgate, 2015), 30–52.

24 John A. O'Brien, *The Vanishing Irish: The Enigma of the Modern World* (London: W. H. Allen, 1954), 59.

25 Walter, *Outsiders Inside: Whiteness, Place and Irish Women*, 80.

26 Edna O'Brien, *The Light of Evening* (London: Weidenfeld and Nicolson, 2006), 250.

27 Anne Enright, *What Are You Like?* (London: Vintage, 2001), 135.

28 Juanita Casey, *The Horse of Selene* (London: The Dolmen Press, 1971), 41.

29 In addition to these collections, Ann Rossiter's study of the 'abortion trail' includes first-person testimonies of women forced to seek abortions in England in *Ireland's Hidden Diaspora: The 'Abortion Trail': and the Making of a London-Irish Underground, 1980–2000* (London: Iasc, 2009). Furthermore, the archive of the London Irish Women's Centre offers its own insights into the material realities of Irish women's lives in Britain in this period. The LIWC papers are held at the Archive of the Irish in Britain at the Irish Studies Centre, London Metropolitan University.

30 Moy McCrory, '"This Time and Now": Identity and Belonging in the Irish Diaspora – The Irish in Britain and Second-Generational Silence', in *Land and Identity: Theory, Memory, and Practice*, ed. Christine Berberich, Neil Campbell and Robert Hudson (Amsterdam: Rodopi, 2012), 197.

31 Gray, *Women and the Irish Diaspora*, 9–10.

32 Brennan, 'A Blessing', in *The Rose Garden* (Berkeley, CA: Counterpoint, 1997), 267.

33 Mary McCarthy, *How I Grew* (London: Weidenfeld and Nicolson, 1987), 217–18.

34 Susanna Moodie, *Roughing It in the Bush, or Forest Life in Canada* (Toronto: McClelland and Stewart, 1970), 24–5.

35 Emma Donoghue, 'Going Back', in *Ireland in Exile: Irish Writers Abroad* (Dublin: New Island, 1993), 160.

36 Susan Cahill, *Irish Literature in the Celtic Tiger Years 1990–2008: Gender, Bodies, Memory* (London: Continuum, 2011), 7.

37 Fitzgerald and Lambkin, *Migration in Irish History*, 43.

38 Gray, *Women and the Irish Diaspora*, 94.

39 Kate O'Riordan, *The Memory Stones* (London: Simon & Schuster, 2003), 191–2.

40 Alice McDermott, *Charming Billy* (New York, NY: Picador, 1998), 231.

CHAPTER 22

Celtic Tiger Fiction

Susan Cahill

A recent article in *The Guardian*, 'A new Irish literary boom: the post-crash stars of fiction', pitted a new wave of experimental, radical and innovative Irish literature against the Celtic Tiger years, characterized in the article as a conservative period inhospitable to artistic creation. Claire Kilroy acknowledges the difficulties of the Celtic Tiger years for an artist: 'Back then, by becoming a literary writer, you were pretty much setting yourself in opposition to the dominant ideology of the time, which was to make money, buy property and spend ostentatiously. I would suggest that a large proportion of my generation has been artistically neutered, for the time being at least.'[1] While it is true that more recent years have seen an extraordinary number of exciting literary debuts, such as those by Eimear McBride, Sara Baume, Kevin Barry, Colin Barrett, Lisa McInerney, Louise O'Neill, Paul Murray and Donal Ryan, and the success of independent presses and smaller literary magazines in fostering emerging talent, the definition of the preceding decade as offering little in the way of significant literary talent does a major disservice to this period which produced Anne Enright, Claire Kilroy, Anne Haverty and Éilís Ní Dhuibhne, among others. The article cites Julian Gough's dismissal of the Celtic Tiger period in his 2010 blog post as a writing that looked backward, 'cut off from the electric current of the culture'.[2] He repeats these sentiments for the *Guardian* article: 'Irish literature had gotten smug and self-congratulatory during the boom; lots of novels about how terrible Ireland's past was, with all its sexual repression and poverty ... Heritage literature, and very conservatively told. All old-fashioned lyrical realism, not a trace of the wild experimentalism of Beckett, Joyce and Flann O'Brien.'[3] However, as I argued in *Irish Literature in the Celtic Tiger Years 1990–2008: Gender, Bodies, Memory*, although Gough joined a chorus of voices including Declan Kiberd, John Banville and Fintan O'Toole, who all decried the state of Celtic Tiger literature as disconnected from its contemporary economic and social dynamics, the literature produced by the period was deeply engaged with its present moment, even if it seemed to be focusing on Ireland's past.[4]

What is also apparent in these condemnations of the state of contemporary Irish fiction is that the critics were simply not reading the women, not reading the wealth of novels that incisively mapped the socio-economic and cultural transformations that marked the years of the Celtic Tiger. One of the writers to do so, Éilís Ní Dhuibhne, pointed out this neglect in response to Gough's invective, noting the wealth of novels by women on her bookshelves that focused on contemporary Ireland:

> Maybe that's what the fuss is about? Not enough men – famous men – have written fiction dealing with contemporary Ireland? Well then. But of course. Good fiction about contemporary Ireland does not exist. QED.[5]

Patricia Coughlan had earlier noted a similar critical neglect of writers such as Enright, Ní Dhuibhne, Haverty and Mary Morrissy, and had also cautioned against the jettisoning of the past that was advocated in these articles bemoaning contemporary Irish fiction. For Coughlan in 2004, 'much unfinished business remains to be done in Irish psyches' particularly when it comes to women's narratives or those of other silenced and elided voices.[6] Furthermore, Coughlan details the active experimentation of style and postmodern deconstruction of the individual subject that women writers of the Celtic Tiger excelled at, highlighting the ways in which women's writing was at the forefront of literary innovation during this period. This chapter, then, surveys the wealth of Irish women's writing between the years 1994–2008 and argues that this era is notable for the increased range and quality of Irish women's writing, and a renewed willingness to experiment that ushered in the current boom in Irish publishing.

The period of time under examination is roughly the years between 1994, when the term 'Celtic Tiger' was coined by an economist in Morgan Stanley to describe Ireland's rapid economic growth,[7] and 2008, when the recession was officially declared. These years in Ireland marked a period of unprecedented economic prosperity that was also accompanied by significant transformations in the ways in which Ireland conceived of itself. The established landscapes of rural, Catholic, traditional Ireland were put under much strain in an era of rapid social change that ushered in the decriminalization of homosexuality in 1993, the legalization of divorce in 1995, the closing of the last Magdalene Laundry in 1996, and real and profound changes in women's economic power and position in public life. Mary Robinson's assumption of the presidency in 1990, the first woman to hold this position, was for many a symbolic recognition of the shifting grounds of social change around gender and sexuality as Robinson had previously been instrumental in changing legislation around the legalization of contraception, and had also been strongly involved in the campaign for Homosexual Law Reform. The Celtic Tiger years saw the fall of the old order, in particular the Catholic Church and the political elite. These decades of the 1990s and 2000s witnessed a series of revelations about and investigations into the sexual behaviour of Catholic clergy, child-abuse scandals and the cruelty of the Magdalene Laundries, or mother-and-baby homes, where unmarried mothers were sent. The period was also marked by a series of tribunals investigating the financial dealings of politicians, developers and businessmen highlighting the levels of corruption that would later emerge as fuelling the boom-and-bust of Ireland's economy. It seemed that conservative, Catholic Ireland was changing, and changing rapidly.

Pasts

One of the consequences of the perception of this rapid change was a tendency to invest in rigid breaks with the past – the present moment which ushered in a new modern Ireland had shucked off the shackles of the conservative Catholic past and wanted to disassociate from types of narratives that still inhabited this temporal space. This is satirized in Frank Stapleton's film, *The Fifth Province* (1997), in which a workshop leader cautions would-be scriptwriters: 'When it comes to the story, I'll tell you what we don't want. We don't want any more stories about Irish mothers, priests, sexual repressions and the miseries of rural life. We want stories that are upbeat, that are urban, that have pace and verve, and that are going places.'[8] In articulating this tendency to disavow the past, Claire Bracken borrows Nietzsche's idea of 'active forgetting' in her analysis of a Gen X category in Ireland – whose coming-of-age coincided with the Celtic Tiger – to describe this drive towards amnesia. As Bracken writes: 'Active forgetting is a critical response to an Irish postcolonial nation dominated, for most of the twentieth century, by an official discourse of conservative nationalism, which idealized the traditional values of a rural Ireland, prioritizing acts of remembrance and an unhealthy obsession with the past.'[9] Anne Haverty neatly captures the consciousness of 'active forgetting' in her novel, *The Free and Easy* (2006), which hilariously pillories the boom years. One character declares:

> You can forget the last century. And you can definitely forget the century before. Ireland as we know it – and let's thank whoever and whatever – was born some time around nineteen ninety-four. Or ninety-six?[10]

The amnesiac drive in Irish cultural production was an understandable response to the rapidity of social change, yet feminist critics, particularly, alerted us to the problematics of this type of forgetting, which elided the work that still needed to be done in relation to the persistent cultural constructions of woman as mother, the regulatory regimes that continue to govern women's bodies, and the continued exclusion of women writers from canon formation and official literary spaces.[11] Although the Celtic Tiger ushered in a socio-cultural milieu that profoundly changed Irish life and the meanings of Irishness, and transformed the ideological land-scapes in turn of twenty-first-century Ireland, easy categorizations of past and present need to be approached with caution. As Coughlan astutely pointed out in 2004, there was still 'unfinished business' that troubled the neat progress narratives insisting that the new Ireland was global, modern and cosmopolitan and bore no connection to the Ireland that had preceded it. Coughlan reminds us that:

> it would be misleading to accept a simple before-and-after narrative of enlightenment, or to posit a completely clear liberal-conservative and urban-rural divide in Ireland, especially where questions of women's status and freedoms are concerned.[12]

Periodic debates concerning abortion during these years pointed to the repressive and regulatory ideologies surrounding women bodies. The 2004 Citizenship Referendum highlighted the nation's investment in rac-ist constructions of Irish identity. Ireland continues to demonstrate one of the worst imbalances in gender representation in politics.[13]

Thus, fiction by women writers during these years is particularly astute to the discontinuities, fissures and snags in such narratives of progress and development and women authors are at the forefront of interrogating fixed representations of the past and present throughout these decades. Themes of time, history, memory and national identity recur in women's writing of this period. Anne Enright's first novel, *The Wig My Father Wore* (1995), ostensibly takes place in this urban, cosmopolitan, media-driven, fast-paced environment of early 1990s Ireland, set as it is in the world of television production. Yet the novel alerts us to the complexities of past-present relationships. Grace, the protagonist, is the producer of a reality-type TV show called the *LoveQuiz* and the novel plays with ideas of memory, time, authenticity and the synthetic. The central objects of the artificial wig and the television – which enter Grace's childhood simul-taneously – draw our attention to constructions of self and memory. Grace's 'childhood rearranges itself, the phantom Apollo 8 is regulated to a kind of misalignment of the pixels, the shadow of another channel breaking through' when she encounters a TV guide for her first night's viewing that does not map onto her memories.[14]

As Bracken argues, against the 'active forgetting' common to the Celtic Tiger imaginary, an Irish, feminist aesthetic like Enright's privileges 'creative remembering'; the 'dominant motif of the television configures an idea of the past as constructed, contradictory, and multiple. It allows ... Grace to creatively play and engage with technologically mediated memories'.[15] The past is shown to be flexible, plugged into the present in the recurring imagery of electric currents, airwaves and flows, and is creatively and explosively disruptive. This becomes particularly apparent in a central episode in which Grace tears strips of the wallpaper away to reveal the house's buried history – fragments of religious instruction, a playbill dating from the Free State, a recipe, a shopping list, a letter, a poem about childbirth – items relating to women's history, women's writing, and women's bodies. These fragments all represent those voices and narratives silenced in a conservative Catholic past and re-muted in the amnesiac drive of the present. This is exemplified in the desire of Stephen (the angel who arrives on Grace's doorstep at the beginning of the novel) to whitewash Grace's house and to return her body to a smooth, child-like state, effectively erasing her history and her maternal genealogies: 'I missed my mother's knees and my Granny's hammer toes.'[16]

The feminist aesthetic of this novel, and many others of the time, is not to disavow the past as disconnected from the contemporary new, but actively to reengage with the past, with the histories buried under the wallpaper, to let the madwomen speak.

> I yanked up the carpet with the newspaper underneath, stuffed it all out the window and when it lodged in the frame, went into the front garden and pulled, like a vet pulling out a dead calf ... Let them read something for a change. I didn't care what they thought. They had been living with a madwoman for years and never told me.[17]

Similarly, Enright's *The Gathering* (2007) excavates the troubled histories of the Celtic Tiger present – highlighting those discontinuities that trouble the affluent surface of the boom years as the novel explicitly engages with the child sex-abuse scandals that marked these years.

Éilís Ní Dhuibhne's *The Dancers Dancing* (1999) reinhabits 1970s Ireland to reveal traces of darker histories that persist into the present – in a significant moment, Orla, the teenage protagonist, discovers a dozen baby skulls hidden in a river, evidence of a history of infanticide literally buried in the landscape. Ní Dhuibhne's earlier novel, *The Bray House* (1990), is a future archaeology of the present. Set in a world in which a nuclear disaster has wiped out Ireland, a team of Swedish archaeologists travel to Bray and excavate the eponymous house. The novel calls linear models of past-present relations into question through the problematic historiography enacted by the main protagonist as well as through the novel's use of folk and fairytale motifs which open up alternate temporal spaces to challenge traditional historiographical thought. Both of Ní Dhuibhne's novels place constructions of Ireland under pressure: *The Dancers Dancing* problematizes the possibility of a journey west into the Gaeltacht as a return to authenticity, while *The Bray House* resists an ability to accurately represent the history of the house and, by implication, Ireland more generally. Both novels pay attention to the bodies and voices that are obscured by particular constructions of Irishness and the relationships to official histories that underpin such configurations.

Edna O'Brien's novels throughout the Celtic Tiger period also engage in this act of creative re-engagement with Ireland's problematic past (and present) in relation to women's bodies. Her novel, *Down by the River* (1996), is based on the actual events of the 1992 X-case in which a teenage girl, pregnant as a result of rape, was prevented from travelling to England for an abortion by a High Court ruling (which was then overturned by the Supreme Court). O'Brien's novel, like Ní Dhuibhne's, draws our attention to the uncomfortable realities of infanticide in a society that continues to deny women control over their own bodies. In *Down by the River*, a midwife remembers 'the silenced creatures she had found in drawers and wardrobes and in bolster cases, like sleeping dolls: a little baby boy in a lavatory bowl, twins with binding twine around their necks'.[18] Her novel, *In the Forest* (2002), is also based on events from Ireland's recent past, the horrific triple-murder of a young mother, her three-year-old son and a local priest who were then buried in the forest of O'Brien's title. The novel raises questions concerning the Ireland that produced such a killer.

Of note too is the recurrent trope of the family and, even more particularly, of the traumatized dysfunctional family. Since the 1937 Constitution enshrined the family as 'the natural primary and fundamental unit group of Society', fictional depictions of the family often extend metaphorically towards commentary on the state of the nation itself. Eve Patten, in her survey of contemporary Irish fiction, notes '[t]he fictional dismembering of the body of the family, as it were, indicates a state at odds with itself, riven with discrepancies and misfit traditions'.[19] Irish women's fiction, particularly, troubled the conventional family and the predominance of motifs of doubles and of pregnant bodies is to be noted, as well as a sustained focus on the ways in which families contained and facilitated trauma and often failed to protect the most vulnerable members. In Enright's *What Are You Like?* (2000), the pregnant body is shown to be a mere incubator (a commentary on the status of the right to life of the mother in the Irish Constitution) when the pregnant Anna is allowed to die of a brain tumour to facilitate the birth of her twins. As I have previously argued, the novel registers trauma at all levels of the family; it is 'a novel populated with abandoned children, dead mothers, missing siblings, uncanny doubles, and separated twins'.[20] Enright's families expand towards the exaggerated family of *The Gathering*, a family which is structured by the trauma of child abuse: 'I don't know what wound we are showing to them all, apart from the wound of family. Because, just at this moment, I find that being part of a family is the most excruciating possible way to be alive.'[21] Yet the novel is also a celebration of the family, of Veronica learning how to live in her family having borne witness to 'the uncertain event' of her brother's abuse at the hands of her grandmother's landlord. Lia Mills's *Another Alice* (1996) also concentrates on the negotiation of repressed memories of paternal incest. And incest is a central feature of numerous novels by women writers across these years, including Edna O'Brien's *Down by the River* and Jennifer Johnston's *The Invisible Worm* (1991) and *Grace and Truth* (2005).[22]

The family reshapes itself through these novels. *The Wig My Father Wore* ends with a single pregnant woman, and many of these novels seek to repair mother-daughter relationships. One of the main emotional drives in Kilroy's *Tenderwire* (2006) is the tentative healing of the dynamic between the protagonist, Eva, and her mother. This relationship is also at stake in Enright's fiction in general; *What Are You Like?*, in particular, allows the silenced mother to speak back from beyond the grave. Anne Fogarty in her astute analysis of such relationships in Irish literature commented on the potential of the representation to engender new paradigms for the female self: 'The very turbulence of the mother-daughter bond becomes paradoxically the means by which feminine identity with all its painful intergenerational entanglements can be reimagined.'[23] The exploration of this relationship in fiction spoke to a larger feminist drive to retrieve and repair women's literary genealogies as evidenced in the necessity for *The Field Day Anthology of Irish Writing, Volumes IV and V: Women's Writing and Traditions* (which aimed to redress the exclusion of women from the canon formation exercise of the first three volumes). This period also saw the development of exciting projects such as the *Dictionary of Munster Women Writers 1800–2000*, the 'Women in Modern

Irish Culture' database and the 'Inventing and Reinventing the Irish Women' project which produced a series of datasets cataloguing Irish women's cultural contributions.[24]

The recovery of women's obscured histories is similarly a major concern for women writers of this moment. Anne Haverty's *The Far Side of a Kiss* (2000) imagines William Hazlitt's *Liber Amoris* (his 1824 fictionalized account of falling in love with his 19-year-old housemaid) from the point of view of the maid. Emma Donoghue's historical novels, *Slammerkin* (2000), *Life Mask* (2004) and *The Sealed Letter* (2008), also stage narratives that illuminate neglected and overlooked women's stories and Annabel Davis-Goff's novels inhabit the disappearing world of the Anglo-Irish. In light of this focus on the retrieval of silenced histories, it is notable how many narratives of this period are structured around amnesia. Claire Kilroy's *All Summer* (2003) and Mary Morrissy's *The Pretender* (2000) both engage in issues relating to history and memory through amnesiac protagonists and narratives concerning the creative reconstruction of memory. Similarly, Jennifer Johnston's *Foolish Mortals* (2007) and Lia Mills's *Another Alice* (1996) circulate around memory loss, secrets and revelations. Neither the past nor the self is ever stable in these narratives. All of these novels register buried historical trauma, particularly around women's bodies and women's histories. The novels also highlight the unreliability of historical discourses and the creative potentials of remembering.

Presents

As well as actively engaging in creative encounters with Ireland's past in ways that trouble the present, and despite Gough's and others' pronouncements to the contrary, Irish women writers articulated critiques of the consumer-driven climate of the Celtic Tiger in their fiction. Two groups of novels are identifiable here – those that obliquely comment on the boom years and those that explicitly satirize or critique its excesses. Enright's earlier novel, *The Pleasure of Eliza Lynch* (2002) and Kilroy's *Tenderwire* (2006) belong to this first group. While *The Pleasure of Eliza Lynch* is a historical novel set in nineteenth-century Paraguay and focusing on the life of Eliza Lynch, an Irish courtesan who became paramour to the future dictator of Paraguay, Francisco Solano López (1826–70), the novel largely considers the ethics of consumption, which cannot be disconnected from the socio-economic climate during which it was written. Eliza's life sees her move from obscure circumstances to become 'the

richest woman in the world' with 'a talent for shipping'.[25] Her excesses of
consumption are mirrored in the narrative investment in images of food,
eating, hunger and desire which Enright places in a deliberately uneasy
dialogue with images of war, wounding, decay and trauma that are also
part of the economy of consumption in the novel. As one of the narrative
voices says of Eliza, 'And when her dress falls away there is nothing under
the whalebone but more bone, and then more bones.'[26]

Similarly, although Kilroy's *Tenderwire* takes place in the classical
music world of contemporary New York, focusing on a young Irish
violinist, Eva, and her growing obsession with a violin of dubious origins, the novel also has much to say about the Celtic Tiger world that
haunts the margins of the narrative. Eva's father's disappearance, his
wealth, his large property and his association with the Taoiseach (Irish
prime minister) all link him with a dubious underbelly of Celtic Tiger
dealings that will lead to the economic collapse in 2008. The unsettling
space of Eva's family home, which bookends the novel's main plot, can
be read as a symbol of this fragile economic state. The violin in the novel
becomes resonant of loss, abandonment and trauma: personally, in its
connection to the major but unacknowledged loss of Eva's miscarriage,
and more broadly, in its naming - the Magdalena. This name raises the
spectre of Ireland's past of Magdalene Laundries, the shame and stigma
surrounding sex and pregnancy, and the loss experienced by the women
in these institutions – loss of their subjectivity, their agency, their child (if
pregnant). The novel asks us to confront Ireland's ghosts, historical and
recent, and asks us to acknowledge the absent – the traumatic histories
– and the void at the centre of the economic bubble, which by now has
become a recession. The novel is prescient.

Novels such as Anne Haverty's *The Free and Easy* (2006), Éilís Ní
Dhuibhne's *Fox, Swallow, Scarecrow* (2007) and Anne Enright's *The
Forgotten Waltz* (2011) are more visibly set in the affluent world of the
Celtic Tiger and clearly satirize (Ní Dhuibhne and Haverty) or decon-
struct (Enright) the dominant modes of consumerism, individualism
and entitlement that characterize the moment. Although published
after the official years of the Celtic Tiger, Kilroy's novel, *The Devil
I Know* (2012), focuses squarely on the years of Ireland's economic
boom, which becomes reimagined as a Faustian pact between property speculators and builders and a sinister character called Monsieur
Deauville. Haverty's novel, *The Free and Easy*, pillories with biting wit
the ways in which consumption governs the ethos of the Celtic Tiger in
which everything is subject to commodification and exploitation. One

character, Eimear, works in 'heritage management', packaging Ireland's traumatic history for contemporary entertainment and the production of 'authentic' Irish identity, which is continuously shown to be highly constructed. Eimear explains her work:

> 'I produce spectacles to illustrate and celebrate the glories and the sorrows of our heritage. I call them shows.'
> 'Spelled S-e-o-s', Doll interjected.
> 'As in the Irish ... I've put on several evictions. The evictions are very popular.'[27]

One storyline of the novel builds towards the production of a Famine 'seo' in which the almost unrepresentable event[28] of the mid-nineteenth-century Famine becomes another consumable object for the present, hungry for the veneer of authenticity. Set alongside this is the world of excess, material goods, politicians, property developers and financiers. The art world proves to be equally implicated in the capitalist drive – an exhibit, 'Home', becomes an accidental political statement – rebellion and subversion are shown to be media-produced and toothless. The novel brings into sharp focus the ways in which the capitalist postmodernity of the Celtic Tiger world incorporates and consumes even the potentially radical. The artists, Frog and Aaron, show themselves to be apathetic and characters in the novel are not concerned with an ethical engagement with history (Famine, eviction) or with their contemporary social-economic issues (homelessness); rather these elements are important only insofar as they serve the products that generate money and attention. This is a world in which art is not ethically engaged, but rather valuable only in terms of its marketability.

Where art turns commodity in *The Free and Easy*, so too does literature in Ní Dhuibhne's novel, set as it is in the literary world of book launches. Novelists are more concerned about celebrity than art; poets see the potential of 'the first black Irish language woman poet' in terms of economic value – 'If he couldn't sell her work, he was worse than useless' – rather than the potential for new creative energies that such a figure might generate.[29] *Fox, Swallow, Scarecrow* links an idiom of consumption with a dominant imagery of speed, glossiness, glass and surface to critique an ethos of isolation and disconnection. In a similar move to the ways in which the horrors of the Famine haunt the excesses of Dublin in Haverty's *The Free and Easy*, Ní Dhuibhne skilfully brings the inequities of the Celtic Tiger into clear view, such as the homeless man that the main character, Anna, constantly encounters; the deprived areas of the city which become merely a backdrop to her affair and the ways in which the idiom of speed in the novel is troubled by those not served by the Celtic Tiger's ethos of affluence. What is significant about much women's writing during this period is that, unlike the place of art in the Celtic Tiger ethos it depicts, this writing is ethically engaged, rooted in highlighting the problematics of an isolationist and consumerist ideology.

While Enright's *The Gathering* certainly engages with the Celtic Tiger moment and the ghosts that haunt its surfaces, her 2011 postmodern love story, *The Forgotten Waltz*, more directly inhabits the years just before the collapse of the economic boom. The novel chronicles this climate through the lens of an extra-marital affair. As Enright comments, 'It seemed to me that adultery was a great subject for a boom, partly because it's about authority: the old authorities had lost their credibility, so people had to make their own way.'[30] *Fox, Swallow, Scarecrow* also uses an affair as its main plot device. Enright's novel, narrated by Gina Moynihan, a thirty-four-year-old married woman, charts with acerbic acuity the ways in which houses (symbolic of the property boom) are bound up with desire and articulations of identity. Gina's introduction of the husband she is about to betray focuses on the disappointments of their house purchase potential, describing their love as 'Mortgage love. Shagging at 5.3 per cent.'[31] Similarly, Gina's articulation of her affair with Seán is interwoven with this architectural imagery: 'it took almost another year before we did the bold thing; before we pulled the houses down around us; the townhouse and the cottage and the semi-d. All those mortgages'.[32] The novel is interested in the relationship between the things we do and how we talk and think about them, about the gap, for example, between the discourse of love and the act of loving. Each chapter is named for the title or lyric of popular love songs. Gina, who has been very invested in being in love throughout the novel, must confront different types of realities at the novel's conclusion as she walks with Seán's daughter through a silent, snow-filled Dublin on the eve of the recession:

> I say, 'I know it's hard about your parents, Evie.'
> She does not reply.
> 'I just think, it [the affair] was going to happen one way or
>   another. I mean it could have been anyone, you know?'
> She slides on; one scraping step after the other.
> 'But it wasn't,' she says.
> I can't quite see her face.
> 'It was you.'[33]

The starkness of Evie's reminder to Gina that actions have consequences also plays out against the broader economic climate in which the false promises of the boom are punctured.

These novels which comment directly on the Celtic Tiger all circulate around an emotional problem of connection, or rather, disconnection. As Bracken notes in *Irish Feminist Futures*, much writing of the Celtic Tiger was characterized by 'a general cultural condition in which intensely isolated subjects are not just separated and isolated from others, but also from their own embodied selves, caught up as they are in a powerful late capitalist system that aggressively manages and controls the desires of the supposedly individualistic self'.[34] At stake in these narratives is the dismantling of a politics of disconnection and isolation towards an embedded and interconnected ethical subjectivity. This drive towards interconnection is often paralleled with the interest in intergenerational female relationships and an interrogation of history, narrative and forgetting as outlined above. Enright's *The Gathering* is a clear example of this, in the novel's self-consciousness about the relationship between fiction and history and Veronica's movement towards connection, towards 'falling into my own life'.[35]

Chick Lit and Crime Fiction

Although much women's writing of the Celtic Tiger period critiqued the late-capitalist privileging of the consuming subject, one genre of women's writing is produced from and works within the context of Celtic Tiger consumerism – the commercial and international success of Irish chick lit, portraying the lives of young urban women. Irish chick lit, which became internationally popular in these years – Claire Lynch labels its success a 'global phenomenon'[36] – is associated with such names as Marian Keyes, Patricia Scanlan, Cathy Kelly and Cecilia Ahern. Maggie O'Neill identifies the Celtic Tiger period as a second phase of popularity for the genre (the first flourished during the 1980s), and notes the dominance of narratives concerned with material goods and sexual freedoms.[37] One of the defining features of the Irish chick lit of these years is its interest in narratives of consumerism, buoyed up by the climate of the Tiger years. As Lynch argues, 'Conceptually, the economic boom permitted, or rather encouraged, the glorification of spending.'[38] The genre then operates, as does much popular fiction, as a type of barometer for its contemporary moment. Chick lit's effect on gender stereotypes has been much debated, and while feminist responses to chick lit have noted the gender bias of pejorative attitudes based on the fact that this is commercial fiction aimed at women, concern is also expressed about the prioritization of a particular type of subject and attitudes to feminism found in many of these novels. As O'Neill notes, the genre often 'centralizes the white, middle-class subject and emphasizes freedom of choice in the spheres of personal, family and professional life under the assumption that feminism has succeeded'.[39] Marian Keyes is of major importance here, particularly as a writer whose popularity maps onto the Tiger period – her first novel *Watermelon* was published in 1995 – and as a globally and commercially successful author whose work both does and does not fit neatly into the conventions of chick lit. Keyes has been lauded both for her engagement with serious issues, such as depression and addiction, as well as for her articulation of a changing Ireland in her representations of homosexuality and of race.[40] Yet, as O'Neill points out, 'without underestimating the importance of representation, it might be argued that these depictions offer individualized solutions to problems of discrimination, containing little critique of systems of institutional power and privilege'.[41] Lynch argues, however, that Irish chick lit offers formal and content innovations in terms of a narrative engagement with technology and social media.[42]

A second area of genre fiction in which women writers excelled during the Celtic Tiger years was that of crime fiction, part of a general flourishing of the genre in an Irish context and much linked to the social change of the time. Writers associated with 'Celtic Crime', 'Hibernian Homicide' or 'Emerald Noir' as it has been dubbed,[43] include Tana French, Niamh O'Connor, Ruth Dudley Edwards and Arlene Hunt. As Shirley Peterson notes in an exploration of Tana French's novels, 'Social critique has long been a hallmark of the detective novel, particularly in police procedurals' and the intense socio-economic changes of the Celtic Tiger offered a particularly potent climate to writers of this genre.[44] Peterson's analysis of French's crime novels links her work directly to the concerns of writers such as Enright, Kilroy, Ní Dhuibhne, Mills, O'Brien and Morrissy in relation to an interest in occluded histories and haunted presents as outlined above. Peterson writes, 'in French's novels, homicide investigations also double as "home-icide" investigations, targeting Ireland's reconstruction of itself on the ruins of a homeland scarred by unredressed loss and injustice. The novels' literal corpses, then, signal the symbolic corpse of Ireland's past: buried, exhumed, and finally resuscitated in the style of the detective story'.[45] The novels also draw attention to the social injustices and inequalities generated by the socio-economic climate of the Tiger years and use a focus on crime to diagnose the traumatic pulses of the affluent surface of the Tiger. French's novel, *Broken Harbour* (2012), for instance, places the central murder in one of Ireland's 'ghost estates', deeply symbolic of the excesses and losses of the boom period. Furthermore, French often frustrates generic conventions to discover the identity of the murderer, registering the persistence of the trauma beyond the confines of the novel.

Artistic Creation

Given that many of the novels of the Celtic Tiger period circulate around traumatic, repressed histories and the reparation of intergenerational maternal relationships, ideas of voice, narrative, storytelling and truth are of profound importance and are also put under major pressure in these novels. A dominant mode of these novels is a self-consciousness about narrative itself. From *The Wig My Father Wore*, which draws attention to itself as text through visual representations of textual fragments ripped from the wallpaper, reproductions of TV guides and the representation of closing credits blurring past the viewer, to the insistence on unreliability and ambiguity in novels such as Morrissy's *The Pretender*, Kilroy's *All Summer* and Enright's *The Gathering*, women's writing of the Tiger period is heavily invested in a foregrounding of creativity. Interestingly, Lynch notes a pattern in Irish chick lit for the protagonist to reject an unfulfilling office job to pursue a writing career.[46] At the end of Ní Dhuibhne's critique of literature as commodity in *Fox, Swallow, Scarecrow*, the main character Anna, who had equated creativity with economic gain, is refigured through a changed attitude to art: 'I need to see what art is, what artists do ... No talk of advances, bestsellers, pricing your book. I want to write what I have not yet written, something deep inside me, not yet seen, not yet felt, not yet known, to me. Myself. I want to write. Real, I want to write, and unreal.'[47] This reconceptualization of art forms part of the dismantling of the isolationist subject. For Ní Dhuibhne, writing becomes an integral part of seeing and reshaping the landscape: 'Anna writes, tries to write, writes, tries to write. Lets the words float to the top like spawn on the water, lets the words sit like a hare on the tract, lets the words leap like a trout in the lake, lets the words sing like the finches. Lets the words. Lets the words. Lets the words.'[48] The novel's ending opens up a space for an eco-poetics, drawn from the land and initiates connectivity and innovation.

Deirdre Madden's *Authenticity* (2002) and *Molly Fox's Birthday* (2008) also belong to this group of novels in which the life of the creative artist is a central theme; painting and art in *Authenticity* and acting and play-writing in *Molly Fox's Birthday*. Set in contemporary Dublin, *Authenticity* focuses on three artists, Julia, William and Roderic, and *Molly Fox's Birthday* uses the confines of a single day to explore the relationship between the unnamed playwright narrator and the eponymous Molly Fox, an actress. Like Ní Dhuibhne and Haverty, Madden is particularly interested in the place of art in the commercially driven world of the Celtic Tiger, and in *Molly Fox's Birthday*, in the way in which art and self are built through intersubjective engagement ('I would not be the writer I am without Molly,' admits the narrator).[49] Madden speaks to the themes of connectivity and embeddedness that characterize women's writing of the Celtic Tiger period.

Collaborative practice is also at stake in Kilroy's *Tenderwire* in which Vivaldi's concertos for two violins become an important model for a move away from creation in isolation to a more open dialogic relationship. As the narrative tells us, Vivaldi became the musical director of the Pieta, 'an institution' as Eva tells us 'for female orphans, bastards, and the just plain abandoned. A building full of girls nobody wanted'.[50] These girls became virtuosos, yet were always hidden from view, and Vivaldi often composed more and more elaborate scores in order to facilitate two solo violins in dialogue.[51] In the novel, the musical motif which structures and resonates through the narrative is also positioned as a reformative energy. The Magdalena violin, Eva's double and a symbol for traumatic histories around loss and life, is also a figure for the power of art to heal. The violin appears to Eva in the form of a young woman in a dream-vision at the end of the novel, praying for her.[52] This personification of the violin as a young woman comes just before Eva's revelation that she had not lost the violin to Daniel – he had merely stolen an empty violin case. Eva instead dismantles the violin and smuggles it home to finally confront the loss of her father and to finally listen to her mother: '*My mother might actually be telling the truth.* She might actually have been telling the truth all along. She might actually know no more than I know.'[53] Art is shown here to have the potential to heal. The novel concludes with Eva in transit, the Magdalena at her feet, on their way to a 'full restoration' of the violin.[54] Eva has confronted her ghosts and is on her way to her own full restora-tion, on the way to a reunion with the orchestra both actual and meta-phorical. In this we can see the combination of the overriding concerns of the Celtic Tiger novel – reparation of the mother-daughter relationship, attention to persistent traumatic histories, acknowledgment of obscured women's histories (particularly evident in Eva's meditation on Vivaldi's orphan violinists) and the foregrounding of art.

Futures

This mobile immigrant subject at the end of Kilroy's novel also takes on extra significance in the context of Ireland's changing demographics during this era. The years of the Celtic Tiger saw a shift away from out-migration towards an increase of new migrants to Ireland, coming largely from Eastern European and African countries. The 2004 Citizenship Referendum, which effectively revealed the racist and exclusionary nature of conceptions of Irishness, removed the right to citizenship for children of non-Irish parents. Passed by a majority of 79.8 per cent, the referendum exposed Irish attitudes around race and the regulation of the pregnant body – the hysterical tone of the debates centred on a perceived influx of pregnant African women taking advantage of a 'loophole' in the constitution. Enright, with her focus on a pregnant migrant woman in *The Pleasure of Eliza Lynch*, stages a critical engagement with the racial and gender dynamics of the Irish subject. Scholars have begun to analyse representations of mobile female subjects in fiction by Irish writers as well as explore the emerging field of new writers to Ireland, which signals exciting energies for Irish fiction and examinations of the intersections between subjectivity, nation, race, gender and narrative that such interventions will generate.[55] Most recently, Claire Bracken's sensitive exploration of such initiatives as the Women Writers in the New Ireland network, founded in University College Dublin (UCD) in 2007 to support the work of migrant writers, and anthologies such as *Embers of Words: An Irish Anthology of Migrant Poetry* (2012), *Landing Places: Immigrant Poets in Ireland* (2010) and *Herstory: Migration Stories of African Women in Ireland* (2006), draws our attention to a wealth of fresh creative paradigms emerging from these new demographics.[56]

Although the creative work is predominantly performed through poetry and memoir, Bracken and Mulhall and Feldman highlight the potentials of these new configurations of artistic practice and collective engagement that speak to new futures, new languages and new discourses that will creatively remember and re-energize Irish literary landscapes. While the dominant form for these new Irish writers was poetry during the Tiger period, the post-Tiger years are seeing the emergence of fiction, and often narratives that bring into stark focus the realities of asylum and Ireland's inhumane Direct Provision system. Ifedinma Dimbo's short story, 'Grafton Street of Dublin', from the collection *Dublin: Ten Journeys, One Destination* (2010), published by the Irish Writers Exchange, comments directly on the asylum experience. Dimbo has also written a novel, *She Was Foolish?* (2012), which explores migration and sex work. Other writers include Ebun Akpoveta, whose novel *Trapped: Prison Without Wall* (2013), focuses on an abusive relationship. It remains to be seen how these new influences will reshape and reform the Irish novel in new and exciting ways. The current rise of independent presses like Tramp Press and the plethora of new literary journals, both print and online, such as *gorse*, *The Moth*, *The Penny Dreadful*, *Banshee*, *Winter Pages*, *wordlegs*, *The Bohemyth* and *The South Circular*, all contribute to a climate supporting new and innovative writing in the post-Tiger period.

Notes

1 Justine Jordan, 'A New Irish Literary Boom: The Post-Crash Stars of Fiction', *The Guardian*, 17 October 2015, sec. Books, www.theguardian.com/books/2015/oct/17/new-irish-literary-boom-post-crash-stars-fiction

2 Julian Gough, *The State of Irish Literature 2010* (London, Galway, Berlin: Julian Gough, 10 February 2010), www.juliangough.com/journal/2010/2/10/the-state-of-irish-literature-2010.html.

3 Jordan, 'A New Irish Literary Boom'.

4 Susan Cahill, *Irish Literature in the Celtic Tiger Years 1990 to 2008: Gender, Bodies, Memory* (London: Continuum, 2011), 6–9.

5 Éilís Ní Dhuibhne, 'Irish Literary Writers "Cut Off" from Current of Culture', *The Irish Times*, 11 March 2010, www.irishtimes.com/opinion/letters/irish-literary-writers-cut-off-from-current-of-culture-1.636167

6 Patricia Coughlan, 'Irish Literature and Femininity in Postmodernity', *Hungarian Journal of English and American Studies* 10, nos. 1–2 (2004): 180.

7 Kevin Gardiner, the economist, uses the term Celtic Tiger to compare Ireland's fiscal development with that of East Asia's 'Tiger' economies which experienced high levels of growth since the 1960s. See Kevin Gardiner, 'The Irish Economy: A Celtic Tiger', *MS Euroletter* 31 (1994).

8 Frank Stapleton, *The Fifth Province* (Ocean Films, 1997).

9 Claire Bracken, 'An Irish Feminist GenX Aesthetic: Televisual Memories in Anne Enright's *The Wig My Father Wore*', in *Generation X Goes Global: Mapping a Youth Culture in Motion*, ed. Christine Henseler (New York, NY: Routledge, 2013), 159.

10 Anne Haverty, *The Free and Easy* (London: Chatto & Windus, 2006), 112.

11 See discussions of the *Field Day Anthology* such as Claire Bracken, 'Becoming-Mother-Machine: The Event of Field Day Vols IV; V', in *Irish Literature: Feminist Perspectives*, ed. Patricia Coughlan and Tina O'Toole (Dublin: Carysfort Press, 2008), 223–44; Margaret Kelleher, '"The Field Day Anthology" and Irish Women's Literary Studies', *The Irish Review (1986–)*, 30 (1 April 2003): 82–94; Margaret Kelleher, 'Writing Irish Women's Literary History', *Irish Studies Review* 9, no. 1 (2001): 5–14; Gerardine Meaney, 'Engendering the Postmodern Canon? The Field Day Anthology of Irish Writing, Volumes IV & V: Women's Writing and Traditions', in *Opening the Field: Irish Women, Texts and Contexts*, ed. Patricia Boyle Haberstroh and

Christine St Peter (Cork: Cork University Press, 2007), 15–29. This work is far from done – as I write this in November 2015, the #wakingthefeminists campaign is challenging the Abbey's exclusion of female playwrights in its programming for the 1916 centenary.

12 Coughlan, 'Irish Literature and Femininity in Postmodernity', 176.

13 Claire McGing and Timothy J. White, 'Gender and Electoral Representation in Ireland', *Études Irlandaises*, 37, no. 2 (2012): 33.

14 Anne Enright, *The Wig My Father Wore* (London: Jonathan Cape, 1995), 31.

15 Bracken, 'An Irish Feminist GenX Aesthetic: Televisual Memories in Anne Enright's *The Wig My Father Wore*', 160.

16 Enright, *The Wig My Father Wore*, 126–7.

17 Ibid., 90.

18 Edna O'Brien, *Down by the River* (London: Weidenfeld & Nicholson, 1996), 17.

19 Eve Patten, 'Contemporary Irish Fiction', in *The Cambridge Companion to the Irish Novel*, ed. John Wilson Foster (Cambridge: Cambridge University Press, 2006), 269.

20 Cahill, *Irish Literature in the Celtic Tiger Years 1990 to 2008*, 114–15.

21 Anne Enright, *The Gathering* (London: Jonathan Cape, 2007), 243.

22 See Claire Bracken, *Irish Feminist Futures* (New York, NY: Routledge, 2016), 45 for further discussion of these novels.

23 Anne Fogarty, '"The Horror of the Unlived Life": Mother–Daughter Relationships in Contemporary Irish Women's Fiction', in *Writing Mothers and Daughters: Renegotiating the Mother in Western European Narratives by Women*, ed. Adalgisa Giorgio (New York, NY: Berghahn Books, 2002), 89.

24 Tina O'Toole, ed., *Dictionary of Munster Women Writers, 1800–2000* (Cork: Cork University Press, 2005); Maria Luddy and Gerardine Meaney, 'Women in Modern Irish Culture', accessed 18 March 2016, www2.warwick.ac.uk/fac/arts/history/irishwomenwriters/; Gerardine Meaney, Bernadette Whelan and Mary O'Dowd, 'Inventing & Reinventing the Irish Woman', accessed 18 March 2016, www.ul.ie/inventing/.

25 Anne Enright, *The Pleasure of Eliza Lynch* (London: Jonathan Cape, 2002), 225.

26 Ibid., 141.

27 Haverty, *The Free and Easy*, 95.

28 See David Lloyd, 'The Indigent Sublime: Specters of Irish Hunger', in *Memory Ireland: The Famine and Its Troubles*, ed. Oona Frawley, Vol. 3 (Syracuse: Syracuse University Press, 2014), 17–58.

29 Éilís Ní Dhuibhne, *Fox, Swallow, Scarecrow* (Belfast: Blackstaff Press, 2007), 142.

30 Miranda Popkey, 'Anne Enright on *The Forgotten Waltz*', *Paris Review Daily*, 25 October 2011, www.theparisreview.org/blog/2011/10/25/anne-enright-on-the-forgotten-waltz/

31 Anne Enright, *The Forgotten Waltz* (London: Jonathan Cape, 2011), 15.

32 Ibid., 23.

33 Ibid., 230.

34 Claire Bracken, *Irish Feminist Futures* (New York, NY: Routledge, 2016), 25.

35 Enright, *The Gathering*, 261.
36 Claire Lynch, *Cyber Ireland: Text, Image, Culture* (Basingstoke: Palgrave Macmillan, 2014), 97.
37 Maggie O'Neill, 'Assuming Gender: You Still Can Have It All, But Just in Moderation: Neoliberal Gender and Post-Celtic Tiger "Recession Lit"', *Assuming Gender* 5, no. 1 (2015): 65.
38 Lynch, *Cyber Ireland*, 97.
39 O'Neill, 'Assuming Gender', 59.
40 Mary Ryan, 'Trespassing on Ireland's "Norms": Irish Chick Lit and Ireland's "Others"', *Trespassing Journal: An Online Journal of Trespassing Art, Science, and Philosophy* 1 (2012), http://trespassingjournal.com/?page_id=170.
41 O'Neill, 'Assuming Gender', 67.
42 Lynch, *Cyber Ireland*, 13.
43 Gerard O'Donovan, 'Val McDermid: Why Irish Crime Fiction Is All the Rage', *The Telegraph*, 3 August 2011, www.telegraph.co.uk/culture/tvandra-dio/8368248/Val-McDermid-why-Irish-crime-fiction-is-all-the-rage.html
44 Shirley Peterson, 'Homicide and Home-Icide: Exhuming Ireland's Past in the Detective Novels of Tana French', *Clues: A Journal of Detection* 30, no. 2 (2012): 97.
45 Ibid., 98.
46 Lynch, *Cyber Ireland*, 99.
47 Ní Dhuibhne, *Fox, Swallow, Scarecrow*, 351.
48 Ibid., 354.
49 Deirdre Madden, *Molly Fox's Birthday* (London: Faber, 2008), 45.
50 Claire Kilroy, *Tenderwire* (London: Faber, 2006), 249.
51 Ibid., 250.
52 Ibid., 290.
53 Ibid., 286.
54 Ibid., 294.
55 Alice Feldman and Anne Mulhall, 'Towing the Line: Migrant Women Writers and the Space of Irish Writing', *Éire-Ireland* 47, no. 1 (2012): 201–20; Borbála Faragó, '"I Am the Place in Which Things Happen": Invisible Immigrant Women Poets of Ireland', in *Irish Literature: Feminist Perspectives*, ed. Patricia Coughlan and Tina O'Toole (Dublin: Carysfort Press, 2008), 145–66.
56 Bracken, *Irish Feminist Futures*, 147.

Select Bibliography of Secondary Works

Addis, Jeremy. 'Publishing for Children in Ireland'. In *The Big Guide to Irish Children's Books*, edited by Valerie Coghlan and Celia Keenan, 14–19. Dublin: Irish Children's Book Trust, 1996.

Agnew, Kate. 'The Troubled Fiction of the "Troubles" in Northern Ireland: Focus on Joan Lingard and Catherine Sefton'. In *The Big Guide 2: Irish Children's Books*, edited by Valerie Coghlan and Celia Keenan, 116–19. Dublin: Children's Books Ireland, 2000.

Akenson, Donald Harman. *The Irish Diaspora*. Belfast: Institute of Irish Studies, 1996.

Alcobia-Murphy, Shane and Richard Kirkland, eds. *The Poetry of Medbh McGuckian: The Interior of Words*. Cork: Cork University Press, 2010.

Allen-Randolph, Jody. *Eavan Boland*. Cork: Cork University Press, 2014.

Allen-Randolph, Jody and Anthony Roche, eds. 'Special Issue-Eavan Boland'. *Irish University Review* 23, no. 1 (1993).

Almqvist, Bo. 'Of Mermaids and Marriages'. *Béaloideas* 58 (1990): 1–74.

Annat, Aurelia. 'Class, Nation, Gender and Self: Katharine Tynan and the Construction of Political Identities, 1880–1930'. In *Politics, Society and the Middle Class in Modern Ireland*, edited by Fintan Lane, 194–211. Houndmills: Palgrave Macmillan, 2010.

Anselment, Raymond. 'Seventeenth-Century Manuscript Sources of Alice Thornton's Life'. *Studies in English Literature 1500–1900* 45 (2005): 135–55.

Armstrong, Isobel and Virgina Blain, eds. *Women's Poetry, Late Romantic to Late Victorian: Gender and Genre, 1830–1900*. Basingstoke: Palgrave Macmillan, 1999.

Auge, Andrew J. A. *Chastened Communion: Modern Irish Poetry and Catholicism*. Syracuse, NY: Syracuse University Press, 2013.

Backus, Margot Gayle. *The Gothic Family Romance: Heterosexuality, Child Sacrifice, and the Anglo-Irish Colonial Order*. Durham, NC: Duke University Press, 1999.

Backus, Margot and Joseph Valente. '*The Land of Spices*, the Enigmatic Signifier and the Stylistic Invention of Lesbian (in) visibility'. *Irish University Review*, ed. Anne Mulhall, 43, no. 1 (Spring/Summer 2013): 55–74.

Banville, John. 'In Praise of Elizabeth Bowen'. *Irish Times*, Saturday 7 March 2015.

Barker Benfield, G. *The Culture of Sensibility: Sex and Society in Eighteenth-Century Britain*. Chicago, IL: University of Chicago Press, 1992.

Barnard, Toby. 'Children and Books in Eighteenth Century Ireland'. In *That Woman! Studies on Irish Bibliography. A Festschrift for Mary 'Paul' Pollard*, edited by Charles Benson and Siobhán Fitzpatrick, 214–38. Dublin: Lilliput Press, 2005.

Barr Ebest, Sally. *Banshees: A Literary History of Irish American Women Writers*. Syracuse, NY: Syracuse University Press, 2013.

Beatty, John D., ed. *Protestant Women's Narratives of the Irish Rebellion of 1798*. Dublin: Four Courts Press, 2001.

Behrendt, Stephen. 'Placing "Irish" and "Romanticism" in the Same Frame: Prospects'. In *Ireland and Romanticism: Publics, Nations and Scenes of Cultural Production*, edited by Jim Kelly, 207–20. London: Palgrave, 2011.

Bennett, Andrew and Nicholas Royle. *Elizabeth Bowen and the Dissolution of the Novel: Still Lives*. Basingstoke: Macmillan, 1995.

Benson, Charles. 'The Dublin Book Trade'. In *The Oxford History of the Irish Book. Volume IV: The Irish Book in English, 1800–1891*, edited by James H. Murphy, 27–46. Oxford: Oxford University Press, 2011.

Blair, Kirstie. *Form and Faith in Victorian Poetry and Religion*. Oxford: Oxford University Press, 2012.

Bloom, Harold, ed. *Elizabeth Bowen: Modern Critical Views*. New York, NY: Chelsea House, 1987.

Boehmer, Elleke. *Colonial and Postcolonial Literature: Migrant Metaphors*. Oxford: Oxford University Press, 2005.

Boland, Eavan. *Object Lessons: The Life of the Woman and the Poet in Our Time*. London: Vintage, 1995.

Bourke, Angela. 'Bean an Leasa: Ón bPiseogaíocht do dtí Filíocht Nuala Ní Dhomhnaill'. In *Leath na Spéire*, edited by Eoghan Ó hAnluain, 74–90. Baile Átha Cliath: An Clóchomhar, 1992.

     Maeve Brennan: Homesick at the 'New Yorker'. London: Jonathan Cape, 2004.

Bourke, Angela and Borbála Faragó, eds. *Landing Places: Immigrant Poets in Ireland*. Dublin: Dedalus, 2010.

Bourke, Angela, et al., eds. *Field Day Anthology of Irish Writing, Volumes IV and V: Women's Writing and Traditions*. Cork: Cork University Press, 2002.

Bourke, Evan. 'Female Involvement, Membership, and Centrality: A Social Network Analysis of the Hartlib Circle'. *Literature Compass* 14 (2016). doi: 10.1111/lic3.12388.

Bowen, Elizabeth. *Pictures and Conversations*, Foreword by Spencer Curtis Brown. London: Allen Lane, 1974.

     Love's Civil War: Elizabeth Bowen and Charles Ritchie: Letters and Diaries from the Love Affair of a Lifetime, edited by Victoria Glendinning with Judith Robertson. London: Simon and Schuster, 2009.

     Listening In: Broadcasts, Speeches and Interviews, edited by Allan C. Hepburn. Edinburgh: Edinburgh University Press, 2010.

Bracken, Claire. 'An Irish Feminist GenX Aesthetic: Televisual Memories in Anne Enright's *The Wig My Father Wore*'. In *Generation X Goes Global:*

Mapping a Youth Culture in Motion, edited by Christine Henseler, 159–78. New York, NY: Routledge, 2013.

Irish Feminist Futures. New York, NY: Routledge, 2016.

Bracken, Claire and Susan Cahill, eds. *Anne Enright*. Dublin: Irish Academic Press, 2011.

Brady, Deirdre. 'Literary Coteries and the Irish Women Writers' Club (1933–1958)'. Unpublished PhD thesis. University of Limerick, 2013.

'Modernist Presses and the Gayfield Press'. *Bibliologia*, 9, no. 24 (2014): 103–18.

Breathnach, Diarmuid and Máire Ní Mhurchú. www.ainm.ie.

Brooke, Stopford and T. W. Rolleston, eds. *A Treasury of Irish Poetry in the English Tongue*. London: Macmillan, 1915.

Brouckmans, Debbie. 'The Short Story Cycle in Ireland: From Jane Barlow to Donal Ryan'. Unpublished PhD thesis. University of Leuven, 2015.

Brown, Karen. *The Yeats Circle, Verbal and Visual Relations in Ireland, 1880–1939*. Burlington: Ashgate Publishing Company, 2011.

Buchanan, Averill. *Mary Blachford Tighe: The Irish Psyche*. Cambridge: Cambridge Scholars Publishing, 2011.

Butler, Marilyn. *Maria Edgeworth: A Literary Biography*. Oxford: Clarendon Press, 1972.

Buttimer, Neil. 'Literature in Irish, 1690–1800: From the Williamite Wars to the Act of Union'. In *The Cambridge History of Irish Literature*, edited by Margaret Kelleher and Philip O'Leary, 1: 320–71. 2 vols. Cambridge: Cambridge University Press, 2006.

Cahalan, James M. 'Forging a Tradition: Emily Lawless and the Irish Literary Canon'. In *Border Crossings: Irish Women Writers and National Identities*, edited Kathryn Kirkpatrick, 38–57. Tuscaloosa, AL: University of Alabama Press, 2000.

Cahill, Susan. *Irish Literature in the Celtic Tiger Years 1990 to 2008: Gender, Bodies, Memory*. London: Continuum, 2011.

Campbell, Matthew. *Irish Poetry under the Union, 1801–1924*. Cambridge: Cambridge University Press, 2013.

Campo del Pozo, Mercedes del. 'Alternative Ulsters: Troubles Short Fiction by Women Writers, 1968–1998'. Unpublished PhD thesis. University of Ulster, 2015.

Canning, Richard, ed. *Hear Us Out: Conversations with Gay Novelists*. New York, NY: Columbia University Press, 2003.

Carey, Vincent. '"What's Love Got to Do with It?" Gender and Geraldine Power on the Pale Border'. In *Dublin and the Pale in the Renaissance c.1540–1660*, edited by Michael Potterton and Thomas Herron, 93–103. Dublin: Four Courts, 2011.

Carlson, Julia, ed. *Banned in Ireland: Censorship and the Irish Writer*. London: Routledge, 1990.

Carpenter, Lynette. 'Tragedies of Remembrance, Comedies of Endurance: The Novels of Edna O'Brien'. In *Essays on the Contemporary Irish Novel*, edited by Albert Wertheim and Hedwig Brock, 263–81. Munich: Max Hueber, 1986.

Casal, Teresa. "'Words Bursting, Words Witnessed": Language and Violence in Jennifer Johnston's War Novel'. In *New Voices in Irish Criticism*, edited by P. J. Mathews, 99–105. Dublin: Four Courts Press, 2000.

Casway, Jerrold. 'Heroines or Victims? The Women of the Flight of the Earls'. *New Hibernia Review: Irish Éireannach Nua* 7 (2003): 56–74.

Chambers, Anne. *Eleanor, Countess of Desmond, c.1545–1638*. Dublin: Wolfhound, 1986.
    Granuaile: The Life and Times of Grace O'Malley c.1530–1603. Dublin: Wolfhound, 1988.

Chambers, Lilian, et al., eds. *Theatre Talk*. Dublin: Carysfort Press, 2001.

Chansky, Ricia A. and Emily Hipchen, eds. *The Routledge Auto Biography Studies Reader*. New York, NY and London: Routledge, 2015.

Chedgzoy, Kate. *Women's Writing in the British Atlantic World: Memory, Place and History, 1550–1700*. Cambridge: Cambridge University Press, 2007.

Christensen, Lis. *Elizabeth Bowen: The Later Fiction*. Copenhagen: Museum Tusculanum, 2001.

Clarke, Norma. "'The Cursed Barbauld Crew": Women Writers and Writing for Children in the Late Eighteenth Century'. In *Opening the Nursery Door: Reading, Writing and Childhood 1600–1900*, edited by Mary Hilton, Morag Styles and Victor Watson, 91–103. London: Routledge, 1997.
    Queen of the Wits: A Life of Laetitia Pilkington. London: Faber, 2008.

Clear, Caitriona. "'I Can Talk About It, Can't I?" The Ireland Maura Laverty Desired, 1942–46'. *Women's Studies* 30, no. 6 (2001): 819–35.

Cliff, Brian and Eibhear Walshe, eds. *Representing the Troubles: Texts & Images, 1970–2000*. Dublin: Four Courts, 2004.

Clutterbuck, Catriona. 'Good Faith in Religion and Art: The Later Poetry of Eiléan Ní Chuilleanáin'. *Irish University Review* 37, no. 1 (2007): 131–56.

Coates, John. 'The Misfortunes of Eva Trout'. *Essays in Criticism* 48, no. 1 (1998): 59–79.

Coghlan, Valerie. 'Ireland'. In *The International Companion Encyclopaedia of Children's Literature*, Vol. 2, 2nd edition, edited by Peter Hunt, 1099–1103. London: Routledge, 2004.
    'Questions of Identity and Otherness in Irish Writing for Young People'. *Neohelicon* 36, no. 1 (2009): 91–102.
    "'A Homesick Love": Emigrant Echoes of Maternal Loss in the Novels of Siobhan Dowd'. In *Children's Literature on the Move: Nations, Translations, Migrations*, edited by Nora Maguire and Beth Rodgers, 87–99. Dublin: Four Courts Press, 2013.

Colletta, Lisa and Maureen O'Connor, eds. *Wild Colonial Girl: Essays on Edna O'Brien*. Madison, WI: University of Wisconsin Press, 2006.

Collins, Lucy. *Sheila Wingfield: Poems*. Dublin: Liberties Press, 2013.
    ed. *Poetry by Women in Ireland: A Critical Anthology 1870–1970*. Liverpool: Liverpool University Press, 2014.

Colman, Anne Ulry. *A Dictionary of Nineteenth-Century Irish Women Poets*. Galway: Kenny's, 1996.

Connolly, Claire. *A Cultural History of the Irish Novel, 1790–1829*. Cambridge: Cambridge University Press, 2012.

Connolly, Linda. *The Irish Women's Movement: From Revolution to Devolution*. London: Palgrave Macmillan, 2002.

Connolly, Ruth. 'A Proselytising Protestant Commonwealth: The Religious and Political Ideals of Katherine Jones, Viscountess Ranelagh'. *The Seventeenth Century* 23 (2008): 244–64.

Connolly, S. J. 'A Woman's Life in Mid-Eighteenth-Century Ireland: The Case of Letitia Bushe'. *The Historical Journal* 43, no. 2 (2000): 433–51.

Government of Ireland. *Constitution of Ireland*. Dublin: Government Publications, 2015.

Coogan, Tim Pat. *De Valera: Long Fellow, Long Shadow*. New York, NY and London: Random House, 1993.

Coolahan, Marie-Louise. 'Ideal Communities and Planter Women's Writing in Seventeenth-Century Ireland'. *Parergon* 29 (2012): 69–91.

Women, Writing, and Language in Early Modern Ireland. Oxford: Oxford University Press, 2010.

Corcoran, Neil. *Elizabeth Bowen: The Enforced Return*. Oxford: Clarendon Press, 2004.

Coté, Jane M. *Fanny and Anna Parnell: Ireland's Patriot Sisters*. London: Macmillan, 1991.

Coughlan, Patricia. 'Women and Desire in Elizabeth Bowen'. In *Sex, Nation and Dissent*, edited by Eibhear Walshe, 104–34. Cork: Cork University Press, 1997.

'An Léiriú ar Shaol na mBan i dTéacsanna Dírbheathaisnéise Pheig Sayers'. In *Ceiliúradh an Bhlascaoid 3: Peig Sayers Scéalaí 1873–1958*, edited by Máire Ní Chéilleachair, 20–57. Baile Átha Cliath: Coiscéim, 1999.

'Irish Literature and Femininity in Postmodernity'. *Hungarian Journal of English and American Studies* 10, nos. 1–2 (2004): 175–202.

'Rereading Peig Sayers: Women's Autobiography, Social History and Narrative Art'. In *Opening the Field: Irish Women, Texts and Contexts*, edited by Patricia Boyle Haberstroh and Christine St. Peter, 58–73. Cork: Cork University Press, 2007.

'"Not Like a Person at All": Bowen, the 1920s, and "The Dancing-Mistress"'. In *Elizabeth Bowen*, edited by Eibhear Walshe, 40–65. Dublin: Irish Academic Press, 2009.

Coughlan, Patricia and Tina O'Toole, eds. *Irish Literature: Feminist Perspectives*. Dublin: Carysfort Press, 2008.

Couser, G. Thomas. *Vulnerable Subjects: Ethics and Life Writing*. Ithaca, NY: Cornell University Press, 2003.

Cousin, Geraldine. *Women in Dramatic Space and Time: Contemporary Female Characters on Stage*. London: Routledge, 1996.

Cowell, John. *No Profit but the Name*. Dublin: O'Brien Press, 1988.

Craig, Layne Parish. 'Passion's Possibilities: Kate O'Brien's Sexological Discourse in *Without my Cloak*'. *Eire Ireland* 44, no. 3/4 (Winter 2009): 117–39.

Cullen, L. M. 'The Contemporary and Later Politics of Caoineadh Airt Uí Laoire'. *Eighteenth-Century Ireland* 8 (1993): 7–38.

'Refiguring the Popular in Charlotte Brooke's *Reliques of Irish Poetry*'. In *Romanticism and Popular Culture in Britain and Ireland*, edited by Philip Connell and Nigel Leask, 72–87. Cambridge: Cambridge University Press, 2009.

Cullingford, Elizabeth. 'Our Nuns are Not a Nation'. *Éire-Ireland* 41, no. 1/2 (Spring/Summer 2006): 9–39.

D'Arcy, Kathy. '"Almost Forgotten Names:" Irish Women Poets of the 1930s, 1940s and 1950s'. In *Irish Literature: Feminist Perspectives*, edited by Patricia Coughlan and Tina O'Toole, 99–124. Dublin: Carysfort Press, 2008.

D'hoker, Elke, ed. *Mary Lavin*. Dublin: Irish Academic Press, 2013.

Irish Women Writers and the Modern Short Story. New York, NY: Palgrave, 2016.

D'hoker, Elke and Stephanie Eggermont, eds. *The Irish Short Story: Traditions and Trends*. Bern: Peter Lang, 2015.

Dalsimer, Adele. *Kate O'Brien: A Critical Study*. Dublin: Gill and Macmillan, 1990.

Darwood, Nicola. *A World of Lost Innocence: The Fiction of Elizabeth Bowen*. Cambridge: Cambridge Scholars, 2012.

Davey, Maeve. '"You're Dying for Me": Representations of Masculinity in Contemporary Northern Irish Popular Women's Fiction'. In *Irish Masculinities: Reflections on Literature and Culture*, edited by Caroline Magennis and Raymond Mullen, 35–48. Dublin: Irish Academic Press, 2011.

Davis, Alex. 'Wilds to Alter, Forms to Build: The Writings of Sheila Wingfield'. *Irish University Review* 31, no. 2 (2001): 334–52.

Davis, Leith. 'Malvina's Daughters: Irish Women Poets and the Sign of the Bard'. In *Ireland and Romanticism: Publics, Nations and Scenes of Cultural Production*, edited by Jim Kelly, 141–60. Houndsmills: Palgrave Macmillan, 2011.

Day, Angelique. *Letters from Georgian Ireland: The Correspondence of Mary Delaney*, 1731–68. Belfast: Friar's Press, 1991.

De Búrca, Máire. 'Biddy Jenkinson'. In *Filíocht Chomhaimseartha na Gaeilge*, edited by Ríóna Ní Fhrighil, 167–81. Baile Átha Cliath: Cois Life, 2010.

De Paor, Louis. 'Contemporary poetry in Irish: 1940–2000'. In Kelleher and O'Leary, eds. *The Cambridge History of Irish Literature*, 2: 317–56.

De Paor, Louis, ed. *Míorúilt an Pharóiste: Aistí ar fhilíocht Mháire Mhac an tSaoi*. Indreabhán: Cló Iar-Chonnacht, 2014.

De Paor, Pádraig. *Tionscnamh Filíochta Nuala Ní Dhomhnaill*. Baile Átha Cliath: An Clóchomhar, 1997.

'Mo mháistir dorcha: Leathchéad dán le Nuala Ní Dhomhnaill ar théama an bháis'. In *Féilscríbhinn do Chathal Ó Háinle*, edited by Eoin Mac Cárthaigh and Jürgen Uhlich, 87–116. Indreabhán: An Clóchomhar/ Cló Iar-Chonnacht, 2012.

Deane, Seamus, et al., eds. *Field Day Anthology of Irish Writing, Volumes I–III*. Derry: Field Day Publications, 1991.

Denvir, Gearóid. 'Ní Sean go Nua is Ní Nua go Sean: Filíocht Nuala Ní Dhomhnaill agus Dioscúrsa na Gaeilge'. In *Téada dúchais: Aistí in ómós don Ollamh Breandán Ó Madagáin*, edited by Máirtín Ó Briain and Pádraig Ó Héalaí, 59–70. Indreabhán: Cló Iar-Chonnachta, 2002.

Department of Justice and Equality. *Report of the Interdepartmental Committee to Establish the Facts of State Involvement with the Magdalen Laundries*, Chair: Martin McAleese Dublin: Government Publications, 2013.

DiMeo, Michelle. '"Such a Sister Became Such a Brother:" Lady Ranelagh's Influence on Robert Boyle'. *Intellectual History Review* 25 (2015): 21–36.

Doak, Naomi. 'Ulster Protestant Women Authors'. *Irish Studies Review* 15, no. 1 (2007): 37–49.

Doan, Laura, and Jane Garrity, eds. *Sapphic Modernities: Sexuality, Women, and National Culture*. Basingstoke: Palgrave Macmillan, 2006.

Donovan, Katie, A. Norman Jeffares and Brendan Kennelly. *Ireland's Women: Writings Past and Present*. London: Gill and Macmillan, 1994.

Doyle, Maria-Elena. 'A Spindle for the Battle: Feminism, Myth, and the Woman-Nation in Irish Revival Drama'. *Theatre Journal* 51, no. 1 (1999): 33–46.

Dunbar, Carole. 'The Wild Irish Girls of L. T. Meade and Mrs George De Horne Vaizey'. In *Studies in Children's Literature 1500–2000*, edited by Celia Keenan and Mary Shine Thompson, 38–43. Dublin: Four Courts Press, 2004.

Dunbar, Robert. 'Rebuilding Castle Blair: A Reading of Flora Shaw's 1878 Children's Novel'. In *Studies in Children's Literature 1500–2000*, edited by Celia Keenan and Mary Shine Thompson, 31–37. Dublin: Four Courts Press, 2004.

——— '"It's the Way We Tell 'em": Voices from Ulster Children's Fiction'. In *Divided Worlds: Studies in Children's Literature*, edited by Mary Shine Thompson and Valerie Coghlan, 61–75. Dublin: Four Courts Press, 2007.

Dwan, David. 'Cultural Developments: Young Ireland to Yeats'. In *The Princeton History of Modern Ireland*, edited by Richard Bourke and Ian McBride. Oxford: Princeton University Press, 2016.

Eagleton, Terry. *Heathcliff and the Great Hunger*. London: Verso, 1995.

Eckley, Grace. *Edna O'Brien*. Cranbury, NJ: Associated University Presses, 1974.

Edwards, Heather. 'The Irish New Woman and Emily Lawless's *Grania: The Story of an Island*: A Congenial Geography'. *ELT* 51, no. 4 (2008): 421–38.

Eger, Elizabeth, 'Griffith, Elizabeth (1727–1793)'. In *Oxford Dictionary of National Biography*. Oxford: Oxford University Press, 2004-. Accessed 7 March 2016. https://doi-org.ucc.idm.oclc.org/10.1093/ref:odnb/11596

Ellmann, Maud. *Elizabeth Bowen: The Shadow across the Page*. Edinburgh: Edinburgh University Press, 2003.

Engel, Laura. 'Edna O'Brien'. In *British Writers: Supplement V*, edited by George Stade and Sarah Hannah Goldstein. New York, NY: Charles Scribner, 1999.

Epplé, Colette. '"Wild Irish with a Vengeance": Definitions of Irishness in Katharine Tynan's Children's Literature'. In *Divided Worlds: Studies in Children's Literature*, edited by Mary Shine Thompson and Valerie Coghlan, 32–40. Dublin: Four Courts Press, 2007.

Esty, J., ed. 'Virgins of Empire: The Antidevelopmental Plot in Rhys and Bowen'. In *Unseasonable Youth: Modernism, Colonialism, and the Fiction of Development*, 160–94. New York, NY: Oxford University Press, 2012.

Fallon, Ann Connerton. *Katharine Tynan*. Boston, MA: Twayne, 1979.

Faragó, Borbála. *Medbh McGuckian*. Cork: Cork University Press, 2014.

Fauset, Eileen. *The Politics of Writing: Julia Kavanagh, 1824–77*. Manchester: Manchester University Press, 2009.

Feldman, Alice, and Anne Mulhall. 'Towing the Line: Migrant Women Writers and the Space of Irish Writing'. *Éire-Ireland* 47, no. 1 (2012): 201–20.

Ferris, Ina. *The Romantic National Tale and the Question of Ireland*. Cambridge: Cambridge University Press, 2004.

Ferriter, Diarmaid. *Occasions of Sin: Sex and Society in Modern Ireland*. London: Profile, 2012.

Finnegan, Frances. *Do Penance or Perish*. Oxford: Oxford University Press, 2004.

Fitzgerald-Hoyt, Mary. 'Claire Keegan's *Foster*: The Child, the Famine, the Future'. In *The Country of the Young: Interpretations of Youth and Childhood in Irish Culture*, edited by John Countryman and Kelly Matthews, 119–32. Dublin: Four Courts Press, 2013.

Fitzgerald, Jennifer. '"The Queen's Girl": Helen Waddell and Women at Queen's University Belfast, 1908–1920'. In *Have Women Made a Difference?* edited by Claire Rush and Judith Harford. Oxford: Peter Lang, 2010.

Fitzgerald, Patrick and Brian Lambkin. *Migration in Irish History, 1607–2007*. Basingstoke: Palgrave Macmillan, 2008.

FitzSimon, Betsey Taylor. 'Conversion, the Bible, and the Irish Language: The Correspondence of Lady Ranelagh and Bishop Dopping'. In *Converts and Conversion in Ireland, 1650–1850*, edited by Michael Brown, Charles McGrath and Thomas Power, 157–82. Dublin: Four Courts, 2005.

FitzSimon, Betsey Taylor and James Murphy, eds. *The Irish Revival Reappraised*. Dublin: Four Courts Press, 2004.

Fitz-Simon, Christopher. *The Boys: A Biography of Micheál MacLiammóir and Hilton Edwards*. London: Nick Hearn Books, 1994.

Flint, Kate. *The Woman Reader 1837–1914*. Oxford: Clarendon, 1993.

Fogarty, Anne. '"A Woman of the House:" Gender and Nationalism in the Writings of Augusta Gregory'. In *Border Crossings: Irish Women Writers and National Identities*, edited by Kathryn Kirkpatrick, 100–22. Tuscaloosa, AL: University of Alabama Press, 2000.

    '"The Horror of the Unlived Life": Mother-Daughter Relationships in Contemporary Irish Women's Fiction'. In *Writing Mothers and Daughters: Renegotiating the Mother in Western European Narratives by Women*, edited by Adalgisa Giorgio, 85–118. New York, NY: Berghahn Books, 2002.

    ed. 'Special Issue: Lady Gregory'. *Irish University Review* 34, no. 1 (2004).

    ed. 'Special Issue: Eiléan Ní Chuilleanáin'. *Irish University Review* 37, no. 1 (2007).

Foley, Imelda. *The Girls in the Big Picture*. Belfast: Blackstaff, 2003.

Foster, John Wilson. *Fictions of the Irish Literary Revival: A Changeling Art*. Syracuse, NY: Syracuse University Press, 1987.

ed. *The Cambridge Companion to the Irish Novel.* Cambridge: Cambridge University Press, 2006.

Irish Novels 1890–1940. Oxford: Oxford University Press, 2008.

Foster, R. F. 'The Irishness of Elizabeth Bowen'. In *Paddy and Mr Punch: Connections in Irish and English History*, 102–33. London: Allen Lane, 1993.

'Prints on the Scene: Elizabeth Bowen and the Landscape of Childhood'. In *The Irish Story: Telling Tales and Making It Up in Ireland*, 148–63. London: Allen Lane, 2001.

Fulmer, Jacqueline. *Folk Women and Indirection in Morrison, Ní Dhuibhne, Hurston and Lavin.* New York, NY: Ashgate, 2007.

Gagnier, Regenia. *Individualism, Decadence, and Globalization: On the Relationship of the Part to the Whole, 1859–1920.* London: Palgrave Macmillan, 2010.

Gallagher, Bláithín. 'Sexing the Bisto'. *Children's Books Ireland* 9 (1993): 15.

Gavin, Adrienne E. and Carolyn Oulton, eds. *Writing Women of the Fin de Siècle: Authors of Change.* London: Palgrave, 2011.

Gildersleeve, Jessica. *Elizabeth Bowen and the Writing of Trauma: The Ethics of Survival.* Amsterdam: Rodopi, 2014.

Gillespie, Raymond and Andrew Hadfield, eds. *The Oxford History of the Irish Book. Vol III: The Irish Book in English, 1550–1800.* Oxford: Oxford University Press, 2006.

Gilmore, Leigh. *Autobiographics: A Feminist Theory of Women's Self-Representation.* Ithaca, NY: Cornell University Press, 1994.

The Limits of Autobiography: Trauma and Testimony. Ithaca, NY: Cornell University Press, 2001.

Tainted Witness: Why We Doubt What Women Say About Their Lives. New York, NY: Columbia University Press, 2017.

Glaser, Marisa. 'Dethroning the Goddess, Crowning the Woman: Eva Gore-Booth and Augusta Lady Gregory's Mythic Heroines'. In *New Voices in Irish Criticism 4*, edited by Fionnuala Dillane and Ronan Kelly, 96–104. Dublin: Four Courts Press, 2003.

Gleeson, Sinéad. 'A Long Gaze Back at Norah Hoult on her 117th Birthday'. *The Irish Times*, 10 September 2015.

ed. *The Long Gaze Back: An Anthology of Irish Women Writers.* Dublin: New Island, 2015.

ed. *The Glass Shore: Short Stories by Women Writers from the North of Ireland.* Dublin: New Island, 2016.

Glendinning, Victoria. *Elizabeth Bowen: Portrait of a Writer.* Harmondsworth: Penguin, 1977.

González-Arias, Luz Mar. 'In Dublin's Fair City: Citified Embodiments in Paula Meehan's Landscapes'. *An Sionnach: A Journal of Literature, Culture and the Arts* 5, no. 1–2 (2009): 34–49.

Gough, Julian. 'The State of Irish Literature 2010'. Julian Gough: London, Galway, Berlin, 10 February 2010. www.juliangough.com/journal/2010/2/10/the-state-of-irish-literature-2010.html.

Gray, Breda. *Women and the Irish Diaspora*. London: Routledge, 2004.
  'Breaking the Silence: Emigration, Gender and the Making of Irish Cultural Memory'. In *Modern Irish Autobiography: Self, Nation and Society*, edited by Liam Harte, 111–31. Basingstoke: Palgrave Macmillan, 2007.
Gray, Catharine. 'Katherine Philips in Ireland'. *English Literary Renaissance* 39 (2009): 557–85.
Greene, Velma O'Donoghue. 'Writing Women for a Modern Ireland: Geraldine Cummins and Susanne Day'. In *Women in Irish Drama: A Century of Authorship and Representation*, edited by Melissa Sihra, 42–54. New York, NY: Palgrave Macmillan, 2007.
Greenwood, Amanda. *Edna O'Brien*. Plymouth: Northcote House, 2003.
Gregory, Lady. *Lady Gregory's Journals, 1916–1930*, edited by Lennox Robinson. New York, NY: The Macmillan Company, 1947.
  Lady Gregory's Journals, edited by Daniel Murphy. New York, NY: Oxford University Press, 1987.
  Lady Gregory's Diaries, 1892–1902, edited by James Pethica. New York, NY: Oxford University Press, 1996.
Grenby, M. O. *The Child Reader 1700–1840*. Cambridge: Cambridge University Press, 2011.
Grubgeld, Elizabeth. *Anglo-Irish Autobiography: Class, Gender and the Forms of Narrative*. Syracuse, NY: Syracuse University Press, 2004.
Gupta, Nikhil. '"No Man Can Face the Past:" Eva Gore-Booth and Reincarnation as Feminist Historical Understanding'. *Women's Studies: An inter-Disciplinary Journal* 44, no. 2 (2015): 224–38.
Haberstroh, Patricia Boyle. *Women Creating Women: Contemporary Irish Women Poets*. Syracuse, NY: Syracuse University Press, 1996.
  My Self, My Muse: Irish Women Poets Reflect on Life and Art. Syracuse, NY: Syracuse University Press, 2001.
  The Female Figure in Eiléan Ní Chuilleanáin. Cork: Cork University Press, 2013.
Haigh, Susan. 'An Interview with Colette Bryce'. In *Dundee University Review of the Arts*, edited by Gail Low. Accessed 6 September 2016. https://dura-dundee.org.uk
Hand, Derek. 'Being Ordinary: Ireland from Elsewhere: A Reading of Éilís Ní Dhuibhne's *The Bray House*'. *Irish University Review* 30, no. 1 (2000): 103–16.
  A History of the Irish Novel. Cambridge: Cambridge University Press, 2011.
Hanley, Evelyn. 'Dora Sigerson Shorter: Late Victorian Romantic'. *Victorian Poetry* 3, no. 4 (1965): 223–34.
Hanson, Clare, ed. *Re-reading the Short Story*. London: Macmillan, 1989.
  'Little Girls and Large Women: Representations of the Female Body in Elizabeth Bowen's Later Fiction'. In *Body Matters: Feminism, Textuality, Corporeality*, edited by Avril Horner and Angela Keane, 185–198. Manchester: Manchester University Press, 2000.
  Hysterical Fictions: The 'Woman's Novel' in the Twentieth Century. New York, NY: St Martin's Press, 2000.

Hansson, Heidi. *Emily Lawless 1845–1913: Writing the Interspace*. Cork: Cork University Press, 2007.

'Selina Bunbury, Religion, and the Woman Writer'. In Murphy, *History of the Irish Book*, 322–330.

Harris, Mary N. '"Beleaguered but determined:" Irish Women Writers in Irish'. *Feminist Review* 51 (1995): 26–40.

Harte, Liam, ed. *Modern Irish Autobiography: Self, Nation and Society*. Basingstoke: Palgrave Macmillan, 2007.

Harte, Liam and Michael Parker, eds. *Contemporary Irish Fiction: Themes, Tropes, Theories*. New York, NY: Palgrave Macmillan, 2000.

Hartigan, Anne Le Marquand. *To Keep the Light Burning: Reflections in Times of Loss*. Co. Clare: Salmon, 2008.

Haughton, Miriam and Maria Kurdi, eds. *Radical Contemporary Theatre Practices by Women in Ireland*. Dublin: Carysfort Press, 2015.

Hickman, Mary. 'Migration and Diaspora'. In *The Cambridge Companion to Modern Irish Culture*, edited by Joe Cleary and Claire Connolly, 117–136. Cambridge: Cambridge University Press, 2005.

Hill, Judith. *Lady Gregory: An Irish Life*. Cork: The Collins Press, 2011.

Hipsky, Martin. *Modernism and the Women's Popular Romance in Britain, 1885–1925*. Athens, OH: Ohio University Press, 2011.

Hoeveler, Diane Long. 'Regina Maria Roche's *The Children of the Abbey*: Contesting the Catholic Presence in Female Gothic Fiction'. *Tulsa Studies in Women's Literature* 31, nos. 1/2 (2012): 137–58.

Hoogland, Renée. *Elizabeth Bowen: A Reputation in Writing*. New York, NY: New York University Press, 1994.

Howes, Marjorie. 'Blood and Tears: Lady Wilde'. In *Colonial Crossings: Figures in Irish Literary History*. Dublin: Field Day, 2006.

Hughes, Barbara. *Between Literature and History: The Diaries and Memoirs of Mary Leadbeater and Dorothea Herbert*. New York, NY: Peter Lang, 2009.

Hughes, Sarah. 'Déjà vu in Dublin and New York'. Review of *The Light of Evening* by Edna O'Brien. *The Observer* Sunday 15 October 2006.

Ingman, Heather. *Women's Fiction between the Wars: Mothers, Daughters, and Writing*. New York, NY: St Martin's Press, 1998.

'Edna O'Brien: Stretching the Nation's Boundaries'. *Irish Studies Review* 10, no. 3 (2002): 253–65.

'Nation and Gender in Jennifer Johnston: A Kristevan Reading'. *Irish University Review* 35, no. 2 (2005): 334–48.

Twentieth-Century Fiction by Irish Women: Nation and Gender. Aldershot; Burlington, VT: Ashgate, 2007.

Irish Women's Fiction: From Edgeworth to Enright. Dublin: Irish Academic Press, 2013.

Innes, C. L. '"A Voice in Directing the Affairs of Ireland:" *L'Irlande libre*, *The Shan Van Vocht and Bean na h-Eireann*'. In *Irish Writing, Subversion and Exile*, edited by Paul Hyland and Neil Sammells, 146–58. London: Macmillan, 1991.

Jaffe, Aaron. *Modernism and the Culture of Celebrity*. Cambridge: Cambridge University Press, 2005.

Jaillant, Lisa. *Modernism, Middlebrow and the Literary Canon: The Modern Library Series, 1917–55*. London: Pickering & Chatto, 2014.

Jaros, Michael. 'Image-Makers and Their Discontents: Lady Gregory and the Abbey Theatre Audience'. *Theatre Symposium* 20 (2012): 56–65.

Jordan, Heather Bryant. *How Will the Heart Endure? Elizabeth Bowen and the Landscape of War*. Ann Arbor, MI: University of Michigan Press, 1992.

Jordan, Justine. 'A New Irish Literary Boom: The Post-Crash Stars of Fiction'. *The Guardian*, 17 October 2015, sec. Books www.theguardian.com/books/2015/oct/17/new-irish-literary-boom-post-crash-stars-fiction.

Kahn, Helena Kelleher. *Late Nineteenth-Century Ireland's Political and Religious Controversies in the Fiction of May Laffan Hartley*. Greensboro, NC: ELT Press, 2005.

Kauffmann, Stanley. 'Night'. Review of *Night* by Edna O'Brien. *World* January 30 1973: 78.

Keane, Maureen. *Mrs S. C. Hall: A Literary Biography*. Gerrards Cross: Colin Smythe, 1997.

Kearney, Richard. *On Stories*. London: Routledge, 2002.

Keenan, Celia. 'Maeve Friel'. In *Irish Children's Writers and Illustrators. A Selection of Essays 1986–2006*, edited by Valerie Coghlan and Siobhán Parkinson, 46–52. Dublin: Children's Books Ireland and CICE Publications, 2007.

Kelleher, Margaret. 'Writing Irish Women's Literary History'. *Irish Studies Review* 9, no. 1 (2001): 5–14.

'*The Cabinet of Irish Literature*: A Historical Perspective on Irish Anthologies'. *Éire-Ireland* 38, nos. 3–4 (2003): 68–89.

'"The Field Day Anthology" and Irish Women's Literary Studies'. *The Irish Review* 30 (April 1 2003): 82–94.

ed. 'Special Issue: New Perspectives on the Irish Literary Revival'. *Irish University Review* 33, no. 1 (2003).

'Representations of Ireland, 1830–1880'. In *Palgrave History of Women's Writings 1830–1880*, edited by Lucy Hartley. London: Palgrave Macmillan, forthcoming.

Kelleher, Margaret, and Philip O'Leary, eds., *The Cambridge History of Irish Literature*. 2 vols. Cambridge: Cambridge University Press, 2006.

Kelleher, Margaret and James H. Murphy, eds. *Gender Perspectives in Nineteenth-Century Ireland: Public and Private Spheres*. Dublin: Irish Academic Press, 1997.

Kelly, A. A. *Pillars of the House: An Anthology of Verse by Irish Women from 1690 to the Present*. Dublin: Wolfhound, 1987.

Kennedy-Andrews, Elmer. *Fiction and The Northern Ireland Troubles Since 1969*. Dublin: Four Courts, 2003.

Kennedy, Catriona. '"Womanish epistles"? Martha McTier, Female Epistolarity and Late-Eighteenth-Century Irish Radicalism'. *Women's History Review* 13, no. 4 (2004): 649–67.

Kenney, Edwin. *Elizabeth Bowen*. Lewisburg: Bucknell University Press, 1975.

Kent, Brad. 'Literary Criticism and the Recovery of Banned Books: The Case of Kate O'Brien's *Mary Lavelle*'. *Ariel* 41, no. 2 (2011): 47–74.

Kernowski, Alice Hughes, ed. *Conversations with Edna O'Brien*. Jackson, MS: University of Mississippi Press, 2013.

Keyes, Marian Thérèse. 'Paratexts and Gender Politics: A Study of Selected Works by Anna Maria Fielding Hall'. In *Politics and Ideology in Children's Literature*, edited by Marian Thérèse Keyes and Áine McGillicuddy, 141–56. Dublin: Four Courts Press, 2014.

Kiberd, Declan. *Inventing Ireland: The Literature of the Modern Nation*. London: Jonathan Cape, 1995.

Kiely, Benedict. 'The Whores on the Half-Doors'. In *Conor Cruise O'Brien Introduces Ireland*, edited by Owen Dudley-Edwards, 148–61. New York, NY: McGraw-Hill, 1969.

Kilfeather, Siobhán. 'Origins of the Irish Female Gothic'. *Bullán* 1, no. 2 (1994): 35–45.

'Terrific Register: The Gothicization of Atrocity in Irish Romanticism'. *Boundary 2* 31, no. 1 (2004): 49–71.

'The Profession of Letters, 1700–1810'. In *The Field Day Anthology of Irish Writing Vols IV and V: Women's Writing and Traditions*, edited by Angela Bourke et al., 5: 772–832. Cork: Cork University Press, 2002.

King, Jeannette. *Discourses of Ageing in Fiction and Feminism*. Basingstoke: Palgrave Macmillan, 2013.

Kirwan-Keane, Siobhán. 'Sinéad De Valera agus Drámaíocht Ghaelach na nÓg'. In *Codladh Céad Bliain: Cnuasach Aistí ar Litríocht na nÓg*, edited by Ríona Nic, Congáil, 45–61. Baile Átha Cliath: LeabhairCOMHAR, 2012.

Kristeva, Julia. 'Modern Theater Does Not Take (A) Place'. *Sub-Stance* 18/19 (1977): 131–34.

Kuti, Elizabeth. 'Rewriting Frances Sheridan'. *Eighteenth-Century Ireland* 11 (1996): 120–8.

Laing, Kathleen, Sinéad Mooney and Maureen O'Connor, eds. *Edna O'Brien: New Critical Perspectives*. Dublin: Carysfort Press, 2006.

Laird, Mark, and Alicia Weisberg-Roberts, eds. *Mrs Delany and Her Circle*. New Haven, CT: Yale Centre for British Art, 2009.

Lane, Leann. '"In My Mind I Build a House:" The Quest for Family in the Children's Fiction of Patricia Lynch'. *Éire-Ireland* 44, no. 1 & 2, Spring/Summer (2009): 169–93.

Lassner, Phyllis. *Elizabeth Bowen*. Basingstoke: Macmillan, 1990.

Lawless, Emily. *Maria Edgeworth*. London: Macmillan, 1904.

Lawrenson, Sonja. 'Frances Sheridan's "The History of Nourjahad" and the Sultan of Smock Alley'. *Eighteenth-Century Ireland* 26 (2011): 24–50.

Ledger, Sally. *The New Woman: Fiction and Feminism at the Fin de Siècle*. Manchester: Manchester University Press, 1997.

Lee, Hermione. *Elizabeth Bowen: An Estimation*. London: Vision, 1981. Reprinted London: Vintage, 1999.

Leeney, Cathy. *Irish Women Playwrights 1900–1939: Gender and Violence on Stage*. New York, NY: Peter Lang, 2012.

Leeney, Cathy and Anna McMullan, eds. *The Theatre of Marina Carr*. Dublin: Carysfort Press, 2003.

Levenson, Leah. *The Four Seasons of Mary Lavin*. Dublin: Marino Books, 1998.

Lewis, Gifford. *Somerville and Ross: The World of the Irish R.M.* Harmondsworth: Penguin, 1987.

Lilley, Kate. 'Katherine Philips, "Philo-Philippa" and the Poetics of Association'. In *Material Cultures of Early Modern Women's Writing*, edited by Patricia Pender and Rosalind Smith, 118–39. Basingstoke: Palgrave Macmillan, 2014.

Lloyd, David. 'The Indigent Sublime: Specters of Irish Hunger'. In *Memory Ireland: The Famine and Its Troubles*, edited by Oona Frawley, 17–58. Syracuse, NY: Syracuse University Press, 2014.

Loeber, Rolf, and Magda Loeber. *A Guide to Irish Fiction, 1650–1900*. Dublin: Four Courts, 2005.

Longley, Edna. *The Living Stream*. Newcastle upon Tyne: Bloodaxe Books, 1994.

Luddy, Maria. 'William Drennan and Martha McTier: A "Domestic" History'. In *The Drennan-McTier letters Vol. 1, 1776–1793*, edited by Jean Agnew, 29–51. Dublin: Women's History Project/Irish Manuscripts Commission, 1998.

Luddy, Maria and Gerardine Meaney, eds. *A Database of Irish Women's Writing 1800–2005*, 2007. www2:warwick.ac.uk.

'Women in Modern Irish Culture', 2007. www2.warwick.ac.uk/fac/arts/history/irishwomenwriters/.

Lynch-Brennan, Margaret. *The Irish Bridget: Irish Immigrant Women in Domestic Service in America, 1840–1930*. Syracuse, NY: Syracuse University Press, 2009.

Lynch, Claire. *Irish Autobiography: Stories of Self in the Narrative of a Nation*. Oxford: Peter Lang, 2009.

Cyber Ireland: Text, Image, Culture. Basingstoke: Palgrave Macmillan, 2014.

Lynch, Rachel Jane. '"A Land of Strange, Throttled, Sacrificial Women": Domestic Violence in the Short Fiction of Edna O'Brien'. *The Canadian Journal of Irish Studies* 22, no. 2 (1999): 37–48.

Lysaght, Patricia. 'Caoineadh Os Cionn Coirp: The Lament for the Dead in Ireland'. *Folklore* 108 (1997): 65–82.

McAreavey, Naomi. '"This is that I may remember what passingis that happind in watirfort": Inscribing the 1641 Rising in the Letters of the Wife of the Mayor of Waterford'. *Early Modern Women* 5 (2010): 77–109.

'An Epistolary Account of the Irish Rising of 1641 by the Wife of the Mayor of Waterford [with text]'. *English Literary Renaissance* 42 (2012): 77–109.

'Re(-)Membering Women: Protestant Women's Victim Testimonies during the Irish rising of 1641'. *Journal of the Northern Renaissance* 2 (2010): www.northernrenaissance.org/re-membering-women-protestant-womens-victim-testimonies-during-the-irish-rising-of-1641/.

'Reading Conversion Narratives as Literature of Trauma: Radical Religion, the Wars of the Three Kingdoms, and the Cromwellian Reconquest of Ireland'. In *Region, Religion and English Renaissance Literature*, edited by David Coleman, 153–70. Burlington, VT: Ashgate, 2013.

McBreen, Joan, ed. *The White Page, An Bhileog Bhán*. Co. Clare: Salmon, 1999.

McCormack, W. J. *Dissolute Characters: Irish Literary History through Balzac, Le Fanu, Yeats and Bowen*. Manchester: Manchester University Press, 1993.

Mac Craith, Mícheál. 'Fun and Games among the Jet Set: A Glimpse of Seventeenth-Century Gaelic Ireland'. In *Memory and the Modern in Celtic Literatures*, edited by Joseph Falaky Nagy, 15–36. Dublin: Four Courts, 2006.

Mac Craith, Mícheál. 'Literature in Irish, c.1550–1690'. In *The Cambridge History of Irish Literature*, edited by Margaret Kelleher and Philip O'Leary, 1: 191–231. 2 vols. Cambridge: Cambridge University Press, 2006.

McCrory, Moy. '"This Time and Now": Identity and Belonging in the Irish Diaspora – The Irish in Britain and Second Generational Silence'. In *Land and Identity: Theory, Memory, and Practice*, edited by Christine Berberich, Neil Campbell and Robert Hudson, 165–90. Amsterdam: Rodopi, 2012.

MacCurtain, Margaret, and Mary O'Dowd, eds. *Women in Early Modern Ireland*. Edinburgh: Edinburgh University Press, 1991.

McDiarmid, Lucy, and Maureen Waters, eds. *Selected Writings by Lady Augusta Gregory*. London: Penguin, 1995.

McDiarmid, Lucy. *Poets and the Peacock Dinner: The Literary History of a Meal*. Oxford: Oxford University Press, 2014.

Mac Éinrí, Piaras. 'Introduction'. In *The Irish Diaspora*, edited by Andrew Bielenberg, 1–15. Harlow: Pearson, 2000.

McGing, Claire, and Timothy J. White. 'Gender and Electoral Representation in Ireland'. *Études Irlandaises* 37, no. 2 (2012): 33–48.

Mac Giolla Léith, Caoimhín. 'Metaphor and Metamorphosis in the Poetry of Nuala Ní Dhomhnaill'. *Éire-Ireland* 35, no. 1–2 (2000): 150–72.

McMahon, Sean. 'A Sex by Themselves: An Interim Report on the Novels of Edna O'Brien'. *Éire-Ireland* 2, no. 1 (1967): 79.

McMahon, Timothy. *Grand Opportunity: The Gaelic Revival and Irish Society, 1893–1910*. Syracuse, NY: Syracuse University Press, 2008.

McManus, Antonia. *The Irish Hedge School 1695–1831*. Dublin: Four Courts Press, 2002.

Mac Mathúna, Liam. 'Getting to Grips with Innovation and Genre Diversification in the Work of the Ó Neachtain Circle in Early Eighteenth-Century Dublin'. *Eighteenth-Century Ireland* 27 (2012): 53–83.

McNulty, Eugene. 'The Place of Memory: Alice Milligan, Ardrigh, and the 1898 Centenary'. *Irish University Review* 38, no. 2 (Autumn–Winter 2008): 203–21.

McWilliams, Ellen. *Women and Exile in Contemporary Irish Fiction*. Basingstoke: Palgrave Macmillan, 2013.

Markey, Anne, ed. *Children's Fiction 1765–1808*. Dublin: Four Courts Press, 2011.

'Irish Children's Books 1696–1810: Importation, Exportation and the Beginnings of Irish Children's Literature'. In *Children's Literature Collections: Approaches to Research*, edited by Keith O'Sullivan and Pádraic Whyte, 33–52. London: Palgrave Macmillan, 2017.

'Irish Children's Fiction, 1727–1820'. *Irish University Review* 41, no. 1 (2011): 115–32.

Martin, Peter. *Censorship in the Two Irelands 1922–1939*. Dublin: Irish Academic Press, 2006.

Mathews, P. J. *Revival: The Abbey Theatre, Sinn Fein, The Gaelic League and the Co-operative Movement*. Cork: Cork University Press, 2003.

Mattar, Sinéad Garrigan. *Primitivism, Science, and the Irish Revival*. Oxford: Oxford English Monographs, 2004.

Matthews, Kelly. *The Bell Magazine and the Representation of Irish Identity*. Dublin: Four Courts, 2012.

May, Charles, ed. *The New Short Story Theories*. Athens, OH: Ohio University Press, 1994.

Meaney, Gerardine. 'Engendering the Postmodern Canon? *The Field Day Anthology of Irish Writing, Volume IV & V: Women's Writing and Traditions*'. In *Opening the Field: Irish Women, Texts and Contexts*, edited by Patricia Boyle Haberstroh and Christine St. Peter, 15–29. Cork: Cork University Press, 2007.

Meaney, Gerardine, Bernadette Whelan and Mary O'Dowd. 'Inventing & Reinventing the Irish Woman', 2010. www.ul.ie/inventing/.

Meaney, Gerardine, Mary O'Dowd and Bernadette Whelan, *Reading the Irish Woman: Studies in Cultural Encounters and Exchange, 1714–1960*. Liverpool: Liverpool University Press, 2014.

Mentxaka, Aintzane L. *Kate O'Brien and the Fiction of Identity*. New York, NY: McFarland, 2011.

Mhac an tSaoi, Máire. 'Biddy Jenkinson: sampla d'imaistriú anama?' In *Leath na Spéire*, edited by Eoghan Ó hAnluain, 61–74. Baile Átha Cliath: An Clóchomhar, 1992.

Montefiore, Jan. 'The 1930s: Memory and Forgetting'. In *Women Writers of the 1930s: Gender, Politics and History*, edited by Maroula Joannou, 16–32. Edinburgh: Edinburgh University Press, 1999.

Mooney, Sinéad. 'Unstable Compounds: Bowen's Beckettian Affinities'. 'Special Issue: Elizabeth Bowen'. *MFS: Modern Fiction Studies* 53, no. 2 (2007): 238–56.

Morash, Chris. *Writing The Irish Famine*. Oxford: Oxford University Press, 1995.

'Theatre in Ireland, 1690–1800: From the Williamite Wars to the Act of Union'. In *The Cambridge History of Irish Literature*, edited by Margaret Kelleher and Philip O'Leary. 1: 372–406. 2 vols. Cambridge: Cambridge University Press, 2006.

Morin, Christina. 'Forgotten Fiction: Reconsidering the Gothic Novel in Eighteenth-Century Ireland'. *Irish University Review* 41, no. 1 (2011): 80–94.

'Theorizing Gothic in Eighteenth-Century Ireland'. In *Irish Gothics: Genres, Forms, Modes and Traditions, 1760–1890*, edited by Christina Morin and Niall Gillespie, 13–33. Houndmills: Palgrave Macmillan, 2014.

Morris, Catherine. 'Becoming Irish? Alice Milligan and the Revival.' *Irish University Review* 33, no. 1 (2003): 79–98.

Alice Milligan and the Irish Cultural Revival. Dublin: Four Courts Press, 2013.

Muldoon, Paul. *To Ireland, I. An Abecedary of Irish Literature*. London: Faber, 2011.

Mulhall, Anne. 'Memory, Poetry and Recovery: Paula Meehan's Transformational Aesthetics'. *An Sionnach: A Journal of Literature, Culture and the Arts* 5 no. 1–2 (2009): 142–55.

'"The Well-Known, Old, but Still Unbeaten Track:" Women Poets and Irish Periodical Culture in the Mid-Twentieth Century'. *Irish University Review* 42, no. 1 (2012): 32–52.

Murphy, James H. *Catholic Fiction and Social Reality in Ireland, 1873–1922*. Westport, CT: Greenwood, 1997.

Irish Novelists and the Victorian Age. Oxford: Oxford University Press, 2011.

ed. *The Oxford History of the Irish Book. Volume IV: The Irish Book in English, 1800–1891*. Oxford: Oxford University Press, 2011.

'The Dark Arts of the Critic: Yeats and William Carlton'. In *Yeats and Afterwords*, edited by Marjorie Howes and Joseph Valente, 80–99. Notre Dame: Notre Dame University Press, 2014.

Murphy, Sharon. *Maria Edgeworth and Romance*. Dublin: Four Courts Press, 2004.

Murray, Christopher. 'Lady Gregory: Coming to Terms'. In *Twentieth-Century Irish Drama: Mirror Up to Nation*, edited by Christopher Murray, 37–63. New York, NY: Manchester University Press, 1997.

Murray, Tony. *London Irish Fictions: Narrative, Diaspora and Identity*. Liverpool: Liverpool University Press, 2012.

Naipaul, V. S. Review of *The Country Girls* by Edna O'Brien. *New Statesman* 16 July 1960: 97.

Napier, Taura A. *In Search Of a Country: Literary Autobiographies of Twentieth-Century Irishwomen*. New York, NY: University Press of America, 2001.

Ní Annracháin, Máire. 'Ait Liom Bean ina File'. *Léachtaí Cholm Cille* 12 (1982): 145–82.

'Biddy Jenkinson: File na Saighead agus an tSlánaithe'. *Oghma* 4 (1992): 32–39.

'Biddy agus an Bandia'. In *Saoi na hÉigse: Aistí in Ómós do Sheán Ó Tuama*, edited by Pádraigín Riggs, Breandán Ó Conchúir and Seán Ó Coileáin, 339–58. Baile Átha Cliath: An Clóchomhar, 2000.

Ní Bhaoighill, Caoimhe. 'An Drámaíocht Ghaeilge 1954–89'. *Irisleabhar Mhá Nuad* (1991): 131–61.

Ní Bhrádaigh, Siobhán. *Máiréad Ní Ghráda: Ceannródaí Drámaíochta*. Indreabhán: Cló Iar-Chonnachta, 1996.

Ní Bhroin, Ciara. 'A Divided Union: Reformation and Reconciliation in Maria Edgeworth's Orlandino'. In *Divided Worlds: Studies in Children's Literature*, edited by Mary Shine Thompson and Valerie Coghlan, 22–31. Dublin: Four Courts Press, 2007.

Ní Chinnéide, Máiréad. 'Mna Breatha an Chonartha'. *Comhar: Conradh na Gaeilge 1893–1993: Móreagrán Comórtha* 52, no. 8 (August 1993): 18–22.

Ní Chuilleanáin, Eiléan, ed. *Irish Women: Image and Achievement*. Dublin: Arlen House, 1985.

Nic Congáil, Ríona. *Úna Ní Fhaircheallaigh agus an Fhís Útóipeach Ghaelach*. Gaillimh: Arlen House, 2010.

Nic Dhiarmada, Bríona. 'An Bhean Is an Bhaineann: Gnéithe den Chritic Fheimineach'. In *Téacs agus Comhthéacs: gnéithe de chritic na Gaeilge*, edited by Máire Ní Annracháin and Bríona Nic Dhiarmada, 152–182. Corcaigh: Cló Ollscoile Chorcaí, 1998.

'Bláthú an Traidisiúin'. *Comhar* (Bealtaine 1987): 23–9.

'Ceist na Teanga: Dioscúrsa na Gaeilge, an Fhilíocht, agus Dioscúrsa na mBan'. *Comhar* (Bealtaine 1992): 160–7.

'Immram sa tSíce: Filíocht Nuala Ní Dhomhnaill agus Próiseas an Indibhidithe'. *Oghma* 5 (1993): 78–s94.

'Máire Mhac an tSaoi'. In *Filíocht Chomhaimseartha na Gaeilge*, edited by Ríóna Ní Fhrighil, 15–27. Baile Átha Cliath: Cois Life, 2010.

Téacs Baineann Téacs Mná: Gnéithe de fhilíocht Nuala Ní Dhomhnaill. Baile Átha Cliath: An Clóchomhar, 2005.

Nic Eoin, Máirín. '"Na Murúcha a Thriomaigh" le Nuala Ní Dhomhnaill: An Scéalaíocht, an Fhilíocht agus Trámaí na Staire'. In *Trén bhFearann Breac: An Díláithriú Cultúir agus Nualitríocht na Gaeilge*, 284–320. Baile Átha: Cois Life, 2005.

'Athscríobh na Miotas: Gné den Idirthéacsúlacht i bhFilíocht Chomhaimseartha na Gaeilge'. *Taighde agus Teagasc* 2 (2002): 23–47.

'Filíocht Mháire-Áine Nic Gearailt: Ag cur friotail ar an eolchaire'. In *Aimsir Óg Cuid a Dó*, edited by Micheál Ó Cearúil, 179–84. Baile Átha Cliath: Coiscéim, 2000.

'Gender's Agendas'. *Graph* (Summer/Autumn 1992): 12: 5–8.

'Léiriú na mBan sna Leabhair'. In *Leath na Spéire*, edited by Eoghan Ó hAnluain, 13–41. Baile Átha Cliath: An Clóchomhar, 1992.

'Máire Mhac an tSaoi'. In *The UCD Aesthetic: Celebrating 150 Years of UCD Writers*, edited by Anthony Roche, 130–9. Dublin: New Island, 2005.

'Maternal Wisdom: Some Irish Perspectives'. *Irish Journal of Feminist Studies* 4 (2002): 1–15.

B'ait leo bean: Gnéithe den Idé-eolaíocht Inscne i dTraidisiún Liteartha na Gaeilge. Dublin: An Clóchomhar, 1998.

Nic Fhearghusa, Aoife. *Glór Baineann, Glór an Léargais: An tSochaí, an Bheith agus Dánta Dheirdre Brennan*. Baile Átha Cliath: Coiscéim, 1998.

Ní Dhomhnaill, Nuala. 'Tidal Surge (1990–1999)'. In *Flowing, Still*, edited by Pat Boran, 71–80. Dublin: Dedalus, 2009.

Ní Dhonnchadha, Aisling. *Idir Dhúchas agus Dualgas: Staidéar ar Charachtair Mhná sa Ghearrscéal Gaeilge 1940–1990*. Baile Átha Cliath: An Clóchomhar, 2002.

Ní Dhonnchadha, Máirín. 'Courts and Coteries I: c.900–1600' and 'Courts and Coteries II: c.1500–1800'. In *Field Day Anthology*, 4: 358–66.

Ní Dhuibhne, Éilís, ed. *Voices on the Wind: Women Poets of the Celtic Twilight*. Dublin: New Island Books, 1995.

Ní Eaghra, Érin. 'Úna Bean Uí Dhiosca: Síochánaí na Réabhlóide'. *Comhar* (August 2011): 305.

Ní Fhrighil, Ríóna. 'Nuala Ní Dhomhnaill'. In *Filíocht Chomhaimseartha na Gaeilge*, edited by Ríóna Ní Fhrighil, 142–166. Baile Átha Cliath: Cois Life, 2010.

'Scéal na Murúch i bhFilíocht Nuala Ní Dhomhnaill'. In *Aistí ag iompar Scéil: In ómós do Shéamus P. Ó Mórdha*, edited by Breandán Ó Conaire, 37–56. Baile Átha Cliath: An Clóchomhar, 2004.

Briathra, Béithe agus Banfhilí: Filíocht Eavan Boland and Nuala Ní Dhomhnaill. Baile Átha Cliath: An Clóchomhar, 2008.

Ní Ghairbhí, Róisín and Ríóna Ní Fhrighil. 'Filíocht Ghaeilge na linne seo'. In *Filíocht Chomhaimseartha na Gaeilge*, edited by Ríóna Ní Fhrighil, 289–305. Baile Átha Cliath: Cois Life, 2010.

Nordin, Irene Gilsenan. *Reading Eiléan Ní Chuilleanáin : A Contemporary Irish Poet*. Lewiston, NY: Edwin Mellen Press, 2008.

O'Brien, Darcy. 'Edna O'Brien: A Kind of Irish Childhood'. In *Twentieth-Century Women Novelists*, edited by Thomas F. Staley, 179–90. London: Macmillan, 1982.

O'Brien, John A. *The Vanishing Irish: The Enigma of the Modern World*. London: W. H. Allen, 1954.

O'Brien, Máire Cruise. *The Same Age as the State*. Dublin: The O'Brien Press, 2003.

O'Brien, Peggy, ed. *The Wake Forest Book of Irish Women's Poetry*. Winston-Salem, NC: Wake Forest University Press, 1999.

Ó Ciosáin, Éamon. 'Máiréad Ní Ghráda agus a Saothar Liteartha'. In *An Triail/ Breithiúnas: Dhá Dhráma*, by Máiréad Ní Ghráda, 171–96. Baile Átha Cliath: Oifig an tSoláthair, 1978.

Ó Coileáin, Seán. 'The Irish Lament: An Oral Genre'. *Studia Hibernica* 24 (1988): 97–17.

Ó Conchubhair, Brian. 'Éilís Ní Dhuibhne: Is Minic Ciúin Athchruthaithe'. In *Éilís Ní Dhuibhne: Perspectives*, edited by Rebecca Pelan, 171–96. Galway: Arlen House, 2009.

O'Connell, Helen. *Ireland and the Fiction of Improvement*. Oxford: Oxford University Press, 2006.

O'Connor, Frank. *The Lonely Voice: A Study of the Short Story*. Cork: Cork City Council, 2003.

O'Connor, Laura. 'The "War of the Womb:" Folklore and Nuala Ní Dhomhnaill'. In *That Other World: The Supernatural and the Fantastic in Irish Literature and its Contexts*, edited by Bruce Stewart, 186–204. Gerrards Cross: Colin Smythe, 1998.

O'Connor, Sarah. 'Female Maturation in Éilís Ní Dhuibhne's *Cailíní Beaga Ghleann na mBláth*'. In *Éilís Ní Dhuibhne: Perspectives*, edited by Rebecca Pelan, 113–128. Galway: Arlen House, 2009.

O'Donovan, Gerard. 'Val McDermid: Why Irish Crime Fiction Is All the Rage'. *The Telegraph*, 3 August 2011. www.telegraph.co.uk/culture/tvandradio/8368248/Val-McDermid-why-Irish-crime-fiction-is-all-the-rage.html.

O'Dowd, Mary. *A History of Women in Ireland, 1500–1800*. Harlow: Pearson Longman, 2005.

Ó Drisceoil, Proinsias. '"Eolus na Céirde:" Filíocht Áine Ní Fhoghludha'. In *An Linn Bhuí: Iris Ghaeltacht na nDéise 12*, edited by Pádraig Ó Macháin and Aoibheann Nic Dhonnchadha (2008): 100–109.

O'Faolain, Julia. 'A Scandalous Woman', review of a *Fanatic Heart: Selected Stories by Edna O'Brien*. *New York Times*, 22 September 1974: 5.

O'Faolain, Sean. *The Vanishing Hero: Studies in Novelists of the Twenties*. London: Eyre and Spottiswoode, 1956.

O'Flaherty, Emily. 'Patrons, Peers and Subscribers: The Publication of Mary Barber's *Poems on Several Occasions*'. Unpublished NUIG PhD Thesis. 2013.

Ó Gallchoir, Clíona. *Maria Edgeworth: Women, Enlightenment and Nation*. Dublin: University College Dublin Press, 2005.

'Foreign Tyrants and Domestic Tyrants: the Public, the Private, and Eighteenth-Century Irish Women's Writing'. In *Irish Literature: Feminist Perspectives*, edited by Patricia Coughlan and Tina O'Toole, 17–38. Dublin: Carysfort Press, 2008.

Ó Háinle, Cathal. 'Flattery Rejected: Two Seventeenth-Century Irish Poems'. *Hermathena* 138 (1985): 5–27.

O'Hanlon, Eilis. 'What Shall We Tell the Children?' In *The Irish Times*, 8 May 1993.

O'Leary, Philip. *The Prose Literature of the Gaelic Revival, 1881–1921: Ideology and Innovation*. Pennsylvania, PA: The Pennsylvania State University Press, 1994.

O'Neill, Maggie. 'Assuming Gender: You Still Can Have It All, But Just in Moderation: Neoliberal Gender and Post-Celtic Tiger "Recession Lit"'. *Assuming Gender* 5, no. 1 (2015): 59–83.

Osborn, Susan. 'Introduction. Elizabeth Bowen: New Directions for Critical Thinking'. In '*Special Issue: Elizabeth Bowen*'. *Modern Fiction Studies* 53, no. 2 (2007): 225–37.

ed. *Elizabeth Bowen: New Critical Perspectives*. Cork: Cork University Press, 2009.

O'Sullivan, Emer. *Comparative Children's Literature*. London: Routledge, 2005.

'Insularity and Internationalism: Between Local Production and the Global Marketplace'. In *Irish Children's Literature and Culture, New Perspectives on Contemporary Writing*, edited by Valerie Coghlan and Keith O'Sullivan, 183–96. London: Routledge, 2011.

O'Sullivan, Keith. '"Binding with Briars": Romanticizing the Child'. In *Irish Children's Literature and Culture: New Perspectives on Contemporary Writing*, edited by Valerie Coghlan and Keith O'Sullivan, 99–113. London: Routledge, 2011.

O'Toole, Fintan. 'A Fiction too Far'. *Irish Times Weekend Review*, 2 March 2002: 1.

O'Toole, Tina, ed. *Dictionary of Irish Munster Writers 1800–2000*. Cork: Cork University Press, 2005.

'Angels and Monsters: Embodiment and Desire in *Eva Trout*'. In *Elizabeth Bowen*, edited by Eibhear Walshe, 162–78. Dublin: Irish Academic Press, 2009.

'Unregenerate Spirits: the Counter-Cultural Experiments of George Egerton and Elizabeth Bowen'. In *Irish Women Writers: New Critical Perspectives*, edited by Elke D'hoker, Raphael Ingelbien and Hedwig Schwall, 227–44. Oxford: Peter Lang, 2011.

The Irish New Woman. London: Palgrave Macmillan, 2013.

'George Egerton's Translocational Subjects'. *Modernism/Modernity* 21, no. 3 (2014): 827–42.

'The New Woman Flâneuse or Streetwalker? George Egerton's Urban Aestheticism'. In *Reconnecting Aestheticism and Modernism*, edited by Bénédicte Coste et al. London: Routledge, 2016.

Ó Tuama, Seán. 'Filíocht Nuala Ní Dhomhnaill: An Mháthair Ghrámhar is an Mháthair Ghránna ina cuid filíochta'. *Léachtaí Cholm Cille* 17 (1986): 95–116.

Oulton, Carolyn, ed. *New Woman Fiction, 1881–1899*. London: Pickering and Chatto, 2010.

Pal, Carol. *Republic of Women: Rethinking the Republic of Letters in the Seventeenth Century*. Cambridge: Cambridge University Press, 2012.

Palko, Abigail 'Colonial Modernism's Thwarted Modernity: Elizabeth Bowen's *The House in Paris* and Jean Rhys's *Voyage in the Dark*'. *Textual Practice* 27, no. 1 (2013): 89–108.

Parker, Michael. 'Shadows on a Glass: Self-Reflexivity in the Novels of Deirdre Madden'. *Irish University Review* (Spring/Summer 2000): 82–102.

Northern Irish Literature, 1956–2006. Basingstoke: Palgrave Macmillan, 2007.

Parkes, Susan. *The Kildare Place Society*. Dublin: CICE Publications, 2011.

Pašeta, Senia. *Irish Nationalist Women 1900–1918*. Cambridge: University Press, 2013.

Patten, Eve. 'Women and Fiction 1985–1990'. *Krino* 8–9 (1990): 1–7.

Peach, Linden. *The Contemporary Irish Novel*. Basingstoke: Palgrave Macmillan, 2004.

Pearson, Nels. *Irish Cosmopolitanism: Location and Dislocation in James Joyce, Elizabeth Bowen, and Samuel Beckett*. Gainesville, FL: University of Florida Press, 2015.

Pelan, Rebecca. 'Edna O'Brien's "Stage-Irish" Persona: An "Act" of Resistance'. *Canadian Journal of Irish Studies* 19, no. 1 (1993): 67–78.

'Edna O'Brien's "World of Nora Barnacle"'. *Canadian Journal of Irish Studies* 22, no. 2 (1997): 49–61.

Two Irelands: Literary Feminism North and South. Syracuse, NY: Syracuse University Press, 2005.

Perrick, Penny. *Something to Hide: The Life of Sheila Wingfield, Viscountess Powerscourt*. Dublin: Lilliput Press, 2007.

Peterson, Shirley. 'Homicide and Home-Icide: Exhuming Ireland's Past in the Detective Novels of Tana French'. *Clues: A Journal of Detection* 30, no. 2 (2012): 97–108.

Phelan, Peggy. *Unmarked: The Politics of Performance*. London: Routledge, 1993.

Phillips, Áine. *Performance Art in Ireland: A History*. London: Live Art Development Agency and Intellect Books, 2015.

Piesse, A. J. 'Islands, Ireland and the Changing State of Writing for Children'. In *Treasure Islands. Studies in Children's Literature*, edited by Mary Shine Thompson and Celia Keenan, 153–60. Dublin: Four Courts Press, 2006.

Pine, Emilie. *The Politics of Irish Memory: Performing Remembrance in Contemporary Irish Culture*. Basingstoke: Palgrave Macmillan, 2011.

Plain, Gill. *Women's Fiction of the Second World War: Gender, Power, and Resistance*. Edinburgh: Edinburgh University Press, 1996.

Pollard, Mary. *A Dictionary of Members of the Dublin Book Trade 1550–1800 Based on the Records of the Guild of St Luke the Evangelist*. Dublin; London: Bibliographical Society, 2000.

Pomeroy, Laura. '"Undisturbed by Leaves": Constructions of Nature in Mary Devenport O'Neill's Poetry'. In *Engendering Ireland: New Reflections in Modern History and Literature*, edited by Rebecca Anne Barr, Sarah-Anne Buckley and Laura Kelly, 177–95. Cambridge: Cambridge Scholars Publishing, 2015.

Popkey, Miranda. 'Anne Enright on *The Forgotten Waltz*'. *Paris Review Daily*, 25 October 2011. www.theparisreview.org/blog/2011/10/25/anne-enright-on-the-forgotten-waltz/.

Prendergast, Amy. '"The Drooping Genius of Our Isle to Raise:" The Moira House Salon and Its Role in Gaelic Cultural Revival'. *Eighteenth-Century Ireland* 26 (2011): 95–114.
  Literary Salons across Britain and Ireland in the Long Eighteenth Century. London: Palgrave, 2015.

Pryce, Alex. 'Ambiguous Silences? Women in Anthologies of Contemporary Northern Irish Poetry'. *Peer English* 9 (2014). Accessed 28 September 2016. www2.le.ac.uk/offices/english-association/publications/peer-english/9/6.pdf.

Purdon, James. *Modernist Informatics: Literature, Information and the State*. New York, NY: Oxford University Press. 2015.

Pykett, Lyn. *Engendering Fictions: The English Novel in the Early Twentieth Century*. London: Edward Arnold, 1995.

Quinn, Antoinette. 'Cathleen ni Houlihan Writes Back: Maud Gonne and Irish Nationalist Theater'. In *Gender and Sexuality in Modern Ireland*, edited by Anthony Bradley and Maryann Valiulis, 39–59. Amherst, MA: University of Massachusetts Press, 1997.

Radford, Jean. 'Late Modernism and the Politics of History'. In *Women Writers of the '30s: Gender, Politics and History*, 33–45. Edinburgh: Edinburgh University Press, 1999.
  'Race and Ethnicity in White Women's Modernist Literature'. In *Cambridge Companion to Modernist Women Writers*, edited by Maren Tova Linett, 110–28. Cambridge: Cambridge University Press, 2010.

Rafroidi, Patrick and Terence Brown, eds. *The Irish Short Story*. Gerrards Cross: Colin Smythe, 1979.

Rankin, Deana. '"If Egypt Now Enslav'd or Free a Kingdom or a Province Be:" Translating Corneille in Restoration Dublin'. In *Culture and Conflict in Seventeenth-Century France and Ireland*, edited by Sarah Alyn Stacey and Véronique Desnain, 194–209. Dublin: Four Courts, 2004.

Rau, Petra. 'Telling it Straight: The Rhetorics of Conversion in Elizabeth Bowen's *The Hotel* and Freud's *Psychogenesis*'. In *Sapphic Modernities: Sexuality, Women, and National Culture*, edited by Laura Doan and Jane Garrity, 217–28. Basingstoke: Palgrave Macmillan, 2006.

Read, Charles A., and Katharine Tynan Hinkson, eds. *The Cabinet of Irish Literature*. [Revised and Greatly Extended.] 3 vols. London: Gresham, 1902.

Reddin, Kenneth. 'Children's Books in Ireland. Were We All Brought Up Behind a Half-door?' *Irish Library Bulletin* 7 (1946): 74–6.

Reynolds, Kimberley. *Girls Only? Gender and Popular Juvenile Fiction in Britain 1880–1910*. Hemel Hempstead: Harvester/Wheatsheaf; Philadelphia, PA: Temple University Press, 1990.

Reynolds, Lorna. *Kate O'Brien, A Literary Portrait*. Gerrard's Cross: Colin Smyth, 1987.

Reynolds, Paige. 'The Making of a Celebrity: Lady Gregory and the Abbey's First American Tour'. *Irish University Review* 34, no. 1 (2004): 81–93.

  Modernism, Drama, and the Audience for Irish Spectacle. Cambridge: Cambridge University Press, 2007.

Rich, Adrienne. *On Lies, Secrets, and Silence: Selected Prose 1966–1978*. London: Virago, 1980.

Rives, Rochelle. 'Chapter 5: A Solicitude for Things: Elizabeth Bowen and the Bildungsroman'. In *Modernist Impersonalities: Affect, Authority and the Subject*, 149–81. New York, NY: Palgrave Macmillan, 2012.

Robinson, Mary. 'Cherishing the Irish Diaspora'. *An Address to the Houses of the Oireachtas*, 2 February 1995.

Roche, Anthony. 'Reworking *The Workhouse Ward*: McDonagh, Beckett and Gregory'. *Irish University Review* 24 (2004): 171–84.

  The Irish Dramatic Revival 1899–1939. London: Bloomsbury, 2015.

Roos, Bonnie. 'Unlikely Heroes: Katharine Tynan's *The Story of Bawn*, the Irish Famine, and the Sentimental Tradition'. *Irish University Review* 43, no. 2 (2013): 327–43.

Rose, Jacqueline. 'Bizarre Objects: Mary Butts and Elizabeth Bowen'. In *On Not Being Able to Sleep: Psychoanalysis and the Modern World*, 89–104. London: Chatto, 2003.

Ross, Ian Campbell. '"One of the principal Nations in Europe": The Representation of Ireland in Sarah Butler's *Irish Tales*'. *Eighteenth-Century Fiction* 7 (1994): 1–16.

Ross, Sarah C. E. *Women, Poetry, and Politics in Seventeenth-Century Britain*. Oxford: Oxford University Press, 2015.

Rule, Jane. *Lesbian Images*. Garden City: Doubleday, 1976.

Ryan, Mary. 'Trespassing on Ireland's "Norms": Irish Chick Lit and Ireland's "Others"'. *Trespassing Journal: An Online Journal of Trespassing Art, Science, and Philosophy* 1 (2012). http://trespassingjournal.com/?page_id=170.

Sage, Lorna. *Women in the House of Fiction: Post-War Women Novelists*. Basingstoke: Macmillan, 1992.

Schaffer, Kay, and Sidonie Smith. *Human Rights and Narrated Lives: The Ethics of Recognition*. New York, NY; Basingstoke: Palgrave Macmillan, 2004.

Schirmer, Gregory. 'Tales from Big House and Cabin: The Nineteenth Century'. In *The Irish Short Story: a critical history*, edited by James Kilroy, 21–44. Boston: Twayne, 1984.

 Out of What Began: A History of Irish Poetry in English. Ithaca, NY: Cornell University Press, 1998.

Schneider, Karen. *Loving Arms: British Women Writing the Second World War*. Lexington, KY: University Press of Kentucky, 1997.

Schreibman, Susan. 'Irish Women Poets 1929–49: Some Foremothers'. *Colby Quarterly* 37, no. 4 (2001): 309–36.

Scolnicov, Hanna. *Woman's Theatrical Space*. Cambridge: Cambridge University Press, 2004.

Sewell, Frank. 'Nuala Ní Dhomhnaill: Journeying to the Shrine'. In *Modern Irish Poetry: A New Alhambra*, 149–98. Oxford: Oxford University Press, 2000.

Shovlin, Frank. *The Irish Literary Periodical 1923–1958*. Oxford: Oxford University Press, 2003.

Showalter, Elaine, ed. *New Feminist Criticism*. New York, NY: Pantheon Books, 1985.

 ed. *Daughters of Decadence: Women Writers of the fin de siècle*. London: Virago, 1993.

Siegfried, Brandie. 'Queen to Queen at Check: Grace O'Malley, Elizabeth Tudor, and the Discourse of Majesty in the State Papers of Ireland'. In *Elizabeth I: Always Her Own Free Woman*, edited by Carole Levin, Jo Eldridge Carney and Debra Barrett-Graves, 149–75. Aldershot: Ashgate, 2003.

Sihra, Melissa, ed. *Women in Irish Drama: A Century of Authorship and Representation*. New York, NY: Palgrave Macmillan, 2007.

Simpson, Janet Madden, ed. *Woman's Part: An Anthology of Short Fiction by and about Irish Women 1890–1960*. Dublin: Arlen House, 1984.

Smith, James. *Ireland's Magdalen Laundries and the Nation's Architecture of Containment*. Notre Dame, IN: University of Notre Dame Press, 2007.

Smith, Michelle. *Empire in British Girls' Literature and Culture: Imperial Girls 1880–1915*. London: Palgrave Macmillan, 2011.

Smith, Sidonie and Julia Watson. *De/Colonizing the Subject: Politics of Gender in Women's Autobiography*. Minneapolis, MN: University of Minnesota Press, 1992.

 Reading Autobiography: A Guide for Interpreting Life Narratives, 2nd edn. Minneapolis, MN: University of Minnesota Press, 2010.

Smyth, Ailbhe. *Wildish Things: An Anthology of New Irish Women's Writing*. Dublin: Attic, 1989.

St. Peter, Christine. *Changing Ireland: Strategies in Contemporary Women's Fiction*. Basingstoke: Palgrave, 2000.

Steele, Karen. 'Editing Out Factionalist: The Political and Literary Consequences in Ireland's *Shan Van Vocht*'. *Victorian Periodicals Review* 35, no. 2 (Summer 2002): 113–32.

'Reading Maud Gonne: Gendered Poetics in the Advanced Nationalist Press'. *Prose Studies: History, Theory, Criticism* 25, no. 2 (2002): 102–21.

Maud Gonne's Irish Nationalist Writing, 1895–1946. Dublin: Irish Academic Press, 2004.

Women, Press, and Politics During the Irish Revival. Syracuse, NY: Syracuse University Press, 2007.

Stetz, Margaret Diane. 'The New Grub Street and the Woman Writer of the 1890s'. In *Transforming Genres: New Approaches to British Fiction of the 1890s*, edited by Nikki Lee Manos and Meri-Jane Rochelson, 21–45. New York, NY: St. Martin's, 1994.

'Feminist Politics and the Two Irish "Georges": Egerton versus Shaw'. In *Shaw and Feminisms: On Stage and Off*, edited by D. A. Hadfield and Jean Reynolds, 133–43. Gainesville, FL: University Press of Florida, 2013.

Stevens, Julie Ann. *The Irish Scene in Somerville and Ross*. Dublin: Irish Academic Press, 2007.

'The Little Big House: Somerville and Ross's Work for Children'. In *Divided Worlds: Studies in Children's Literature*, edited by Mary Shine Thompson and Valerie Coghlan, 41–49. Dublin: Four Courts Press, 2007.

Stevenson, Jane. *Women Latin Poets: Language, Gender, and Authority from Antiquity to the Eighteenth Century*. Oxford: Oxford University Press, 2005.

Sullivan, Megan. '"Instead I Said I Am A Home Baker": Nationalist Ideology and Materialist Politics in Mary Beckett's *Give Them Stones*'. In *Border Crossings: Irish Women Writers and National Identities* edited by Kathryn Kirkpatrick, 227–49. Tuscaloosa, AL: The University of Alabama Press, 2000.

Sullivan, Moynagh. 'Looking at Being Somebody: Class and Gender in the Poetry of Rita Ann Higgins'. *Irish University Review* 15 (2001): 112–33.

'"The Woman Gardener:" Transnationalism, Gender, Sexuality and the Poetry of Blanaid Salkeld'. *Irish University Review* 42, no. 1 (2012): 53–71.

Sweeney, Bernadette. *Performing the Body in Irish Theatre*. Basingstoke: Palgrave, 2008.

Thompson, Lynda M. *The 'Scandalous Memoirists': Constantia Phillips, Laetitia Pilkington and the Shame of 'publick fame'*. Manchester: Manchester University Press, 2002.

Thuente, Mary Helen. 'Liberty, Hibernia, and Mary Le More: United Irish Images of Women'. In *The Women of 1798*, edited by Dáire Keogh and Nicholas Furlong, 9–25. Dublin: Four Courts Press, 1998.

Thurschwell, Pamela, and Sian White. 'Introduction: Elizabeth Bowen and Textual Modernity'. *Textual Practice Special Issue* 27, no. 1 (2013): 1–6.

Tiernan, Sonja. *Eva Gore-Booth: An Image of Such Politics*. Manchester: Manchester University Press, 2012.

The Political Writings of Eva Gore-Booth. Manchester: Manchester University Press, 2015.

Todd, Janet. *Sensibility: An Introduction*. London: Routledge, 1986.

Toomey, Deirdre. 'Elizabeth Bowen'. *New Oxford Dictionary of National Biography*. Oxford: Oxford University Press, 2004. https://doi-org.ucc.idm .oclc.org/10.1093/ref:odnb/30839. Accessed 19 February 2018.

Trotter, Mary. *Ireland's National Theaters*. Syracuse, NY: Syracuse University Press, 2001.

Tucker, Amanda. 'A Space Between: Transnational Feminism in Kate O'Brien's *Mary Lavelle*'. *New Hibernian Review* 12, no. 1 (2008): 82–95.

Tucker, Bernard. '"Our chief poetess:" Mary Barber and Swift's Circle'. *Canadian Journal of Irish Studies* 19, no. 2 (1993): 31–44.

United Nations Convention Against Torture. 'Consideration of Reports Submitted by States Parties under Article 19 of the Convention, Concluding Observations: Ireland'. (17 June 2011). UN Doc CAT/C/IRL/Co/1.

Valente, Joseph. 'The Mother of All Sovereignty'. In *The Myth of Manliness in Irish National Culture, 1880–1922*. Chicago, IL: University of Illinois, 2011.

Vulliamy, Ed. 'At last O'Brien has her country under her spell'. *The Independent* 11 November 2015.

Wallace, Diana. *Sisters and Rivals in British Women's Fiction 1914–1939*. Basingstoke: Macmillan 2000.

Walshe, Eibhear, ed. *Ordinary People Dancing: Essays on Kate O'Brien*. Cork: Cork University Press, 1993.

     ed. *Sex, Nation and Dissent in Irish Writing*. Cork: Cork University Press, 1997.

     Kate O'Brien: A Writing Life. Dublin: Irish Academic Press, 2006.

     ed. *Elizabeth Bowen: Visions and Revisions*. Dublin: Irish Academic Press, 2009.

Walter, Bronwen. *Outsiders Inside: Whiteness, Place and Irish Women*. London: Routledge, 2000.

     'Personal lives: Narrative Accounts of Irish Women in the Diaspora'. *Irish Studies Review* 21, no. 1 (2013): 37–54.

Ward, Margaret, ed. *In Their Own Voice: Women and Irish Nationalism*. Cork: Attic Press, 1995.

Watson, Barbara Bellow. 'Variations on an Enigma: Elizabeth Bowen's War Novel'. In *Elizabeth Bowen: Modern Critical Views*, edited by Harold Bloom, 81–102. New York, NY: Chelsea House, 1987.

Weekes, Ann Owens. *Irish Women Writers: An Uncharted Tradition*. Lexington, KY: University of Kentucky, 1990.

Whitlock, Gillian. *Soft Weapons: Autobiography in Transit*. Chicago, IL: University of Chicago Press, 2007.

Whitney, Standlee. *'Power to Observe': Irish Women Novelists in Britain, 1890–1916*. Oxford: Peter Lang, 2015.

Whyte, Pádraic. 'Children's Literature'. In Murphy, *The Oxford History of the Irish Book*, 4: 518–28.

     Irish Childhoods: Children's Fiction and Irish History. Newcastle upon Tyne: Cambridge Scholars Publishing, 2011.

Williams, Leslie. '"The stone recalls its quarry": An Interview with Eiléan Ní Chuilleanáin'. In *Representing Ireland: Gender, Class, Nationality*, edited by Susan Shaw Sailer, 37–38. Gainesville, FL: University Press of Florida, 1970.

Wills, Clair. *Improprieties: Politics and Sexuality in Northern Irish Poetry*. Oxford: Oxford University Press, 1993.

'Neutrality and Popular Culture'. In *The Art of Popular Culture: From 'The Meeting of the Waters' to Riverdance*, edited by P. J. Mathews, Series 1, no. 5, 1–13. Dublin: UCDscholarcast, 2008.

That Neutral Island: A Cultural History of Ireland during World War II. London: Faber, 2008.

Winterson, Kieron. 'Green Flags on Their Bayonets: Winifred Letts and the Great War'. In *Irish Women at War: The Twentieth Century*, edited by Gillian McIntosh and Diane Urquhart, 17–34. Dublin: Four Courts Press, 2010.

Woolf, Virginia. *The Letters of Virginia Woolf*. Vol 5, edited by Nigel Nicolson and Joanne Trautmann. London: Hogarth Press, 1975.

Wright, Julia M. *Ireland, India, and Nationalism in Nineteenth-Century Literature*. Cambridge: Cambridge University Press, 2007.

Wyatt-Brown, Anne M. 'The Liberation of Mourning in Elizabeth Bowen's *The Little Girls* and *Eva Trout*'. In *Ageing and Gender in Literature: Studies in Creativity*, edited by Anne M. Wyatt-Brown and Janice Rossen, 164–86. Norfolk, VA: University Press of Virginia, 1993.

Wyndham, Horace. *Speranza: A Biography of Lady Wilde*. London: Boardman, 1951.

Zeilig, Hannah. 'The Critical Use of Narrative and Literature in Gerontology'. *International Journal of Ageing and Later Life* 6, no. 2 (2012): 7–37.

Index

Page numbers in bold indicate a detailed reference